Daly City Public Library
7 9
D0534553

Creating
Web Pages
ALL-IN-ONE
FOR
DUMMIES®
4TH EDITION

by Richard Wagner

Wiley Publishing, Inc.

W

Creating Web Pages All-in-One For Dummies®, 4th Edition

Published by
Wiley Publishing, Inc.
111 River Street
Hoboken, NJ 07030-5774

www.wiley.com

Published by Wiley Publishing, Inc., Indianapolis, Indiana

Published simultaneously in Canada

For general information on our other products and services, please contact our Customer Care Department within the U.S. at 877-762-2974, outside the U.S. at 317-572-3993, or fax 317-572-4002.

For technical support, please visit www.wiley.com/techsupport.

Wiley also publishes its books in a variety of electronic formats. Some content that appears in print may not be available in electronic books.

Library of Congress Control Number: 2010943055

ISBN: 978-0-470-64032-6

Manufactured in the United States of America

10 9 8 7 6 5 4 3 2 1

About the Author

Richard Wagner is Lead Product Architect, Web/Mobile at MAARK and author of several Web and mobile-related books, including *Safari and WebKit Development for iPhone OS 3.0, XSLT For Dummies, Web Design Before & After Makeovers,* and more. Richard has also authored several books outside of the field of technology, including *The Myth of Happiness* and *The Expeditionary Man.*

Dedication

To Kimberly and the boys

Publisher's Acknowledgments

We're proud of this book; please send us your comments at `http://dummies.custhelp.com`. For other comments, please contact our Customer Care Department within the U.S. at 877-762-2974, outside the U.S. at 317-572-3993, or fax 317-572-4002.

Some of the people who helped bring this book to market include the following:

Acquisitions and Editorial

Project Editor: Rebecca Senninger *(Previous Edition: Nicole Sholly)*

Executive Editor: Steven Hayes

Copy Editor: Barry Childs-Helton

Technical Editor: Claudia Snell

Editorial Manager: Leah Cameron

Editorial Assistant: Amanda Graham

Sr. Editorial Assistant: Cherie Case

Cartoons: Rich Tennant (`www.the5thwave.com`)

Composition Services

Project Coordinator: Patrick Redmond

Layout and Graphics: Vida Noffsinger, Lavonne Roberts

Proofreader: Laura Bowman

Indexer: BIM Indexing & Proofreading Services

Publishing and Editorial for Technology Dummies

Richard Swadley, Vice President and Executive Group Publisher

Andy Cummings, Vice President and Publisher

Mary Bednarek, Executive Acquisitions Director

Mary C. Corder, Editorial Director

Publishing for Consumer Dummies

Diane Graves Steele, Vice President and Publisher

Composition Services

Debbie Stailey, Director of Composition Services

Contents at a Glance

Table of Contents

Book VI: Graphics 345

Chapter 1: Understanding Web Graphics 347

Chapter 2: Optimizing Your Graphics 353

Chapter 3: Image Rollovers 361

Book VII: Microsoft Expression Web 369

Chapter 1: Getting to Know Microsoft Expression Web 371

Introduction

If you're interested in creating a Web site, chances are that you've at least seen the terms *HTML, XHTML, CSS, JavaScript,* and *Flash* floating around. Maybe your friends talk about their WordPress blogs or Facebook pages and you don't know whether you should do the same or dive into using a more powerful tool, like Adobe Dreamweaver or Microsoft Expression Web.

However, unless you're a professional Web designer, you might be a bit unsure of — and maybe even a little intimidated by figuring out — where to start. You have to know which of these technologies is important to know and which ones can be left to the techie-geek crowd. What's more, you need to know the *least* amount of information you need to have to create a decent Web site.

Along the way, you will need to dig into the code of your Web page and at least make sense of what's going on behind the scenes. However, when possible, you may want to use Dreamweaver or Expression Web to handle most of that lower-level coding for you.

If these sorts of issues ring true for you, you have the right book in hand.

About This Book

In *Creating Web Pages All-in-One For Dummies,* 4th Edition, I take you on a tour around the Web. The nine minibooks packed inside these pages cover all the "required" technologies that you need to know about to create Web pages. Here are some tasks that I show you how to do in this reference book:

- ✦ Create attractive, professional-looking Web pages.
- ✦ Enjoy some of the most popular Web services, including WordPress and SquareSpace.
- ✦ Use Adobe Dreamweaver or Microsoft Expression Web to create Web sites.
- ✦ Make sense of HTML code.
- ✦ Use Cascading Style Sheets (CSS) to style your Web site.
- ✦ Use graphics and multimedia effectively.
- ✦ Make your pages interactive, by adding JavaScript or Ajax scripts.
- ✦ Use Adobe Flash to add animated Flash movies to your site.

Foolish Assumptions

In *Creating Web Pages All-in-One For Dummies,* 4th Edition, I don't assume that you already know how to create a Web page or that you're familiar with the technologies I cover, such as HTML, Cascading Style Sheets, and JavaScript. However, I assume that you have surfed the Web and know what a Web site is. I also assume that you have a working knowledge of either a Windows or Mac computer and have used Microsoft Word or a similar word processing program.

Conventions Used in This Book

By *conventions,* I simply mean a set of rules I use in this book to present information to you consistently:

- **Screen shots:** All of the browsers and Web-site software (except for Microsoft Expression Web) that I cover in this book run on both the Microsoft Windows and Mac OS X platforms. The screen shots in this book feature both the Mac and Windows versions, but all the instructions are for both operating systems.
- **Special formatting:** When you see a term *italicized,* look for its definition, which is included so that you know what words mean in the context of Web-site design and creation. Web-site addresses and e-mail addresses appear in `monofont` so that they stand out from regular text. Code appears in its own font, set off from the rest of the text, like this:

```
<p class="normalPara">
It's a <em>brave</em> new world.
</p>
```

- **HTML terminology:** A Web page is created by using HTML, which is a *markup programming language* used for organizing and displaying the information you present. HTML is composed of many *elements,* such as a `p` (paragraph) that looks like this:

```
<p>Here is a paragraph</p>
```

  The `<p>` is the *start tag,* and the `</p>` is the *end tag.* The text between them is the *content.* The entire piece of code is referred to as the `p` *element,* or *tag.* The terms are synonymous.

- **HTML and XHTML:** In Book III, you explore what HTML and XHTML (Extensible HTML) are and how the technologies differ from each other. However, for the rest of the book, when I speak of HTML, I speak in a generic sense and am speaking of both HTML and XHTML in the discussion.

What You Don't Have to Read

I structured this book modularly: It's designed so that you can easily find just the information you need and so that you don't have to read anything that doesn't pertain to your task at hand. I include sidebars here and there throughout the book that contain interesting information that isn't necessarily integral to the discussion at hand; feel free to skip over them. You also don't have to read the Technical Stuff icons, which parse out ubertechie tidbits (which might or might not be your cup of tea).

How This Book Is Organized

Creating Web Pages All-in-One For Dummies, 4th Edition, is split into nine minibooks. You don't have to read the book sequentially, you don't have to look at every minibook, you certainly don't have to read every chapter, and you don't even have to read all the sections in any particular chapter. (Of course, you can if you want to; I hope you find the book to be a good read!) And, the table of contents and the index can help you quickly find whatever information you need. In this section, I briefly describe the topics that each minibook contains.

Book I: Establish a Web Presence

In this minibook, I show you how to get started making a presence online by exploring the choices you have, but focusing on online blogging tools and full Web-site-building solutions. I also show how you can connect your blog or Web site to Twitter and Facebook.

Book II: Web Design

Start off right by exploring proven Web page design principles. Book II covers such topics as organizing an effective site, designing with white space, using the rule of thirds, and avoiding the eight most common Web-site mistakes.

Book III: HTML/XHTML

Web pages are written in the special tag-based languages HTML (Hypertext Markup Language) or XHTML (Extensible HTML). Online blogging tools (such as WordPress) and desktop Web-site software (such as Dreamweaver) generally do a good job of hiding the complex HTML code from you. However, in some cases, you can't avoid peeking "under the hood." Book III comes in handy to help you know what's going on in the midst of the source code.

Book IV: Style with CSS

I don't think it's an overstatement to say that Cascading Style Sheets (or CSS, for short) is an essential technology to understand and work with as you begin to create Web sites. CSS helps revolutionize the way you structure a Web site by separating your page's content from the formatting rules you create. That may not sound like a big deal, but it makes your job as a Web-site creator *much* easier. In this minibook, you discover the power of this technology by exploring all its major features, including inheritance, selectors, and cascades.

Book V: JavaScript and Ajax

In this minibook, you discover the world of JavaScript. Using JavaScript, you can write scripts for your Web pages to make them interactive and respond to user events (button clicks, for example). I introduce you to the key concepts you need to know to be productive with scripting and then show you how to seamlessly add scripts into your Web page and make them work. I also show you how to add Ajax to your Web site to enable live refreshes of content without refreshing the entire page.

Book VI: Graphics

Graphics can make or break your Web-site design. Book VI shows you how best to obtain images, optimize them, and explore other important graphics techniques, such as hotspots, image maps, and rollovers.

Book VII: Microsoft Expression Web

Expression Web is the flagship Web design tool from Microsoft. This integrated Web-site design and authoring environment sports a visual page designer. In Book VII, I walk you through the steps required to design, create, and publish a Web site by using Expression Web.

Book VIII: Adobe Dreamweaver

Available for both Windows and Mac, Dreamweaver has long been the industry-standard, Web design software package. Book VIII introduces you to the key features of Dreamweaver and shows you how to quickly become productive using it.

Book IX: Adobe Flash

A Flash movie is by far the most important add-in to a Web page. In fact, Flash movies are so widespread and popular that some sites are written entirely by using Flash. With Flash, you can add interactivity and animation that goes far beyond what HTML and JavaScript can do by themselves. In this minibook, you discover how to be productive in the Flash authoring environment and how to create basic movies.

Icons Used in This Book

For Dummies books are known for using helpful icons that point you in the direction of useful information. This section briefly describes the icons used in this book.

The Tip icon points out helpful information or key techniques that can save you time and effort.

The Remember icon is used to point out something particularly important in the text to help you in your understanding of the technology.

The Warning icon is synonymous with saying "Hey, you — be careful!" When you see this icon, pay attention and proceed with caution.

This icon denotes nearby techie information. If you're not feeling very technical, you can skip this info.

Where to Go from Here

You can begin by starting out with Book I. Or, if you want to dive into a specific topic right away, consider any of these jumping-off points:

- To create an immediate Web presence, check out Book I.
- To create cool, well-designed pages, check out Book II, Chapter 1.
- To master style sheets, take a look at Book IV.
- To find out the basics of creating an HTML document, check out Book III, Chapter 1.
- To gain a working knowledge of the HTML source code, check out Books III, IV, and V.
- To create interactive Web sites, go to Books V and IX.

Book I

Establish a Web Presence

"Just how accurately should my Web site reflect my place of business?"

Contents at a Glance

Chapter 1: Getting Up and Running

In This Chapter

- **Getting to know the lingo for creating Web sites**
- **Understanding how a Web site is published**
- **Discovering Web sites that work (and some that don't)**

Perhaps you created a simple Web site in the past and are now ready for the next step. Or maybe you always wanted to build your first site but didn't know where to start.

Either way, you'll get started toward your Web-site goals in this chapter, as I introduce you to key terms and technologies that you use along the way. I also explore the three major options available to you for creating your Web site.

Knowing the Lingo and the Basics

Any time you start doing something new, one challenge is picking up the lingo. The Web has so many new terms floating about every day that you can easily pick up some terms, but you might find that other, more techie concepts or technologies go right over your head. So here's a crash course to make sure that you know the linga franca of Web-site building.

Navigating the Web

A *Web site* is a collection of pages, usually formatted in HTML (Hypertext Markup Language), that contains text, graphics, and multimedia elements, such as Flash, audio, or video files. The main page of a site is known as a *home page,* which links to other documents in the site by using hyperlinks. All these pages are stored on a *Web server,* which is the name for a computer that hosts the site.

A variety of sites are on the Web, including

- Corporate sites
- Personal home pages
- Blogs
- Facebook profiles
- Special-interest sites

Every Web site has a unique address, known as a *URL* (Uniform Resource Locator). A URL looks like

```
http://www.cnn.com
http://www.facebook.com/richwagner
http://richwagner.posterous.com
```

The main part of the URL (`cnn.com`, `facebook.com`) is known as a *domain name.*

A user enters the URL in a browser, such as Microsoft Internet Explorer. The browser sends the request across the Internet; it winds up at the doorsteps of the Web server. The Web server then responds by sending the requested page back to the browser.

The Web server is often hosted by an Internet service provider (ISP) or Web hosting provider. Some providers are free, but generally most of the more reliable ones charge a fee, typically ranging from $5 to $20 a month, for their services.

Browsing the browsers

The software you use to navigate the Web is a *browser,* and you can choose from a few:

- **Firefox** is one of the most popular browsers. It not only works on all major platforms (Windows, Mac, and Linux), but also has an amazing number of free extensions you can add to greatly enhance your browsing experience. To download Firefox and its extensions, visit `www.mozilla.org`.
- **Microsoft Internet Explorer** is not as popular as it was ten years ago, but it remains a dominant browser for Windows users. If you have a Windows-based computer, it probably came pre-loaded with IE. If not, you can find it at `www.microsoft.com`.
- **Google Chrome** is a relatively new kid on the block, but it has quickly become a favorite among many Web-site builders (including me) and casual users for its speed, stability, and extensions. Available on Windows and Mac platforms at `www.google.com/chrome`.
- **Safari** is the dominant browser on the Mac platform and is available for Windows as well. Download it at `www.apple.com/safari/download`.
- **Opera** (`www.opera.com`) is a commercially available browser that sports powerful functionality.

No matter which browser you prefer, install on your computer at least two or three browsers that you can use for testing your Web site. Each browser has idiosyncrasies that can occasionally affect your page design. Having a selection of these on hand helps you catch problems before your visitors do!

For example, I usually work with Google Chrome to test my pages initially, and then later check them against Internet Explorer and Firefox.

Creating and publishing a Web site

When you create a Web site, you work with HTML (Hypertext Markup Language) documents. The HTML tag-based markup language is used for presenting information. It intermixes content with instructions that tell the computer how and where to present the content on the Web page.

These pages, which have a `.html` or `.htm` extension, look different depending on the software you use to view them. When you view an HTML document in a text editor like Notepad, you see a bunch of weird-looking code, as shown in Figure 1-1. However, a browser knows what all these instructions mean and can then *render* (a fancy word for *process and display*) the document in all its visual glory, as shown in Figure 1-2.

Figure 1-1: HTML documents can look intimidating "under the hood."

If you're used to working with Microsoft Word or other word processors, you've probably added a graphical image to a document. When you perform this action in Word, it grabs a copy of the graphic image from its original file and embeds the copy in the document. Therefore, if you were to e-mail the file to a friend, the image would be displayed on your friend's computer when the document is opened.

Figure 1-2: HTML documents, however, can look visually attractive when viewed in a browser.

In contrast, although HTML documents display graphics, video, and other types of media files as content, this media is never stored inside the HTML file itself. Instead, the HTML document links to external image files or Flash media. Therefore the Web site includes not only HTML documents but also any other media files that you add to your page layout.

The other common types of files you work with include

- Cascading Style Sheets (`.css`); see Book IV
- Graphics (`.jpg`, `.gif`, and `.png`); see Book VI
- JavaScript files (`.js`); see Book V
- Flash movies (`.swf`); see Book IX

Finally, when you're done creating your Web site, you *publish* your files to your Web-site hosting server. If you're creating the pages on your own computer, publishing involves uploading all the HTML, graphic, and other media files. When the files have been successfully added to the Web server, the Web site is considered *live* — that is, open for all the world to see.

Exploring Your Web-Site Choices

When you create a presence on the Web, you now have a variety of sophisticated and powerful choices to choose from — blogging tools, desktop Web-site-building software, and online Web builders.

Exactly which solution you decide to use depends on your individual needs. I maintain a couple of blogs (tech and personal) on Posterous because they work great for publishing articles. I recently used Adobe Dreamweaver to build a Web site for a nonprofit organization whose needs were too customized to work well within a blog structure.

Convenience of online blogging tools

Perhaps the most convenient solution available to creating a Web presence is to start off with one of several online blogging tools, such as WordPress, Posterous, or Tumblr. Blogging sites are a great choice because of the ease of getting started and the low cost (the major ones are available completely free of charge). You also can take advantage of pre-built design themes to style and color your site, which is especially helpful if you consider yourself design-challenged.

Because of their sequential, list-based structure, blogs work best when you are publishing articles or posting pictures (see Figure 1-3). Some blogging tools, such as WordPress, do have an extensive set of plug-ins you can add that enable you to create quite sophisticated and robust Web sites.

In Chapter 2 of this minibook, I walk you through how to create a free WordPress blog.

Most flexibility: Building your own site

On the other end of the scale, you can create your own site from scratch using a Web-site-building software application, such as Adobe Dreamweaver or Microsoft Expression Web. These tools enable you to work inside of a visual environment (see Figure 1-4) to design your pages and create your site.

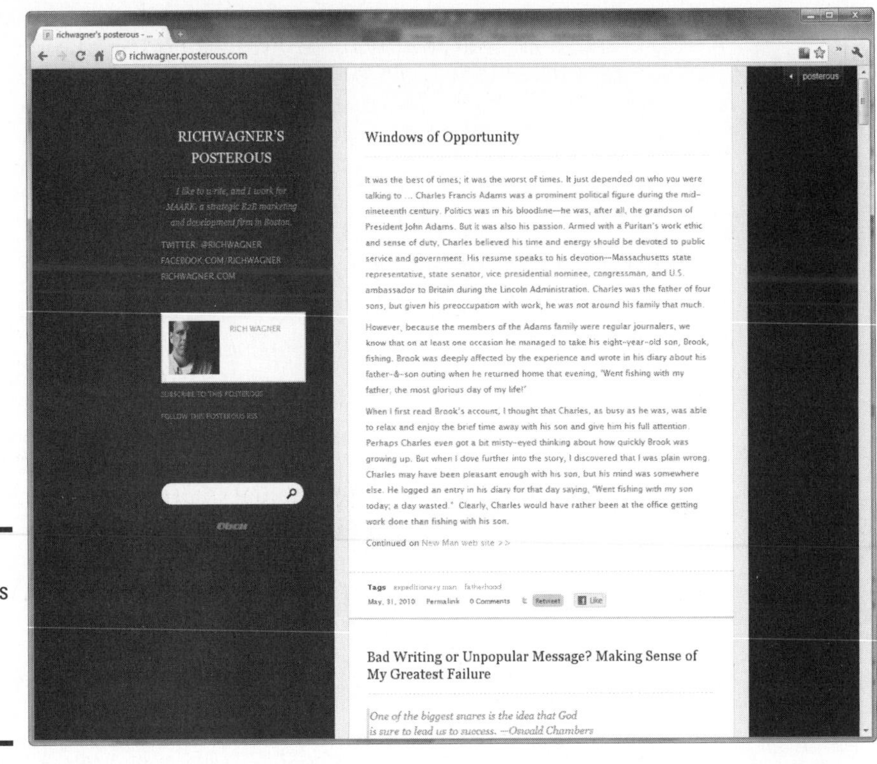

Figure 1-3: A Posterous blog is easy to set up and maintain.

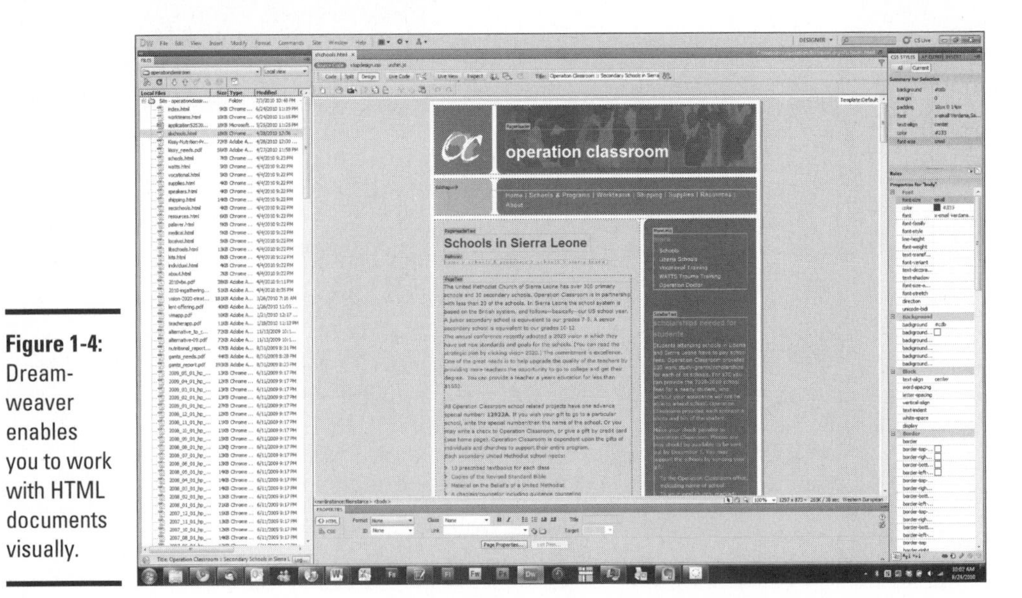

Figure 1-4: Dreamweaver enables you to work with HTML documents visually.

The great advantage to the software solution is that you have the most flexibility in the ways you can structure your site, lay it out, and design its individual pages. The downside is that building a Web site from scratch requires a lot more effort than the other solutions.

Books VII (Microsoft Expression Web) and VIII (Adobe Dreamweaver) are devoted to the two most popular desktop Web-site-building applications.

Compromise: Using an online site builder

A final option is a compromise between the more rigid structure of an online blogging tool and the complete freedom of a desktop-based software application. Online site builders have been around for years, and although they're not as popular as blogging tools, they remain a viable option for some people.

Squarespace.com is a great example of a commercial Web-site-building tool that is also a blog service. You can create powerful, customized Web sites, but still take advantage of using a service that manages many site tasks rather than being forced to do it all yourself. Figure 1-5 shows a site built with Squarespace.

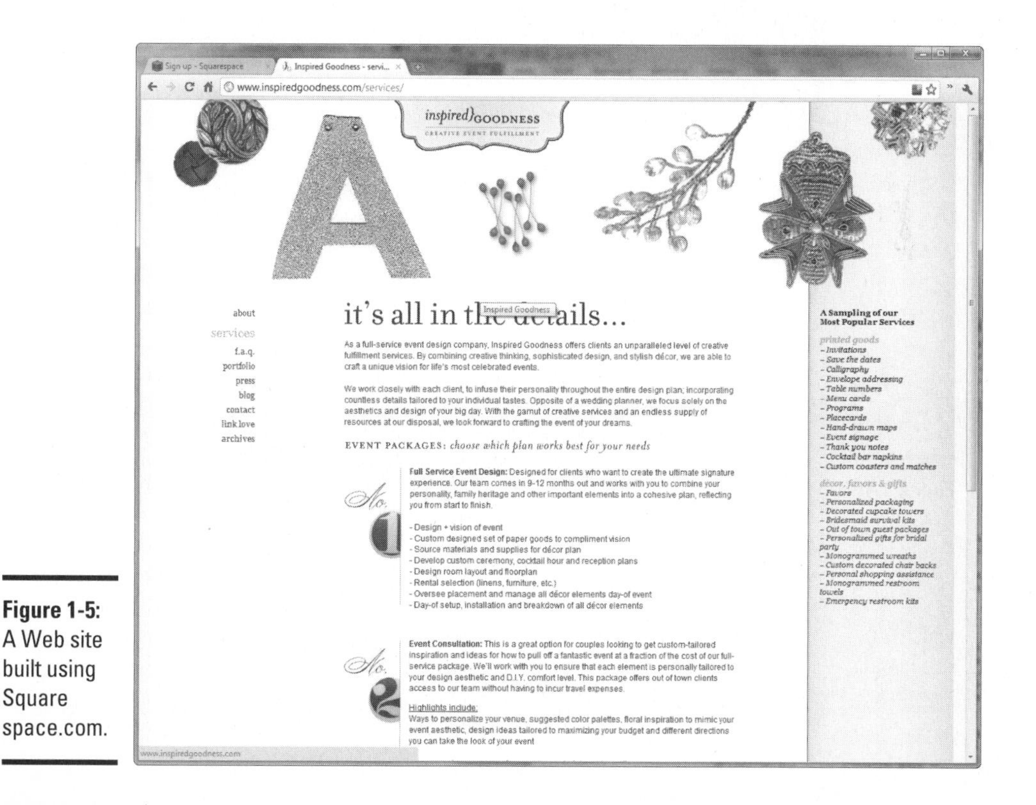

Figure 1-5: A Web site built using Square space.com.

Chapter 3 of this minibook walks you through how to create a Web site using Squarespace.

Surf and Study: Discovering What Works and What Doesn't

Before you begin creating your Web site, spend some time browsing various Web sites, making notes about what you see. In other words, rather than surf the site, *study* it. Consider each of these issues:

- **Identify what you like and dislike about the design of the site.** If you like it, jot down styling concepts you want to emulate. If you dislike it, make sure to avoid these mistakes yourself. (See Book II for more on design strategy.)
- **Consider the overall "tone" of the site.** Does the site look overly formal or informal? Professional or amateurish? You should set a tone for your site and make sure that your content, design, color, and font selection all work together in support of it.
- **Look for the overall messaging of the site.** What's being communicated through the design, graphics, and text of the home page? Is there a single theme? Are you getting mixed messages? Is it successful? For your Web site, develop a consistent, coherent theme or message and then create the site around it.
- **Check out the site's navigation.** Can you easily find the information you're looking for? Can you get lost in the site? You should develop a site that's easy to navigate. (See Book II for more on site organization.)
- **Identify the technologies being used.** When you come across an effect or interactive feature that you really like, dive under the hood and identify the technology that the site is using to pull off the effect.

To peek under the hood, right-click the page and choose View Source from the pop-up menu that appears (this feature is available in most browsers). Inside the HTML source code, you can find all the nitty-gritty details of the technology behind the scenes. Be sure to read Book III first, however, to help you navigate your way through the source code.

When you come across a site you really like, don't blatantly copy its design or (especially) its actual files. Instead, use it as inspiration to spawn your own creative ideas.

If you get into a rut trying to find interesting Web sites to explore, check out `www.coolhomepages.com` and `www.cssbeauty.com/gallery`. Both sites feature a gallery of well-designed sites that can inspire you.

If you feel intimidated by the high level of expertise necessary to pull off a good Web-site design, don't sweat it. Most of these sites are created by design professionals. The idea is to learn from their designs and techniques, not to try to copy or compete with them.

Chapter 2: WordPress

In This Chapter

- Exploring the world of blogging
- Creating a blog by using WordPress
- Managing your blog entries
- Changing the theme
- Blogging from e-mail and voice
- Dealing with comments

Journalists. College students. Authors. Politicians. Techies. Almost anyone. You name someone's profession or interest, and I can find a blog written by someone about it. Blogging continues to take the world by storm, and it's time for you to get on board.

In this chapter, I introduce you to the world of blogging and show you how to create your own WordPress blog in a just a matter of minutes.

WordPress has a lot more to offer than I can cover in this chapter. To find out more about WordPress, check out *WordPress For Dummies,* by Lisa Sabin-Wilson.

Understanding Blogging

A *blog,* short for We*b log,* can be an online journal, a news-oriented site, or a place to post your vacation pictures. Blogs enable you to easily publish your thoughts, ideas, and opinions on the Web without using a traditional site.

Technically speaking, a blog is a more structured form of a traditional Web site. Standard Web sites are usually one-of-a-kind creations — each one is structured to meet the unique needs of its owner. In contrast, a blog is a Web site with these specific organizational elements:

- **Blog listing:** Made in the style of a journal and shown in reverse chronological order.
- **Home page:** Shows the latest postings, but individual entries are archived and usually organized by date.

- **Individual entries:** Normally these appear in journal format in the blog listing (on the home page or in an archives section). However, blogging software can also assign a specific URL (a *permalink)* to a blog entry to enable it to appear on its own, individual page.
- **Comments:** This feature allows readers to express their thoughts about an entry and have them posted as part of the blog. As you would expect, blogs that use comments can thus form an interactive community of participants.

A variety of blogs are on the Web, each with its own moniker. A *photoblog* is a photo-based blog, a *vlog* is a video-based blog, a *moblog* is a blog written using a mobile device, and a *liveblog* features real-time journaling. The collection of all blogs in the world is the *blogosphere*. A variety of free and paid blogging sites are available on the Web.

Popular free blogging services include these:

- WordPress (`www.wordpress.com`)
- Posterous (`www.posterous.com`)
- Tumblr (`www.tumblr.com`)
- Blogger (`www.blogger.com`)

Creating a Blog with WordPress

WordPress is the most popular blogging service on the Web. You can download WordPress software on your own server space. Or you can create a blog on a WordPress hosted service. I show you how to sign up for the hosted service — all you need to get started is a name for your blog.

Using WordPress, you can get up and running with a blog in a matter of minutes. Follow these steps:

1. **Go to** `www.wordpress.com`**.**

   The WordPress home page, shown in Figure 2-1, showcases several blogs that use it and basic information on how to get started.
2. **Click the Sign Up Now link and sign up using the form that is provided.**
3. **Enter a username, a password, and your e-mail address in the form that appears and click the Next button.**

   Be sure to select the I Accept the Terms of Service check box before continuing.

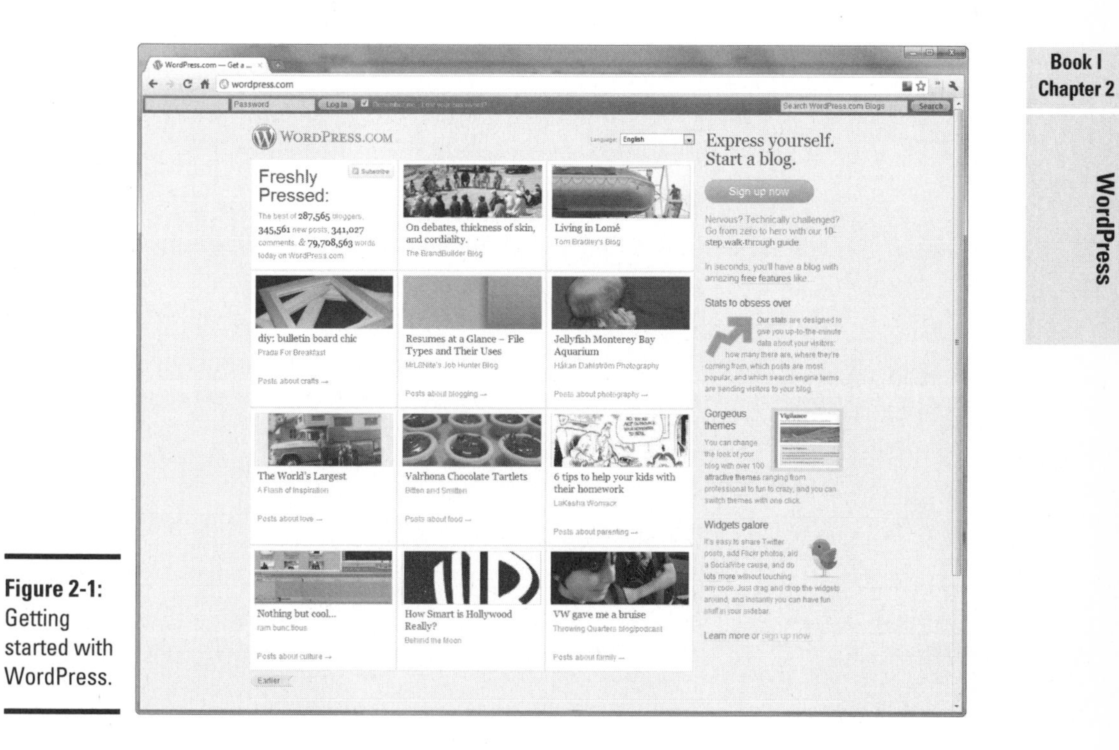

Figure 2-1: Getting started with WordPress.

Leave the Gimme a Blog radio button checked.

After you click the Next link, you're asked to customize the domain and title of your blog (see Figure 2-2).

4. **Enter the desired blog domain in the space provided.**

   WordPress hosts your blog for you, freeing you from dealing with another Web host. As a result, the name you enter here is the start of the Web address for your blog, followed by the `.wordpress.com` suffix.

   You often want to use a portion or all of your blog title as the name for your domain. (I decided to choose `everestleaders` as the domain.)

   Alternatively, if you already have a Web-hosting provider that provides WordPress support, you may want to host the blog yourself. The advantage to this route is that you can specify your own, unique domain name. Sign up at `www.wordpress.org` if you'd like to find your own hosting.

5. **Enter a title for your blog.**

   Some people opt for descriptive titles (Rich Wagner's Blog); others prefer creative ones (Tales from the Cheese Monkey Soup or Encapsulate Obscurity).

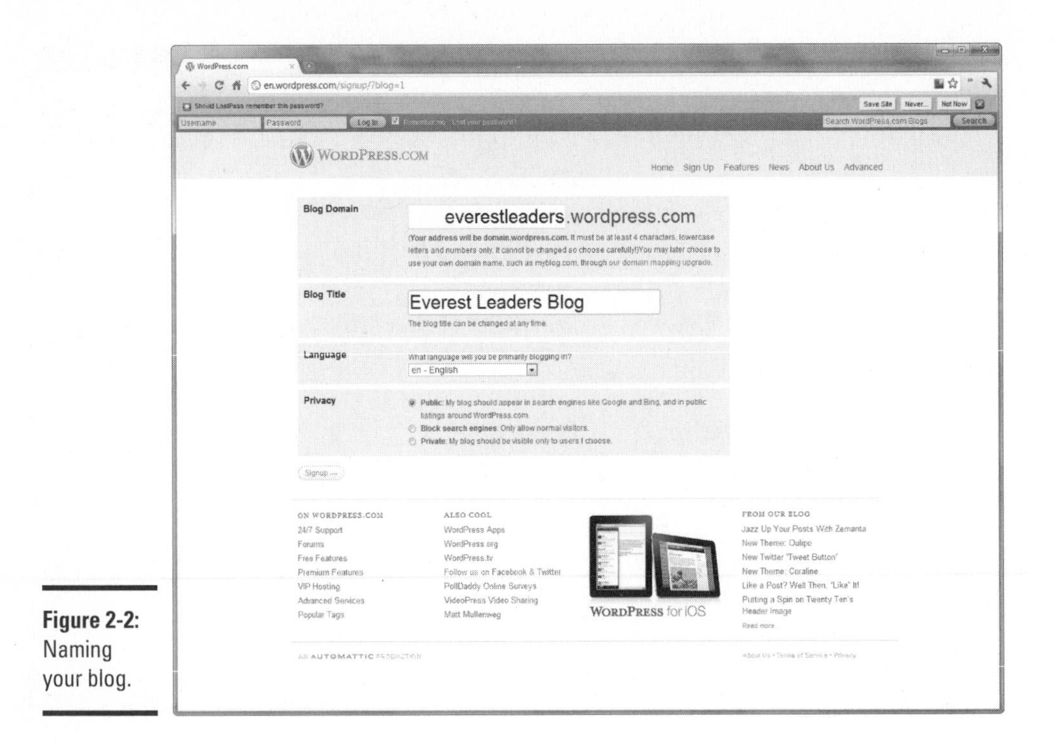

Figure 2-2: Naming your blog.

6. **Specify the language and privacy settings for your blog and click Signup.**

   A confirmation e-mail is sent to your e-mail address.

7. **Click the link in the e-mail address to activate your WordPress account.**

   Be sure to activate your account by clicking the link in your e-mail message within 48 hours or you'll have to sign up again.

   After you click the link, you go to a Web page that confirms your activation and allows you to view your blog (which will contain one dummy entry) or log in.

8. **Click the Login link.**

   You're taken to the login page.

9. **Log in to your newly activated account by entering your username and password and clicking Login.**

   Once logged in, your Dashboard appears, which is the command-and-control center for your blog (see Figure 2-3).

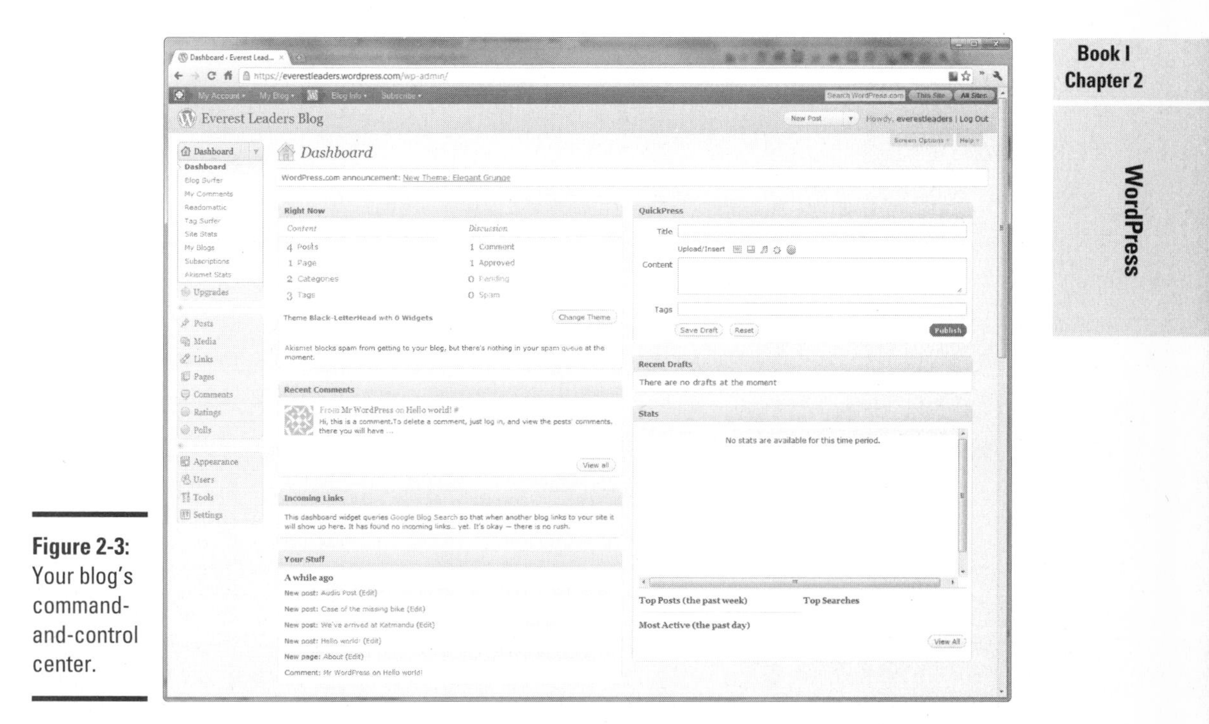

Figure 2-3: Your blog's command-and-control center.

Creating a Post

Your blog looks really empty when you create it; the first thing you'll want to do is add some posts. Follow these steps.

1. **Click the New Post button at the top of the page to begin creating a post.**

   The Add New Post page appears, as shown in Figure 2-4.

2. **Enter the title of your post in the Title box.**
3. **Type your post in the text box.**
4. **Format your text as you want.**

   The WYSIWYG editor acts as a mini word processor, so you can use the toolbar to format your text the way you want (refer to Figure 2-3). If you're familiar with word processors, you'll recognize most of these. Here are some you might not know:

   - *Blockquote:* Offset a paragraph as a quote.
   - *Add and Remove Link:* Add, edit, or remove a hyperlink.

- *Insert More Tag:* Allows you to divide your blog entry so that only the first part of the post is displayed on the home page. If you add the More tag, a link enables readers to go to the full content of the article.
- *Proofread Writing:* Check your spelling before you post your blog entry.
- *Toggle Fullscreen Mode:* Enables you to expand the editor to take up the full page.
- *Show/Hide Kitchen Sink:* Displays an additional row of formatting controls.

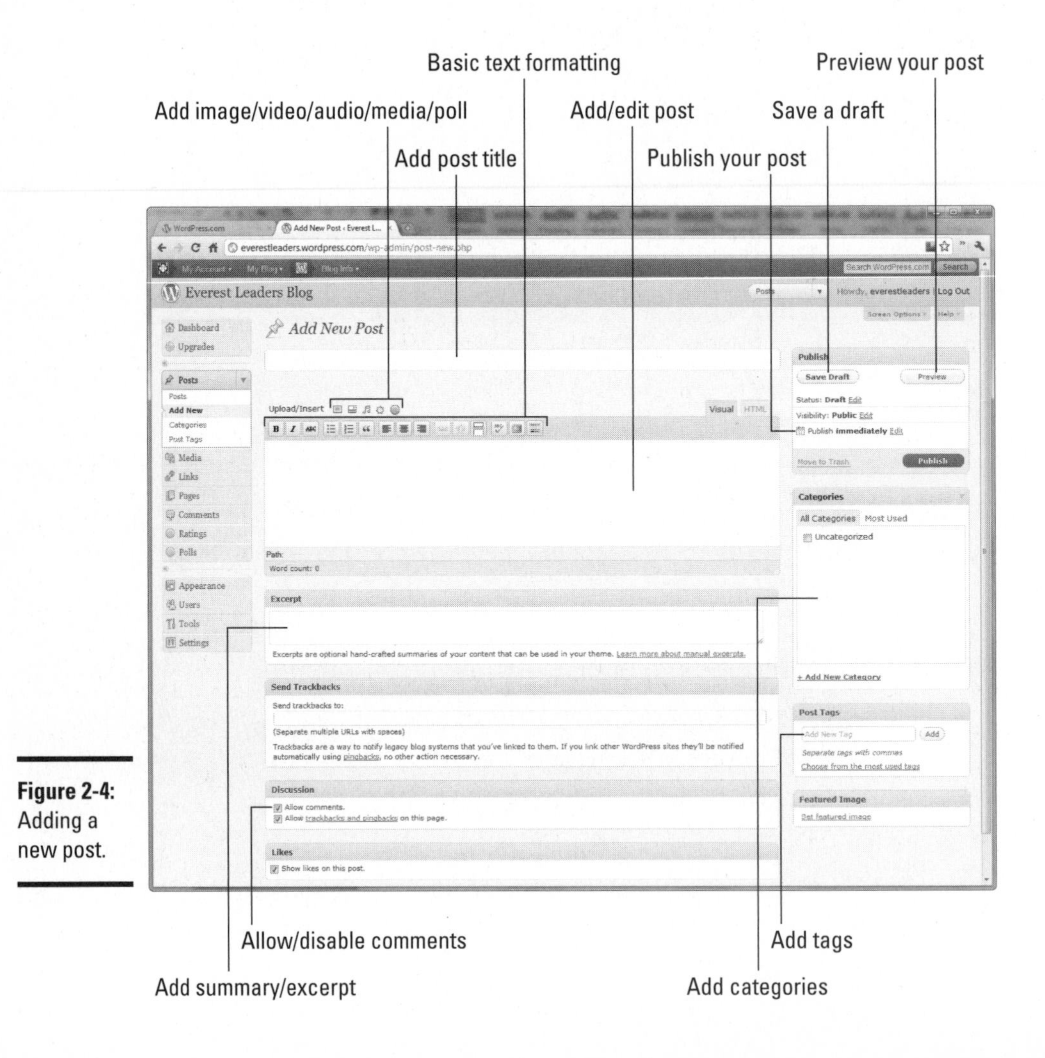

Figure 2-4: Adding a new post.

WARNING!

Legacy (that is, old and usually obsolete) browsers will not support the WYSIWYG editor. If your browser doesn't provide support, a plain-text-only version appears.

5. **(Optional) To add a clickable URL to your post, select the text that will contain the link and then click the Link button.**

   For example, suppose you are defining a topic and would like to reference the Wikipedia entry for that term. You could add a link to the Wikipedia page in your blog post.

   A dialog box (see Figure 2-5) appears for you to enter the URL of the link.

6. **Enter your URL in the dialog box and click Insert.**

   The link is added to your entry.

7. **(Optional) To insert an image, position your text cursor where you want the image to appear and then click the Add an Image button.**

   The Add an Image box appears, as shown in Figure 2-6.

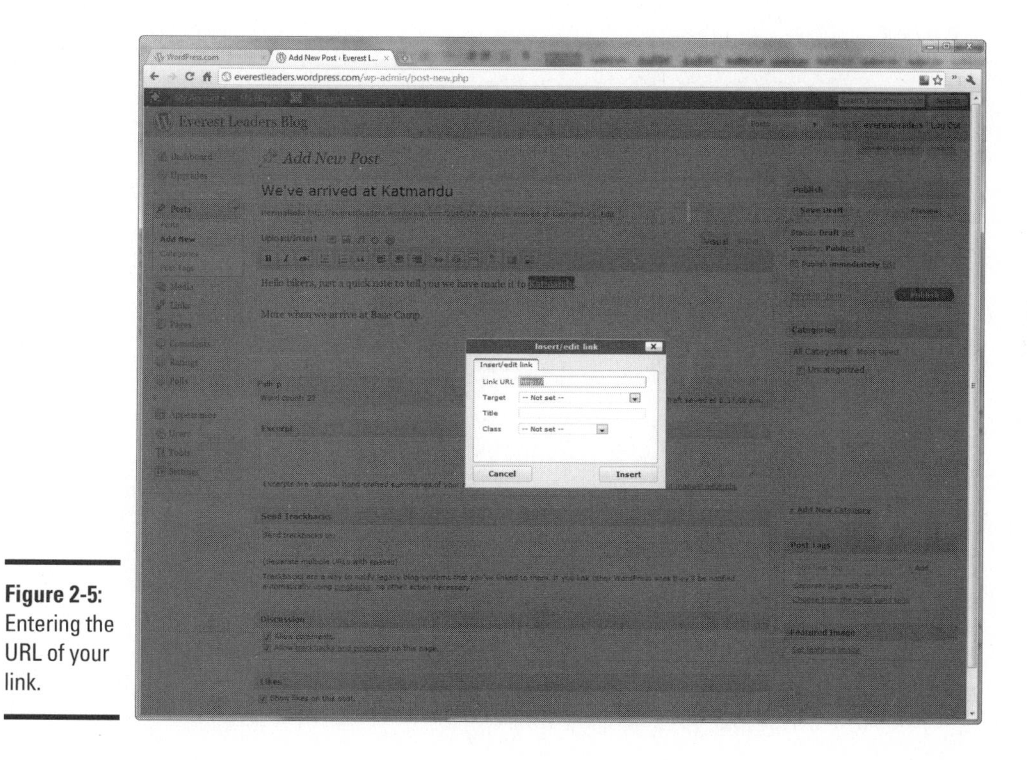

Figure 2-5: Entering the URL of your link.

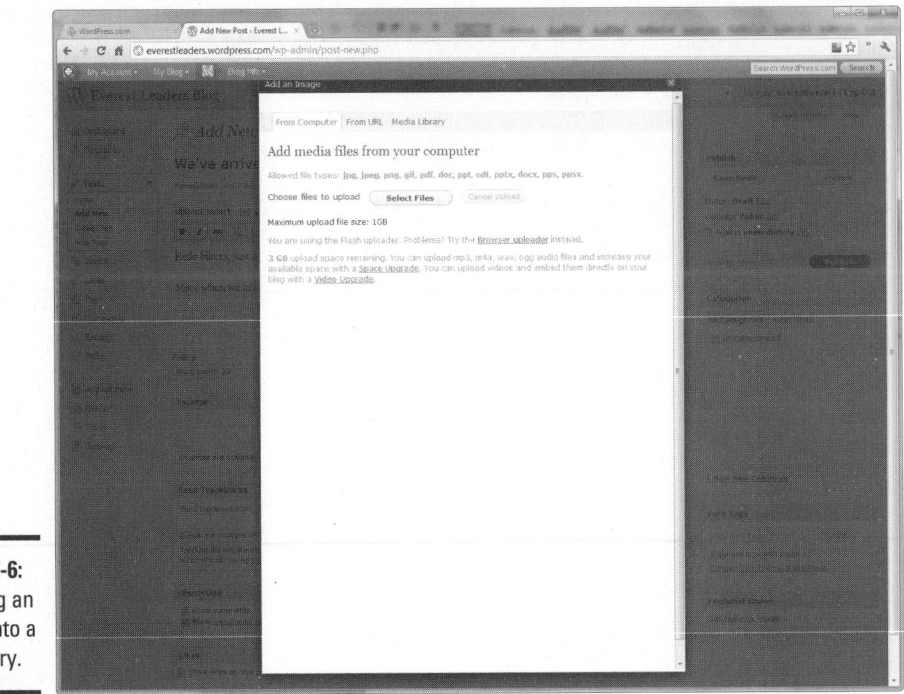

Figure 2-6: Inserting an image into a blog entry.

8. **Click the Select Files button and locate the file on your drive.**

   - If you have multiple images, you can click the Add Another Image link to upload each of these images at the same time.
   - You can also add an image posted elsewhere on the Web by clicking the From URL and then entering the image's URL in the space provided.

   WordPress uploads your image(s); then you can specify more properties of the image (see Figure 2-7).

9. **Click the Insert Into Post button to add the image to your post.**

   The image is inserted into your post; see Figure 2-8.

10. **Click the Add New Category link and enter a category for the post.**

    Categories are usually top-level bins in which you wish to organize your posts, such as News, General, and so on.

11. **In the Post Tags section, enter one or more tags for this post, and separate each entry with a comma.**

    Tags are posted with each blog entry (usually at the bottom). Readers of your blog can then click a label to display a page that lists each blog entry containing that label.

    Labels are optional and are especially useful if you blog on a wide variety of topics.

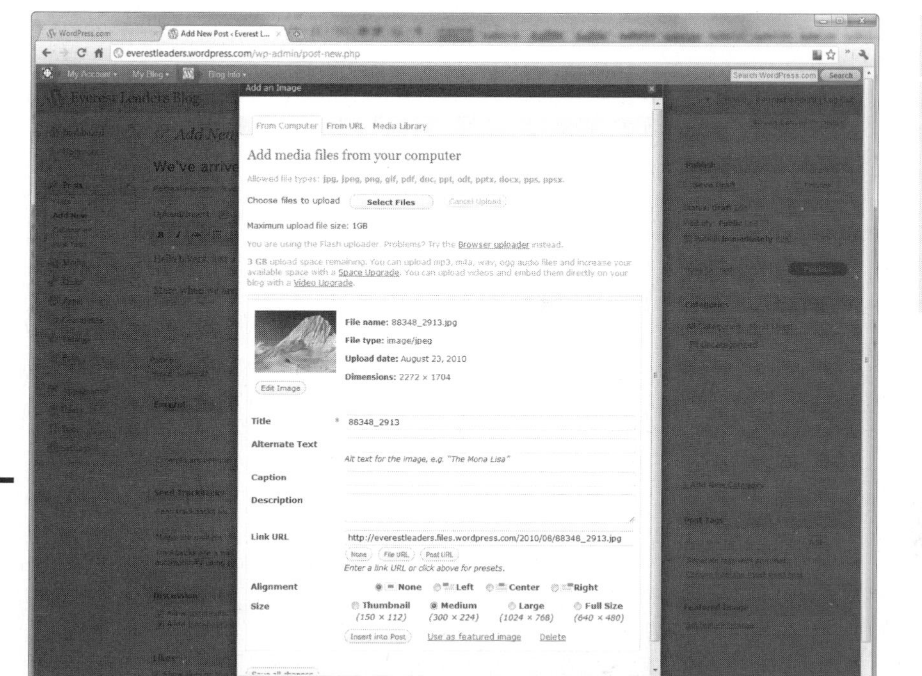

Figure 2-7: Specifying size and other properties of image.

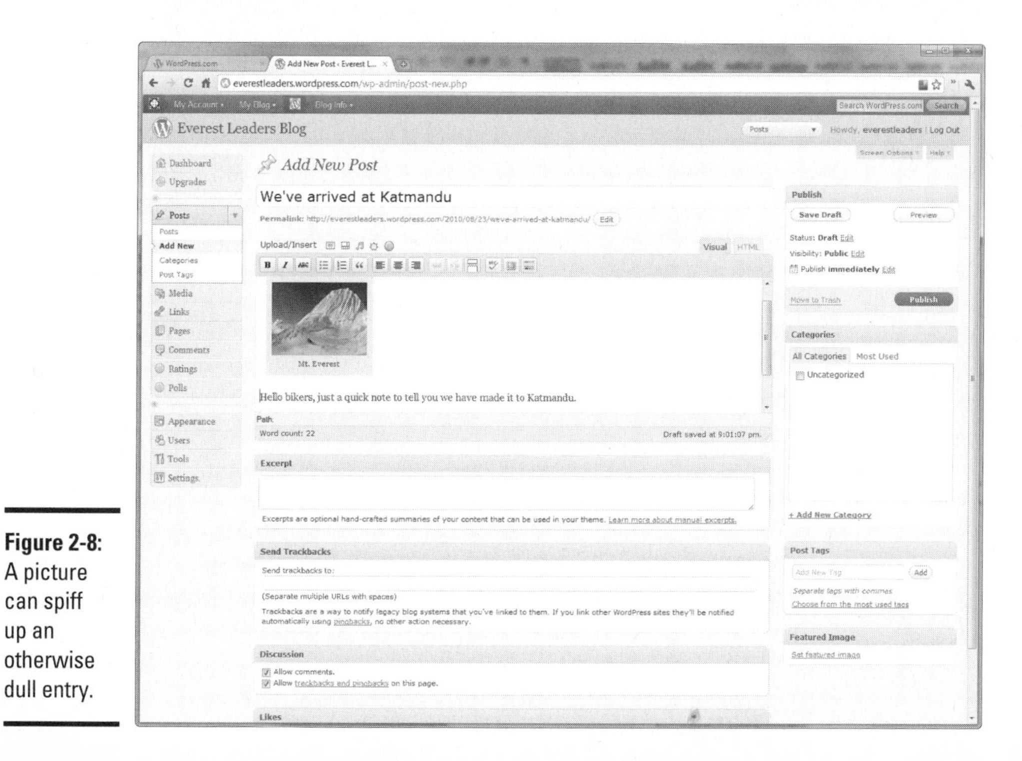

Figure 2-8: A picture can spiff up an otherwise dull entry.

12. **Click the Publish button.**

    WordPress publishes your blog to the Permalink URL defined below the title and informs you when the process is complete.

    A *permalink* is the URL that refers to your blog post after it has scrolled off of the home page of your blog.

13. **Click the View Blog link.**

    WordPress displays your blog with the default theme. Figure 2-9 shows my results.

As you can see, WordPress displays a toolbar at the top that enables you to search other WordPress blogs as well as to access your own account and blog.

You can return to the Dashboard by choosing My Blog⇨Dashboard from the WordPress menu.

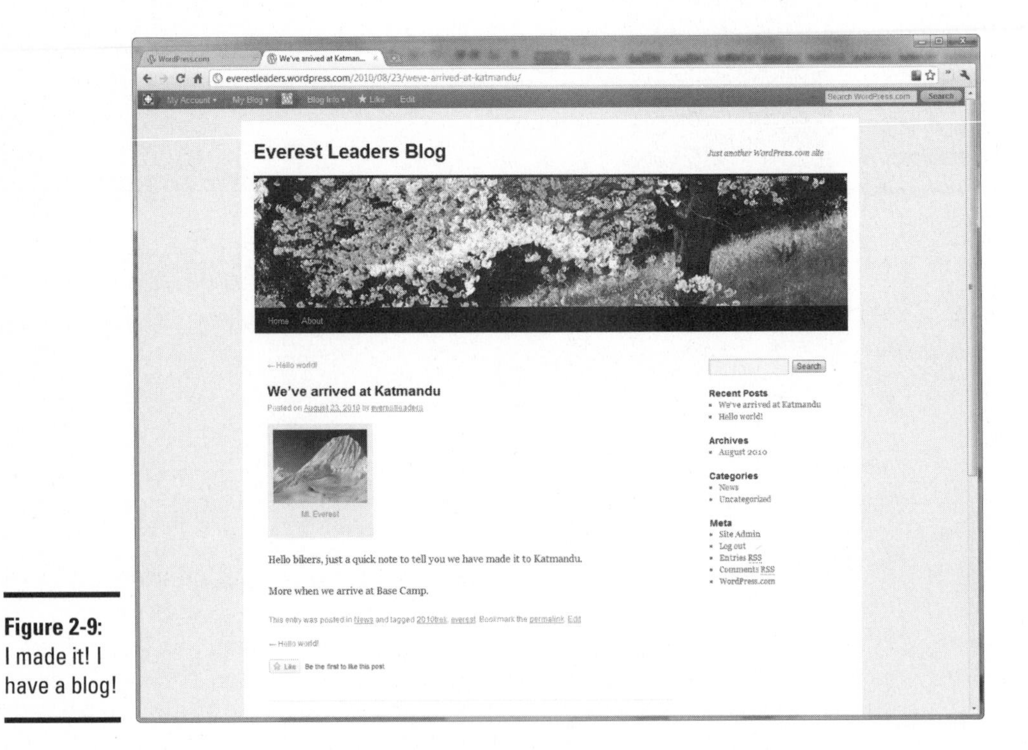

Figure 2-9: I made it! I have a blog!

Managing Your Blog Posts

Each of your blog entries is available in the Posts list, as shown in Figure 2-10. To access the Posts window, click the Posts link on the left side of the Dashboard.

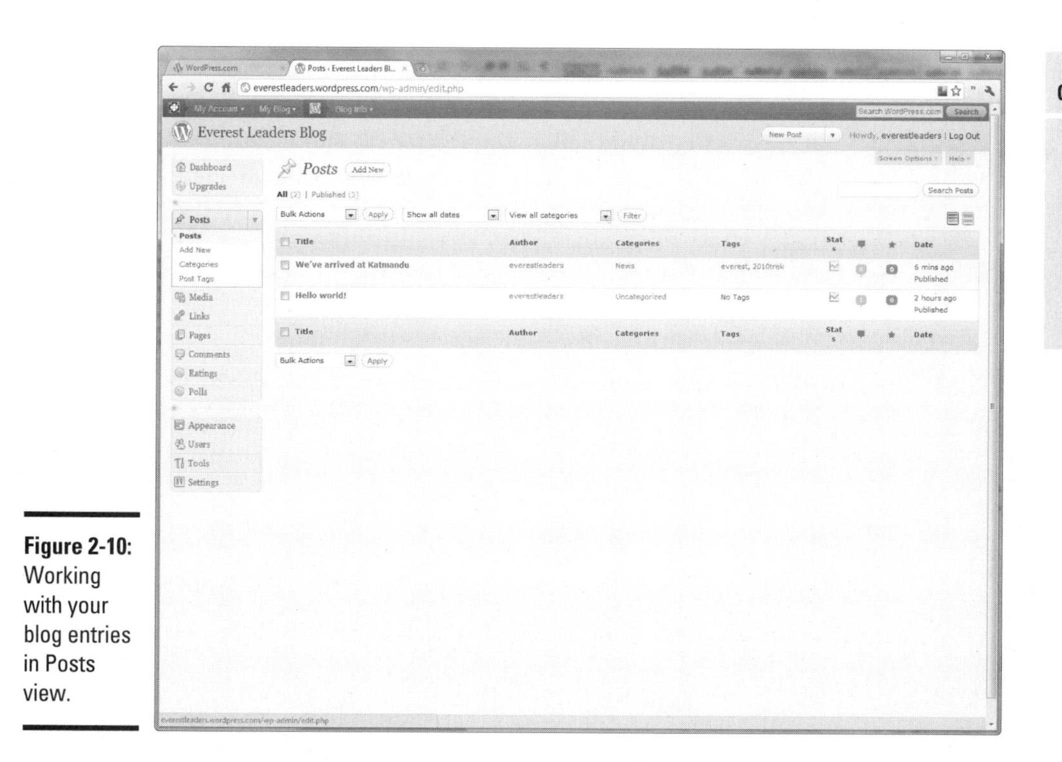

Figure 2-10: Working with your blog entries in Posts view.

You can perform several tasks here:

✦ **Edit a post.** Hover your cursor over the blog title and select the Edit link to display the post in the WYSIWYG editor.

✦ **View the live version of a post.** Hover your cursor over the blog title and select the View link to see the individual post on your blog.

✦ **Edit post details.** You can edit the post details (such as title, category, and tags) by hovering your cursor over the title and selecting Quick Edit.

✦ **Delete posts.** Hover your cursor over the blog title and select the Trash link to banish the post from your blog.

✦ **Search for posts.** When you first start with a new blog, you can easily locate a particular entry you want to work with. However, when your blog grows to include a large number of entries, finding one in particular can be a challenge. Use the Search box to look up an entry.

Designing Your Blog Look

WordPress gives you considerable control over the template, fonts, colors, and layout of your blog. Just as important, modifying your blog design is a breeze.

Perhaps the most important decision you make in your blog design is the template you decide to use. You can choose from several templates with different looks and feels.

1. **In the Dashboard, click the Appearance link on the left side.**

   The Manage Themes page appears (see Figure 2-11).

2. **Browse the themes and look for your favorites.**

3. **When you find a candidate, click the Preview to see what your blog looks like with the theme.**

4. **When you find a theme you like, click the Activate link to change your theme.**

   Your blog is updated to reflect the new look (see Figure 2-12).

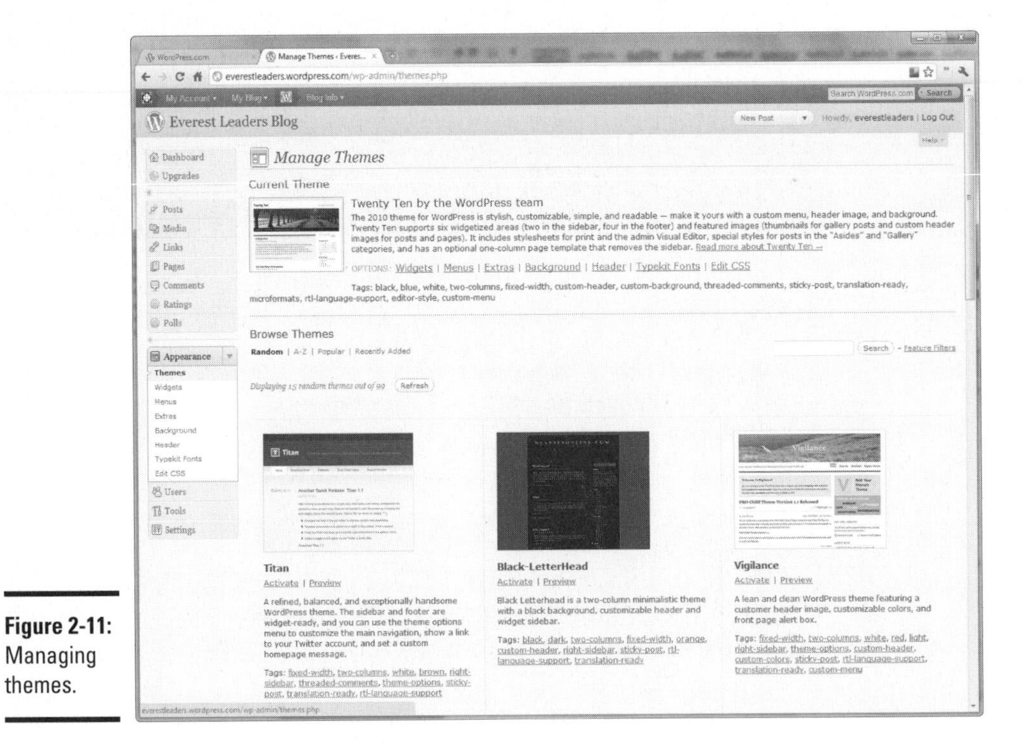

Figure 2-11: Managing themes.

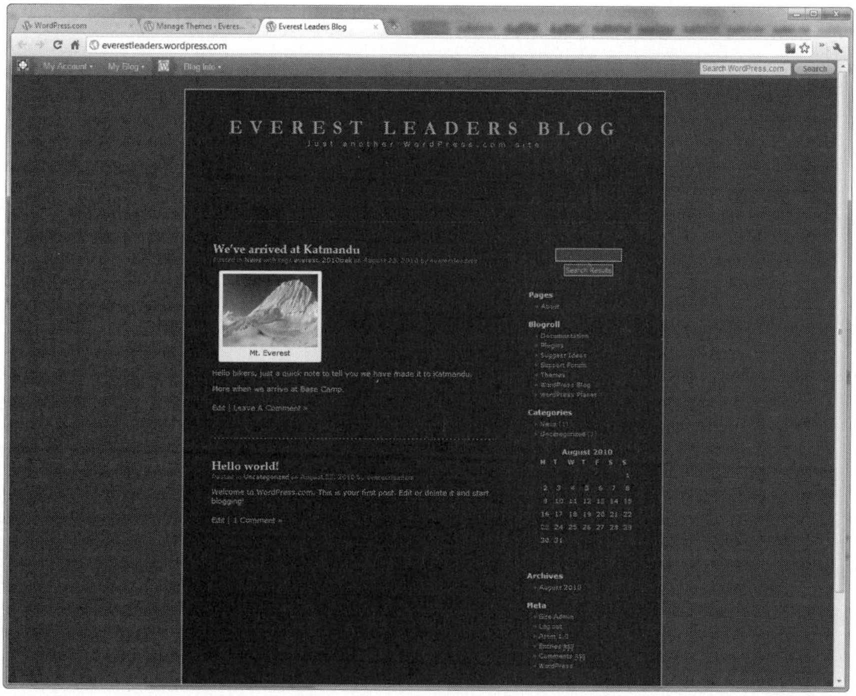

Figure 2-12: Blog with a new template.

WordPress enables you to do a lot of additional customizing beyond the themes; you can add such niceties as these:

- *Widgets,* components that you can add to your blog for additional functionality
- Menus
- Extras, including a Tweet This button, mobile theme, and so on
- Header
- Typekit Fonts, if you want to utilize non-standard fonts on your Web site
- Edit CSS capability (See Book IV for more on Cascading Style Sheets.)

If you want to start tweaking, click the Appearance link in the Dashboard.

Making Posts Outside of WordPress

Although you can make entries to your blog by using the Add Post page that I discussed earlier in this chapter, you might find it more convenient to post using e-mail or by voice.

After these e-mail entries are posted, you can edit them just as you would any other blog entry inside your WordPress Dashboard.

Posting by e-mail

Posting to your blog can be as easy as sending an e-mail message. To post by e-mail, you set up a special e-mail address to send your posts to. Configure it by clicking the My Blogs link in the Dashboard. Figure 2-13 shows the page that's displayed.

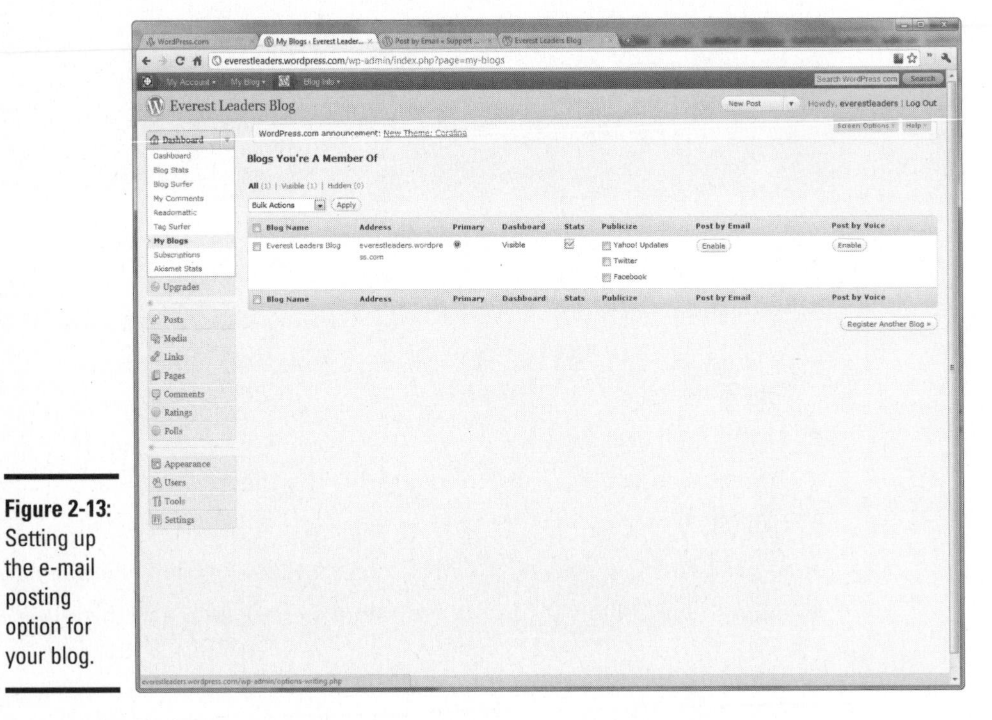

Figure 2-13: Setting up the e-mail posting option for your blog.

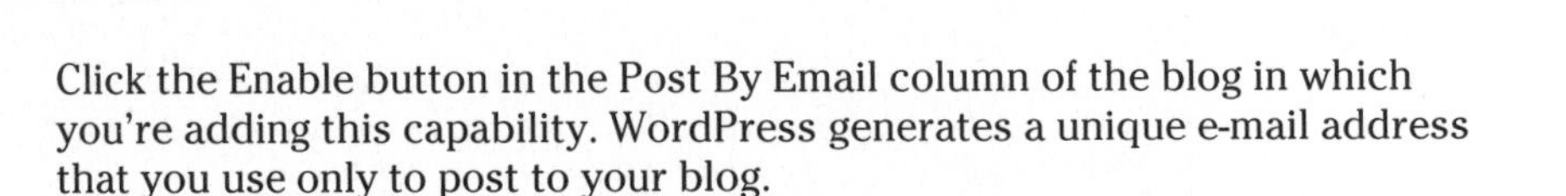
Click the Enable button in the Post By Email column of the blog in which you're adding this capability. WordPress generates a unique e-mail address that you use only to post to your blog.

After you enable e-mail posting, go to your e-mail software and compose a post as an e-mail message (see Figure 2-14). After you send the message, it's posted on your blog in a matter of moments (see Figure 2-15).

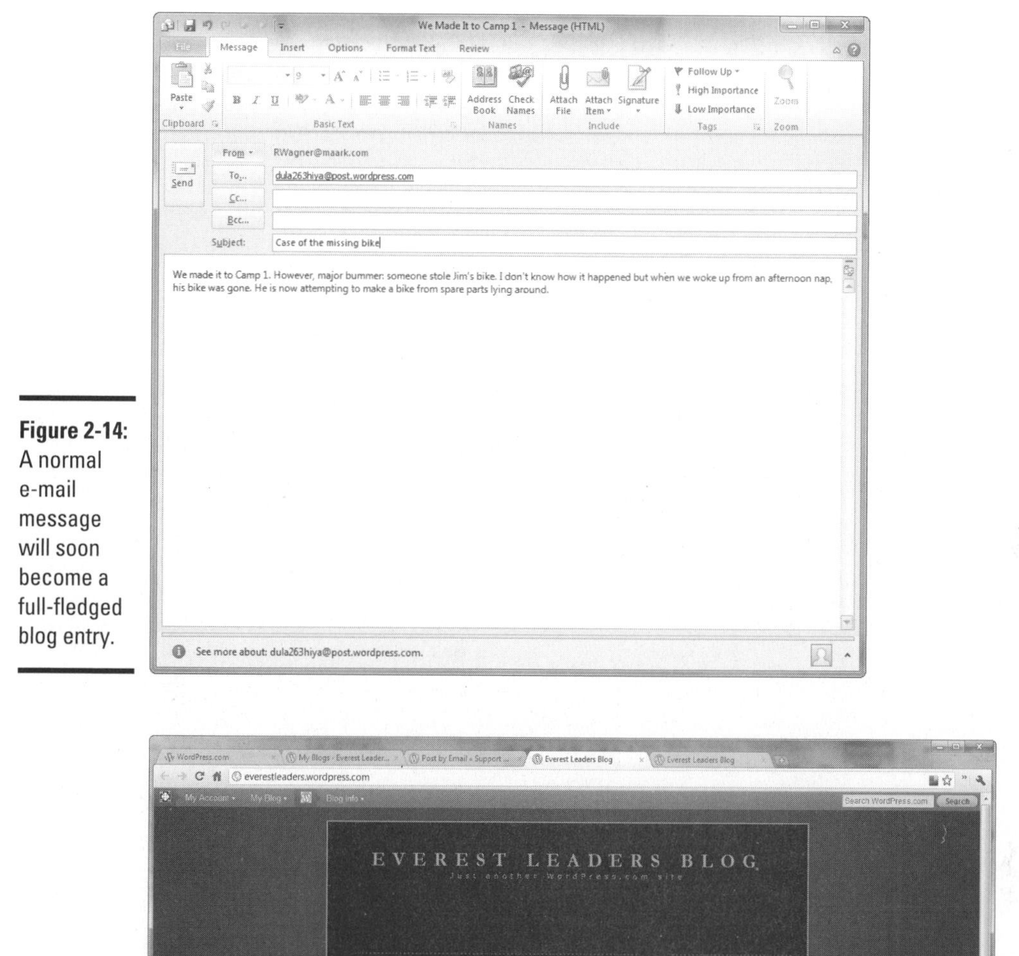

Figure 2-14: A normal e-mail message will soon become a full-fledged blog entry.

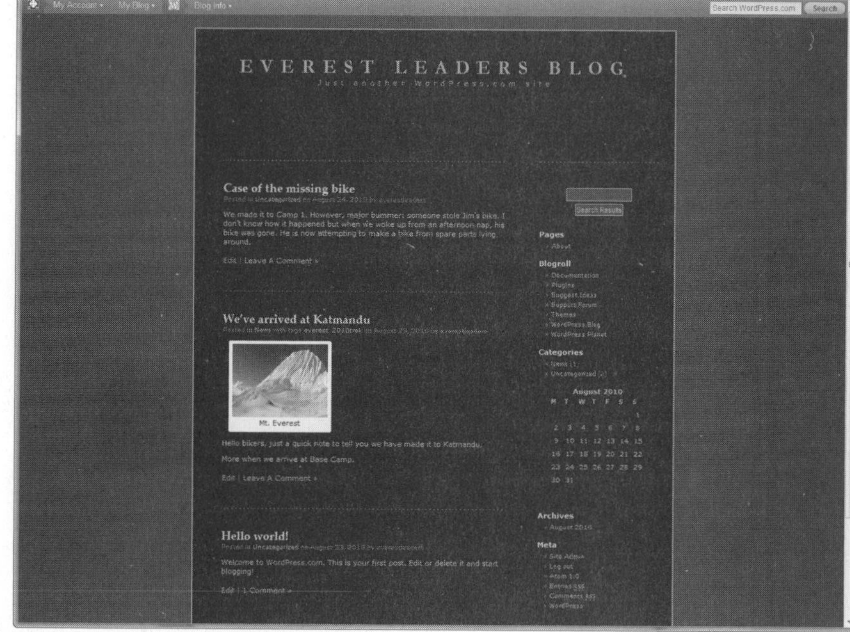

Figure 2-15: Blog post is added seconds later to the WordPress blog.

Creating audio blog entries

In addition to text posts, WordPress allows you to create audio posts as well. To enable this functionality, click the My Blogs link in the Dashboard box (refer to Figure 2-13). Click the Enable button in the Post By Voice column. WordPress displays a phone number and a blog key code that you use to identify your blog.

When you call the phone number and enter your key code, you can then record a voice blog post. When you're done, the audio clip is added as a new post on your blog; Figure 2-16 shows an example.

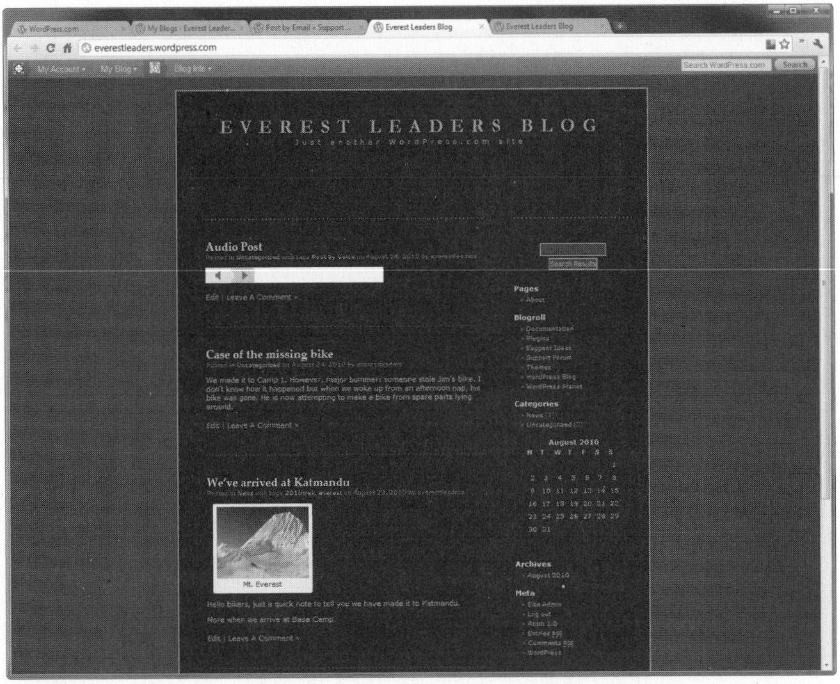

Figure 2-16: Blog posts aren't just text anymore.

By default, the title of the blog entry is simply "Audio Post" — but you can edit the entry to update its title, tags, and category as needed.

Working with Comments

One important issue you have to consider is comments. Readers' comments are a major component of many blogs because they provide

- Interaction between you and your audience
- A sense of community for people coming to your site

To configure comments, click the Discussion link in the Dashboard. The Discussion Settings page appears, as shown in Figure 2-17.

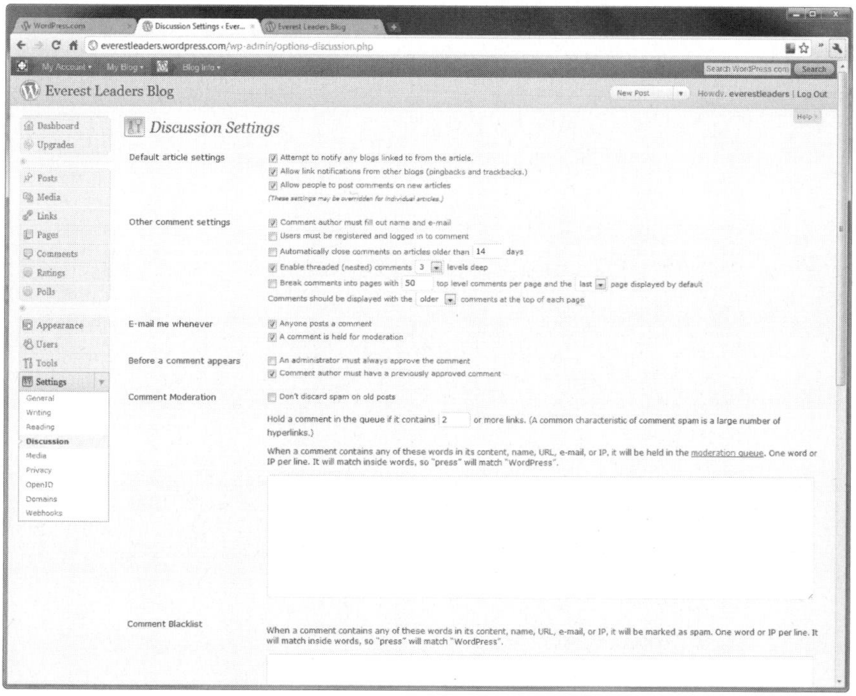

Figure 2-17: Discussion Settings page.

Here some questions to consider as you configure your comment support:

✦ **Do you want to allow comments?** The biggest decision you need to make is whether you want to allow people to comment on your blog entries. By default, this feature is enabled. However, if you prefer to disable comments, deselect the "Allow people to post comments on new articles" check box in the Default Article Settings section. You can also enable/disable comments on a per-article basis in the settings for a blog entry.

✦ **Who do you want to be able to make comments?** After you decide to allow comments, decide who can post: anonymous users, users with a visible username and e-mail address, or only registered WordPress users. Use the options in the Other Comment Settings section to specify further user qualifications.

✦ **Do you want to review comments before they're posted?** By default, a comment is posted publicly and automatically, within moments after the reader saves it provided he/she has commented before. If not, then the blog administrator (you) must approve the comment before it's made public.

This basic level of protection enables you to deter spam comments or inappropriate comments from being posted on your site.

You can modify the default settings in the Before a Comment Appears section of the Discussion Settings page.

The Comments page, accessible from the Comments link on the Dashboard, is the location for reviewing new comments.

Chapter 3: Squarespace

In This Chapter

- ✔ **Understanding what Squarespace can do**
- ✔ **Signing up for Squarespace**
- ✔ **Creating a basic Web site**
- ✔ **Changing the look and layout of a page**
- ✔ **Working with images and text**
- ✔ **Linking your pages**
- ✔ **Publishing your site**

Online Web-site creators are everywhere. You can find plenty of free ones across the Web. Your Internet service provider (ISP) probably has one. Most of the big names of the Web have one, too. A few of these browser-based tools try hard to do almost everything that Adobe Dreamweaver or Microsoft Expression does. (Trust me — they can't.) Other online builders are so limited that you can't do much of anything. However, arguably the most common attribute of these builders — other than that they work inside your browser — is that they can often produce bland, unremarkable, or even downright ugly sites.

Enter Squarespace. While it may not have all of the power of Dreamweaver, you can use it to create a rather impressive Web site, have a strong degree of customization, and have access to your site's HTML and CSS. Although Squarespace does charge a monthly fee, the cost is the equivalent of a typical Web-hosting solution. (Don't worry, they have a free 14-day trial period you can use to try out the service.)

In this chapter, I introduce you to Squarespace and walk you through building a basic Web site. Perhaps the initial site you create is a steppingstone for you — a temporary site as you begin working with Expression (see Book VII) or Dreamweaver (see Book VIII). Or you may find Squarespace to be just the site builder you're looking for.

I should note that this chapter is meant as a primer for Squarespace. Squarespace has many, many more features that couldn't quite be shoehorned into this chapter.

Signing Up for Squarespace

To sign up for Squarespace, go to `squarespace.com` and click the Sign Up button or link. You're taken to a sign-up page, as shown in Figure 3-1. Enter the information in the boxes provided and you're all set. Click the Finish button to be taken to your new Web site.

After you sign in, you see your initial Web site, as shown in Figure 3-2. By default, the URL is `yourdomainname.squarespace.com`, based on what you entered on the sign-up page. In my case, I signed up as `everestleaders`, so my URL is `everestleaders.squarespace.com`.

You're now ready to begin customizing the site for your particular needs.

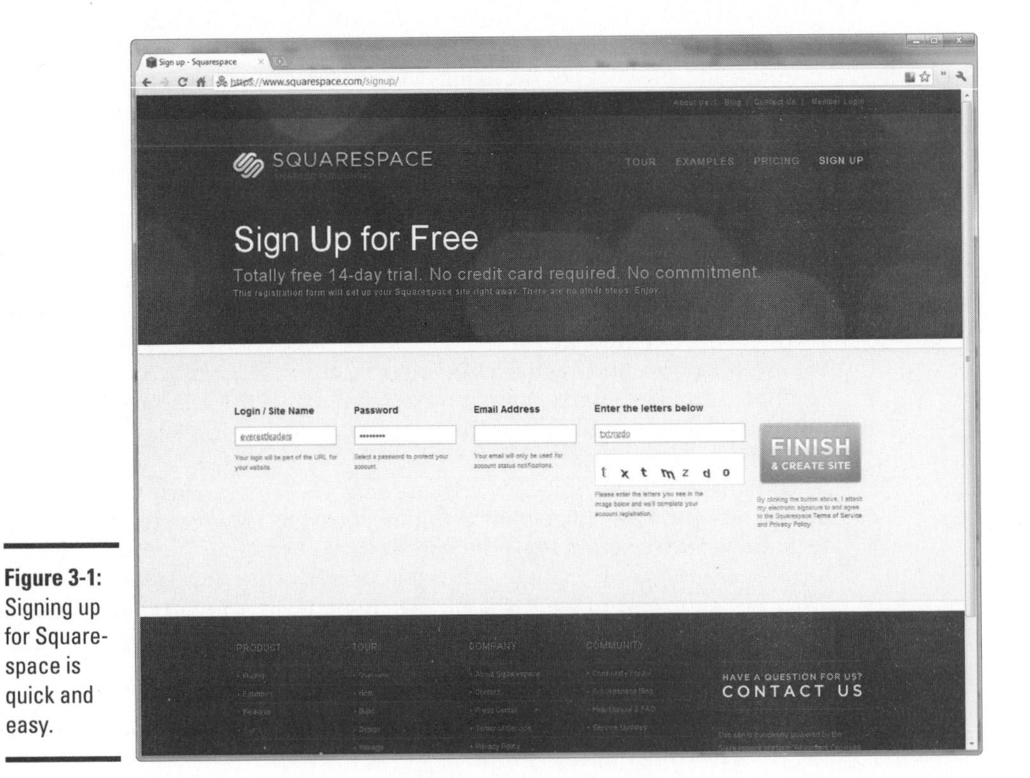

Figure 3-1: Signing up for Squarespace is quick and easy.

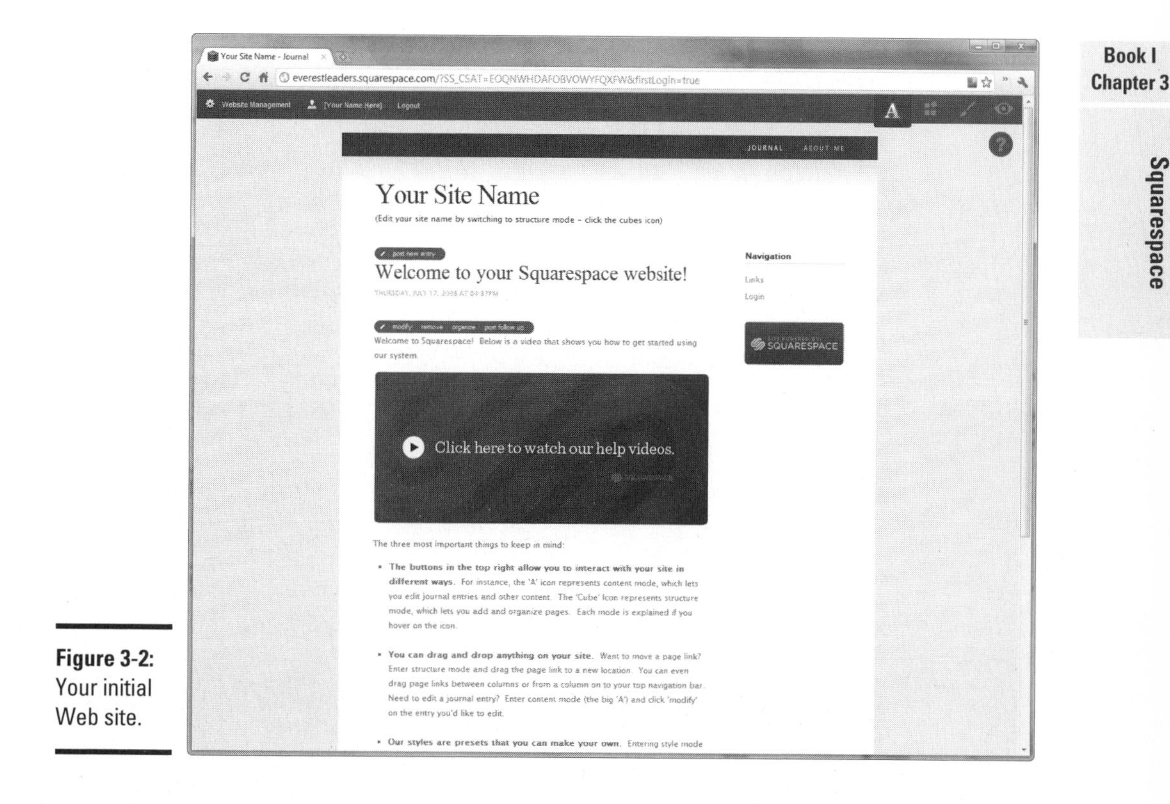

Figure 3-2: Your initial Web site.

Creating a Basic Web Site

Squarespace sets up your site in a blog-style format, but it's equally suitable for creating normal Web sites as well. In the following sections, I show you how to turn your blog into a Web site.

Getting started with your site

The following steps show how you can customize your newly created Web site. When you have the default site that Squarespace gives you when you sign up (refer to Figure 3-2), follow these steps:

1. **Click the Structure Editing button (the cubes icon) in the top toolbar.**
2. **Change the title of your site by clicking the Edit Website Header link at the top of the page.**

   An Edit Website Header dialog box appears; see Figure 3-3.

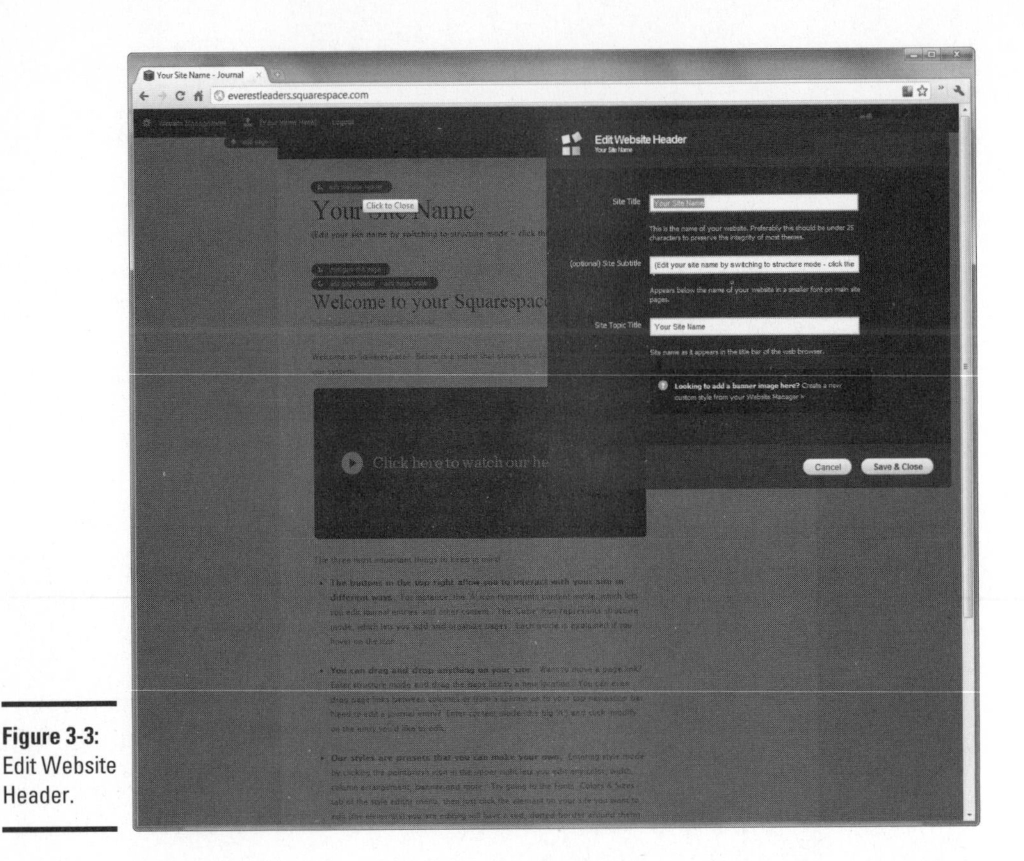

Figure 3-3: Edit Website Header.

3. **Enter your site name in the Site Title box.**

   I typed `Everest Leaders`.

4. **Enter a slogan or subtitle for your page in the Site Subtitle box.**

   If you don't have anything to put in this box, just leave it blank. The dummy text isn't displayed in the actual Web page.

   I entered `World Leaders in Mount Everest Biking Expeditions`. (And you thought that there was no such leader!)

5. **Enter the title as you want it to appear in the browser's title bar.**

   I typed `Everest Leaders - Experts in Expedition Biking`.

6. **Click the Save & Close button to save your changes.**

Creating a home page

The default page is set up as a blog-style journal. To create a traditional-looking Web site, you'll have to make some changes. Follow these steps to add a home page:

1. **Click the Add Page link beside the navigation bar.**

   Squarespace displays the Add New Page page, giving you several page types to choose from (see Figure 3-4). There are many to choose from, but the two standard entries are

   - *Journal* is a standard blog-style entry
   - *HTML* is a standard Web page.

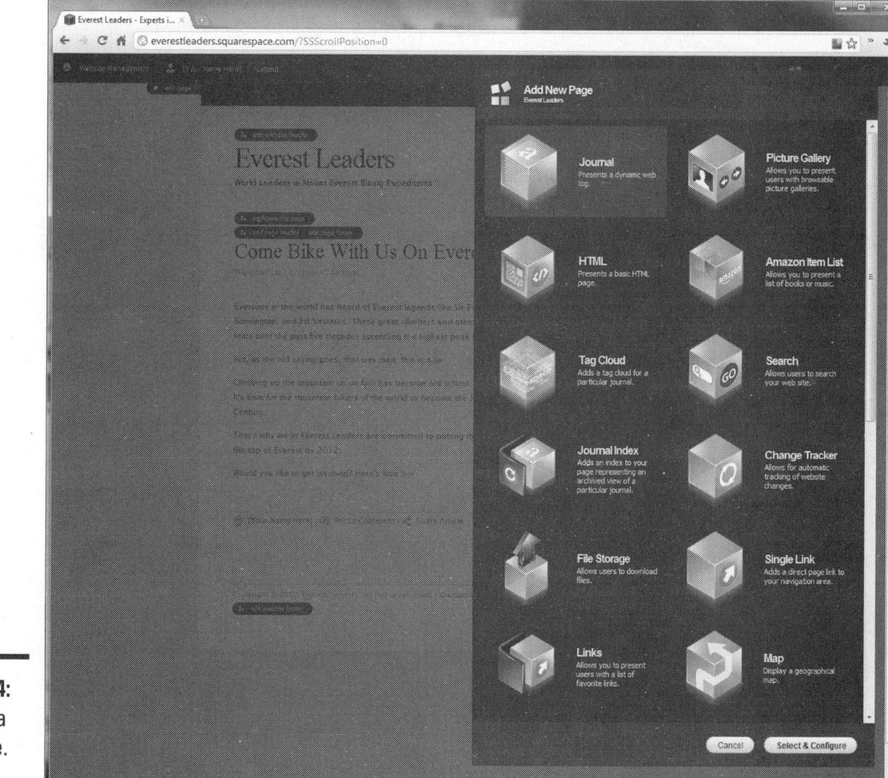

Figure 3-4: Creating a new page.

2. **Select the HTML option and then click the Select & Configure button.**

   The New HTML Page Configuration page appears (see Figure 3-5).

3. **Enter the title of the new page in the Page Title box.**

   As you do so, the Navigation Bar Title and URL Identifier fields are automatically completed, though you can modify those as needed.

   I entered `Everest Leaders` as my Page Title, but changed the Navigation Bar Title to `Home` and the URL identifier to `home`.

   The Navigation Bar Title is shown in the navigation bar for the current page, while the URL identifier allows you to customize the URL for this page.

4. **Click the Create Page button.**

   You return to your initial page. The navigation bar has been updated to include your new page.

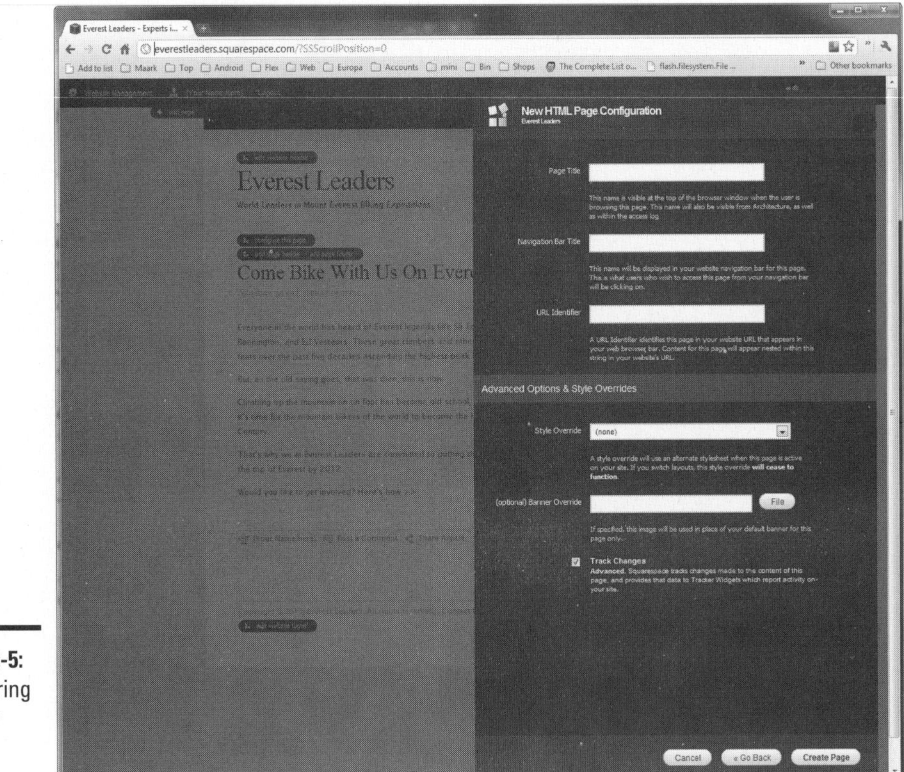

Figure 3-5: Configuring the new page.

5. **Hover your mouse pointer over the New Page link and then click Enable.**
6. **Hover your mouse pointer over the New Page link and then click Configure.**

   The HTML Page Configuration page appears.
7. **Click the Set as Front Page button.**

   Doing so sets this page as the main page for your site.

   Although the vertical navigation bar displays the home page, I actually want to display the home page at the top *horizontal* navigation bar.
8. **(Optional) Drag the Home link from the vertical navigation bar to the far left of the horizontal navigation bar.**

   The Home link is added to the top.

Repeat this process to add new pages to your site. In my case, I also added a Tours page that provides updated information on the tours for the year.

Renaming a page

If you don't like the standard name Squarespace gives a page — for example, you prefer "Blog" instead of "Journal," you can rename your page.

Follow these steps to rename the page:

1. **Click the Structure Editing button.**
2. **Hover the mouse pointer over the Blog link on the top horizontal navigation bar and then click the Configure link.**

   The Journal Page Configuration page appears.
3. **Change the name of the page title and the navigation bar title in the boxes provided.**

   I changed the page title and navigation bar title to `Blog`.
4. **Click the Save Page Configuration button.**

Figure 3-6 shows the navigation bar with the Home link added and two pages — Blog and About Us — renamed.

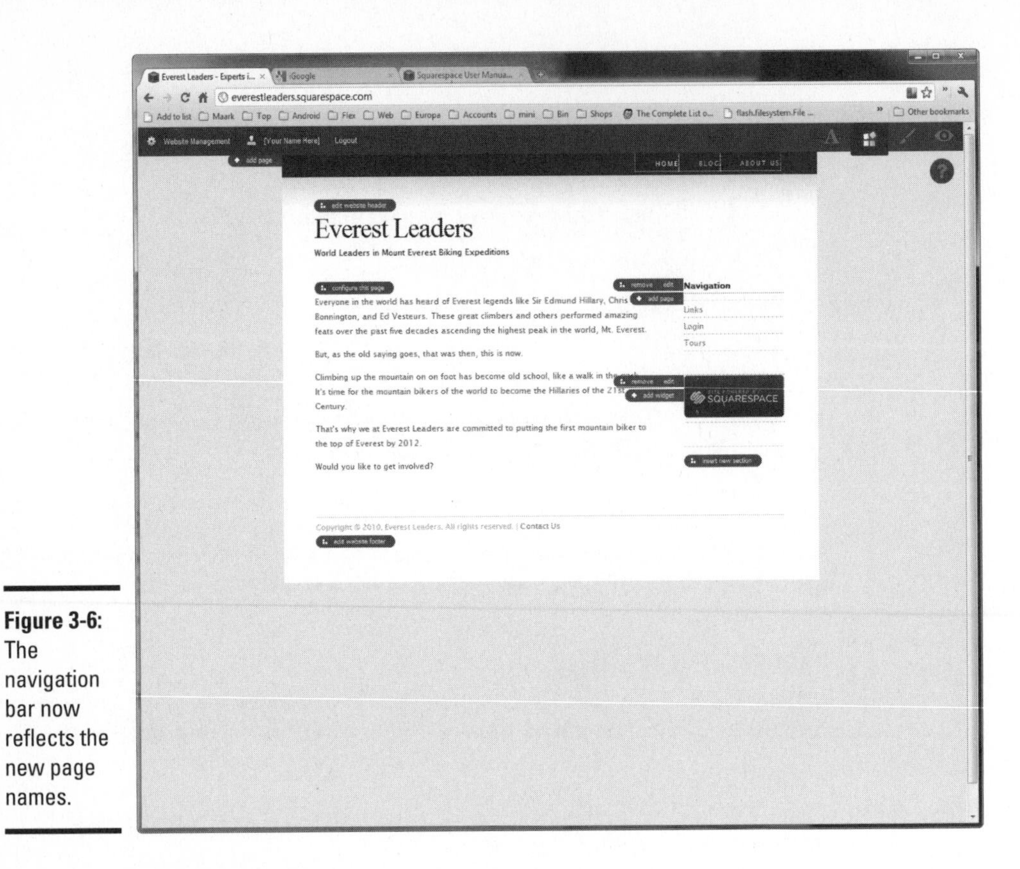

Figure 3-6: The navigation bar now reflects the new page names.

Modifying a page's content

You probably don't want to keep the boilerplate text provided by Squarespace. Follow these steps to change the text.

1. **Click the Content Editing button.**
2. **Click the desired link in the top horizontal navigation bar.**

   In my case, I chose Blog.
3. **Click the Modify Link button just above the post.**

   The Modify Post page appears, as shown in Figure 3-7.

   The page is presented in Raw HTML. If you find HTML intimidating, switch to the WYSIWYG view by selecting it from the View drop-down list.
4. **Update the title and entry text.**

   The content you enter is your visitors' introduction to your Web site. Therefore you should provide a good introduction to who you are and the purpose of your Web site.

   I added a brief blog entry for my Web site (see Figure 3-8).

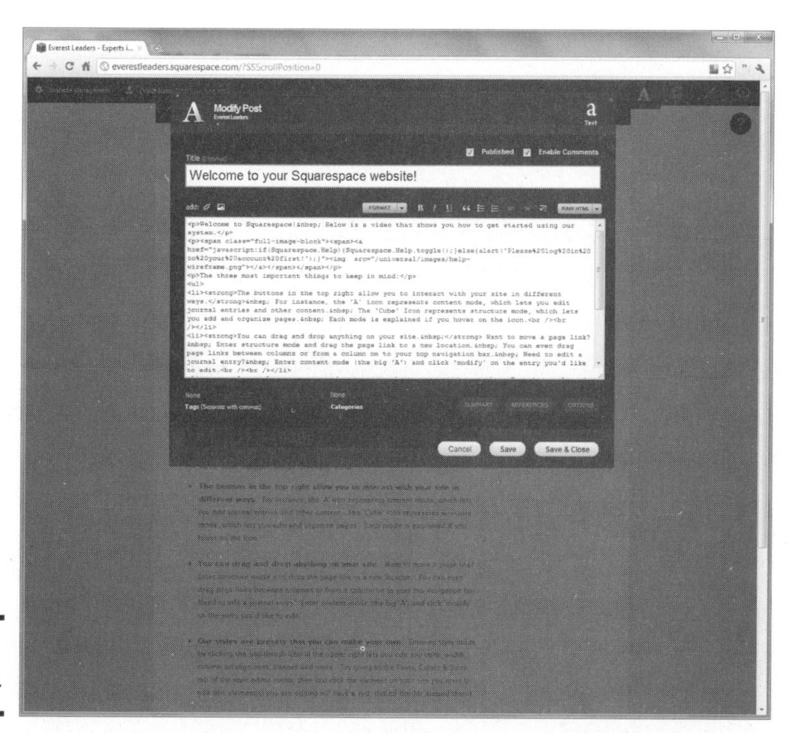

Figure 3-7: Modify Post.

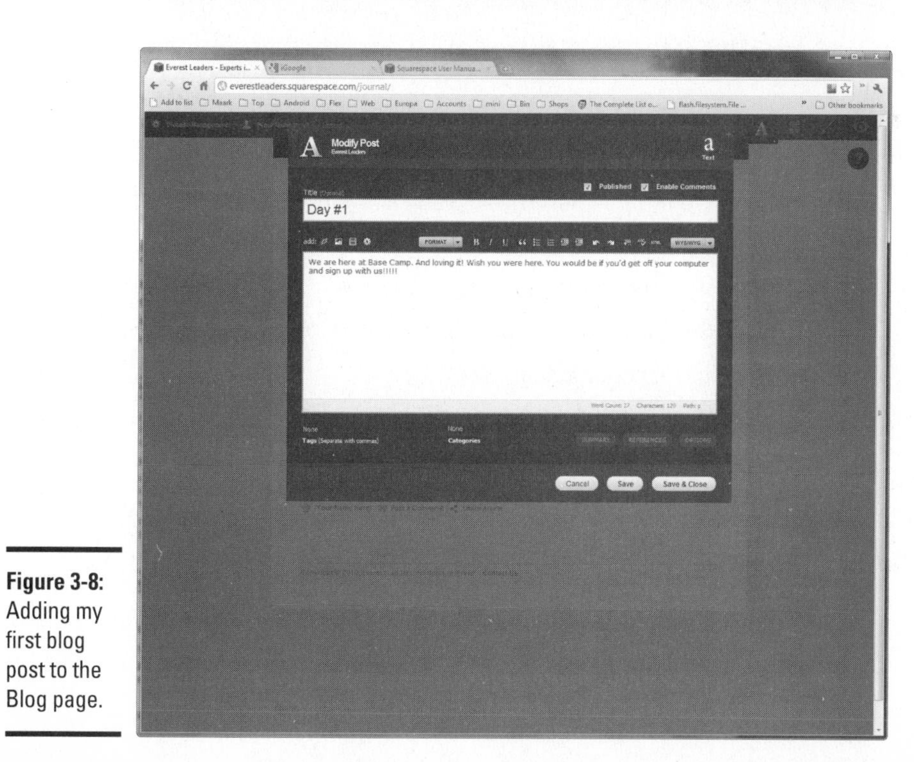

Figure 3-8: Adding my first blog post to the Blog page.

5. **Click the Save & Close button.**

   You return to the Content Editing view.

Adding a footer

A footer is the standard location to add basic copyright information, a usage policy, and often a contact link. You can add a footer to any of your Web site's pages by following these steps:

1. **Click the Structure Editing button.**
2. **Click the Edit Website Footer link at the bottom of the page.**
3. **In the Edit Website Footer page, click Generate Standard Copyright.**

   Standard boilerplate text is added.
4. **Update the text as needed with your company, organization, or personal name.**
5. **(Optional) Add a Contact Us link to the footer by adding the following HTML to the end of your copyright message:**

   ```
   <a href="mailto:youremail@address.com"/>Contact Us</a>
   ```

   Replace `youremail@address.com` with your own address.
6. **Click the Save & Close button.**

   You return to the Home page again.

Changing the Look of Your Site

Squarespace has 15, attractive, well-designed themes you can choose from as you develop your Web site. Each theme has 4 variants, which gives you some 60 template possibilities.

To change the look of your site, follow these steps:

1. **Open your home page.**
2. **Click the Style Editing link in the upper-right corner of the page.**

   The Appearance Editor appears, as shown in Figure 3-9.

   The Appearance Editor enables you to select variances to the basic theme. Or, if you want a completely different look, you can change the theme altogether.

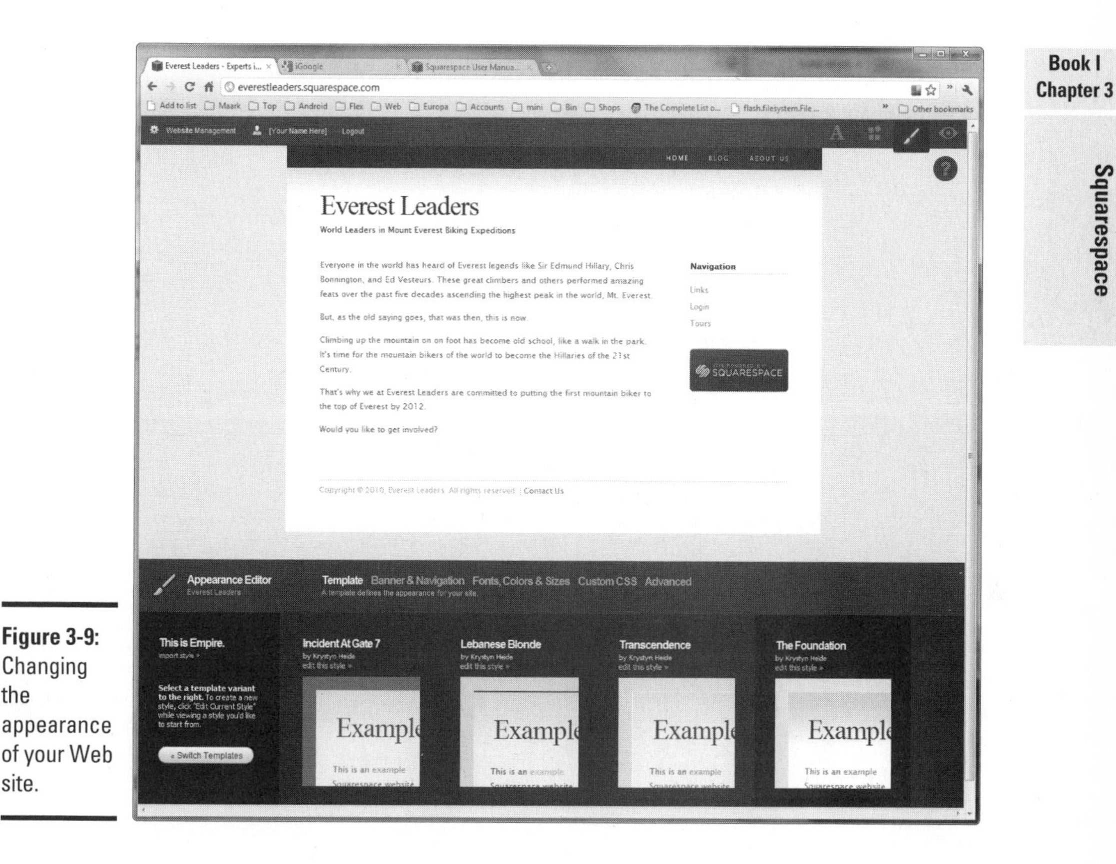

Figure 3-9: Changing the appearance of your Web site.

3. **Click the Switch Templates button.**

   The Appearance Editor now displays thumbnails of different themes that you can use.

4. **Select the theme that looks most appealing.**

   Browse through the designs until you find the one you want to use. You can click any of the templates to preview it. (In my case, I chose `Periodika!`.)

5. **Select the variant you want to use.**

   You can click each of the variants to see a preview of the look as it would appear on your home page.

   I tested each, but settled on `Dirty Rollers`. (See Figure 3-10.)

6. **Click the Enable Style button to make the change.**

   Squarespace updates your Web site with the new design.

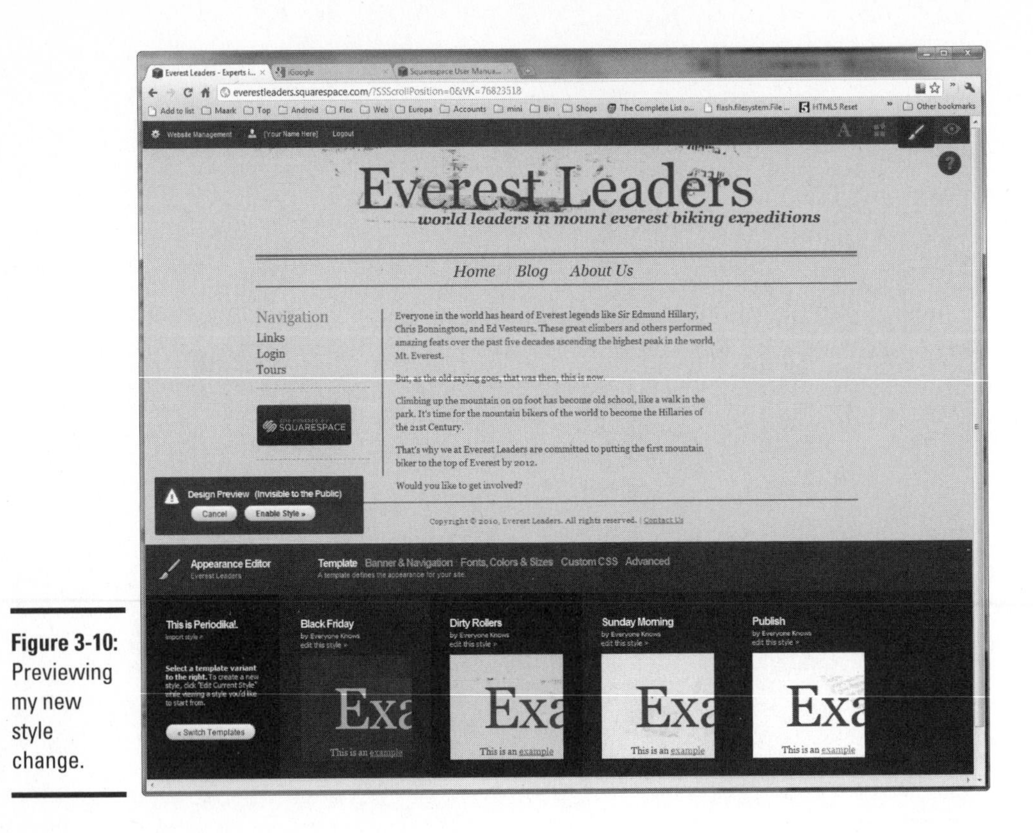

Figure 3-10: Previewing my new style change.

Adding and Removing Sections

Although each template deals with sidebar sections differently, typically you have a sidebar section on the left or right side of a site page's content, and that's where you can display sections. A *section* is a small container of content that can be stacked on top of other such containers. By default, you get a Navigation section and a "Powered by Squarespace" graphic section.

Removing a section

You can remove sections that you don't want to appear on your Web site. For example, if you have the horizontal navigation bar across the top of the Web pages, you may not need the vertical Navigation section in the sidebar. Here's how to remove a section:

1. **Click the Structure Editing button.**

   The site changes to Structure Editing view.

2. **Click the Remove link next to the section you want to remove.**

You're asked to confirm your action.

3. **Click the Confirm button in the Confirm Removal dialog box.**

   The section is removed.

Repeat as needed for other sections. (I also deleted the "Powered by Squarespace" graphic.)

Inserting a section

You can add a variety of *widgets* (components that add functionality to your Web site) and content to serve as a section, including:

- Text or HTML
- "Tag cloud" which is used for blogs
- List of links
- Amazon item list
- RSS feed
- Send e-mail
- Search
- Change tracker
- Journal index
- Form
- Twitter feeds
- Flickr pictures

To use these features, first you want to create a new section and then specify its content. Follow these steps:

1. **Click the Structure Editing button.**

   The site changes to Structure Editing view.

2. **Click the Insert New Section button.**

   The New Section Configuration page appears, as shown in Figure 3-11.

3. **Enter the title for your section.**

   I want to add the Everest Leaders Twitter feed as a section, so I entered `Everest Tweets`.

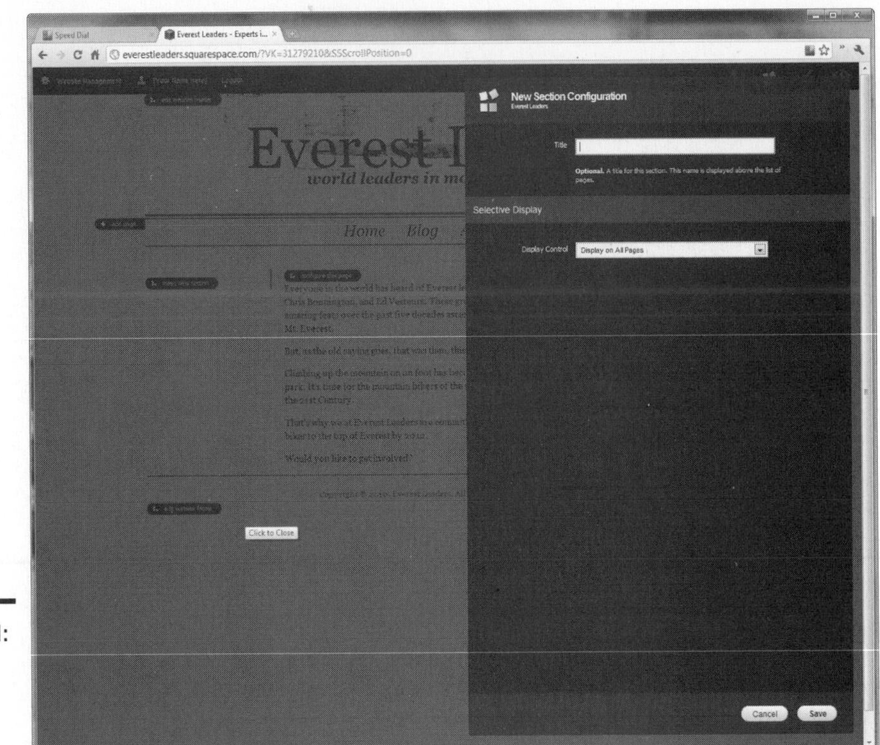

Figure 3-11: Adding a new section.

4. **Select the scope of the section by selecting the desired option in the Display Control list.**

   I kept mine at the default `Display on All Pages`.

   You can also specify whether you want to display the section when specific pages are active.

5. **Click Save.**

6. **Add content to your new section by either clicking the Add Page link or the Widget link.**

   I want to add an RSS feed, so I clicked the Widget link.

   The Add New Squarespace Widget page appears, as shown in Figure 3-12.

   The page displays both Squarespace Widgets and Social Widgets.

7. **Click the Social Widgets tab.**

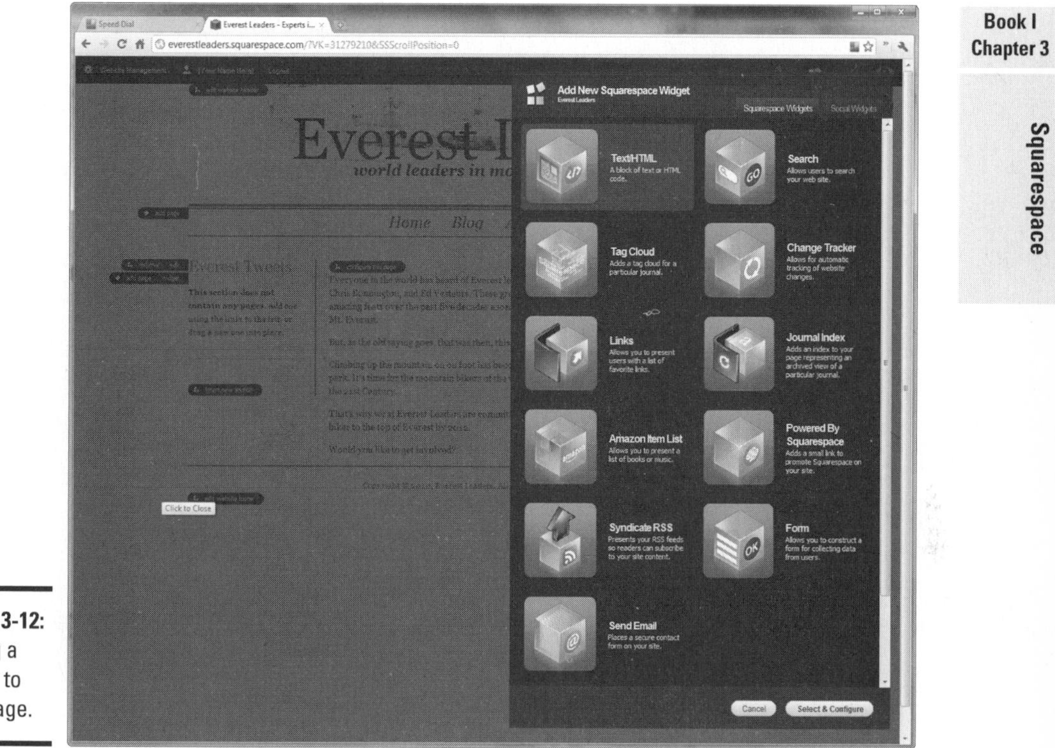

Figure 3-12: Adding a widget to your page.

8. **Click the widget you want and then click the Select & Configure button.**

   The exact configuration page that appears depends on the widget you choose. Figure 3-13 shows the New Twitter Widget Configuration page. You can use this page to specify the Twitter account to follow, the widget's look, and the keyword-filter options.

9. **Click the Create Widget button to add the widget to your Web site.**

   The widget is added to the section, but you have to enable it before it becomes usable.

   You can also configure the widget by hovering your mouse pointer over it and clicking the Configure link.

10. **Click the Enable the Widget button.**

    Figure 3-14 shows the Web site with the new section added.

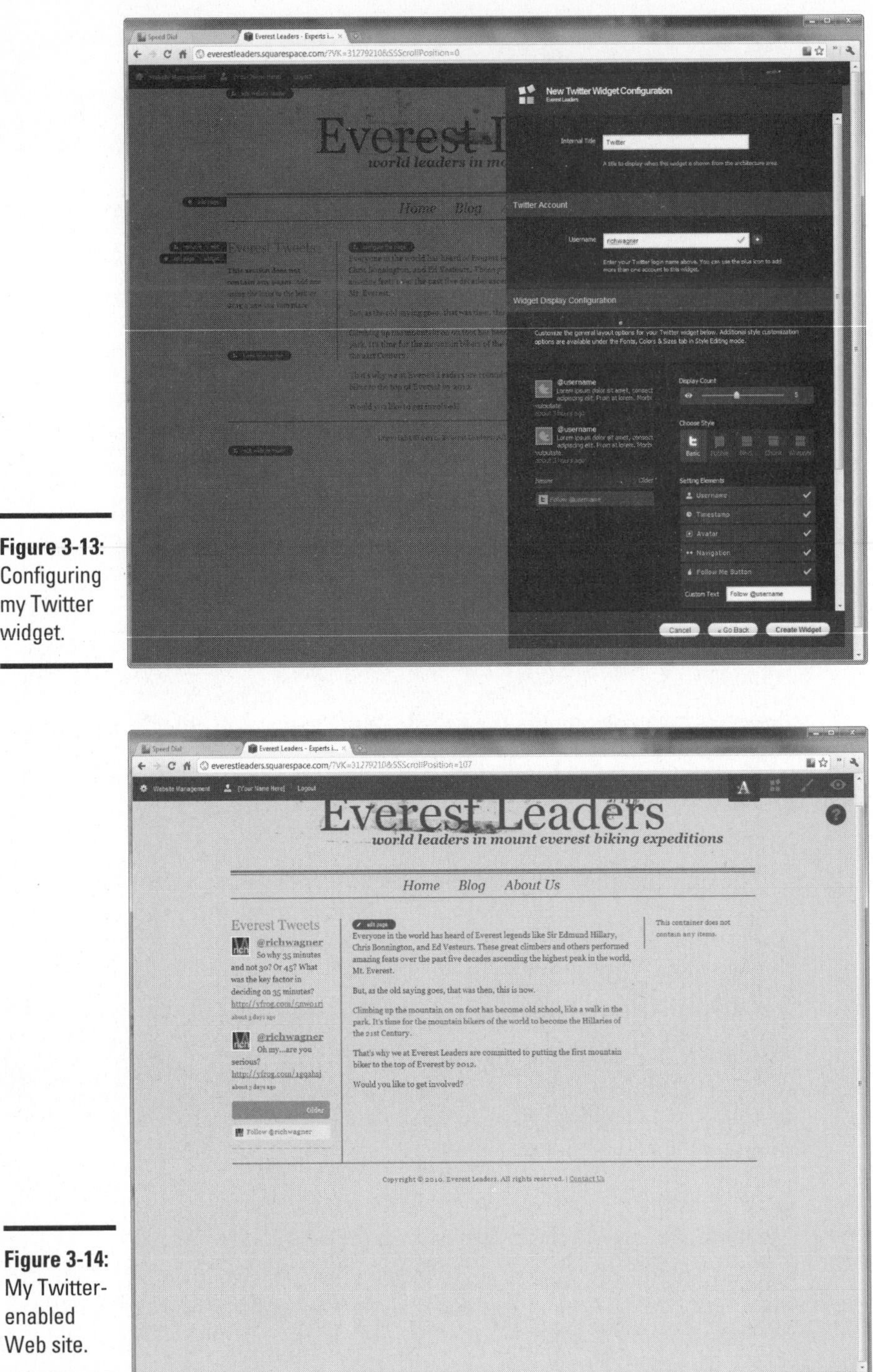

Figure 3-13: Configuring my Twitter widget.

Figure 3-14: My Twitter-enabled Web site.

Adding an Image to Your Page

You can add an image that's stored on either your desktop computer or a Web server to your Web page. Here's how to add a locally stored image:

1. **Open the page where you want to add an image.**
2. **Click the Content Editing button.**
3. **Click the Edit Page link at the top of the page.**

   The Edit Page Content page appears.
4. **Place your cursor at the location in which you want the image displayed.**
5. **Click the Insert an Image button on the toolbar.**

   The Insert Image dialog box appears (see Figure 3-15).
6. **Click the Upload an Image link.**
7. **Click the Choose File button.**

   A dialog box appears for picking the image file.

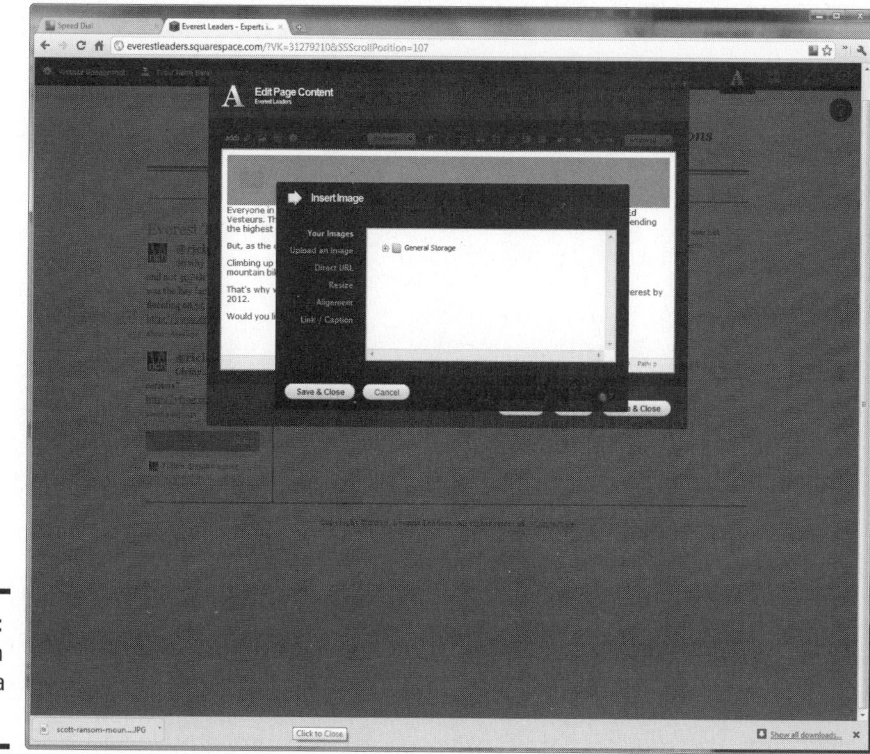

Figure 3-15: Inserting an image into a page.

8. **Select the image you want to add to your Web site and click OK.**
9. **Click the Upload button.**

   Squarespace will ask you if you want to create a thumbnail to the image. If you want to, specify the thumbnail size in pixels and click the Resize Original Image button.
10. **Click the Alignment link.**
11. **Decide how you want the text to wrap around the image.**

    I chose the Left Alignment option.
12. **(Optional) Click the Link/Caption to specify additional options.**
13. **Click the Save & Close button when you're done.**

    You return to the Edit Page Content window.

    If you want to make changes, hover your mouse pointer over the image and select from its menu.
14. **Click Save & Close to save your changes.**

    Figure 3-16 shows the image added to the page.

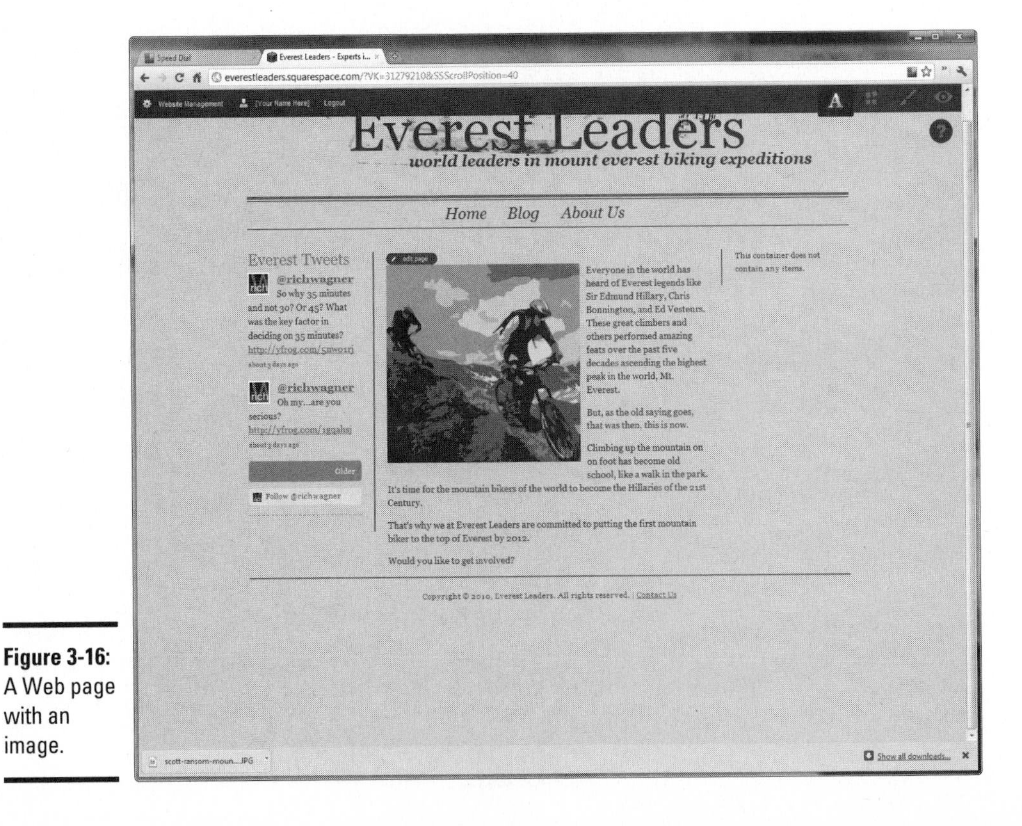

Figure 3-16: A Web page with an image.

Viewing Your Web Site

If, while creating your Web site, you want to preview the site at any time, you can do so by clicking the Preview Website link (the "eye" icon) on the top navigation bar. This action simply prevents all the various edit links from being displayed, although the top Squarespace Website Management toolbar remains where it is.

Alternatively, you can open another browser window and view the Web site as a visitor would (see Figure 3-17).

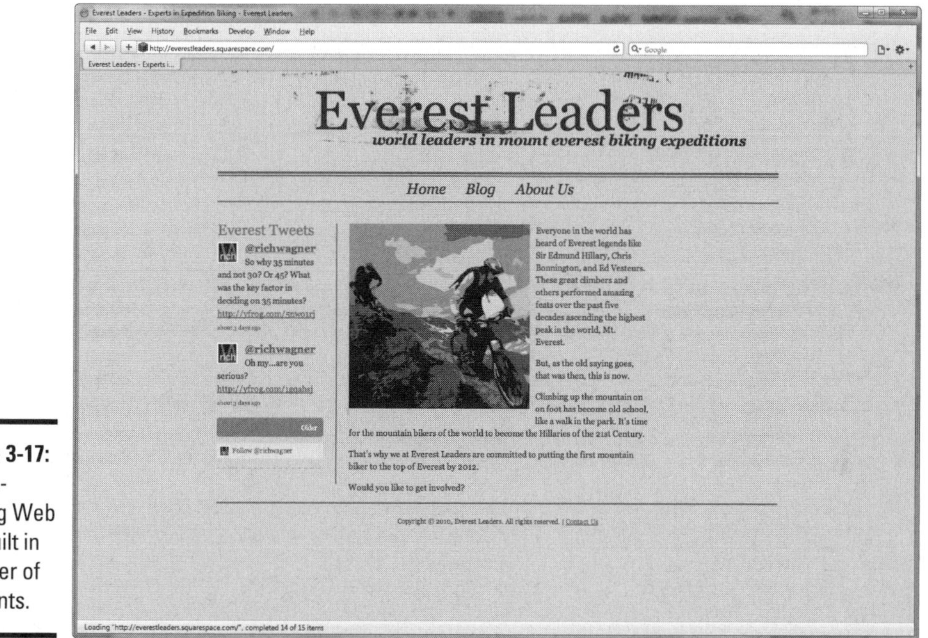

Figure 3-17: A nice-looking Web site built in a matter of moments.

Chapter 4: Connecting Your Site to the Social Web

In This Chapter

- **Adding a Facebook Like button to your site**
- **Using a Tweet button to promote your site**
- **Adding a Google Friends gadget to your page**

A decade ago, Web sites that you created and promoted were your "digital home" on the Internet. However, with the rapid rise of social Web sites such as Facebook and Twitter, you can go beyond your Web site to reach out to people. As a result, as you design and build your Web site, you want to be sure to integrate any of your social Web presences with your Web site.

In this chapter, I show you how you can connect your site to Facebook, Twitter, and Google Friends.

When you integrate with other sites, typically you're pasting HTML or JavaScript code into your Web pages. If that sounds intimidating or alien to you, see Books III and V first and then come back when you're comfortable working with HTML and JavaScript.

Connecting to Facebook

Facebook, the popular social Web site for connecting to friends and family, allows you to integrate your Web site with your Facebook wall. You can add what Facebook calls "social plugins" to your pages or blog postings. Small HTML snippets are easy to configure and paste into your Web page. These include the following:

- **Like Button:** This button allows your Web-site viewers to share your page/post on their Facebook profiles. See `http://developers.facebook.com/docs/reference/plugins/like`.
- **Like Box:** You can have your Web-site viewers like your Facebook wall from your Web site. See `http://developers.facebook.com/docs/reference/plugins/like-box`.

- **Activity Feed:** Shows your Web-site viewers the most interesting activity on your Facebook wall. See `http://developers.facebook.com/docs/reference/plugins/activity`.
- **Recommendations feed:** Shows your suggestions for pages or content on your Facebook wall. See `http://developers.facebook.com/docs/reference/plugins/recommendations`.
- **Facepile:** Shows profile pictures of other users who have signed up for your Web site. See `http://developers.facebook.com/docs/reference/plugins/facepile`.
- **Login Button:** Like Facepile, displays profile pictures of your friends who are logged in to your Web site. It has a login button as well. See `http://developers.facebook.com/docs/reference/plugins/login`.
- **Comments:** Enables your Web-site viewers to comment on your site via their Facebook profiles. See `http://developers.facebook.com/docs/reference/plugins/comments`.
- **Live Stream:** Allows you to share activity and comments in real-time. See `http://developers.facebook.com/docs/reference/plugins/live-stream`.

You must be registered as a Facebook developer to enable the Comments and Live Stream plugins. Go to `http://developers.facebook.com`.

In the following sections, I walk you through how to add two of the most popular of these plugins to your site.

Adding a Like button

You can add a Facebook Like button to your Web site to share your content on the visitor's Facebook profile. To quickly add a Like button, follow these steps:

1. **Open your Web page in the editor of your choice.**

   If you're using Adobe Dreamweaver or Expression Web, open the HTML page on your desktop. Or, if you're using an online site builder or blog, open the online editor.

2. **View HTML code for your page.**
3. **Locate the location in your page in which you want to add the Like button.**

4. **Paste the following code into your page:**

```
<iframe src="http://www.facebook.com/widgets/like.
   php?href=http://yourdomain.com"
    scrolling="no"
    frameborder="0"
    style="border:none; width:450px; height:80px">
</iframe>
```

Replace *yourdomain.com* with the name of your domain. Figure 4-1 shows the code inserted into a page on my Squarespace Web site.

5. **Save the changes.**
6. **Preview your Web page.**

The Like button appears, as shown in Figure 4-2.

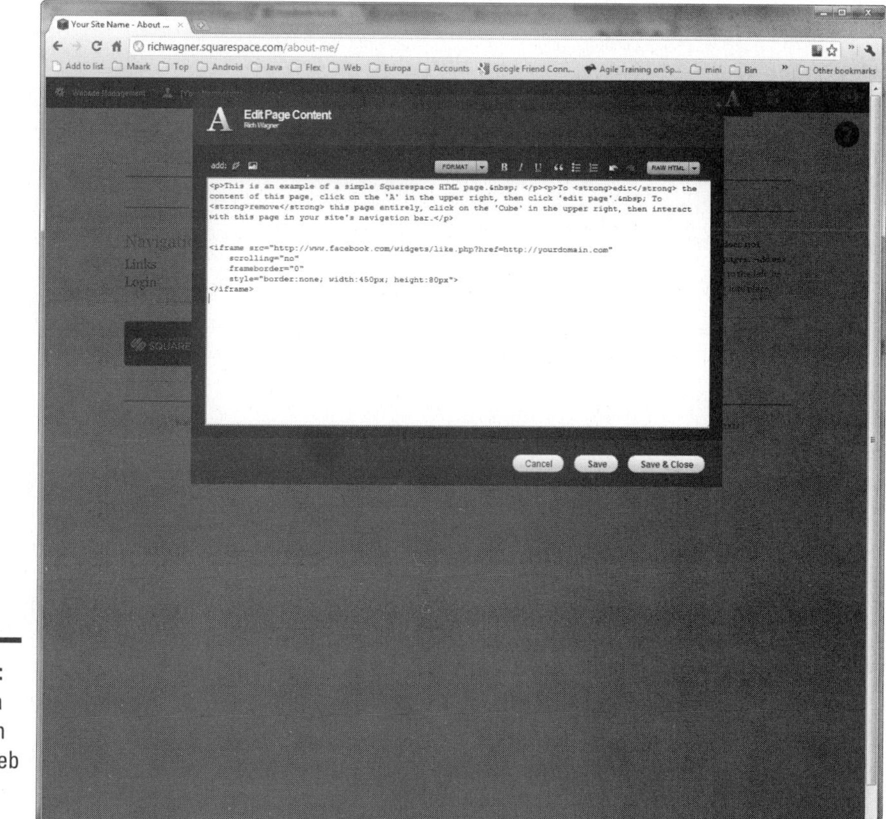

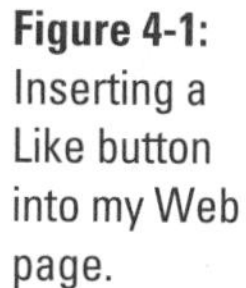

Figure 4-1: Inserting a Like button into my Web page.

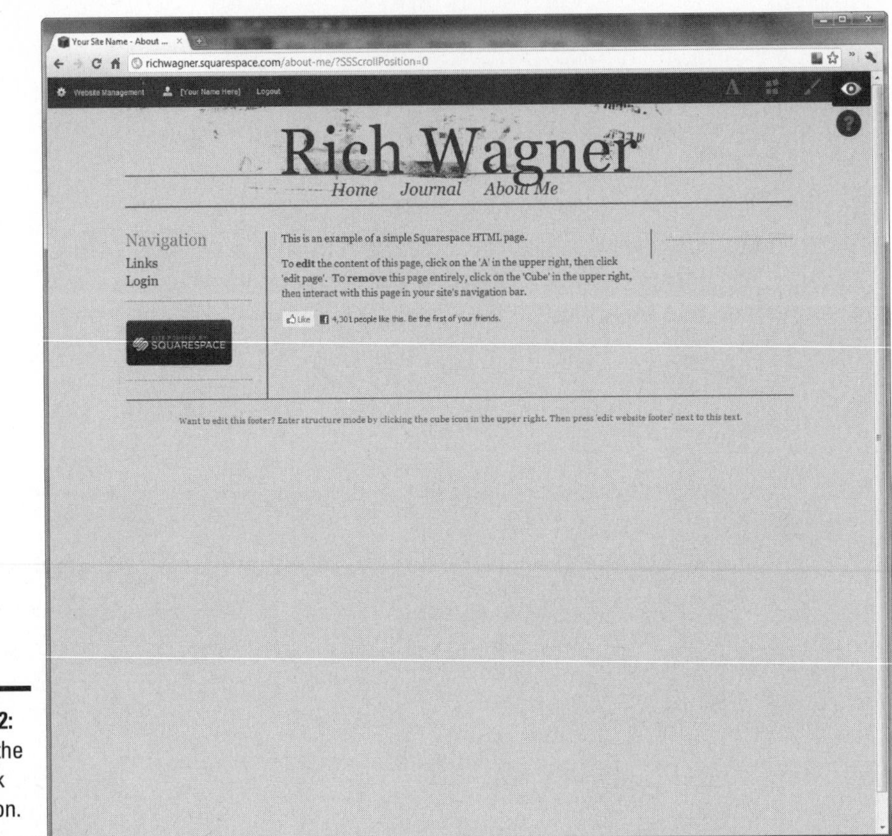

Figure 4-2: Viewing the Facebook Like button.

If you'd like to do more customizing, go to `http://developers.facebook.com/docs/reference/plugins/like` and fill out the form shown in Figure 4-3. You can then copy and paste that HTML code into your Web page.

Adding a Like box

You can also add a Facebook Like Box plugin to a Web page or blog post to promote your Facebook wall. To do so, follow these steps:

1. **Go to `http://developers.facebook.com/docs/reference/plugins/like-box`.**

   Figure 4-4 shows the Like Box configuration page.

2. **Enter the URL of your Facebook wall in the space provided.**

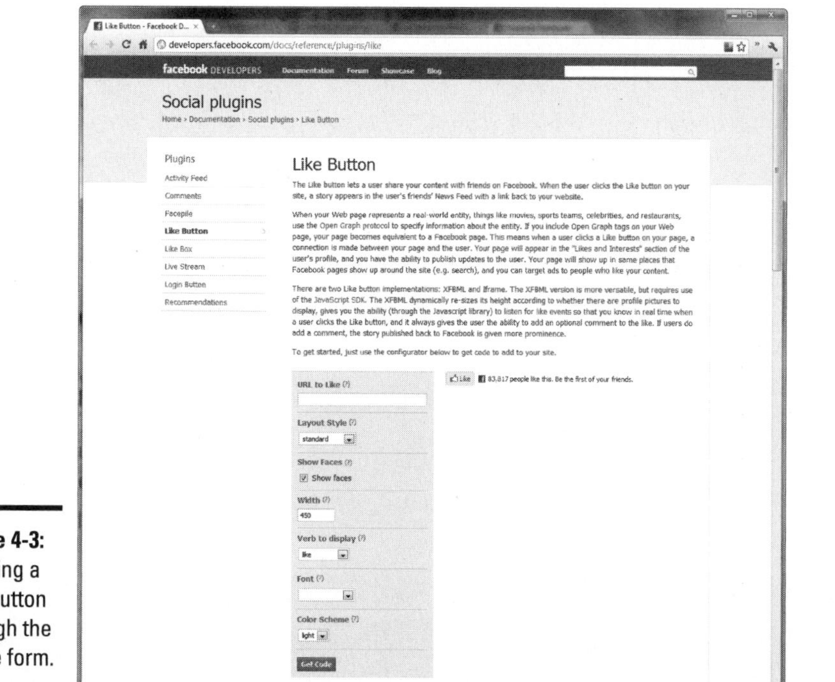

Figure 4-3: Creating a Like button through the online form.

Figure 4-4: Configure your Like Box.

3. **Specify the desired width in the Width box.**

The size you choose depends entirely on where you plan to place it on your Web page. Go to your Web page and measure the width of the column or area in which you're inserting your box. If you need a tool to measure your page, download a free utility at `www.spadixbd.com/freetools/jruler.htm`.

In my case, I chose 292px.

4. **Customize the Connections, Stream, and Header options as you want.**

I chose 10 connections and enabled the stream and header options.

5. **Click the Get Code button.**

Your plugin code appears in the dialog box, as shown in Figure 4-5.

6. **Copy the HTML code provided in the I-frame box.**

The XFBML is generally for more advanced usage.

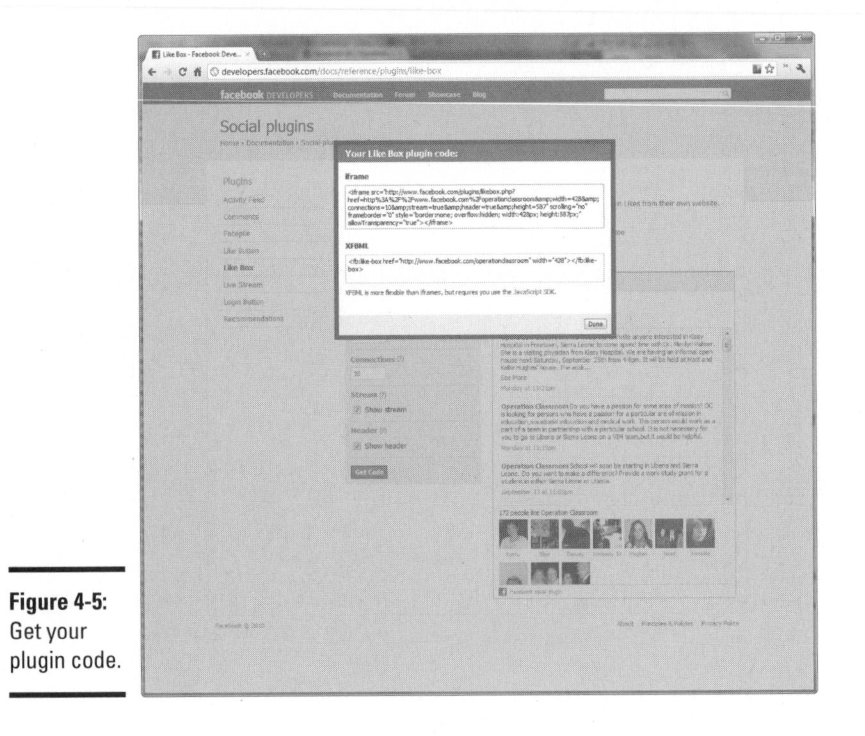

Figure 4-5: Get your plugin code.

7. **Open your Web page in the editor of your choice.**

   If you're using Adobe Dreamweaver or Expression Web, open the HTML page on your desktop. Or, if you're using an online site builder or blog, open the online editor.

8. **View HTML code for your page.**

9. **Locate the place you want to add the Like Box.**

10. **Paste the plugin code from the Clipboard into your page.**

    Figure 4-6 shows the plugin code pasted into my Dreamweaver page.

11. **Save your page.**

12. **Preview your Like box on your Web site.**

    Figure 4-7 shows the Like box on a Web page.

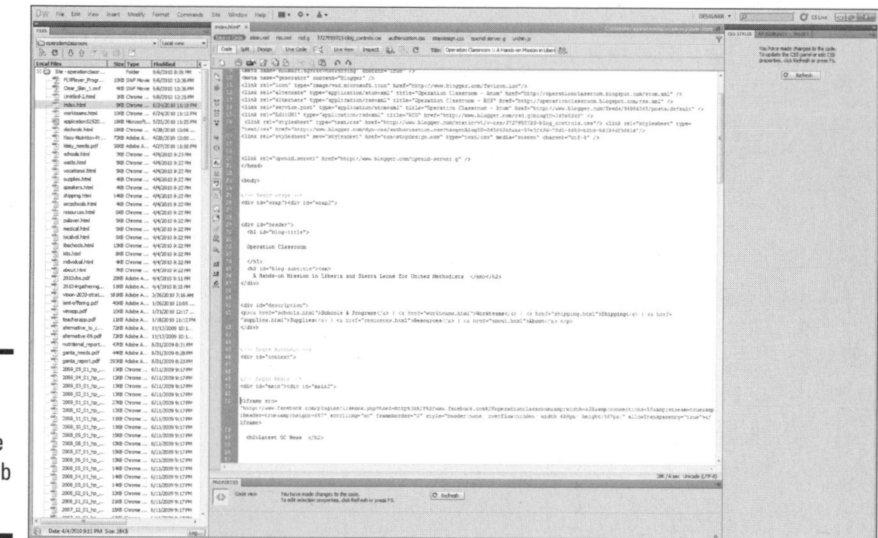

Figure 4-6: Adding plugin code into my Web page.

You can also perform more advanced integration, such as enabling visitors to log in to your Web site using their Facebook accounts. For more details, visit `http://developers.facebook.com/docs/guides/web`.

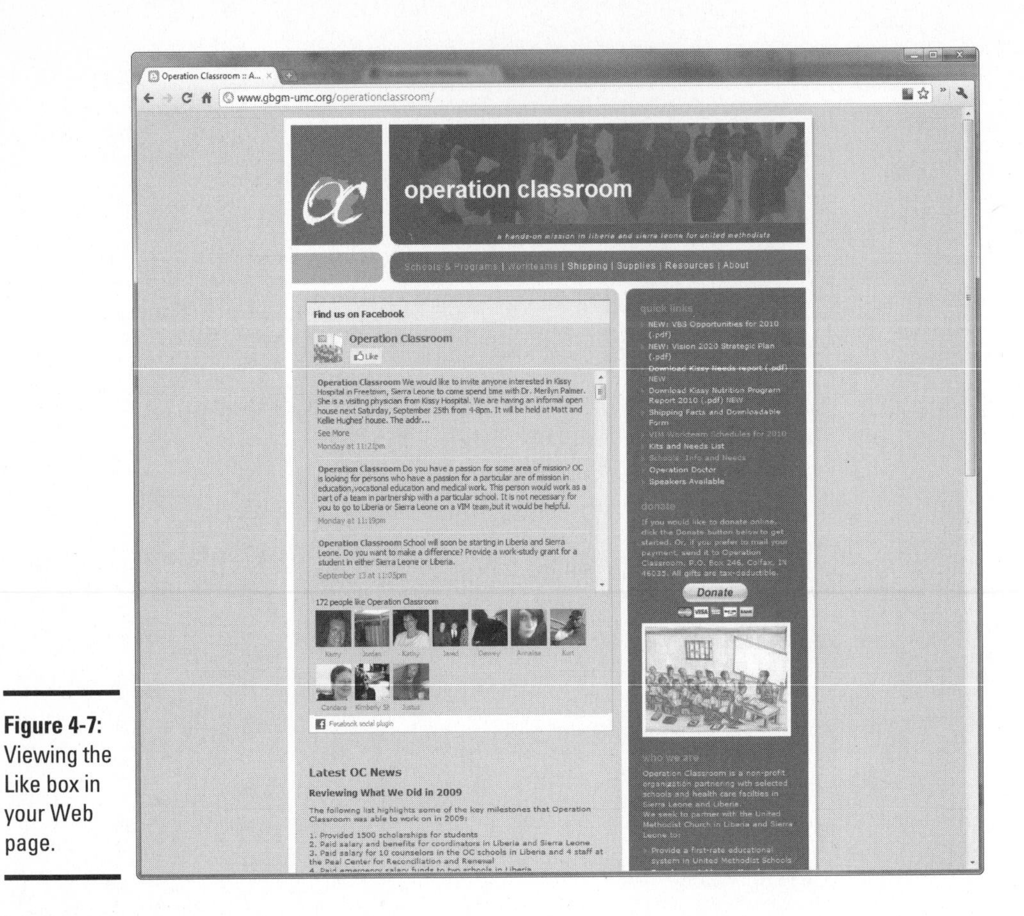

Figure 4-7: Viewing the Like box in your Web page.

Connecting to Twitter

Twitter is a social networking service that enables you to send short text messages (called *tweets*) to people who follow you and to read tweets from people you follow.

You can connect your Web site to Twitter to encourage your Web-site viewers to share your Web pages or blog posts via tweeting. Then, when visitors tweet your content, they'll drive their followers to your Web site.

To add a Tweet button to your Web site, follow these steps:

1. **Go to** `http://twitter.com/goodies/tweetbutton`**.**

   Figure 4-8 shows the Tweet Button editor page.

2. **Choose the style of button that you want to use from the Button tab.**
3. **Click the Tweet Text tab.**

4. **(Optional) Specify the text to use in the tweet.**

   If you don't specify the text, then the title of the page the button is on is what appears in the tweet.

   Customize this text so you can easily target your message.

5. **Click the URL tab.**
6. **(Optional) Enter a URL for the tweet.**

   If you don't specify a URL, then the current page is used for the URL.

7. **(Optional) Click the Language tab and specify a language.**
8. **(Optional) To recommend your Twitter account, add your Twitter account name in the Recommend section.**

   You can suggest an additional account as well.

Figure 4-8: Customize your Tweet button.

9. **Preview your button in the Preview area.**
10. **Copy the HTML code from the code box to your Clipboard.**
11. **Open your Web page in the editor of your choice.**

    If you're using Adobe Dreamweaver or Expression Web, open the HTML page on your desktop. Or, if you're using an online site builder or blog, open the online editor.
12. **View HTML code for your page.**
13. **Locate the place in your page in which you want to add the Tweet button.**
14. **Paste the plugin code from the Clipboard into your page.**
15. **Save your page.**
16. **Preview your Tweet button on your Web site.**

    Figure 4-9 shows the Tweet button when it appears on a Web page.

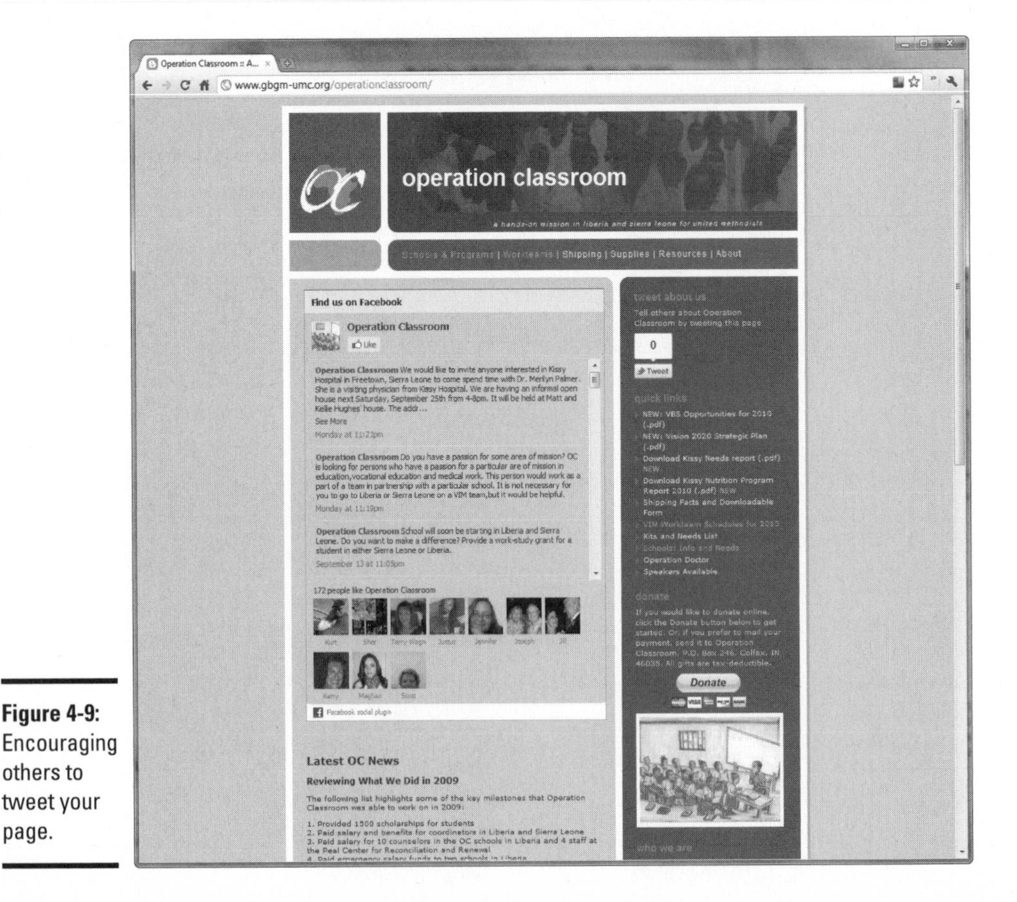

Figure 4-9: Encouraging others to tweet your page.

Connecting to Google Friends

Google Friends Connect is a service provided by Google that allows visitors of your Web site to connect with their friends on your Web site. It allows Web-site visitors to add comments to your blog with their Google Profile or to communicate with their friends using your Web site as a hub.

To add Google Friends to your Web site, sign in to your Google account and follow these steps:

1. **Go to** `www.google.com/friendconnect`**.**
2. **Click the I Agree button to agree to the terms of service.**

   After you agree, the Tell Us About Your Web Site page appears, as shown in Figure 4-10.
3. **Enter your Web site's name and URL in the spaces provided.**
4. **Click Continue.**
5. **Click the Add the Members Gadget button.**

   The Gadget editor appears.

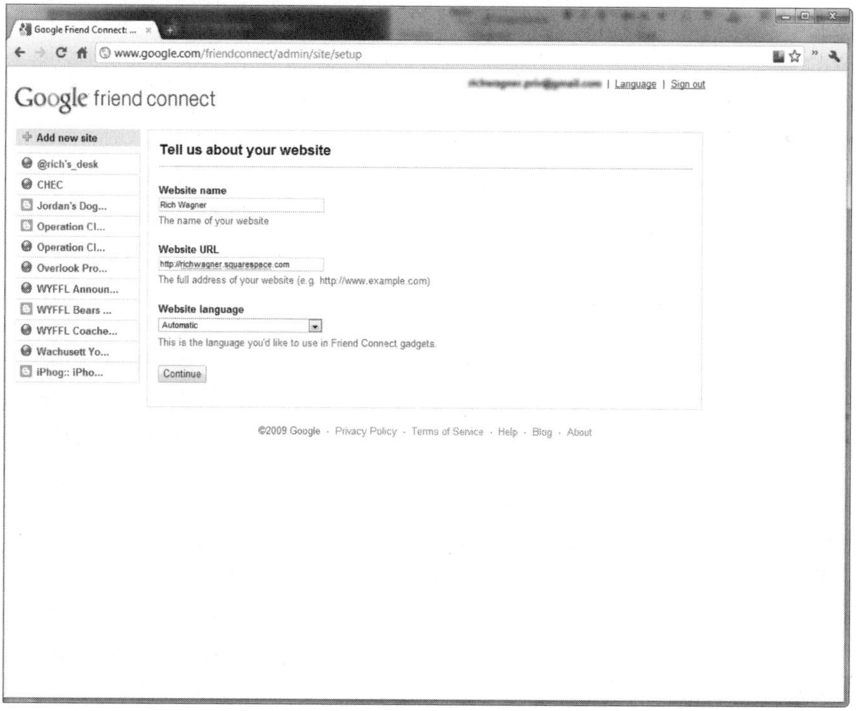

Figure 4-10: Connecting with Google Friends.

6. **In the first section, enter the width of the gadget and the number of rows that you want to display faces.**
7. **(Optional) Modify the colors in the second section.**
8. **Click the Generate Code button.**

   The code that you'll copy and paste into your Web site is generated and displayed in the box, as shown in Figure 4-11.
9. **Copy the code.**
10. **Open your Web site and paste the HTML code into the location in which you'd like to add it.**

    The exact instructions depend on the Web-site software or site you're using. In my example, I am adding it on the home page of my Squarespace Web site (see Figure 4-12).
11. **Preview the changes on your site.**

    Figure 4-13 shows the gadget as it appears to your site users.

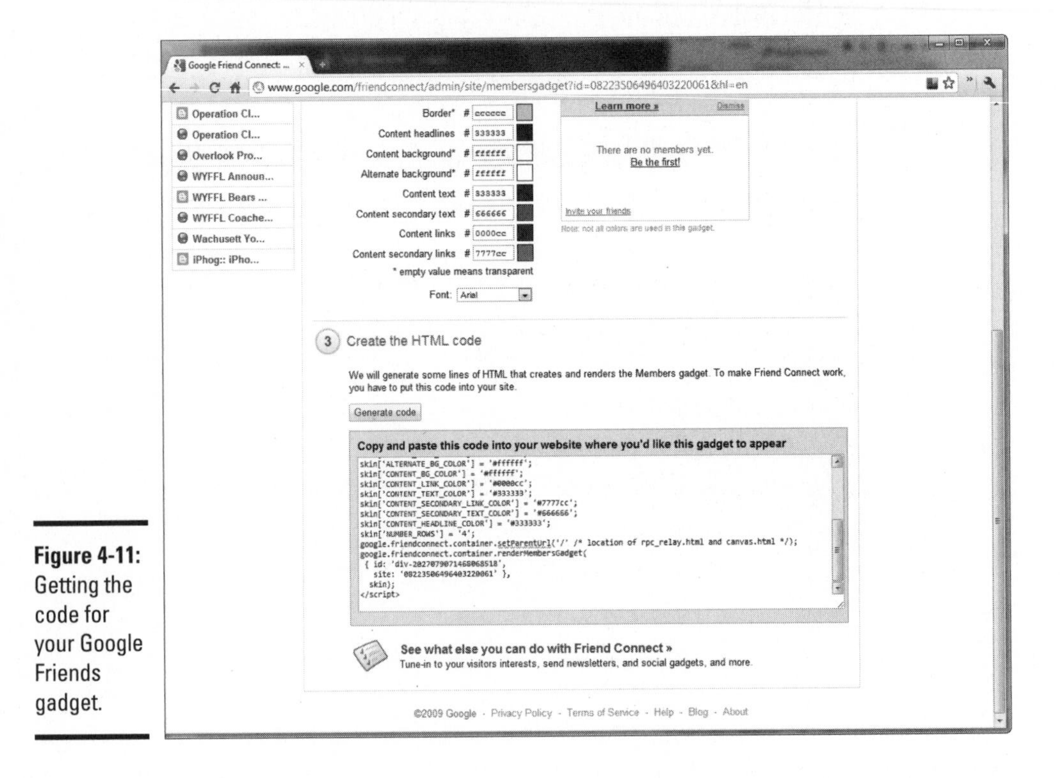

Figure 4-11: Getting the code for your Google Friends gadget.

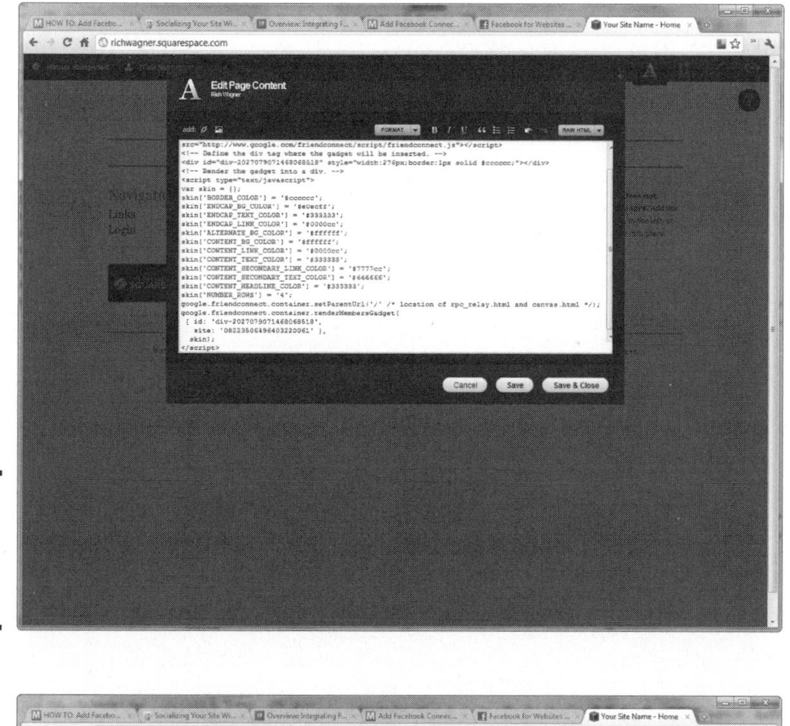

Figure 4-12: Pasting a gadget into my site.

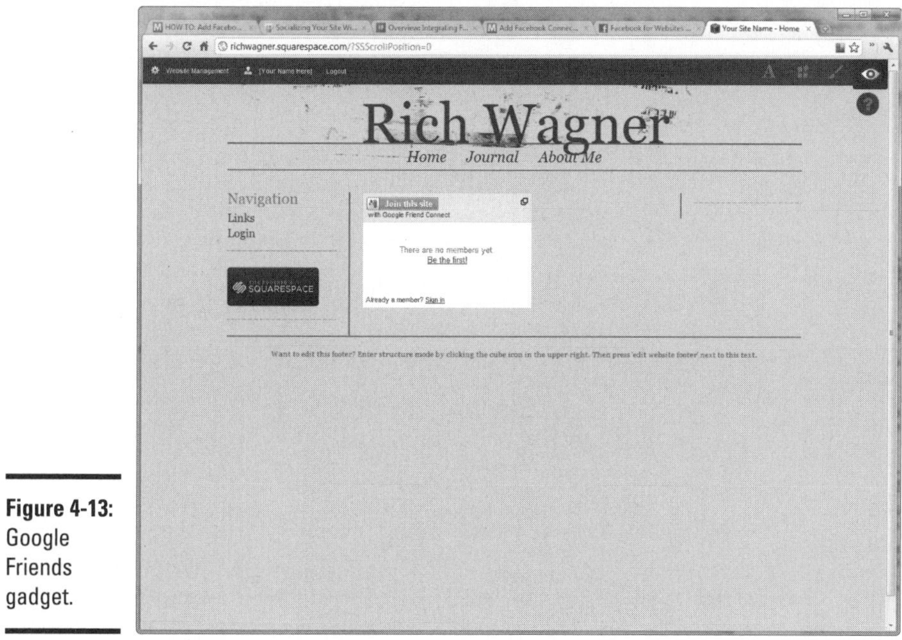

Figure 4-13: Google Friends gadget.

Chapter 5: Analyzing Your Web-Site Traffic with Google Analytics

In This Chapter

- Signing up for Google Analytics
- Getting your tracking code
- Viewing tracking data

Google Analytics is a free Google tool that you can use to track how visitors use your site, no matter how large or small your Web site is. You can use it to identify how much time people spend on different pages and how they navigate through your site, and to evaluate the success of various marketing campaigns.

In this chapter, I show you how to add Google Analytics to your Web site. I then highlight some of the data you can mine from it.

If you're using WordPress, check out the Google Analytics for WordPress plugin at `http://wordpress.org/extend/plugins/google-analytics-for-wordpress`.

Adding Google Analytics Code to Your Web Site

Google Analytics uses a small snippet of JavaScript code to collect usage data from your visitors. You add it to the Web pages whose activity you want to track. To get this code, follow these steps:

1. **Go to** `www.google.com/analytics`**.**

   The Getting Started page appears, as shown in Figure 5-1.

2. **Click the Sign Up Now button.**
3. **Sign in with your Google account.**

   If you don't have a Google account, click the Create an Account Now link and follow the instructions.

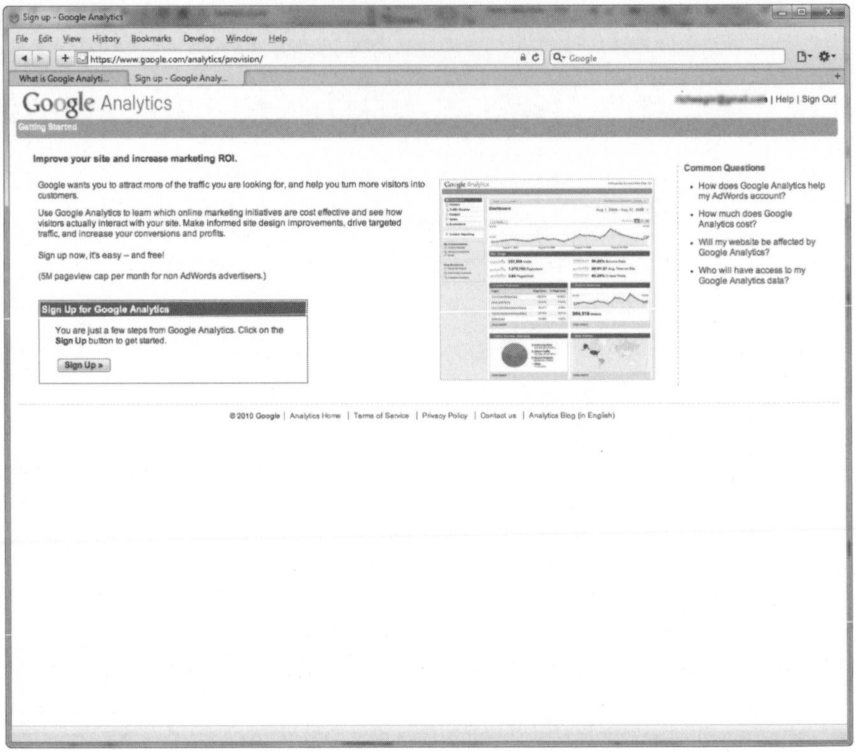

Figure 5-1: Getting started in the sign-up process.

4. **Click the Sign In button.**

   The Analytics: New Account Signup page appears (see Figure 5-2).

5. **Enter the URL for your Web site.**

   Enter your main domain URL in the space provided.

6. **Enter an Account Name.**

7. **Enter your country and time-zone information.**

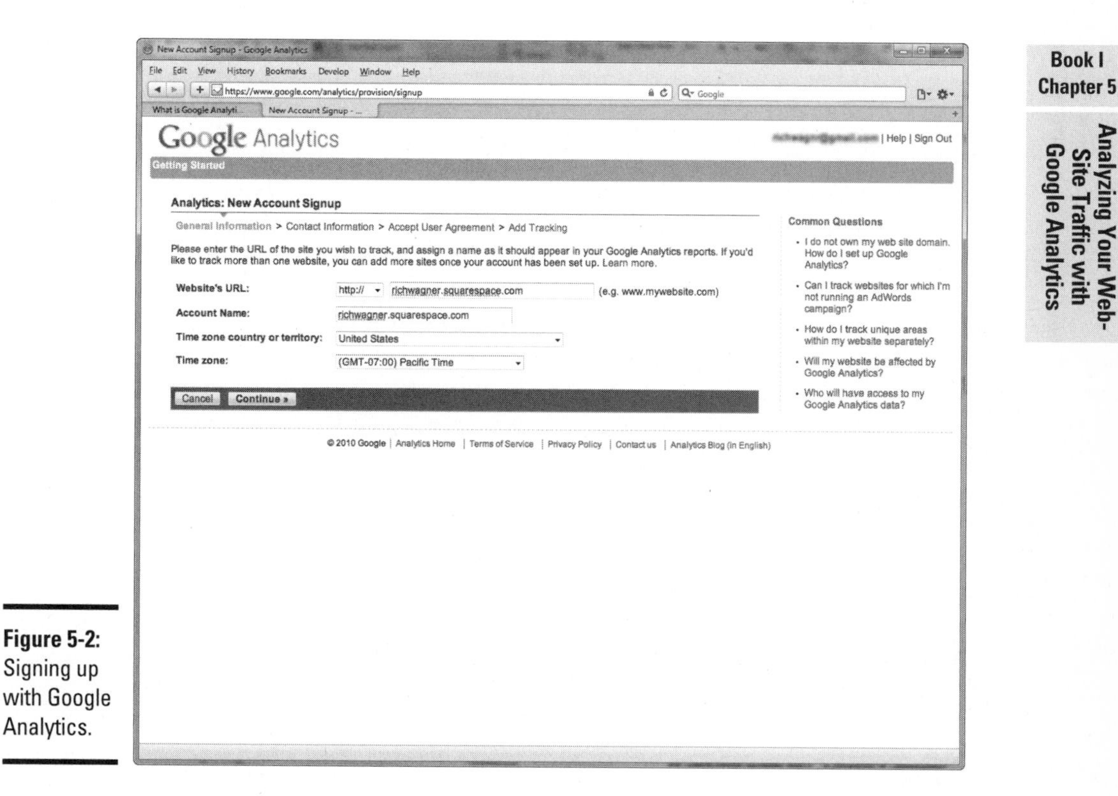

Figure 5-2: Signing up with Google Analytics.

8. **Click Continue.**

   The Contact Information page appears (see Figure 5-3).

9. **Enter your contact name and country.**

10. **Click Continue.**

    The Terms of Service page appears.

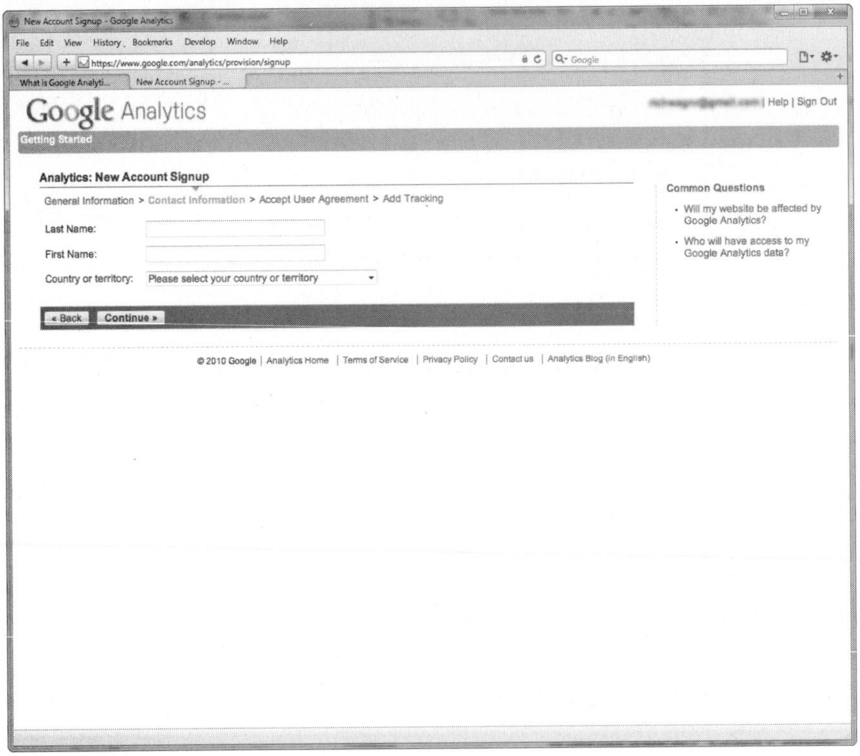

Figure 5-3: Contact Information page.

11. **Select the Yes check box and then click the Create New Account button.**

    The Analytics: Tracking Instructions page appears (see Figure 5-4).

12. **Copy all of the code in the box to your Clipboard.**

    This is the tracking code that Google will use to track your usage data.

13. **Click the Save and Finish button.**

    The main control panel of Google Analytics opens, as shown in Figure 5-5.

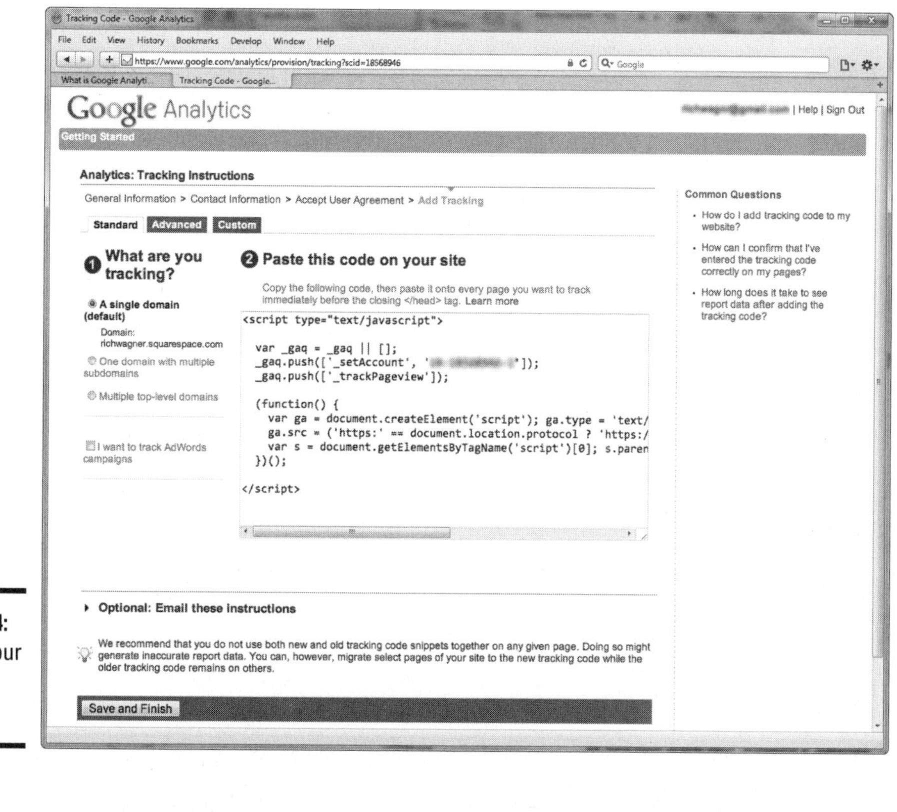

Figure 5-4: Getting your tracking code.

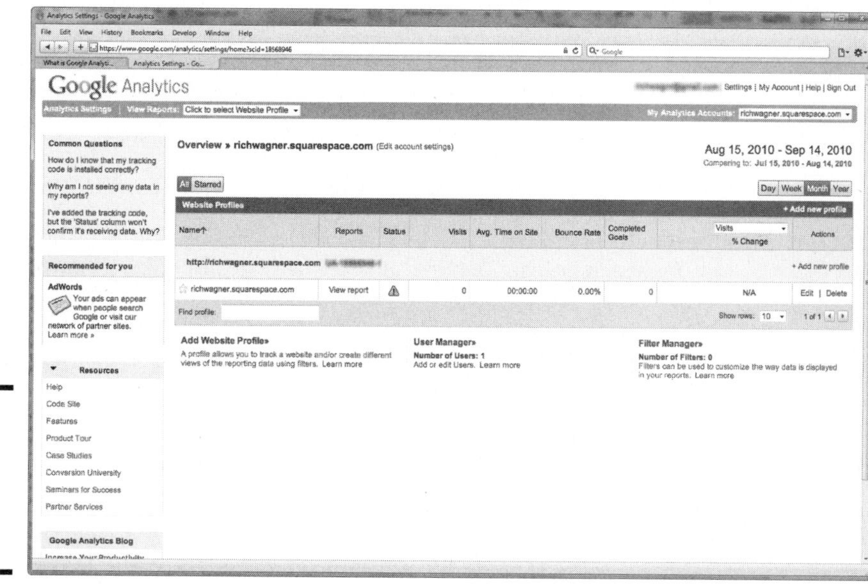

Figure 5-5: Control panel for Google Analytics.

14. **Add the tracking code at the very end of the </head> section of your Web pages.**

    The exact instructions for inserting this code varies for each Web-site builder or blog you're using:

    - *Adobe Dreamweaver, Microsoft Expression Web, or another software package:* View the HTML code of your pages and insert the tracking code just before the </head> tag.

      You must add the code to each of your Web pages. If you use a template, add the tracking code to your template file. If you don't have a template, you have to add the code manually to each of your Web pages.

    - *Online builder:* Look for an option to view the HTML code for your page and insert the tracking code just before the </head> tag.

      If your Web-site builder (such as Squarespace) doesn't allow you to add it in the <head> section of your page, then add it just after the </body> tag at the very bottom of the document. However, for best performance, placing it just before the closing </head> tag is preferred.

Working with the Admin Console

When you've inserted the tracking code into your Web pages, you can begin to track usage data.

Give Google Analytics a few days, weeks, and maybe months (depending on how popular your Web site is) so it can collect data and provide useful trends and insights.

To get to your main console, go to `www.google.com/analytics` and log in, if needed.

From the main console, click the View Report link. The View Reports section of Google Analytics gives you access to all your site information.

The initial view is your Dashboard (see Figure 5-6), which provides a summary view of all of the tracking data.

From the Dashboard, you can use the left-side navigation bar to discover tracking information. The amount of statistics that you can tap into is extensive enough to warrant a complete book by itself, but here's a survey of the kind of data you can discover once you add Google Analytics tracking to your Web site.

Figure 5-6: The Google Analytics Dashboard.

For example, here are a few reports Analytics gives you:

- **New versus returning visitors** (see Figure 5-7): This can help you know how many people like your site enough to return to it.
- **The amount of time visitors are spending on your site** (see Figures 5-8 and 5-10): You can use this to gauge how interesting your site is to people.
- **Frequency of visitors returning to your site** (see Figure 5-9): This stat is a good measure of how useful your site is to people on a regular basis.

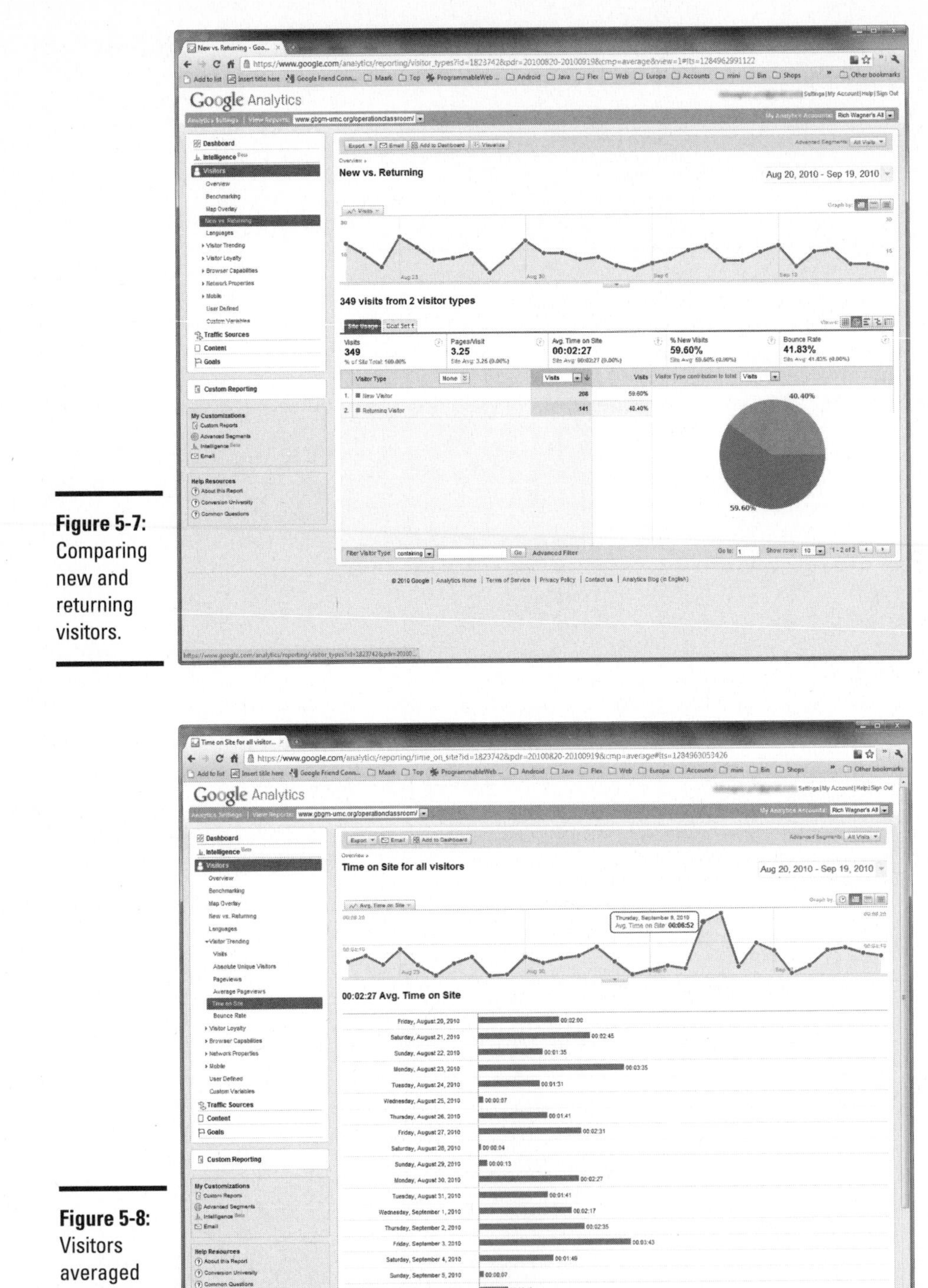

Figure 5-7: Comparing new and returning visitors.

Figure 5-8: Visitors averaged 2:27 minutes on this site.

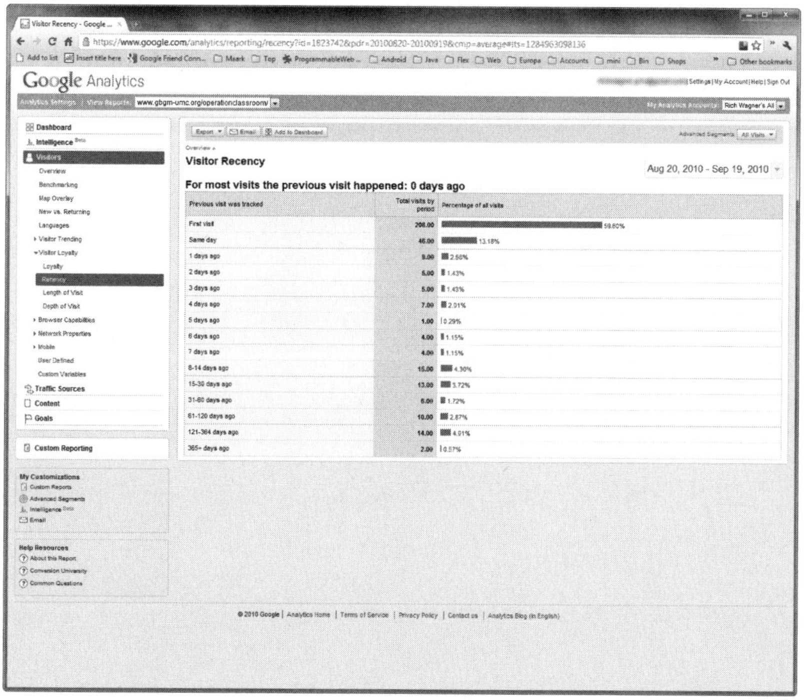

Google Analytics

Settings | My Account | Help | Sign Out

www.gbgm-umc.org/operationclassroom/

Rich Wagner's All

Dashboard
Intelligence Beta
Visitors
Overview
Benchmarking
Map Overlay
New vs. Returning
Languages
Visitor Trending
Visitor Loyalty
Loyalty
Recency
Length of Visit
Depth of Visit
Browser Capabilities
Network Properties
Mobile
User Defined
Custom Variables
Traffic Sources
Content
Goals

Custom Reporting

My Customizations
Custom Reports
Advanced Segments
Intelligence Beta
Email

Help Resources
About this Report
Conversion University
Common Questions

Export | Email | Add to Dashboard

Advanced Segments: All Visits

Overview »

Visitor Recency

Aug 20, 2010 - Sep 19, 2010

For most visits the previous visit happened: 0 days ago

Previous visit was tracked	Total visits by period	Percentage of all visits
First visit	208.00	59.80%
Same day	46.00	13.18%
1 days ago	9.00	2.58%
2 days ago	5.00	1.43%
3 days ago	5.00	1.43%
4 days ago	7.00	2.01%
5 days ago	1.00	0.29%
6 days ago	4.00	1.15%
7 days ago	4.00	1.15%
8-14 days ago	15.00	4.30%
15-30 days ago	13.00	3.72%
31-60 days ago	6.00	1.72%
61-120 days ago	10.00	2.87%
121-364 days ago	14.00	4.01%
365+ days ago	2.00	0.57%

© 2010 Google | Analytics Home | Terms of Service | Privacy Policy | Contact us | Analytics Blog (in English)

Figure 5-9: Recency of visitors (how recently they accessed your site).

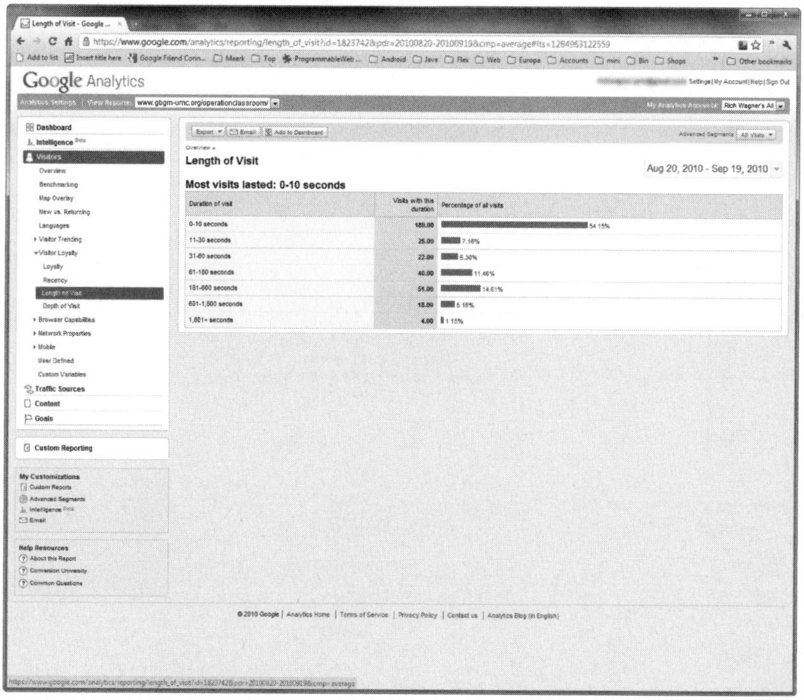

Google Analytics

Settings | My Account | Help | Sign Out

www.gbgm-umc.org/operationclassroom/

Rich Wagner's All

Export | Email | Add to Dashboard

Advanced Segments: All Visits

Overview »

Length of Visit

Aug 20, 2010 - Sep 19, 2010

Most visits lasted: 0-10 seconds

Duration of visit	Visits with this duration	Percentage of all visits
0-10 seconds	189.00	54.15%
11-30 seconds	25.00	7.16%
31-60 seconds	22.00	6.30%
61-180 seconds	40.00	11.46%
181-600 seconds	51.00	14.61%
601-1,800 seconds	18.00	5.16%
1,801+ seconds	4.00	1.15%

© 2010 Google | Analytics Home | Terms of Service | Privacy Policy | Contact us | Analytics Blog (in English)

Figure 5-10: Average length of visit.

- **How many pages people navigate in your site** (see Figure 5-11): You can see if people come to the home page and leave or whether they stick around and browse.
- **How each user came to your site — search engine, direct URL, or referring site** (see Figure 5-12): This is a good indicator of how people are finding you on the Web.
- **The most popular pages in your site** (see Figure 5-13): You can judge what works and what doesn't on your site.
- **The types of users coming to your site** — that is, mobile versus desktop, Windows versus Mac, and so on (see Figure 5-14).

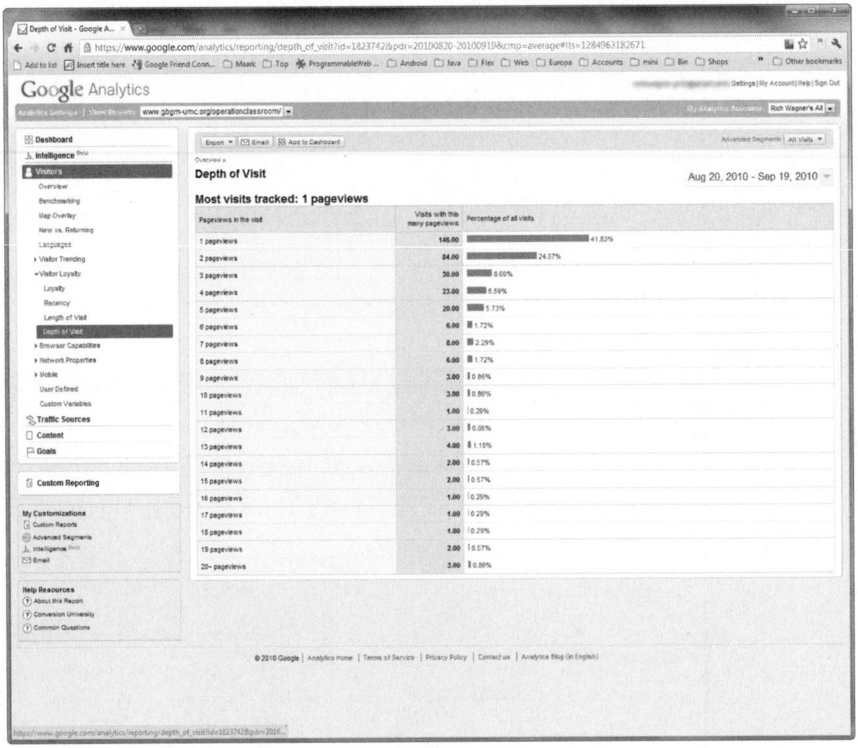

Figure 5-11: The depth of the visitors' visits.

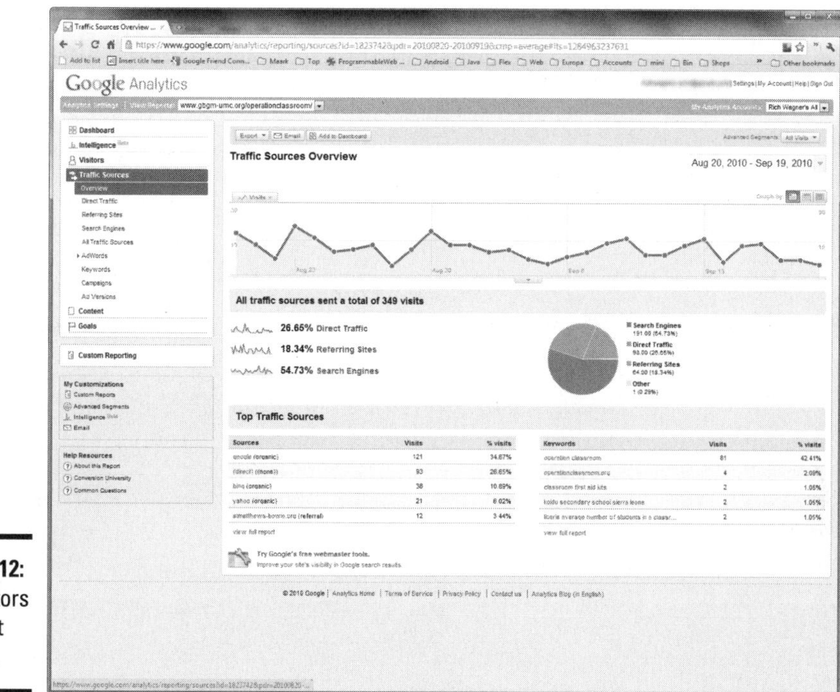

Figure 5-12: How visitors arrived at your site.

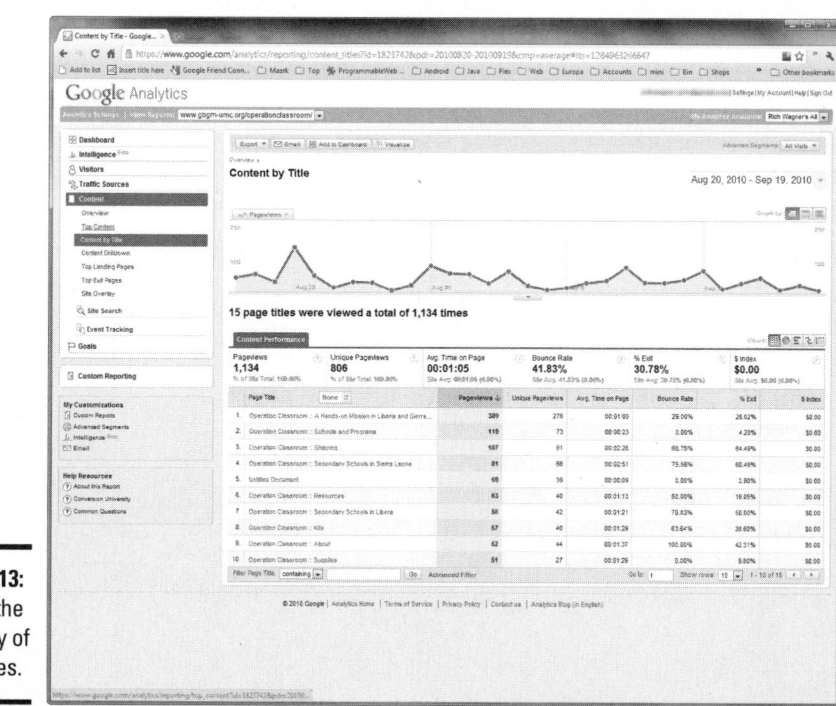

Figure 5-13: Ranking the popularity of your pages.

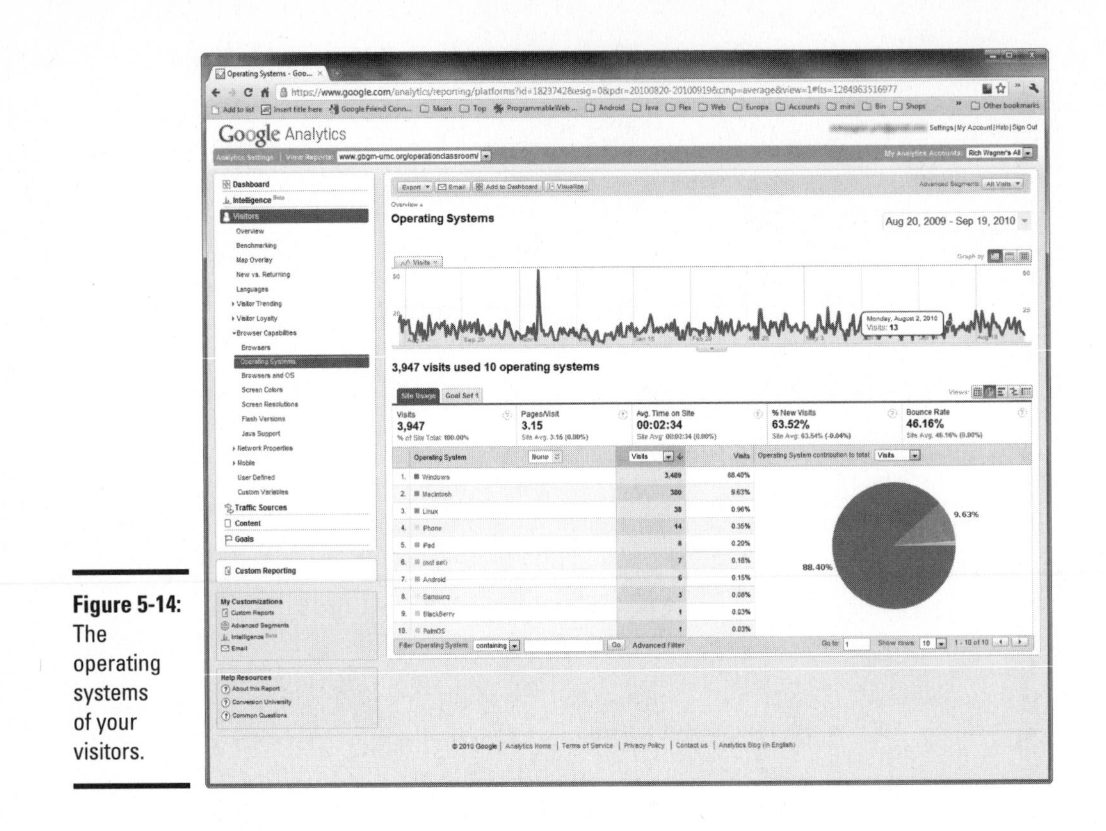

Figure 5-14: The operating systems of your visitors.

Book II

Web Design

Contents at a Glance

Chapter 1: Best Practices in Web Design

In This Chapter

- Keeping your design simple
- Maintaining consistency
- Applying the rule of thirds to your site design
- Avoiding the eight most common site-design problems

Because the Web is a visual medium, the design of your Web site can be as important as the content you offer on your site. If your design is tacky, amateurish, and annoying, visitors might not treat you seriously or might hit the Back button before you can cry out "But I tried!"

Therefore, in this chapter, I explore several proven design principles that you should understand. In addition, I also talk about what not to do — those errors that you should avoid from the start.

Applying Three Proven Design Principles to Your Site

The early days of the Web were filled with sites dense with information. They were functional, but they often looked liked they had been designed by a trash compactor — smashing as much content inside the page as possible. However, the world of design soon caught up with the Web and transformed ugly pages into works of art.

Before you start designing your Web site, spend some time analyzing other well-designed sites. If you find several candidates, I'm willing to bet that in spite of their visual differences, they employ many of the same proven design principles.

Simplicity: Less is more

If the past century has stressed any single aesthetic principle, it is that less is more. You see it in glass-box architecture, Hemingway's sparse sentences, Minimalist painting — and, indeed, throughout the Web. The fashion designer Raoul (`raoul.com`) offers a good example of applying the simplicity principle to the home page to keep the visitors' full attention on the company's fashions. (See Figure 1-1.)

Figure 1-1: Raoul.com conveys simplicity in its Web site.

Figure 1-1 shows how minimal content can create a highly effective Web page: one main photo, one thumbnail image, small menu, and corporate logo. Note the use of few words here. Most of the page is, in fact, white space (discussed in the next section).

Or consider Apple.com. While Apple has a multitude of products that it sells and markets, its home page will always feature a single, clear message that the company wants to communicate at a given time. (See Figure 1-2.)

Figure 1-2: Apple.com delivers a single message, not several.

Contrast that with a site like Dell.com (see Figure 1-3). While the page actually does a pretty good job taming things down, when you consider all of the customers that a large corporation like Dell must cater to, it remains far less simple than Apple.com.

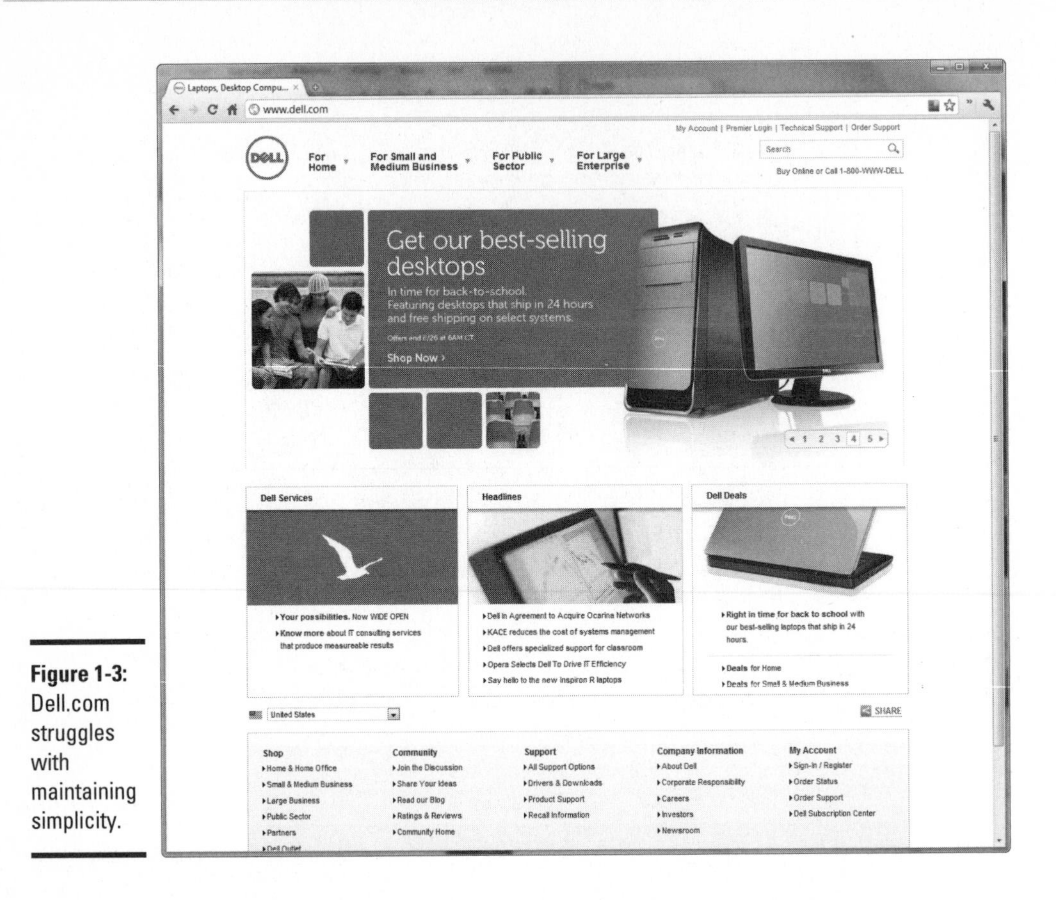

Figure 1-3: Dell.com struggles with maintaining simplicity.

One of the best-known examples of minimalist design is Google (`www.google.com`). The search engine's home page is famous for its refusal to include anything considered unnecessary.

Even heavy information sites are transforming their sites to become simpler. A few years ago, BBC News and CNN both had complex Web sites, putting dense amounts of news and pictures on their home pages (see Figure 1-4). Today, both Web sites are far more restrained. While a strictly minimalist Web site design wouldn't make any sense for a news organization, BBC (see Figure 1-5) removed a lot of info from the home page to make it much more pleasing to the eye.

Figure 1-4: The BBC News home page from 2006.

Figure 1-5: The BBC News home page in 2010.

The reality is, however, that most of us aren't Raoul, Apple, Google, or the BBC. You probably can't get by with just placing a couple words here or there on the page and living with a minimalist design. But you also don't need to deal with the constant barrage of content that a worldwide news service has to manage. Your aim, therefore, should be to strike a balance by following the age-old advice to *keep it simple.*

Here are some ideas to consider:

- **Have a center point of focus, particularly for your home page.** Your primary focus — the thing that catches a visitor's eye first — should have considerable punch. Make it big, sharp, and forceful. By contrast, other elements of the page can tend toward the paler, softer-focused, and smaller. In other words, the majority of your page should be visually gentle, with one main exception.

  For example, your eye naturally is attracted to the main photo of the Raoul.com site that shows off the fashion designer's wares. In contrast, the BBC Web site uses the top-left corner to display its major story and headline.
- **Include lots of white space, and also try to simplify the organization of the page.** I discuss using white space in the next section.
- **Limit the overall number of links.**
- **Use two or three columns.**
- **Give the visitor a simple, obvious pathway to navigate through your page.** Don't allow your visitors to get the deer-in-the-headlights look because your page is confusing and complex.
- **Consider putting your main symbol (whether an image or a headline) in a vibrant color.**

Keeping things clean with white space

White space, also called *negative space,* is a design term that refers to regions that are empty of text or graphics. It doesn't necessarily mean that the space is colored white. Empty areas can be any color, or even a *gradient* (a visual transition between colors). White space serves several purposes:

- **Increase readability:** Text on computer screens can be more difficult to read than text on paper. Give your viewers plenty of white space, to make the content more readable.
- **Keep things clean:** Viewers aren't overwhelmed with the feeling that they must buckle down and work to get through all the information you're cramming into their view.
- **Emphasize your content:** When your page is less crowded, each image and paragraph has greater value and doesn't compete with the others.
- **Free you for an effective design:** By using more white space, you have greater freedom to move items around, which helps build an effective design.

The standard tech-specifications page on the Web usually calls for a densely packed page of technical content. Apple shows how the effective use of white space can make even a tech-spec page as readable as possible (see Figure 1-6).

Being consistent across the site

Although the home page of a site often has a page layout that's different from that used for the rest of the pages, the overall site design should be consistent in terms of colors, fonts, font sizes, margins, and other elements.

Several technologies are available that can help you simplify this task. In particular, Cascading Style Sheets (CSS) will allow you to set styles and formatting rules for your site in one central location and attach every page of your site to those rules. (I cover CSS fully in Book IV.)

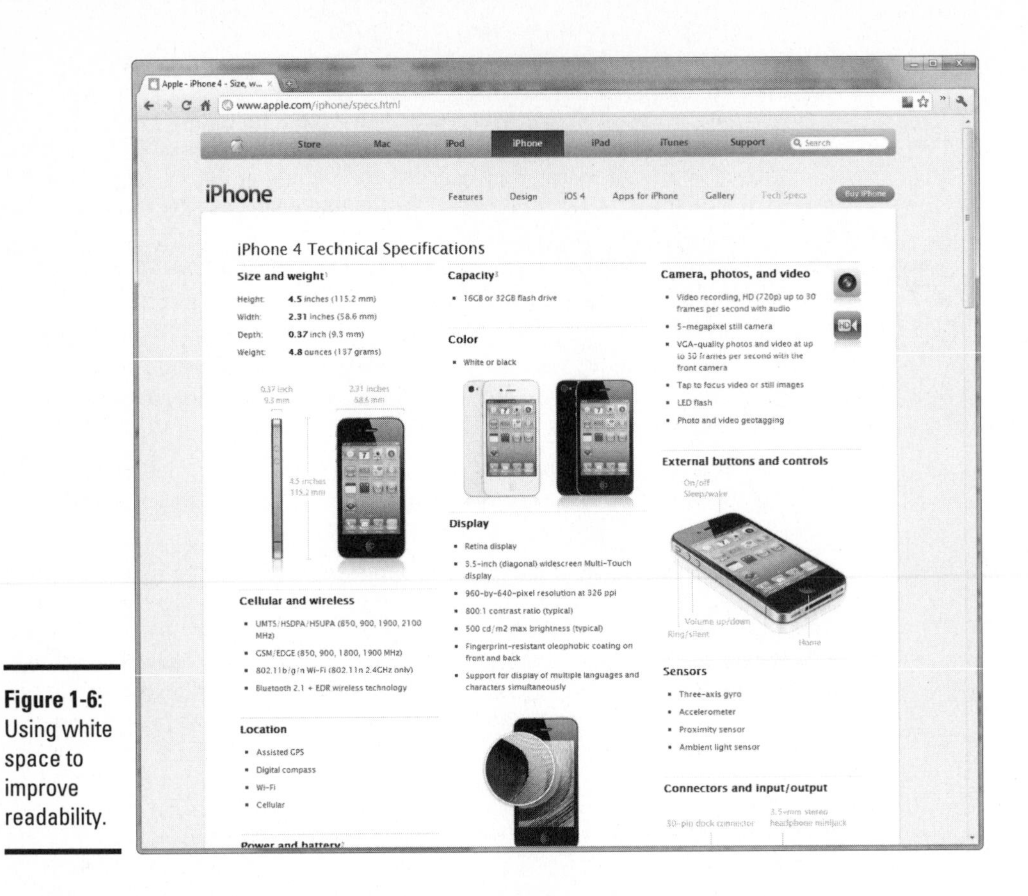

Figure 1-6: Using white space to improve readability.

Understanding the Rule of Thirds

The *rule of thirds* is one of the most persistent and pervasive tenets of Western art: This rule has been employed successfully by everyone from brilliant Greek sculptors to contemporary greeting-card designers, with good reason: When an image or a page is divided into thirds vertically and horizontally — and objects are positioned on those lines — the image is simply more pleasing to the eye.

For example, in Figure 1-2, the iPhone banner add takes up two-thirds of the page, while the bottom thumbnails take up the remaining third. Or notice the content-driven pages shown in Figures 1-5 and 1-6. They both divide the content across three columns.

When you apply the rule of thirds to your Web site, the main subject is rarely in the center of your page or image. Too much symmetry makes for a bad overall composition. In addition, you avoid centering the horizon line — that is, equal amounts of sky and land — which would divide the visual in the middle horizontally, instantly turning it static and visually dull.

Experiment as you design a page. Move elements around. Tweak your original ideas and see what happens. When you feel pretty good about a page, pull back to take a dispassionate look at it with the rule of thirds in mind. More likely than not, you'll find that adjusting your page design to harmonize with the rule of thirds improves its overall look.

REMEMBER

You don't need to employ the rule of thirds in every last photograph you take or Web page you design. If you regularly follow this rule of composition, though, your designs will benefit.

Tweaking your page design with the rule of thirds

Consider how a page design can be modified by following the rule of thirds. To start, you need a focal point. Like any good painting or photograph, your Web pages benefit from having an object that's the main topic or the most prominent visual element — whatever the viewer is supposed to notice first.

Figure 1-7 illustrates a Web page displayed in an abstract way to highlight its primary zones: some text (gray blocks), some bold text (the dark block), and headlines (black bars). Overall, this isn't a bad design — it has variety and is also balanced. Note that it's not symmetrical: It's *balanced.* That's an important difference.

Figure 1-7: This nicely balanced page lacks a focus.

However, Figure 1-7 lacks a focal point. Nothing really punchy or extraordinary exists on the page to draw the viewer's attention. Remember that a focal point stands out from the rest of the page. It can even be as simple as an unusual shape — something that doesn't match the other shapes on the page, as shown in Figure 1-8.

Figure 1-8 looks like an improvement over Figure 1-7, but invoking the rule of thirds can strengthen the composition even more. To apply the rule, draw imaginary lines dividing your Web page into thirds vertically and horizontally, as shown in Figure 1-9.

Place straight lines (walls and horizons, for example) along any of these lines.

Figure 1-8: A new shape provides a focus.

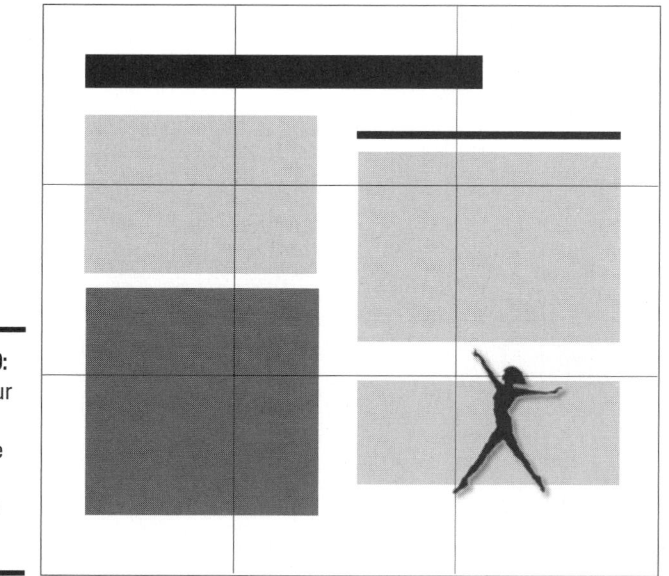

Figure 1-9: Divide your image or Web page into nine imaginary zones.

The points in which these lines intersect are the best places to put your focus: the subject of the picture. The four spots where the lines intersect are *hotspots.* Figure 1-10 is a further improvement to the design: It moves the dancer to a hotspot.

Avoiding background noise

One of the most important parts of a page to follow the *keep it simple* rule is your background. It should be a single color (often white, gray, or black) or a gradual gradient (a gradual blend from one color or shade to another) that doesn't compete visually with the content of your page. Nothing is more annoying to visitors than having bright colors or flashing images in the background. The only way a site like Raoul.com (refer to Figure 1-1) can get away with it is to put very little else on the page to compete with it.

Figure 1-10: Moving the focal point onto a hotspot.

Remember that you have four hotspots to experiment with. In Figure 1-11, the dancer is positioned in the upper-left hotspot. Also notice that the dancer has been reversed from her position in Figure 1-10; now, she dances *into* the page, as shown in Figure 1-11.

When you have *motion* in your composition (an arrow, a dancer, or anything that points or "moves"), good design emphasizes ensuring that the motion moves into — not out of — your page. The focal point is the first thing the viewer sees, and it should lead the eye into the page.

Photoshop support

To help you apply the rule of thirds with your images, Adobe Photoshop CS5 provides you with a crop option in which you can use rule-of-thirds gridlines. Older editions have no built-in feature for the rule of thirds, but `powerretouche.com` offers a helpful *plug-in* (third-party component that can add functionality), which you can add into Photoshop for this purpose.

Figure 1-11: The dancer looks good in this other hotspot.

Balancing the rule of thirds with the background

When you're tinkering with placing your focal-point object according to the rule of thirds, pay attention to the background you use. You can see that the design shown in Figure 1-12 isn't nearly as successful as the one in Figure 1-11, even though the dancer is positioned on a hotspot. With this design, the focal point is swallowed by the dark background.

Another rule of good composition is that you *should* violate white space: That is, move a focal point so it isn't framed or sunk into its background but instead pokes into the surrounding white space. In Figures 1-10 and 1-11, the dancer leaps out of the background into the white space. That's the better choice.

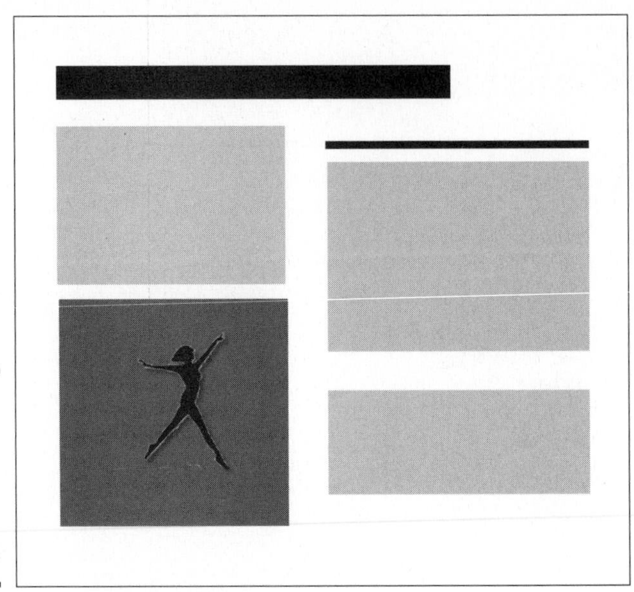

Figure 1-12: The focal point is swallowed by the dark background.

Of all these page designs, Figure 1-10 is arguably the best. It's the most balanced because the dancer counteracts the weight of the large headline at the top of the page. But, keep in mind, Web design is an art, not a science. In the end, the final choice is, of course, up to you.

Positioning the background image

You should also employ rule-of-thirds hotspots with your background images. Even though Raoul.com features a full-page image, note that the subject positioning occupies the first two thirds of horizontal space; the man and woman aren't centered.

When you move your background over to a rule-of-thirds hotspot, you maintain balance while adding interest to your composition.

Finessing graphics

Using the rule of thirds applies to more than the overall design on your page. For added visual appeal, remember to apply it with the graphics that you add to the page.

Avoiding Eight Common Web-Design Problems

As you consider the good design principles I discuss in this chapter, I also want to tell you about the "bad stuff," the common mistakes that Web designers often make. Sometimes these problems occur from the start, and sometimes they creep in slowly as you update and modify your site over time.

Clutter eats your site alive

Clutter makes visitors uncomfortable and gives them the impression that your site is disorganized. Avoid it. You want your site to make it easy for visitors to get the information they're looking for — not feel like they're trapped in a dream within a dream within a dream.

If you have a tendency to create a cluttered design, take the reins and throw out everything possible. Then throw out even more, or move items to pages deeper within the site.

Overwhelming your visitors at the start

This error sometimes results from being so enthusiastic about what's on your site that you overwhelm your visitors by throwing everything at them on the home page. The fix (as Apple.com does so well), is to determine what's *most essential* and highlight it, and be disciplined enough to place other content on other pages. As long as you have a good navigation scheme (see Chapter 2 of this minibook), you'll be fine.

Confusion comes with complexity

Visitors make instant decisions the moment they arrive on your site. If they're confused or annoyed, they click the Back button and never return. If you can't simplify by eliminating clutter (see the "Clutter eats your site alive" section), you have to employ your design skills to clarify by design.

Divide your page into logical areas, to make clear what goes with what. Traditionally, horizontal and vertical lines used to fence off various areas on a Web page, just as newspapers continue to do now. However, contemporary Web design often eliminates lines in favor of bars of color zones in the background, multimedia areas (audio and animation using Flash, for example), navigation bars, and other visually distinct areas. Figure 1-13 illustrates how a variety of textures, colors, and multimedia zones can separate content into recognizable categories.

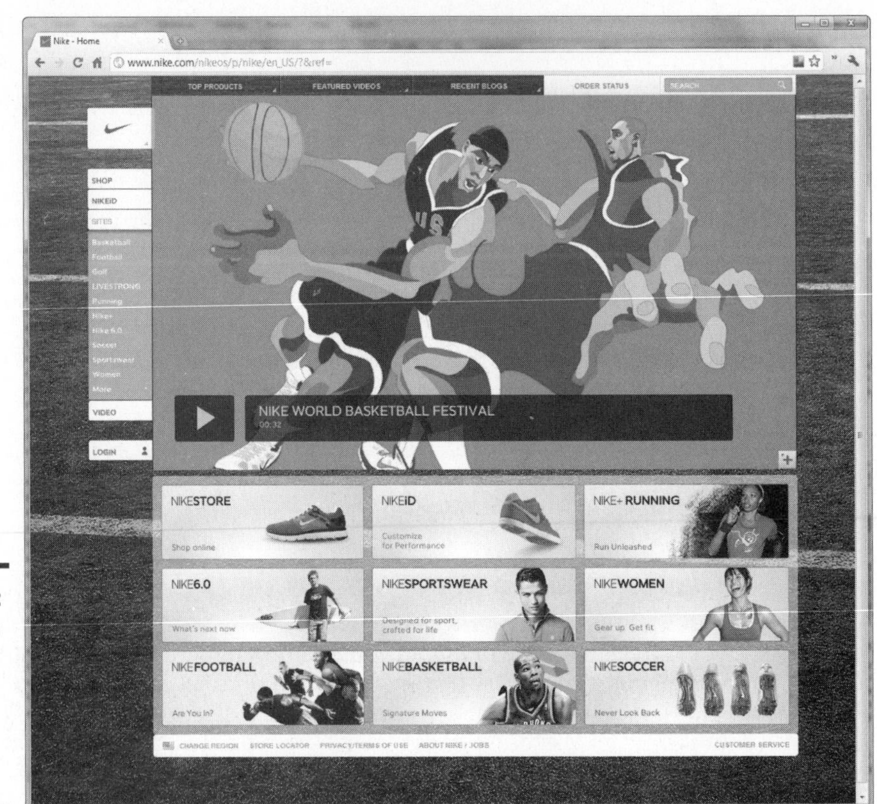

Figure 1-13: Nike.com is organized with zones of texture, color, and animation.

Mixing and matching design ideas never works

Avoid creating a Web design that mixes and matches various styles, no matter how strong they are by themselves. Instead, use a visual theme that's coherent and organized and helps give you a unique identity. Whether it's the *New York Times* with its famous gothic typeface, Martha Stewart's beloved pale aquamarine, or the NBC peacock, visual themes are indispensable to identifying a person or organization.

By carefully selecting graphics, font typefaces, and colors that work together and match your tone and messaging, you can create a design that holds together visually and gives your site an attractive personality.

For deciding which colors work well together, check out `www.colorschemer.com/schemes` and `www.colourlovers.com`.

For comparing and contrasting font typefaces, check out `typetester.org`.

Extreme symmetry is a yawner

As I mention in the rule-of-thirds discussion earlier in the chapter, a major graphical design rule — for magazine ads, interior decorating, photography, Web pages, and many other fields — is to avoid using extreme symmetry. Simply, don't position the *focus* (the main item) of your page or photo smack dab in the center. If a lit Christmas tree is the focus of a snapshot, don't have the tree right in the middle of the picture. If you're photographing the sea, don't have the horizon line where water meets sky in the middle of your shot.

The problem with symmetry is that it removes quite a bit of the life, the subtle conflict, that is necessary for successful contemporary design. It's the visual equivalent of headlining a newspaper story with "People Strolled through the Park Yesterday."

If you need one more example to convince you, check out Oakley.com (see Figure 1-14). The sunglass maker's Web site employs the rule of thirds well, drawing attention to the top third as a hotspot and avoiding symmetry.

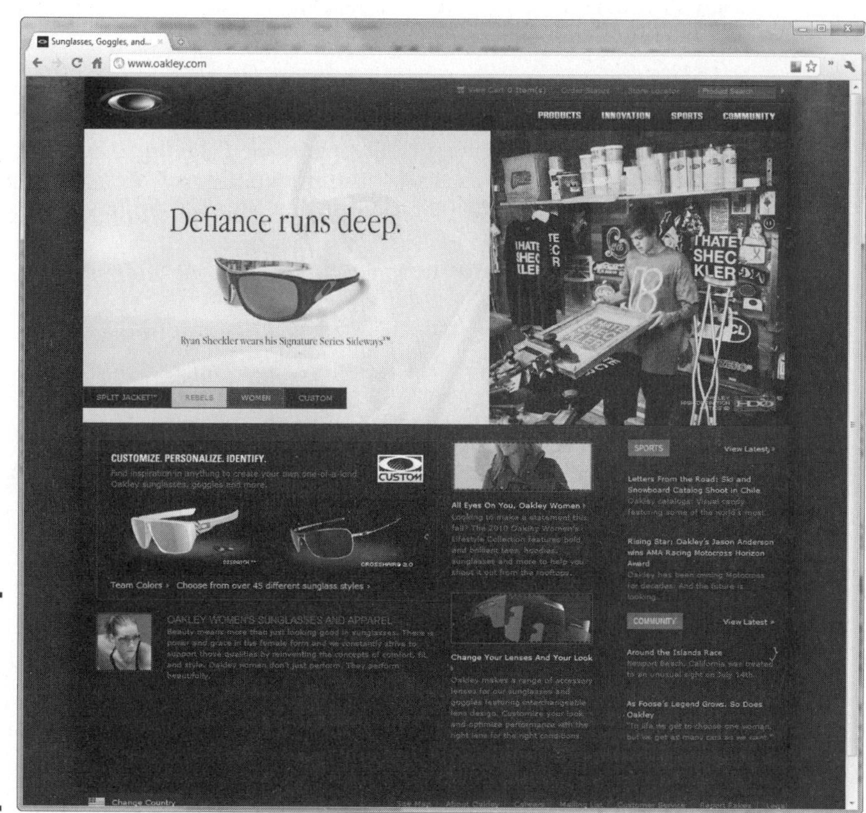

Figure 1-14: Oakley.com's use of proven design principles.

Forgetting about the visitor

Some site-design errors result from an inadequate site-navigation structure. As you might recall from the earlier section "Overwhelming your visitors at the start," you should resist the urge to put all your eggs in the home-page basket. Divide what you're selling into categories and create separate pages (or whole groups of pages) for those categories.

Double-check your page's navigation features. Having links to pages that don't exist is sloppy. Ask outsiders who are unfamiliar with your site to see whether they can quickly and intuitively locate precisely what they're after. Although a Search feature can be helpful, your customer should ideally be able to click visual cues — icons, photos, and navigation bars — to locate subcategories, such as Antique Quilts or Under–$200 Quilts. For example, if your major categories group products by cost, even something as simple as four tabs with $, $$, $$$, and $$$$ symbols on them can assist visitors. Then, when they click one of these selections, perhaps they'll find their chosen cost group further divided by tabs indicating age, size, color, or whatever. The idea is to let them get to their particular wishes — perhaps the page displaying your second-most-expensive, large, blue quilts — with only two or three mouse clicks.

Negligence is like moldy bread

Don't work hard creating your Web site and then forget about it and let it waste away. Just as successful stores keep themselves continually up to date, you need to do the same with your Web site. Follow these tips:

- **Update your blog or news section.** If you have a blog or What's New section, be sure to regularly post new information. At minimum, even if you don't add new material, be sure to take off content that's outdated.
- **Keep your copyright date current.** Few things date your site more than an old copyright date at the bottom of the page. If visitors see a two-year-old date on your site, they assume that you've stopped updating it.
- **Check links.** Periodically test both internal and external links you provide. Delete broken links or update them to the new URLs.

Insecurity makes people nervous

You wouldn't enjoy shopping at a nasty store where suspicious characters are peeking over your shoulder as you enter your PIN code, or are stuffing copies of your Visa charge receipt into their pockets. Likewise, if you're selling goods on eBay or directly on your Web site, you must reassure your customers on the Internet that you're trustworthy and will provide secure financial transactions.

Chapter 2: Organizing and Navigating Your Web Site

In This Chapter

- **Deciding between random and sequential access**
- **Combining structures**
- **Navigating via bars**

I've always thought that a well-organized Web site is much like a GPS for your automobile. A road map or atlas throws all the possible routes and destinations at you, leaving you all alone to figure out where you are and how to best get where you're going. A GPS, on the other hand, gives you just the facts you need to navigate successfully to your intended destination.

In much the same way, your Web site needs to be GPS-enabled, so to speak. Visitors should feel like they're navigating your Web site with a GPS in hand rather than simply being tossed a road atlas. They need an intuitive way to locate the content they're looking for without feeling bombarded with every possible option.

In this chapter, you explore the important concepts to consider as you organize your site.

Creating a Site Hierarchy

Web sites usually have a logical, tree-like hierarchy to them. A home page branches out into four to six section pages, some of which might have subpages or even subsections under those. Larger sites might have several of these subsections, whereas smaller sites might have little beyond the original section pages.

When you organize your site as a tree-like structure, some branches quickly and easily fall into place. However, other pages might take much more work before you can figure out exactly where they fall into place.

As you organize your site, make sure that you put on a visitor's hat and look at the overall structure as a newcomer would. As the creator of the site, you have the "inside scoop" and understand the various interrelationships that exist among the various items of content. However, be aware of how this content fits together logically from the viewpoint of the uninformed.

To organize your site structure, follow these steps:

1. **Make a flat list of all the pages you want to add to your Web site.**

   If you have an existing site, don't reuse the same hierarchy automatically. Start from scratch this time around and see where you end up.

2. **Put the pages into broad topical groups.**

   Organize the pages into various groups that naturally fit together.

   For example, a small consulting firm that sells goods and services might have 30 pages that the owners want to include on their site. The pages might naturally fall under just five distinctive topics, such as News, About Us, Services, Portfolio, and Products.

   Avoid using too many groups because they turn into the main sections of your site, and you want a manageable number of those. You should be able to organize your site into five to eight clearly defined and distinct topical categories.

3. **Label the group with a prosaic name that clearly and effectively describes it.**

   These group names will be the names of your Level 2 pages (just under the home page) that you'll want to include on the navigation menu of the site. (See the next section for more about navigation menus.)

   Avoid being too clever, abstract, vague, or generic in your labeling. You simply want a term that people can understand intuitively without having to think much about it. For example, if you're selling cars, label it Cars, not Automatic Transport Vehicles or Your New Transportation Device.

4. **Identify subgroups within each broad group.**

   Check to see whether your topics can be further subdivided. If so, group them together and name the subgroup according to the conventions described in Step 3.

   If you have a really large Web site, you can repeat this step as needed. However, work to limit the number of tiers on your site structure to no more than three under the home page. When visitors have to plunge much deeper than that, they easily get lost.

5. **Go through each page on your site and identify pages that must be linked directly from the home page, even if the link doesn't neatly fit within the hierarchy you established.**

   Web sites normally function best when you have a well-defined site organization, but never be so rigid that you hurt the site's usefulness.

Analyze each of the pages you identified and determine their overall importance. If they're *very* important, you might want to move them to a separate first-level category. If they're not all that important, you can highlight these special pages in various places on the home page, even if they don't work as items on the main navigation menu.

6. **Create each of the pages in the software package you're using.**

   If you're using Expression Web, flip over to Book VII. Or, if you're using Dreamweaver, you can find what you're looking for in Book VIII.

When you finish organizing your Web site's navigation hierarchy, get a friend (or a friendly person off the street) to look it over and provide feedback.

Navigating Your Site with a Navigation Menu

Web-site design goes beyond the page layout, colors, fonts, and other visual elements. Your design should also encompass the organization of your site.

Sites almost always display a *navigation menu* (or *menu bar*), which is a set of graphical or textual links to the major sections of your site. Although the home page might have its own navigation scheme, the rest of the Web site usually has a common navigation bar found at one of two locations on each page:

- A horizontal menu bar is located at the top of the page, usually under a banner or logo.
- A vertical menu bar is placed along the left side.

Whichever main navigation you decide to use, a text-only menu bar is traditionally placed at the bottom of the page to eliminate the need to scroll up to change pages. (In Book VI, Chapter 3, I show you how to create a navigation menu bar with rollovers.)

Figure 2-1 illustrates how a well-organized, top-level, navigation menu can drive the entire Web site's flow. What's more, much of the content on the home page is meant to highlight a particular page within that hierarchy. New visitors will have no trouble understanding how to use this site or how to navigate it.

You can create a navigation menu manually by using HTML and CSS (see Books III and IV). What's more, Dreamweaver and Expression Web offer features that create navigation menus for you.

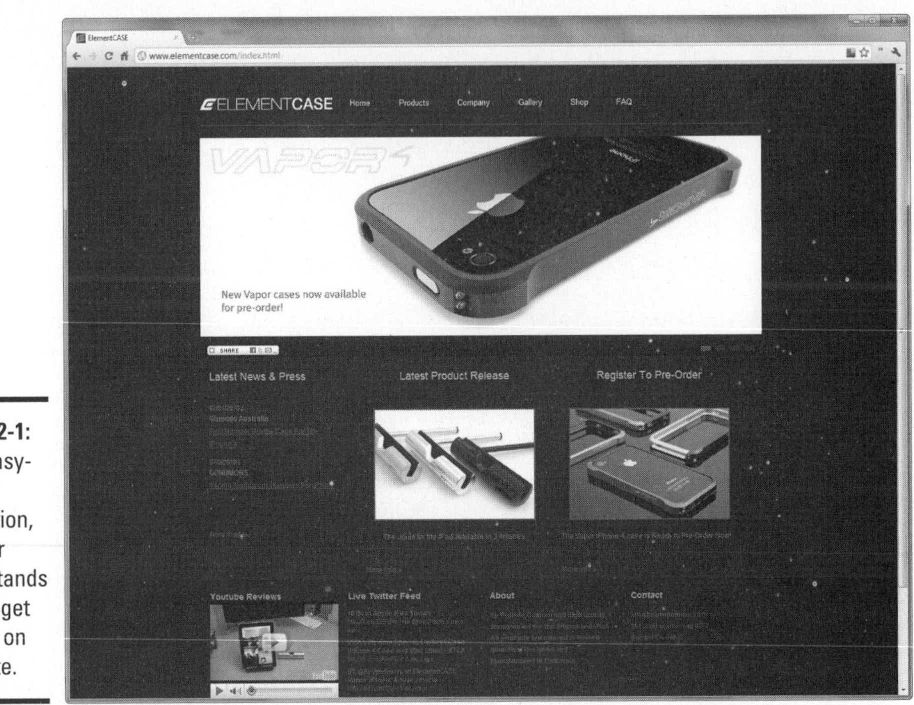

Figure 2-1: With easy-to-find navigation, a visitor understands how to get around on your site.

From the Dept. of Redundancy Dept.: Self-linking pages

Avoid linking to the same page in your Web site. If, for example, you display a common navigation bar at the top of each page, make sure to highlight the link for the current page through special formatting. This effect helps visitors easily identify their current location in the Web site visually. At the same time, disable that link so that nothing happens if the user clicks it. Self-linked pages confuse people.

Chapter 3: Designing for Mobile Visitors

In This Chapter

- **Simulating mobile devices**
- **Designing a mobile-compatible site**
- **Mobile-friendly design techniques**

Five years ago, the idea of designing your Web site for mobile visitors was either never a consideration or just an afterthought. You could simply design a text-only version of your Web site that the occasional cell-phone user could use.

All that changed with the release of the iPhone, iPad, Android devices, and other smartphones. Now, with the power of these devices and their fully functional mobile browsers, mobile visitors expect to have a satisfying browsing experience.

Whether you create your Web site with WordPress, Squarespace, Dreamweaver, or whatever, you'll want to fully consider the mobile user in your design and determine the level of support you want to provide for these mobile devices — compatibility, "mobile-friendly" features, or even a separate mobile site.

In this chapter, I walk you through these options as you consider them. Note that I do occasionally touch on more technical solutions that involve using HTML and CSS, so read Books III and IV before tackling a mobile version of your site.

Previewing Your Mobile Site

Your first step toward mobile compatibility and friendliness is simply to preview what your own Web site and/or other Web sites you visit look like when a visitor browses from a mobile device.

You'll want to view your Web site on as many devices as you can; just as with desktop operating systems, your Web site's going to look different from phone to phone. To preview your site — without going broke buying every smartphone on the market — download a simulator. Simulator software mimics the look of a particular phone's operating system and browser. Here's what's available:

- **iOS devices (iPhone, iPod touch, iPad):** You can download this simulator at `www.puresimstudios.com/ibbdemo`.
- **Android devices:** The freely downloadable Android Software Developers Kit (SDK) is a bit on the techie side for most folks, but it does include an emulator that allows you to check out how Web sites behave on various Android devices. Check out `http://developer.android.com/sdk` for details.
- **BlackBerry:** The BlackBerry Web Development Web page contains a list of available simulators you can use to test how your site performs on various BlackBerry smartphone devices. Go to `http://na.blackberry.com/eng/developers/browserdev/`.

Using your own phone, phones you borrow, and these simulators, you can develop a solid understanding of how your Web site will look to mobile visitors.

Four Levels of Mobile Web-Enabling

There are four basic levels of enabling your Web site for mobile devices:

- Compatibility
- Mobile-friendly site design
- Mobile styling
- Companion site

Determining the path you want to choose comes down to a personal or business decision. You have to decide how important it is for your site to work well for mobile users — and how much time you have to implement the changes needed for mobile support.

In this section, I walk you through each of these levels.

Basic compatibility

The first level of support is simply making sure that your Web site will at least be viewable and operable with a mobile device's browser. If your Web site is using standard CSS formatting and HTML structures or if it was built using popular online tools (WordPress, Posterous), you're probably fine in terms of iPhone, Android, and BlackBerry support.

However, even with basic compatibility, there is one thorny issue to consider: While Flash is supported on newer versions of Android (and future BlackBerry versions), it is not supported on any iOS device (iPhone, iPod touch, and iPad).

On the desktop, Web-site builders usually take for granted that Flash is appropriate (97 percent of all browsers have Flash installed), so they use Flash without hesitation (see Book IX for more on Flash). These days, however, a major percentage of mobile-device users come to your site without Flash support — so this assumption now bears rethinking. If you use Flash on your site, iOS users will see a Lego block in place of the Flash object (see Figure 3-1).

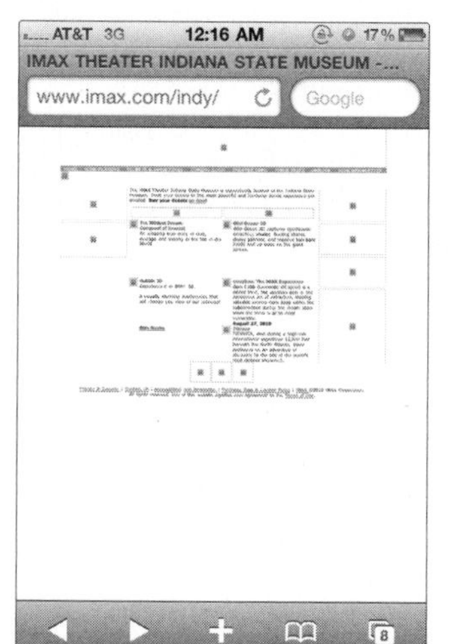

Figure 3-1: This movie site is unusable on an iPhone.

If you do decide to add Flash to your Web site, you should either accept the fact that iOS visitors will not see that content or you should consider an alternative HTML-only or companion mobile site.

Mobile-friendly site design

The second level of mobile enablement is to make sure your Web site is easy to navigate on a small screen. Trying to navigate Web sites on a mobile device can be a painful exercise in frustration — it may be possible, but it's not easy. For example, wide sections of text can be hard to read if horizontal panning is required.

Gaining mobile-friendliness with a viewport metatag

A second way to make your Web site mobile-friendly is to add a viewport metatag to each page of your Web site as a way to deal with layout issues for normal HTML pages.

The *viewport* is a rectangular area of the screen in which a Web page is displayed. It's much like looking through a camera lens at a city skyline. If you want to see the entire skyline, then you use a wide-angle lens. But when you do that, the individual buildings become smaller and more difficult to detect. Or, if you want to see a close-up picture of one of the towers, then you might zoom in with a telephoto lens. The viewport metatag works much the same way; it tells the mobile browser how much of the page to display, the "zoom" factor, and whether you want the user to zoom in and out or browse your page using only one scale factor.

To add a metatag, include this code in the `<head>` section of your Web page:

```
<meta name="viewport"
    content="width=device-
    width; initial-scale=1.0;
    user-scalable=1;" />
```

When you add this tag to the page, the device's browser automatically sizes the page to the screen width (320px for an iPhone, 480px for a Nexus One, and so on) and zooms to a 1.0 scale. Then, if the user flips the device and changes the orientation to landscape, the browser adjusts the zoom factor, basing the adjustment on the new width of the viewport.

One of the most important ways to make your site mobile-friendly is to structure the pages in columns. Columns don't force the user to read wide chunks of text that require scrolling left and right.

Take an iPhone or iPad, for example. When a Web-page element is double-tapped, Safari zooms the page to fit the content of that "block" of the page and centers it. Or, if the element is already zoomed in, then Safari zooms it out. Other mobile devices offer similar functionality. But this interaction is made possible by structuring the page in columns of a reasonable (and legible) size.

Mobile styling

A third, richer and deeper, level of support that you can provide mobile users is to actually provide styling specifically targeted for mobile devices.

If you wish to specify a style sheet for iOS, Android, and several other mobile devices, you can use a *CSS3 media query* through two rules:

- **A special CSS `@media` rule:** You can specify mobile-specific rules inside of CSS style sheets by using a `@media` rule. For example, you could add the following to your Web site's style sheet:

```
@media only screen and (max-device-width: 480px)
{
  /* Add mobile specific styles here */
}
```

- **A special `<link>` tag:** You can also place a `<link media="">` tag inside the `<head>` section of a Web page; it would look something like this:

```
<link media="only screen and (max-device-width: 480px)"  rel="stylesheet"
    type="text/css" href="mobile-device.css"/>
```

  This `link` element tells the browser to use the `.css` style sheet if (and only if) the page is displayed on a viewport of a maximum of 480px. Older desktop browsers that don't support the `only` keyword used in the `media` attribute simply bypass this rule.

One caveat to using a `<link>` tag: In some circumstances, older versions of Internet Explorer (7 and lower) on the desktop don't bypass the CSS3 media query; they apply the mobile-device `.css` file. You can prevent this by enclosing the link tag in special conditional comments that are supported by IE. Here's what it would look like:

```
<!--[if !IE]>-->
<link media="only screen and (max-device-width: 480px)"
    rel="stylesheet" type="text/css" href="mobile-device.
    css"/>
<!--<![endif]-->
```

As a result, if you want to add mobile-specific styling to your Web site pages, here's a recommended way to do so:

```
<head>
...
<!-- Desktop styles -->
<link media="screen and (min-device-width: 481px)"
  rel="stylesheet" type="text/css" href="default.css"/>

<!-- Mobile styles -->
<!--[if !IE]>-->
<link media="only screen and (max-device-width: 480px)"
  rel="stylesheet" type="text/css" href="mobile.css"/>
<!--<![endif]-->
...
</head>
```

WordPress blogs are a great example of how mobile styling can be utilized. Figure 3-2 shows a blog styled normally, designed for the desktop. Then Figure 3-3 displays the same blog, using a mobile-specific style sheet.

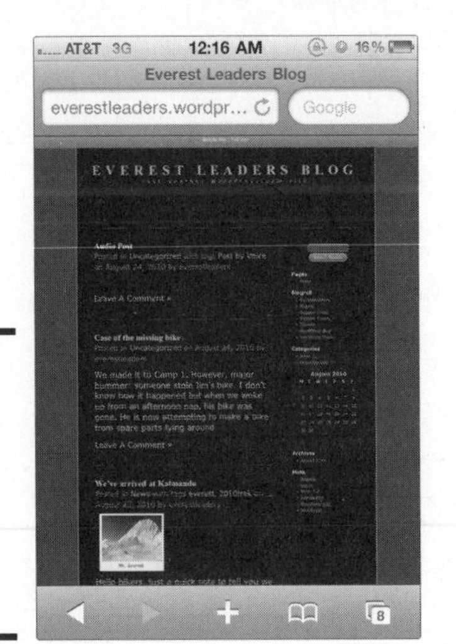

Figure 3-2: Viewing a blog with a default design on a mobile device.

Figure 3-3: Much more usable styling for mobile devices.

One important point to keep in mind if you're using mobile-specific styling (and a mobile companion site, which is discussed in the next section): If you offer a mobile version of your site, always allow the users the freedom to choose between the mobile and normal versions of the Web site. Although your site may default to the mobile style sheet for your mobile users, be sure to provide the functionality on each page to view the site normally.

Creating a companion site

For the vast majority of Web sites, providing a mobile-friendly site or a mobile styling design is a fully satisfactory way to support mobile devices. However, there may be some specific cases in which you need to go beyond the page structure and styling — for example, if you're creating a Web site or Web application that specifically targets mobile users. In such a case, you can offer the highest level of support designing and structuring a site *from the ground up* in a manner that's optimized for mobile devices.

Book III

HTML/XHTML

"Give him air! Give him air! He'll be okay. He's just been exposed to some raw HTML code. It must have accidently flashed across his screen from the server."

Contents at a Glance

Chapter 1: Exploring HTML and XHTML Documents

In This Chapter

- Understanding HTML tags and formatting
- Knowing why XHTML is important to use
- Finding out about DOCTYPE declarations
- Exploring the structure of a Web page

If I were to sit down with James Cameron and watch *Avatar,* the film I would view would be quite different from the one he would see. Through "movie magic," I would be transported to Pandora as I root for Jake and the Na'vi people to succeed in their quest to defeat the greedy corporation and hired guns. In contrast, James surely would not look at what was on-screen as much as he would replay what was going on behind the scenes. He would likely remember the exact special effect that was used in a particular shot, the last-minute script edit that was made, or the specific camera angle someone suggested.

In the same way, you can view Web pages differently, depending on your point of view. You can look at the page as it's presented to you in the browser. Or, if you have an understanding of HTML and XHTML, you can consider what's going on "under the hood." In this chapter, you discover the basic tasks that go on behind the scenes of any Web page.

Before starting on your journey, open your favorite text editor and browser so you can try out the examples in this chapter.

Under the Hood: Understanding HTML

A Web page is written in *Hypertext Markup Language (HTML),* a tag-based programming language used for presenting information. It consists of two types of data:

- **Content:** Text and graphics that you want to display on the page.
- **Instructions:** A defined set of formatting elements, or *tags,* that determine how text and graphics are displayed and arranged on a page. These instructions are invisible when the page is displayed in a browser.

Most of the elements you normally work with format content: They specify the font or style of a paragraph of text, the exact placement of a JPG photo, or the number of rows in a table, for example. However, a few other elements apply more generally to the entire HTML document: They specify the title of the page or the structure of the document, for example.

When a browser opens a Web page, the browser presents the content based on the instructions contained in the page.

Opening and closing tags

An HTML element usually consists of a pair of *tags* — made up of text inside angle brackets — that enclose a piece of content:

```
<element>Content</element>
```

The *opening tag* (`<element>`) declares the start of an instruction to be performed. The *closing tag* (`</element>`) specifies the end of the instruction. Everything inside the opening and closing tags is considered the element's *content*. As you can see from this example, the opening and closing tags are nearly the same, except that the closing tag has a forward slash (/) just before the element name.

Suppose you want to format a sentence in a Web page so it looks like this:

> **Phil:** There is no way this winter is *ever* going to end as long as that groundhog keeps seeing his shadow.

The HTML code you write looks like this:

```
<p><strong>Phil:</strong>There is no way this winter is
   <em>ever</em>going to end as long as that groundhog keeps
   seeing his shadow.</p>
```

Because the `p` element is used to define a paragraph, everything inside the start and end `p` tags is considered to be in it. The `strong` element declares bold text, so text inside it is bolded. The `em` element is for italicized words, so all the text inside the `em` element is formatted in italic.

As you can see in the previous example, you often need to nest or enclose elements inside other elements. When you do so, you apply multiple elements to some or all of the same content. The `p` element contains all the text of the paragraph as well as the nested `strong` and `em` elements, both of which apply to only a single word of the paragraph.

Now suppose you want to make a piece of text both bold and italic. You surround the text with both elements:

```
<strong><em>Mind over matter.</em></strong>
```

In well-written HTML, the element that appears first in the code must close last. As you develop Web pages, follow this rule: *First in, last out; last in, first out.* (Older-style HTML was somewhat flexible about closing your elements in varying orders.)

Case doesn't matter — sort of

In traditional HTML, tags are case-insensitive. Therefore all the following lines of HTML code are treated identically by a browser:

```
<strong>Phil:</strong>
<STRONG>Phil:</STRONG>
<Strong>Phil:</Strong>
<sTRONG>Phil:</StRoNg>
```

In years past, personal preference usually determined the case of tags. SOME PEOPLE LIKED UPPERCASE; others preferred lowercase. A Few Oddballs Liked Mixed Case.

In XHTML, all elements must be in lowercase. Although case doesn't matter to HTML, it makes a *big* difference with XHTML, HTML's successor (which is discussed later in this chapter). To avoid problems later, use lowercase for your HTML coding.

The devil is in the attributes

If the expression "The devil is in the details" is true, watch out for attributes. Most elements also include additional information inside the opening tag. These *attributes* further define the behavior of the HTML element. An attribute is expressed as a *name-value pair,* with the attribute name on the left side of the equal sign and the value on the right side:

```
<element attributename="attributevalue">Content</element>
```

The attribute value is normally enclosed in quotes. And, although traditional HTML considers quotation marks optional, I recommend getting used to using them because XHTML requires them.

Consider the `a` element as an example. It declares a hyperlink:

```
<a>Visit my home page.</a>
```

You can see that the `a` opening and closing tags used by themselves are insufficient. I specified which text should be hyperlinked but didn't tell the browser where to go when the text is clicked. The `href` attribute provides that vital piece of information:

```
<a href="http://www.richwagnerwords.com">Visit my home
   page.</a>
```

Although many attributes are optional, some elements (such as the a element example) have required attributes.

Blanks are blanked

HTML doesn't do much with blank spaces, tabs, and empty lines when formatting text on a page. In fact, it ignores them! As a result, both of the following paragraphs are presented the same way in a browser:

```
<p><strong>XHTML</strong> is the next big thing.</p>
```

is equivalent to

```
<p>            <strong>XHTML</strong>    is      the       next
big
thing.</p>
```

Both lines are displayed this way:

```
XHTML is the next big thing.
```

HTML's way of dealing with spaces lets you be flexible in writing your HTML documents, but you can't resort to good old-fashioned tabs and spaces for manual formatting and text alignment. Instead, you need to use CSS instructions for that sort of thing. See Book IV for more.

XHTML: An Extreme HTML Makeover

The HTML markup language spawned the Web revolution, back in the 1990s. However, as the popularity of the Web grew, the shortcomings of the markup language became increasingly apparent to Web designers. The biggest problem with HTML is its *laissez-faire* flexibility: inconsistent rules and sloppy shortcuts, for example. The laxness of HTML is reminiscent of a grandfatherly teacher not in control of his classroom: He sees his students turning in papers late and only partially answering questions. However, rather than discipline them, he simply shrugs his shoulders and says, "I'm sure they mean well."

The problem is that HTML's flexibility leads to ambiguity and other problems in trying to process more complex pages in more complex platforms and environments, such as cellphones and handheld devices.

Enter XHTML. Built on the Extensible Markup Language (XML) technology, XHTML is a better-organized-and-structured version of HTML.

Because all future Web development will focus on XHTML, I strongly recommend using XHTML to develop your Web pages.

Fortunately, the exact differences between HTML and XHTML are fairly straightforward, so distinguishing between them shouldn't be traumatic for even an old-fogey HTML coder:

- **XHTML elements and attributes must be lowercase.** As I say earlier in this chapter, HTML is case-insensitive: `<table>`, `<TABLE>`, and `<tAbLe>` are considered identical. In XHTML, however, all elements and attribute names must be in lowercase letters.
- **XHTML elements must always be closed.** In HTML, several tags were often used with just the opening tag, such as `<p>` (paragraph), `<br>` (line break), and `<hr>` (horizontal line). But in XHTML, every start tag needs to have a matching end tag. A starting `<p>` tag, for example, needs a `</p>` tag to close it.
- **Empty XHTML elements can be written using shorthand notation — a single tag closed with `/>`.** Although every element must be properly closed, an element with no content between the opening and closing tags can close by itself. For example, the `hr` element adds a horizontal line to the page. But because it never would have any text or other content inside it, it would always have to be expressed as

  ```
  <hr></hr>
  ```

  You can, however, use the shortcut notation to reduce this example; it looks like this:

  ```
  <hr/>
  ```

  Typically, the XHTML elements that you self-close include `br`, `hr`, `img`, `input`, `link`, and `meta`.

- **XHTML documents must have one root element that encloses all the others.** Although most HTML pages always enclosed the code inside an `html` element, technically you can get by without one. However, an XHTML document must always enclose all XHTML elements inside the `html` root element.
- **Images must have an alternative text attribute.** In HTML, `img` elements (used to display images) had an *optional* `alt` attribute for supplying an alternative text description for a graphical image. In XHTML, this attribute is required.
- **XHTML documents must have a valid `DOCTYPE`.** Although later versions of HTML encouraged the use of a `DOCTYPE` element (see "The `DOCTYPE` element," later in this chapter), XHTML requires it.

Table 1-1 shows several examples of HTML code and the same code after it's cleaned up in XHTML.

Table 1-1 Converting Old HTML into XHTML

HTML	*XHTML*
`<p>Go to the hill, ye sluggard.`	`<p>Go to the hill, ye sluggard.</p>`
` `	`<br/ >`
`<img src="photo1.jpg">`	`<img src="photo1.jpg" alt="Portrait" />`
`<Table></TABLE>`	`<table></table>`

Throughout this book, I often use *HTML* in a generic sense to refer to the markup code of a Web page. However, even as I do so, I always follow the XHTML conventions.

Surveying the Document Structure of a Page

An HTML document uses special elements to define and describe the structure of a page. You can generally break any document into two parts: the head and the body. The *head* contains important document-level information about the page, and the *body* contains the content and the formatting elements. A skeleton HTML page looks something like this:

```
<!DOCTYPE html PUBLIC "-//W3C//DTD XHTML 1.0 Transitional//
   EN" "http://www.w3.org/TR/xhtml1/DTD/xhtml1-transitional.
   dtd">
<html xmlns="http://www.w3.org/1999/xhtml">
<head>
<meta http-equiv="Content-Type" content="text/html;
   charset=ISO-8859-1" />
<title>Untitled Document</title>
</head>
<body>
Content goes here.
</body>
</html>
```

Each of these elements is described in the following sections.

The DOCTYPE element

The first element you encounter in any Web page is perhaps the most confusing to look at. The DOCTYPE declaration looks something like this:

```
<!DOCTYPE html PUBLIC "-//W3C//DTD XHTML 1.0 Transitional//
   EN" "http://www.w3.org/TR/xhtml1/DTD/xhtml1-transitional.
   dtd">
```

That's a no-no in a Strict DOCTYPE

The Web may be an ideal platform to express yourself, but if you're using a Strict DOCTYPE, you have to mind your Ps and Qs — or at least your elements and attributes. The following list outlines the general restrictions of the Strict DOCTYPE:

- **Elements not allowed with a Strict** DOCTYPE: center, font, iframe, strike, and u.
- **Attributes not allowed with a Strict** DOCTYPE: align (except with certain table elements, such as td, th, and tr), alink, background, bgcolor, border (except on the table element), height (except for img and object), hspace, language, link, name, noshade, nowrap, target, text, vlink, vspace, and width (except for the col, colgroup, img, object, and table elements).

A few differences also exist in the placement of certain elements inside other elements:

- Text and images aren't allowed immediately inside the body element and must be contained in a p, div, or other block-level element.
- Text placed inside blockquote elements must be enclosed in a p or other block-level element.
- An input element must not be directly placed inside a form element.

Okay, I admit it, the DOCTYPE element just looks weird. Everyone was just getting comfortable with the conventions of HTML and XHTML elements, and then DOCTYPE comes along and seems to break all the rules. A DOCTYPE begins with an exclamation point. The name is all in uppercase. Its attributes don't follow the name-value pair rules that I describe earlier in this chapter. To top it off, it has no closing tag.

The DOCTYPE element doesn't follow the normal markup rules because, technically speaking, it isn't an HTML *or* XHTML element. Instead, it's a *document type declaration*. The DOCTYPE element's purpose is to declare the type of document that the file contains and the version of HTML or XHTML that's used. A browser looks at this information to determine how to render the page as accurately and efficiently as possible. A document type declaration appears only at the top of an HTML or XHTML document — before the html element.

Whether you're working with HTML or XHTML, you find three basic DOCTYPE varieties:

- **Strict:** This type is the most restrictive; it requires you to code your presentation instructions in Cascading Style Sheets (CSS), not in HTML or XHTML. (See Book IV for more on CSS.) See the nearby sidebar, "That's a no-no in a Strict DOCTYPE" for a listing of features not allowed with a Strict DOCTYPE.

- **Transitional:** Provides more flexibility, allowing you to retain some older-style HTML presentation elements and attributes. However, the term *Transitional* specifies that it's a temporary solution for transferring old, legacy HTML code into the newer markup standards. The W3C expects this DOCTYPE to be phased out eventually.
- **Frameset:** Used when you want to place frames inside your document.

Use the Strict DOCTYPE unless you have a compelling reason to use one of the other alternatives. Using Strict now helps ensure that your Web page doesn't (from a coding standpoint) become outdated. It also helps ensure that the browsers processing the document will use the strictest rendering available (which ensures that you get the greatest level of control over how the page is displayed to users).

Table 1-2 lists the typical DOCTYPE declarations for XHTML and HTML. As you can see in the example, the !DOCTYPE element declaration is somewhat technical. Fortunately, most Web site applications, such as Dreamweaver and Expression, add this declaration for you automatically when you create a new HTML page.

Table 1-2 DOCTYPE Declarations

DTD	*Declaration*
XHTML 1.0 Strict	<!DOCTYPE html PUBLIC "-//W3C//DTD XHTML 1.0 Strict//EN" "http://www.w3.org/TR/xhtml1/DTD/xhtml1-strict.dtd">
XHTML 1.0 Transitional	<!DOCTYPE html PUBLIC "-//W3C//DTD XHTML 1.0 Transitional//EN" "http://www.w3.org/TR/xhtml1/DTD/xhtml1-transitional.dtd">
XHTML 1.0 Frameset	<!DOCTYPE html PUBLIC "-//W3C//DTD XHTML 1.0 Frameset//EN" "http://www.w3.org/TR/xhtml1/DTD/xhtml1-frameset.dtd">
HTML 4.01 Strict	<!DOCTYPE HTML PUBLIC "-//W3C//DTD HTML 4.01//EN" "http://www.w3.org/TR/html4/strict.dtd">
HTML 4.01 Transitional	<!DOCTYPE HTML PUBLIC "-//W3C//DTD HTML 4.01 Transitional//EN" "http://www.w3.org/TR/html4/loose.dtd">
HTML 4.01 Frameset	<!DOCTYPE HTML PUBLIC "-//W3C//DTD HTML 4.01 Frameset//EN" "http://www.w3.org/TR/html4/frameset.dtd">

The html element

The `html` element is much like an envelope: It exists only to provide a neat bundle for all the content inside it. In an HTML or XHTML document, only the `DOCTYPE` declaration appears outside of it. In traditional HTML, the `html` element had no parameters. With XHTML, however, the XML namespace declaration should be declared as an attribute:

```
<html xmlns="http://www.w3.org/1999/xhtml">
</html>
```

If the term *XML namespace* makes your head spin, don't worry about what it means (not just now, anyway). It's just more technical jargon that the browser uses to understand which kind of document it's working with.

The head element

The `head` element serves as a place to store information related to the document, although it doesn't appear as content inside the browser itself. The `head` section contains the document title, links to external style or script files, and other meta-information, such as the character set or document author.

The title element

The `title` element is located inside the `head` element. The text that appears inside the element provides a descriptive title for the document. The browser typically displays the title text in the browser window or tab:

```
<title>Digitalwalk :: About Digitalwalk</title>
```

The title is also one of the most important pieces of content on your Web page for search engines. Google and other search engines factor in the document title heavily when they evaluate the Web page. In addition, the title is what identifies each main entry in listings of search results.

Therefore, although you should limit your title to fewer than 80 characters, make sure that it's expressive and descriptive enough to adequately describe your page. Moreover, savvy Web designers creatively incorporate specific keywords that they want associated with their pages in search results.

The meta element

The `meta` element is a general-purpose element to specify meta (that is, related descriptive) information about the document — such as author, date, keywords, a description of the content, and character set. Tags that enclose such information are often referred to as *metatags*. Here are two general rules for using the `meta` element:

- It must be placed inside the `head` element.
- It never contains any of the content it describes, and is always self-closed (ends with `/>`).

The following sections describe the most commonly used metatags.

Content type declaration

This type of metatag is often used to declare the content of the document to the browser:

```
<meta http-equiv="Content-Type" content="text/html;
   charset=ISO-8859-1" />
```

Most Web site builders automatically add this information when you create a new document.

Meta description

A *meta description tag* is often used by search engines as the source of the summary text that's displayed for the page in search engine listings. Here's an example:

```
<meta name="description" content="Wimbly Tech Online solves
   all of your technology needs in 5 seconds or less."/>
```

However, the content in your meta description tag matters only for search engines that support it. Google, for example, ignores this tag. Instead, Google generates the summary text automatically, based on the content of your document.

If you use the meta description tag, use as your descriptor the text from the first couple of sentences in your HTML page's content.

Meta keywords

The *meta keywords tag* is a popular way to provide search engines with specific keywords to index as they process your Web page. However, because of misuse by Web-site designers over the years, this tag is much less important now. In fact, most major search engines ignore it! Even so, if you want to supply it to search engines that still use the tag, the code looks like this:

```
<meta name="keywords" content="Waterslides,Hoses,Water
   fun,HydroDance" />
```

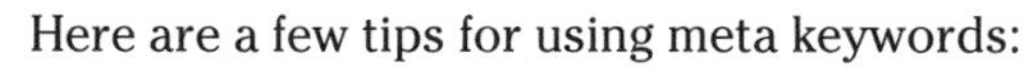

Here are a few tips for using meta keywords:

- Limit the number of keywords to fewer than 20.
- Avoid repeating words, even if a word appears in more than one term.
- Use only keywords that are relevant to the content of your document.

The body element

The `body` element encloses the content of the Web page — and is where most of your real work takes place. Any text that's placed between the opening and closing `body` tags is displayed in the browser. For example, consider this HTML document:


```
<!DOCTYPE html PUBLIC "-//W3C//DTD XHTML 1.0 Transitional//
   EN" "http://www.w3.org/TR/xhtml1/DTD/xhtml1-transitional.
   dtd">
<html xmlns="http://www.w3.org/1999/xhtml">
<head>
<meta http-equiv="Content-Type" content="text/html;
   charset=ISO-8859-1" />
<title>Creating Web Pages</title>
</head>
<body>
All of the text I place inside the document body is shown in
   the browser.
</body>
</html>
```

When this page is viewed in a Web browser (see Figure 1-1), the text inside the browser is displayed and everything else remains hidden from the user's view. Notice that the content of the `title` element is displayed in the browser window's title bar.

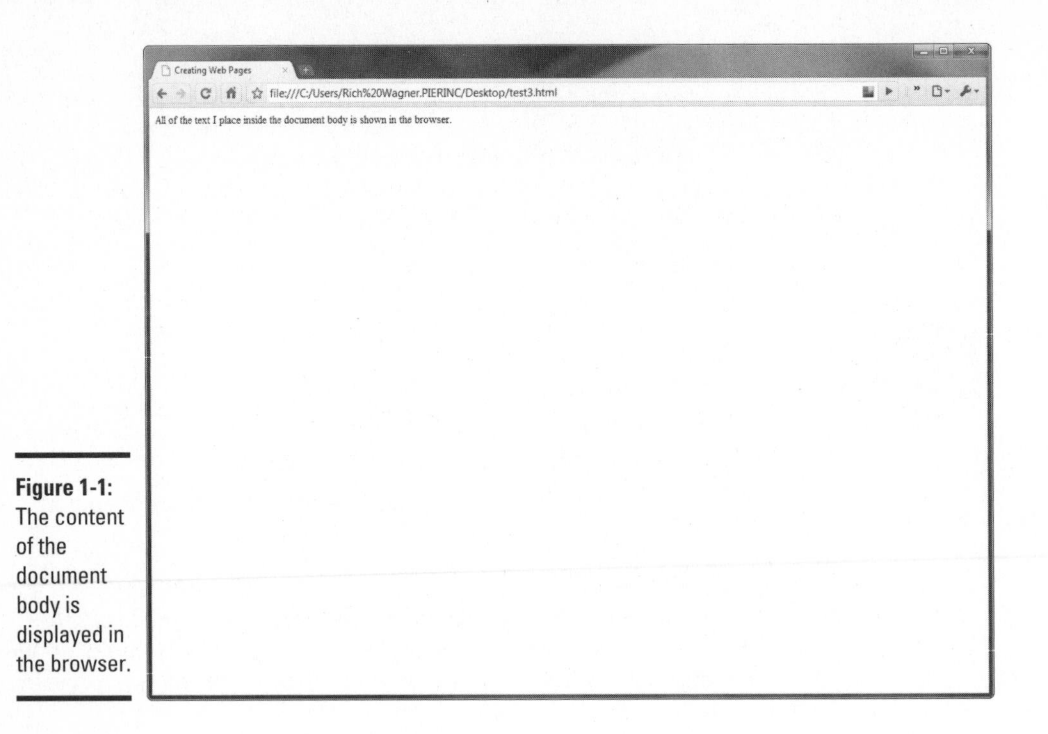

Figure 1-1: The content of the document body is displayed in the browser.

Chapter 2: Working with Text and Links

In This Chapter

- **Working with paragraphs and other document elements**
- **Adding bold and italic text**
- **Specifying font properties for your pages**
- **Creating links to Web pages and e-mail addresses**

While images and video garner much of the attention, the heart and soul of the Web remains something more vanilla: text and links. In this chapter, I show you how to work with the most common HTML elements to display and format text on your Web pages. I also show you how to create links to other Web pages.

Giving Your Document Structure

Any document you compose and edit contains at least a basic structure and formatting. Without these basic formatting techniques, text is extremely difficult to read. You already divide a page of text into distinct paragraphs, often grouping related paragraphs with a single heading. For special words or phrases, you emphasize the text by changing its text style. In fact, this sort of practice is probably second nature, to the point that you don't even think about doing it when you're writing e-mail messages or creating Word documents.

However, when you work with the source of an HTML document, you need to think about giving the document some built-in structure — because you can't format it as you would with an old typewriter by merely pressing Enter and Tab.

Making a paragraph

The `p` element is used to contain a paragraph of text. The opening tag (`<p>`) is placed at the beginning of the paragraph, and the closing tag (`</p>`) serves as the caboose. For example, the following HTML code shows two paragraphs of text:

```
<p>"Not much of a blowing up, I am sure," Mrs. Ellison said;
   "and as likely as not, a shilling at the end of it."</p>
<p>"Well, Mary, I must own," the squire said pleasantly,
   "that a shilling did find its way out of my pocket into
   his."</p>
```

Each paragraph appears as a block of text with an extra blank line at the end to divide it from the next paragraph. Figure 2-1 shows this code in a browser window.

Figure 2-1: The browser adds space between paragraphs.

When you use traditional HTML, be sure to add the closing tag (</p>) to the end of a paragraph — even though you don't have to. Traditional HTML allows you not to add the closing tag; however, as I discuss in Chapter 1 of this minibook, this practice isn't compatible with XHTML.

Adding a line break

The `br` element serves as a way to end a line manually or create an empty line of text. It's the equivalent of pressing Enter in your e-mail message or word processing document and starting a new line.

The br element forces a new line when it's used and does not add space around other paragraphs. Unlike the p element, br never contains any content by itself and, in fact, is often located inside a p element, as shown in this example:

```
<p>"Not much of a blowing up, I am sure,"<br/>
Mrs. Ellison said.<br/>
"And as likely as not, a shilling at the end of it."</p>
```

The two self-closing br elements force new lines to be added, as shown in Figure 2-2.

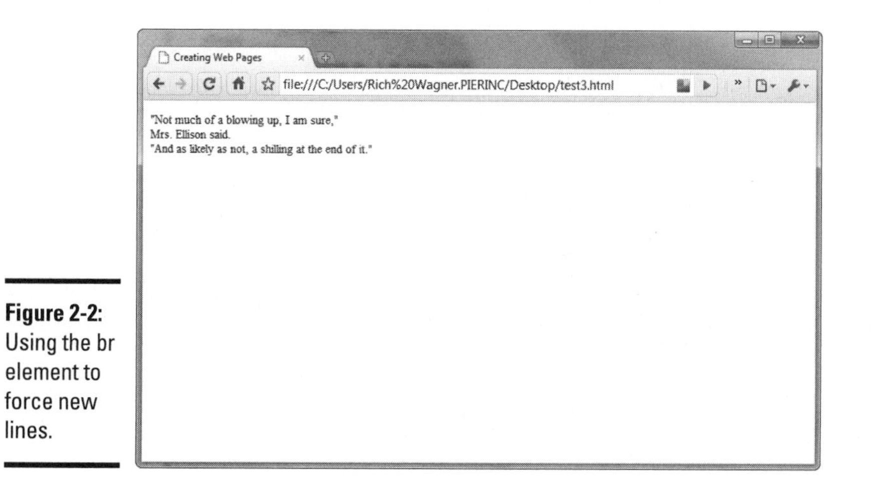

Figure 2-2: Using the br element to force new lines.

Making a heading

Most Web pages have a paragraph or groups of paragraphs offset by headings. HTML supports six levels of headings with the h1, h2, h3, h4, h5, and h6 elements. The h1 element is the topmost and largest; the h6 element is the smallest heading. Here are some examples:

```
<h1>This is heading 1</h1>
<h2>This is heading 2</h2>
<h3>This is heading 3</h3>
<h4>This is heading 4</h4>
<h5>This is heading 5</h5>
<h6>This is heading 6</h6>
```

The HTML is displayed in the browser, as shown in Figure 2-3.

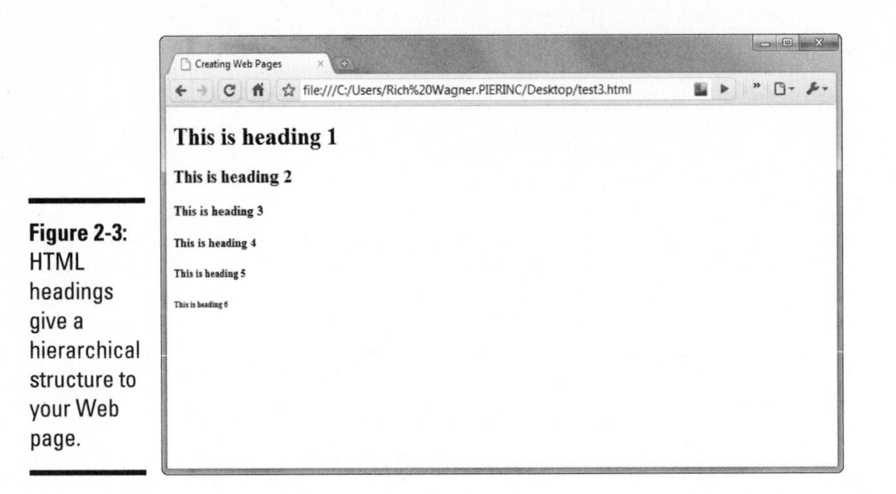

Figure 2-3: HTML headings give a hierarchical structure to your Web page.

Adding a horizontal line

You may want to visually offset one block of text from another. One way to do this is to use an `hr` element, which adds a horizontal line (or rule) to your document. For example, the following self-closing `hr` tag separates two sections of a page:

```
<p>The next day Mrs. Whitney and Reuben moved, with all their
   belongings, to Lewes.</p>
<hr/>
<h1>Chapter 3: The Burglary At The Squire's.</h1>
<p>"What is that woman Whitney going to do with her boy?" the
   squire asked the schoolmaster, when he happened to meet
   him in the village about a month after she had left. "Have
   you heard?"</p>
```

Figure 2-4 shows the horizontal line in the browser.

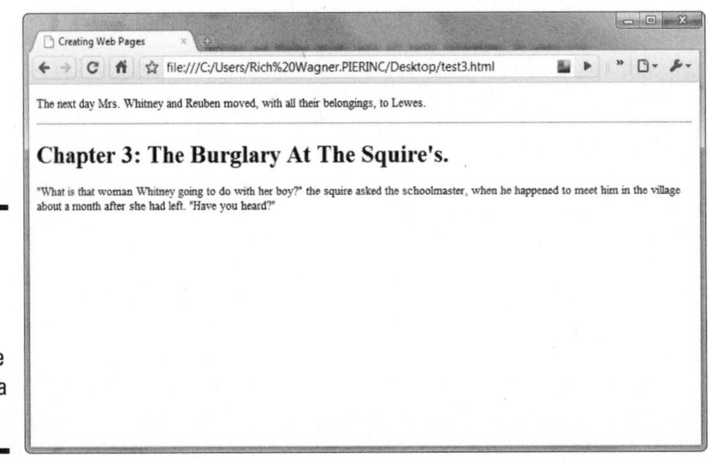

Figure 2-4: Horizontal lines are a great way to divide the content on a Web page.

Grouping inline text

Within a paragraph, you may have a reason to group part of the text so that you can add styling only to it rather than to the entire paragraph. The `span` element is what you use to perform this sort of behind-the-scenes grouping, as shown in this example:

```
<p>One morning in the spring, <span>the squire looked</span>
   in at Mrs. Whitney's shop.</p>
```

Without any attributes, the `span` element does nothing to the text. Instead, you typically use it with the `style` attribute, as shown a little later in this chapter, in the section "Fontastic! Specifying the Typeface, Size, and Color."

Emphasizing Your Text with Bold and Italics

Whether the Web site you're creating is megahuge or teeny-weeny, your most common formatting task is emphasizing text with bold and italics. This section describes the two elements you use for adding these two popular text effects.

Bolding text

Use the `strong` element when you want to **strongly emphasize** a portion of text. Strong text is displayed in the browser with a bold typeface, as shown in this example:

```
<p>I told the daring skater to <strong>stop</strong> ice
   dancing with scissors.</p>
```

Use the `strong` element to ensure compatibility with future browsers. Traditional HTML had a `b` tag for bolded text, but this element is being phased out in newer versions of HTML and XHTML.

Heading elements (`h1` to `h6`) apply bold to the text automatically, if you use them, you don't need to add `strong` tags.

Italicizing text

The `em` element is used when you want to emphasize text with italics, as shown in this example:

```
<p>A <em>tilde</em> is popularly known as a "squiggly
   mark."</p>
```

Traditional HTML sported an `i` tag for italics. However, the `em` element is now recommended as a better way to mark text that you wish to emphasize.

Fontastic! Specifying the Typeface, Size, and Color

Until now in this chapter, all the HTML formatting you looked at uses HTML elements to change the look of the text. However, after you begin to work with font properties — such as typeface, size, and color — you begin styling your Web pages with Cascading Style Sheets (CSS). (See Book IV for full details on CSS.) In years gone by, HTML designers used a `font` tag to set character formatting. However, the `font` tag is obsolete in newer versions of HTML and XHTML, so I strongly recommend that you avoid using it.

In this section, I show you the basics of using CSS to format text with the `style` attribute of the `p` and `span` elements. You can use the `style` attribute to set a style rule for all the content within a single element. The generic code looks like this:

```
<element style="css-property:value;another-css-
   property:value">Content</element>
```

CSS properties are declared as name-value pairs, separated by colons. Semicolons are used to separate more than one CSS property.

In addition to applying inline styles, you can apply style rules globally with the `style` element or by using an external stylesheet. (For the full scoop on these items, be sure to flip to Book IV.)

Setting the typeface

You can set the typeface or font face for a block of text by using the CSS property `font-family`. The `font-family` property is a comma-separated list of fonts you want to use. The browser uses the first font in the list that's available on the user's system. Here's an example that specifies three typefaces:

```
<span style="font-family:Arial, Helvetica, sans-serif">"Is
   this the road to Lewes?" Reuben asked.</span>
```

In this example, the browser looks for the Arial typeface first and then for Helvetica if Arial isn't located. If neither is available, the browser uses any sans serif (smooth-looking) font.

Multiple-word font names must be placed within quotation marks. Therefore, when using inline styles with the `style` attribute, be sure to use single quotation marks. For example, if you specify Times New Roman as the font, here's what the style declaration looks like:

```
<p style="font-family:'Times New Roman', Times, serif">"Is
   this the road to Lewes?" Reuben asked.</p>
```

```
<p style="font-family:Arial, Helvetica, sans-serif">"Lewes?
   Noa, this baint the road to Lewes. I don't know nothing
   about the road to Lewes. This bee the road to Hastings,
   if you goes further. So they tell me; I ain't never been
   there."</p>
```

Figure 2-5 shows the two paragraphs as displayed in the browser.

However, there's a better way to define formatting for paragraphs using CSS styles. See Book IV, Chapter 3 for full details.

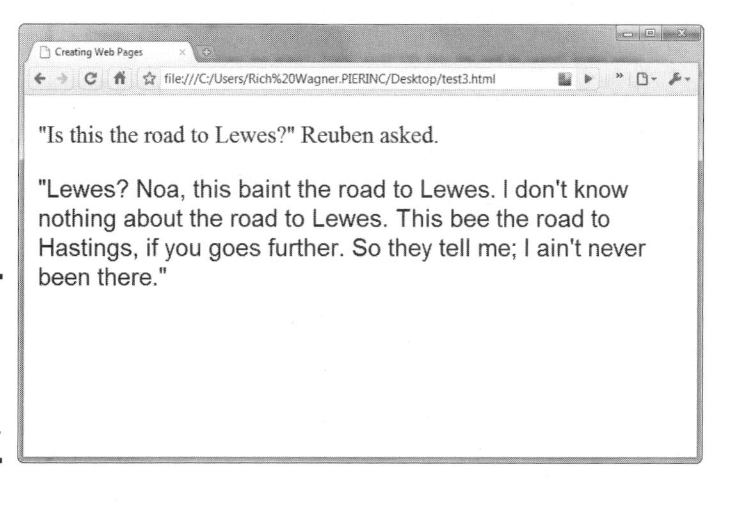

Figure 2-5: Setting the font typeface in a Web page.

Sizing the text

The size of the text is set using the CSS property `font-size`. You can set an *absolute* font size or have the size be *relative* to the browser's default font size.

Absolute sizes

To set the absolute font size, you can use a collection of constants: `xx-small`, `x-small`, `small`, `medium` (default), `large`, `x-large`, and `xx-large`. The following bit of code sets the sentence font to extra-small, which is roughly three sizes smaller than the normal, default size:

```
<span style="font-size:x-small">Reuben told the story of his
   adventures from the time of leaving.</span>
```

You can also set the font size by specifying it in points or pixels:

```
<p style="font-size:12pt">Reuben told the story of his
   adventures from the time of leaving.</p>
```

```
<p style="font-size:12px">Reuben told the story of his
   adventures from the time of leaving.</p>
```

Although point size is the unit of measurement that people are most comfortable with, point size is less precise than the collection of size constants. Different computers render point sizes differently, giving you less control of the text appearance if you specify font size in points.

Here's a code listing of several absolute-size paragraphs:

```
<p style="font-size:xx-small">xx-small</p>
<p style="font-size:x-small">x-small</p>
<p style="font-size:small">small</p>
<p style="font-size:medium">medium</p>
<p style="font-size:large">large</p>
<p style="font-size:x-large">x-large</p>
<p style="font-size:xx-large">xx-large</p>
<p style="font-size:8pt">8 point</p>
<p style="font-size:10pt">10 point</p>
<p style="font-size:12pt">12 point</p>
<p style="font-size:14pt">14 point</p>
<p style="font-size:8px">8 pixels</p>
<p style="font-size:10px">10 pixels</p>
<p style="font-size:12px">12 pixels</p>
<p style="font-size:14px">14 pixels</p>
```

Figure 2-6 shows this HTML code as displayed in the browser.

However, keep in mind, fonts can be adjusted by the user in a browser. Therefore, be careful about using small text or it could be unreadable if a user already has his or her default browser font set to a small size.

Relative sizes

To set the size of the text relative to the base font size, you can use the constants `smaller` and `larger`. In addition, you can specify a percentage of the base font size. This bit of code shows several relative size options:

```
<p style="font-size:smaller">Smaller</p>
<p style="font-size:90%">90% of Normal</p>
<p>Default font size - the standard bearer</p>
<p style="font-size:larger">Larger</p>
<p style="font-size:300%">300% of Normal</p>
```

The browser displays the code snippet, as shown in Figure 2-7.

Creating Web Pages
file:///C:/Users/Rich%20Wagner.PIERINC/Desktop/test3.html
xx-small
x-small
small
medium
large
x-large
xx-large
8 point
10 point
12 point
14 point
8 pixels
10 pixels
12 pixels
14 pixels

Figure 2-6: Working with various absolute font sizes.

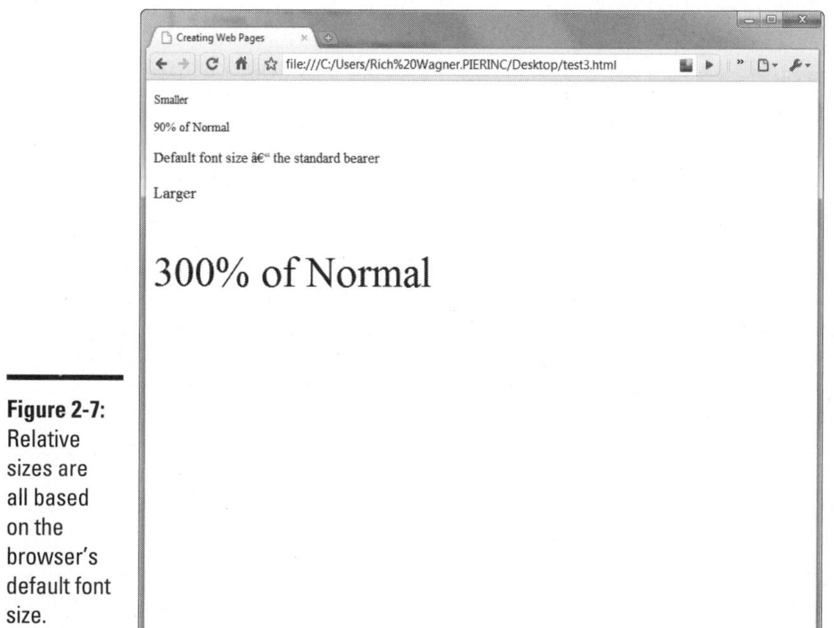

Figure 2-7: Relative sizes are all based on the browser's default font size.

Giving your text some color

You can specify the color of your text by using the CSS property `color`. You can assign a color by using a predefined color keyword, a hexadecimal (hex) value, or an RGB value.

HTML and CSS define 17 color constants for standard colors: `aqua`, `black`, `blue`, `fuchsia`, `gray`, `green`, `lime`, `maroon`, `navy`, `olive`, `orange`, `purple`, `red`, `silver`, `teal`, `white`, and `yellow`, as shown in this example:

```
<p style="color:navy">Can I see my mother?" Reuben asked
   next.</p>
```

However, because you can use millions of colors, you often want to use a hexadecimal color value, which is a technical-looking hex number prefixed with a hash character (#). It can be either three or six digits long, as shown in this example:

```
<p class="color:#ffffff">White</p>
<p class="color:#000000">Black</p>
<p class="color: #66FFCC">Spindrift</p>
```

Fortunately, most of the software applications you use in Web design and development allow you to copy these hex values easily from color selector dialog boxes and paste them directly into your code.

Creating Links

Links, links, links — it's all about links. In a very real way, links make the Web go 'round. Links drive everything people do on the Web. You read a Web page and then click a hyperlink to jump to another page on the site for more details. Or you search for a term on Google.com and then click the top result to jump to the associated site.

As you construct your Web site, think carefully about how you want to use links to help increase its usefulness to your visitors. Ask yourself these types of questions:

- ✦ What other information on your site is relevant to your current page?
- ✦ What other sites can you link to that provide more details about a particular topic?

Dissecting a URL

After you have any link-related decisions worked out, you're almost ready to create links in your document. However, before I jump into the HTML instructions, I give you an overview of URLs. A Uniform Resource Locator (URL) is the technical term for a Web address. A *URL* (pronounced either "you-are-ell" or "earl") is the unique identifier that's used to access any Web page, graphical element, or other resource.

Here's an example:

```
http://www.digitalwalk.net/more/about.html
```

URLs are composed of these three main parts:

- **Protocol:** Most Web links use the `http://` protocol, which simply tells the Web server that a document or other Web resource is being requested by the browser. Other protocols you might encounter include `mailto` (for creating a new e-mail message to the specified e-mail address), `ftp` (for a file on an FTP server), and `https` (for a Secure Sockets Layer transaction).
- **Domain name:** The domain name, such as `www.digitalwalk.net`, identifies the Web site containing the document. The domain name points to a particular Web server that hosts the site itself.
- **Path:** The path points to the exact location of the page on the Web server. This part (such as `/more/about.html`) often looks similar to a folder-and-filename combination that you work with on your local computer. The path can also include an anchor (prefixed with the # character), which indicates a link to a specific bookmark on a page. (See the later section "Linking to a location inside a page.")

Although you don't need to worry about case when you're working with the protocol and domain name, the path portion of a URL is often case-sensitive on many Web servers.

Distinguishing between absolute and relative URLs

Two types of URLs exist: absolute and relative. Here's a description of both types:

- **Absolute URL:** Provides the full address (including protocol, domain name, and path) of the page or other resource you're pointing to. Here's an example:

  ```
  http://www.wiley.com/resources/extras.html
  ```

- **Relative URL:** Also an address to a Web page, but described in relationship to the current page. For example, if the `extras.html` page is linking to another page (`more.html`) that sits in the same domain and directory (`www.wiley.com/resources/`), the relative URL is simply

  ```
  more.html
  ```

  Or, if you want to point to a file that's in the directory above the current file location, you can use this relative URL:

  ```
  ../index.html
  ```

You might find it helpful to think of an absolute URL as much like a full mailing address that you give to someone who lives far away from you: "I live at 122 Reed Lane, Fremont, MS 34531." A relative URL, on the other hand, is much like an informal address that you give to someone who lives in your neighborhood: "I live on the corner of Reed and Lamotte."

When you add a link to your Web page, use absolute URLs for all resources you point to that aren't part of your site. For links to other pages on your domain, you can use either absolute or relative paths, although relative URLs are often easier to work with.

Making a link

The HTML anchor element (`a`) is used to define a link on your page to another document. To use the anchor, you enclose text inside the `<a>` and `</a>` tags and then specify the URL by using the `href` attribute. Follow these steps to make a link:

1. **Inside the HTML page's body, locate or enter the text that you want to serve as the link on your page.**

   Here's an example:

   ```
   <p>
   Go to CNN for more information.
   </p>
   ```

2. **Enclose the link text with the a element.**

   In the following example, I use only part of the text:

   ```
   <p>
   <a>Go to CNN</a> for more information.
   </p>
   ```

3. **Specify the URL you want to link to inside the `href` attribute:**

```
<p>
<a href="http://www.cnn.com">Go to CNN</a> for more
   information.
</p>
```

The browser jumps to the `www.cnn.com` URL when the `Go to CNN` text is clicked in the Web page.

If the page you're linking to is on your site, you can use a relative URL instead, as shown in this example:

```
<p>
<a href="index.html">Home</a>
</p>
```

To make a link from an image, see Chapter 4 of this minibook.

To customize the visual look of your links by using CSS, see Book IV.

Linking to a location inside a page

Although most links you create link to other pages on the Web, you might occasionally want to link to a specific section on the same page. Typical examples are a Return to Top link at the bottom of a page or a table of contents that links to each section of the document.

To link to a specific location on a page, you first define a *named anchor,* an invisible HTML element that serves as the placeholder bookmark. Don't be confused: The named anchor uses the same `a` element as normal links. However, rather than use the `href` attribute, a named anchor uses the `name` attribute. After the named anchor is defined, you can link to the named anchor by using the `a` element.

When you link to a named anchor, you specify the named anchor as the value of the `href` attribute, prefixed with a pound sign (#). For example, to link to the named anchor `topofpage`, you use the following code:

```
<a href="#topofpage">Return to top</a>
```

Here's how to set up a link to a named anchor:

1. **Create a named anchor at the destination you want to jump to by using the link with the `a` element. Enter a value in the name attribute that effectively describes the location:**

```
<a name="section1"></a>
```

Note that you don't need to place text inside the named anchor.

2. **Create a link to the named anchor, by specifying its name (prefixed with a # sign) in the `href` attribute:**

```
<a href="#section1">Section 1: Understanding Political
   Reform</a>
```

Linking to an e-mail address

You can link to an e-mail address from your Web page, to provide an easy and direct way for site visitors to send e-mail to you. To do so, use the `mailto` protocol (rather than the familiar `http://`) inside the `href` attribute, as shown in this example:

```
<a href="mailto:info@digitalwalk.net">Email me</a>
```

If you want to add a subject line, you can specify it inside the `href` value after the e-mail address. To do so, add `?subject=` followed by the subject text. Here's an example:

```
<a href="mailto:info@digitalwalk.net?subject=Question for You"> Email me </a>
```

Note that `mailto:` links are good only when users use e-mail clients on their computers. They don't work with browser-based e-mail.

Linking to a picture, PDF document, or file

You can link to other resources, besides HTML pages, that are on the Web. You can use the `a` element to jump to JPG or PNG images, Adobe Acrobat documents (PDF files), Microsoft Word or Excel documents, ZIP files, and more. To link to one of these file types, you simply point to the URL of the file:

```
<a href="manuals/netspud_102.pdf">Read user manual</a>
```

Depending on the type of document you're pointing to, the file is either downloaded on the user's computer or displayed like another Web page inside the browser itself. For example, a picture or PDF document is usually opened in the browser.

You need to link to a file on a Web server, not to a file on your computer's hard drive.

Opening the link in a new browser window

When you click a link on a Web page, the normal action is to replace the existing page with the destination page inside the browser window. However, you may occasionally want to define a link that opens in a new browser window and leaves the existing page unchanged. This technique is especially helpful when you're linking to an external site. To do this, add a `target` attribute to your link code, as shown in this example:

```
<a href="http://www.cnn.com" target="_blank">Go to CNN</a>
   for more information.
```

Chapter 3: Presenting Information with Lists and Tables

In This Chapter

- Creating bulleted and numbered lists
- Using images for bullets
- Working with nested lists
- Creating tables to organize tabular data
- Formatting tables

The typical Web page contains large amounts of text. But there's more to organizing text on a page than just positioning sentences and paragraphs. A Web page filled with lines of text may contain good content, but the eyes of a visitor quickly glaze over if you don't break the text into readable chunks. Lists and tables are therefore excellent organizational tools that help make your Web pages easier and quicker to read. In this chapter, you discover how to create lists and tables.

Creating a Bulleted List

A *bulleted list* is one of the most common ways to organize a series of items, whether it's a single word, phrase, sentence, or occasionally even an entire paragraph: Each item in the list is indented and prefixed with a *bullet* (normally a black dot). In the HTML world, a bulleted list is the same as an *unordered list*.

Making a normal unordered list

To create a bulleted list, you use the `ul` and `li` elements. The `ul` element defines an unordered list, and its start and end tags enclose the items on the list. The `li` element is used to define each item in the list. Here's a simple example:

```
<ul>
<li>Patriots</li>
<li>Jets</li>
<li>Bills</li>
<li>Dolphins</li>
</ul>
```

Figure 3-1 shows the result in the browser.

Figure 3-1: Round bullets for a list.

Using alternative bullets

When you use HTML by itself, your bullet choices are limited. However, if you add just a bit of CSS, you can customize the look of the bullets themselves. (See Book IV for full details on what CSS is and how it works.)

The `list-style-type` CSS property is used to set the type of list-item marker. When you're working with unordered lists, you can use `square`, `circle` (a doughnut-like circle), `disc` (the default black circle), or `none`. For example, to use square bullets for a simple list, you can add a `style` attribute to the list definition:

```
<ul style="list-style-type:square">
<li>Patriots</li>
<li>Jets</li>
<li>Bills</li>
<li>Dolphins</li>
</ul>
```

Alternatively, if you want to change the style of all unordered lists on your page, you can add the following property definition to a `style` element in the page's document head:

```
<style>
ul { list-style-type: square }
</style>
```

Using images for bullets

Although CSS provides some alternative bullet styles with its `list-style-type` property, images can be the best way to go when you want to use a unique bullet style or specific color that complements your overall Web-page design.

To create an image-based bullet list, turn to CSS (again). Although you have a couple of ways to create the list, the best method to ensure consistent results is to use the `background-image` property for the image and then tweak the padding and margin settings for the `ul` and `li` elements.

The following CSS rules are added to the document head in a `style` element. The padding and margin rules push the content to the right to ensure that the text doesn't overlap the background image:

```
<style>
ul {
    list-style-type: none;
    padding-left: 0;
    margin-left: 0;
}
li {
    padding-left: 1.2em;
    background-image: url('images/arrow.png');
    background-repeat: no-repeat;
    background-position: 0 .1em;
}
</style>
```

Figure 3-2 shows the results in a browser.

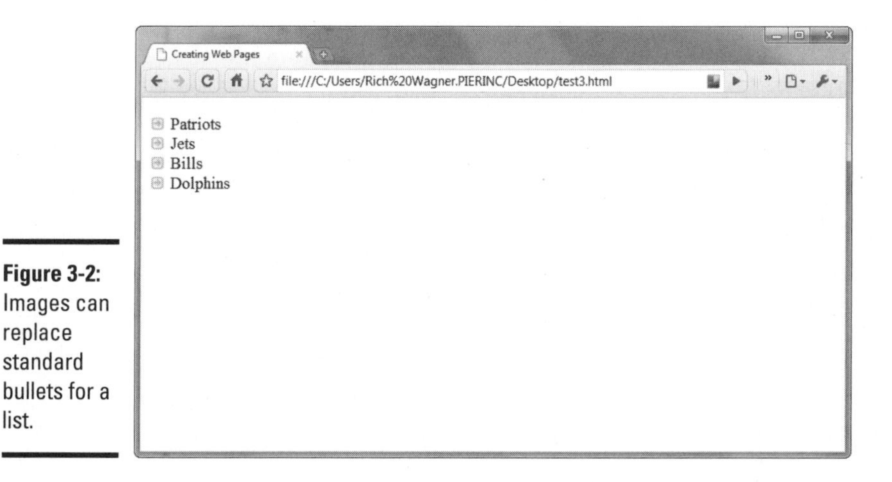

Figure 3-2: Images can replace standard bullets for a list.

Creating a Numbered List

HTML also allows you to create numbered lists with the `ol` element. Numbered (or ordered) lists enclose the list with an `<ol>` start tag and `</ol>` end tag, and they use the `li` elements for each numbered list item. Here's an example:

```
<ol>
<li>Get up at 6:00am.</li>
<li>Take a shower.</li>
<li>Eat breakfast.</li>
<li>Drive to work.</li>
</ol>
```

The result is a numbered list of items:

1. Get up at 6:00am.
2. Take a shower.
3. Eat breakfast.
4. Drive to work.

As with unordered lists, you can use `list-style-type` to change the numbering style for ordered lists. Some of the possible values you can use are in Table 3-1.

Table 3-1 Common Number-Related Values for list-style-type

Value	*Numbering Styles*
`decimal`	1, 2, 3, 4, 5
`decimal-leading-zero`	01, 02, 03, 04, 05
`lower-roman`	i, ii, iii, iv, v
`upper-roman`	I, II, III, IV, V
`lower-alpha`	a, b, c, d, e
`upper-alpha`	A, B, C, D, E

For example, to change the numbering to lowercase Roman numerals, you can add a style attribute to the `ol` list:

```
<ol style="list-style-type:lower-roman">
<li>Get up at 6:00am.</li>
<li>Take a shower.</li>
<li>Eat breakfast.</li>
```

```
<li>Drive to work.</li>
</ol>
```

The result looks like this:

i. Get up at 6:00am.

ii. Take a shower.

iii. Eat breakfast.

iv. Drive to work.

Working with Nested Lists

You can nest ordered and unordered lists, and intermix them as necessary to produce the desired results. Here's an ordered list with three bulleted lists nested inside:

```
<ol>
<li>Europe
 <ul>
  <li>United Kingdom</li>
  <li>France</li>
  <li>Netherlands</li>
 </ul>
</li>
<li>North America
 <ul>
  <li>Canada</li>
  <li>United States</li>
 </ul>
</li>
<li>South America<ul>
  <li>Brazil</li>
  <li>Peru</li> </ul>
</li>
</ol>
```

Nested lists can get complicated when you're opening and closing tags everywhere. The best principle to remember is the adage *first in, last out; last in, first out.*

Working with Tables

Since the early days of the Web, HTML tables have had a tough life. The `table` element was created as a way to organize tabular data into rows and columns. However, as page design became more important, HTML tables were initially the only way to structure a sophisticated page design; only this method enabled you to position elements at specific locations on the page. But as time went on — and designs became more and more sophisticated — the shortcomings of the `table` element as a layout tool became painfully evident.

Fortunately, innovations such as CSS and `div` elements (see Chapter 5 in this minibook) have replaced HTML tables as the best way to structure and organize the layout of your entire page. As a result, the `table` element is free to return to its original purpose: organizing tabular data.

You use four main elements when creating an HTML table. These elements are shown in Table 3-2.

Table 3-2 Principal Elements of HTML Tables

Element	*What It Does*
`table`	Defines a table and encloses all table-related elements and content
`tr`	Serves as a table row
`td`	Serves as a table cell
`th`	Identifies headings

The following steps show you how to create a table in HTML, such as this one, with four columns and five rows:

Team	*Wins*	*Losses*	*GB*
Browns	7	0	--
Giants	5	2	2
Colts	5	2	2
Bills	4	3	3

Here's what you do:

1. **Type the text of the table in your document, and separate the columns with a space:**

```
Team Wins Losses GB
Browns 7 0 --
Giants 5 2 2
Colts 5 2 2
Bills 4 3 3
```

2. **Enclose the table text with** `<table>` **tags:**

```
<table>
Team Wins Losses GB
Browns 7 0 --
Giants 5 2 2
Colts 5 2 2
Bills 4 3 3
</table>
```

3. **Enclose each of the rows with** `<tr>` **tags:**

```
<table>
<tr>Team Wins Losses GB</tr>
<tr>Browns 7 0 --</tr>
<tr>Giants 5 2 2</tr>
<tr>Colts 5 2 2</tr>
<tr>Bills 4 3 3</tr>
</table>
```

4. **Surround header text for each cell with** `<th>` **tags.**

   To make the code easier to read, format the text in a more hierarchical format, using new lines and indentations:

```
<table>
<tr>
 <th>Team</th>
 <th>Wins</th>
 <th>Losses</th>
 <th>GB</th>
</tr>
<tr>Browns 7 0 --</tr>
<tr>Giants 5 2 2</tr>
<tr>Colts 5 2 2</tr>
<tr>Bills 4 3 3</tr>
</table>
```


5. **Surround the text of your table cells with** `<td>` **tags.**

   If a cell has no content, place ` ` in the cell; it's a special HTML code that indicates a nonbreaking space. For example, if you want to use an empty cell rather than the double hyphen in the last column of the `Browns` row, you can substitute ` ` instead:

```
<table>
<tr>
 <th>Team</th>
 <th>Wins</th>
 <th>Losses</th>
 <th>GB</th>
</tr>
<tr>
 <td>Browns</td>
 <td>7</td>
 <td>0</td>
```

```
  <td> </td>
 </tr>
 <tr>
  <td>Giants</td>
  <td>5</td>
  <td>2</td>
  <td>2</td>
 </tr>
 <tr>
  <td>Colts</td>
  <td>5</td>
  <td>2</td>
  <td>2</td>
 </tr>
 <tr>
  <td>Bills</td>
  <td>4</td>
  <td>3</td>
  <td>3</td>
 </tr>
 </table>
```

Figure 3-3 shows the result in the browser.

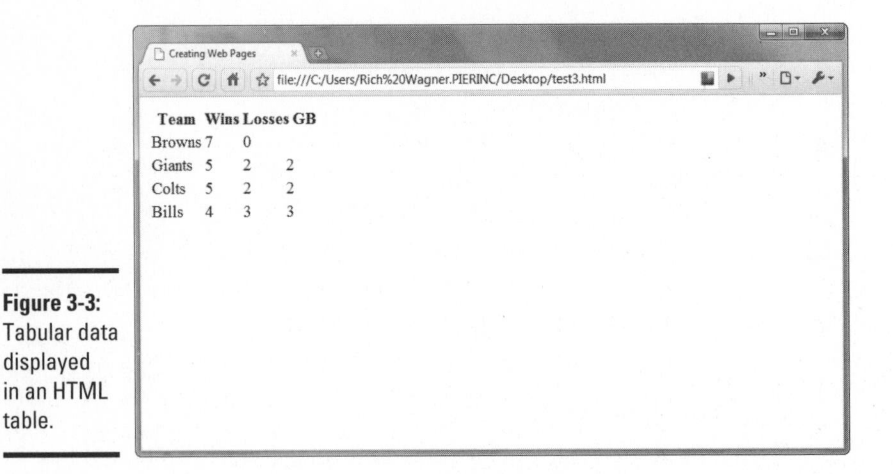

Figure 3-3: Tabular data displayed in an HTML table.

Adding a border to the table

The `table` element has a `border` attribute that allows you to add borders to your table. The higher the number, the thicker the border. Here's a mini-table with a thin border:

```
<table border="1">
<tr>
 <th>Team</th>
```

```
  <th>Wins</th>
  <th>Losses</th>
  <th>GB</th>
</tr>
<tr>
  <td>Browns</td>
  <td>7</td>
  <td>0</td>
  <td>--</td>
</tr>
</table>
```

Figure 3-4 shows the table defined here.

Removing the `border` attribute is equivalent to `border="0"`.

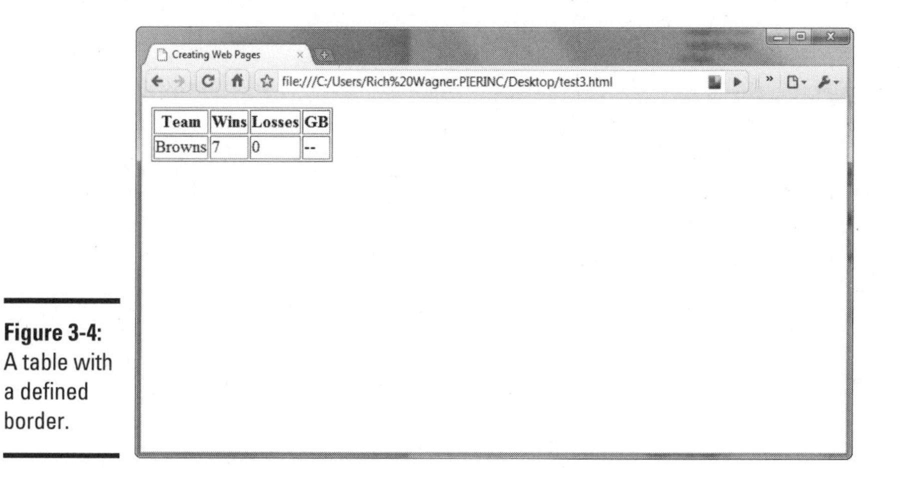

Team	Wins	Losses	GB
Browns	7	0	--

Figure 3-4: A table with a defined border.

You can also use CSS to style your borders (see Book IV for more details).

Sizing your table

By default, the width of a table is sized according to its content and the width of the browser window. However, you can set the size of the table by using the `width` attribute. As shown in Figure 3-5, the value of this attribute can be shown either in pixels or as a percentage of the browser window.

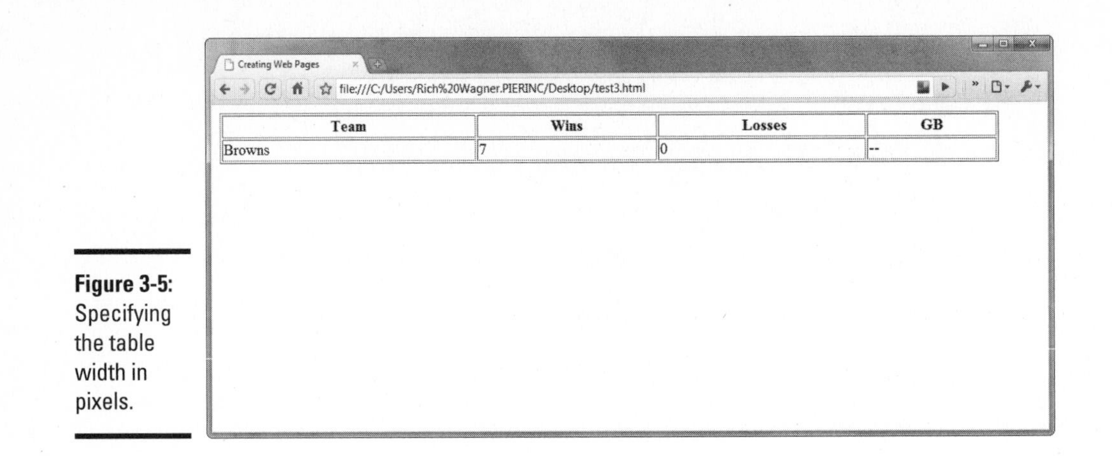

Figure 3-5: Specifying the table width in pixels.

Here's an example of a pixel-sized table:

```
<table border="1" width="700px">
<tr>
 <th>Team</th>
 <th>Wins</th>
 <th>Losses</th>
 <th>GB</th>
</tr>
<tr>
 <td>Browns</td>
 <td>7</td>
 <td>0</td>
 <td>--</td>
</tr>
</table>
```

A second example demonstrates a percentage-based table — no matter the size of the browser window, the table is always 90 percent of the width of the window:

```
<table border="1" width="90%">
<tr>
 <th>Team</th>
 <th>Wins</th>
 <th>Losses</th>
 <th>GB</th>
</tr>
<tr>
 <td>Browns</td>
 <td>7</td>
 <td>0</td>
 <td>--</td>
</tr>
</table>
```

Figures 3-6 and 3-7 show the table sized automatically according to the changing size of the browser window.

Figure 3-6: The table sizes itself as a percentage of a large browser window.

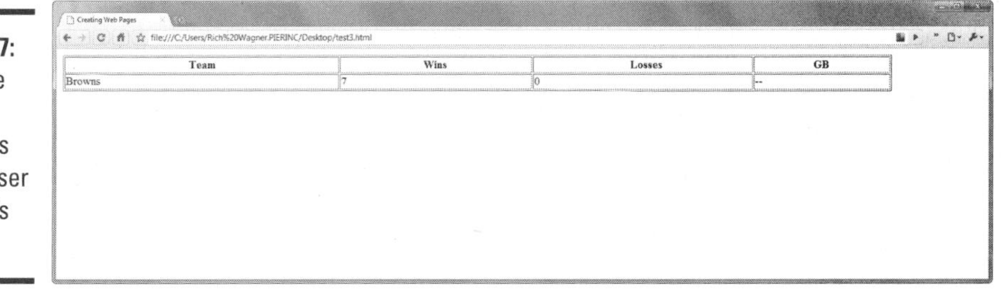

Figure 3-7: The same table is resized as the browser window is resized.

Sizing the columns of a table

Using the `width` attribute of a `th` or `td` element, you can adjust not only the table element, but also the width of each column. The value can be either a pixel value or a percentage of the table width.

When you adjust one of the cells in a table column, you adjust, in effect, *all* of them. However, the code is often easier to manage if you add the same attribute to each cell of the column.

The following chunk of code widens the first column in the table to 200 pixels:

```
<table border="1" width="90%">
<tr>
 <th width="200px">Team</th>
 <th>Wins</th>
 <th>Losses</th>
 <th>GB</th>
</tr>
<tr>
 <td width="200px">Browns</td>
 <td>7</td>
 <td>0</td>
 <td>--</td>
</tr>
</table>
```

Spacing your table

The `table` element has two attributes that enable you to space the content inside the table cells: `cellspacing` and `cellpadding`. The `cellspacing` attribute defines the space between cells, and `cellpadding` defines the space between a cell's walls and its content. Both values are in pixels.

When these values aren't specified in the code, most browsers set the value of `cellpadding` to 1 and `cellspacing` to 2. Therefore, if you want to eliminate any spacing between cells, set them both explicitly to `0`.

The following chunk of code adds padding and spacing for the table's cells:

```
<table width="90%" border="1" cellpadding="2"
    cellspacing="4">
<tr>
 <th width="100px">Team</th>
 <th>Wins</th>
 <th>Losses</th>
 <th>GB</th>
</tr>
<tr>
 <td width="100px">Browns</td>
 <td>7</td>
 <td>0</td>
 <td>--</td>
</tr>
</table>
```

Chapter 4: Adding Images

In This Chapter

- **Adding an image by using HTML**
- **Positioning your image on a page**
- **Adding padding around an image**
- **Specifying the dimensions of an image**
- **Using an image as a link**

Many adages stress the importance of visual images over textual information: *Image is everything. A picture equals a thousand words. A photo in hand is worth two documents in the bush.* Okay, I made up that last one, but you get the idea.

Because of the importance of images, you have to be ready to add them to your Web pages. Graphics not only make your site look more attractive, they also make your documents easier to browse and read.

In this chapter, I show you how to work with images by using HTML. Be sure to check out Book VI for full details about the different types of Web graphics.

Adding an Image

When you add an image to a Web page, you don't embed it into the document, as you'd do in an application like Microsoft Word. Instead, you link a separate image file into the HTML code. The browser then pulls the image when the page is loaded and displays the image as part of the page.

JPG, PNG, and GIF images are the common types of graphics that you typically add to your pages.

The `img` element is used to define an image and has two basic attributes: `src` and `alt`. The basic code looks like this:

```
<img src="http://www.digitalwalk.net/wally.jpg" alt="Portrait
   of Wally"/>
```

The `src` attribute indicates the URL of the image file. The `alt` attribute specifies the text to display if the image isn't displayed.

Always use `alt` (commonly referred to as an *alt tag*) when working with images. Using `alt` tags ensures that people using alternative ways of accessing your Web site (screen readers or text-only browsers, for example) can understand the content of the image.

The following chunk of code shows a basic Web page with an image:

```
<!DOCTYPE html PUBLIC "-//W3C//DTD XHTML 1.0 Transitional//
   EN" "http://www.w3.org/TR/xhtml1/DTD/xhtml1-transitional.
   dtd">
<html xmlns="http://www.w3.org/1999/xhtml">
<head>
<meta http-equiv="Content-Type" content="text/html;
   charset=ISO-8859-1" />
<title>HBC Chess Time</title>
</head>
<body>
<p>Chess Time: This Week</p>
<p><img src="images/DSC02669-01.jpg" alt="Justus playing
   chess"/></p>
</body>
</html>
```

Figure 4-1 shows the page displayed in a browser. Figure 4-2 shows the alternative text that's displayed when the image isn't found during the loading of the form.

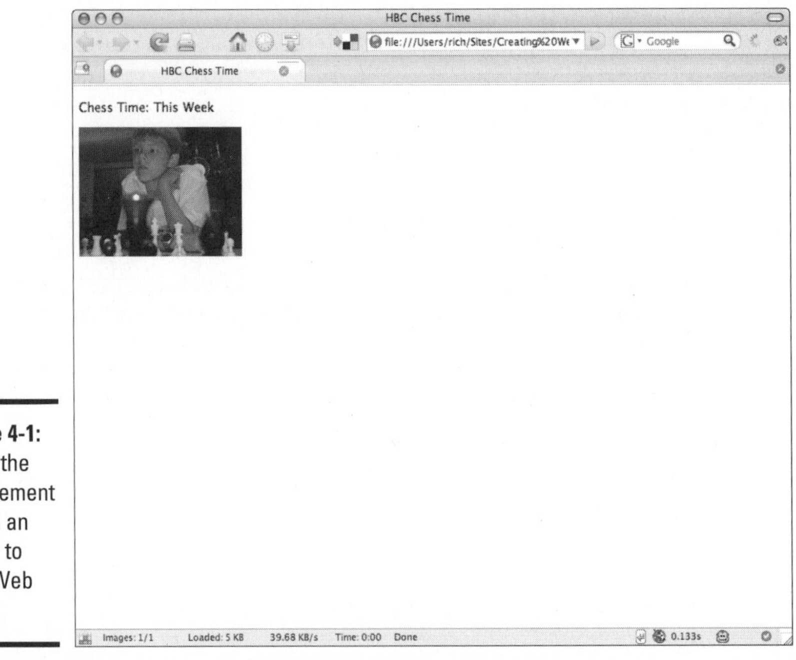

Figure 4-1: Using the img element to add an image to your Web page.

Figure 4-2: Using the img element's alt attribute to show alternative text if the image isn't displayed.

Positioning an Image on the Page

When you add an image to your page, it's added *inline:* It's displayed in the document at any location you specify, even in the middle of a line of text. However, you can control the alignment of the image by using CSS styles. (See Book IV if you need a primer on CSS.)

In the past, you could control the alignment of the image by using the `img` element's `align` attribute. Because this attribute has been deprecated in the latest HTML and XHTML specifications, however, avoid using it.

Suppose you want to position a picture alongside the first paragraph of a page. As a result, you place the `img` element just before the paragraph text begins. Here's the code:

```
<!DOCTYPE html PUBLIC "-//W3C//DTD XHTML 1.0 Transitional//
   EN" "http://www.w3.org/TR/xhtml1/DTD/xhtml1-transitional.
   dtd">
<html xmlns="http://www.w3.org/1999/xhtml">
<head>
<meta http-equiv="Content-Type" content="text/html;
   charset=ISO-8859-1" />
<title>War and Peace</title>
</head>
<body>
```

```
<p><img src="images/tolstoy.jpg" alt="Author Leo
   Tolstoy"/>&quot;Well, Prince, so Genoa and Lucca are now
   just family estates of the Buonapartes. But I warn you, if
   you don't tell me that this means war, if you still try
   to defend the infamies and horrors perpetrated by that
   Antichrist--I really believe he is Antichrist--I will
   have nothing more to do with you and you are no longer
   my friend, no longer my 'faithful slave,' as you call
   yourself! But how do you do? I see I have frightened you--
   sit down and tell me all the news.&quot;</p>
<p>It was in July, 1805, and the speaker was the well-known
   Anna Pavlovna Scherer, maid of honor and favorite of the
   Empress Marya Fedorovna. With these words she greeted
   Prince Vasili Kuragin, a man of high rank and importance,
   who was the first to arrive at her reception. Anna
   Pavlovna had had a cough for some days. She was, as she
   said, suffering from la grippe; grippe being then a new
   word in St. Petersburg, used only by the elite.</p>
</body>
</html>
```

The problem is that the `img` is set inline to the text by default, which extends the text line so that it's the same size as the height of the image. Figure 4-3 shows the result.

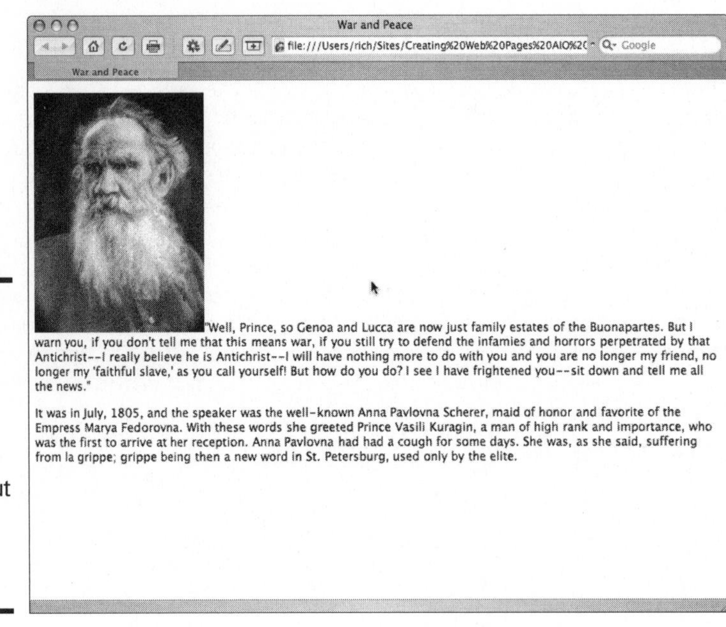

Figure 4-3: An image displayed inline with the paragraph text, without using an align attribute.

However, you can use the `float` CSS property to align the image to the left of the text of the paragraph and wrap the text around it. Here's an updated `img` element definition:

```
<img src="images/tolstoy.jpg" alt="Author Leo Tolstoy"
   style="float:left"/>
```

When the updated page is loaded in a browser, the image is left-aligned and wraps the text. See Figure 4-4.

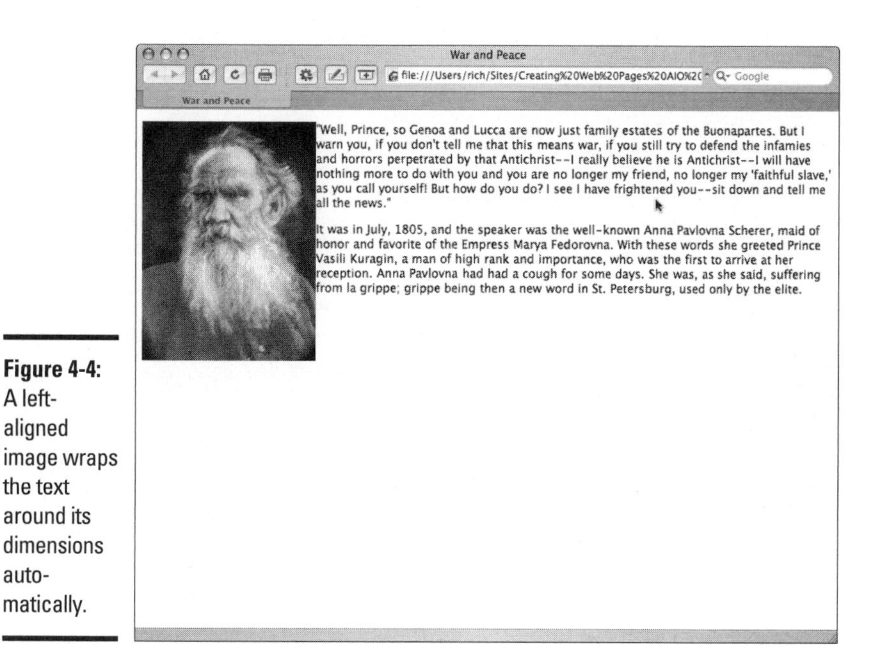

Figure 4-4: A left-aligned image wraps the text around its dimensions automatically.

Although the image placement looks better using the `float` CSS property, it's still too close to the paragraph text that surrounds it. Therefore, in the next section, I show you how to add padding around the image.

Adding Padding Around Your Image

Typically you *pad* an image with extra spacing to offset it from other visual elements. As shown in Figure 4-4 (refer to the preceding section), the lack of padding makes the image appear crowded next to the text around it.

The CSS set of margin properties comes to the rescue. As Book IV explains in greater detail, these properties define the space between an element and the elements around it. The margin property sets the margin for all four sides of the element. The margin-left, margin-right, margin-top, and margin-bottom properties define the margin for the corresponding side.

To fix the margin in Figure 4-4, you need to offset only the right margin. Therefore you add a margin-right property to the style declaration, and set the value to 15 pixels:

```
<img src="images/tolstoy.jpg" alt="Author Leo Tolstoy"
   style="float:left;margin-right:15px"/>
```

Figure 4-5 shows the results you're looking for.

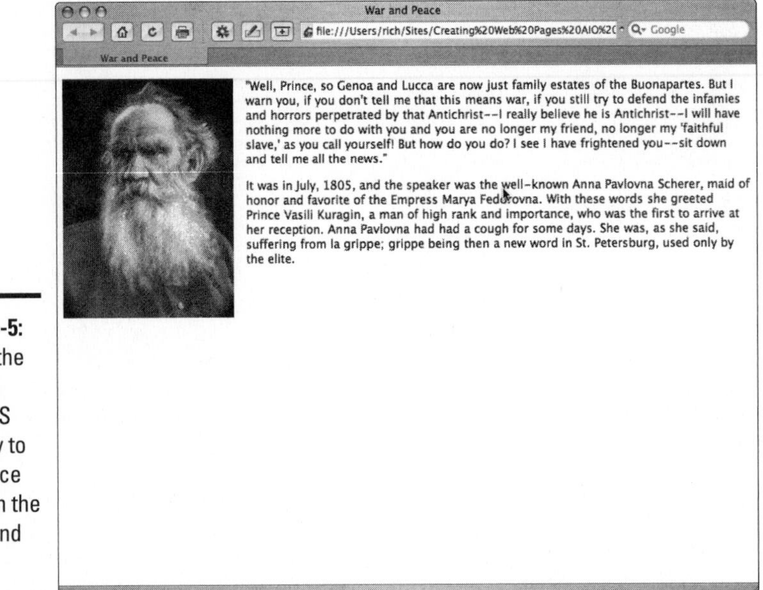

Figure 4-5: Setting the margin-right CSS property to add space between the image and the text.

Earlier versions of HTML used hspace and vspace attributes to provide spacing around an img element. However, as with the align attribute, these properties have gotten the boot from the newer HTML and XHTML specifications. Use CSS styles instead: They offer much greater control.

Specifying the Dimensions of the Image

The img element also has width and height attributes that you can use to define the specific dimensions of the image. Browsers no longer require these attributes because they automatically set the size to be equal to the size of the image itself. However, there's a reason for adding them: These dimensions allow the browser to create a placeholder space as it loads the image and the rest of the document, which can result in a faster rendering of the HTML file. Additionally, if you want to enlarge or shrink the size of the image, these attributes can come in handy. Here's an example:

```
<img src="images/tolstoy.jpg" alt="Author Leo Tolstoy"
   width="150" height="300"/>
```

Be careful when you use height and width values that differ from the actual physical size of the image. If you enlarge the values significantly, the image quality is degraded. If you shrink the values significantly, you needlessly add to the size of the Web page. (A better alternative is to shrink the image in an image-editing software program first and *then* add it to your Web page.) Finally, if you tweak the height and width proportions, the image can become skewed.

Linking Your Image

In Chapter 2 of this minibook, I show you how to create text links to other Web pages by using the anchor (a) element. However, you can use the a element to create clickable images as well.

One handy use for linking images is to display a smaller thumbnail image on your page and allow the user to click it to display a full-size version of the same picture.

Be sure to only link to images that are uploaded to your Web server or are accessible over the Internet, not images on your local hard drive.

To create a thumbnail-linked image, follow these steps:

1. **Add an img element to your document:**

```
<!DOCTYPE html PUBLIC "-//W3C//DTD XHTML 1.0
   Transitional//EN" "http://www.w3.org/TR/xhtml1/DTD/
   xhtml1-transitional.dtd">
<html xmlns="http://www.w3.org/1999/xhtml">
<head>
<meta http-equiv="Content-Type" content="text/html;
   charset=ISO-8859-1" />
<title>Coming Soon</title>
</head>
```

```
<body>
<h2>Coming Soon to a Theater Near You</h2>
<img src="images/cracked_mini.jpg" alt="Thumbnail of
   Cracked poster"/>
<p style="font-style: italic;font-size: x-small">Click
   to view a full-sized image of the movie poster </p>
</body>
</html>
```

2. **Add the `<a>` start and `</a>` end tags before and after the `img` element:**

```
<a><img src="images/cracked_mini.jpg" alt="Thumbnail of Cracked
   poster"/></a>
```

The image should be enclosed in the a element.

3. **Add an `href` attribute that points to the document or file that you want to link to:**

```
<!DOCTYPE html PUBLIC "-//W3C//DTD XHTML 1.0
   Transitional//EN" "http://www.w3.org/TR/xhtml1/DTD/
   xhtml1-transitional.dtd">
<html xmlns="http://www.w3.org/1999/xhtml">
<head>
<meta http-equiv="Content-Type" content="text/html;
   charset=ISO-8859-1" />
<title>Coming Soon</title>
</head>
<body>
<h2>Coming Soon to a Theater Near You</h2>
<a href="images/cracked_full.jpg"><img src="images/
   cracked_mini.jpg" alt="Thumbnail of Cracked
   poster"/></a>
<p style="font-style: italic;font-size: x-small">Click
   to view a full-sized image of the movie poster </p>
</body>
</html>
```

Figure 4-6 displays the page in a browser; Figure 4-7 shows the result when the image thumbnail is clicked.

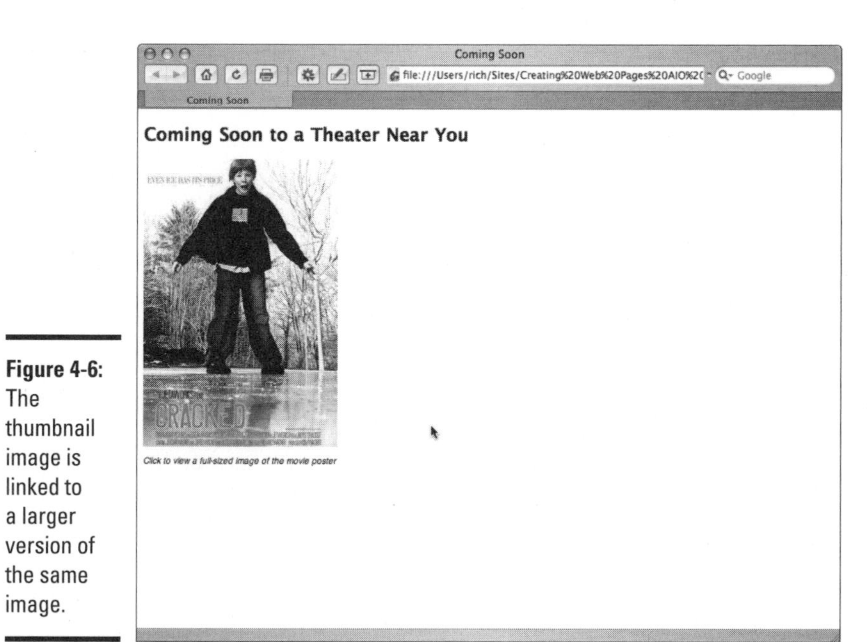

Figure 4-6: The thumbnail image is linked to a larger version of the same image.

Figure 4-7: Clicking the thumbnail image displays the full-size version of the image.

Chapter 5: Divvying Up the Page with divs

In This Chapter

- **Understanding what `div` elements can do**
- **Positioning and sizing a `div` element**
- **Adding border and background settings to a `div` element**
- **Creating a `div`-based page layout**

In the early days of the Web, the average Web page resembled a typical word-processing document — a single-column, text-based layout that flowed from top to bottom and from left to right. An element appeared on the page after the element that came before it. You could shake things up slightly with line breaks and alignment properties, but that was about it.

However, Web designers longed to transfer the same kind of sophisticated layouts that they were using for print publications to desktop publishing tools. The designers wanted to create Web sites that looked Madison Avenue slick, not MIT geeky.

To get around this problem of page flow, designers came up with a "band-aid" solution — HTML tables. Although the `table` element was intended as a container for spreadsheet-like data, they found that they could do almost anything with it. A visual Web page may look sleek inside the browser, but viewing its source code would reveal the complex grid system of rows and columns, sometimes nested inside each other, to achieve the visual effect. Unfortunately, these page layouts were a pain to work with and became difficult to manage.

The `div` element was introduced into HTML as a solution to the layout problem. In this chapter, I show you how to use the `div` element as a core element to use as you design your Web site.

Read Book IV before you work through this chapter. When you lay out `div` elements on your page, you make heavy use of CSS.

Introducing the div Element

The `div` element (short for *division*) is a rectangular block used for grouping other HTML elements. By default, a `div` element occupies 100 percent of the available width of the browser window and adds line breaks between other elements. A `div` element is visible only if you color its borders or background. Otherwise it's perfectly content to serve as a behind-the-scenes layout device for content contained inside it.

Using CSS, you can position the `div` element anywhere you want on a page. That flexibility gives the `div` element its layout power. Here are some elements you can easily create with `div` elements; without `div` elements, they're quite difficult to create in HTML:

- **A three-column Web page:** Create left, right, and center `div` elements.
- **A text sidebar, alongside the main text:** Float the `div` element to the side of the main body text.
- **A table or set of images:** They appear in the center of the document body, with the text wrapping itself around it.

The `div` element, by itself, creates a rectangular block where it's positioned on the page. Consider the following bare-bones document:

```
<!DOCTYPE html PUBLIC "-//W3C//DTD XHTML 1.0 Transitional//
   EN"
    "http://www.w3.org/TR/xhtml1/DTD/xhtml1-transitional.
   dtd">
<html xmlns="http://www.w3.org/1999/xhtml">
<head>
<title>The Broken Window</title>
</head>
<body>
<p>"I am not troublesome, ma'm," the boy said sturdily.
   "That is, I wouldn't be if they would let me alone; but
   everything that is done bad, they put it down to me."</p>
</body>
</html>
```

Suppose that you enclose the paragraph of content inside a `div` element, like this:

```
<html xmlns="http://www.w3.org/1999/xhtml">
<head>
<title>The Broken Window</title>
</head>
<body>
<div>
```

```
<p>"I am not troublesome, ma'm," the boy said sturdily.
   "That is, I wouldn't be if they would let me alone; but
   everything that is done bad, they put it down to me."</p>
</div>
</body>
</html>
```

Just adding a div element here doesn't do much. In fact, it has no noticeable visual effect on the page, as shown in Figure 5-1.

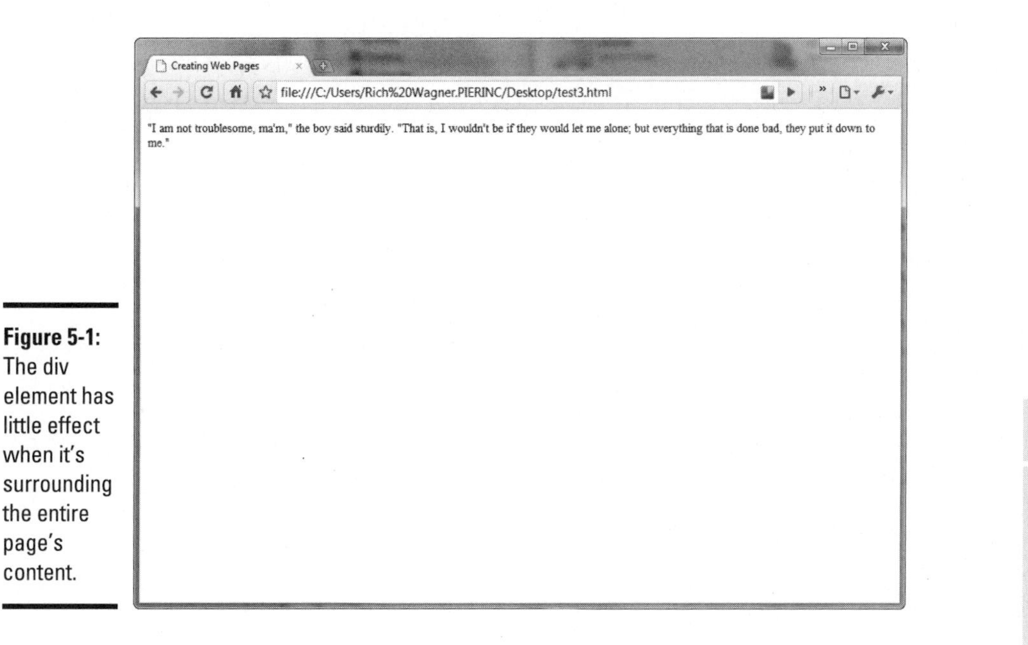

Figure 5-1: The div element has little effect when it's surrounding the entire page's content.

However, suppose you move the div to contain just a portion of the paragraph:

```
<html xmlns="http://www.w3.org/1999/xhtml">
<head>
<title>The Broken Window</title>
</head>
<body>
<p>"I am not troublesome, ma'm," <div>
the boy said sturdily.</div>
 "That is, I wouldn't be if they would let me alone; but
   everything that is done bad, they put it down to me."</p>
</body>
</html>
```

The blockish nature of the div element creates a rectangular block around its content, separating it from the other text in the paragraph. A line break is added to separate it from the following element (see Figure 5-2).

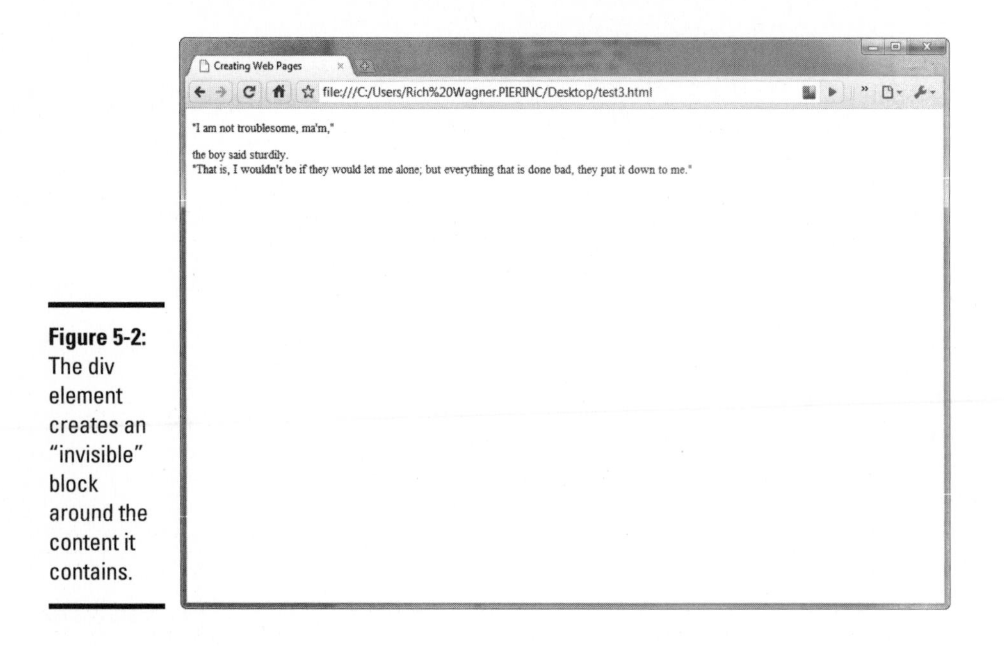

Figure 5-2: The div element creates an "invisible" block around the content it contains.

Positioning and Sizing a div Element on a Page

A div element might not look much like a big deal when you're working with plain HTML (as shown in the previous section). However, when you combine it with the positioning capabilities of CSS, you begin to tap into its full potential.

Floating a div element on the page left or right

The CSS property float is a handy way to position a div block. You can use it to "float" the div on the right or left side of the page. Suppose that you want to treat a section of content on your Web page as a sidebar to appear alongside the rest of the document text. The way to go is to float your div.

In this example, I use the document shown in Figure 5-3. The objective is to take the table of contents out of the flow of the document and move it to a sidebar on the right side of the page.

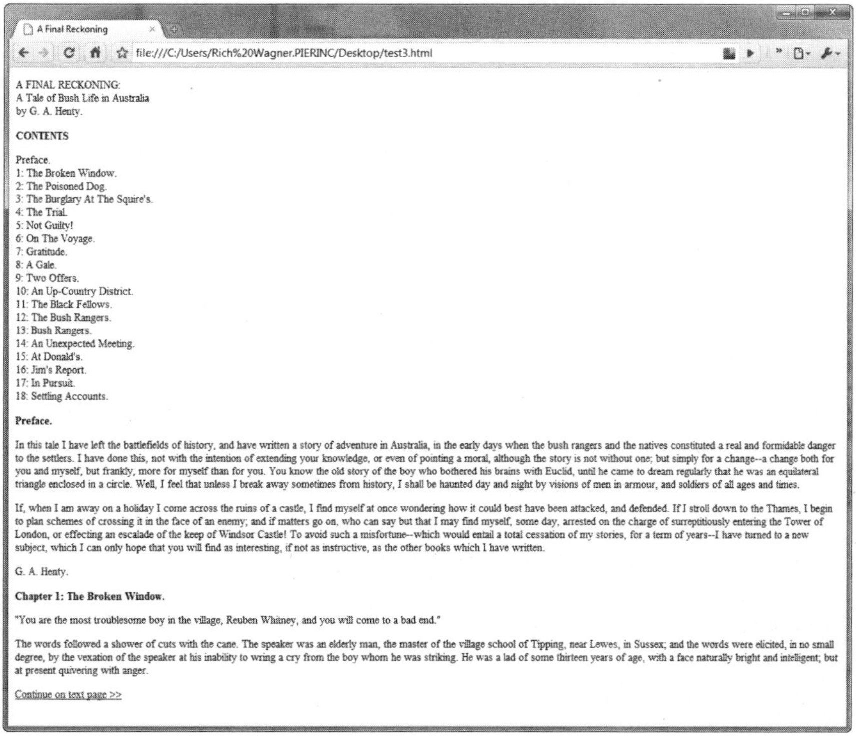

Figure 5-3: Before I make any changes, the table of contents sits as part of the regular document text.

The following steps show you how to use the `float` element with `div`:

1. **Open the HTML file you want to modify.**

   Here's the HTML code for the sample document:

```
<!DOCTYPE html PUBLIC "-//W3C//DTD XHTML 1.0 Transitional//EN" "http://
   www.w3.org/TR/xhtml1/DTD/xhtml1-transitional.dtd">
<html xmlns="http://www.w3.org/1999/xhtml">
<head>
<meta http-equiv="Content-Type" content="text/html; charset=ISO-8859-1"
    />
<title>A Final Reckoning</title>
</head>

<body>
<p>A FINAL RECKONING:<br />
A Tale of Bush Life in Australia<br />
by G. A. Henty.</p>
<p><strong>CONTENTS</strong></p>
<p>Preface.<br />
  1: The Broken Window.<br />
  2: The Poisoned Dog.<br />
  3: The Burglary At The Squire's.<br />
  4: The Trial.<br />
  5: Not Guilty!<br />
  6: On The Voyage.<br />
```

```
  7: Gratitude.<br />
  8: A Gale.<br />
  9: Two Offers.<br />
  10: An Up-Country District.<br />
  11: The Black Fellows.<br />
  12: The Bush Rangers.<br />
  13: Bush Rangers.<br />
  14: An Unexpected Meeting.<br />
  15: At Donald's.<br />
  16: Jim's Report.<br />
  17: In Pursuit.<br />
  18: Settling Accounts.</p>
<p><strong>Preface.</strong></p>
<p>In this tale I have left the battlefields of history, and have written
    a story of adventure in Australia, in the early days when the bush
    rangers and the natives constituted a real and formidable danger to
    the settlers. I have done this, not with the intention of extending
    your knowledge, or even of pointing a moral, although the story is
    not without one; but simply for a change--a change both for you and
    myself, but frankly, more for myself than for you. You know the old
    story of the boy who bothered his brains with Euclid, until he came
    to dream regularly that he was an equilateral triangle enclosed
    in a circle. Well, I feel that unless I break away sometimes from
    history, I shall be haunted day and night by visions of men in
    armour, and soldiers of all ages and times.</p>
<p>If, when I am away on a holiday I come across the ruins of a castle, I
    find myself at once wondering how it could best have been attacked,
    and defended. If I stroll down to the Thames, I begin to plan
    schemes of crossing it in the face of an enemy; and if matters go
    on, who can say but that I may find myself, some day, arrested
    on the charge of surreptitiously entering the Tower of London, or
    effecting an escalade of the keep of Windsor Castle! To avoid such a
    misfortune--which would entail a total cessation of my stories, for
    a term of years--I have turned to a new subject, which I can only
    hope that you will find as interesting, if not as instructive, as
    the other books which I have written.</p>
<p>G. A. Henty.</p>
<p><strong>Chapter 1: The Broken Window.</strong></p>
<p>&quot;You are the most troublesome boy in the village, Reuben Whitney,
    and you will come to a bad end.&quot;</p>
<p>The words followed a shower of cuts with the cane. The speaker was
    an elderly man, the master of the village school of Tipping, near
    Lewes, in Sussex; and the words were elicited, in no small degree,
    by the vexation of the speaker at his inability to wring a cry from
    the boy whom he was striking. He was a lad of some thirteen years of
    age, with a face naturally bright and intelligent; but at present
    quivering with anger.</p>
<p><a href="page2.html">Continue on text page >></a></p>
</body>
</html>
```

2. **Enclose the sidebar content inside a `div` element. Add an `id` attribute with a value of `sidebar`:**

```
<div id="sidebar">
<p><strong>CONTENTS</strong></p>
<p>Preface.<br />
  1: The Broken Window.<br />
  2: The Poisoned Dog.<br />
  3: The Burglary At The Squire's.<br />
  4: The Trial.<br />
  5: Not Guilty!<br />
```

```
  6: On The Voyage.<br />
  7: Gratitude.<br />
  8: A Gale.<br />
  9: Two Offers.<br />
  10: An Up-Country District.<br />
  11: The Black Fellows.<br />
  12: The Bush Rangers.<br />
  13: Bush Rangers.<br />
  14: An Unexpected Meeting.<br />
  15: At Donald's.<br />
  16: Jim's Report.<br />
  17: In Pursuit.<br />
  18: Settling Accounts.</p>
</div>
```

The `id` attribute enables you to uniquely identify the `<div>` element for CSS styling later in these steps.

3. **Add a `style` element to the document head:**

```
<head>
<meta http-equiv="Content-Type" content="text/html; charset=ISO-8859-1"
    />
<title>A Final Reckoning</title>
<style>
</style>
</head>
```

The `<style>` element contains CSS styling instructions.

4. **Add a CSS `id` selector for the sidebar `div`, and set the `float` style to `right`.**

An `id` selector contains a # symbol followed by the `id` value of the `div`. This type of CSS selector specifies the formatting for an element with the associated `id` value. The `float` property moves the `div` element to the side of the page, forcing the content of the page to wrap around it:

```
<style>
div#sidebar { float: right; }
</style>
```

5. **Add spacing between the sidebar and the document body by setting the `margin-left` style to `20px`:**

```
<style>
div#sidebar { float: right; margin-left: 20px; }
</style>
```

6. **Adjust the width of the sidebar by setting the `width` sidebar to `200px`:**

```
<style>
div#sidebar { float: right; margin-left: 20px; width: 220px; }
</style>
```

7. **Save your HTML file.**

Figure 5-4 shows the newly created sidebar in a browser.

A Final Reckoning

file:///C:/Users/Rich%20Wagner.PIERINC/Desktop/test3.html

A FINAL RECKONING:
A Tale of Bush Life in Australia
by G. A. Henty.

Preface.

In this tale I have left the battlefields of history, and have written a story of adventure in Australia, in the early days when the bush rangers and the natives constituted a real and formidable danger to the settlers. I have done this, not with the intention of extending your knowledge, or even of pointing a moral, although the story is not without one; but simply for a change--a change both for you and myself, but frankly, more for myself than for you. You know the old story of the boy who bothered his brains with Euclid, until he came to dream regularly that he was an equilateral triangle enclosed in a circle. Well, I feel that unless I break away sometimes from history, I shall be haunted day and night by visions of men in armour, and soldiers of all ages and times.

If, when I am away on a holiday I come across the ruins of a castle, I find myself at once wondering how it could best have been attacked, and defended. If I stroll down to the Thames, I begin to plan schemes of crossing it in the face of an enemy; and if matters go on, who can say but that I may find myself, some day, arrested on the charge of surreptitiously entering the Tower of London, or effecting an escalade of the keep of Windsor Castle! To avoid such a misfortune--which would entail a total cessation of my stories, for a term of years--I have turned to a new subject, which I can only hope that you will find as interesting, if not as instructive, as the other books which I have written.

G. A. Henty.

Chapter 1: The Broken Window.

"You are the most troublesome boy in the village, Reuben Whitney, and you will come to a bad end."

The words followed a shower of cuts with the cane. The speaker was an elderly man, the master of the village school of Tipping, near Lewes, in Sussex; and the words were elicited, in no small degree, by the vexation of the speaker at his inability to wring a cry from the boy whom he was striking. He was a lad of some thirteen years of age, with a face naturally bright and intelligent; but at present quivering with anger.

Continue on text page >>

CONTENTS

Figure 5-4: You can align a div element to different parts of the page and have the text wrap itself around it.

Centering a div element on the page

Although you can use the `float` property to align to the left or right of a page, you can't center a `div` horizontally on a page by using this technique. To center align a `div` block, you need to set the `text-align:center` property of the `body` (or the element container):

```
body {
 margin: 0px;
 padding: 0px;
 text-align:center;
}
```

Note that if you center the text in the body, you need to add `text-align:left` in the `div` elements in the page to left-align your text.

Positioning the div element in an absolute position

The example in the earlier section "Floating a `div` element on the page left or right" shows you one way to position a `div` element by using `float`. However, you can also use the CSS property `position` to set absolute positioning. For example, you might want to change the CSS style from the previous example to

```
div#sidebar { position: absolute; top: 50px; right: 40px; }
```

When you specify `position: absolute`, the `div` element appears at a specific location indicated by the `top` and `right` properties. However (and it's a *big* however!), the document body no longer wraps around the `div` element. As a result, absolute positioning of `div` content isn't nearly as useful for most designers, except for graphical content that you want to place in the background.

Formatting a div Element

Because a `div` element is used as a container for other content, it doesn't have any visible properties by default. However, you can use CSS to format the rectangular shape of the `div`. Typically, you format the border or background.

Adding a border

To add a CSS border to your `div`, use the `border` property (or its related properties — `border-style`, `border-width`, and `border-color`). If you want to add a 1-pixel black border to the sidebar, you add the `border` property to the style definition:

```
div#sidebar { float: right; width: 220px; margin-left: 20px;
   border: 1px black solid; }
```

Figure 5-5 shows the border around the sidebar.

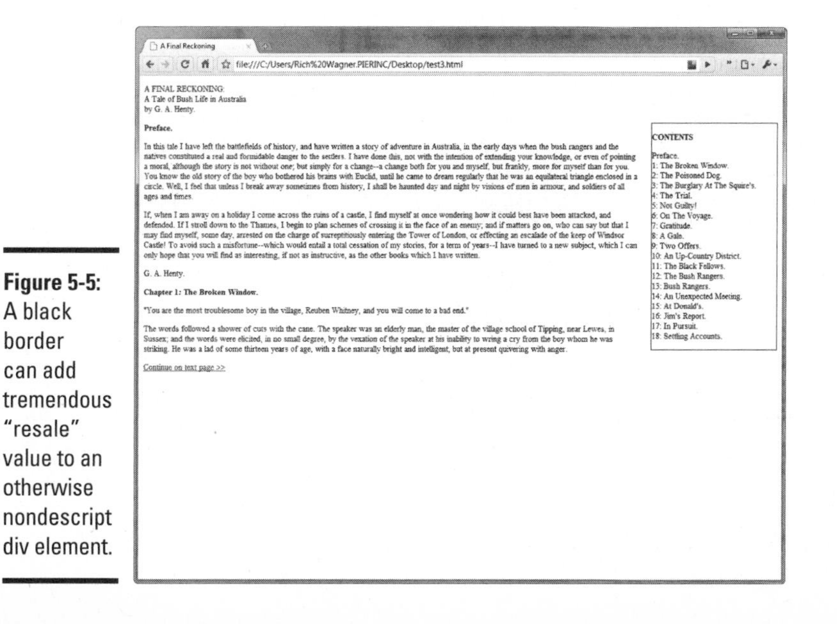

Figure 5-5: A black border can add tremendous "resale" value to an otherwise nondescript div element.

The problem is that the border is too close to the content inside the sidebar. As a result, you need to add padding around the `div` content by using the CSS property `padding` (see Figure 5-6):

```
div#sidebar { float: right; width: 220px; margin-left: 20px;
   border: 1px black solid; padding: 7px; }
```

Adding a background

Adding a shaded background or background image to your `div` involves working with the background properties, usually `background-color` or `background-image`. Here's the code for adding a blue background:

```
div#sidebar { float: right; width: 220px; margin-left: 20px;
   border: 1px black solid; padding: 7px; background-color:
   #99CCFF }
```

Figure 5-7 shows the completed sidebar, now with a border and colored background.

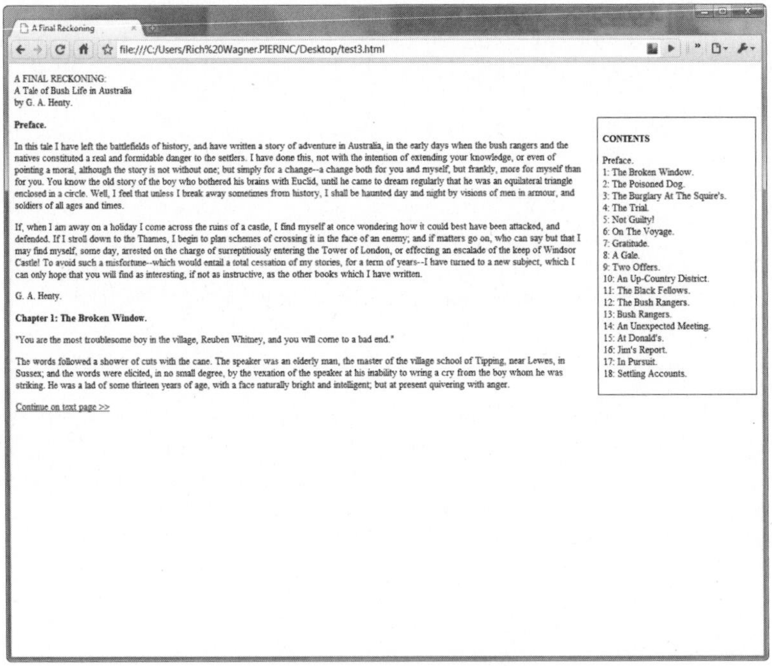

Figure 5-6: Adding padding to the sidebar to separate the div content from the border.

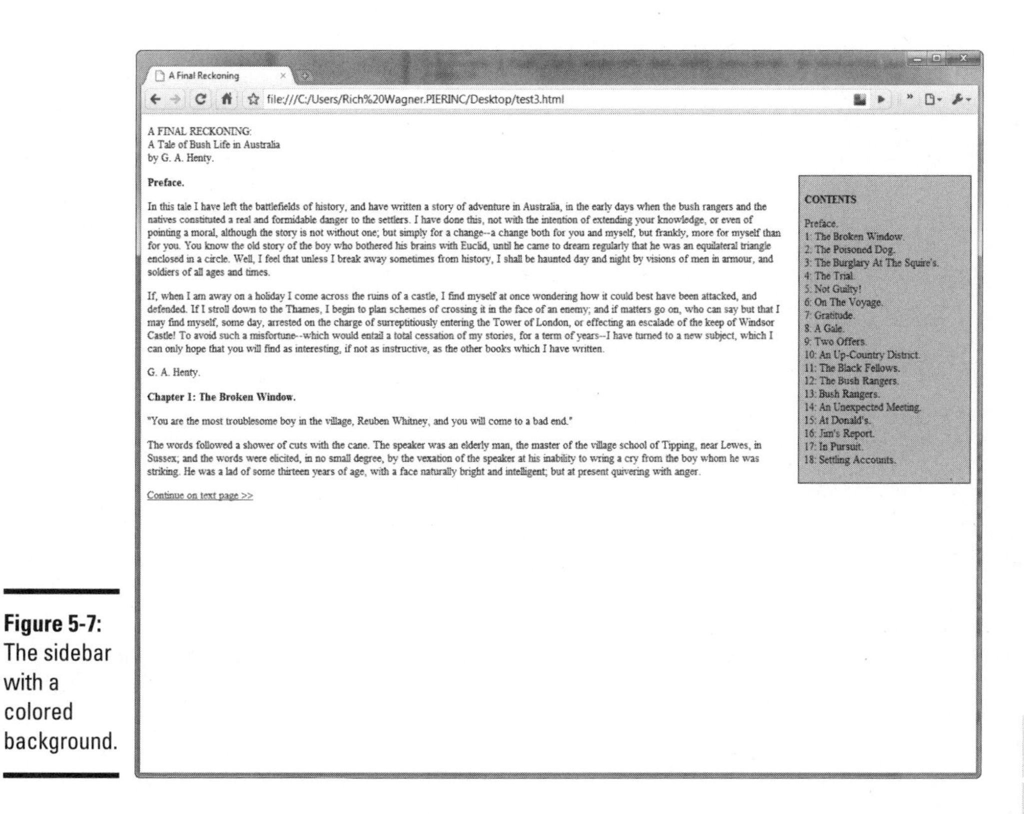

Figure 5-7: The sidebar with a colored background.

Creating a scrollable div

By default, a `div` adjusts its height based on its content. If you specify the CSS property `height`, however, the `div` adjusts its size to this value. The problem is that if the content extends beyond fixed dimensions of the `div`, some content is left "out in the cold" and can't be displayed on the page.

Once again, CSS comes to the rescue with its `overview` property. When `overview: auto` is added to the style definition, scrollbars are added if the content exceeds the available space to display it. Here's the code for the sidebar in Figure 5-7 (note the newly added `height` property to fix the vertical size of the `div`):

```
div#sidebar { float: right; width: 220px; margin-left: 20px;
   border: 1px black solid; padding: 5px; background-color:
   #99CCFF; height: 150px; overflow: auto;}
```

Figure 5-8 shows the result in a browser.

Figure 5-8: A scrollable div element allows you to set a fixed size for the block and then scroll any content that doesn't fit in the space.

Structuring a Basic Two-Column Page Layout

The `div` is the primary building block for page layout because it allows you to carve the page into different regions — yet still format and work with each of them independently of each other.

Here's how to set up a fixed-width, `div`-based layout, using the popular two-column layout:

1. **Create a new HTML document with a skeleton page structure.**

```
<!DOCTYPE html PUBLIC "-//W3C//DTD XHTML 1.0 Transitional//EN" "http://
    www.w3.org/TR/xhtml1/DTD/xhtml1-transitional.dtd">
<html xmlns="http://www.w3.org/1999/xhtml">
<head>
<meta http-equiv="Content-Type" content="text/html; charset=UTF-8" />
<title>Two Column Layout</title>
</head>
<body>

</body>
</html>
```

2. **Add** `div` **elements to represent the major regions of a typical layout — header, body, sidebar, and footer.**

   Use a container `div` element to enclose the body and sidebar.

   Use descriptive `id` attributes to identify each element:

```
<!DOCTYPE html PUBLIC "-//W3C//DTD XHTML 1.0 Transitional//EN" "http://
    www.w3.org/TR/xhtml1/DTD/xhtml1-transitional.dtd">
<html xmlns="http://www.w3.org/1999/xhtml">
<head>
<meta http-equiv="Content-Type" content="text/html; charset=UTF-8" />
<title>Two Column Layout</title>
</head>
<body>
<div id="header">Don't play head games with the header content.</div>
<div id="container">
<div id="sidecolumn">This is the side column. It can go on the right or
    left and still be happy. </div>
<div id="bodytext">This section contains the main body text of the
    document.</div>
</div>
<div id="footer">Not to be stepped upon, the footer content goes inside
    this element.</div>
</body>
</html>
```

   As you can see, I placed dummy text in the `div` elements for this example.

3. **Add a** `style` **element to the document head.**

   To simplify this example, I am adding the CSS rules in the document head of this file. However, if you're using the same style settings for multiple pages, use an external style sheet (see Book IV for more on this subject):

```
<head>
<meta http-equiv="Content-Type" content="text/html; charset=UTF-8" />
<title>Two Column Layout</title>
<style>
</style>
</head>
```

4. **Enter the style definition for the** `header div`**.**

   Set the `header` to a variable width of 90 percent of the browser window and a fixed height of 80 pixels. The left margin is set to 20 pixels, ensuring spacing between the browser's window and the left side of the page:

```
#header {
    width: 90%;
    height: 80px;
    margin-left: 20px;
}
```

5. **Add the style information for the `container` element.**

   The `container` element allows you to work with the main part of the document as one unit rather than always as two pieces (body text and sidebar):

   ```
   #container {
        width: 90%;
        margin-left: 20px;
        min-height: 600px;
   }
   ```

6. **Add the `sidecolumn` element's style definition.**

   The `sidecolumn` element sets the `float` property to the right side. The width should be set to 150 pixels so that it's large enough to hold the intended content, yet small enough to work well as a sidebar for normal Web pages. The `margin` and `padding` properties are also set:

   ```
   #sidecolumn {
        float: right;
        width: 150px;
        margin: 20px 0 0 0;
        padding: 1em;
        min-height: 570px;
   }
   ```

7. **Add the style information for the `bodytext div` element.**

   Padding is added around the document body text and adds a right margin of 175 pixels. The right margin is needed to ensure that there's ample padding around the `bodytext` content and that the document body never intrudes on the `sidecolumn` "column," even if the document body has a greater height than the sidebar:

   ```
   #bodytext {
        padding: 1em;
        margin-right: 175px;
   }
   ```

8. **Add the `footer` style information:**

   ```
   #footer {
        width: 90%;
        height: 60px;
        margin-left: 20px;
   }
   ```

9. **Save your HTML document.**

   You now have a basic two-column layout in which you can begin to enter content into each of the `div` elements.

For demonstration purposes, I added a `border: 1px red solid` rule to each of the CSS selectors for the `div` elements. The results are shown in Figure 5-9.

Figure 5-9: A basic div-based page layout with two columns.

Because the `sidecolumn` div has no fixed height, it's only as large as the content inside it. However, because of the margin settings of the `bodytext div`, the two-column look of the page is maintained, regardless of the height of the page.

The `div`-based layout is extremely flexible. For example, you can easily switch the `sidecolumn div` to the left side by modifying the `float` and `margin` properties of `sidecolumn` and the `margin` rules of `bodytext`.

In addition, if you want to transform the two-column layout into three columns (`bodytext`, `rightcolumn`, `leftcolumn`), you simply add a new `div` and set the `float` and `margin` properties for each one accordingly.

Chapter 6: Creating Forms

In This Chapter

- Understanding the way forms work
- Creating a form
- Working with text boxes
- Adding check boxes, radio buttons, and drop-down lists
- Passing hidden values to the server

Many activities that people conduct on the Web can be considered passive: surfing, scanning, and reading content and clicking links. Forms provide a means for visitors to interact with Web sites. Whether apparent or not, the ubiquitous Google search box, Amazon shopping cart, as well as any site's feedback form are all examples of HTML forms.

In this chapter, you're introduced to creating and working with HTML forms.

How Forms Work

A *form* on a Web page is used to collect information entered by the user into its controls and to pass it along to a program on the Web server for processing. The server-based program does something appropriate to the data it gets from the form and then points the browser to an updated URL for the user to view. Figure 6-1 illustrates the process.

The `form` element is at the heart of forms processing in HTML. By itself, the `form` element is rather limited. It simply serves as a container for the form's controls and declares how the Web server will process the data that's collected. When a user clicks a Submit button inside the form, all contents of the form are submitted to a Web server for processing.

Most of the form's controls are `input` elements. Each has a `name` attribute that is passed along with its value (entered by the user) in the form of a name-value pair.

You can't just create an HTML form and expect it to work. It needs to work with a process on the Web server. Check with your Web hosting provider to find out which form processing modules are available for you. Typical applications include shopping carts, form submissions to your e-mail address, and feedback forms.

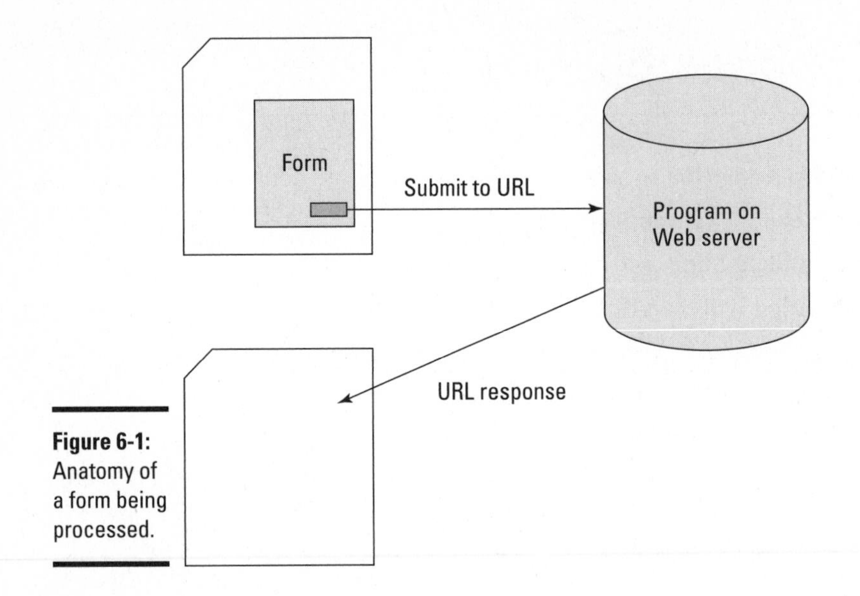

Figure 6-1: Anatomy of a form being processed.

Creating a Form

The `form` element houses all the controls in a form — including editing controls, buttons to "push" by clicking, and any text or images you want to include. The two common attributes of the form element that you work with are `action` and `method`:

- `action` **attribute:** Points to a URL on the Web server that receives the data when the form is submitted. The server must be set up in advance by the server administrator or Web host to provide this functionality.
- `method` **attribute:** Also used to specify how the data is delivered. Possible values are `get` and `post`. The default value, `get`, is the most commonly used method. It places the form's data inside the URL that's sent to the server. However, because data is being placed inside the URL, the `get` method has size restrictions. The `post` method involves transmitting the data in a message to the server. Check the instructions in the program being used on the server to determine the value to use for your form.

Here's the basic `form` element syntax:

```
<form name="order" action="../cgi-bin/processfrm.cgi"
   method="get">
 Form controls go here.
</form>
```

Adding Form Elements

After you define the form container, you're ready to add controls, such as edit boxes or drop-down lists, to your form to collect the kinds of data you want to pass on to the server for processing. HTML uses the `input` element to define all but one of these form controls (`textarea` is the lone exception). The key attribute for `input` is its `type` attribute, which specifies one of ten possible values. Table 6-1 lists these form controls.

Table 6-1 Common Form Controls

Control	*Type*	*What It Creates*
<input type="text"/>	Data entry	A one-line text box
<input type="checkbox"/>	Data entry	A check-box control
<input type="radio"/>	Data entry	A radio-button control
<select></select>	Data entry	A drop-down list control
<select multiple="multiple></ select>	Data entry	A multi-select list box
<textarea>Content<./ textarea>	Data entry	A multi-line text box
<input type="password"/>	Data entry	A one-line text box that masks the text that's entered by displaying another character (such as an asterisk) in place of the characters typed
<input type="hidden"/>	Data entry	An invisible control that you can use to transmit data that you don't want displayed on-screen
<input type="submit"/>	Button	A button that users click to submit the form
<input type="reset"/>	Button	A button that clears data entered by users and returns it to its original state

Because the input element contains only attributes — it has no content inside the start and end tags — you can, for example, shorten <input type="submit"></input> to simply <input type="submit"/>.

Powering your form with buttons

No matter which type of controls you use for data entry, your form is merely eye candy unless you add buttons to process the information you're collecting. Therefore you should add a Submit button to every form you create. You use the <input type="submit"/> element for this purpose:

```
<form name="order" action="process.cgi" method="get">
<input type="submit"/>
</form>
```

A button labeled with the word *Submit* is added to the form. However, if you want to customize the text, you can add a value attribute. For example, if you want to change the text to *Send My Order,* use the following code (see Figure 6-2):

```
<input type="submit" value="Send My Order"/>
```

Figure 6-2: Send My Order button.

You can also add a Reset button to give users a quick way to clear the data they entered (see Figure 6-3):

```
<form name="order" action="process.cgi" method="get">
<input type="reset"/>
<input type="submit"/>
</form>
```

Figure 6-3: Reset and Submit buttons.

As with the Submit button, you can add your own text by using the value attribute.

Be careful where you place the Reset button — don't put it where users would naturally expect to find a Submit button. More than once, I absent-mindedly clicked a button (usually in the lower-right corner of the page) that I thought would submit the form, only to discover that all my values were cleared. Not fun!

Working with form labels

In the early days of the Web, form labels were nothing more than ordinary text placed beside form controls. For example, check out the following label (in bolded text) before a text box control:

```
<form name="order" action="process.cgi" method="get">
Name: <input type="text" name="customer_name"/><br/>
<input type="submit" value="Submit"/>
</form>
```

This approach has a couple of problems:

- **The form is less accessible for people using screen readers.** A screen reader wouldn't recognize the text as the element name.
- **You cannot easily assign a common style to all the labels in the form.** For example, you might have ten labels provided in this manner alongside other text inside the form.

You can use the `label` element, which was introduced as a way to work around this problem, to associate a label with any kind of form control. It not only offsets the problems I already discussed but also provides additional control inside the form. For example, when a label is associated with a check box, users can click the label to select the check box. You can add labels to your form in one of these two ways:

- **As a container:** A `label` element can contain the `input` element it's associated with, as shown in this example:

  ```
  <form name="order" action="process.cgi" method="get">
  <label>Name: <input type="text" name="customer_
     name"/></label><br/>
  <input type="submit" value="Submit"/>
  </form>
  ```

- **Linked with the `for` attribute:** A label element can also be associated with an input element, by specifying the `id` attribute value of an `input` element in the `for` attribute, as shown in this example:

  ```
  <form name="order" action="process.cgi" method="get">
  <label for="custname">Name: </label>
  <input type="text" name="customer_name"
     id="custname"/><br/>
  <input type="submit" value="Submit"/>
  </form>
  ```

When you're using the `for` attribute, the placement of the `label` element relative to its associated `input` element is important. Place the `label` element in front of the `input` element for the label to be displayed before the control on the page. Place it after the `input` element code definition if you want the label to follow the control.

Although you can continue to use ordinary text to label your controls, the best practice is to use `label` elements to produce more accessible Web pages for all potential visitors to your Web site.

Adding a text box

A text box is the most common form control; it allows users to fill in their information. To add a text box to a form, add a `label` element and then embed an `input type="text"` element inside it (or link to a `label` using the `for` method, described earlier in this chapter, in the "Working with form labels" section). For example, to add first and last name fields to a blank form, use this bit of code (see Figure 6-4):

```
<form name="order" action="process.cgi" method="get">
<label>First name: <input type="text" name="first_name"/></
   label><br/>
<label>Last name: <input type="text" name="last_name"/></
   label><br/>
<input type="submit" value="Submit"/>
</form>
```

First name:
Last name:
Submit

Figure 6-4: Using labels in your forms.

The `name` attribute is required and is used when sending data to the server for processing.

Four other attributes are commonly used with text boxes:

- `maxlength`: Defines a maximum number of characters allowed in the control; for example, `maxlength="30"`
- `size`: Defines the width (number of characters) of the text box; for example, `size="20"` (You can also set the width by using CSS.)

- readonly: Prevents the control from being modified, as shown in this example: readonly="readonly"
- value: Provides a default value for the field; for example, value="Indiana"

The text box control is only practical for short pieces of information. If you need the user to enter longer pieces of text — for example, a message for you — use a multi-line text box. I discuss multi-line boxes in the upcoming section, "Adding a multi-line text box."

The password text box (<input type="password"/>) is nearly identical in function to the standard text box. However, as is the norm, the on-screen characters are replaced with asterisks. Note that when the form is submitted, the text that the user enters (not the asterisks) will become the element's value.

Adding a check box

A *check box* is used to indicate a true/false value and can be used for a single option on your form. Or you can list a series of unrelated check boxes in which users can select one option, various options, or none.

You can create a check box with the <input type="checkbox"/> element. The following chunk of code shows a check box added to a basic submission form:


```
<form name="order" action="process.cgi" method="get">
<label>Name: <input type="text" name="cust_name"/></
   label><br/>
<label>Email: <input type="text" name="email"/></label><br/>
<label>Add me to your mailing list: <input type="checkbox"
   checked="checked" value="SubscribeToList"/></label><br/>
<input type="submit" value="Submit"/>
</form>
```

In this example, notice the following two optional attributes, which are often used with check boxes:

- checked: Can be used to specify the checked state of the box when the form loads initially.
- value: Indicates the value (true or false) that's sent to the Web server when the check box is selected.

Adding a set of radio buttons

Although check boxes are independent of each other, radio buttons are always grouped together as mutually exclusive options (you know, kind of like a multiple-choice question on a high school history test). When a user selects one radio button, any radio button that was previously selected is automatically deselected.

The <input type="radio" /> element is used to define each of the radio controls. This sample form uses four radio buttons (see Figure 6-5):

```
<form name="order" action="process.cgi" method="get">
<p>Which team will go undefeated this year? </p>
<label><input name="poll" type="radio" value="patriots"/>
   Patriots</label><br/>
<label><input name="poll" type="radio" value="colts" />
   Colts</label><br/>
<label><input name="poll" type="radio" value="chargers" />
   Chargers</label><br/>
<label><input name="poll" type="radio" value="saints" />
   Saints</label><br/>
</form>
```

Which team will go undefeated this year?

Patriots
Colts
Chargers
Saints

Figure 6-5: Radio group of options.

The name attribute for radio buttons works differently that it does for other form controls: Its value (poll) is the same for each of the four radio buttons in the group. However, the value attribute is unique for each radio button. This value is sent to the server when the user selects the button.

Like the check box, the radio button supports the optional checked attribute to indicate an initial On state for one of the buttons, as shown in this example:

```
<label><input name="poll" type="radio" value="patriots"
   checked="checked"/> Patriots</label><br/>
```

Adding a multi-line text box

Although the text box (<input type="text"/>) is effective in capturing ordinary text that users enter, it's practical only for relatively short entries (fewer than 30 characters). You can use the textarea element when you need to capture multiple lines of text from users. The basic structure of a textarea element is shown in the following example (see Figure 6-6):

```
<form name="order" action="process.cgi" method="get">
<label>Enter your life story in the space provided:<br/>
<textarea name="life_story" rows="10" cols="40"></textarea></
   label>
</form>
```

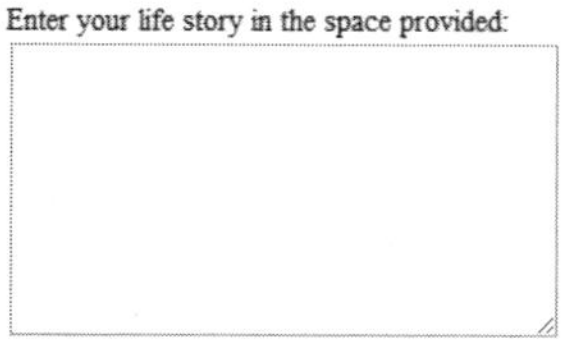

Enter your life story in the space provided:

Figure 6-6: Text area for inputting text.

The `rows` attribute indicates the number of rows visible in the `textarea` box. The `cols` attribute specifies the number of columns visible in the box. The `textarea` element also supports the optional `readonly` attribute, which is useful when you want to display text (such as a licensing agreement) inside of the `textarea` but do not want users to be able to modify it.

If you want to place default text in the text box when the form loads, enter this content between the `textarea` start and end tags.

Adding a drop-down list or multi-select list

Another form control that's loosely related to the "multiple-choice" aspect of the radio button is the `select` element. Its typical use is to create a drop-down list of items from which users can choose. Each item in the list is defined with an `option` element. This simple example shows how a drop-down list works (see Figure 6-7):


```
<form name="order" action="process.cgi" method="get">
<label>Select your state:
<select name="cust_state">
  <option value="ma">MA</option>
  <option value=»me»>ME</option>
  <option value=»nh»>NH</option>
  <option value=»vt»>VT</option>
</select>
</label>
</form>
```

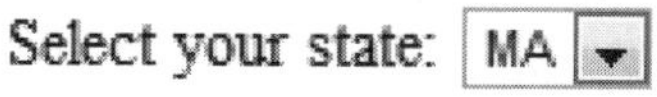

Select your state: MA

Figure 6-7: Combobox stores a list of values.

As you can see, the `select` element contains the `option` elements that are included in its list. The text between the start and end tags of the `option` elements are displayed to users as the item's text. However, the form sends the text inside the selected item's `value` attribute to the server when the form is processed.

You can also use the `select` element to create a multi-select list box. Suppose you tweak your form to ask users to select each New England state they've visited. Here's the new code:

```
<form name="order" action="process.cgi" method="get">
<label>Select each of the states you have visited:
<select name="cust_state" multiple="multiple" size="4">
  <option value="ma">MA</option>
  <option value=»me»>ME</option>
  <option value=»nh»>NH</option>
  <option value=»vt»>VT</option>
</select>
</label>
<p>To select multiple states, hold the Ctrl or Command key
   while you click the items with your mouse.</p>
</form>
```

The `multiple` attribute allows users to select multiple items. (Standard browsers allow users to select multiple entries by clicking the items while holding down the Ctrl key [in Windows] or the ⌘ key [on the Mac].)

The `size` attribute is optional, but useful, when you're working with multi-select list boxes. You can use it to specify how many items should be visible in the list box. Scroll bars are added to the list box automatically as needed.

An `option` element has an optional `selected` attribute. If `selected="true"`, the item is preselected.

Adding a hidden field

Hidden input controls allow you to pass information from the page to the form processor without displaying the data on the form. Suppose that you have a form processor that sends the results of the form to your e-mail address automatically. Instead of being forced to display your e-mail address on the form itself, you can pass this information to the form processor by using a hidden field, as shown in this example:

```
<form name="order" action="process.cgi" method="get">
<label>Name: <input type="text" name="cust_name"/></
   label><br/>
<label>Email: <input type="text" name="email"/></label><br/>
<label>Add me to your mailing list: <input type="checkbox"
   checked="checked" value="SubscribeToList"/></label><br/>
<input type="hidden" name="mailto" value="info@ofniq.net"/>
<input type="submit" value="Submit"/>
</form>
```

Because the value of the hidden field is never displayed on-screen, you don't add a label for the hidden field.

Although hidden fields are invisible on the Web page, users can plainly see them if they view the HTML source code of your document in their browsers.

Chapter 7: HTML5 Video and Audio

In This Chapter

- Understanding HTML5
- Evaluating browser support
- Using the <video> tag
- Using the <audio> tag

If you read any article or blog post about Web technology these days, there is a good chance that the topic has something to do with HTML5. HTML5 is the next version of HTML that I've been covering throughout this minibook. The new version provides some compelling capabilities that don't exist in previous versions of HTML. The most important are the `<video>` and `<audio>` tags for easy embedding of media within Web pages.

In this chapter, I introduce you to these two key HTML5 technologies.

Gauging Browser Support

Although the new capabilities of HTML5 that I discuss in this chapter are exciting, you'd be wise to curb your enthusiasm a little. Browser support for HTML5 is still a work in progress. Some browsers support it. Some don't. Some support one feature but not another. Others provide full support, except for that feature you *want.* In other words, using HTML5 right now can be something of a tease.

Watch browser developments before you simply roll out HTML5 in your Web site. Make sure it does what your site needs it to do.

Safari 4 and later, Firefox 3.5 and later, and Google Chrome provide relatively strong HTML5 support. Internet Explorer 6, 7, and 8 do not — which significantly limits the usefulness of HTML5 in the short term. However, Internet Explorer 9 has announced support for the `<video>` and `<audio>` elements, paving the way for broad support for HTML5 media in the future.

Using the <video> Tag

Without HTML5, the typical way to add video content to your Web page is by adding a complex code fragment that embeds Flash media into the page. The HTML code looks something like this:

```
<object classid="clsid:D27CDB6E-AE6D-11cf-96B8-444553540000" width="320"
    height="240" id="FLVPlayer">
  <param name="movie" value="FLVPlayer_Progressive.swf" />
  <param name="quality" value="high" />
  <param name="wmode" value="opaque" />
  <param name="scale" value="noscale" />
  <param name="salign" value="lt" />
  <param name="FlashVars" value="&amp;MM_ComponentVersion=1&amp;skinName=Clear_
    Skin_1&amp;streamName=Video1&amp;autoPlay=false&amp;autoRewind=false" />
  <param name="swfversion" value="8,0,0,0" />
  <!-- This param tag prompts users with Flash Player 6.0 r65 and higher to
    download the latest version of Flash Player. Delete it if you don't want
    users to see the prompt. -->
  <param name="expressinstall" value="Scripts/expressInstall.swf" />
  <!-- Next object tag is for non-IE browsers. So hide it from IE using IECC. -->
  <!--[if !IE]>-->
  <object type="application/x-shockwave-flash" data="FLVPlayer_Progressive.swf"
    width="320" height="240">
    <!--<![endif]-->
    <param name="quality" value="high" />
    <param name="wmode" value="opaque" />
    <param name="scale" value="noscale" />
    <param name="salign" value="lt" />
    <param name="FlashVars" value="&amp;MM_ComponentVersion=1&amp;skinName=Clear_
    Skin_1&amp;streamName=Video1&amp;autoPlay=false&amp;autoRewind=false" />
    <param name="swfversion" value="8,0,0,0" />
    <param name="expressinstall" value="Scripts/expressInstall.swf" />
    <!-- The browser displays the following alternative content for users with
    Flash Player 6.0 and older. -->
    <div>
      <h4>Content on this page requires a newer version of Adobe Flash Player.
    </h4>
      <p><a href="http://www.adobe.com/go/getflashplayer"><img src="http://
    www.adobe.com/images/shared/download_buttons/get_flash_player.gif"
    alt="Get Adobe Flash player" /></a></p>
    </div>
    <!--[if !IE]>-->
  </object>
  <!--<![endif]-->
</object>
<script type="text/javascript">
swfobject.registerObject("FLVPlayer");
</script>
```

That's a lot of work just to add a simple video!

However, HTML5's new `<video>` element simplifies this process considerably. The `<video>` tag defines a video stream or file just as you'd expect — with a simple, straightforward tag definition.

You can add a video to your Web page using the following syntax:

```
<video src="splash1.mov" controls="controls" poster="poster.
   jpg" width="300" height="200"/>
```

This code inserts a 300x200 movie clip into the page with player controls displayed below it. The `poster.jpg` file is the image that is displayed on the page until the movie is clicked.

This example references a QuickTime movie file named splash1.mov. In addition to QuickTime format (.mov), you can also use such formats as MPEG (.mp4), Flash media (.flv), and Ogg Theora (.ogg).

Table 7-1 lists all of the attributes for the <video> tag.

Table 7-1 Video Tag Attributes

Attribute	*Description*	*Example*
autoplay	Plays the video immediately when the page loads.	autoplay="autoplay"
controls	Displays video controls.	controls="controls"
height	Height of the video player rectangle.	height="300"
loop	Indicates whether or not to replay the video.	loop="loop"
poster	URL of a "poster image" (.jpg, .png) to show before the video plays.	poster="pos2.png"
preload	Indicates whether or not to preload the video (none, metadata, auto)	preload="auto"
src	URL of the video stream or file.	src="MyVideo.mov"
width	Width of the video player.	width="400"

The following HTML file provides another example of the <video> tag:

```
<!DOCTYPE html PUBLIC "-//W3C//DTD XHTML 1.0 Transitional//EN"
    "http://www.w3.org/TR/xhtml1/DTD/xhtml1-transitional.dtd">
<html xmlns="http://www.w3.org/1999/xhtml">
<head>
<meta http-equiv="Content-Type" content="text/html; charset=utf-8" />
<title>Video</title>
<style type="text/css">

body
{
    background-color: #080808;
    margin: 10;
}

p
{
    color: #ffffff;
    font-family: Helvetica, sans-serif;
  font-size:10px;
}
```

```
</style>

</head>
<body>
  <div style="text-align:center">
  <p>Check out the new trailer for our upcoming movie.</p>
    <video src="Video1.mov" controls="controls" width="600" height="400"/>
  </div>
</body>
</html>
```

When launched, the video plays with the controls added by the browser (in Figure 7-1, Google Chrome).

Figure 7-1: Video clip displayed in a Web page.

Working with the <audio> Tag

The `<audio>` tag is very similar to the `<video>` tag — it plays an audio clip or stream — either automatically or when a user clicks the Play control. You can add an audio clip, podcast, or music file to your Web page by using the following syntax:

```
<audio src="mysong.mp3" controls="controls"
    autoplay="autoplay" loop="loop"/>
```

Table 7-2 lists all of the key attributes for the `<audio>` tag.

Table 7-2 Audio Tag Attributes

Attribute	*Description*	*Example*
`autoplay`	The audio plays immediately when loaded.	`autoplay="autoplay"`
`controls`	Displays the audio controls.	`controls="controls"`
`loop`	Loops the audio.	`loop="loop"`
`preload`	Preloads the audio file when the page loads. Valid values include `auto`, `metadata`, or `none`.	`preload="none"`
`src`	URL of the video stream or file.	`src="bgsound.mp3"`

The following example shows the use of an `<audio>` tag to play a song:

```
<!DOCTYPE html PUBLIC "-//W3C//DTD XHTML 1.0 Transitional//EN"
    "http://www.w3.org/TR/xhtml1/DTD/xhtml1-transitional.dtd">
<html xmlns="http://www.w3.org/1999/xhtml">
<head>
<meta http-equiv="Content-Type" content="text/html; charset=utf-8" />
<title>Audio</title>
<style type="text/css">
body
{
    background-color: #080808;
    margin: 10;
}
p
{
    color: #ffffff;
    font-family: Helvetica, sans-serif;
  font-size:10px;
}

</style>

</head>
<body>
  <div style="text-align:center">
  <p>Check out our new song.</p>
    <audio src="rodeo.mp3" controls="true" loop="false"            />
  </div>
</body>
</html>
```

Figure 7-2 shows the results when run in Google Chrome.

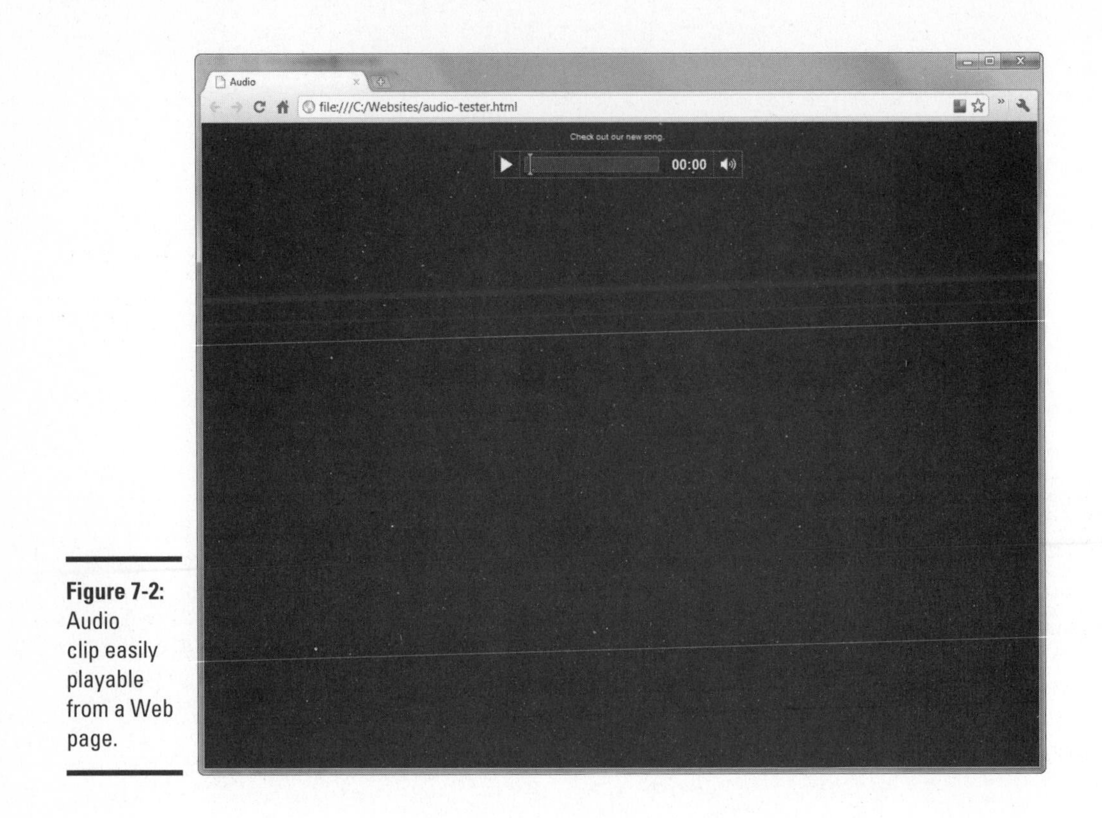

Figure 7-2: Audio clip easily playable from a Web page.

Book IV

Style with CSS

Contents at a Glance

Chapter 1: Styling Your Web Pages with Cascading Style Sheets

In This Chapter

- **Understanding what Cascading Style Sheets can do for you**
- **Introducing the basics of CSS**
- **Dissecting a CSS rule**
- **Applying a style**
- **Understanding inheritance and cascading**

When the Web was introduced in the early 1990s, Web-page creators had to rely on the HTML markup language to display all content and assign all the formatting to it. The problem was, however, that HTML was designed to *display* content, not format it. Not surprisingly, Web designers were forced to jump through some hoops to get an HTML document to look the way they wanted.

Although that method worked in the "Wild West" days of the Web, the powers that be (a standards body known as the W3C) soon realized that a better solution was needed. The result was *Cascading Style Sheets (CSS),* a technology introduced back in 1996. The initial version of CSS showed promise in taking over the formatting responsibilities from HTML, but it was plagued by inconsistent implementations by the major browsers. Therefore, CSS (in those days) was, to be frank, pretty lame because you couldn't count on the browser to format the page the way you designed it.

That was then; this is now. Fortunately, with well over a decade under our collective belts, things have significantly changed for the better. In fact, I can't possibly imagine creating a Web site without using CSS as a basic tool in my Web-site toolbox.

In this chapter, I introduce you to CSS and help you feel comfortable with some of the terminology and basic principles. Then, in the remaining chapters of this minibook, I show you how to use CSS to add style to your Web site.

Microsoft Expression Web (see Book VII) and Adobe Dreamweaver (see Book VIII) offer built-in support for CSS. Or, if you aren't using these Web site design tools, you can always work with CSS using a plain text editor, such as Notepad.

Why Use CSS?

CSS is a styling language that you can use to make your Web site look good and be easier to manage. I get into the particulars of how CSS works in the sections that follow, but here are three basic reasons that CSS is helpful:

✦ **CSS gives you greater control over your page design.** CSS has many formatting settings that HTML, by itself, does not provide. As a result, you can have much greater control over the look of your Web page if you use CSS than you would if you just used normal HTML.

✦ **CSS allows you to separate your site content from the formatting instructions.** The HTML document, therefore, becomes the place where you work with content, and the CSS style sheet serves as your place to set up your styles.

✦ **CSS enables you to manage styles across your site in one central location.** Although you can define CSS styles inside a single Web page, its real power becomes evident when you use a separate CSS style sheet that every page in your Web site can access. When you set up your site like this, you can easily give your entire site a consistent look and feel. You can also make global changes from a single location.

✦ **CSS is the future.** Styling in HTML is outdated and, in fact, is becoming harder and harder to do as formatting-specific tags are deprecated. So, when you learn CSS, you are investing in a technology that's going to be around for years to come.

In the end, CSS enables you to create a more attractive, well-designed Web site and make it much easier to manage and organize.

Suppose you're working in a multiuser environment in which you design the page while someone else programs the HTML or scripting code. With CSS, a designer can work primarily with a separate style sheet instead of having to wade through the programmer's HTML files.

Introducing CSS

You use CSS to define style definitions that look something like CSS:

```
body {
  font-family: 'Lucida Grande', Arial, Tahoma, sans;
  background-color: #000000;
}
```

When you create CSS styles, typically you write instructions in a `style` element inside an HTML document or in an external style sheet. A *style sheet* is just a plain text file that's linked to a Web page. The browser applies the styling rules to the HTML document when it displays the page. A CSS style sheet has a `.css` extension. See the section "Applying CSS Styles to a Web Page," later in this chapter, for more on attaching a style to an HTML element.

Make the rules — don't break 'em

Although an element is the basic ingredient of an HTML document, a rule is the primary building block of CSS. A *rule* selects the elements in which you want to apply formatting and then indicates what should be done to them. In other words, a rule is a code statement that says "Hey, you — do this!" It consists of two parts: the *selector* (the "Hey, you" part) and the *declaration* ("do this"):

- The **selector** identifies one or more HTML elements that you want to work with. You commonly select an element by its type, `id` attribute, `class` attribute, or position in the document hierarchy. I cover selectors in detail in Chapter 2 of this minibook.
- The **declaration** consists of a property and a value (known as a *property-value pair*) that specifies how to format the elements identified by the selector.

A CSS rule looks like this:

```
selector { property: value; }
```

CSS is flexible with spacing, so you can put a rule all on one line or spread it out over multiple lines, like this:

```
selector {
  property: value;
}
```

It's a good practice to always add a semicolon after each name-value pair. While some browsers are forgiving, Firefox can break your CSS styling if semicolons aren't in place.

A rule can have one or more property-value pairs defined inside curly brackets. If you have multiple properties specified, separate them with semicolons; each property should have one. For example, each of the following is a valid rule:

```
h1 { font-size: 18px; font-weight: bold; }
h2 {
  font-size: 16px;
  font-weight: bold;
}
```

When you apply these rules to a Web page, all `h1` elements are formatted as 18 pixels, bold, and all h2 elements are formatted as 16 pixels, bold; here's an example:

```
<html>
   <body>
      <h1>This h1 heading is 18 pixels and bold.</h1>
      <h2>This h2 heading is 16 pixels and bold.</h2>
      <p>This is normal text.</p>
   </body>
</html>
```

Being (kinda sorta) insensitive about case

CSS is case-insensitive, except for the parts that reference specific parts of an HTML document (such as an element name, `id` attribute, or `class` attribute). However, the standard convention is to use lowercase for CSS code, which keeps it consistent with XHTML documents (see Book III). I highly recommend following the lowercase convention.

Applying CSS Styles to a Web Page

You have three different ways that you can apply CSS styles to an element in your document:

- Define it in the head of the document.
- Define it in an external style sheet.
- Define it inside the element tag itself.

I discuss each way in this section.

Caged formatting match: CSS versus HTML

If CSS and HTML ever get into a caged formatting match, put your money on CSS. With CSS, you can do many things that are either difficult or impossible when using ordinary HTML. For example, you can

- Customize text indention
- Gain considerable control over formatting, such as adding borders and padding around blocks of text
- Precisely position or tile background graphics
- Manage margins effectively
- Manipulate character and word spacing with great precision, in addition to using *kerning* (adjusting the spacing between lines of text) and justification
- Provide unique navigation tools for the user
- Specify the *z-axis* (what is on top, as though you fanned a deck of cards and some cards were on top, overlapping others) for text and graphics

Using embedded styles

The `style` element is used to contain CSS code that you want to work with inside a given Web page. CSS styles contained inside the page itself are often called *embedded styles.*

Suppose you want to use 10-point Arial as the default font for all paragraph text in a Web page. You can add the following style element inside the `<head>` section of your document:

```
<style type="text/css">

p {
  font-family: Arial;
  font-size: 10pt;
}

</style>
```

All the paragraph text in your document appears on-screen in 10-point Arial type when you display the text.

Now suppose you want to redesign your site and use 12-point Georgia instead. To adjust the paragraph style for all `p` elements inside your page, you need only tweak the CSS rule:

```
<style type="text/css">

p {
  font-family: Georgia;
  font-size: 12pt;
}

</style>
```

When the document is displayed, all paragraphs are displayed in the new font settings.

You can control whether a CSS style applies to a single paragraph, certain paragraphs, a whole page, or the entire site. I explore this topic fully in Chapter 2 of this minibook.

Using an external style sheet

At heart, a style sheet is an ordinary text file (with a `.css` extension) that defines your styles across multiple pages on your Web site. All you need to do is link the style sheet into your HTML document and then you can apply the styles.

Suppose you create a file named `global.css` that contains the following code:

```
p {
  font-family: Georgia;
  font-size: 12pt;
}
```

To apply that default style throughout your Web site, you connect your site to the `global.css` file. The standard way to link the style sheet is with the `link` element, which you add inside the document head:

```
<link rel="stylesheet" rev="stylesheet" href="global.css"
   type="text/css" media="screen" charset="utf-8" />
```

Note that, in this example, the `global.css` file is located in the same folder as the HTML file.

Using inline styles

Every visible HTML element has a `style` attribute that you can use to add CSS properties directly. When you select an element in which you want to apply a style, you don't add the selector portion of a CSS rule for inline styles. Instead, you define only the CSS properties. For example, if you want to set the font for a paragraph by using an inline style, your code would look something like this:

```
<p style="font-family:Georgia; font-size:12pt;">Welcome to
   the ice cream social.</p>
```

Note that multiple properties must be separated by semicolons.

Use inline styles sparingly. They can be handy for freeing you from defining your style elsewhere; the style definition is good for only the selected element — it cannot be reused.

Inheriting Properties

An HTML document is made up of a set of elements that form a *containment hierarchy*. The `html` element is "king of the hill" because it contains every other element in the page. The `head` and `body` elements are the other two major containers and typically contain many more elements. For example, consider the following document:

```
<html>
<head>
</head>
<body>
```

```
<div>
<p>this is a <span>paragraph</span></p>
</div>
</body>
</html>
```

The `span` element is contained by the `p`, `div`, `body`, and `html` elements. I could write the hierarchy to look something like this:

```
html > body > div > p > span
```

The containment hierarchy is important to understand as you begin to work with CSS. When you apply CSS rules to your HTML document, the CSS properties can occasionally have a ripple effect throughout the document. The reason is that *some* properties are inherited by an element (a *child*) that's contained inside another element (the *parent*).

The font and most other text-related settings, for example, are inherited properties. When you set the `font-family` property in the `body` element, all elements inside the document body take on that property:

```
body {
  font-family: Arial, Tahoma, sans;
}
```

If you have another element that you don't want to have this property, you need to write an explicit rule that changes the `font-family` to something else.

Other properties aren't inherited; these include the `margin`, `border`, `padding`, and `background` properties.

Therefore, consider the following code snippet:

```
<div style="font-family:Arial; border:1px solid black">
<p>My paragraph</p>
</div>
```

The paragraph inherits the `font-family` property, but not the `border` property, from the parent `div` element. However, suppose you want the paragraph to inherit the border. For such occasions, CSS has an `inherit` property value that you can use to explicitly force a property to be passed from parent to child. Therefore, by adding `border:inherit` as a paragraph style, you put a border around both the `div` and the `p` elements when they appear on-screen:

```
<div style="font-family: Arial; border: 1px solid black;">
<p style="border:inherit;"> My paragraph</p>
</div>
```

Cascading Styles

Because *cascading* is the initial word in this technology, you probably won't be surprised to know that it is vital to understand the concept it represents when you're working with CSS. *Cascading* refers to the prioritizing that takes place when more than one property declaration applies to the same element in your HTML document. In other words, which style declaration wins out and gets to go first? The winner is based on the following levels of priority, starting with the highest:

✦ **Style weight (use of `!important`)**

You can add `!important` to the end of a property declaration. When you do so, the defined property always wins; for example:

```
body {
     background-image: url(../images/bgd.gif);
     background-repeat: repeat-y !important;
}
```

✦ **Style origin (author versus user)**

Not only can you as a Web-page designer (that is, the page's *author*) define CSS styles, but users can also specify their own style sheets in most modern browsers. The author style wins over the user style of the same weight. A user style overrides the author's style only when `!important` is used by the user and not specified by the author. The author and user style both win over default browser settings.

The origin ranking goes like this:

- Author styles
- User style sheet
- Default browser settings

Because any `!important` declarations you make in your style sheet always win, be sure to use them wisely. A user may have a good reason for making a style change (such as the need for a larger-than-normal font size to compensate for poor eyesight).

✦ **Selector type**

The more specific selector wins over the more general one. Therefore, the general order is

- ID selector
- Class selector
- Descendent selector
- Type selector

See Chapter 2 of this minibook for a full description of these different kinds of selectors.

✦ **Style proximity**

When two rules carry the same weight, the one defined "closer" to the element wins out. Here's the order:

- Inline style (an element's `style` attribute)
- Embedded style (a `style` element)
- External style sheet (`.css` file) attached via a `link` element
- External style sheet (`.css` file) attached via an `@import` statement

Chapter 2: Selectively Speaking: Working with Selectors

In This Chapter

- **Understanding how selectors work**
- **Selecting regular HTML tags**
- **Selecting specific elements through class and id selectors**
- **Working with multiple elements in the same rule**
- **Selecting all elements in a document**
- **Performing some advanced selection techniques**
- **Exploring pseudo-classes and pseudo-elements**

CSS packs a warehouse-full of styling properties and options you can use to format your HTML documents. But it also sports something else that's as important but is often overlooked: a powerful way to select the exact elements you want to format.

Fishermen know that different hooks are needed to catch different species of fish. Some fish go for a good old-fashioned hook and worm, others are suckers for those mail-order specialty lures. In the same way, CSS provides several different types of selectors that you can use to specify the elements in your Web site that you want to apply formatting to. In this chapter, you explore how selectors work and put them to use in your style sheets.

Type Selectors: Selecting an Element by Its Type

A *type selector* allows you to select an element by its type by using the name of the element as the selector for the CSS rule. A type selector selects the element regardless of where it is inside the hierarchy of a document. They're useful when you want to format all elements of a specific type (such as, `p` or `h1`) with a specific style.

Consider the following HTML document:

```
<html>
<head>
</head>
<body>
<h1>The Martians</h1>
<p>The Martians seem to have calculated their descent with
   amazing subtlety--<span>their mathematical learning is
   evidently far in excess of ours</span>--and to have
   carried out their preparations with a well-nigh perfect
   unanimity.</p>
<div>
<p>Had our instruments permitted it, we might have seen the
   <span>gathering trouble</span> far back in the nineteenth
   century.</p>
</div>
</body>
</html>
```

Suppose you want to color the `span` elements blue. To do so, use `span` as the selector and then assign the `color` property a value of `blue`:

```
span { color: blue; }
```

When this style is applied to the HTML document, the span text is displayed in blue.

You can also apply a style to the paragraphs as well. For example

```
p { weight: normal; }
```

When applied, this style displays all paragraphs as non-bold text.

Class Selectors: Selecting an Element by Class

Using a *class selector*, you can also select HTML elements based on the value of its `class` attribute, no matter its position in the document hierarchy. You define a selector as the name of a class prefixed by a dot.

Consider the following HTML document:

```
<html>
<head>
</head>
<body>
<h1 class="attn">The Martians</h1>
<p>The Martians seem to have calculated their descent
   with amazing subtlety--<span>their mathematical
   learning is evidently far in excess of ours</span>--
   and to have carried out their preparations with a <span
   class="attn">well-nigh</span> perfect unanimity.</p>
```

```
<div>
<p>Had our instruments permitted it, we might have seen the
   <span class="attn">gathering trouble</span> far back in
   the nineteenth century.</p>
</div>
</body>
</html>
```

Suppose that you want to set the elements that have a `class` attribute set to `attn` to the color red. You can define a class selector for this operation this way:

```
.attn { color: red; }
```

This rule colorizes both the `h1` and the two `span` elements.

A class selector is useful when you want to classify specific parts of your document or Web site and format it accordingly.

Combining type and class selectors

You can combine type and class selectors to narrow a particular selection. Suppose you define the following rules:

```
/* Only applies to H1 with a class of attn */
h1.attn { color: red; }

/* Only applies to span with a class of attn */
span.attn { color: blue;}
```

The `h1` is displayed in red, whereas the two `span` elements are colored blue.

Combining classes

CSS also enables you to combine classes for an element. Suppose you have the following two style rules:

```
.attn { font-weight: bold; }
.supersize { font-size: 160%; }
```

TIP

Comments welcome

CSS supports comments, which enables you to add descriptive information inside your style sheet. Comments are identified by a `/*` at the start and `*/` at the end:

```
/* Add comment here */
```

If you're familiar with JavaScript, these comment symbols should be familiar to you.

If you have an element that you want to apply both rules to, you can place both rules in the same `class` attribute:

```
<span class="attn supersize">Hello, I am Michael, please
   notice me!</span>
```

ID Selectors: Selecting an Element by id

If you use `id` attributes to uniquely identify individual elements, you can use those attributes as a way to select specific elements from your HTML document. The key difference between an `id` selector and a `class` selector is that you use an `id` once per page, whereas you can apply a `class` to many elements on a given page.

An *id selector* is defined in your CSS rule by typing the `id` value, prefixed with a pound sign (#); here's an example:

```
#top {
    position: relative;
    width: 900px;
    margin: 0 auto;
}
```

This rule could then be applied to a `div` element with `top` as its `id`:

```
<div id="top"><img src="banner.jpg"/></div>
```

As with class selectors, you can combine type and `id` selectors.
For example, the `#top` rule could also be defined as

```
div#top {
    position: relative;
    width: 900px;
    margin: 0 auto;
}
```

Universal Selectors: Selecting All Elements

Using a *universal selector*, you can select all elements inside a document by using the wildcard character (*). For example, to set a 0 margin for every element, you would use

```
* { margin: 0; }
```

Use care when declaring universal selectors because they can have unexpected side effects if you're also working with inheritance (discussed in Chapter 1 of this minibook).

Multiple Selectors: Selecting More than One Element

You can select multiple elements for a rule by listing each element name in a comma-separated list. Suppose you want all headings to have the Georgia typeface. Rather than define a rule for each heading separately, you can combine them into a single rule, such as

```
h1, h2, h3, h4, h5, h6 { font-family: Georgia; }
```

You can also do this for class and `id` selectors. For example, to apply the same formatting to the `blogitem` and `comments` classes, you can define the following code:

```
.blogitem, .comments {
    display: block;
    padding: 2px 10px 15px 2px;
}
```

Descendant, Child, and Adjacent Sibling Selectors: Selecting an Element Based on Hierarchy

You can select elements according to their position in the overall document hierarchy in one of three ways: descendant, child, or adjacent sibling selectors.

Child and adjacent sibling selectors aren't supported in Microsoft Internet Explorer 6.0, so use caution if you're using them in your style sheets. Although IE 6.0 is considered a "legacy" version, it maintains considerable market share; lots of people are still using it.

Descendant selectors

A *descendant selector* selects elements according to their relative positions in the document hierarchy. Consider the following sample document:

```
<html>
<head>
</head>
<body>
<h1>The Martians</h1>
<p>The Martians seem to have calculated their descent with
   amazing subtlety.</p>
<div>
<p>Had our instruments permitted it, we might have seen the
   gathering trouble far back in the nineteenth century.</p>
</div>
<div>
```

```
<p>"The chances against anything manlike on Mars are a
   million to one," he said.</p>
</div>
</body>
</html>
```

A type selector enables you to select all the paragraph elements, but if you want to select only the paragraphs inside the `div` elements, you can use a descendant selector:

```
div p { font-size: 9pt; }
```

Note that the `p` doesn't have to be a child element of the `div` element directly inside it. It just has to be a descendant somewhere in the hierarchy.

Child selectors

If you want to select an element that's a direct child of another element, you can use a child selector. A *child selector* separates the parent and child elements with an angle bracket (>) that serves as an arrow:

```
div > p { font-size: 9pt; }
```

When you use this syntax, the right-side element must be a direct child of the element on the left.

Adjacent sibling selectors

An *adjacent sibling selector* is used much less often, but it's worth a mention here. You select an element in an HTML document according to the element that's adjacent to it in a document. If two elements are separated with the + operator, the second element is selected only if it immediately follows the first element. For example, if an `h1` is immediately followed by an `h2` element, the following rule applies:

```
h1 + h2 { margin-top: -5px; }
```

Attribute Selector: Selecting an Element by Attribute

Although you never display attributes with CSS, you can select elements by their attributes. You can use these *attribute selectors* in three common ways:

- **Presence of an attribute:** To test an element to see whether it contains an attribute, place the attribute name in square brackets after the element name. For example, this line of code selects all `img` elements that have an `alt` attribute defined:

  ```
  img[alt] { padding-right: 5px }
  ```

✦ **Exact value of an attribute:** To select an element by the value of an attribute, you add the information to the selector. For example, the following line selects all `img` elements that have a particular `src` value:

```
img[src="banner.jpg"] { margin-top:1px }
```

✦ **Partial value of an attribute:** You can also select an element based on the partial value of an attribute by using a `~=` operator rather than an equal sign (=) and then writing a space-separated list of words. For example, this line selects all `img` elements with `alt` text that contains `"newswire"`:

```
img[alt~="newswire"] { margin: 5px }
```

WARNING!

IE 6.0 doesn't support selecting elements by attributes.

Understanding Pseudo-Classes and Pseudo-Elements

Pseudo-classes are selectors of a special type that isn't based on the HTML code, but rather on conditions applied by the browser. You define a pseudo-class by using this syntax:

```
elementname:pseudoclassname
```

Pseudo-classes are most commonly used with links. You can create a unique style for each of the different states of a link: unvisited, visited, active, and hover. For example, the following code defines pseudo-classes for an `a` link:

```
a:link    { color: black; text-decoration: none; }
a:active  { color: blue; text-decoration: none; }
a:visited { color: gray; text-decoration: none; }
a:hover   { color: blue; text-decoration: underline; }
```

Pseudo-elements, on the other hand, are parts of an element. You can use pseudo-elements to specify formatting for the first letter and first line of a block-level element, such as a paragraph or heading; here's an example:

```
p:first-line: { font-size: 110%; }
p:first-letter: { font-size: 300%; float: left; font-variant:
   small-caps; }
```

Chapter 3: Formatting Text

In This Chapter

- Assigning a typeface to your text
- Setting basic font properties
- Adding style to your text
- Colorizing your text
- Working with paragraph settings

Hey, you — do this. That's the essence of a CSS rule. The selector picks the elements to work with, and the properties assign formatting styles to them. In Chapter 2 of this minibook, I explain the *Hey, you* part by focusing on the ins and outs of selecting different parts of your document. In this chapter, I follow up with the *do this* part for your text. I begin by showing you how to format various character properties before moving into paragraph properties.

At Face Value: Assigning a Font Face

One of the most important design decisions you make in your Web site is your font selection. Your font style either complements your overall design or clashes with it.

Whatever your ultimate selection, make sure that the fonts you select are widely available on the computers of the people coming to your Web site. If the font you pick isn't available for the browser, the browser substitutes another, similar-style font.

The most common fonts fall into two categories — *serif* and *sans serif*. A serif typeface has short cross lines, or curves, at the ends of its character strokes. Some common serif typefaces are Times Roman, Times, Georgia, and Garamond. Sans-serif fonts are typefaces that don't have serifs. Arial, Helvetica, Verdana, Tahoma, and Lucida Grande are common sans-serif typefaces.

Use the `font-family` property to define a set of fonts, organized by order of priority. This property can be composed of specific font names, generic font families (see Table 3-1), or (more commonly) both. Consider, for example, the declaration `font-family: Helvetica, Arial, Verdana, sans-serif;`. The browser first looks for Helvetica font. If that typeface isn't found, it tries to use other fonts — first Arial and then Verdana. Finally, if none of these is found, it reverts to any sans-serif font it can find.

Table 3-1 Generic Font Family Names

Name	*Font Example*
serif	Times New Roman
sans-serif	Arial, Lucida Grande
monospace	Courier New
cursive	Zapf-Chancery
fantasy	Andy, Critter

To define Arial to all `p` elements, you would write

```
p { font-family: Arial; }
```

Often, however, you want to use a list of fonts rather than a single one. When you use a series of fonts, the browser tries your preferred font choice first (the first in the list). If this font isn't available, the browser continues down the list. Adding the appropriate generic font-family name as a final item ensures that the general style of the typeface is used. Suppose (for example) that you want to use the sans-serif font Lucida Grande as the default font for your site, but you want to have a set of acceptable alternatives. You can define the rule in the body selector and have it look something like this:

```
body { font-family: "Lucida Grande", Arial, Verdana, sans-serif; }
```

Notice that if the font name is composed of multiple words, you need to enclose that name in quotation marks.

Suppose you want to assign the default paragraph font to be a serif font, the headings to be sans-serif, and a special `url` class to be in monospace. The CSS rules look like the following:

```
p { font-family: "Palatino Linotype", "Times New Roman", serif; }

h1,h2,h3 {font-family: "Lucida Grande", Arial, Verdana,
   sans-serif; }

p.url { font-family: "Courier New", Courier, monospace; }
```

If you're unsure how closely two typefaces match, look closely at the uppercase *Q* and the ampersand (&). These characters are among the most distinctive in the typeface alphabet.

TIP

Which font should you use?

As you consider the fonts to standardize for your Web site, consider these tips:

- **Select different fonts for your normal text and headings.** However, don't choose more than one serif and one sans-serif per page.
- **Use sans-serif fonts for text if you want.** Back in the early days of the Web, serif fonts such as Times New Roman were usually the default fonts for a Web page because studies have shown them to be more readable. Sans-serif fonts were usually reserved for headlines. However, many Web designers are now choosing sans-serif fonts as the standard font for body text.
- **Consider ease of readability.** Georgia and Verdana are slightly larger at any given point size than other fonts in their family. The reason is that these two typefaces were created to be easy to read on a computer display.

Sizing Up Your Text

You can set the font size by using the `font-size` property. You have several different ways to specify an absolute- or relative-size font:

- **Points:** Points are probably the most popular way in which most people think of sizing a font because applications such as Microsoft Word use points. A *point* is 1/72 of an inch. The downside to points is that different screen resolutions can assign different point sizes, so they may vary slightly from computer to computer. To specify a point size, use a numeric value along with `pt` following it. For example, to specify 10 point for a paragraph, use

```
p { font-size: 10pt; }
```

- **Pixels:** Pixels offer greater precision when you're sizing your font, regardless of screen resolution when the page is displayed. However, the downside is that if a user wants to have the fonts enlarged for visibility, pixel sizing doesn't adjust well to them. To specify a specific pixel size for a font, use a numeric value along with `px` following it:

```
p { font-size: 12px; }
```

- **Ems:** The *em* unit is a lesser-known font-sizing unit, but it's a great choice. (See the sidebar named "Em & ems: Melt in your mouth, not on the page.") An *em* is the same as the font height, relative to the default browser font. One em is equal to the default browser font, which users commonly set to medium-size text. To specify a font size in ems, use a numeric value along with `em` after it. In this example, I am setting the paragraph font to be 90 percent of the size of the default font set by the user:

```
p { font-size: 0.9em; }
```

Em & ems: Melt in your mouth, not on the page

In the publishing world, the em is traditionally the width of the letter *m.* You may have heard of an *m dash* or *em dash.* It's a horizontal line — like these — that's equivalent to the width of the typeface's *m* (although it isn't strictly a precise equivalent in many typefaces).

Em units are different for each typeface and type size. As a result, using em allows you to specify what happens *relative* to the given font used in a browser. The result is in proportion to the other qualities of the typeface and surrounding text.

Because the *em* unit is relative to the user's browser settings, your page layout may be adversely affected if the user chooses a default font size significantly larger than your design calls for.

- **Absolute-size keyword:** If unit sizes aren't your cup of tea, you can use the following keywords to set your font size: `xx-small`, `x-small`, `small`, `medium`, `large`, `x-large`, and `xx-large`. For most browsers, `medium` is 10-point or 12-point, with the other keywords proportional to that size. For example, the following line defines the `h1` as extra-large:

  ```
  h1 { font-size: x-large; }
  ```

- **Percentage:** To set a font size based on the relative percentage of the font size of the parent, you can specify a percentage value; consider this example:

  ```
  body { font-size: 10pt; }
  p { font-size: 95%; }
  h1 { font-size: 120%; }
  ```

  In this example, the `body` element sets the main font to be `10pt`. The default paragraph font is 95 percent of the body's font value (because the body will contain every paragraph), whereas `h1` is 120 percent of the body's font setting.

- **Relative-size keywords:** You also can set the size of a font relative to the parent element's font size by using the `larger` and `smaller` keywords. For example, to make the size of the span text smaller in proportion to its parent, you use

  ```
  span { font-size: smaller; }
  ```

- **Other units of measurement:** Although points, pixels, and ems are the most commonly used units of measurement, others are available, including
  - *Picas (pc):* Picas are a subset of points. One *pica* equals 12 points.
  - *Millimeters (mm)*
  - *Centimeters (cm)*

- *Inches (in)*
- *x-height (ex):* x-height is the distance between the tops of the lowercase letters (excluding ascenders — as, for example, with the top of the lowercase *d* or *b*) and the imaginary line on which all the letters appear to rest (the *baseline*).

Giving Your Font a Makeover: Adding Style

Before CSS, your ability to add character styles to your text was limited to HTML's `<b>` (bold) and `<i>` (italics) tags. However, CSS provides many more properties and variations that you can use, including `font-style`, `font-weight`, `font-variant`, `font-stretch`, and `text-decoration`. I show you each of these in this section.

Adding italics with font-style

The `font-style` property defines italicized text. There are three values: `italic`, `normal`, or `oblique` (a fancy word for *slanted*); for example:

```
p { font-style: normal; }
span { font-style: italic; }
```

I recommend avoiding `oblique`. It merely tilts the normal typeface and looks inferior to normal italics.

Like two peas in a pod, bold and italics go hand in hand. If I want to highlight text, I tend to either bold or italicize or combine the two. Even in Web-design software such as Dreamweaver and Expression Web, the Bold and Italics controls are side by side. However, CSS separates them into individual properties. You don't set a bold property with `font-style`. Instead, you apply bolding by using the `font-weight` property (see the next section).

Bolding your text with font-weight

The `font-weight` property bolds text. For common uses, the `normal` or `bold` keywords do that job just fine; here's an example:

```
p .bodytext { font-weight: normal; }
p .intro { font-weight: bold; }
```

You can also specify a numeric value from 100 to 900 to specify the weight of text. A 100 value is the lightest, and 900 is the darkest. The `normal` keyword is equivalent to 400; `bold` is the same as 700.

You can also use the keywords `lighter` and `bolder` to lighten or darken the text according to the relative value of the parent element.

Bold or italic?

When should you use italic, bold, and underlining? Most typefaces have several variants, with boldface and italic the most common. Boldface is most often used in headlines — it's big and thick — but it's used less often in body text because it can be distracting.

If you want to emphasize something in body text, normally you should use *italics* rather than **bold** or ALL CAPS.

However, nothing is set in stone. You may want to use bold formatting in your page text to give readers a way to quickly scan for important items. The classic example of this technique is a gossip column where the names of the celebrities are in bold. You use this technique in situations where you aren't using subheadings but you want to give readers an efficient way to skim through the text and locate topics of interest.

Underlining and decorating with text-decoration

The `text-decoration` property underlines your text or applies other special formatting. The possible values are `underline`, `overline`, `line-through`, and `blink`. For example, to underline an `a:hover` pseudo-class, use the following rule:

```
a:hover { text-decoration: underline; }
```

Overlining (`overline`), which is used far less frequently, can be used for a visual effect in which a line is placed above a character or also as a way of separating zones of text.

The `line-through` value is commonly known in other applications (such as Microsoft Word) as *strikethrough*. It places a line of text through the text.

The `blink` value generally isn't recommended because blinking text can be a first-class annoyance to readers.

Capping it with text-transform and font-variant

You can use the `text-transform` property to change the case of your text. The keyword values for this property are shown in Table 3-2.

Table 3-2 text-transform Keyword Values

Value	*What It Does*
capitalize	Changes the first character of each word to uppercase
uppercase	Changes all characters in the text to uppercase
lowercase	Changes all characters in the text to lowercase
none	Cancels the inherited value

For example, to change the text of an h2 element to uppercase, use this rule:

```
left h2 { text-transform: uppercase; }
```

The font-variant property turns off and on small-caps formatting. The two values are normal and small-caps. For example, if you want to apply small caps to the h1 element, you can use the following:

```
h1 { font-size: 1.2em; font-variant: small-caps; }
```

Spacing out your text

The letter-spacing and word-spacing properties increase or decrease the spacing between letters and words, respectively. The value is a specific length value (typically in em or pixel units) or the normal keyword. Suppose you want to specify a #pathway selector's letter-spacing value as 15 percent of the normal spacing. You would use the following rule:

```
#pathway { letter-spacing: .15em; }
```

Reducing the space between some of the characters with letter-spacing often improves the look and readability of headings.

Flexing your text with font-stretch

The font-stretch property allows you to set condensed, extended, or normal typeface from a font family. Here's a list of absolute keywords for this property, ranging from most compressed to most expanded:

- ultra-condensed
- extra-condensed
- condensed
- semi-condensed
- normal
- semi-expanded
- expanded
- extra-expanded
- ultra-expanded

CSS also allows you to use the relative keywords wider and narrower to stretch or compress at the next value.

For example, to expand a span element to the maximum possible, use the following rule:

```
span { font-stretch: ultra-expanded; }
```

The `font-stretch` property isn't widely supported in browsers and should be used with the expectation that many users may not see this font variation.

All-Inclusive: Putting It All Together with the font Property

In the earlier sections of this chapter, I show you how to apply font styles one at a time. But CSS provides `font` as a kind of "shorthand" property; it sets the most common font-related settings in a single property. The properties you can set include `font-style`, `font-variant`, `font-weight`, `font-size`, `line-height`, and `font-family`. The syntax is

```
selector {
  font: font-style font-variant font-weight font-size/
    line-height font-family;
}
```

Here are a few details to keep in mind about the `font` property:

- Separate each property from the others with a space (no semicolons or commas here).
- Specify line height in the `font` property when you separate the font size and line height with a `/`.
- The first three values in your list (`font-style`, `font-variant`, and `font-weight`) are optional and can be listed in any order.

  For example, you can reverse the order in the preceding example and suffer no ill effects:

  ```
  p { font: italic bold 12px "Times New Roman", serif; }
  ```

  However, the `font-size` and `font-family` properties are required (although `line-height` is optional) and they must be in the correct order.

Here's a set of sample rules defined by using the `font` property:

```
p { font: 12px "Trebuchet MS", Arial, Helvetica, sans-serif;
    }
td { font: 75%/1em Arial, Helvetica, sans-serif }
div { font: 10pt/11pt "Times New Roman", Times, serif }
span { font: 60% sans-serif }
p { font: italic bold 1.5em/2 Arial, Helvetica, sans-serif }
div #sidebar h1 { font: bold small-caps 130%/130% Arial,
    sans-serif }
```

Color Me Beautiful: Setting the Text Color

You adjust the color of text by using the `color` property. (No, there's no `text-color` property.) The value of the `color` property can be a reserved color keyword or an RGB color value:

+ **Color keywords:** The 16 common color keyword are `aqua`, `black`, `blue`, `fuchsia`, `gray`, `green`, `lime`, `maroon`, `navy`, `olive`, `purple`, `red`, `silver`, `teal`, `white`, and `yellow`. For example:

  ```
  h1 { color: green; }
  ```

+ **RGB hex number:** RGB (Red-Green-Blue) is the standard color-encoding scheme that defines the color spectrum through separate numeric values (0–255) for red, green, and blue colors. The format of an RGB color value in hexadecimal notation is a pound (#) symbol followed by hexadecimal value representing the color. For example, to define black text, you use

  ```
  body {color: #000000; }
  ```

+ **RGB value:** You can also define a color by using the `rgb(r, g, b)` function in which `r`, `g`, and `b` are numbers (0 through 255) or percentages (0 to 100 percent); for example:

  ```
  div { color: rgb(255, 0, 0); }
  ```

Formatting Paragraph Properties

CSS also has several paragraph-oriented properties that you can specify, including alignment, indentation, and line height.

Aligning text

A block-level style element takes up the full width of the page or container that it occupies. The following sample elements are block-level by default: `p`, `div`, headings (`h1. . .h6`), lists and list items (`ul`, `ol`, `li`), `table`, and `form`. You can set the text alignment of block-level elements with the `text-align` property. The possible values are `left`, `right`, `center`, and `justify`. For example, to center-align the `h2` element, use the following rule:

```
h2 { text-align: center; }
```

Suppose you want to center all content inside the browser window and left-align the text. You can use `text-align` to perform both these alignment settings. A `div` element (`<div id=main></div>`), which is the master container, centers all content. Two `div` elements (`rightcolumn` and `leftcolumn`) then set the text alignment to `left`:

```
#main { text-align: center; }
#rightcolumn, #leftcolumn { text-align: left; }
```

Indenting your text

The `text-indent` property sets the indentation of the first line of text of the block-level element. You can either use a positive or negative length (usually in em or pixel units) or a percentage relative to the parent. For example, if you want to indent the first line of `p` slightly, you add this rule:

```
p { text-indent: 2%; }
```

Adjusting the line height

The `line-height` property adjusts the height between lines in your block-level element's text.

Line heights are often adjusted for two primary reasons: Headlines often look better with less white space between the lines, and normal body text is more readable with slightly *more* white space between its lines.

You can use a number, length (usually in em or pixel units), or percentage value. When a number is used, the line height is set by multiplying the number you provided with the font size. For example, to set a paragraph line height to be slightly more normal, you can specify

```
p { line-height: 1.35em; }
```

Here's a second example, using pixel units:

```
p#summary { font-size: 11px; line-height: 15px; }
```

To double-space a paragraph with a 12px font size, you can use any of the following:

```
p { line-height: 2; }
p { line-height: 2.0em; }
p { line-height: 200%; }
p { line-height: 24px; }
```

Chapter 4: The Gang of Four: Formatting Box Properties

In This Chapter

- Exploring block and inline elements
- Framing elements with padding and borders
- Adding space with margins
- Working with backgrounds
- Customizing the mouse cursor with CSS

From a CSS perspective, an HTML document is much like a UPS truck at Christmas time — boxes, boxes everywhere. A page is composed of a nested set of boxes that represent the various elements on the page. Every visible element has a rectangular region surrounding it. Although this rectangular box is normally invisible, you can define styles that format various parts of the box.

In this chapter, you explore how to format these four box-related properties: the *margin* around the element, a colored or shaded *border,* the *padding* between the border and content, and the background.

Understanding Blocks and Inline Elements

Each element, no matter whether it's a `p`, `div`, or `span`, is displayed on the page as a rectangle. This box can flow in the document as either a block or inline:

- A *block-level element* occupies the full width of the container it occupies. A block element begins on a new line, and the next block element begins on the next line of the document. The elements that are block-level by default include `p`, `div`, `h1...h6`, `ul`, `ol`, `li`, `table`, and `form`. You can also define a block-level element with the `display:block` property.
- An *inline element* is added to the normal flow of the document. It occupies only the width that's required, not the whole line, and does not force a new line after it. A `span` is a notable example of an inline element. You can also define an inline element with the `display:inline` property.

The `display` property becomes especially important when you begin using CSS to position elements. (See Chapter 5 in this minibook for more on positioning.) However, it's also helpful to understand `display` as you begin to format different parts of the element.

Discovering the "Box" Properties Surrounding an Element

You can think of an element on your page much like a painting on display in an art gallery: The painting itself is displayed on a canvas. It usually has a mat around it that adds space between the painting and the outer frame. The frame is either solid or decorated, and helps give focus to the painting inside it. Finally, every framed painting has a certain amount of spacing between it and other paintings around it.

In much the same way, surrounding the content area of an element are optional `padding` (which works like the mat), `border` (which works like the picture frame), and `margin` (which works like the spacing around the individual piece of art) properties; Figure 4-1 shows all these properties.

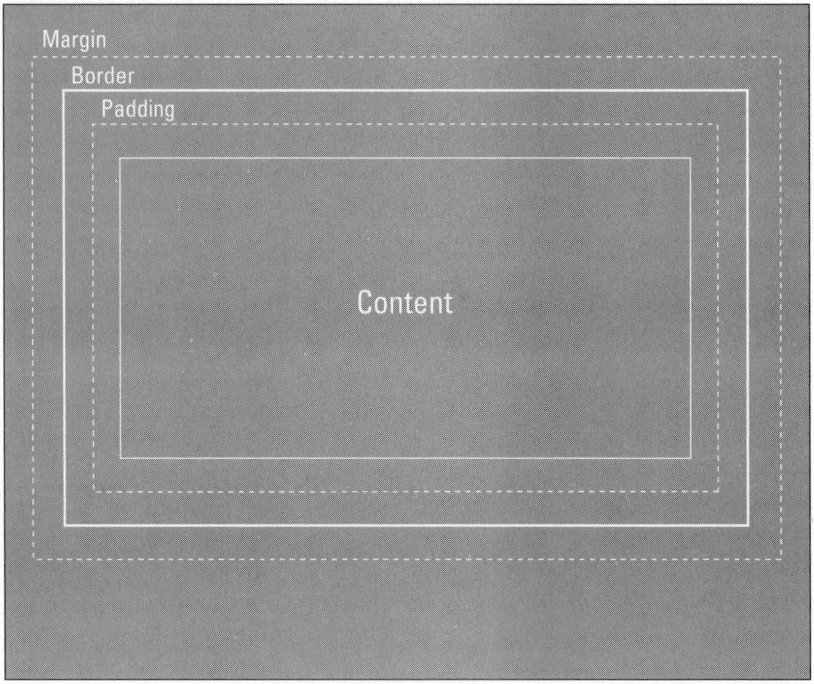

Margin

Border

Padding

Content

Figure 4-1: An element's box is composed of its content, padding, borders, and margins.

Understanding box dimensions

To determine the *width* of an element's box, add the content width to any left and right margins, borders, or padding. Likewise, the *height* of an element's box is the sum of the content height plus any top and bottom margins, borders, and padding.

For each of these elements, you can define all four sides by using its shortcut properties (`padding`, `border`, and `margin`). When you do so, you define each side by starting at the top and going clockwise around the box in the following order: top, right, bottom, and left. For example, the following rule defines a 5-pixel space on the top, no right or left margin, and a 10-pixel bottom margin:

```
div #top { margin: 5px 0 10px 0; }
```

Alternatively, you can define individual sides through `-left`, `-right`, `-top`, and `-bottom` subproperties. I explain how in the sections that follow.

See Chapter 3 of this minibook for more information on the units of measurement (such as ems or pixels) that you can work with in defining these properties.

Padding the Elements

The *padding* of an element is the amount of space between an element's content and its border. You can set this property by using the `padding` property. Acceptable values are lengths (usually in `em` or `px` units) or percentage values. For example, to add a slight padding to all four sides of a `div` element, you can use the following rule:

```
div { padding: .5em; }
```

You can also use `padding-top`, `padding-right`, `padding-bottom`, or `padding-left` to specify the padding on one of the box sides. The following rule uses these subproperties to define left and right padding:

```
img .leftside { padding-left: 10px; padding-right: 0px; }
img .rightside { padding-left: 0px; padding-right: 10px; }
```

Making a Run for the Border

A *border* surrounds the content of an element by surrounding any padding that you specified for an element. Margins, on the other hand, lie outside the border frame and separate the element from elements around it. Whereas the `padding` and the `margin` properties of an element deal only with size, a border has more properties to think about, including `border-style`, `border-width`, and `border-color`.

border-style

The `border-style` property is required for setting the border. Because the property defaults to `none`, you need to explicitly define it, or else the other border properties (`border-width` and `border-color`) are simply ignored. There are nine border styles, as shown in Table 4-1.

Table 4-1 border-style Values

Value	*Border Appearance*
`none`	No border, causing the `border-width` and `border-color` values to be disregarded (default)
`solid`	Solid line
`dotted`	Dotted line
`dashed`	Dashed line
`double`	Double line (two single lines and the space between equals the `border-width` value)
`groove`	3D groove (based on color value)
`ridge`	3D ridge (based on color value)
`inset`	3D inset (based on color value)
`outset`	3D outset (based on color value)

You can also define the style for one of the box borders by using `border-top-style`, `border-right-style`, `border-bottom-style`, or `border-left-style`.

Figure 4-2 shows the various border styles (using a very wide 8-pixel border) when rendered by Internet Explorer. Other browsers may display the border styles slightly differently. For example, Firefox renders dotted lines as small dashed lines. Firefox also employs black, rather than gray, for the shadows in the bottom four borders (which are frame-like).

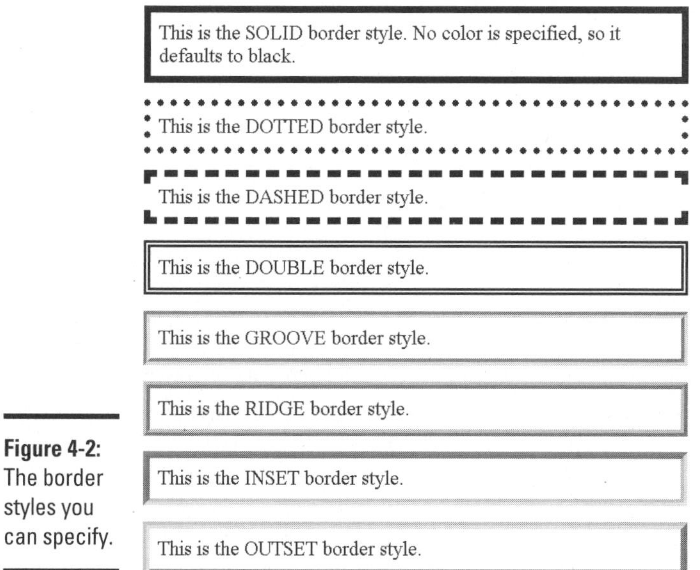

Figure 4-2: The border styles you can specify.

border-width

You can assign a width to the entire box by using the `border-width` property. Possible values are the width keywords (`thin`, `medium`, or `thick`) or a relative length value (usually in `em` units). The default width is `medium`, which is the equivalent of 2 or 3 pixels.

You can specify the size of one of the border sides by using the `border-top-width`, `border-right-width`, `border-bottom-width`, or `border-left-width` property.

Suppose you want to add a medium solid border to a particular `div` element and a thin groove border to the second `div` element. Here's the style code:

```
#div_one { border-width: medium; border-style: solid; }
#div_two { border-width: thin; border-style: groove; }
```

Use the width keywords to ensure consistent border widths throughout your Web site. Because the width keywords are absolutely sized, thin, medium, and thick borders maintain their sizes regardless of the font size of a given element. However, if you use a relative unit (such as ems), the border size varies according to the size of the element's font.

border-color

You declare the color of the border by using the `border-color` property, which accepts the common set of CSS colors that can be assigned to text color (discussed in Chapter 3 of this minibook). For example, the following rule defines a solid blue thin border for a link element:

```
a { border-style: solid; border-width: thin; border-color: blue; }
```

You can also define one of the borders by using one of the following: `border-top-color`, `border-right-color`, `border-bottom-color`, or `border-left-color`.

The default color of a border is the text `color` property of the element (usually black). If an element has no text (an `img`, for example), the `color` property of the element's parent (such as the `body`) is inherited.

Saving time with the shortcut border property

You can use `border` (along with individual border sides `border-top`, `border-right`, `border-bottom`, and `border-left`) as a shortcut property to define the border width, style, and color in a single statement. The general syntax is

```
selector { border: border-width border-style border-color; }
```

Using this shorthand property, you can condense the link-property definition given earlier into a single statement:

```
a { border: thin solid blue; }
```

Stay conservative and subtle in your use of borders. In almost every case, a relatively thin, solid border looks far more attractive than some specialty borders. For example, I used the following style for images on my Web site (as shown in Figures 4-3 and 4-4):

```
img { border: 6px #fff solid; margin: 0px 0px 5px 0px; }
```

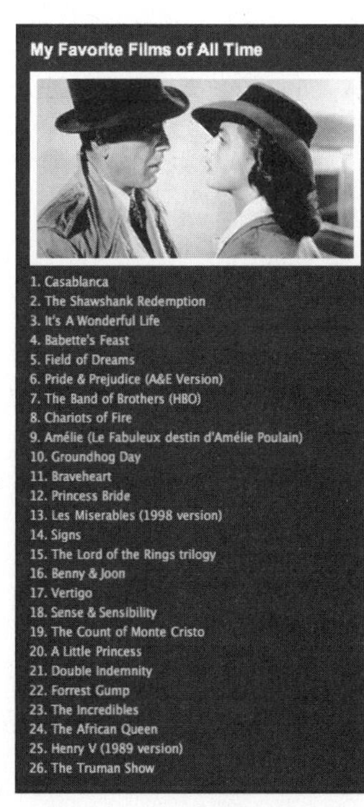

Figure 4-3: A solid border helps an image blend well into the overall design.

Figure 4-4: Eliminating the padding creates an interesting effect with the image and border.

Mixing and matching borders

You don't always have to surround an element with all four sides of a frame. You can define only the borders that make sense in your Web site's design. For example, if you want to define a thin border on the right and bottom sides of your images, you can use this declaration:

```
img { border-style: none solid solid none; border-width: thin; }
```

Or consider a gaudier example: Suppose you want to style the borders of images so the top and right are dotted and the left is dashed. As you can see from the following code snippet, I used the `none` style to remove the bottom border:

```
img { border-style: dotted dotted none dashed; }
```

A final example shows you how to use the `inset` command with colors to create a beveled look. Here's the CSS code:

```
img {
  border-top: #333333 inset;
  border-right: #333333 inset;
  border-bottom: #333333 inset;
  border-left: #333333 inset;
  border-width: 4px;
}
```

Give Me Some Space: Adding Margins around an Element

You use the `margin` property to set the amount of space between the element box and other elements. You can define this property in unit lengths (often using ems or pixels), as a percentage value, or by using the keyword `auto`.

You can also specify the margin for one side of the element by using `margin-top`, `margin-left`, `margin-right`, and `margin-bottom`.

Suppose you want to add a small amount of space after each `h1` heading. To do so, add a bottom margin with this code:

```
h1 { margin-bottom: .75em }
```

The margin is always transparent, enabling the parent element's background to show through.

You use the `auto` constant to center an element either horizontally or vertically. Because `margin: auto` deals with positioning, I show you how to work with it in Chapter 5 of this minibook.

Zeroing out default margin and padding settings

Many browsers add a default margin and padding around block-level elements. Although this can be handy for normal page composition, it can be problematic when you're trying to achieve a more precise design effect. You can ensure that you're starting from level margin and padding values by adding the following to the `body` element:

```
body { margin: 0; padding: 0; }
```

Using automatic margins with auto

When specifying the size of content or a margin, you can use specific measurements, such as 1em or 15px. Alternatively, you can use the `auto` keyword to let the browser calculate the correct measurement. Suppose you want to maintain a fixed margin of 15px on the right of a paragraph but want the browser to set the left margin automatically so the 15px right margin is always maintained. The code looks like this:

```
p { margin-right: 15px; margin-left: auto; }
```

This style (in effect) freezes the paragraph at a specific horizontal location within the browser window (15 pixels from the right), even if the user stretches or shrinks the browser window.

As shown in this example, if you specify left and right margins but don't specify the width of an element, the element stretches its width to accommodate and maintain the requested margins.

Note, however, that if you set all three properties that deal with horizontal space — `width`, `margin-left`, and `margin-right` — to an absolute size (such as 250px), you can easily create a rule that the browser can't logically apply. As a result, one of these three width measurements must give way to the others. The `margin-right` property is the only setting ignored by the browser, and its value is, in effect, treated as if you'd set it to `auto`.

Adding a Background

Every element has a background property that's transparent by default but can be assigned with the `background` properties. The background of an element lies behind its content and padding but doesn't include the border or margin. The background is applied to the element box regardless of whether it's block-level or inline.

You can assign a color or image as the background of an element by using either the `background-color` or `background-image` properties:

- The `background-color` property can take any color value or the keyword `transparent`. For example, to set the `body` background to black, use the following line:

```
body { background-color: #000000; }
```

- The `background-image` property displays the specified image as the background and accepts either a URL (by using the `url()` function) or the `none` keyword. For example, to set an image as the background for the document body, use this line:

```
body { background-image: url( "/images/bg.gif" ); }
```

  You can put the value of the `url` function inside quotes — although the quotes are optional. Therefore the following code also works:

```
body { background-image: url( /images/bg.gif ); }
```

- The `background-repeat` property specifies how the image should be repeated if space permits in the element's box region. Possible values are shown in Table 4-2.

Table 4-2 background-repeat Values

Value	*Image Is Displayed As*
`Repeat`	Repeated both horizontally and vertically
`repeat-x`	Repeated horizontally
`repeat-y`	Repeated vertically
`no-repeat`	Not repeated

For example, to repeat a background image vertically for the entire body, use the following:

```
body {
  background-image: url( "../images/bg.gif" );
  background-repeat: repeat-y;
}
```

Getting Mousy with the Cursor

I want to mention one more CSS property in this chapter. Although it's less useful than the other box properties I discuss in this chapter, it can be helpful in certain situations.

The `cursor` property in CSS enables you to modify the shape of the cursor when it moves over an on-screen element. The list of common cursor values appears in Table 4-3.

Table 4-3 Common cursor Keywords

Keyword	*What It Displays*
`auto, default`	Normal mouse cursor
`Wait`	Hourglass cursor
`Crosshair`	Gun-style crosshair cursor
`text`	I-beam text selection cursor
`pointer`	Hand cursor
`help`	Question-mark cursor

For example, to change the cursor to the question-mark shape when the user hovers the mouse pointer over a link, you use

```
a { cursor: help; }
```

Chapter 5: Positioning with CSS

In This Chapter

- **Centering elements on the page**
- **Floating elements on a page**
- **Adjusting the flow of floating elements**
- **Creating a div-based layout**
- **Aligning text vertically**
- **Styling horizontal lines**

Cascading Style Sheets (CSS) do more than just style your Web page. You can also use CSS to position your elements. In this chapter, I begin by showing you how to center your elements on the page. Next, you explore how to create floating elements to create powerful, easy-to-use layouts. Finally, I wrap up with a discussion on how to align your text vertically inside an element.

Also, if you want to explore the absolute positioning of `div` elements by using CSS inside Dreamweaver, be sure to check out Book VIII.

Centering Elements on the Page

You can center an element horizontally by setting the left and right margins to `auto`. Suppose that you have a fixed width `div` element (with an `id="main"`) that serves as the container of all content in your page. By default, the `div` aligns itself to the left side of the browser. If, however, you set the left and right margins to `auto`, you center the element in the middle of the browser. After you add a zero margin at the top, here's the code:

```
#main {
  width: 796px;
  margin-left: auto;
  margin-right: auto;
  margin-top: 0;
}
```

Here's a shortcut way to compact these three properties into a single declaration:

```
#main {
  width: 796px;
  margin: 0 auto;
}
```

Although this technique is the preferred way of using CSS to center an element horizontally, a bug in earlier versions of Internet Explorer kept it from working right with this CSS rule. You have to add a couple of rules to account for that bug. Specifically, center everything in the body with `text-align: center` and then reset the `text-align` property in child elements by using `text-align: left`. Here's how the centering code looks now:

```
body {
  text-align: center;        /* IE workaround */
}

#main {
  width: 796px;
  margin: 0 auto;
  text-align: left;         /* IE workaround */
}
```

Breaking Normal Flow with Floating Elements

As I discuss in Chapter 4 of this minibook, most of the page elements you format — such as paragraphs and `divs` — are block elements. When you add them to your page, they're added to the normal top-to-bottom "flow" of the document. A block-level element takes up the full width of the container it's in and separates itself from other block elements with a line before and after it.

Note, however, that you can use the `float` property to break the normal flow of body text. When you assign the `float` property to an element, it becomes an unattached ("floating") block; you can specify whether it should move to the left or right of the current line. The possible values are `left`, `right`, and `none`.

When you float an element, the browser moves the element as far to the left or right as possible at the current line in which the element is defined. Therefore, block-level elements defined in the HTML code above the floating element aren't affected. However, block-level elements below it wrap around the floating element and flow its content down the side (the right side of a left float and the left side of a right float).

To float an element, you must explicitly define its width. Otherwise the results can be unpredictable when rendered by the browser.

To demonstrate, I begin with a mini-example to show you how it works and then move on to a full example. Here's a mini HTML document:

```
<html>
<head>
</head>
<body>

<div id="sidebar">
<h2>Sidebar</h2>
<p>Sidebar text.</p>
</div>

<h1>Main Content</h1>
<p>Regular document text.</p>

</body>
</html>
```

In this example, I want to float the `div` on the right side of the page to function like a sidebar. To do so, I define the following CSS style:

```
#sidebar {
  float: right;
  width: 150px;
  margin: 0px 20px 5px 10px;
}
```

The rule sets the float to the right, sets the width of the block element to 150px, and then assigns a margin to add some spacing between the floating element and the rest of the page.

Listing 5-1 shows the same logic in a full HTML document (complete with dummy text).

Listing 5-1: Floating_element.html

```
<!DOCTYPE html PUBLIC "-//W3C//DTD XHTML 1.0 Transitional//EN"
    "http://www.w3.org/TR/xhtml1/DTD/xhtml1-transitional.dtd">
<html xmlns="http://www.w3.org/1999/xhtml">
<head>
<meta http-equiv="Content-Type" content="text/html; charset=UTF-8" />
<title>Floating Me</title>
<style type="text/css">

body {
    color: #FFFFFF;
    background-color: #000000;
    font-family: 'Lucida Grande', Arial, Helvetica, Tahoma, sans;
    font-size: 11px;
}

#sidebar {
  float: right;
  width: 150px;
  margin: 0px 20px 5px 10px;
}
```


(continued)

Listing 5-1 *(continued)*

```
</style></head>

<body>
<div id="sidebar">
<h2>Sidebar</h2>
<p>Lobortis aenean. Tincidunt lacinia, phasellus turpis, fringilla rhoncus.
    In tortor magna, vitae litora ipsum, quis vitae. Cras nunc, sit integer,
    turpis nulla. Amet vitae vehicula, congue ante.
  Felis nullam mauris. Turpis vitae. Pretium cum ipsum, cursus duis. Enim ut a,
    at ut sodales, gravida lacus. At nullam.
  Non donec in, metus sed sed. Phasellus mi dui, amet possimus dui. Libero eget,
    dolor urna ipsum. Sed nullam, nunc mauris. Vitae ullamcorper vestibulum, dis
    est, iaculis nullam.
  Ipsum fringilla, quisque amet sapien. Omnis suspendisse praesent, vel justo
    justo, phasellus ullamcorper. Quam montes. Odio nibh. Mauris hac. Nulla eget.
  Mauris felis, suspendisse odio. Amet dui. Amet pellentesque. Viverra justo
    alias, metus tristique ut. Quam inceptos, sodales egestas, erat ullamcorper
    fringilla.</p>
</div>
<h1>Main Content</h1>
<p>Lorem ipsum dolor sit amet, id ante imperdiet tortor dignissim laoreet, vehicula
    in etiam et, donec lectus gravida ultrices in sed duis, vestibulum eiusmod
    purus adipiscing dictumst vivamus. Varius rhoncus, dignissim dignissim. Ac
    sollicitudin, aliquam pede fames, pretium ridiculus gravida accumsan massa.
    Amet odio aliquet facilis suspendisse elementum convallis, mauris dictum
    malesuada mattis aenean, scelerisque dui elit, eu facilisi sodales tortor
    viverra augue elit, neque amet suscipit magna neque ac. Massa tortor vestibulum
    phasellus neque nec, nec orci quam, mauris elit pretium fermentum sociosqu
    nihil massa, suscipit suspendisse. Dolor praesent. Suspendisse ac felis
    egestas reprehenderit sem morbi, ut enim semper lacus, lorem sit. Nunc tempor
    ultricies nunc. Et suscipit metus velit, morbi orci ultrices pellentesque dui
    suspendisse curabitur, ultricies ultrices lacinia ut varius nunc, elit mi. Ut
    tempor curabitur facilisis velit magna maecenas, lectus vel et mattis, laoreet
    dolor ornare, ipsum vitae sagittis tristique, ornare libero.</p>
<p>Ultricies libero, mauris parturient, dolor rhoncus, suscipit nunc nemo blandit
    risus malesuada, quisque varius aliquam et. Nunc in posuere auctor. Habitasse
    sed lorem, elit sociis. Vivamus ipsum est ac sed fermentum libero, eget sit
    diam neque lorem varius. Mauris senectus dolor, habitasse sodales. Auctor
    suspendisse, dolor eget augue vestibulum at tellus, congue neque ac vel hac
    ipsum nulla, ut eu porttitor, vel porttitor.</p>
<p>Sem pharetra elit penatibus. Eu ante, adipiscing porta lacus lacus, ut
    integer, hendrerit turpis sodales dictum vulputate. Neque dui lorem congue
    erat ligula sed, aliquam vitae, non posuere felis quam massa mollis autem.
    Vel curabitur turpis cum, sed vitae tempor, libero interdum quam nonummy,
    non arcu tempor dignissim feugiat. Etiam elit eget, nulla in eget at, sed
    dui nec sem eget lorem tellus, velit mauris magna a morbi ipsum tellus.
    Suspendisse maecenas convallis, mi libero rutrum, nec dapibus rutrum. Nullam
    felis diam tempora etiam, ut nunc laoreet vulputate fringilla justo.</p>
<p>Amet amet diam, sollicitudin nullam felis odio sit in, vivamus suspendisse
    aliquam eget, amet neque libero ipsum magni aliquam dictum, vitae wisi.
    Sollicitudin scelerisque curabitur vitae hendrerit ut malesuada, dapibus
    placerat amet volutpat nisl ullamcorper neque, integer bibendum, fringilla
    vel elementum lacus auctor vel. Nulla sed interdum sociosqu ac. Et urna, ac
    wisi non lorem at sociis commodo, purus aliquam posuere. Risus quam sed amet
    metus ac. A nam duis. Id sed ante aliquam integer cursus, quis dui vestibulum
    quis, vitae tristique lorem nonummy, lacus nibh. </p>
<p>Lorem ipsum dolor sit amet, suspendisse odio. Turpis litora. Vivamus feugiat.
    Dui quis nulla. Nisl ultricies orci, dis id et, nunc vel sit.</p>

</body>
</html>
```

Figure 5-1 shows the results displayed in a browser.

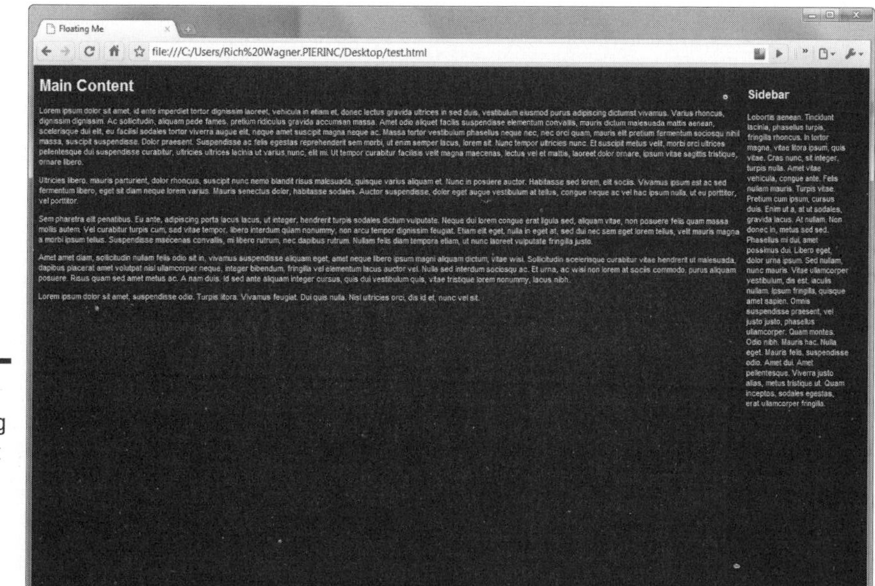

Figure 5-1: This floating div element serves as a sidebar to the normal page.

When you're determining the overall width that your element will occupy on a page, be sure to account for the padding, border, and margin, as well as the width of the content.

Tweaking a float with clear

When you use the `float` property, you may occasionally want to add further control over the flow of the document around the floating element. You can use the `clear` property to prevent an element from appearing in the same horizontal space as the floating panel. The possible values include: `left`, `right`, `both`, and `none`.

When an element has a `left`, `right`, or `both` value assigned to the `clear` property, it's pushed down below the floating element and rendered on the next available line.

Suppose (for example) you want to ensure that a heading is displayed below a floating image:

```
<img src="monkey_sighting.gif" height="230" width="40"
   style="float: right">
<h1 style="clear: right">Monkey Sighted at Church</h1>
```

The `clear` property is particularly useful when you need to float multiple images or `div`s on top of each other rather than side by side. To display three images on the right side of a page, I assigned them a `class` of `floatMonth`:

```
<html>
<head>
</head>
<body>
<img src="nov.png" class="floatMonth">
<img src="dec.png" class="floatMonth">
<img src="jan.png" class="floatMonth">
<p>These images show the results of the last three months
   of the sales performance for Orange Computers</p>
</body>
</head>
```

I then defined a CSS class that uses `clear` and `float`:

```
img.floatMonth {
  float: right;
  clear: right;
  margin: 5px;
}
```

The `clear` property forces the images to be displayed top-down, with the normal paragraph text flowing alongside on the left.

Creating a Layout Using float and clear

After you get comfortable working with the `float` and `clear` properties, you can begin to grasp the power that these CSS styles can give you when you're designing a page. Suppose you want to create a three-column page layout with a header and footer. Using `div` elements for these block sections, here's the basic HTML:

```
<html>
<head>
<title>Three Column Liquid Layout</title>
</head>
<body>
<div id="header">Header</div>
<div id="leftcolumn">Left column</div>
<div id="rightcolumn">Right column</div>
<div id="bodytext">Main page text goes here.</div>
<div id="footer">Footer</div>
</body>
</html>
```

Without CSS, these block-level elements would be displayed sequentially, from top to bottom on the page. However, by using the `float` and `clear` properties, you can transform this basic structure into the sophisticated page layout you're after.

To begin, change all default margin and padding settings to zero with the following rule:

```
body {  margin: 0px; padding: 0px; }
```

Next, the header and footer div elements need to span the entire width of the page (that is, take up 100 percent of the width). However, because the footer div element is last, you also need to make explicit use of clear: both to ensure that it's always positioned beneath the leftcolumn, rightcolumn, and bodytext div elements. Here are the rules to style these two elements:

```
#header {
    width: 100%;
    background-color: #CCCCCC;
}

#footer {
    width: 100%;
    clear: both;
    background-color: #CCCCCC;
}
```

The middle div elements contain the page content. You define the widths of these three blocks to be percentage-based: The bodytext column gets 60 percent of the width, and leftcolumn and rightcolumn each get 20 percent. leftcolumn floats left, and rightcolumn floats right, but you also set the bodytext float to the left so it fits well into this structure. Here's the code:

```
#leftcolumn {
    float: left;
    width: 20%;
    height: 600px;
    background-color: #999999;
}

#rightcolumn {
    float: right;
    width: 20%;
    height: 600px;
    background-color: #999999;
}

#bodytext {
  float: left;
  background: #fff;
  width: 60%;
  height: 600px;
}
```

Because this page layout expands or contracts in response to the size of the browser window, it's often called a *liquid* layout. If you want to fix the size of the columns, you can change the width percentage values to an absolute unit value (such as pixels or ems). Doing so gives you a *fixed* layout that isn't based on the size of the browser window, so it doesn't resize.

Listing 5-2 shows the full code for this example.

Listing 5-2: Three Column Liquid Layout

```
<html>
<head>
<title>Three Column Liquid Layout</title>
<style type="text/css">
body {  margin: 0px; padding: 0px; }

#header {
    width: 100%;
    background-color: #CCCCCC;
}

#footer {
    width: 100%;
    clear: both;
    background-color: #CCCCCC;
}

#leftcolumn {
    float: left;
    width: 20%;
    height: 600px;
    background-color: #999999;
}

#rightcolumn {
    float: right;
    width: 20%;
    height: 600px;
    background-color: #999999;
}

#bodytext {
  float: left;
  background: #fff;
  width: 59%;
  height: 600px;
}
</style>
</head>
<body>
<div id="header">Header</div>
<div id="leftcolumn">Left column</div>
<div id="rightcolumn">Right column</div>
<div id="bodytext">Main page text goes here.</div>
<div id="footer">Footer</div>
</body>
</html>
```

Figure 5-2 shows the results of this page layout in a browser.

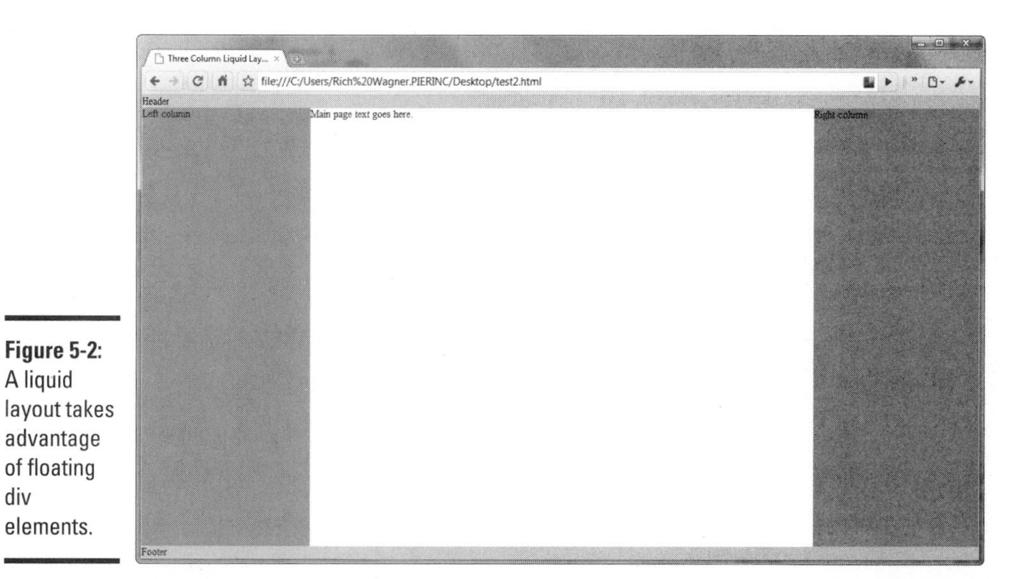

Figure 5-2: A liquid layout takes advantage of floating div elements.

Aligning Text Vertically

The `vertical-align` property specifies how text aligns vertically in relation to another element, such as other text (superscripting, for example) or an image (captioning, for example).

You can give the `vertical-align` property any of the following eight descriptive values: `bottom`, `baseline`, `middle`, `sub`, `super`, `text-top`, `text-bottom`, and `top`. Or you can supply a specific measurement (such as 4px, which places the superscript four pixels above the baseline) or a percentage.

The alignment is made relative to any `line-height` property used with the text. Most of the values you can use with `vertical-align` are self-describing, but `text-bottom` means that the baseline is ignored and that the imaginary line is drawn at the bottom of the typeface's descenders (such as a line at the bottom of the letters *p* and *y*, which both have descenders).

The *baseline* is an imaginary line drawn between characters that have no descenders. The baseline is the default to which everything aligns unless you specify otherwise with the `vertical-align` property.

Superscripting

You can achieve superscripting (such as adding a degree symbol to a temperature) by modifying the vertical alignment. Superscripted (and subscripted) characters are often printed in a smaller typeface than the surrounding text (think of footnote numbers, for example). However, if you superscript (or subscript) a character by using the `vertical-align` property, the character's text size isn't automatically reduced. If you want that effect, you can add a font size specification to your style. To get the effect you want — both superscription and text-size reduction — you should combine the `super` value with a percentage of downsizing for the `font-size` property.

Here's an example:

```
<html>
<head>
<style type="text/css">
  span.super { vertical-align:
    super; font-size: 70%; }
</style>
</head>
<body>
<p>Hello, I am here to
    stay<span class="super">
    SUPERSCRIPT</span>.
</p>
</body>
</html>
```

Book V

JavaScript and Ajax

"Great goulash, Stan. That reminds me, are you still scripting your own Web page?"

Contents at a Glance

Chapter 1: Understanding How Scripting Works

In This Chapter

- **Working with the `script` element**
- **Connecting a script with an HTML element**
- **Understanding how JavaScript can add content to your document**
- **Triggering a script with event handlers**
- **Adding a ready-made script to your Web page**

We're off to see the wizard, the wonderful Wizard of Oz. Scripts inside of your Web pages can serve much like Oz's "man behind the curtain." You can use them to provide logic and control for everything you want to do on your Web site. Therefore, as you begin to develop more and more sophisticated Web sites, you'll find that a key part of that solution is JavaScript.

In this chapter, I don't dive into the details of JavaScript programming just yet. Instead, I introduce you to how JavaScript works, how it's added to a Web page, and how it's called when a certain event occurs.

Surveying the JavaScript Scripting Language

HTML is actually a *markup* language — essentially a set of tags that you place around blocks of content to categorize it or describe how to display it in a browser. However, when an HTML document is sent by a Web server for display in a browser, the document can't change.

HTML documents are used to create interactive Web pages with features such as image rollovers, self-validating forms, and dynamic visual effects. By itself, an HTML document is much like an inanimate statue. JavaScript "code" transforms this statue into a full-fledged moving robot.

JavaScript is similar to traditional programming languages, such as C++ or Java. However, JavaScript is easier to use and is designed for specific tasks specifically inside Web pages.

JavaScript allows you to access different parts of a Web page, such as a form, an image, the entire document, or even the browser window. These parts are actually programming objects; taken together, they make up the *Document Object Model (DOM),* which I discuss more fully in Chapter 4 of this minibook. As you work with JavaScript, you create *scripts* — mini-programs — that can control, modify, and transform various objects on your page.

JavaScript is universally supported by all major Web browsers, including Internet Explorer, Firefox, Google Chrome, and Safari. The DOM is standardized by the W3C standards body, but not all browsers (particularly older versions) are fully compliant with it. Therefore, as you work with JavaScript, you should test your work regularly in multiple browsers to ensure that the functionality of your page works as you intend.

Although it's not normally an issue, users can disable JavaScript in their browsers. Be sure, therefore, that your Web site doesn't depend entirely on scripts to let users function on the site.

Oh, and one last thing I should mention . . . though the names are familiar, JavaScript has nothing to do with Java (another programming language).

Working with the script Element

JavaScript code can exist inside an HTML document in two locations:

- Inside a `script` element
- Inside the event handlers of HTML elements. I discuss how to do this in the section, "Enabling JavaScript with an Event Handler."

The `script` element serves as a container for JavaScript code that you want to execute. A `script` element is normally placed inside the document head, although in certain instances you place it inside the body. It has one required attribute, `type`, which indicates the MIME type (`text/javascript`) of the script:

```
<script type="text/javascript">
</script>
```

In older versions of HTML, the `script` element sported a `language` attribute to indicate the version of JavaScript. Note, however, that this attribute is *deprecated* (abandoned as obsolete) in newer specifications; avoid using it.

Executing JavaScript automatically on load

JavaScript code is inserted as content in the `script` element, as shown in this example:

```
<script type="text/javascript">
alert( 'Welcome to the world of scripting.' );
</script>
```

This script displays an alert message box. JavaScript commands, such as `alert()`, inside a `script` element are processed when the script is loaded by the browser. In this case, the browser displays the alert message box when the user opens the page.

If the code inside the `script` element makes no sense, flip to Chapter 2 of this minibook, which deals with the basics of writing a JavaScript script.

Executing JavaScript on demand

Not all code is executed when the script is loaded. If JavaScript code is placed inside a function, the function must be specifically called by name to execute. A *function* is a block of code that begins with the keyword `function` and has the following structure:

```
function functionname() {
 // code goes here
}
```

For example, consider the following HTML file:

```
<!DOCTYPE html PUBLIC "-//W3C//DTD XHTML 1.0 Transitional//EN"
    "http://www.w3.org/TR/xhtml1/DTD/xhtml1-transitional.dtd">
<html xmlns="http://www.w3.org/1999/xhtml">
<head>
<meta http-equiv="Content-Type" content="text/html;
    charset=UTF-8" />
<title>Scripting test</title>
<script type="text/javascript">
alert( 'I show up when this script loads' );

function alertOnDemand() {
 alert( 'I show up only when I am triggered.' );
}
</script>
</head>
<body>
</body>
</html>
```

In this example, the first `alert()` command is triggered when the document head loads (see Figure 1-1). However, because the `alertOnDemand()` function is never explicitly called, the second alert message box isn't displayed to the user.

Figure 1-1: A JavaScript message box is displayed when the script is processed.

Therefore, although a `script` element contains the JavaScript code, you often want to trigger it from other HTML elements on the page.

Enabling JavaScript with an Event Handler

An *event,* which is at the heart of scripting in Web pages, is anything that happens to any object in the DOM — including all HTML elements, the document, and even the browser window. The page's loading is an event. So too is a button being clicked by a user or a user moving the mouse pointer on top of a button.

JavaScript and HTML allow you to assign a piece of JavaScript code to execute when a particular event occurs in your Web page. The event-driven nature of JavaScript gives the scripting language the capability to interact dynamically with the user.

To connect the pieces, HTML elements have event handler attributes that essentially bridge the HTML world and the JavaScript world. For example, an `img` element has an `onclick` handler:

```
<img src="images/suki.jpg" onclick="openPreview()"/>
```

The image is displayed as normal, but when a user clicks the image with the mouse, the `openPreview()` function is called, which is a piece of code you can write to display an enlarged view of the picture in a special preview window.

The code inside an event handler doesn't have to consist only of calls to functions you've created in a script elsewhere in the document. You can also put any kind of JavaScript calls in there. If you want to display an alert message box when a user clicks an image, you can write this bit of code:

```
<img src="images/jboys.jpg" onclick="alert('J-boys love
   eating macaroni and cheese.')"/>
```

Figure 1-2 displays the results.

Figure 1-2: This message box is displayed from a JavaScript command inside the `onclick` handler.

See Chapter 4 in this minibook for complete details on working with event handlers.

Embedding Ready-Made Scripts into Your Web Pages

As you're getting up to speed with JavaScript, be sure to check out several Web sites that provide ready-made JavaScript scripts that you can quickly copy and paste into your pages. These sites, however, are more than just useful for people who don't know how to use JavaScript. They're also excellent resources for even advanced scripters who don't want to reinvent the wheel to use popular scripting techniques.

You can find a variety of repository sites for JavaScript scripts, but keep in mind that many of those sites are dated and not well maintained. Two that do a good job of keeping current are Dynamic Drive (`www.dynamicdrive.com`) and dhtmlgoodies.com (`www.dhtmlgoodies.com`).

Chapter 2: Programming in JavaScript

In This Chapter

- Dissecting a script
- Knowing the basic syntax rules of JavaScript
- Discovering what variables do
- Exploring conditional expressions and loops
- Working with functions and operators

If you're new to scripting, looking at JavaScript code can resemble trying to find an exit door in a dark room: It's confusing. It's hard to take even a step without bumping something or knocking something over. However, as your eyes slowly begin to adjust to the dark surroundings, you can start to discern the vague outline of an obstacle right in front of you.

As you begin to work with JavaScript, making sense of a script can seem daunting. However, as you begin to let your eyes adjust to your new environs, you begin to gradually see the shadows and outlines of the obstacles.

In this chapter, I help light your path through those dark alleys and cracks of JavaScript. After an introduction to object-based programming, you take a close look at a script and dissect the pieces of it. As you do so, you pick up on the key syntax rules of JavaScript, and then can better understand the code you're working with. I then talk about key programming constructs, including variables, conditional expressions, and loops.

It's All about Objects

When you write scripts, you work primarily with different objects in an HTML document and in the JavaScript language. An object in the real world is anything you see lying around your office or house: a desk, a cup of coffee, or a cat, for example.

In the same way, an *object* in a script is any element that might be found inside a Web page, such as a `table` element, a collection of `a` links, or even the document itself. In general, you can work with two groups of objects:

✦ **DOM objects:** The scripting equivalents of HTML elements and other parts of a Web page. When an HTML element is created by the browser, a corresponding DOM object is created at the same time. As a result, you don't need to do anything explicitly to create the DOM objects in your script before using them.

You're likely to spend most of your scripting time working with DOM objects. That's why you want to be sure to thumb over to Chapter 4 in this minibook for full details on how to work with the DOM.

✦ **Built-in JavaScript objects:** A set of objects that don't directly relate to an HTML document. These objects are used for working with data types (such as strings and dates) or for performing certain utility functions, such as math calculations. Unlike DOM objects, built-in JavaScript objects aren't created by default. Therefore you have to create them by using the `new` operator.

For full information on built-in objects, see the online JavaScript Reference at Mozilla.org: `http://developer.mozilla.org/en/docs/JavaScript`.

An object in JavaScript contains both properties and methods:

✦ **Property:** An attribute associated with an object that helps describe it. For example, the `document` object has a `url` property that specifies the location of the Web page.

✦ **Method:** An action or behavior that can be performed by the object. The `document` object has a `getElementById` method that retrieves a reference to the first element that has a specific `id` value.

Making Sense of JavaScript Syntax

As you begin, I want to avoid immediately explaining how a script code works. (The rest of this book does that!) Instead, begin by looking at the following code in the script:

```
<script type="text/javascript">

/* getParaCount()
          Last modified: 3/29/07
          Developer:           R. Wagner
          Purpose:             Counts the total number of paragraphs in the
    document
                               and displays the results in a message box.
*/
function getParaCount()
{
```

```
  var paraCollection = document.getElementsByTagName( 'p' );
  var paracollection = 'dummy variable';
  var count = paraCollection.length;
  // If I find a match, then display count and then the first paragraph
  if ( count > 0 ) {
     alert("There are exactly " + count + " paragraphs in this HTML document.");
    alert( 'In fact, just for fun, here is first one: ' + paraCollection[0].
    childNodes[0].nodeValue );
  }
  // Otherwise...
  else {
     alert( 'Sorry, no paragraphs were found. Try writing one first!' );
  }
}

</script>
```

If this code sample looks terribly confusing, don't worry. In this section, I dissect various aspects of the script as I explain some basic "rules of the road" for JavaScript programming. Read this section to understand how to read the script for yourself.

Case is all-important

Just like XHTML, JavaScript is case-sensitive. The `paraCollection` variable is a different variable from the dummy variable that has all-lowercase letters (`paracollection`). In addition, `var` is a valid keyword for defining a variable, and using `VAR` gives you a syntax error.

Semicolons mark the end of a statement

A normal statement in JavaScript can be almost any command, expression, or assignment operation. Take a look at the code and you can see that each of the normal statements end with the most neglected punctuation mark: the semicolon. Truth be told, JavaScript is flexible and doesn't force you to use semicolons (as long as each new statement is on a new line). However, it's considered good programming practice to include the semicolon anyway.

Objects do dots

In the scripting code, JavaScript uses a syntax convention called *dot notation* when it's working with objects and its own properties and methods. In dot notation, the object name is listed first, followed by a dot, followed by the name of the property or method. For example, the following code snippet shows how the `document` object's `url` property and `getElementById` method are written:

```
var myUrl = document.url;
var myLink = document.getElementById( 'newslink' );
```

A second example is taken from the sample script. Check out this code snippet:

```
document.getElementsByTagName( 'p' );
```

`getElementsByTagName()` is a method of the `document` object that returns a collection of all the specified elements in the current Web page.

Curly braces are used to enclose blocks of code

In JavaScript, curly braces serve as containers for sections of a script. A function (for now, think of a function as a module of code with a unique name) uses them to define its starting and ending points. The `getParaCount()` function, for example, contains all its code inside the `{ }` braces. Curly braces are also used by various JavaScript statements (such as `if...else` in the example) to separate code in different branches.

Scripters often debate whether the first brace should be on the same line as the beginning of the statement or on a separate line. In this book, I prefer to keep it on the same line as the first code segment, but it makes no difference to the interpreter.

Collections and arrays are zero-based

A collection and an array are special kinds of objects that can contain multiple items. For example, the `document.all` DOM object is a collection that contains all the HTML elements in a document. An *array* is a type of variable that can also store multiple items. In each case, you can access a particular member of the collection or array by using an index number. In order to access the first item, however, you use 0, not 1. That's because collections and arrays are *zero-based,* meaning that you start counting at 0 rather than at 1. For example, the following line of code that I use in the sample script returns the content of the first paragraph in the `paraCollection` collection:

```
paraCollection[0].childNodes[0].nodeValue;
```

Also, keep in mind that the last item in the collection or array will have an index value of one less than the total number of elements in an array.

White space doesn't matter

The spacing of the code matters to you only as a scripter, not as the JavaScript interpreter. Therefore you can add as much white space as you want (by using tabs, spaces, and even blank lines) between parts of the code. (I have the habit of adding a space after parentheses marks.)

Helpful comments are encouraged

Comments don't execute; instead, they describe what a script (or a specific line in it) does; they're helpful in troubleshooting. You can add your own comments to your scripts in two ways:

- **Single-line comment:** Add two slashes (`//`) to a line. Anything on the rest of the line is considered a comment and is ignored by the interpreter. In the example, I use slash marks to comment on the `if..else` statement.
- **Multi-line comment:** If you want to add a comment that spans multiple lines, enclose it inside `/*` and `*/` marks. The comment at the top describing the `getParaCount()` function shows you how this works.

Quotation marks come in a variety pack

You can use both single quote and double quote marks to indicate a string literal (a fancy term for normal text). As long as both sides of a pair match, it doesn't matter which kind you use. In the sample code, for example, I use double quotes in the first `alert()` command and then single quotes for the remaining two.

makeSureYouUnderstandHungarian NamingConventions

The JavaScript naming convention is popularly known as *Hungarian.* (No, you don't need to travel to Budapest to use it.) The Hungarian convention calls for a name to begin with a lowercase letter, and the first letter of each subsequent new word in a "compound word" should be uppercase, with all other letters lowercase. With a couple of exceptions, both the core JavaScript language and DOM use this convention throughout.

For example, check out the following line of code from the example:

```
var paraCollection = document.getElementsByTagName( 'p' );
```

`document` is the object name for the HTML document and is in all-lowercase letters. Its method, `getElementsByTagName`, is a compound word that gets elements by the specified tag name. Note that the remaining new words in the method name are capitalized.

I follow this convention in variable names (`paraCollection`, `count`) for consistency's sake, even though it isn't required.

Avoid reserved words

JavaScript has a set of *reserved words* that are core parts of the language. You can't use these words when you name variables and functions, for example. Following is a list of JavaScript-reserved words:

```
abstract
boolean
break
byte
case
catch
char
class
const
continue
debugger
default
delete
do
double
else
enum
export
extends
false
final
finally
float
for
function
goto
if
implements
import
in
instanceof
int
interface
long
native
new
null
package
private
protected
public
return
short
static
super
switch
synchronized
this
throw
throws
transient
true
try
typeof
var
void
volatile
while
with
```

Different types of data

In a script, you can work with a variety of basic data types, including string literals, numbers, and Boolean (true/false) values.

Strings

A *string literal* is a string of characters enclosed in single or double quotation marks. The following examples show string literals in the sample script:

```
'p'
 'dummy variable'
"There are exactly "
" paragraphs in this HTML document."
'In fact, just for fun, here is the first one: '
'Sorry, no paragraphs were found. Try writing one first!'
```

Although you normally want to work with strings as literals, JavaScript also allows you to work with strings as objects. This capability can be helpful when you want to perform certain processes on a string. Check out this example:

```
var str = new String( 'my life as a bus boy' );
alert( 'Original string is ' + str );
str.toUpperCase();
alert( 'Updated string is ' + str );
```

In this example, I declared `str` as a new String object by using the `new` operator and assigning it the value of `dummy`. Its original value is shown to the user, and then its `toUpperCase()` method is called. The `toUpperCase()` method converts the string to uppercase text. The updated text is then shown in the `alert` message.

Numbers

A number can be either an integer or a floating-point number. You can even get fancy and use scientific notation, hexadecimal, and octal numbers. The script uses the numeric value `0` for a variety of purposes.

JavaScript supports a `Number` object. Again, although working with plain number values is simpler, a `Number` object is helpful when you need to convert it to different notations, such as exponential or precision.

Boolean values

A Boolean value is either `true` or `false` and is often used to determine whether a condition is true. Here's an example of testing the value of a variable named `confirm`:

```
if ( confirm == true ) {
   alert( 'You have been confirmed. Do not back out now!' );
}
```

JavaScript also provides a built-in Boolean object type, although it's rarely used by most scripters.

Arrays

An *array* is a collection of items that are indexed. The items can be a variety of data types, such as strings, numbers, or even objects. You can even mix and match data types within a single array. An array is defined with the `new` operator:

```
var states = new Array();
```

You can define the items in the array when you create the array by passing the values in as parameters:

```
var states = new Array( 'MA', 'ME', 'RI', 'VT' );
```

Alternatively, you can add items by listing them by their index value or in the order in which they appear in the list. The index value is designated by a zero-based value within brackets, such as

```
states[0]= 'MA';
states[1] = 'ME';
states[2] = 'RI';
states[3] = 'VT';
```

You can then access any value in the array according to its index. For example, to display the fourth item in the array in an alert box, you can use the following line of code:

```
alert( 'Customer is from ' + states[3] );
```

While this example showed how to store strings in an array, you can store any kind of data, including numbers, Boolean values, objects, functions, and even null values. For example, consider the following array that contains a variety of types:

```
var kitchenSink = ["fiabo", 1.31, function(){alert("Get a
   Clue")}, null, false];
```

You can get the number of items in this array by accessing its `length` property:

```
var kitchenSink = ["fiabo", 1.31, function(){alert("Get a
   Clue")}, null, false];
alert(kitchenSink.length));
```

The alert box displays 5.

Working with Variables

Remember the television series *Alias?* Sydney Bristow was a secret agent and master of disguise who dressed in a variety of costumes each week to defeat her evil enemies. JavaScript may not have the same intrigue, tropical locales, and plot twists as the television show, but it does have its own sort of master of disguise: the variable.

A variable is an "alias" for values you want to work with in your JavaScript scripts. In other words, a *variable* is a word that stores another value. For example, you can declare a variable named `myName` to be equal to the value of `Rich`. Then, everywhere that you want to use the word `Rich` in your script, you can use `myName` instead.

Why go to all the trouble? Why not just use the literal string `Rich` throughout? As you see throughout this book, a variety of programming tasks require variables. But, perhaps most noteworthy is that just as Sydney Bristow might wear multiple costumes in an episode, so too a variable can change its values multiple times during the course of a script. As a result, variables enable you to create dynamic scripts rather than have everything defined up front.

Declaring and assigning a variable

To use a variable in your script, you declare it. A variable is formally defined by using the keyword `var`:

```
var myVariable
```

The `var` keyword essentially says, "Hey, the word that follows will be a variable in this script." The variable name that follows needs to begin with either a letter or an underscore (although you can include a number elsewhere in the word).

In traditional programming languages, like C++ or Java, you have to declare the type of data that's stored in the variable: a number, character string, or Boolean (`true` or `false`), for example. The *interpreter,* a program that processes the code, needs to know that sort of thing. However, JavaScript is more flexible, which means that you don't need to specify the type of value that the variable will hold.

After the variable is defined, the variable can receive a value. For example, if you want to assign the value `Rich` to `myName`, here's the code snippet:

```
var myName;
myName = "Rich";
```

Didn't I say that JavaScript is flexible? Rather than declare the variable in one step and then assign it a value in another, you can combine them into a single line of code:

```
var myName = "Rich";
```

As the infomercials say, "Wait — there's more!" JavaScript allows you to use shortcut notation so you can declare a variable and then assign an initial value without using the keyword `var`:

```
myName = "Rich";
```

Although you can use this shorthand notation, the use of the keyword `var` can make your code more readable and easier to understand as you work with it.

Accessing a variable

After a variable is defined, you can reference the variable in your code, and its current value is used. Check out the code in the following brief script. The value of `currentName` starts out as `"Rich"` but is then reassigned to a value that the user enters in a prompt that appears in a dialog box:

```
var currentName = "Rich";
alert( "Hello, my name is" + currentName );
currentName = prompt( "Please enter your name.", "Jimmy
   Crackcorn" );
alert( "Hello, " + currentName + ". That is a really nice
   name. And I don't say that to just anyone." );
```

Scoping out variable scope and lifetime

A variable can have either a global or a local scope. Any variable that's defined outside of a function is a *global variable* — you can access it from any other part of the document. A variable declared inside a function (a *local variable*) is accessible only to the function itself and is destroyed when the function is done processing.

In addition, the location in which a variable is defined matters. A variable is accessible only after it's declared. Therefore you generally want to make sure that all global variables are defined at the start of the first `script` element in the document head.

The following code provides a good illustration of the scope of variables:

```
<!DOCTYPE html PUBLIC "-//W3C//DTD XHTML 1.0 Transitional//EN" "http://www.
    w3.org/TR/xhtml1/DTD/xhtml1-transitional.dtd">
<html xmlns="http://www.w3.org/1999/xhtml">
<head>
<meta http-equiv="Content-Type" content="text/html; charset=UTF-8" />
<title>Scoping out Variables</title>
<script type="text/javascript">
// Global variable
var quote = 'Think global.';

// Function
function quoteme() {
    // Local variable
     var quote = 'Act local.'
     alert( quote );
}

alert( quote ); // called when document opens
</script>
</head>

<body>

<form id="form1" name="form1" method="post" action="">
  <input type="button" name="localvar" value="Local" onclick="quoteme();"/>
  <input type="button" name="globalvar" value="Global" onclick="alert( quote
    );"/>
</form>

<script type="text/javascript">
// Global variable
var quote = 'Think globally with a twist. ';
</script>

</body>
</html>
```

The variable `quote` is defined three different times:

- As a global variable in the top `script` element
- As a local variable in the `quoteme()` function
- As a global variable in a `script` element that's placed at the bottom of the document body

When the document loads, the `alert()` command (the final line of the first `script` element) is called and displays the current value of `quote`, which is `'Think global.'` When the Local button is clicked, it calls the `quoteme()` function, which displays the value of the local version of the `quote` variable, `'Act local.'` Finally, when the Global button is clicked, it displays `'Think globally with a twist.'` because the global variable `quote` was reassigned a new value when the bottom `script` element was processed (on document load).

Working with constants

Not all variables need to change values during the processing of the script. Sometimes a variable is simply a handy way to refer to another value. Many programming languages, in fact, have *constants,* which are essentially variables that don't change values.

JavaScript doesn't have the concept of a constant built into the language. Don't let that stop you. You can create a constant as a normal variable but use a special naming convention to make constants and variables easy to distinguish from each other. To follow the conventions of traditional languages, use all-uppercase words and separate different words with underscores:

```
var COUNTY = "United States of America";
var PI = 3.14159;
var VERSION_NUMBER = "8.02";
```

You can use a constant value in the same manner as you use a variable in your code (which is good because it really is a variable with an uppercase name).

Basic Conditional Expressions

"That depends." How often do you find yourself using that expression during the day? Suppose that the bartender asks, "Would you like another beer?" You look at the friend you drove to the bar with and say, "That depends. Am I driving, or are you?"

JavaScript also allows you to perform conditional logic in your scripts with three types of statements:

- `if`
- `if...else`
- `switch`

The if statement

The `if` statement is used when you want to run a portion of code if the expression you're testing is `true`. The basic structure looks like this:

```
if ( condition ) {
     // code to execute if condition is true
}
```

For example, consider the following code snippet:

```
secretcode = prompt( "Enter the secret code.", "" );
if ( secretcode == "moops" ) {
     alert( "You won the contest." );
}
```

A prompt dialog box is displayed to the user when the script is executed. The `secretcode` variable stores the value given by the user. The `if` statement then evaluates whether `secretcode` is equal to `"moops"`. If so, a message box is displayed. Otherwise the `alert()` command is bypassed.

Notice the double equal sign in the conditional expression — it isn't a typo. A single equal sign (=) is used to assign a value to a variable, and a double equal sign (==) is used to compare one side of an expression with another.

The if...else statement

The `if...else` statement is similar to the `if` statement, except you can also run code only if the expression evaluates to `false`:

```
if ( condition ) {
    // code to execute if condition is true
}
else {
    // code to execute if condition is false
}
```

Here's an example of the `if...else` statement in action:

```
if ( document.title == 'Home page' ) {
    alert( "Welcome home" );
}
else {
    alert( "Here's where you are instead " + document.title
    );
}
```

This code checks to see whether the document title is equal to `'Home page'`. If so, then a Welcome home alert message is displayed. If not, then the alternative alert message is displayed.

The switch statement

The `if` and `if..else` statements are ideal for evaluating for a single value, but suppose you want to check for multiple values. The `switch` statement comes in handy for exactly this reason.

Its basic structure is shown here:

```
switch ( expression ) {
case label1:
  // code to be executed if expression equals label1
  break;
case label2:
  //code to be executed if expression equals label2
  break;
default:
  // code to be executed if expression is different
  // from both label1 and label2
}
```

The `switch` statement evaluates the condition and looks to see whether the result equals the first `case` value. If so, the program performs the code inside the `case` statement. The `break` statement is used to stop the flow of the `switch` statement from continuing its evaluation in the `case` statements that follow. The `default` statement executes if no matches are found.

Here's an example that uses the `switch` statement to evaluate the current time by using the built-in `Date()` object:

```
var d = new Date()
var hr = d.getHours()

switch ( hr ) {
case 8 :
   document.write( "Good morning sunshine." );
   break;
case 12 :
   document.write( "Lunch time!" );
   break;
case 15 :
   document.write( "Afternoon tea with the queen." );
   break;
case 22 :
   document.write( "Time to hit the sack." );
   break;
default
   document.write( "Come back later." );
}
```

The `hr` variable is assigned the current hour by using the `getHours()` method. The `switch` statement evaluates `hr` by looking at each of the `case` statements in sequence. If it finds a match, the code inside is executed. Otherwise the `default` statement executes.

Getting Loopy: Working with Looping Constructs

A common need when you develop in JavaScript is the ability to loop through a task a number of times or until a specific condition changes. JavaScript provides two programming constructs that allow you to "get loopy": `for` and `while`. The `for` loop cycles through a block of code a specific number of times. The `while` loop loops through a program block as long as a specific condition is `true`.

The for loop

A `for` loop can look rather intimidating because the construct looks much like gibberish. After you understand the pieces, though, it becomes a rather straightforward tool to add to your scripting tool belt. Here's an example of a loop cycling through ten times:

```
for ( var i=1;i<=10;i++) {
   document.write( "Pass number " + i + "<br/>" );
}
```

Here's how the different parts break down:

- **Initialization statement:** The `var i=1` statement is the initializing piece, indicating that the loop declares and then uses a counter variable named `i`, which has a starting value of `1`. (The variable `i` is the standard name for most JavaScript loop counters.)
- **Condition:** The `i<=10` statement indicates the condition that's evaluated each time the loop is cycled through. The condition returns true as long as the `i` value is less than or equal to 10.
- **Update statement:** The `i++` statement is the update statement that's processed after each time through the loop. In this case, the shortcut expression `++` increments the value by `1`.

This `for` loop repeats the code block inside the brackets ten times. After the loop evaluates to `false` on the 11th pass, the script goes on to the next line of code. The output for the script is shown here:

```
Pass number 1
Pass number 2
Pass number 3
Pass number 4
Pass number 5
```

```
Pass number 6
Pass number 7
Pass number 8
Pass number 9
Pass number 10
```

For the most part, you can copy and paste a `for` loop construct into your script. For most purposes, you need to update only two values (the counter number and the code to process), which I indicate by bolding in this example:

```
for ( var i=1;i<=10;i++) {
    // code
}
```

However, you don't always need to use a number. Here's an example of a loop based on the total number of links in the current document:

```
for ( var i=0;i<document.links.length;i++ ) {
    processLink( document.links[i] );
}
```

The while loop

Like a `for` loop, a `while` loop cycles through a block of code multiple times. However, although `for` loops through a specific number of times, `while` executes a block of code as long as a condition evaluates to `true`. Its generic form is simpler than the `for` loop:

```
while( condition ) {
  // code to process when condition is true
}
```

Here's an example:

```
while( items > 10 ) {
   document.writeln( "Current item count is " + items );
   processOrder( items ); // Fictional custom function
   items++;
}
```

In this example, the code block loops through as long as the `items` variable is less than 10. Inside the block, the current item count is written, followed by a call to a fictional function named `processOrder()`, which can be used to act on the current state of the order. Finally, the value of the `items` variable is incremented by 1; `items++` does that job.

Working with Functions

A *function* is a named group of JavaScript commands and statements that has to be explicitly called by an event or your script before it's executed. Suppose you have a miniscript that performs a validity check on a form text field. You can create a function to handle this process and then call the function by name every time the user leaves any text field in your form.

You can think of a function as a factory that processes stuff. A real-world factory receives raw material (such as steel), does something to it inside the factory (molds the steel into components, for example), and then sends a finished product (such as a car). In the same way, a function can accept optional input values (called *arguments* or *parameters*), can perform a specific process, and can optionally send back a *return value* to whichever event handler or line of code called it.

To define a function, you use the following structure:

```
function myFunctionName( [param1,param2...] ) {
    // Function code goes here
}
```

To illustrate, here's a function for creating a cookie. The function is named `addCookie()` and accepts three arguments, the last of which is optional:

```
function addCookie( cookieName, cookieValue, days ) {
    if ( days ) {
         var dt = new Date();
         dt.setTime( dt.getTime()+ ( days*24*60*60*1000 ) );
         var expdate = "; expires=" + date.toGMTString();
    }
    else {
         var expdate = "";
    }
    document.cookie = cookieName + "=" + cookieValue +
   expdate + "; path=/";
}
```

To call this function, here's what the statement looks like:

```
addCookie( 'username', 'rayman', 90 );
```

The `addCookie()` function processes its code, according to the arguments that are supplied, and creates a cookie. In this example, no result is sent back to the statement that called the code. Instead, `addCookie()` simply performs its job and then quits.

A second example demonstrates how a value is returned to the calling statement by using the `return` command:

```
function calcTotal( netTotal ) {
   var t = ( netTotal * .05 );
   return t;
}
```

Note: This bit of code is expanded for clarity. You can combine the two into a single line: `return ( netTotal * .05 );`.

When the `return` command is encountered, the function stops executing and returns program control to the statement that called the function. Therefore, if you place statements after the `return` command, the interpreter ignores them.

A method of an object is basically the same thing as a function. The only difference is that a method is designed to perform an action on its associated object, and a function is a more generic piece of code that you can create to do anything you please.

Operators Are Standing By: Connecting with JavaScript Operators

In this digital age, the role of the telephone operator is long forgotten for all except special needs. However, if you think back to the early years of the telephone, the operator played an important role in connecting the caller to another phone line. A JavaScript operator acts something like the old-time phone operator by connecting different JavaScript pieces of code. You use operators (for example) to add numbers, connect two strings, assign values to variables, or evaluate expressions.

Tables 2-1, 2-2, 2-3, and 2-4 list the major operators in JavaScript. The ones you most often use are shown in bold.

Table 2-1 Assignment Operators

Operator	*Example*	*Description*
=	**x=y**	**The value of y is assigned to x**
+=	**x+=y**	**Same as x=x+y**
–=	x–=y	Same as x=x–y
*=	x*=y	Same as x=x*y
/=	x/=y	Same as x=x/y
%=	x%=y	Same as x=x%y (modulus)

Table 2-2 Comparison Operators

Operator	*Example*	*Description*
==	x==y	x is equal to y
!=	x!=y	x is not equal to y
===	x===y	Evaluates both for value and data type (for example, if x = "5" and y = 5, then x==y is true, but x===y is false)
<	x<y	x is less than y
<=	x<=y	x is less than or equal to y
>	x>y	x is greater than y
>=	x>=y	x is greater than or equal to y
?:	x=(y<5) ? –5 : y	If y is less than 5, then assign –5 to x; otherwise, assign y to x (known as the conditional operator)

Table 2-3 Logical Operators

<table>
<tr><th>Operator</th><th>Example</th><th>Description</th></tr>
<tr><td>&&</td><td>if (x > 3 && y=0)</td><td>logical and</td></tr>
<tr><td>||</td><td>if (x>3 || y=0)</td><td>logical or</td></tr>
<tr><td>!</td><td>if !(x=y)</td><td>not</td></tr>
</table>

Table 2-4 Mathematical Operators

Operator	*Example*	*Description*
+	x+2	Addition
–	x–3	Subtraction
*	x*2	Multiplication
/	x/2	Division
%	x%2	Modulus (division remainder)
++	x++	Increment (same as x=x+1)
--	x--	Decrement (same as x=x–1)

Postmodern JavaScript

In the early days of JavaScript, scripters needed to account for browsers that didn't support scripting. Therefore, to prevent JavaScript code from screwing up an older browser's processing of the document, a common practice was to enclose all the scripting code with HTML comments:

```
<script>
<!--
 // JavaScript code
-->
</script>
```

All browsers now deal with the `script` element. What's more, using HTML comments inside a `script` tag violates XHTML standards. Avoid this practice when you're writing your own JavaScript.

Chapter 3: JavaScript Libraries and Frameworks

In This Chapter

- **Why use a JavaScript library?**
- **Introducing Prototype**
- **Exploring jQuery**
- **Noting other libraries and frameworks**

Perhaps you heard something like this from a parent or grandparent when you were growing up: *When I was your age, I had to walk 5 miles to school in 2 feet of snow in my bare feet at 5:30am each day.* It's common for everyone to talk about how hard it was for them and how easy it is in comparison for someone else — even in the Web world. In fact, if you work around some long-time Web developers, you might get a similar-sounding story: *Back in the day, we worked with pure JavaScript. There was none of this fancy-schmancy stuff you guys work with today.*

I'm not giving those old-timers a hard time. Hey, I was working with JavaScript back in the "good ol' days"! But as I look around at JavaScript in the Web 2.0 landscape, I am amazed at how far this "Little Scripting Language That Could" has come. And perhaps nowhere is this maturation process more keenly seen than in the rich libraries and frameworks that are available for JavaScript developers today.

In this chapter, I show you the major JavaScript libraries available on the Web. While there's not enough space in this book to explore the full extent of the capability contained in these amazing libraries, this chapter gives you a foretaste of what is possible with them.

Why Use a JavaScript Library?

Up until recently, JavaScript developers kept their own personal JS libraries and pulled occasional canned scripts from the Web. But large numbers of developers didn't use *JavaScript frameworks,* shared code libraries that handle many tasks you'd otherwise have to write on your own. All that has changed within the past few years. As the core language has matured, so too have the third-party libraries that now dot the Web developer landscape.

Developers are turning to libraries and frameworks for two primary reasons:

- **Simpler, more efficient code:** Many of the frameworks encapsulate core language functionality within shortcut methods. This allows you to write less code and simplify scripts that could normally become repetitive and complex in traditional JavaScript.
- **Avoid reinventing the wheel:** The available libraries and frameworks solve technical problems that developers have faced over and over. So, rather than coming up with your own solution, you can take advantage of the work other experts have done.

Working with Prototype

Prototype is a JavaScript framework that focuses on object-oriented extensions to the language as well as providing a very popular Ajax library.

For full details on all of the capabilities of Prototype, visit `www.prototypejs.org`.

Prototype supports Internet Explorer 6.0 and higher, Firefox 1.5 and higher, Safari 1.0 and higher, Google Chrome 1.0 and higher, and Opera 9 and higher.

Your first step in working with Prototype is to download the latest version from `www.prototypejs.org`. All you need to download is the `.js` library file and save it on your hard drive. Prototype includes its version number in the filename. So, for example, the version I am working with is 1.6.1, so the filename is `prototype-1.6.1.js`.

While you want to keep a master version of that file on your hard drive, copy it as well to a `prototype.js` file, which links to your Web pages. That way, when Prototype updates, you simply update the `prototype.js` file rather than having to update references to it throughout your site.

Then you include the `.js` file in your HTML files with a `script` tag:

```
<script type="text/javascript" src="scripts/prototype.js"/>
```

Using the all-purpose $() method

Prototype refers to its `$()` utility method as its "Swiss Army knife" because you can do so many things with it. By adding an `id` value as its parameter, you can use it as a shortcut replacement for `document.getElementById()`, which I discuss in Chapter 4 of this minibook. For example, consider the document shown in Listing 3-1.

Listing 3-1: example.html

```
<html>
  <head>
    <title>My title</title>
  </head>
  <body>
    <div id="container" class="special">
      <h1 id="header1">Container</p>
      <p id="p1" class="special">Paragraph 1</p>
      <p id="p2">Paragraph 2</p>
      <p id="p3">Paragraph 3/p>
      <p id="p4" class="special">Paragraph 4</p>
    </div>
  </body>
</html>
```

You can get a reference to the `p1` element with the following line of code:

```
var para = $("p1");
```

Or, if you want to get an array of elements based on the elements' `id` values, you could add multiple `id` values to it:

```
var eArr = $("container", "header1", "p1");
```

Using ordinary JavaScript, the equivalent code looks something like this:

```
var co = document.getElementById("container");
var he = document.getElementById("header1");
var pa = document.getElementById("p1");
var eArr = new Array( co, he, pa);
```

Starting to get the clue to why Prototype can be useful?

Using the $$() method

The `$$()` method is a second handy-dandy utility method that Prototype provides. You can use it as a shortcut replacement for `document.getElementsByTagName()` (see Chapter 4 of this minibook).

Suppose, for example, you wanted to get all the `p` elements in the `example.html` file shown in Listing 3-1. Here's the code that does the trick:

```
var pArr = $$("p"); // returns p1, p2, p3, and p4
```

You can also use the `$$()` method to select elements using CSS selector syntax. For example, to retrieve all of the `p` elements inside the `container` `div`, you use this code:

```
var pArr = $$("#container p"); // returns p1, p2, p3, and p4
```

Or, to get all paragraphs with the class `special`, you use

```
var pArr = $$("p.special"); // returns p1 and p4
```

Using the $F() method

Another shortcut utility method that Prototype provides is `$F()`. It returns the value of any form field, as specified by the parameter. Because retrieving the values of various form elements (such as inputs or combo boxes) can get confusing, the `$F()` provides a common interface to make getting their values easier. For example, consider the following form:

```
<form action="dosomething.php">
<select id="menu">
<option value="0" selected>(please select:)</option>
<option value="1">Pizza</option>
<option value="2">Grilled Cheese</option>
<option value="3">Big Salad</option>
</select>
<input type="text" id="fullName">
<input type="submit" value="submit">
</form>
```

To use the value for the `select` element, you use this code:

```
alert("You selected the following " + $F("menu"));
```

Or, to get the value for the text input, you use

```
alert("I think your name is " + $F("fullName"));
```

Trying out Try.these

Prototype provides a `Try.these()` utility method that takes multiple function calls as parameters and returns the result of the first function call that does not throw an error. This method then comes in very handy when (say) you're determining the browser support for a particular feature. Here's an example:

```
var result = Try.these(
supportVersion9(),
supportVersion8(),
supportLegacy()
)

if (result != undefined)
{
    // do something
}
```

In this example, the `Try.these` block tries to call the `supportVersion9()` method. If that returns `true`, then the `Try.these` stops the execution of method calls after it. However, if `supportVersion9()` causes problems, then the `Try.these` block moves on to `supportVersion8()` and tries again. However, if `supportLegacy()` is called and it has problems too, then `Try.these` returns a value of `undefined`.

Binding functions

Prototype supports the concept of *function binding,* which enables you to bind a function to an object so you can use `this` to reference the bound object.

This technique can be very effective when you're working with event handlers.

Consider the following example:

```
var obj = new Object();
obj.name = "my object";
obj.doSomething = function() { alert(this.name); }

$("button1").click = obj.doSomething.bind(obj);
```

In this example, the `doSomething()` method of `obj` is assigned as the `click` handler for the `button1` element. However, without function binding, `doSomething()` has problems when executed by the `button1` element. That's because, in traditional JavaScript, `this` would always refer to the button, because it was the one that triggered the event. However, the `bind()` method binds the associated object to the method — which enables the `this` keyword used in `doSomething()` to refer to `obj`.

Exploring jQuery

If you consider Prototype as a way to extend and streamline your JavaScript, jQuery actually gets you to rethink how you write your scripts. jQuery is a framework that is extremely powerful, but it does take some getting used to.

jQuery is compatible with Internet Explorer 6.0 and higher, Firefox 3 and higher, Safari 3.0 and higher, Google Chrome 1.0 and higher, and Opera 9.0 and higher.

To begin working with jQuery, download the latest version from `www.jquery.com`. You can download the latest version and save it on your hard drive. Like Prototype, jQuery includes the version number as part of its `.js` filename. The version I worked with at the time of writing is `jquery-1.4.2.min.js`.

While you want to keep a master version of the file on your hard drive, copy it to a `jquery.js` file to link to your Web pages.

When you have the library file, include it in the HTML files of your Web site by using a `script` tag:

```
<script type="text/javascript" src="scripts/jquery.js"/>
```

Selecting elements with the jQuery function

With syntax similar to Prototype, one of jQuery's most basic and useful utility methods is `$()`, which is referred to as the *jQuery function.* You can use it as a replacement for `document.getElementById()` to select an element according to the `id` you specify as its parameter.

To get the `h1` element with an `id` of `header1` (refer to Listing 3-1), use this code:

```
var header = $("#header1");
```

Note the use of # preceding the `id` value. If you're familiar with CSS, you'll recognize it (see Book IV for info on Cascading Style Sheets). And that's by design, because jQuery enables you to use CSS selector type syntax inside the `$()` parameter to retrieve all sorts of elements in return. For example, to return all the elements inside `example.html` (refer to Listing 3-1) that have a class name of `special`, you use this code:

```
$(".special"); // returns container, p1, and p4
```

Or, to return all the paragraphs inside the `container div`, you can use

```
$("#container p")
```

Or, to find any `p` (one or more of them) inside any `div`, you can use

```
$("div p")
```

Chaining with jQuery

One of the key concepts of jQuery is its capability to chain together multiple commands in a single call. Start with a three-line script:

```
$("#container").empty();
$("#container").append("<p>Previous text was removed.</p>");
$("#container").css("border", "1px solid black");
```

Because every jQuery method returns the calling object, you can chain these calls together into one line of code:

```
$("#container").empty().append("<p>Previous text was removed.</p>").css("border",
    "1px solid black");
```

Adding CSS styling

jQuery has different ways to add CSS styling to your elements. If the style is already defined, then you can add the class to one or more elements with the `addClass()` method. For example, suppose you have the following CSS style defined in a style sheet:

```
.highlight { color:#38312; font-weight:bold; }
```

Using the jQuery function, add it to all the elements you select. To add the `.highlight` style to all `p` elements in `example.html` (refer to Listing 3-1), use this code:

```
$("p").addStyle("highlight");
```

jQuery also provides a handy `css()` method that enables you to add CSS styling on the fly. You can specify the style properties as a *key/value object* as the parameter. It takes this form:

```
{"name" : "value", "name2" : "value2", ...}
```

For example, to add a border and change the text color of all `div` elements, you could use

```
$("div").css({"border":"1px solid black", "color", "#cccccc"});
```

Or, if you have a single style property to change, you can add a name/value pair as a parameter. Here's an example:

```
$("p").css("margin", "0px 3px 6x 0px");
```

Creating elements

jQuery enables you to take a piece of arbitrary HTML and add it to the DOM, avoiding the complexity of core DOM methods such as `createElement()` or `appendChild()` (see Chapter 4 of this minibook). To do so, simply add an HTML string as the parameter to `$()`. Then, to add that parameter to another element, use `appendTo()`. Here's an example:

```
$("<p>I can't believe adding this to the page is so easy!</p>").
    appendTo("#container");
```

This line adds the HTML you specified to the end of the `container div` of Listing 3-1.

Creating callbacks

A *callback* is a feature that has long been a fixture of traditional programming languages. It's essentially a function that's passed to another function and is triggered when the parent function is finished. Up until jQuery, however, a callback wouldn't even have been considered possible in standard JavaScript. In jQuery, it is.

For example, the following loads an external `.js` file and then calls the `processComplete()` function when it finishes:

```
$.getScript("processnightly.js", processComplete);
```

Other Libraries and Frameworks

While Prototype and jQuery are the most popular JavaScript frameworks, there are additional ones to consider.

Mootools

Mootools is another popular JavaScript framework, known for its object orientation as well as an Effects component that allows you to perform Flash-like transitions and easing.

Mootools works with Internet Explorer 6.0 and higher, Firefox 2.0 and higher, Safari 2.0 and higher, Google Chrome 1.0 and higher, and Opera 9 and higher.

You can download the Mootools framework at `mootools.net`.

Script.aculo.us

While the frameworks I've talked about in this chapter are more focused on core language and DOM extensions, Script.aculo.us is a library that focuses on user-interface widgets and effects. You can use it to add drag-and-drop, animation, auto-completion, and user interface controls to your Web pages.

Script.aculo.us is built on the Prototype framework and works well with it.

For more info, go to `http://script.aculo.us`.

jQuery UI

jQueryUI is to jQuery what Script.aculo.us is to Prototype. jQueryUI is built on the core jQuery library and focuses its attention on the user interface. It is focused on core user interface effects, widgets, and animation.

For details, go to `http://ui.jquery.com`.

moo.fx

Some of the libraries, such as Script.aculo.us, are avoided by some developers because the library can be quite extensive and heavy. The same can't be said for `moo.fx` — because `moo.fx` is a very lightweight (only 3K) library for effects, animation, and extensive CSS property controls. It is compatible and works well with both Prototype and Mootools frameworks.

For full details, go to `http://moofx.mad4milk.net`.

Chapter 4: Understanding the Document Object Model

In This Chapter

- **Understanding the DOM**
- **Accessing objects in the DOM**
- **Working with properties and methods**
- **Adding and removing DOM objects**
- **Exploring DOM objects**

At no cost to you, it's time to discover the DOM!

But wait . . . don't get *too* excited. Before you get out your James Bond tux and two champagne glasses, I need to say that I am not speaking of giving you a complimentary bottle of Dom Perignon, the prestigious French sparkling wine. Instead, I am actually talking about the Document Object Model (DOM), which allows you to work with an HTML document as a hierarchical tree structure.

However, once you understand the power that you have when you're working with and mastering the DOM, I think you'll be more excited about it than you would be about a bottle of 1963 Dom Perignon.

In this chapter, I guide you through the DOM and help you explore how to work with it to create interactive scripts for your Web pages.

What Is the DOM?

The *Document Object Model (DOM)* is a scripting interface to HTML and XML documents. That's a geeky way of saying that the DOM allows you to access, tap into, and even modify the structure of your Web page by using scripting. As its name suggests, the DOM is a modeled structure that describes the relationships of all elements in a document through a hierarchy. The DOM also defines which properties, methods, and events are available for each of its objects.

DOM and DOMER

The DOM is a W3C standard that has three levels:

- ***Level 1:*** Contains the core functionality to be able to script the DOM for a Web page. All current browsers support DOM1.
- ***Level 2:*** Extends support to include new functionality, such as event listeners and DOM support for Cascading Style Sheets (CSS). Modern browsers typically provide good support for the major parts of DOM2.
- ***Level 3:*** Adds new core capabilities, including keyboard events and an XML-related technology called XPath. Individual browsers provide various levels of support for DOM3.

The DOM is a standard set by the W3C, the Web standards body. All newer browsers (Chrome, Firefox, Safari, Internet Explorer, and Opera, for example) support the Level 1 and Level 2 versions of the DOM. (Level 1 focused on HTML; Level 2 refined the standard to support XML and XHTML documents.) See the "DOM and DOMER" sidebar for more.

The cross-browser support of the DOM that you can now enjoy is a relatively new phenomenon. When the DOM was introduced in the late 1990s, different browsers provided various levels of support and often had their own idiosyncratic additions to the standard. Fortunately, these problems have largely disappeared in newer generations of browsers.

Think of the DOM as a tree-like structure that organizes the parts of the HTML document as a hierarchy of object nodes. A *node* can be an element, an attribute, some content, or any part of a Web page. A node can contain other nodes. The DOM uses family terminology to describe the relationships of these nodes. A parent contains child nodes, and two nodes on the same hierarchical level are considered siblings.

The `document` object serves as the "trunk" of this document tree. Because this object has no HTML element equivalent, you can think of it as a "superobject" of sorts, as it contains every document element, including `html`, `head`, and `body`. All remaining elements and other parts of the Web page are descendent nodes of `document`.

For most common purposes, you work exclusively with HTML elements in the DOM. But, technically speaking, the nodes in a document tree consist of elements and content. (The content of an element is a child node of the container element.) Attributes aren't considered part of the document tree, but are accessed as properties of the element object.

Consider, for example, the following code snippet for a basic Web page:

```
<html>
<head>
<title>Great Novelists Online</title>
</head>
<body>
<h1>Best Opening Lines</h1>
<p id="p1">It was the best of times. It was the worst of
   times.</p>
</body>
</html>
```

Figure 4-1 shows what this HTML code looks like as a DOM document tree.

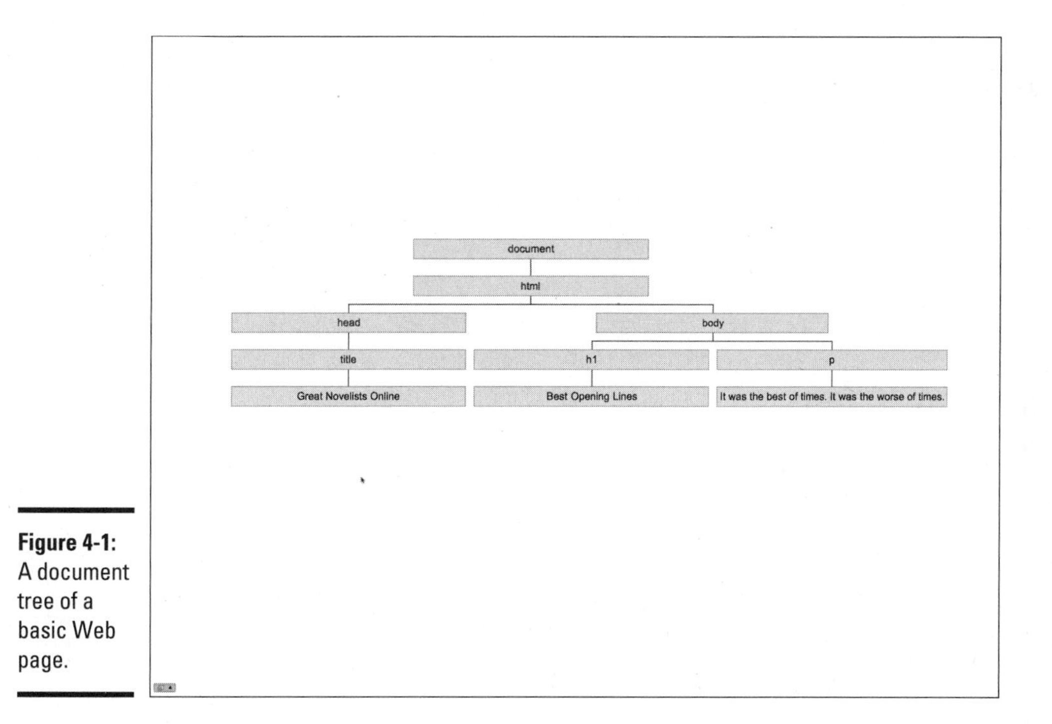

Figure 4-1: A document tree of a basic Web page.

Accessing DOM Objects

As you work with DOM objects in your scripts, one of the most important tasks is being able to access the particular object or collection of objects that you want to manipulate. The DOM provides several ways to reference a particular DOM object.

Using dot notation

To access a particular object, you need to refer to it in your code relative to the document's object hierarchy by using *dot notation*. Consider the following HTML snippet:

```
<form id="shippingForm" method="post" action="">
<input type="text" id="firstName" />
</form>
```

To reference the text input element inside the form and assign it to a variable, you use this line:

```
var fn = document.shippingForm.firstName;
```

When you use dot notation, be aware of the document's hierarchy. The following line of code, for example, doesn't successfully return the text input element because I left out the containing form reference:

```
var fn = document.firstName; // This reference doesn't work
```

A significant shortcoming to using dot notation is that because the object name is "hard-coded," it cannot change when you run your script. The techniques shown in the next four sections provide greater flexibility.

Using square brackets

You can also access an object by using square brackets instead:

```
document.shippingForm['firstName']
```

The object identifier (the input element's `id` value) is placed inside brackets and is surrounded by quotes.

Using DOM arrays

You can reference several built-in collections of objects. Perhaps the most notable is `document.forms`, which returns a collection of `form` elements from the document. You can access it by index (the order in which it occurs in the source). For example, to access the first form in a page, you use this line:

```
document.forms[0]
```

However, this technique is problematic because moving forms around on a page ruins your script. A much better practice is to reference the form's `id` (or `name`) attribute instead:

```
var cf = document.forms['customer_form'];
```

Similarly, to access a `form` element, you can use the `elements` collection:

```
var ln = document.form['customer_form'].elements['last_name'].value;
```

Accessing an element by its id value

The `document` object's `getElementById()` method retrieves the element that has a specific `id` attribute value. It eliminates the need to worry about hierarchy and get straight to it:

```
document.getElementById("elementID")
```

Suppose that you have the following line of HTML:

```
<div id="main_text"></div>
```

You can access the `div` by using the following line of code:

```
var main = document.getElementById( 'main_text' );
```

The main variable now references the `main_text div`. You can now use `main` to access its properties and perform methods on it.

Accessing an element by its tag name

The `getElementById()` is ideal to use if the element you're trying to retrieve has an `id` value that's defined in the HTML code. However, when an `id` doesn't exist or you need to access multiple elements of the same kind, you can use `document.getElementByTagName()`.

The `document` object's `getElementByTagName()` method allows you to return all elements with a particular tag name as a collection (officially, a *nodeList*). For example, to retrieve all `div` elements in your document, you can use this command:

```
var divList = document.getElementByTagName( 'div' );
```

After you have the collection of elements, you can access a particular `div` in the list by using its index number. For example, to access the first `div` in the document, write this line:

```
var div1 = divList[0];
```

Alternatively, if you don't need to work with the collection, you can simply combine the two lines of code into one:

```
var div1 = document.getElementByTagName('elementId')[0];
```

If you want to retrieve a collection of all elements in a document, you can use an asterisk in place of a tag name:

```
var allElements = document.getElementsByTagName('*');
```

The `allElements` variable references all elements in the order in which they occur in the HTML source.

Accessing and Modifying Properties

As I discuss in Chapter 2 in this minibook, a *property* is an attribute associated with an object that helps describe it. Many common properties of a DOM object correspond to an HTML element's attributes. For instance, `bgColor` is a property of the `body` object, and `action` is a property of `form`.

JavaScript gives you access to those properties in your scripts. Suppose you define the following `img` element:

```
<img id="houseImage" alt="Your future home" src="images/
   default.jpg">
```

You can change the `src` value of this image in JavaScript by using the following code:

```
document.getElementById( 'everestImage').src = "images/
   Colonial22.jpg";
```

Alternatively, you can also use the `setAttribute()` method for any DOM object to perform the same task. For example, consider the following line of HTML code:

```
<p id="intro">This is a test</p>
```

You can set the `align` attribute to the right by using either of the following commands:

```
// Set property by calling a method
document.getElementById( 'intro' ).setAttribute('align', 'right');
// Set a property through direct access
document.getElementById( 'intro' ).align = 'right';
```

Calling Object Methods

A *method* defines an action or a behavior of an object. A method's name is an action-oriented word that indicates what happens when it's called. For example, the `submit()` method triggers a form to be submitted to the server for processing, and the `write()` method of the `document` enables you to "write" new content to the Web page.

Again, use dot-notation syntax to reference the object you want to work with. Here are a few examples:

```
document.write( 'I am adding new text from my script.' );
document.forms['form1'].submit();
document.forms['form1'.elements['moreButton'].click();
```

Adding and Removing Nodes from the DOM

The DOM provides the ability to add and remove elements and content from JavaScript.

Adding new nodes

Each HTML element in the DOM has `appendChild()` and `insertBefore()` methods that you can use for adding new elements into the document tree. Consider the following HTML snippet:

```
<h1>Welcome to World@Large</h1>
<div id="sidebar"></div>
```

Suppose that you want to add a new paragraph inside the `div` and a new paragraph just above it. Here's the code you use to perform this function:

```
// Create p node (I'll put it in the right place later)
var p1 = document.createElement( 'p' );
// Assign an id attribute
p1.setAttribute( 'id', 'insideDiv' );
// Create a text node for the paragraph content
var p1_content = document.createTextNode( 'This web site is
   used for...' );
// Add content to the paragraph
p1.appendChild( p1_content );
// Add paragraph as a child node under the sidebar div
document.getElementById( 'sidebar' ).appendChild( p1 );
```

To add that second paragraph before the `div` element, do this:

```
var p2 = document.createElement( 'p' );
p2.setAttribute( 'id', 'subheading' );
var p2_content = document.createTextNode( 'I hope you enjoy
   your stay' );
p2.appendChild( p2_content );
document.getElementById( 'sidebar' ).insertBefore( p2 );
```

Removing a DOM object

You can remove a DOM object by referencing an element's `parentNode` property and calling its `removeChild()` method.

For example, to remove a paragraph with an `id="intro"`, you use the following code snippet:

```
var para = document.getElementById( 'intro' );
para.parentNode.removeChild( para );
```

In this example, the `para` variable references the `intro` paragraph. You then need to work with its parent by using the `parentNode` property. After you reference the parent, you call its `removeChild()` method, specifying `para` as the node to remove. The paragraph is then removed from the DOM (and from the live version of the Web page inside the browser).

You can remove all child nodes of an element by looping through all the child nodes, deleting them one at a time as you go:

```
while ( div_content.childNodes[0] ) {
  div_content.removeChild( div_content.childNodes[0];
}
```

Or, much like Indiana Jones simply shooting the fierce swordsman rather than sword-fighting him, you can simply get the big guns out and clear all the HTML by using the `innerHTML` property instead:

```
div_content.innerHTML = '';
```

Note, however, that `innerHTML` isn't part of the W3C DOM standard (although it's generally supported in the major browsers).

Exploring the DOM

An unabridged, get-every-last-bit-and-byte DOM reference is a rather formidable beast. You just have to consider so many variables when working with the DOM, including the ones in this list:

- ✦ Three W3C standards (Level 1, Level 2, and Level 3)
- ✦ Some objects, properties, or methods introduced only in one browser but not in the others
- ✦ Some objects, properties, or methods implemented across all the major browsers, but not officially part of the W3C standard
- ✦ Parts supported in the latest browsers, but not in older versions

This section, therefore, focuses on the parts of the DOM that are used mainly by Web-page designers — like yourself — to create scripts that work in all the major browsers. To get additional details online, check out these four sources:

- **Mozilla.org (Firefox) DOM Reference:**

  `http://developer.mozilla.org/en/docs/Gecko_DOM_Reference`
- **Microsoft DHTML Reference:**

  `http://msdn.microsoft.com/en-us/library/ms533050.aspx`
- **JavaScript Kit DOM Reference:**

  `www.javascriptkit.com/domref/index.shtml`
- **Quirksmode.org:**

  `www.quirksmode.org/dom/contents.html`

HTML elements

Every HTML element in the DOM has properties that correspond to the element's attributes. (For example, the `body` element in the DOM has `alink` and `bgColor` properties, and an `a` element has `href` and `target` properties.) However, all the HTML elements have a set of common properties, methods, and events, as shown in Tables 4-1, 4-2, and 4-3, respectively. ***Note:*** The events listed in Table 4-3 are defined in Chapter 5 of this minibook (which covers event handlers).

Table 4-1 HTML Element DOM Properties

Property Name	*Applies To*
`Attributes`	All attributes of element (read-only)
`childNodes`	All child nodes of element (read-only)
`className`	Element's class
`clientHeight`	Inner height of element (read-only)
`clientWidth`	Inner width of element (read-only)
`Dir`	Directionality of element
`firstChild`	First direct child node (read-only)
`id`	`id` attribute
`innerHTML`	Markup and content of element
`lang`	Language of element's attributes, text, and element contents
`lastChild`	Last direct child node (read-only)

(continued)

Table 4-1 *(continued)*

Property Name	*Applies To*
`localName`	Local part of qualified element name (read-only)
`name`	Name attribute
`namespaceURI`	Namespace URI of this node (read-only)
`nextSibling`	Node immediately following the given one in the tree (read-only)
`nodeName`	Name of the node
`nodeType`	Number representing node type — 1 for elements (read-only)
`nodeValue`	Value of node; null for elements (read-only)
`offsetHeight`	Height of element (read-only)
`offsetLeft`	Distance from element's left border to its `offset Parent`'s left border (read-only)
`offsetParent`	Element from which all offset calculations are calculated (read-only)
`offsetTop`	Distance from element's top border to its `offset Parent`'s top border (read-only)
`offsetWidth`	Width of element (read-only)
`owner Document`	Document that this node is in (read-only)
`parentNode`	Parent element (read-only)
`prefix`	Namespace prefix of node (read-only)
`previous Sibling`	Node immediately before element in tree (read-only)
`scrollHeight`	Scroll view height (read-only)
`scrollLeft`	Left scroll offset of element
`scrollTop`	Top scroll offset of element
`scrollWidth`	Scroll view width of element (read-only)
`style`	Style attributes (read-only)
`tabIndex`	Position of element in tab order
`tagName`	Name of tag for element (read-only)
`textContent`	Text content of element (and descendants)

Table 4-2 HTML Element DOM Methods

Method Name	*What It Does*
`addEventListener( type, handler, bubble )`	Register a special event handler
`appendChild( appendedNode )`	Insert a node as the element's last child node (returns a Node)
`blur()`	Remove keyboard focus from the element
`click()`	Simulate a click
`cloneNode( deep )`	Clone a node (and all of its contents if `deep = true`) (returns a Node)
`dispatchEvent( event )`	Dispatch an event to this node (returns a Boolean)
`getAttribute( name )`	Get the value of an attribute (returns an Object)
`getAttributeNS( namespace, name )`	Get the value of an attribute with the specified name and namespace (returns an Object)
`getAttributeNode( name )`	Get the node of the named attribute (returns an Attr)
`getAttributeNodeNS( namespace, name )`	Get the node representation of the attribute with the specified name and namespace (returns an Attr)
`getElementsByTagName( name )`	Get a set of all descendant elements of a specific tag name (returns a NodeSet)
`getElementsByTagNameNS ( namespace, name )`	Get a set of all descendant elements of a specific tag name and namespace (returns a NodeSet)
`hasAttribute( name )`	Check if the current element has the specified attribute (returns a Boolean)
`hasAttributeNS( namespace, name )`	Check if the current element has the specified attribute in the specified namespace (returns a Boolean)

(continued)

Table 4-2 (continued)

Method Name	*What It Does*
`hasAttributes()`	Check if the current element has any attributes (returns a Boolean)
`hasChildNodes()`	Check if the current element has any child nodes (returns a Boolean)
`insertBefore( insertedNode, adjacentNode )`	Insert the first node before the second node (returns a `Node`)
`normalize()`	Clean up all the text nodes contained by element (combine adjacent, remove empty)
`removeAttribute( name )`	Remove the named attribute
`removeAttributeNS( namespace, name )`	Remove the attribute with the specified name and namespace
`removeAttributeNode( name )`	Remove the node representation of the named attribute
`removeChild( removedNode )`	Remove a child node (returns a Node)
`removeEventListener( type, handler )`	Remove an event listener
`replaceChild( insertedNode, replacedNode )`	Replace a child node with another (returns a Node)
`scrollIntoView( alignWithTop )`	Scroll the document until the current element gets into the view
`setAttribute( name, value )`	Set the value of the specified attribute
`setAttributeNS( namespace, name, value )`	Set the value of the specified attribute with the name and namespace provided
`setAttributeNode( name, attrNode )`	Set the node representation of the named attribute
`setAttributeNodeNS ( namespace, name, attrNode )`	Set the node representation of the attribute with the specified name and namespace

Table 4-3	HTML Element DOM Events
Event Name	
onblur	
onchange	
onclick	
ondblclick	
onfocus	
onkeydown	
onkeypress	
onkeyup	
onmousedown	
onmousemove	
onmouseout	
onmouseover	
onmouseup	
onresize	

The document object

The document object is the root node of the DOM tree and has no corresponding HTML element — for example, the html, head, and body elements are all contained by document. It serves as the chief controller of everything related to the HTML document. Tables 4-4 and 4-5 describe its properties and methods, respectively.

Table 4-4	document Properties
Property Name	*Applies To*
alinkColor	Color of active links (deprecated)
anchors	List of anchors in document
applets	Ordered list of applets in document
bgColor	Background color (deprecated)
body	A reference to body element (read-only)
contentType	Content-Type from the MIME header
cookie	Semicolon-separated list of cookies

(continued)

Table 4-4 (continued)

Property Name	*Applies To*
`defaultView`	Reference to the window object
`doctype`	Document Type Definition (DTD) of current document (read-only)
`documentElement`	Element that is a direct child of the document — the `html` element (read-only)
`domain`	Domain of current document
`embeds`	List of embedded objects within document
`fgColor`	Foreground or text color (deprecated)
`firstChild`	First node in list of children
`forms`	List of form elements within document
`images`	List of images in document
`lastModified`	Date that document was last modified
`linkColor`	Color of hyperlinks (deprecated)
`links`	List of hyperlinks in document
`plugins`	List of available plug-ins
`referrer`	URI of page that linked to this document
`styleSheets`	List of stylesheets associated with document
`Title`	Title of current document
`URL`	URL of current document
`vlinkColor`	Color of visited hyperlinks (deprecated)

Table 4-5 document Methods

Method Name	*What It Does*
`close()`	Closes document stream (after writing)
`createAttribute()`	Creates new attribute
`createDocumentFragment()`	Creates new document fragment
`createElement(tagName)`	Creates new element with supplied tag name
`createEvent()`	Creates event
`createRange()`	Creates `Range` object
`createTextNode()`	Creates text node

Method Name	*What It Does*
`getElementById()`	Returns reference to specified element
`getElementsByName()`	Returns list of elements with the given name
`getElementsByTagName()`	Returns list of elements with specified tag name
`importNode()`	Returns a clone of a node from an external document
`write()`	Writes text to document
`writeln()`	Writes a line of text to document

The window object

The `window` object is the controller for working with the browser window rather than with the document inside the window. Because the window doesn't interact with documents, the W3C has shied away from adding the `window` object into its standards. Although various browsers provide individually supported properties, methods, and events, Tables 4-6, 4-7, and 4-8 list which ones generally work across all the major browsers.

Table 4-6 window Properties

Property Name	*Applies To*
`defaultStatus`	Status bar text for window
`document`	Reference to associated document
`frames`	Array of frames in window
`history`	Reference to history object
`length`	Number of frames in window
`location`	URL of window
`name`	Name of window
`navigator`	Reference to navigator object
`opener`	Reference to window that opened current window
`parent`	Reference to parent of current window (or subframe)
`self`	Reference to window object (itself)
`status`	Text in status bar at bottom of browser
`top`	Reference to topmost window in window hierarchy
`window`	Reference to current window

Table 4-7 window Methods

Method Name	*What It Does*
`alert()`	Displays an alert dialog box
`blur()`	Sets focus away from window
`clearInterval()`	Cancels repeated execution set when using `setInterval()`
`clearTimeout()`	Ends previously set delay
`close()`	Closes window
`confirm()`	Displays message box for the user to respond to
`focus()`	Sets focus on window
`moveBy()`	Moves window by specified amount
`moveTo()`	Moves window to specified coordinates
`open()`	Opens new window
`openDialog()`	Opens new dialog window
`print()`	Displays Print dialog box to print document
`prompt()`	Displays dialog box and then returns text entered by user
`resizeBy()`	Resizes current window by specified amount
`resizeTo()`	Resizes window
`scroll()`	Scrolls window to specific place in the document
`scrollBy()`	Scrolls document in window by specified amount
`scrollTo()`	Scrolls to specific set of coordinates in document
`setInterval()`	Executes function to occur each *xx* milliseconds
`setTimeout()`	Specifies delay for executing function

Table 4-8 window Events

Event Name
`onblur`
`onerror`
`onfocus`
`onload`
`onresize`
`onunload`

The form object

The `form` object is the scripting equivalent of the `form` element. You use a form to obtain information from users and to submit the data to the Web server for processing. Tables 4-9 and 4-10 list its properties and methods, respectively.

Table 4-9 form Properties

Property Name	*Applies To*
`elements`	List of form controls contained in form element (read-only)
`length`	Number of controls in form element (read-only)
`name`	Name of current form element
`acceptCharset`	List of supported character sets for current form
`action`	Action of form element
`enctype`	Content type of form element
`encoding`	Content type of form element
`method`	HTTP method used to submit form
`target`	Target of the action

Table 4-10 form Methods

Method Name	*What It Does*
`submit()`	Submits form
`reset()`	Resets form

The table object

The `table` object is the scripting interface to a `table` element. You can use the DOM interface to add and remove parts of the table. Tables 4-11 and 4-12 show the supported properties and methods, respectively.

Table 4-11 table Properties

Property Name	*Applies To*
`align`	Alignment of table
`bgColor`	Background color (deprecated)
`border`	Border of table
`caption`	Table caption (read-only)
`cellPadding`	Cell padding
`cellSpacing`	Spacing
`rows`	A collection of the rows in the table (read-only)
`summary`	Table summary (read-only)
`tBodies`	A collection of table bodies (read-only)
`tFoot`	Table footer (read-only)
`tHead`	Table head (read-only)
`width`	Width of table

Table 4-12 table Methods

Method Name	*What It Does*
`createCaption()`	Creates new caption for table
`createTFoot()`	Creates table footer
`createTHead()`	Creates table header
`deleteCaption()`	Removes table caption
`deleteRow()`	Removes a row
`deleteTFoot()`	Removes table footer
`deleteTHead()`	Removes table header
`insertRow()`	Inserts new row

Chapter 5: Adding Event Handlers to Your Web Page

In This Chapter

- **Linking a JavaScript event to an HTML element**
- **Connecting an event handler in code**
- **Getting familiar with JavaScript event handlers**

In Chapter 1 of this minibook, I talk about the usefulness of scripting in creating dynamic, interactive pages. However, scripting can do this because it's driven by events that take place inside the browser window: A mouse moves. A key is pressed. A document loads. A form value changes. JavaScript can trap for each of these events and then allow you to perform any script you want when these events occur.

In this chapter, you discover how to assign a script-based event handler to a document event. You also survey the variety of events available in JavaScript.

Assigning Event Handlers

Event handlers in JavaScript are defined in two different ways:

- **From an HTML element:** Link a JavaScript function or expression with the event-handling attribute of an HTML element.
- **In JavaScript code:** Assign a JavaScript function to an event handler in your script.

I go into more detail on each of these strategies in the following sections.

Linking from an HTML element

Many elements in HTML have events that are associated with them. The `img` element, for example, has an `onmouseover` event. The `a` link element has an `onclick` event. You can tell the browser to run a piece of script code whenever one of these events occurs. To do so, you add an attribute (the event name) to an element. The value of the attribute is a call to a JavaScript function or a snippet of JavaScript code:

```
<element onevent="myFunction()" />
```

or

```
<element onevent="alert( 'event fired' )" />
```

For example, the body element supports the onload attribute, and the form element supports the onsubmit attribute. If you want to trigger actions based on these events, here's how you can connect the two HTML elements with JavaScript code:

```
<head>
<script type="text/javascript">
function init() {
  // Initialize something
}

function checkFormValues() {
  // Check form values
}
</script>
</head>
<body onload="init()">
<form id="myform" onsubmit="checkFormValues()">
</form>
</body>
```

When the document body loads, the init() function is called. Then, when the form is submitted by the user, the checkFormValues() function is also executed.

A second example uses JavaScript statements inside the event handlers:

```
<span onmouseover="this.style.backgroundColor='yellow';this.style.border='2px
    solid black';" onmouseout="this.style.backgroundColor='white';this.style.
    border='none';">"Why do you suppose it was Reuben?" Mrs. Ellison asked the
    master.
</span>
```

When a mouse pointer hovers over the span element, the background turns yellow and a border is displayed. When the mouse pointer exits the area of the span element, the styling returns to normal. The this keyword refers to the object that triggered the event, which in this case is the span element.

Connecting an event handler in code

You can also assign a function to be the event handler of an event in the code itself. For example, rather than add an onload attribute to the body and an onsubmit attribute to the form element (as I did earlier), you can add the following snippet of code instead, inside your script:

```
<head>
<script type="text/javascript">
function init() {
  // Initialize something
}
function checkFormValues() {
  // Check form values
}

window.onload = init;
var iform = document.getElementById( 'myform');
iform.onsubmit = checkFormValues;
</script>
</head>
<body>
</body>
```

The `window.onload` event is assigned the `init()` function. However, notice that when you assign an event handler in code, you don't add the closing parentheses. The form follows in the same manner.

When you assign an event handler by linking it to an HTML element, you can add JavaScript statements directly inside the handler (as shown in the preceding example). However, when you assign event handlers inside your code, you must assign the event to a function name.

Surveying the Events

You can work with a variety of different events in JavaScript. Tables 5-1, 5-2, 5-3, 5-4, and 5-5 list these events in five separate categories.

Table 5-1 User Interface Events

Event	*Occurs When*	*Applies To*
`Onload`	Document has been fully loaded (including images and other external content)	`window`
`Onunload`	Document has been unloaded (for example, going to another page or closing the browser window)	`window`
`Onresize`	Browser window has been resized	`window`

(continued)

Table 5-1 *(continued)*

Event	*Occurs When*	*Applies To*
`Onscroll`	Page or any element with the CSS property `overview:flow` is being scrolled	`document` and any element that can have scroll bars (`div`, for example)
`Onblur`	Object loses input focus	`window`, form elements, any element with a tab index attribute, link (some browsers)
`Onfocus`	Object receives input focus	`window`, form elements, any element with a tab index attribute, and `link` (some browsers)
`Oncontextmenu`	User triggers the right-click pop-up menu	`document` and all visible elements (not supported in all browsers)

Table 5-2 Mouse Events

Event	*Occurs When*	*Applies To*
`onmousedown`	User depresses the mouse button on an element	Any visible element
`onmouseup`	User releases the mouse button on an element	Any visible element
`onclick`	Both a mouse-down and mouse-up action occur on the same element (triggers after `mousedown` and `mouseup` events)	Any visible element
`ondblclick`	Mouse button is rapidly clicked twice on an element	Any visible element
`onmousemove`	User rolls the mouse pointer over an element (fires repeatedly)	Any visible element
`onmouseover`	User first moves the mouse pointer inside the area of an element (fires once)	Any visible element
`onmouseout`	User moves the mouse pointer outside the border of an element	Any visible element

Table 5-3 Keyboard Events

Event	*Occurs When*	*Applies To*
`onkeydown`	User presses a key	`window`, `document`, and all visible elements that can receive focus
`onkeyup`	User releases a key	`window`, `document`, and all visible elements that can receive focus
`onkeypress`	User both presses and releases a key (triggers *after* `keydown` and `keyup` events)	`document` and all visible elements that can receive focus

Table 5-4 Form Events

Event	*Occurs When*	*Applies To*
`onchange`	A `form` element loses focus and its value has changed	Text-based `input`, `textarea`, `select` elements
`onselect`	User selects text in a text field	`onmouseup` fired when selection action completed Text-based `input`, `textarea`
`onsubmit`	User submits the form (by clicking a Submit button); not triggered when submit is done through a scripting call	`form`
`onreset`	User or script resets the form	`form`

Table 5-5 Other Events

Event	*Occurs When*	*Applies To*
`error`	An image isn't loaded properly or a script error occurs	`window`, `img`
`abort`	A page loading is stopped before an image has finished loading (little practical use of this event)	`img`, `object`

Chapter 6: Useful Things to Know When Scripting

In This Chapter

- Reusing scripts across your site with `.js` files
- Opening browser windows from a script
- Executing a script from a link
- Updating a Web page on the fly
- Validating form values
- Scrambling e-mail addresses to avoid spam
- Testing for features, not for browser type
- Using regular expressions

After you have a basic introduction to JavaScript, it's time to get practical and apply some of that newfound knowledge to developing scripts for your Web site. As you do so, you'll encounter some common tasks that you want to perform using JavaScript. Use this chapter as a guide to find helpful tips and techniques as you work on your scripts.

Storing Scripts in an External Script File

You can place all your scripting code for a document inside a `script` element. And until now in this minibook, that's what I've shown you for all the examples. However, the `script` element has an optional `src` attribute that can reference an external `.js` file. A *.js* file is simply a plain-text file that houses JavaScript code. Here's a reference to a `.js` file that contains general validity-checking routines for forms:

```
<script type="text/javascript" src="valform.js"></script>
```

When the `src` attribute is present, any code placed between the start and end tags of the `script` element is ignored.

The biggest advantage of placing your script code in `.js` files is that you can then easily reuse the same routines throughout your Web site. Suppose you have a script for creating rollover buttons. You can either copy and paste the code throughout your pages or create the code in a single `.js` file and then simply point to the code by using a `<script src=""/>` reference.

The contents of the `.js` file are pure JavaScript. Just as you cannot place HTML elements inside a `script` tag, you cannot add any markup in an external script file.

Creating a New Browser Window

You may occasionally need to open a new browser window when the user enters your site or performs a specific action. You can use JavaScript to create a new browser window by using the `window` object's `open()` method. The syntax is

```
window.open( 'url', 'windowName' [, 'featuresList'] )
```

The `url` argument is a string specifying the URL to point to. The `windowName` argument is a string literal that is the name to give to the new window. You can reference this name elsewhere in your code. Here's a basic call to open a new window:

```
window.open( 'http://www.digitalwalk.net/more.html',
    'moreWin' );
```

The `open()` method has a return value that references the new `window` object that's created. Although you don't *have* to do anything explicit to the return value, I strongly recommend it. Doing so enables you to handle references to the new window properly. For example, the following snippet opens a new window and then performs a `document.write` command in the new window:

```
var moreWindow = window.open( 'http://www.digitalwalk.net/
    more.html', 'moreWin' );
moreWindow.document.write( 'Peek-a-boo. I am writing this
    from a different window' );
```

Never leave the `windowName` argument as an empty string because different browsers give you different results.

However, if you're just opening a new, ordinary window, you can just as easily do that without scripting by using a `target="_blank"` attribute on an `a` link. That's why the real power of `window.open()` lies in its optional list of features. With this argument, you can specify what the new browser window looks like when it opens. The argument is a comma-delimited string literal that contains name-value pairs for some or all of the features shown in Table 6-1.

Table 6-1 Features for `window.open()`

Argument	*What It Does*
`Status`	Shows or hides the status bar at the bottom of the window
`Toolbar`	Shows or hides the standard browser toolbar (with Back and Forward buttons, for example)
`Location`	Shows or hides the Address/URL box
`menubar`	Shows or hides the menu bar
`directories`	Shows or hides the standard browser directory buttons
`resizable`	Allows the user to resize the window or prevents such resizing
`scrollbars`	Enables or disables the scrollbars if the document is bigger than the window
`height`	Specifies the height of the window in pixels
`width`	Specifies the width of the window in pixels
`top`	Specifies the y coordinate of the upper-left corner of the window
`left`	Specifies the x coordinate of the upper-left corner of the window

The `height`, `width`, `top`, and `left` arguments are assigned a pixel value. The remaining arguments are assigned a value of `1` to explicitly enable or show the feature and `0` to specifically disable or hide the feature. Here's an example:

```
var myWin = window.open( 'second.html', 'secWin',
   'left=20,top=10,width=400, height=250,toolbar=1,resizable=
   0,menubar=0,location=0' );
```

In this example, a new window is opened displaying the `second.html` Web page. The display is at the 20, 10 coordinates of the browser with a size of 400 x 250 px.

Attaching a Script to a Link

One of the confusing tasks that many scripters struggle with is attaching a script to the clicking of an `a` link. After all, HTML allows you to place a JavaScript command as the `href` attribute value by using the `javascript:` protocol (`<a href="javascript:alert('click')">Click me</a>`). However, a much better practice is to use the `onclick` event handler instead.

Here are a couple of scenarios. First, suppose you want to use the capability of an a link to kick off a script but you don't really want to send the user to another page. To execute a JavaScript statement and prevent the normal link functionality, add an onclick handler that calls the function or statement you want to perform, and add a return false statement at the end to tell the browser to ignore the href value. Then you can assign a # as the href value. Here's what it looks like:

```
<a href="#" onclick="checkPage();return false">Check now</a>
```

A second scenario is when you want to perform a conditional check when the link is clicked. If the check passes, the browser continues to the supplied href value. If not, the user remains on the current page. The a element code looks something like this:

```
<a href="continue.html" onclick="checkPage();">Continue</a>
```

The checkPage() function that's called performs validity checking on the page. If the test passes, a true value is returned from checkPage(). If something needs user attention before continuing, a false value is returned. The false value causes the href value to be ignored.

Modifying a Web Page on the Fly

In addition to reacting to existing HTML elements on a page, JavaScript allows you to add your own content on the fly — without having to go to the Web server for a page refresh. In Chapter 4 of this minibook, I show you how to do this by using DOM methods, such as createElement() or appendChild(). However, you also have an easier way to add content, by using the innerHTML property. The innerHTML property isn't endorsed by W3C, the Web's standards body, but it's still supported widely enough in all modern browsers to make this a viable alternative (even if purists disagree).

The innerHTML property allows you to set and retrieve the HTML content between the start and end tags of a given element. You can also work with either text content or markup.

Suppose you want to update the contents of a div, span, p, or other element without refreshing the entire page. A simple call to innerHTML does the trick. Consider the simple page shown in Figure 6-1.

When you look at the document source, you see that the span element is updated based on the text that the user enters in the text box. Check out the code:

```
<html>
<head>
<script type="text/javascript">
function refreshText(){
   var txt = document.getElementById( 'userText' ).value;
   document.getElementById('ontheflyupdate').innerHTML = txt;
}
</script>
</head>
<body>
<p>Did you know that the <span id='ontheflyupdate'>cowboy sat
   on his horse</span>?</p>
<input type='text' id='userText' value='Enter your own text
   here' />
<input type='button' onclick='refreshText()' value='Update'/>

</body>
</html>
```

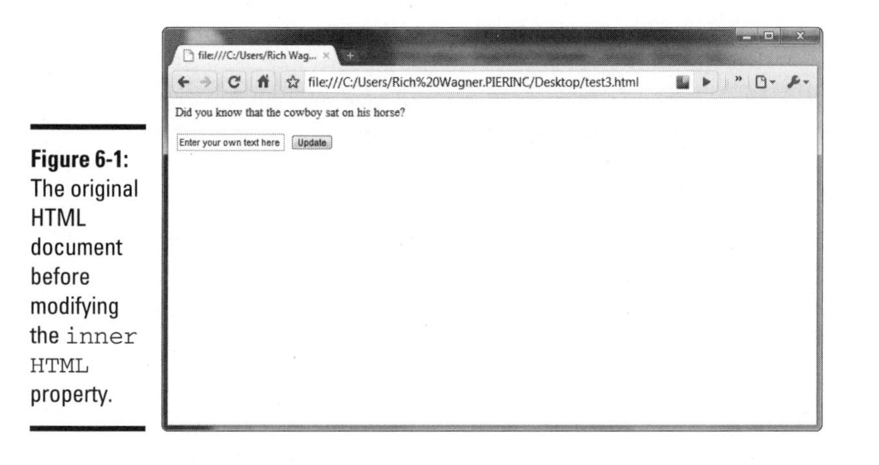

Figure 6-1: The original HTML document before modifying the `innerHTML` property.

Therefore, whenever the user enters new text, the span content is updated when the user clicks the Update button. Figure 6-2 shows the results.

Don't use `innerHTML` for tables. Instead, use the DOM methods discussed in Chapter 4 in this minibook to add rows and other table parts. `innerHTML` is not a Web standard, but was introduced by Microsoft for Internet Explorer.

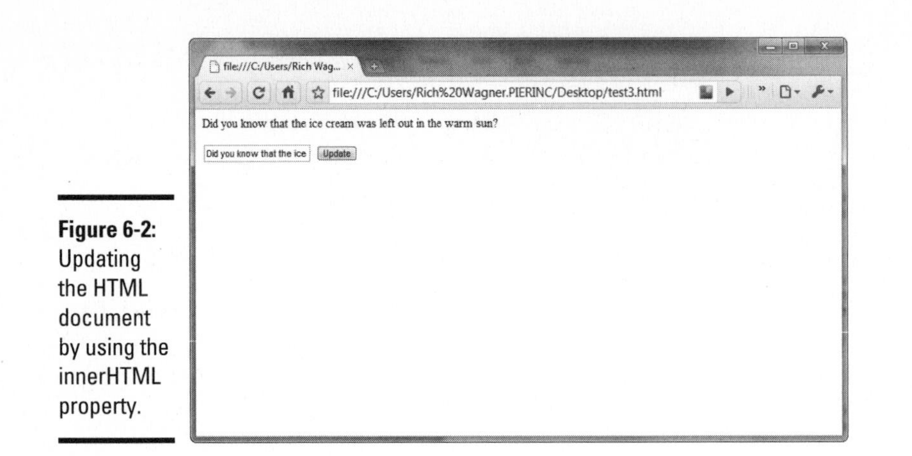

Figure 6-2: Updating the HTML document by using the innerHTML property.

Validating Forms

Data validation has always been one of JavaScript's most useful capabilities within an HTML document. Using JavaScript, you can check the quality of the data to be submitted by the user before sending it over the Internet for processing. You might want to perform various types of validation:

- Check for values in required fields.
- Check for numeric values for number fields (for example, age or five-digit zip code).
- Check to ensure that the entry matches a certain format (for example, e-mail address or telephone number).

Some techniques that scripters have implemented for validation have been frustrating for users filling out the form. Figure 6-3 shows you one technique you can use to display error information (rather than those annoying alert-message boxes) to the user. It uses a `span` element beside the text box.

Note: Before beginning this process, place the `validate.js` file in the same folder as your HTML page.

To set up data validation, follow these steps:

1. **Open a Web page in your editor that contains form fields to which you want to add validation.**
2. **Add a reference to the** `escrambler.js` **file in the document head:**

```
<script src="validate.js" type="text/javascript"></
   script>
```

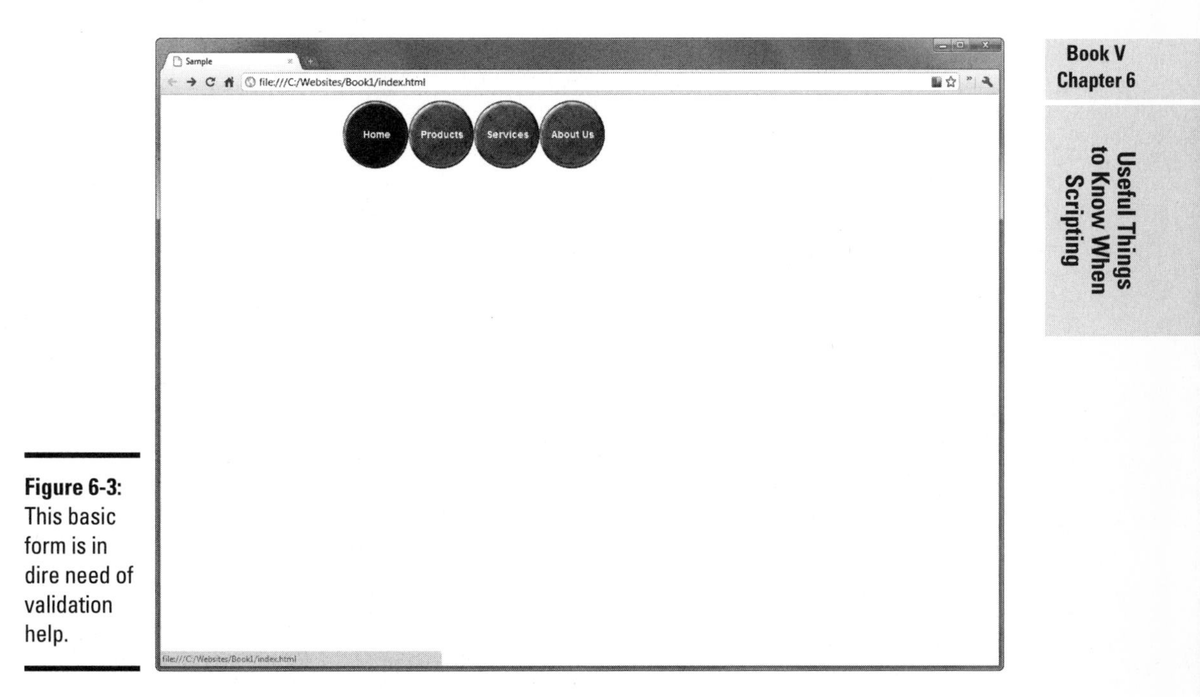

Figure 6-3: This basic form is in dire need of validation help.

This instruction loads the `validate.js` routines into the Web page. Here's the source code for the script file:

```
MSG_REQUIRED_ERROR = 'Value is required';
MSG_INVALID_NUMBER_ERROR = 'Invalid number entered. Please try again.';
MSG_INVALID_EMAIL_ERROR = 'Invalid email address. Please try again.';

function checkRequired( valField, displayID ) {
  var displayHandler = document.getElementById( displayID );

  if ( valField.value == null || valField.value == '' ) {
    displayHandler.innerHTML = MSG_REQUIRED_ERROR;
    valField.focus();
    return false;
  }
  else {
    displayHandler.innerHTML = '';
    return true;
  }
}

function isValidNumber( valField, displayID )  {
  var displayHandler = document.getElementById( displayID );
  if ( isNaN( valField.value ) ) {
     displayHandler.innerHTML = MSG_INVALID_NUMBER_ERROR;
     valField.focus();
     return false;
  }
```

```
  else {
    displayHandler.innerHTML = '';
    return true;
  }
}

function checkEmail( valField, displayID ) {
  var displayHandler = document.getElementById( displayID );
  var emailFormat = /^[^@]+@[^@.]+\.[^@]*\w\w$/; // Regular Expression
    string
  var emailStr = valField.value;
  if ( !emailFormat.test( emailStr ) ) {
    displayHandler.innerHTML = MSG_INVALID_EMAIL_ERROR;
    valField.focus();
    return false;
  }
  else {
    displayHandler.innerHTML = '';
    return true;
  }
}
```

3. **In the document head, add a** `style` **element. Inside it, add a class selector named** `.msg_container`**.**

   This style rule is applied to your error message containers:

   ```
   <style>
     .msg_container { color: #FF0000 }
   </style>
   ```

4. **Next to each field you're validating, add an empty** `span` **element.**

   Be sure to give each `span` element a unique `id` value and add `class="msg_container"` to associate the CSS class selector that you defined in Step 3.

   Here's how the form looks with the `span` elements added:

   ```
   <div style="width:500px">
   <p>Please provide the following information so we can spam you better:</
       p>
   <form id="customer_form" name="customer_form" method="post" action="">
     <label>First name:<input  type="text" name="first_name" id="first_name"
       size="15"/></label>
       <span class="msg_container" id="first_name_msg"> </span><br/>
     <label>Last name:<input type="text" name="last_name" id="last_name"
       size="25"/></label>
       <span class="msg_container" id="last_name_msg"> </span><br/>
     <label>Age:<input type="text" name="age" id="age" size="3"/></label>
       <span class="msg_container" id="age_msg"> </span><br/>
     <label>Email address:<input type="text" name="email" id="email"
       size="25"/></label>
       <span class="msg_container" id="email_msg"> </span><br/>
     <input name="submit" type="submit"/>
   </form>
   </div>
   ```

   These `span` elements are used to provide error feedback to the user as needed.

5. **For every field you want to require the user to fill in, add an** `onblur` **handler that attaches to the** `checkRequired()` **function.**

   The `checkRequired()` function requires two arguments:

   - The keyword `this`, which points to the calling object (the `input` field itself)
   - A string literal that provides the `id` value of the error message container

   I added this check on the first name and last name fields for the form:

```
<div style="width:500px">
<p>Please provide the following information so we can spam you better:</
    p>
<form id="customer_form" name="customer_form" method="post" action="">
  <label>First name:<input  type="text" name="first_name" id="first_name"
    size="15" onblur="checkRequired( this, 'first_name_msg' )"/></label>
     <span class="msg_container" id="first_name_msg"> </span><br/>
  <label>Last name:<input type="text" name="last_name" id="last_name"
    size="25" onblur="checkRequired( this, 'last_name_msg' )"/></label>
     <span class="msg_container" id="last_name_msg"> </span><br/>
  <label>Age:<input type="text" name="age" id="age" size="3"/></label>
     <span class="msg_container" id="age_msg"> </span><br/>
  <label>Email address:<input type="text" name="email" id="email"
    size="25"/></label>
     <span class="msg_container" id="email_msg"> </span><br/>
  <input name="submit" type="submit"/>
</form>
</div>
```

6. **For every field you want to check for valid numbers, add an** `onblur` **handler that attaches to the** `isValidNumber()` **function.**

   Like the `checkRequired()` function, `isValidNumber()` also requires two arguments: `this` and a string of the `id` value of the error message's container.

   For this example, I added this validity check for the age field:

```
<div style="width:500px">
<p>Please provide the following information so we can spam you better:</
    p>
<form id="customer_form" name="customer_form" method="post" action="">
  <label>First name:<input  type="text" name="first_name" id="first_name"
    size="15" onblur="checkRequired( this, 'first_name_msg' )"/></label>
     <span class="msg_container" id="first_name_msg"> </span><br/>
  <label>Last name:<input type="text" name="last_name" id="last_name"
    size="25" onblur="checkRequired( this, 'last_name_msg' )"/></label>
     <span class="msg_container" id="last_name_msg"> </span><br/>
  <label>Age:<input type="text" name="age" id="age" size="3"
    onblur="isValidNumber( this, 'age_msg' )"/></label>
     <span class="msg_container" id="age_msg"> </span><br/>
  <label>Email address:<input type="text" name="email" id="email"
    size="25"/></label>
     <span class="msg_container" id="email_msg"> </span><br/>
  <input name="submit" type="submit"/>
</form>
</div>
```

7. **For e-mail address fields, add an `onblur` handler that attaches to the `checkEmail()` function.**

   The `checkEmail()` function uses the same two arguments as the other two validity check routines. Here's the code:

```
<div style="width:500px">
<p>Please provide the following information so we can spam you better:</
    p>
<form id="customer_form" name="customer_form" method="post" action="">
  <label>First name:<input  type="text" name="first_name" id="first_name"
     size="15" onblur="checkRequired( this, 'first_name_msg' )"/></label>
      <span class="msg_container" id="first_name_msg"> </span><br/>
  <label>Last name:<input type="text" name="last_name" id="last_name"
     size="25" onblur="checkRequired( this, 'last_name_msg' )"/></label>
      <span class="msg_container" id="last_name_msg"> </span><br/>
  <label>Age:<input type="text" name="age" id="age" size="3"
     onblur="isValidNumber( this, 'age_msg' )"/></label>
      <span class="msg_container" id="age_msg"> </span><br/>
  <label>Email address:<input type="text" name="email" id="email"
     size="25" onblur="checkEmail( this, 'email_msg' )"/></label>
     <span class="msg_container" id="email_msg"> </span><br/>
  <input name="submit" type="submit"/>
</form>
</div>
```

8. **Save your HTML document and test the results in a browser.**

   You can load the Web page in a browser and check out the validation routines. Figures 6-4 and 6-5 show the results.

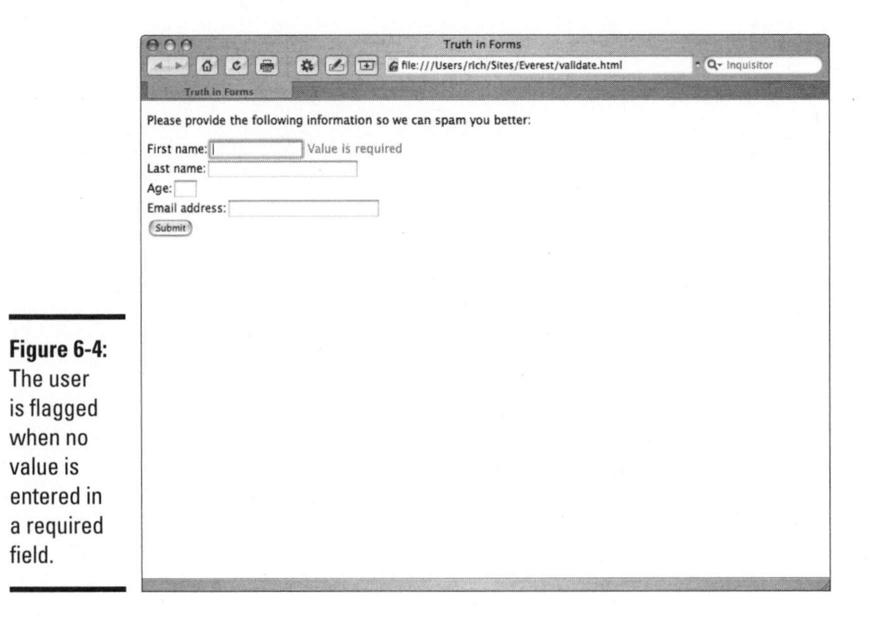

Figure 6-4: The user is flagged when no value is entered in a required field.

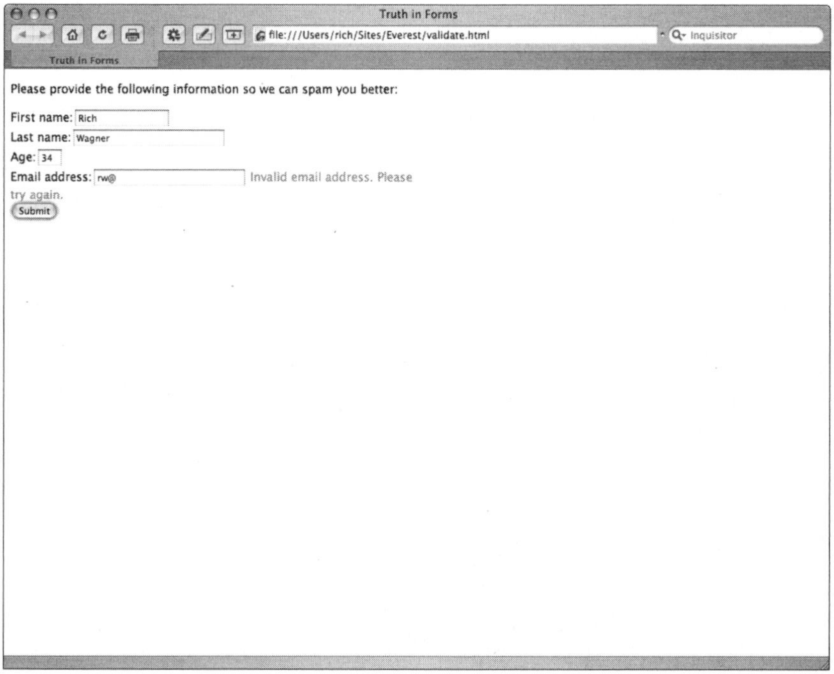

Figure 6-5: The user is prompted when an invalid address is entered.

A closer look at the routines is helpful in understanding how the validation works. The `checkRequired()` function is an example:

```
function checkRequired( valField, displayID ) {
  var displayHandler = document.getElementById( displayID );

  if ( valField.value == null || valField.value == '' ) {
     displayHandler.innerHTML = MSG_REQUIRED_ERROR;
     valField.focus();
     return false;
  }
  else {
    displayHandler.innerHTML = '';
     return true;
  }
}
```

The `displayHandler` variable is defined and references the element with an `id` value that equals the `displayID` value.

The value of the `valField` argument is then evaluated to see whether it's a blank value. If yes, an error message is assigned to `displayHandler.innerHTML`. After the calling input field then receives focus, the function ends with a `false` return value. If no, the `displayHandler.innerHTML` is cleared out and control is returned to the calling field.

Beating the Spammers: Scrambling Your E-Mail Links

A `mailto:` e-mail address link on your Web page is one of the handiest and most effective ways to communicate with people you're trying to reach. Unfortunately, it comes at a significant cost: spam. Spammers scour the Web to look for defenseless e-mail addresses to add to their evil databases. You can fight back with the newest tool in your arsenal: JavaScript.

I show you how to add standard and maximum protection. Standard protection is easier to work with, but spammers might potentially account for it in their Web scouring. Although maximum protection is a pain to work with, spammers almost certainly cannot circumvent it.

Note: Before beginning this process, place the `escrambler.js` file in the same directory as your HTML page.

Follow these steps to scramble your e-mail links with a JavaScript routine:

1. **Open a Web page in your editor that contains one or more e-mail links that you want to scramble.**
2. **For each address, replace the normal e-mail address with a scrambled version.**

   For standard protection, all you need to do is to replace the `@` sign with `_at_` — for example, `steve@acmeinc.com` becomes `steve_at_acmeinc.com`.

   If you want to add maximum protection, replace the `@` sign with `!a!`, the dot with `!d!`, and the domain suffix with `!ds!`. For example, `steve@acmeinc.com` now becomes a bulletproof but confusing-looking `steve!a!acmeinc!d!!ds!`.
3. **Add a reference to the** `escrambler.js` **file in your document head:**

   ```
   <script src="escrambler.js" type="text/javascript"></script>
   ```

   This instruction loads the `escrambler.js` scrambling routines into the Web page. Here's the source code for the script file:

   ```
   // Iterate through each link
   function hrefReplacer( origStr, newStr ) {
        for ( i=0; i<=(document.links.length-1 ); i++ ) {
                if ( document.links[i].href.indexOf( origStr )!=-1 )
                        document.links[i].href= document.links[i].href.
       split( origStr )[0] + newStr +
                        document.links[i].href.split( origStr )[1]
        }
   }
   ```

```
//  ********************************************************
//   unscramble( securityLevel, [domainSuffix] )
//            securityLevel: 0 = Minimal, 1 = Maximum
//            domainSuffix : suffix, if not com
//  ********************************************************
function unscramble( securityLevel, domainSuffix ) {
    // Standard format: me_at_mydomain.com
    if ( securityLevel == 0 ) {
            var separator = '_at_';
            hrefReplacer( separator, '@' );
    }
    // Maximum format: me!a!mydomain!dt!!ds!
    else {
            var separator      = '!a!';
            var dot            = '!dt!';
            var suffix                  = '!ds!';
            if ( domainSuffix == '' ) domainSuffix = 'com';
            hrefReplacer( separator, '@' );
            hrefReplacer( dot, '.' );
            hrefReplacer( suffix, domainSuffix );
    }
}
```

4. **Add a new** `script` **element to the bottom of your page, just above the** `</body>` **end tag.**

   In this script, you call the `unscramble()` function that's located in the `escrambler.js` file. Its syntax is shown here:

   ```
   unscramble( securityLevel [, domainSuffix] )
   ```

   where `securityLevel` is `0` for standard and `1` for maximum protection. If you're using maximum protection, supply a domain suffix if your domain is different from `com`.

   For standard protection, use the following code:

   ```
   <script type="text/javascript">
   unscramble( 0 );
   </script>
   ```

   For maximum protection with a `com` suffix, use the following code:

   ```
   <script type="text/javascript">
   unscramble( 1 );
   </script>
   ```

   For maximum protection with an alternative suffix, add it as the second parameter, as shown in this example:

   ```
   <script type="text/javascript">
   unscramble( 1, 'org' );
   </script>
   ```

5. **Save your file and test the results in a browser.**

   You can load the Web page in a browser and ensure that your e-mail addresses are now properly formatted in your live HTML source.

Testing for Features, Not for Browser Type

In the early days of the Web, it was considered a good programming practice to detect the browser type and version before running a script. Because JavaScript implementation differed strongly back then, a browser detector could reroute your script before it tried doing something that a nonsupporting browser couldn't handle.

To borrow from S. E. Hinton, "That was then, this is now." Nowadays, there's little or no reason to test for a specific browser type. Instead, your best bet — if you're concerned about browser support for a script you want to perform — is to test by feature.

For example, if you want to check to ensure that the browser supports the `getElementById()` method before performing a process that relies on a particular feature, you can perform a conditional check first:

```
if ( document.getElementById ) {
    // Code relying on getElementById goes here
}
```

If the `getElementById()` method is unsupported, the conditional statement returns a null value to the `if` statement. Otherwise the code executes.

You can also perform this test on an object or a property. For example, to test whether the browser supports the `images` collection object (an object often used in rollovers), you can test by using the following statement:

```
if ( document.images ) {
  // Code relying on images collection goes here
}
```

Using Regular Expressions

If you have worked with computers for much time at all, you're probably well familiar with wildcards. Want to search for all the Word documents in a directory? Use `*.doc` in your search. Want to search for all `.xls` and `.xlm` files in a folder? Use `*.xl?`.

Wildcards come in handy when you want to do simple searches with files and directories, but your searching needs will often be more complex inside the world of JavaScript. Suppose you want to look for a specific string pattern inside user content in a `Textarea`. Perhaps you want to test a string to determine whether or not it's a valid U.S. phone number. Or suppose you want to determine whether a URL requested by the user is valid.

That's where regular expressions come in handy. You can think of them as something like "wildcards on steroids." A *regular expression* describes a pattern of characters that you use to evaluate a string to determine whether or not it matches.

Making a direct match

As you begin working with regular expressions, your first step is to get used to the basic syntax. For example, if you wanted to search for the character combination `ball` inside of a string, then you would use the following pattern:

```
/ball/
```

The forward slashes are used to demark the start and end of a regular expression pattern.

```
Therefore, a match would be found in the following stringsDo
   you like baseball?
Football, you bet.
Ballroom dancing rules!
```

However, suppose I changed the pattern to `/bills/`. A match would be found in

```
Did you pay your bills?
```

But not in

```
Bill's mother came to town.
```

You can then use this regular expression pattern in a script in one of two ways. First, you can use a *regular expression literal* as shown in the following example:

```
<script type="text/javascript">
  var pattern = /ball/;
  var str = "Do you like baseball?";
  var t = pattern.test(str);
  if (t)
  {
    alert("Yes, you got a match!");
  }
</script>
```

The `pattern` variable is assigned a regular expression pattern, making it a regular expression literal. The `test()` method is then used to evaluate the `str` text string to look for a match, and it returns a Boolean result to the `t` variable. If a match is found, then the `alert()` message box is displayed.

Second, you can also create an instance of the `RegExp` object in your script:

```
<script type="text/javascript">
  var re = new RegExp("/ball/");
  var str = "Do you like baseball?";
  var t = re.test(str);
  if (t)
  {
    alert("Yes, you got a match!");
  }
</script>
```

In addition to the `test()` method, there are also `exec()`, `search()`, and `replace()` methods (which I discuss in the section "Getting additional information back from the search").

Matching characters

It would be nice if everything you needed to search on could be done with a direct match. However, in most real world situations, you'll need extra searching power. Several sequences of characters have special significance inside a regular expression. These are sometimes called *metasequences.*

For example, consider the following pattern:

```
/person\d/
```

This pattern matches a string that begins with a person followed by any decimal digit, as indicated by the `/d` metasequence. The following would be valid matches:

```
person1
person5
```

Or suppose you wanted to test for any non-decimal digit that followed. You could use:

```
/person\D/
```

The `\D` expression matches any character other than a digit, as shown in the following matches:

```
personal conduct
Person.
person-place-thing
```

Table 6-2 shows a list of all of the metasequence expressions.

Table 6-2 Regular Expression Metasequences

Expression	*Description*
`\b`	Matches at a word boundary (such as a space or newline character). Note that if the first or last character in the string is a word character, then it matches the start or end of the string.
`\B`	Matches a non-word boundary.
`\d`	Matches a decimal digit.
`\D`	Matches any character other than a decimal digit.
`\f`	Matches a form-feed character.
`\n`	Matches a newline character.
`\o`	Matches a null character.
`\r`	Matches a return character.
`\s`	Matches any white-space character, such as a tab, newline, or space.
`\S`	Matches any character other than a white-space character.
`\t`	Matches a tab.
`\unnnn`	Matches the Unicode character with the specified four hexadecimal digits.
`\v`	Matches a vertical tab.
`\w`	Matches any alphanumeric character or underscore (A–Z, a–z, 0–9, or _).
`\W`	Matches any character other than an alphanumeric character.
`\xnn`	Matches the character with the specified ASCII value, as defined by the hexadecimal digits nn.

Adding flags

You can customize your search by adding special flags (as shown in Table 6-3) to the end of your regular expression pattern (outside the closing forward slash). Take, for example, the ignore-case flag. If you'd like to perform a case-insensitive search for the word `snicker`, you would use the following:

```
/snicker/i
```

If you're using more than one flag, they are combined together, like this:

```
/snicker/gimsx
```

Table 6-3 Regular Expression Flags

Flag	Description
G	Global flag to match more than the first match.
I	Ignores case for all A–Z and a–z characters.
M	Indicates a multi-line search. When set, your pattern can search across lines.
S	Known as the dotall flag, this flag enables the . (dot) metacharacter (discussed in the section, "Working with repeaters") to match a newline character (\n).
X	Allows extended regular expressions. You can use spaces to compose the regular expression to make the code easier to read.

Working with repeaters

You can also add certain *metacharacters* to look for repeating patterns inside of the expression. Take the asterisk character *, which acts like the familiar wildcard you are probably already used to:

```
/person\d*/
```

This pattern matches `person` followed by zero or more decimal digits. Each of the following strings would be valid matches:

```
person1
person22
person
person230303030202
```

As you can see from this pattern, a repeater always acts on the item that *precedes* it.

The + character indicates a match of the previous item repeated one or more times, while the ? character denotes a match of the previous item zero or one time.

To match the character `b` that is repeated one or more times, use

```
/b+/
```

To match the character c that is shown zero or one time, use

```
/c?/
```

You can also use the numeric quantifiers or ranges with the use of {} brackets. You can use a numeric quantifier to specify a specific number of repeating items. For example, to match the digit 0 repeated eight times, you would use

```
/0{8}/
```

To match the digit 3 repeated three or more times, use

```
/3{3,}/
```

To define a range, you can set start and end numbers within the curly brackets. Here's an example:

```
/z{2,4}/
```

Table 6-4 lists each of the repeaters you can work with in regular expressions.

Table 6-4 Regular Expression Repeaters

Repeater	*Description*
`*`	Matches the previous item when it's repeated zero or more times.
`+`	Matches the previous item when it's repeated one or more times.
`?`	Matches the previous item when it's repeated zero or one time.

`{n}`
`{n,}`
`{n,n}`
	Indicates a numeric quantifier or a range for the previous item.

Adding more metacharacters

In addition to the repeater or quantity-related metacharacters, you can add other metacharacters to your regular-expression arsenal.

The dot character . matches any single character in an expression. So, consider the following pattern:

```
/ab.d/
```

Each of the following would be valid matches:

```
abcd
ab3d
ab"d
```

You can also perform either/or matches with the pipe character |. If you would like to test for either `Jim` or `Joe`, you could use

```
/Jim|Joe/
```

See Table 6-5 for each of the additional metacharacters.

Table 6-5 Additional Regular Expression Metacharacters

Metacharacter	*Description*
.	Matches any single character, including the newline character if the `s` flag is set.
|	Matches either the part on the left side or the right side of the pipe.
^	Matches at the start of the string. With the `m` flag set, the caret also matches the start of a line.
$	Matches at the end of the string. With the `m` flag turned on, $ matches the position before a newline (`\n`) character.
\	Escapes (or turns off) the special meaning of metacharacters and forward slashes inside regular expressions.

Working with character classes

Character classes, denoted by square brackets `[]`, are used in regular expressions to specify a list of possible characters that can match a single position. For example

```
/8[123]4/
```

In this regular expression, each of the following values would be valid:

```
814
824
834
```

You can use a hyphen to indicate a valid range inside a character class. For example, the following pattern allows for any uppercase character:

```
/[A-Z]/
```

Or, to account for any alphanumeric character, you could combine ranges inside the character class:

```
/[A-Za-z0-9]/
```

When you use the caret (^) metacharacter at the start of a character class, you "negate" those characters — in other words, any character not listed in the class is considered a match. For example, the following pattern allows for any other character except f, g, and h:

```
[^fgh]
```

Working with groups

Use parentheses to group elements in a regular expression so that you can treat those elements as a single unit. As a result, you can use groups to apply a repeater metacharacter, such as *, to more than one character. For example, the following pattern looks for one or more matches of the word cat:

```
/(cat)+/
```

When you use parentheses to group elements, the matched string of the group is remembered for additional uses (see the "Getting additional information back from the search" section).

Combining all the elements

Although you can work with each wildcard type in isolation, typically you'll want to combine wildcards when you are working with real-life scenarios. For example, suppose you would like to test the entry of an e-mail address form field to ensure that it's a valid format. Instead of just looking for text@text, you can use the power of regular expressions to do a really robust job. Here is how an e-mail address validator would look:

```
/([a-zA-Z0-9]+[-._+&])*[a-zA-Z0-9]+@([a-zA-Z0-9]+[.])+
    [a-zA-Z]{2,6}/
```

This pattern combines groups, character classes, repeaters, and other special characters together to form the expression. Using this pattern, the following would be valid e-mail addresses:

```
rich@smileyfacesoup.org
rich.wagner@smileyfacesoup.org
rich_wagner@smileyfacesoup.ak
```

Learning by examples

Sometimes the best way to learn regular expressions is simply by looking at various examples. The following list of snippets shows you a sampling of regular expressions:

```
// U.S. Phone number
var re = /\d{3}\-\d{3}\-\d{4}/

// Integer between 0 and 100
/0|([1-9]|[1-9]\d)|100/

// U.S. Zip Code (+4 is optional)
/\d{5}(-\d{4})?/

//  Windows filename (excludes specific characters)

/[^\\\\./:\*\?\"<>\|]{1}[^\\/:\*\?\"<>\|]{0,254}]/
```

Getting additional information back from the search

The `RegExp` method `test()` performs a simple true/false check on a string for the expression. However, you can also use the `exec()` method to execute a search for a match, but return an array of information based on the results. The results come back as an array containing the matched string and all remembered substrings (denoted by parentheses in your expression).

For example, suppose you want to search a string `F100` and return the `F` and `100` as separate pieces in the array. You could create a script that looks like this:

```
<script type="text/javascript">
var re = /([A-Z]+)(\d+)/g;
var r = r.exec("F100");
alert(r);
</script>
```

Chapter 7: Introducing Ajax

In This Chapter

- ✔ **Understanding Ajax**
- ✔ **Working with XMLHttpRequest**
- ✔ **Updating the page with dynamic content**

In the first six chapters of Book V, I show how you can use JavaScript in your Web pages to add decision-making and programming logic inside the browser (also known as the *client*). However, many times you also rely on data coming from the server. But the problem is that in most normal situations, server updates require the entire page to reload — not optimal from a performance or a user-experience perspective.

There's another way — Ajax (Asynchronous JavaScript And XML). It's a JavaScript-based technology that allows you to exchange and transfer data with a Web server without reloading the entire Web page. Ajax has become such a ubiquitous term that, although it's an acronym, it's often no longer spelled in all caps.

In this chapter, I introduce you to Ajax and show you how you can use this JavaScript-based technology to provide dynamic content to your Web pages.

Note: Ajax requires the use of a server-side technology, such as PHP, Java, or .NET, to provide data back to JavaScript.

What Is Ajax?

In normal situations, when a Web page requests information from the server, it makes what is known as an `HTTP POST` or `GET` request to the application server. The application server processes the request, gets the data, and then reloads the page in the browser that's providing the results. However, using Ajax, you can request and receive data from the server *in the background* and reload part(s) of the page rather than the entire page.

Ajax allows you to build pages that perform faster and save server-side resources, enabling the client to share in the processing of the page.

JavaScript scripts are standalone; they don't depend on an application server. In contrast, Ajax is basically a two-piece solution:

- **Client-side:** JavaScript code that establishes the Ajax connection and listens for data changes.
- **Server-side:** Server-side technology that knows how to respond to the data requests of the client.

Therefore, in order to implement an Ajax solution, you can't just do it on the client side. You need to also program the server-side part of it in a language like PHP or Java.

Exploring XMLHttpRequest

The JavaScript object `XMLHttpRequest` is used for Ajax connections in your Web pages. The `XMLHttpRequest` object sends an HTTP (or HTTPS) request to a Web server and loads the server's response back into an event handler for processing. It's supported in any modern browser. In fact, you'd have to go back many years to find a browser that doesn't support it. For the record, minimum browser requirements include Firefox 1.0 and higher, Internet Explorer 5.0 and higher, Safari 1.2 and higher, Chrome (any version), and Opera 8 and higher.

Tables 7-1 and 7-2 show the properties and methods of the `XMLHttpRequest` object.

Table 7-1 XMLHttpRequest Properties

Properties	*Description*
`readyState`	Indicates the status of the Ajax request from the server (see Table 7-3 for full list)
`responseText`	Response as a string
`responseXml`	Response as an XML or XHTML fragment
`Status`	HTTP status received from server (see Table 7-4 for full list)
`onreadystatechange`	Event that is dispatched when there is a change in status of the `readyState` property.

Table 7-2 XMLHttpRequest Methods

Methods	*Description*
`open(mode, url, boolean)`	Opens an Ajax connection with the server mode: `GET` or `POST` url: URL of file boolean: true (asynchronous), false (synchronous)
`send("string")`	Sends a request to the server (use `null` for a `GET` request)

Creating an Ajax Connection

The basic process of an Ajax request and response is as follows:

- **Client-side JavaScript:** Create an `XMLHttpRequest` object
- **Client-side JavaScript:** Set up an event handler to listen for changes in the request
- **Client-side JavaScript:** Use the `XMLHttpRequest` object to open a conversation and request data from the server
- **Server-side technology:** Respond to the client request and provide data as a string or XML
- **Client-side JavaScript:** When a response is provided, use the response as needed on your page

I walk you through setting up this Ajax connection in the sections that follow.

Creating a request object

The first task is to create an `XMLHttpRequest` object. You can do so with the following code:

```
// Request
var request;

// Normal support
if (window.XMLHttpRequest)
{
    request = new XMLHttpRequest();
}
```

```
// Legacy IE5 support
else if (window.ActiveXObject)
{
    request = new ActiveXObject("Microsoft.XMLHTTP");
}
// Legacy IE6 support
else if(window.ActiveXObject)
{
    request = new ActiveXObject("Msxml2.XMLHTTP");
}
// No support
else
{
    alert("Please upgrade your browser to experience the full
   capabilities of this web page.");
}
```

This code first checks to see whether the browser supports the `XMLHttpRequest` object. If it does, then the request variable is assigned to an instance of the `XMLHttpRequest` object. All modern browsers use this code.

However, to provide support for older versions of Internet Explorer, the next `else` statement creates an `ActiveXObject`, which was the Microsoft version of `XMLHttpRequest` for versions 5.0 and 6.0 of IE.

If a user's browser fails all these conditional statements, then you can inform that user that it's time to enter the twenty-first century and upgrade browsers.

Making the request

Using the `XMLHttpRequest` object, your next step is to initialize the object for a connection with `open()`:

```
request.open(requestType, url, isAsynchronous);
```

The `open()` method takes three parameters:

- `requestType`: Specifies `GET` or `POST` (usually `GET` is used)
- `url`: Provides the URL pointing to the file/resource on the server
- `isAsynchronous`: Indicates whether the connection is asynchronous or synchronous.

When the `isAsynchronous` parameter is set to `true`, the JavaScript continues to process after the `open()` method is called. If set to `false`, the browser suspends execution of the script until a response is received from the server.

In general, keep this parameter set to `true`. If the process takes a while, the user can't do anything on the Web page until the response is provided.

After you initialize the connection, make the request with the `send()` method:

```
request.send("string");
```

For `GET` requests, set the parameter to `null`. For `POST` requests, provide the string in which you want to send to the server.

For example, if you want to make a `GET` request to `ajaxtest.jsp`, you use

```
request.open("GET", "ajaxtest.jsp", true);
request.send(null);
```

Listening for responses

With the send request made, you want to assign a listener for the `XMLHttpRequest` object's `onreadystatechange` event. This event is triggered whenever the server responds to the request. For example

```
request.onreadystatechange = function()
{
    if (request.readyState==4 && request.status == 200)
    {
        var response = request.responseText;
    }
}
```

Inside this handler, the `readyState` property of the `XMLHttpRequest` object is checked to determine the state of the server's response. Table 7-3 displays the possible `readyState` values. In general, because of browser differences in terms of how/when states 0–3 are dispatched, test the 4 state.

Table 7-3 XMLHttpRequest.readyState Values

State	*Description*
0	Request is not initialized (`open()` has not been called)
1	Connection has been established, but request has not been sent
2	Request has been sent
3	Partial response received, still in process
4	Response is finished and connection is closed

You also want to check the HTTP server response with the `XMLHttpRequest` object's `status` property. Table 7-4 displays the common return values.

Table 7-4 XMLHttpRequest.status Values (HTTP Status Values)

State	*Description*
200	OK (no errors)
304	Not modified (data comes from cache, not server)
400	Bad request
401	Unauthorized request
403	Forbidden request
404	Not found
500	Internal server error

If `(readyState == 4)` and `(response == 200)`, then you know that the response from the server was completed successfully.

You can return the response as a string or XML. The `XMLHttpRequest` has a `responseText` property for string values and a `responseXML` property for an HTML fragment or other XML. You can then assign the value to an input text, an HTML fragment to `innerHTML` property, or parse the XML value being returned.

Serving the request

An application server is responsible for taking the request of the Web page, processing it, and returning text or XML to the `XMLHttpRequest` object on the client. You have to use a server-side programming language, such as PHP or Java, to do this processing. For example, to return the current date and time to the client using PHP, the `.php` file contains the following:

```
<?php
echo date("H:i:s");
?>
```

If you're interested in implementing Ajax on your Web site, check out *PHP 5 For Dummies* by Janet Valade or *JavaScript & AJAX For Dummies* by Andy Harris.

Updating the Web page based on the response

When the `XMLHttpRequest` object receives a response from the server, you can do something with it. For example, to display the content received from the server in a `div` element named `dynamicDiv`, you set up a handler:

```
request.onreadystatechange = requestResponseHandler;

function requestResponseHandler()
{
    if (request.readyState == 4 && request.status == 200)
    {
        var responseXML = request.responseXML;
        document.getElementById("dynamicDiv").innerHTML =
    responseXML;
    }
}
```

In this code, the `requestResponseHandler()` is assigned to the handler for the `onreadystatechange` event. As a result, the `requestResponse Handler()` is called when a response is received from the server.

Exploring an Ajax Example

In this section, I show a full example. Suppose you want to allow the user to enter text in a text field and have your code dynamically convert the text that the user types to uppercase and display it in a `div`.

Listing 7-1 displays HTML code that does this job for the main Web page (see Figure 7-1). The `inputTxt` element has an `onkeyup` event listener that calls the `execute()` method for each key typed into the input field. The `execute()` method calls the `ajax-test.php` file on the server and passes the value of the `inputTxt` element. The `.php` file (see Listing 7-2) receives the text and sends it back to the HTML page, converting it to uppercase. Figure 7-2 displays the results.

Listing 7-1: ajax-test.html

```
<!DOCTYPE html PUBLIC "-//W3C//DTD XHTML 1.0 Transitional//
    EN"
 "http://www.w3.org/TR/xhtml1/DTD/xhtml1-transitional.dtd">
<html xmlns="http://www.w3.org/1999/xhtml">
<head>
<meta http-equiv="Content-Type" content="text/html;
    charset=utf-8" />
<title>Ajax Example</title>
</head>
```

(continued)

Listing 7-1 *(continued)*

```
<body>

<script language="javascript" type="text/javascript">

    /**
     * Creates an Ajax request object
     *
     * @returns - XMLHttpRequest object
     *
     */
    function getRequestObject()
    {
       if (window.XMLHttpRequest)
       {
          return new XMLHttpRequest();
       }
       else if (window.ActiveXObject)
       {
          return new ActiveXObject("Microsoft.XMLHTTP");
       }
       else
       {
          alert("Please upgrade your browser.");
          return null;
       }
    }

    /**
     * Handler for the server response
     */
    function responseHandler()
    {
        if (requestObject.readyState == 4)
        {
            renderResponse();
        }
    }

    /**
     * Updates the page based on server response.
     */
    function renderResponse()
    {
        document.getElementById('responseTxt').innerHTML =
   requestObject.responseText;
    }
```

```
    /**
     * Open AJAX conversation
     */
    function execute()
    {
        requestObject = getRequestObject();
        if (requestObject != null)
        {
            requestObject.open("GET", "ajax_test.php?text=" +
   document.getElementById('inputTxt').value, true);
            requestObject.send(null);
            requestObject.onreadystatechange =
   responseHandler;
        }
    }

    var requestObject = null;

</script>

  <form name="form">
     Enter text: <input type="text"  onkeyup="execute();"
   name="inputTxt" id="inputTxt" />
     <br/>
     <br/>
     <div id="responseTxt">Text to be replaced</div>
  </form>
</body>
</html>
```

Listing 7-2: ajax-test.php

```
<?php
    if (isset($_GET['text']))
       echo strtoupper($_GET['text']);
?>
```

Test your pages on your browser with scripting disabled so you can at least be aware of what users might experience on your Web site if they have JavaScript disabled.

Ajax Example

richwagnerwords.com/ajax_test.html

Enter text:

Text to be replaced

Figure 7-1: Ajax-ready Web page.

Ajax Example

richwagnerwords.com/ajax_test.html

Enter text: dynamic

DYNAMIC

Figure 7-2: The server response is displayed dynamically.

Book VI

Graphics

Contents at a Glance

Chapter 1: Understanding Web Graphics

In This Chapter

- Obtaining quality graphics for your site
- Knowing what graphics to avoid
- Looking at graphics software options
- Exploring graphical design trends

The Web is a visual medium of communication. If, therefore, you're going to create a Web site where people will want to visit and spend some time, you must know how to work with graphics. A well-designed site effectively and efficiently uses photos and other images. A poorly designed site, on the other hand, is cheapened and weighed down by them. Your success depends on what images you use, how they fit into your page, and how fast they download over the Web.

In this chapter, I get you started with Web graphics, by showing you how to obtain quality images for your site and what kinds of tools you can use to edit and optimize them, and then I give you some graphical design tips to consider.

It's a Rasterized World: Exploring the Two Types of Graphics

The world of graphics has two basic types of graphics: *raster* (or bitmap) and *vector:*

- **Raster graphics** are composed of tiny pixels that are structured as a rectangle. Each of these pixels has a different color value (or, in some cases, transparency or opaque value). Because raster graphics are pixel-based, they're dependent on monitor resolution. Therefore, you can't resize (and, especially, enlarge) a raster graphic without hurting its image quality. Examples of raster file formats are JPEG, GIF, and PNG, each of which is explored in Chapter 2 of this minibook. Photos and typical Web graphics are examples of raster images.

- **Vector graphics,** in contrast, are geometric shapes composed of angles, curves, and lines. Because vector graphics are based on mathematical calculation, you can scale them up or down without hurting their quality. The best-known vector graphic format for the Web is Adobe Flash SWF. (However, keep in mind that a Flash movie can contain raster images.) SVG is another, lesser-known vector format for the Web. EPS and AI (Adobe Illustrator) are vector formats that aren't supported by browsers.

The Web is now essentially a rasterized world because the vast majority of non-Flash images are raster graphics (JPEG, GIF, or PNG).

It's All about Quality: Finding Good Graphics

I can talk to you until I run out of pages in this book about how to optimize and manage your graphics. But if the quality of the graphics you're using is bad, my advice doesn't do you much good. Therefore, your first stop along the way is the supply store:

- **DIY (Do-It-Yourself):** If you have a digital camera and an eye for taking a good picture, you already have the most hassle-free way to add graphics to your Web site. However, if your snapshots are filled with cut-off portraits, red-eyed people, and boring scenery, perhaps you should turn to other options on the list.
- **Free stock art:** A few years ago, if you wanted to find free graphics online, you were forced to visit tacky-looking sites filled with banner ads that offered cheesy clip art. Fortunately, free stock photography sites now rival commercial sites for the average person's needs.

Two stock art sites in particular that I recommend are stock.xchng (`www.sxc.hu`), shown in Figure 1-1, and `morguefile.com`. However, note that these sites focus on photographic images and offer much less in illustrations.

Each photo has its own license determining what you can do with the image. Sometimes a photo might be restricted to non-commercial purposes only or can be used commercially if you ask the photographer. Be sure to read the license carefully before using.

- **Commercial stock art:** If you have a specific need and can't shoot it yourself or find a good free solution, you have to step up to commercial stock-art sites. These sites typically have royalty-free photos at a moderate price, and often have both photos and illustrations.

Getty Image's Photodisc (`www.gettyimages.com`) is my favorite commercial site, particularly if you need professional-looking illustrations. Another option is `Shutterstock.com`, which offers downloads through a subscription service. For illustrations, I recommend checking out `stockart.com`.

Figure 1-1: The stock.xchng site offers professional-quality photographic images at no cost.

Avoiding Graphics That Lead to No Good

I strongly recommend that you avoid two kinds of graphics at all costs. One can get you into trouble with the law, and the other gets you a visit from the Tacky Police:

- **Copyrighted images:** All images are copyrighted. It's not permissible to take an image from any site (even places like Flickr or Facebook) without the express permission or license to do so by that copyright owner. Be wise in the images you use for your site.
- **Clip art:** Clip art is material for school newsletters and kids' birthday cards. However, it isn't something you should consider using for your Web site. Given all the other preferable graphics-supply options now available, clip art looks amateurish and just plain tacky.

Choosing a Graphics Editor

Although the latest versions of the Windows and Mac operating systems provide a basic capability to crop and resize raster graphics, you quickly outgrow these very limited solutions when you begin working with graphics for your Web site. Here are some options to consider:

- **Web-site software:** You can't edit your graphics, but some Web-site software tools offer modest ways to modify and tweak your images. Dreamweaver, for example, allows you to optimize, crop, resample, adjust brightness and contrast, and sharpen an image — without ever leaving the Dreamweaver environment.

  Even Dreamweaver, however, doesn't allow you to edit your graphics inside its environment. For editing, you need something more advanced.

- **Adobe Photoshop:** If price and learning curve aren't issues, hop on over to your favorite software-buying Web site or store and pick up a copy of Photoshop. It is, by far, the industry standard in image-editing software for Windows and the Mac. When you first start using it, you'll probably use only a fraction of its total capabilities. However, as you continue to use it, you gradually discover more and more of its power.

  As a more casual — although economical — alternative, Adobe also offers Adobe Photoshop Elements, a trimmed-down version of Photoshop.

  Go to `www.adobe.com/products/photoshop/photoshop` for details.

- **Other commercial products:** In addition to Photoshop, you can consider other commercially available products. Microsoft has traditionally never been competitive in the graphics market, but its new Microsoft Expression Design is the company's best offering to date. It serves as a graphics-editing companion to Expression Web (see Book VII for more on Expression Web). Go to `www.microsoft.com/products/expression` for more information.

  Corel's Paint Shop Pro (`www.corel.com`) is another option to consider.

- **GIMP, the open-source alternative:** If you're on a shoestring budget, you can check out GIMP to see whether it meets your needs. GIMP is open-source software, so you're free to use it. And, it has versions for Windows, Mac, and Linux. Some users swear by GIMP; others just swear at it. Given its price, it's probably worth your while to check it out. Go to `www.gimp.org` to download.

Fitting Graphics into Your Design

Imagine you're designing a Web site for a restaurant chain and you need to offer a restaurant-locator utility. You can offer a list of text links for each state. However, a visual solution is much better — displaying a clickable map of the United States. A visitor can click the state in which to locate the restaurant. The map image is then designed to respond to the click and send the visitor to the correct link.

In this section, I explore how you can transform ordinary graphics into clickable links for your Web site.

Using graphical links

As you can explore in Book III, you use a hyperlink in an HTML document to define an a element, as in this example:

```
<a href="http://www.cnet.com">Visit CNET</a>
```

When the browser displays the link, it normally appears as underlined text. You can use Cascading Style Sheets (CSS) to add text styles to links through pseudo-classes (see Book IV). However, as nice as CSS styles can be, occasionally text alone isn't enough. In such cases, you need to use a graphical image as a link.

You can easily define a graphic as a normal hyperlink by simply enclosing the img element in the a link; for example:

```
<a href="http://www.cnet.com"><img src="cnet_logo.png"
   alt="Visit CNET"/></a>
```

If you're using Dreamweaver or Expression Web, you work with graphical links in much the same way you work with text links.

Incorporating hotspots and image maps

Sometimes, a normal graphical link doesn't work. In the United-States-map example I discuss at the beginning of this section, a single link on the map image gets you nowhere. You need, therefore, a hotspot.

A hotspot is an invisible area within a graphical image that, when clicked, behaves like a regular hyperlink. An image that contains clickable hotspots is an *image map*.

You can use any JPEG, GIF, or PNG image as an image map. In fact, the image itself isn't directly involved in the mapping. You define the hotspots within the HTML code by specifying locations (x,y coordinates) inside the image.

The map element represents the image map, and multiple area elements are defined inside the map element, one for each hotspot. The map is linked to the image by adding a usemap attribute to the img element. Here's an example:

```
<html>
<head></head>
<body>

<img src="countrymap.png" usemap="#usa">

<map name="usa">
<area shape="polygon" coords="19,44,45,11,87,37,82,76,49,98"
   href="east.html">
<area shape="rect" coords="128,132,241,179" href="west.html">
<area shape="circle" coords="68,211,35" href="washingtondc.
   html">
</map>

</body>
</html>
```

In this example, the image is linked to the `usa` map through `usemap`. (Notice in the code that the map name is prefixed with a pound sign.)

The `map` element serves as a container for the three `area` elements that define the hotspots. The `area` element has a `shape` attribute that specifies whether the shape of the hotspot is a rectangle, polygon, or circle. The `coords` attribute is used to define the pixel coordinates for the area. When the browser renders the image map, it connects the pixel values provided and displays them in the shape specified, in a geeky game of connect-the-dots.

You can create image maps by using HTML code this way, but using the correct pixel coordinates is a tricky process when you're doing it by hand. At minimum, you have to open the image in an image editor and do a lot of homework on the pixel locations for each hotspot.

Despite this challenge, an image map is, quite frankly, an element you *really* should use in a tool like Expression Web, Dreamweaver, and even Photoshop. Visual tools like these enable you to define hotspots easily with your mouse.

Chapter 2: Optimizing Your Graphics

In This Chapter

- **Optimizing graphics design**
- **Choosing the right graphics format**
- **Improving graphics download speed**

Everything has a trade-off, or so it seems. In Chapter 1 of this minibook, I discuss how to obtain and work with great-looking graphics for your Web site. However, if the graphics you add are roly-poly, megahuge, bandwidth hogs, visitors to your Web will leave your site before you can say "Photoshop."

With the widespread use of broadband connectivity to the Internet, image size is less of an issue than it was a decade ago. At the same time, you should continue to pay attention to minimizing the overall size of your graphics — especially for visitors who access your site from dial-up modems.

In this chapter, you explore *optimization* techniques you can use to minimize the size of your graphics while maintaining an appropriate level of quality. I begin, however, by showing you the different types of Web formats you can use and when you should use each type.

Determining Which Graphics File Type to Use

Web browsers support three popular types of graphics formats:

- JPG/JPEG (`.jpg` or `.jpeg` files)
- GIF (`.gif` files)
- PNG (`.png` files)

Each of these types supports *image compression* (essentially paring down the image data to a practical minimum), making them preferred over other image formats, such as RAW or TIFF. For example, a 15-megabyte TIFF image can be shrunk to as little as 50 kilobytes using JPEG format.

These three formats have their own strengths and weaknesses. In the following sections, I fill you in on the details of each of the three main file types.

JPEG: A great all-around format

JPEG (short for Joint Photographic Experts Group and pronounced "jay-peg") format is your best all-around image format, useful for high-resolution digital photos (up to 16.7 million colors) and normal Web graphics. JPEG uses the *lossy compression* technique for compressing color and grayscale continuous-tone images, which means that it tosses out colors that aren't easily seen by the human eye.

In general, the more complex the image, the better JPEG performs. It doesn't do well with simple graphics, line drawings, or text lettering. Also, unlike GIF and PNG, JPEG doesn't support transparency, so every pixel of a JPEG image must have a color.

One of the most powerful aspects of JPEG images is that you can control precisely the level of optimization you use for any given image. Image-editing software enables you to specify the quality level of a JPEG image (on a scale of 0 to 100, where 0 is most compressed [smaller file] and 100 is no compression [larger file]). Figure 2-1 shows you the JPEG options that are available when you save an image in Adobe Photoshop. As you adjust the Quality value, Photoshop simultaneously updates the graphic and file size — enabling you to determine where the "sweet spot" is between size and image quality.

Figure 2-1: JPEG format allows you to determine the level of compression you want.

In most cases, you should use a quality level of 30–75, depending on the image. I usually find a sweet spot for my images in the 40–60 range. Lower than 30–35, most images show noticeable degradation. Above 75, you don't get much difference in overall quality, even though the file size jumps significantly.

With small images, there isn't much visible difference between a heavily compressed JPEG image and one that's barely compressed. However, if you're displaying a larger photo (one that occupies more than 20 percent of your Web page), you might want to back off on the compression because visitors will notice the difference in quality.

GIF: Great for text and transparencies

GIF (short for Graphics Interchange Format and pronounced "jif") was the standard image format in the early days of the Web and still remains popular. GIF supports only 256 colors, so it isn't a viable alternative for high-resolution photos. However, its *lossless compression* technique is designed to work extremely well with text, lines, and simple graphics in which only a few colors are being used. (Lossless compression doesn't throw away information to shrink the file size.)

GIF also supports *transparency,* enabling you to designate the image's background as transparent. Transparency allows you to get away from simply using rectangular images; you can create rounded corners, different shapes, and so on. GIF also is the only graphics format that supports animation.

Until recently, the biggest problem with GIF wasn't its technology, but rather its legal handcuffs. For decades, Unisys had a patent on the GIF compression algorithm, and companies that used the algorithm in their software were required to license the technology. Although that situation never affected those of us creating Web sites, it did affect software makers like Adobe and Microsoft. As a result, PNG (discussed in the next section) was developed as an open-source alternative to GIF. Fortunately, the legal claims surrounding GIF have recently expired.

PNG: The (relatively new) kid on the block

PNG (short for Portable Network Graphics and pronounced "ping") is the newest graphics format available for the Web and is growing in popularity. All modern browsers support the format, so you can now safely use it on your pages. PNG was developed as an open-source alternative to the proprietary GIF format.

PNG comes in two versions:

- **PNG-8:** The PNG-8 version is similar to GIF in 256-color support and simple transparency. You can often get better compression ratios by using PNG-8 instead of GIF — making it a great option for small, simple graphics.
- **PNG-24:** The PNG-24 version supports 24-bit colors (that's millions of colors) and opacity. However, because PNG uses lossless compression, high-resolution PNG images are much larger than JPEG images.

PNG-24's support for *opacity* (also known as *smooth transparency*) is a step beyond simple on-off transparency: It enables you to specify the level of transparency or opaqueness (on a scale from 0 to 255) for any pixel in the image. Using opacity, you can create translucent effects for your images, allowing the background to show through non-opaque pixels. (Note that earlier versions of Internet Explorer (before 7.0) don't support opacity.)

Table 2-1 compares each of the Web graphic formats.

Table 2-1 Comparing Web Graphic Formats

Format	*Best Use*	*Worst Use*	*Transparency Support?*	*Animation Support?*
JPEG	Photos, continuous color and grayscale images	Simple graphics, images with sharp edges and lines	No	No
GIF	Text, sharp-edged art, line drawings	Continuous color images, photos, images with more than 256 colors	Yes	Yes
PNG-8	Text, sharp-edged drawings, clip art	Continuous color images, photos, images with more than 256 colors	Yes	No
PNG-24	Photos (although much larger than the JPEG equivalent), translucent images	Continuous color photos when file size is important	Yes (support for full-opacity blending)	No

Avoiding Graphic Violence: Speed Up Your Web Graphics

Although 56K modem connections aren't the norm they once were, visitors from rural parts of the country or world still don't have access to broadband. Even more significant: As iPhones, Android phones, and other smartphones become the primary means for accessing the Web, you still need to keep the overall size of your graphics in mind as you design your pages.

In fact, some visitors consider it criminal to leave unoptimized graphics on your site, and they express their frustration by leaving if an image takes too long to appear. To help you avoid the "graphic violence" of a slow page load, I have some suggestions for you. If you put these tips to good use, I may be able to make your graphics download quicker than you can say "Speedy Gonzales."

To ensure that slow connections display your pages rapidly, just reduce the size of your graphics files. You can do this in four ways:

- Reduce the file size.
- Reduce the dimensions of the graphical image.
- Give the appearance of quick performance.
- Define the image size accurately in the Web page.

I discuss each option in the following sections.

A great way to evaluate your page speed is to use the Developer Tools window in Google Chrome and Safari. You can use the Resources section to view the speed at which each resource of a page is downloaded. See Figure 2-2. To access the developer tools in Chrome, click the Tools button and choose Tools⇨Developer Tools; in Safari, choose them from the Developer menu.

Reducing the file size

Consider the following tips as you work to reduce the file size of your image:

- **JPEG files:** The first place to optimize your Web graphics is to open these files in an image editor (such as Photoshop) and reduce their quality level. Start at a low value of quality (as low as 5 to 10 on small images) and work your way upward incrementally until the image quality becomes acceptable. The moment the quality looks good, save the new file.

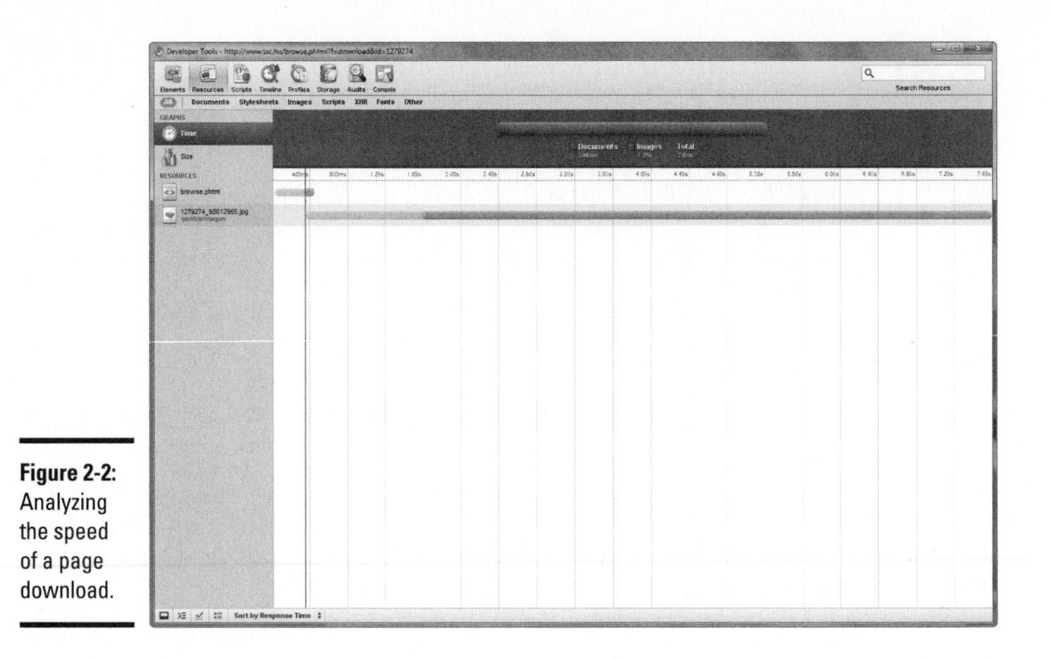

Figure 2-2: Analyzing the speed of a page download.

- ✦ **PNG-24:** If you're working with high-color PNG-24 images, save them as JPEG files instead.
- ✦ **GIF files:** If you're trying to reduce the size of a GIF file, check out the number of colors you're using. If it's more than 200, JPEG becomes a strong option to consider. If the file uses only a few colors, try PNG-8.

Cropping and shrinking the image

You can also reduce the size of a graphics file by *cropping* (lopping off parts of the picture that aren't important to what you want to show). Almost every graphics application has a *crop* tool, and you can experiment with it to see whether you can shave off some of the non-essential parts of the image.

Of course, if you don't want to crop your picture, you can reduce its overall dimensions by resizing it.

A typical graphics application also has an *image size* tool, which you can use to specify either an absolute size (in pixels or inches) or a percentage, whichever is easier.

When you shrink an image to an absolute size, the graphics software often increases the pixels-per-inch (PPI) setting. When this happens, resample the image at 72 or 96 pixels per inch. Note, however, that you can avoid this issue by resizing with percentages.

But be careful that you don't shrink an image too much, or you can lose significant picture quality. Shrink the image to only the dimensions in which you will display it on the Web page.

Making the image download "seem" faster

The final technique you can use to optimize your Web graphics is to make the page *seem* to load faster than it really is. The way to do this is to explicitly define the `height` and `width` attributes in the `img` element; for example:

```
<img src="deer.jpg" width="239" height="148" alt="Bambi's
   return"/>
```


When you specify the dimensions of your image, the browser displays an empty frame as a placeholder *while the text of the page loads first.* As a result, the user can browse the page while waiting for images to download from the Web server.

Ensuring accurate image dimensions

Most Web-site software tools, such as Dreamweaver and Expression Web, allow you to place any image in your document and resize it manually with your mouse. Although resizing an image in this way is handy, avoid doing so. Most tools don't resize the *image* — they simply adjust the `height` and `width` attributes of the `img` element. Therefore, if you shrink an image by performing this action, you shrink only the display dimensions, not the file size of the image.

For example, my father uploaded a picture he took from his digital camera onto his organization's Web site. But, upon visiting his site, I noticed how slow it was loading. When I investigated, I discovered that he uploaded the original image size (3500 x 2300 with a size of over 4MB), but it was resized by his Web software into a small `img` element to fit onto the page. Because the image looked small to my dad, he didn't realize the "hidden weight" behind it.

Therefore, as a general rule, when you need to resize images, use an image editor. Don't let the browser or the Web software do the work for you.

Chapter 3: Image Rollovers

In This Chapter

- Understanding rollovers
- Creating a rollover navigation menu by using CSS
- Creating rollovers with Expression Web

A *rollover* is a visual effect that you can add to your Web page when you want a part of the screen to change without a click: When a mouse pointer hovers over an image, the rollover changes the appearance of the graphical image.

Rollovers are the most popular image effect on the Web, and with good reason: They're relatively easy to create but make your site feel more responsive. They also add visual flavor without going over the top and looking tacky.

You can create rollovers using HTML alone, but why? Instead, these days you can use JavaScript or Cascading Style Sheets (CSS) to create a rollover effect. Or, even easier, if you're using Expression Web or Dreamweaver, you can create rollovers without even having to write any code.

In this chapter, I show you how to create rollovers by using CSS. I then walk you through the process of creating them in Expression Web. To find out how CSS works, turn to Book IV. I cover Expression Web in Book VII.

Creating Rollovers by Using CSS

Traditionally, rollovers have been written in JavaScript: A *script* (small program) is set to swap the normal image with another when the mouse pointer hovers over it. The images usually have text on them to identify the link destination.

You can, however, use CSS to create a rollover. And, unless you're using a tool such as Dreamweaver that does all the work for you, the CSS option is much easier — with CSS, you don't need to write *any* scripting code. Additionally, CSS rollovers are more flexible and extensible — you don't need to create an individual graphical button for each rollover link you're creating. In fact, all you need to do is create two generic buttons (without text) to represent the normal and hover states of the rollover. Then you add the text on top of the button by using CSS.

To show you how to create rollovers, I walk you through the creation of a navigation menu bar. (Or, if you need only a single rollover rather than a complete set, you can still follow along.) Here's how:

1. **Obtain or create two images that will serve as your rollover images.**

   Use two identically shaped images that have different colors — one for when the button is in its default state and another for when the button is in a hover state. Make sure that no text is on the image itself.

   I'm using the two button graphics shown in Figure 3-1.

Figure 3-1: These buttons will serve as my pair of rollover images.

2. **Copy these image files into the root folder or Images folder of your local Web site.**

   I placed my two files (`RoundButtonOver.png` and `RoundButtonDown.png`) into the root folder.

3. **In your Web-page editor, open the HTML document in which you want to add your rollover images.**

4. **In your document source, add a `div` element at the location where you want to place your image.**

   The code for a navigation bar looks like this:

```
<div class="navmenu">
</div>
```

5. **Inside the `div` element, add a new `div` element for each of the buttons you want to add.**

   Here's the code I used for the four menu buttons:

```
<div class="navmenu">
<div class="menuitem"</div>
<div class="menuitem"</div>
<div class="menuitem"</div>
<div class="menuitem"</div>
</div>
```

6. **Add an a link for each of your buttons, and add a URL that each button will access when it's clicked.**

The following code shows what I did:

```
<div class="navmenu">
<div class="menuitem"><a href="index.html"></a></div>
<div class="menuitem"><a href="products.html"></a></div>
<div class="menuitem"><a href="services.html"></a></div>
<div class="menuitem"><a href="aboutus.html"></a></div>
</div>
```

7. **Add an `img` element inside each of the links, each referencing the default-state button.**

   My default-state button is named `RoundButtonDown.png`. The following code shows the navigation bar I'm creating:

```
<div class="navmenu">
<div class="menuitem"<a href="index.html"><img src="RoundButtonDown.png"
    alt="Home" /></a></div>
<div class="menuitem"><a href="products.html"><img src="RoundButtonDown.
    png" alt="Products" /></a></div>
<div class="menuitem"><a href="services.html"><img src="RoundButtonDown.
    png" alt="Services" /></a></div>
<div class="menuitem"><a href="aboutus.html"><img src="RoundButtonDown.
    png" alt="About Us" /></a></div>
</div>
```

8. **Add a `span` element inside each of the links, adding the text that you want to appear on the label.**

   The navigation bar displays the span text on top of the button image.

   Here's my code:

```
<div class="navmenu">
<div class="menuitem"><a href="index.html"><img src="RoundButtonDown.png"
    alt="Home" /><span>Home</span></a></div>
<div class="menuitem"><a href="products.html"><img src="RoundButtonDown.
    png" alt="Products" /><span>Products</span></a></div>
<div class="menuitem"><a href="services.html"><img src="RoundButtonDown.
    png" alt="Services" /><span>Services</span></a></div>
<div class="menuitem"><a href="aboutus.html"><img src="RoundButtonDown.
    png" alt="About Us" /><span>About Us</span></a></div>
</div>
```

   Your HTML code is now complete. You can always add or remove buttons by repeating Steps 5 through 8.

   You're ready to attach CSS styles to the navigation bar.

9. **Copy your file into the root folder or Styles folder of your local Web site.**

   I placed this file into the root folder.

   You can also re-create the CSS style sheet by entering the CSS code shown in Listing 3-1 and saving it as `navmenu.css`.

10. **Open `navmenu.css` in your Web-site software or in a text editor.**

    You need to tweak some of the settings to work with your navigation menu and buttons.

11. **Update the lines marked with** `BUTTON WIDTH` **and** `BUTTON HEIGHT` **to match the sizes of your button images.**

    As you can see in Listing 3-1, you need to modify the `div.navmenu`, `div.menuitem`, and `div.menuitem img` selectors.

12. **Adjust the** `width` **property of the** `div.navmenu` **selector to fit the size of your navigation menu bar.**

    Make sure that the width you define is equal to or greater than the number of buttons you're using, multiplied by the button image's width.

13. **(Optional) Adjust the font, font size, and text color properties in the style sheet.**

    I identified these properties in Listing 3-1 to make them easier to find.

14. **Choose File⇨Save to save the changes to your style sheet.**

15. **Back in your HTML document, add a** `link` **element to the** `head` **section to attach the** `navmenu.css` **style sheet.**

    The code is shown here:

```
<head>
<link href="navmenu.css" rel="stylesheet" type="text/css">
</head>
```

16. **Choose File⇨Save to save your document.**

17. **Open the document in your default browser to check the final results.**

    Figure 3-2 displays my navigation menu.

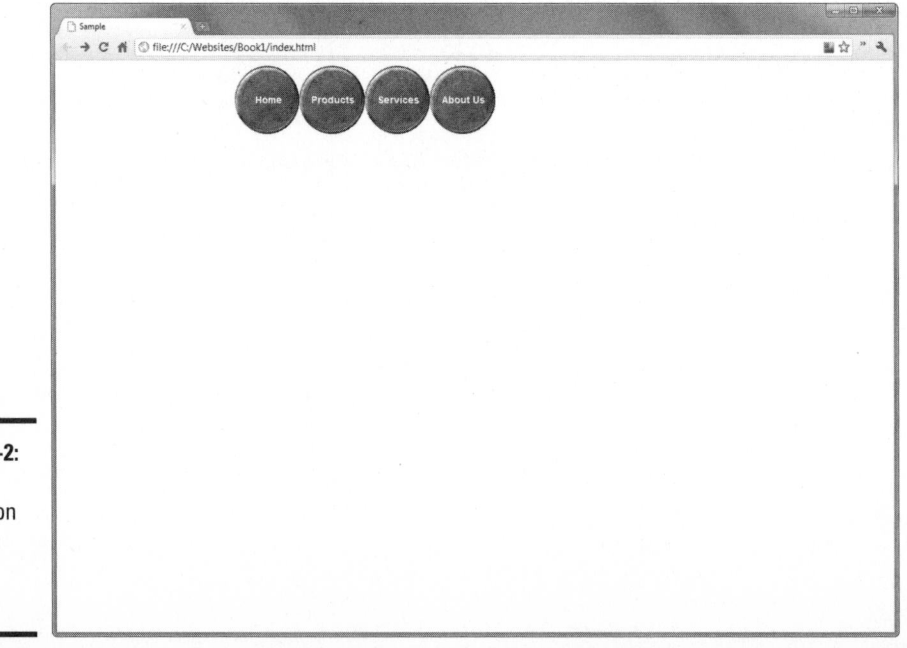

Figure 3-2: A CSS navigation bar in its default state.

18. Move your mouse over the buttons to display the rollover effect.

Figure 3-3 shows my rollover in action.

Figure 3-3: The mouse-pointer-hovering action causes the CSS to change a button's appearance.

Listing 3-1: navmenu.css

```
/* Horizontal Navigation Menu Container */
div.navmenu {
   width: 700px; /* <-- OVERALL LENGTH OF MENU */
   height: 96px;  /* <-- BUTTON HEIGHT */
   margin: 0 auto; /* optional: centers navigation menu in its container */
}

/* Navigation Menu Item */
div.menuitem                                                          {
   font: 14px "Lucida Grande", Helvetica, Arial, sans-serif; /* <-- DEFAULT FONT/
     SIZE */
   background: url( "RoundButtonOver.png" ) no-repeat; /* <--  ROLLOVER HOVER
     IMAGE */
   width: 96px; /* <-- BUTTON WIDTH */
   height: 96px; /* <-- BUTTON HEIGHT */
   position:relative;
   float: left;
   margin: 0;
   padding: 0;
   overflow:hidden;
  text-align:center;
}
```

(continued)

Listing 3-1 *(continued)*

```
/* Menu Link */
div.menuitem a {
   color: ffffff; /* <-- DEFAULT TEXT COLOR */
   display: block;
  text-decoration: none;  /* disables any normal link styles you have set */
   overflow:hidden;
  font-weight:bold;
}

/* Menu Text */
div.menuitem span {
  position: absolute;
  left: 2px;
  top: 40px;
  text-align: center;
  width: 96px;
  cursor: pointer;
  text-decoration: none;
  color: #FFF;
}

/* Menu Link: Hover */
div.menuitem a:hover {
  color: #ffffff; /* <-- DEFAULT HOVER TEXT COLOR */
}

/* Menu Image */
div.menuitem img {
  width: 96px; /* <-- BUTTON WIDTH */
  height: 96px;  /* <-- BUTTON HEIGHT */
  border: 0;
 }

/* Menu Link: Hover Image */
div.menuitem a:hover img { visibility: hidden; }  /* hides default button image
     during hover */

* html a:hover { visibility: visible;}
```

Creating a Rollover with Expression Web

Web site builders such as Expression Web and Dreamweaver have built-in features that can make rollovers even easier. You don't even have to mess around with JavaScript or CSS because you let your design application do that work for you.

In this section, I demonstrate how to add a rollover in Expression Web.

1. **Choose File⇨New⇨HTML in Expression.**

   A blank HTML Web page is created for you. If you aren't in Design mode, click the Design tab at the bottom of the main workspace.

2. **Choose Insert⇨Picture⇨From File.**

   A file browser opens.

3. **Locate an image you wish to use as your default button background, and then click OK to insert the image into your HTML file.**

4. **Click the image to ensure that it has the focus (it has a drag frame around it, and the word *img* appears in its upper-left corner).**

5. **Choose Format⇨Behaviors.**

   The Behaviors pane appears in the workspace, as shown in Figure 3-4. You use this pane to create and manage rollovers in Expression Web.

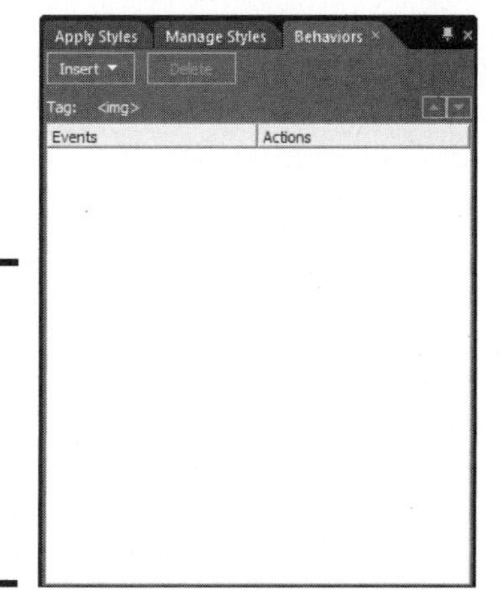

Figure 3-4: Creating and managing rollovers in Expression Web.

6. **Click the Insert button in the Behaviors pane.**

   A menu of behaviors, or actions, appears.

7. **Click the Swap Images option.**

   The Swap Images dialog box appears, as shown in Figure 3-5.

8. **Enter the filename and path of the hover image in the Swap Image URL box.**

9. **Select the Restore on Mouseout Event check box.**

   This option causes the original image to be restored when the hover state returns to normal.

10. **Click OK.**

    The dialog box closes, and you see that two events have been added to the Behaviors pane: `onmouseout` and `onmouseover`.

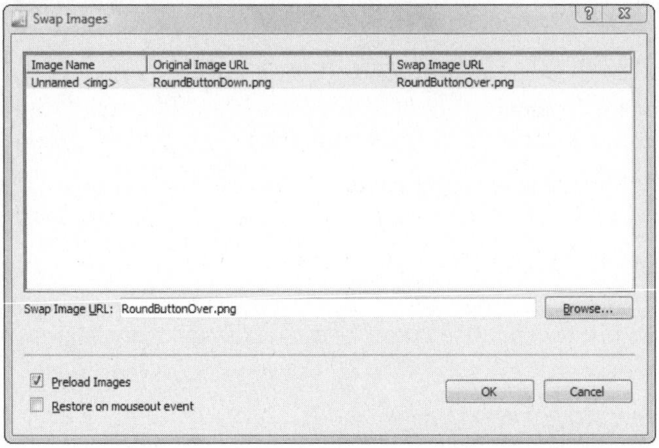

Figure 3-5: Swap Images dialog box.

11. **Press F12 to test your new rollover technique.**

    When you move the mouse cursor over the image element, the image is swapped.

Book VII

Microsoft Expression Web

"Okay, I think I forgot to mention this, but we now have a Web management function that automatically alerts us when there's a broken link on The Aquarium's Web site."

Contents at a Glance

Chapter 1: Getting to Know Microsoft Expression Web

In This Chapter

- **Introducing the Expression Web workspace**
- **Exploring the Editing window**
- **Discovering the panels**
- **Customizing the workspace**

Expression Web is the premier Web site design tool from Microsoft. If you've used Microsoft Office applications, such as Word, you'll find Expression Web fairly easy to pick up. Better yet, if you ever used FrontPage a few years ago, you'll discover many similarities between the two software products. In truth, Expression Web comes from the same software lineage as the older FrontPage.

Expression Web is the flagship product in the new Microsoft Expression Studio. Others products in the software suite include Expression Design (for illustrations and graphic design), Expression Blend (for designing user interfaces), and Expression Media (for organizing your digital assets). In this minibook, I focus on Expression Web.

This chapter introduces you to Expression Web and walks you through the major features of its working environment. In the remaining chapters of this minibook, you'll roll up your sleeves and create pages with it.

Exploring the Expression Web Workspace

When you launch Expression Web, the main workspace (as shown in Figure 1-1) appears in full glory.

An untitled HTML document is created for you automatically. You can immediately begin working with it.

You compose and design your Web pages in the Editing window. Each toolbar and panel that surrounds the editor helps you construct or manage your Web site.

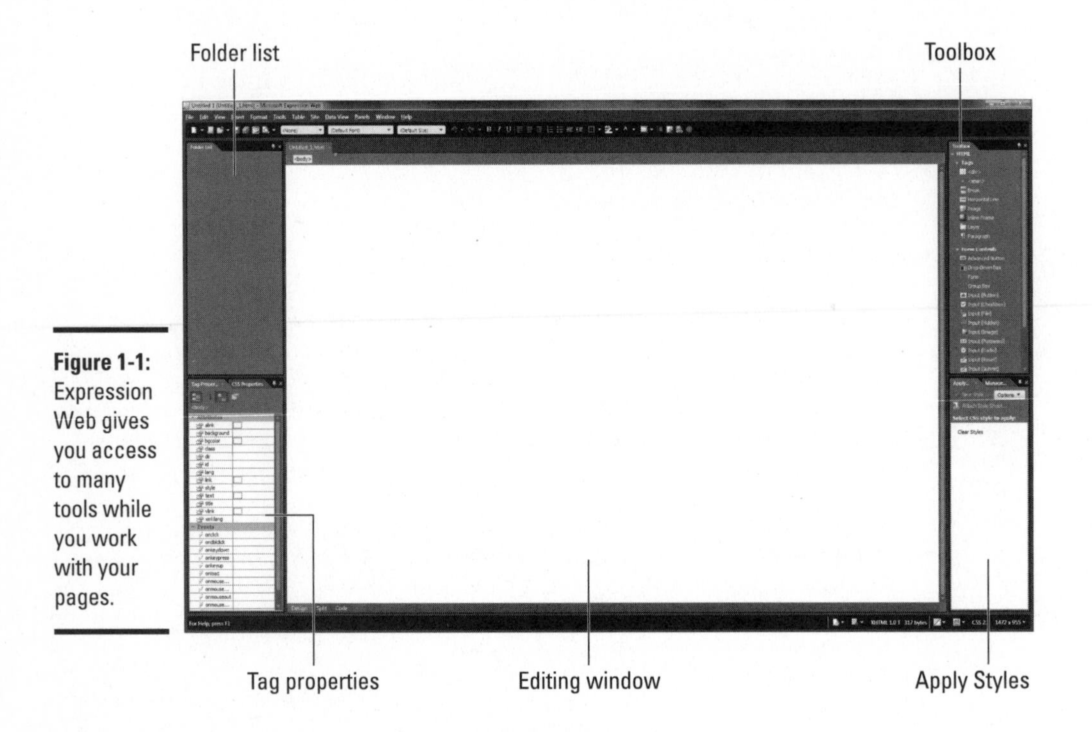

Figure 1-1: Expression Web gives you access to many tools while you work with your pages.

Exploring the Editing Window

The Editing window is the spot inside Expression Web where you'll spend much of your time. Figure 1-2 points out the major features that you can work with.

Pay special attention to the Design, Split, and Code buttons at the bottom of the Editing window. By default, Expression Web displays the document in *Design view* (see Figure 1-2), which features a WYSIWYG look at the Web page that approximates what it will look like in a browser.

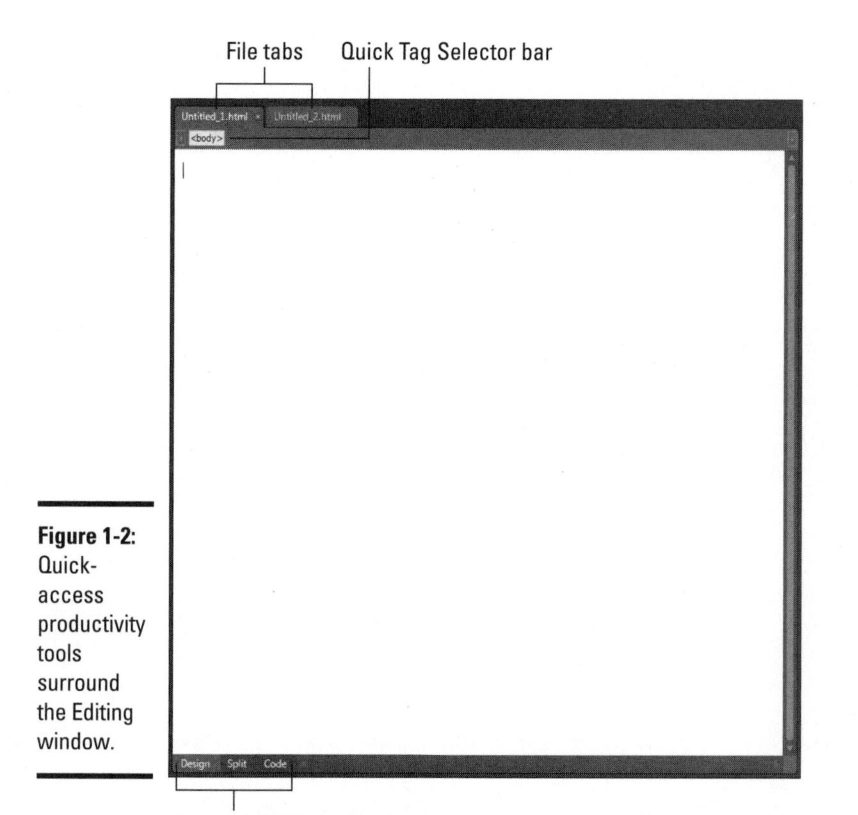

Figure 1-2: Quick-access productivity tools surround the Editing window.

Click the Code button to display the document in *Code view,* which reveals the HTML (Hypertext Markup Language) code of the page (see Figure 1-3). If HTML looks like Greek to you, be sure to check out Book III.

Finally, you can split the difference by viewing the document in Split mode (see Figure 1-4). *Split mode* provides a split screen to display the Code view on top and the Design view on the bottom.

Figure 1-3: Code view displays a document's HTML source code.

Figure 1-4: Split view enables you to see both Design and Code views.

Discovering the Tag Selector

A Web page is written in HTML. Expression Web doesn't force you to hand-code your pages, of course. However, the more you know about the HTML needed for your document, the greater control you can have over it.

When you work in Design view, Expression Web always gives you quick access to the tags you are working with in its Tag Selector, shown just below the file tabs in the Editing window.

When you click your mouse anywhere in the document, the Tag Selector displays a nested-order view of the HTML for that insertion point. For example, Figure 1-5 shows the Tag Selector when the mouse pointer is inside a paragraph of text. The paragraph is contained by several `div` elements and then the `body` element.

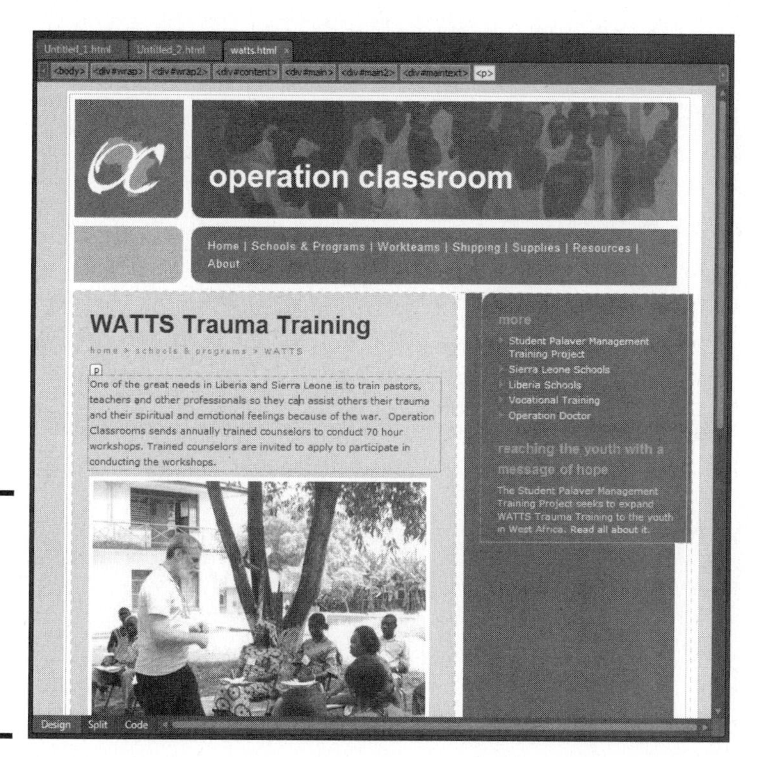

Figure 1-5: Select various HTML tags, using the Tag Selector.

Each tag is a button that, when clicked, selects an element inside the Editing window. Or you can click the down arrow on the right side of the button to display a drop-down list of options (Select Tag, Select Tag Contents, Edit Tag, Remove Tag, Insert HTML, Wrap Tag, Positioning, and Tag Properties), as shown in Figure 1-6.

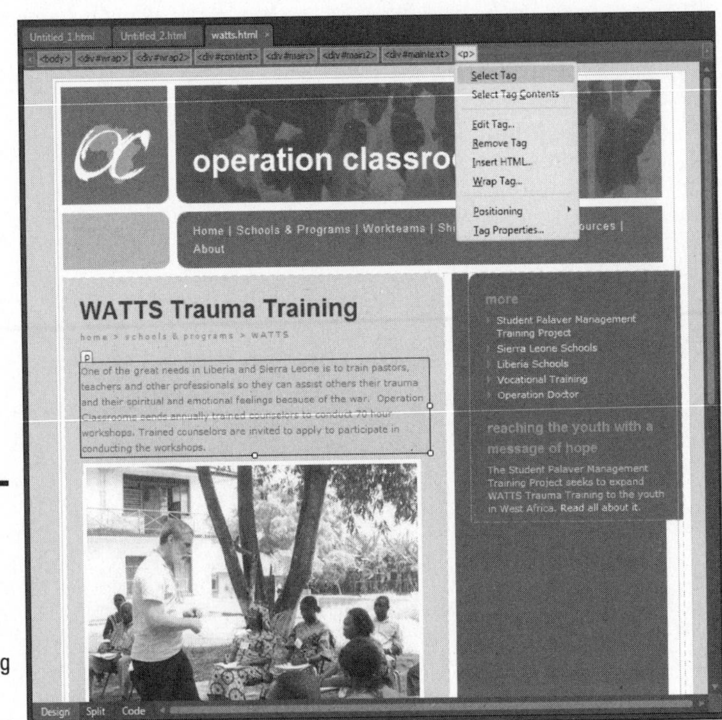

Figure 1-6: You can access several features from the Tag Selector.

Working with Panels

Surrounding the Editing window is a set of panels that provide additional functionality to help you with designing and managing your Web site. These panels are normally displayed on the sides of the Expression Web window, although you can detach each one from the side to display as floating windows.

You can access each of the panels from the Panels menu.

Here are some of the panels that will come in handy as you use Expression Web:

- **Toolbox:** The Toolbox (see Figure 1-7) is used to add HTML tags, form controls, and media elements to your page.

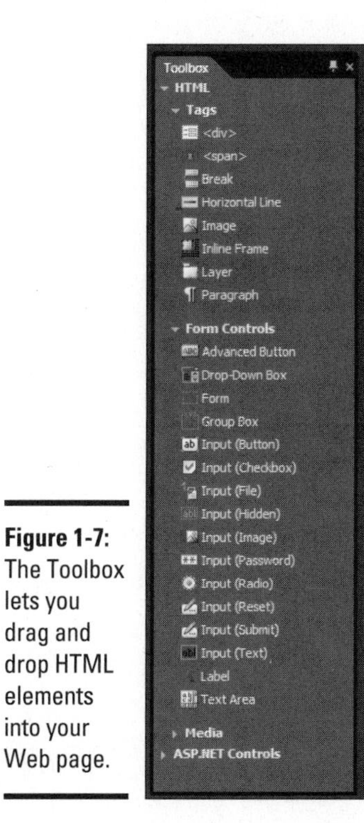

Figure 1-7: The Toolbox lets you drag and drop HTML elements into your Web page.

✦ **Apply Styles and Manage Styles panels:** The Apply Styles and the Manage Styles panels, by default, appear inside the same panel window. Use the Apply Styles panel as a quick way to apply CSS (Cascading Style Sheet) styles to your document; use the Manage Styles panel for managing your style rules and your external style sheets. Figure 1-8 displays the Apply Styles panel.

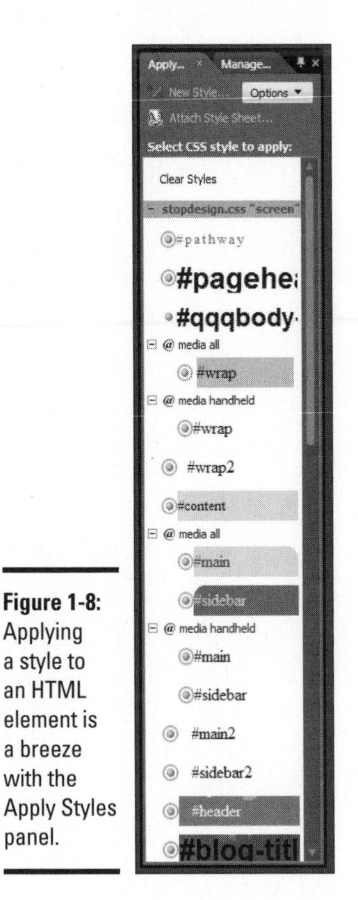

Figure 1-8: Applying a style to an HTML element is a breeze with the Apply Styles panel.

✦ **Folder List panel:** Use the Folder List panel, shown in Figure 1-9, to view and manage the files on your Expression Web site. You can create, open, rename, or delete pages and folders from inside this panel. If you're working on a standalone page outside a site, the panel is empty.

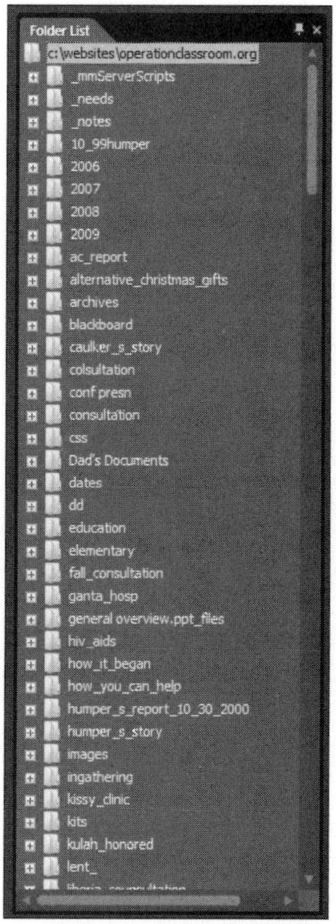

Figure 1-9: The Folder List panel is a mini-Windows Explorer packed inside Expression Web.

✦ **Tag Properties and CSS Properties panels:** By default, the Tag Properties (see Figure 1-10) and CSS Properties (see Figure 1-11) panels are bundled inside the same panel. The Tag Properties panel allows you to view and edit all the available attributes of the current HTML element in your document. The CSS Properties panel displays the CSS rules and properties for the selected element.

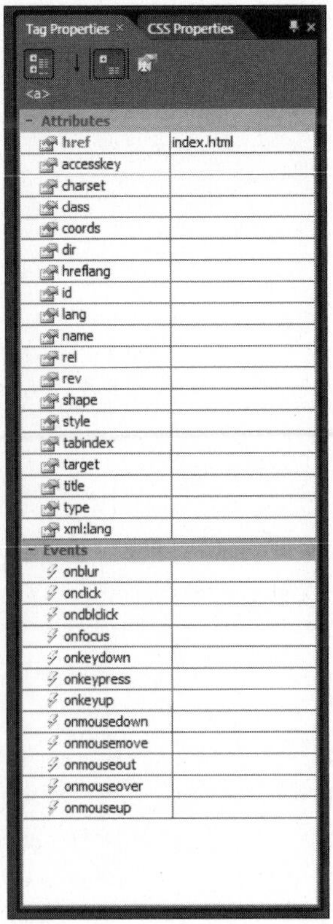

Figure 1-10: Get the inside scoop on any element with the Tag Properties panel.

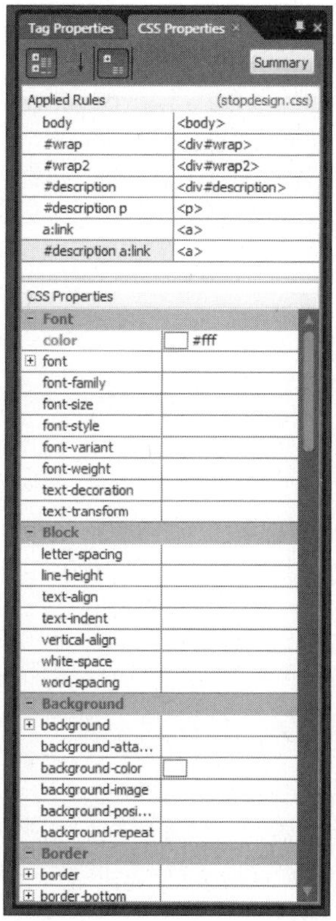

Figure 1-11: The CSS Properties panel allows you to see the current rules applied and the available rule settings.

Viewing Your Web Site

When you open a Web site in Expression Web, a Site View tab appears on the far left of the document tabs. Inside this window is a listing of the site's assets, including local folders, remote Web site(s), reports, and hyperlinks. You can view these different assets through the view buttons at the bottom of the window. Figure 1-12 shows the Site View.

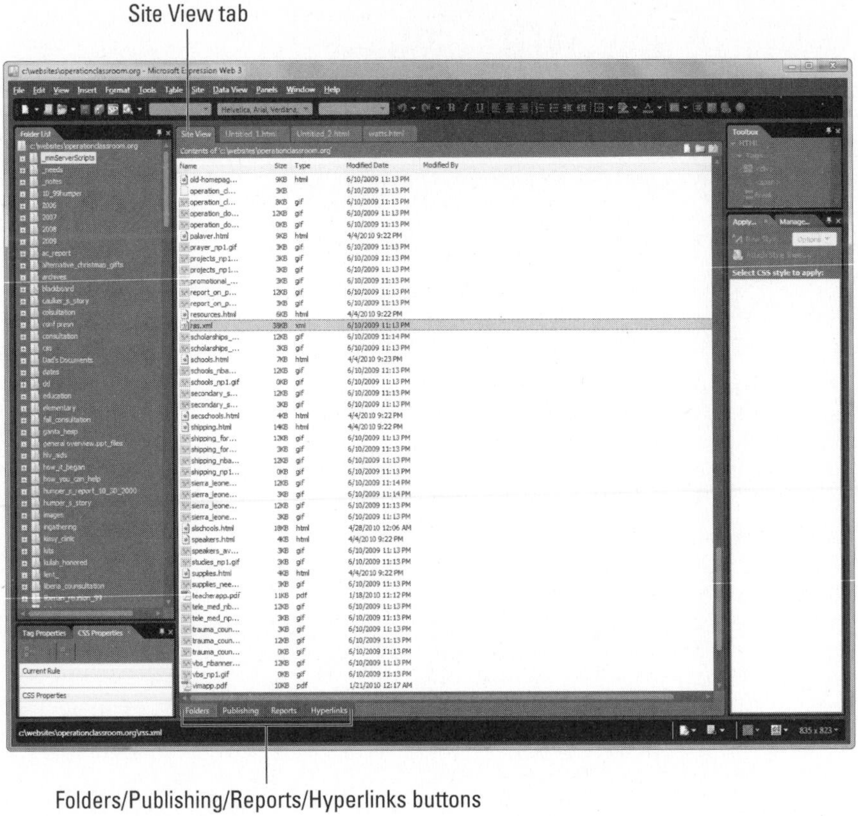

Site View tab

Folders/Publishing/Reports/Hyperlinks buttons

Figure 1-12: Viewing a Web site inside Expression Web.

Customizing Your Working Environment

Expression Web enables you to customize your working environment; you can tailor it just the way you want.

Customizing the panels

Here are several display options that you can perform with the panels:

- **Showing and hiding a panel:** Access all the panels from the Panel menu. You can show or hide a panel by choosing its menu item from the list. You can also hide an open panel by clicking its Close button.

✦ **Maximizing the panel:** You can click the Maximize button on the panel to expand the size of the panel (and shrink any other panels adjacent to it). Click the Restore button to return to the normal size.

✦ **Undocking and docking a panel:** You can undock any of the panels and create a floating window. To do so, drag the caption bar of the panel onto the Editing window: The panel undocks and floats on top of the workspace. You can also right-click and choose Float from the pop-up menu.

To dock a floating panel, drag the panel to the side of the application window: Expression Web docks the panel for you. Or you can right-click the caption bar and choose Dock.

Customizing the Page Editor

The Expression Web Page Editor comes with an impressive assortment of options that you can customize by choosing Tools➪Page Editor Options (as shown in Figure 1-13).

Figure 1-13: The Page Editor can be customized so much that it looks like an aardvark.

Chapter 2: Express Yourself: Creating Your First Site with Expression Web

In This Chapter

- Creating a new Expression Web site
- Adding content to the home page
- Previewing your pages in a browser
- Publishing your site to the Web

It's time to express yourself with Expression Web. As you work your way through this minibook, you'll dive deeper into how to lay out pages and work with content. To get things started, I walk you step-by-step through creating a Web site with Expression Web.

At the end of the chapter, I show you how to publish the Web site you just created to a remote server. Before you get into all this, therefore, you need to have an established account with a Web hosting provider. If you don't, skip the section on publishing.

Creating a New Site

Before you can use Expression Web to work with pages, graphics, and other files as you develop a site, first you have to create the site itself. To create a new site, follow these steps:

1. **Choose Site⇨New Site.**

   The New dialog box appears, as shown in Figure 2-1.

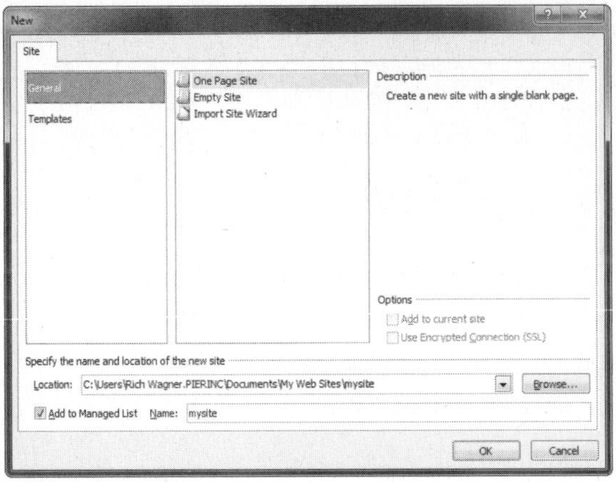

Figure 2-1: Creating a site starts here.

2. **Select the General or the Templates category.**
   - *General:* Select this to begin with a one-page or blank site or to import an existing site into Expression Web.
   - *Templates:* Use this to choose from a list of design templates to get you started.

   If you're importing an existing site, see the "Importing a Site into Expression Web" section at the end of this chapter. If you want to create a template to start your page from, see Chapter 5 of this minibook.

3. **Select the desired site selection from the type list.**

   For this example, I'm choosing the Personal 4 template.

4. **Enter the desired directory in the Location box.**

   You can also click the Browse button and select the desired folder from the dialog box.

5. **Enter a name for your site in the Name box.**

   This name is used in the Managed List of sites. (Unless you uncheck the Add to Managed List check box, the site is added to the Managed List.)

   I entered `My First Site`.

6. **Click OK.**

   Expression Web creates the site and displays the Web Site window, as shown in Figure 2-2.

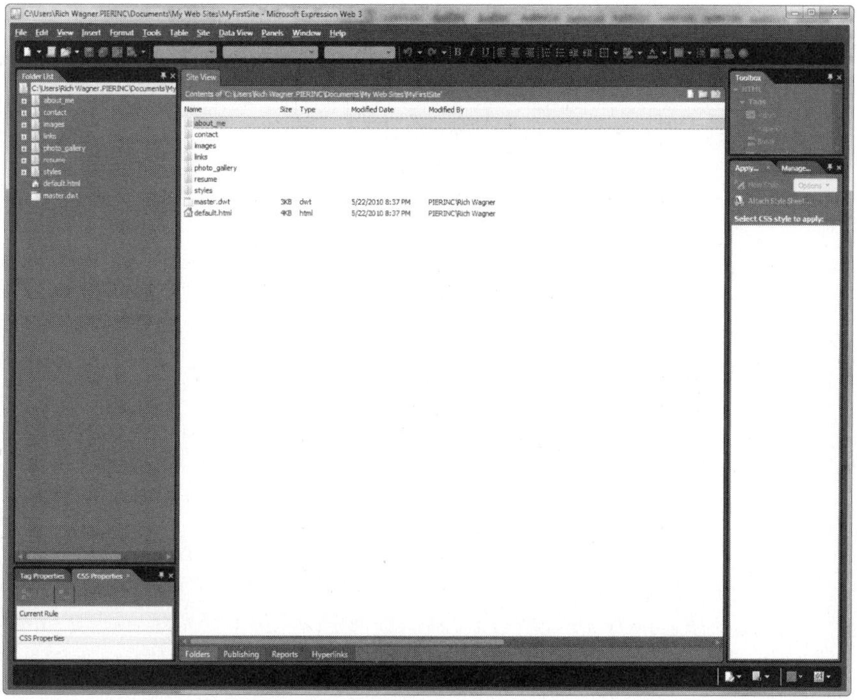

Figure 2-2: The template used by Expression Web creates several folders and pages at the start.

Working with the Home Page

Unless you select an empty site during the site-creation process, Expression Web creates a home page automatically and names it `default.html`.

The home page initially contains canned content, as shown in Figure 2-3. Or, if you choose the blank page, you have a blank document.

To add content to the home page, follow these steps:

1. **Double-click the `default.html` tab in the Editing window.**
2. **Click your cursor at the desired location in the page and begin editing the content.**
3. **(Optional) Add a link.**

   a. *Select the text that you want to link.*

   b. *Click the Insert Hyperlink button on the toolbar.*

   c. *Navigate to the link in the dialog box (or type a URL in the Address box) and then click OK.*

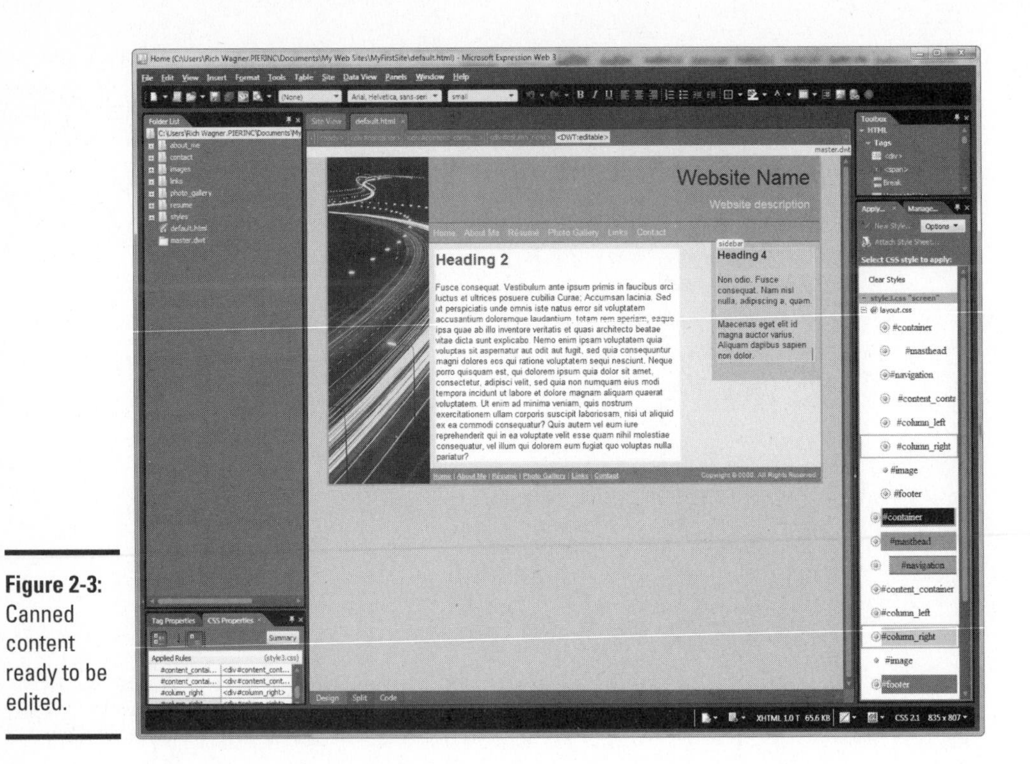

Figure 2-3: Canned content ready to be edited.

4. **(Optional) Add an image.**

   a. *Position your cursor at the location in which you'd like the image to appear.*

   b. *Click the Insert Picture from File button on the toolbar and then select the image you would like to insert from the dialog box that appears.*

   c. *Click OK.*

5. **Add a title to your page.**

   Right-click the page in the Editing window and choose Page Properties from the pop-up menu. In the Page Properties dialog box (see Figure 2-4) that appears, enter a descriptive title in the Title field and then click OK. (The title is displayed in the browser's window or tab title.)

6. **Choose File➪Save.**

   It's not rocket science, but as with other documents you work with, you have to save your Web page before it can be of much use.

7. **Repeat the preceding steps for each of the pages in your Web site.**

   If you use one of the templates, you might have several pages that you want to modify. (Choose File⇨New⇨Page to add new pages.)

Figure 2-4: Modifying the title and other page properties.

Here I've bypassed the many features that Expression Web offers for working with text, links, and images. I save that discussion for Chapter 3 of this minibook.

Previewing Your Page in a Browser

Although Expression Web features a visual editor, some disparities always exist between what you see in Design view and what you actually see in the browser. Therefore, before you finish with a page, be sure to preview your page to see how it looks.

To preview a document, follow these steps:

1. **Click the Preview in Browser button on the toolbar.**

   In the drop-down list, a list of the browsers installed on your computer, and their various window sizes, appears (see Figure 2-5).

   If you prefer the main menu, you can choose an option from the File⇨Preview in Browser submenu instead.

   You can modify the browser list by choosing the Edit Browser List item from the drop-down list. Additionally, you can specify whether you'd like Expression Web to save the current state of the document automatically before you preview it.

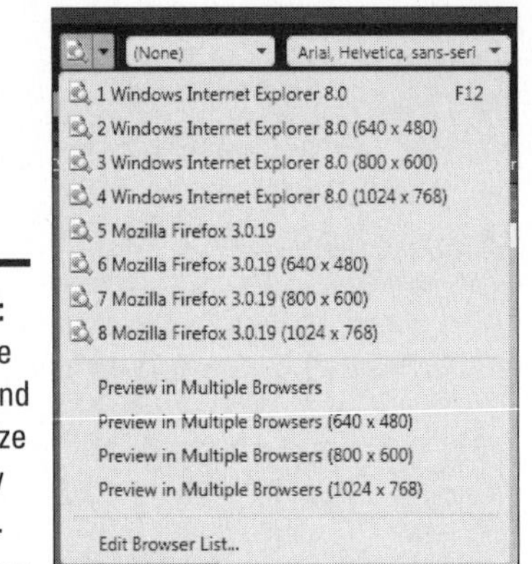

Figure 2-5: Choose the browser and window size to preview your page.

2. **Choose the desired browser and window size from the list.**

   Expression Web opens your page in the browser for you to preview (see Figure 2-6).

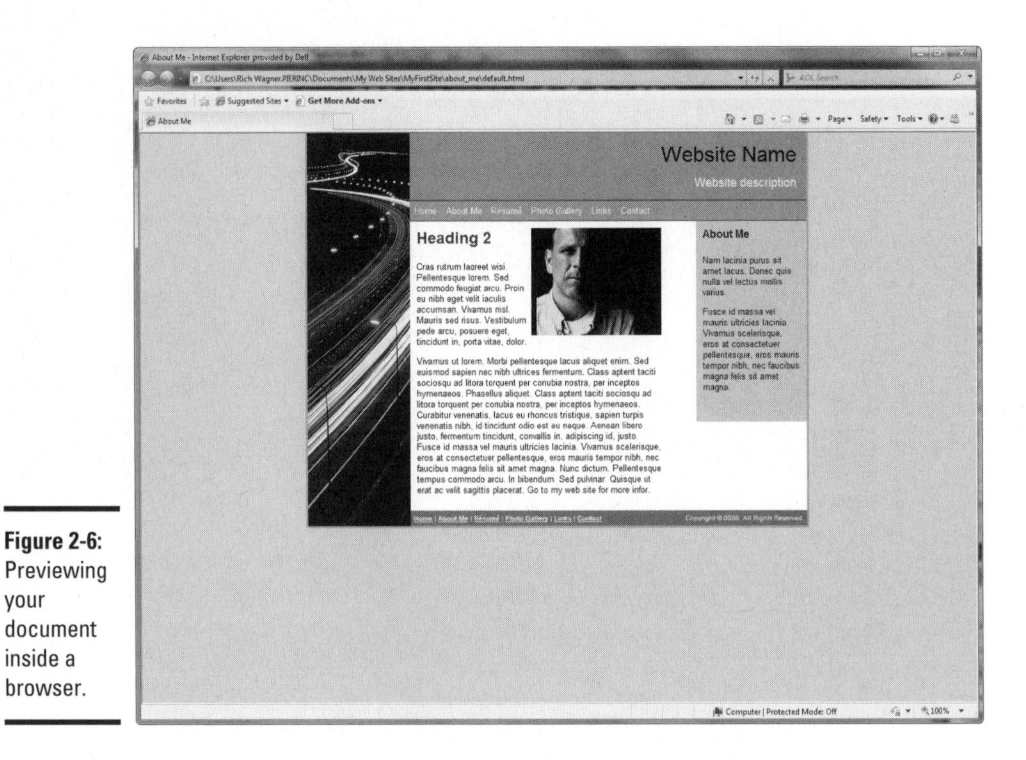

Figure 2-6: Previewing your document inside a browser.

Previewing the Page in SuperPreview

Although the normal preview is certainly functional for a single browser, Expression Web also includes an innovative, powerful feature appropriately called SuperPreview. In SuperPreview, you can preview your page in different browsers and browser versions simultaneously. The left side is intended as the baseline preview; the right side is used for comparison.

Here's how to use it:

1. **Click the SuperPreview button in the toolbar.**

   You can also choose File⇨Display in SuperPreview.

   When you first click the SuperPreview button, the SuperPreview window appears, as shown in Figure 2-7.

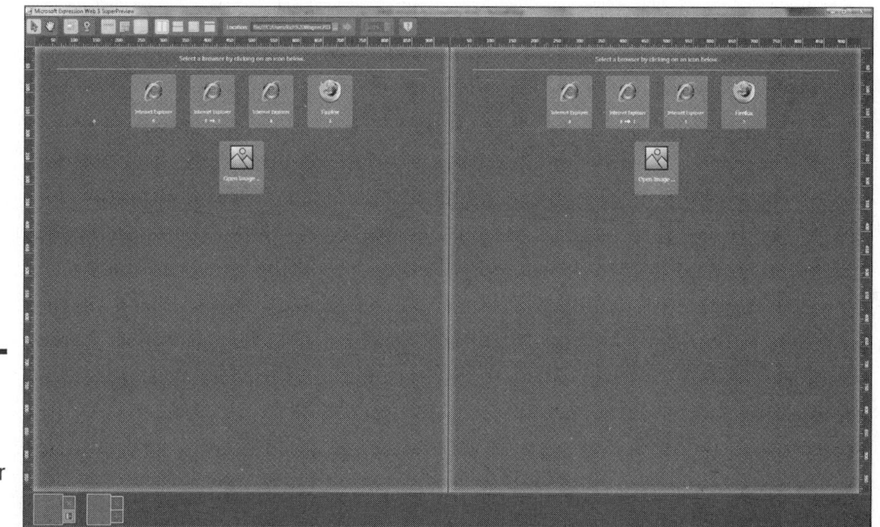

Figure 2-7: It's a bird, it's a plane, no it's Super Preview.

2. **On the left side, select the baseline browser you want to preview you page with.**

   In my case, I chose Internet Explorer 8.

3. **Click the Refresh button to display the page in the baseline panel.**

4. **On the right side, select the browser in which to compare your page with.**

   I chose Firefox.

5. **Click the Refresh button again to update the display.**

   Figure 2-8 shows a page being displayed in SuperPreview.

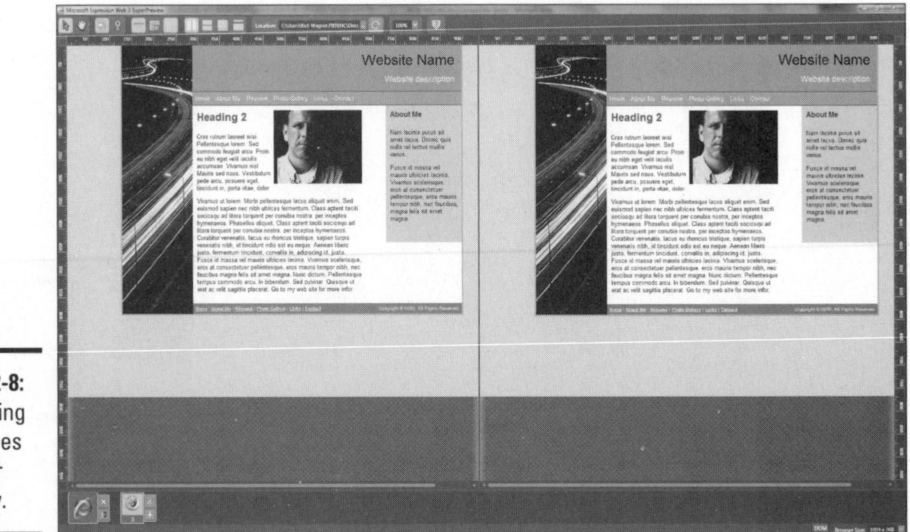

Figure 2-8: Comparing two pages in Super Preview.

Publishing Your Site

After you preview your site and have everything ready to go, you're ready to upload (or publish) it to your remote server.

Here's how to publish your newly created site:

1. **Choose Site⇨Publishing.**

   This feature enables publishing for your site and displays the Publishing tab (see Figure 2-9).

2. **Click the Add a Publishing Destination link.**

   The Connection Settings dialog box appears (see Figure 2-10).

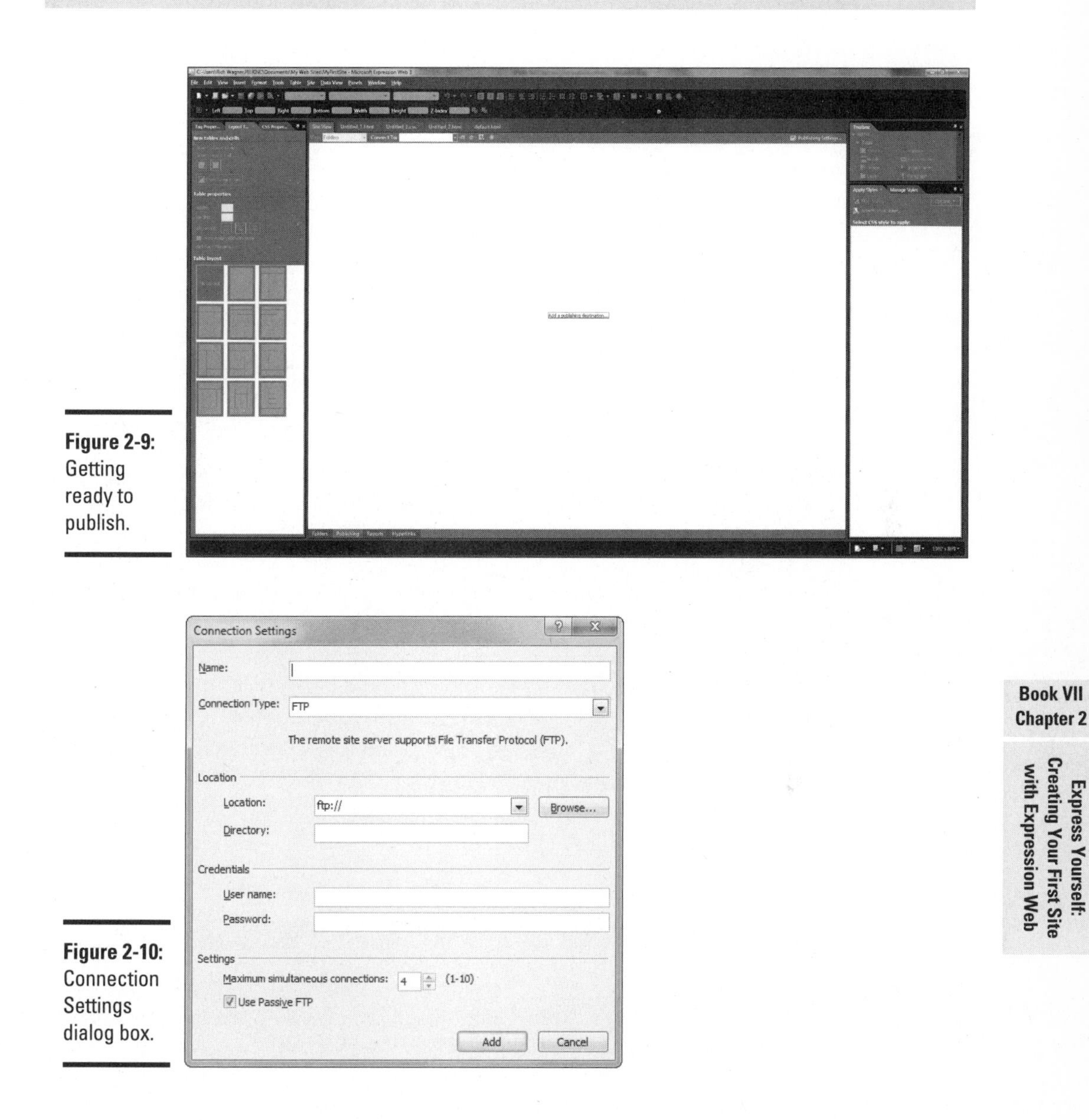

Figure 2-9: Getting ready to publish.

Figure 2-10: Connection Settings dialog box.

3. **Enter a name for the connection in the Name box.**
4. **Select the desired type of connection from the Connection Type drop-down list.**

   If you have a typical Web-hosting provider, you use FTP (File Transfer Protocol) to connect to the server. (If you are using another option, fill in the settings and then skip to Step 8.)

5. **In the Location field, enter the FTP server information for your hosting provider.**
6. **If you have a special directory to place the site files in, add that to the Directory field.**
7. **Fill in the Username and Password fields.**
8. **Click Add.**

   Expression Web attempts to connect to the server, using the information that you provide.

   Expression Web connects to the server and displays a live view of the server, as shown in Figure 2-11.

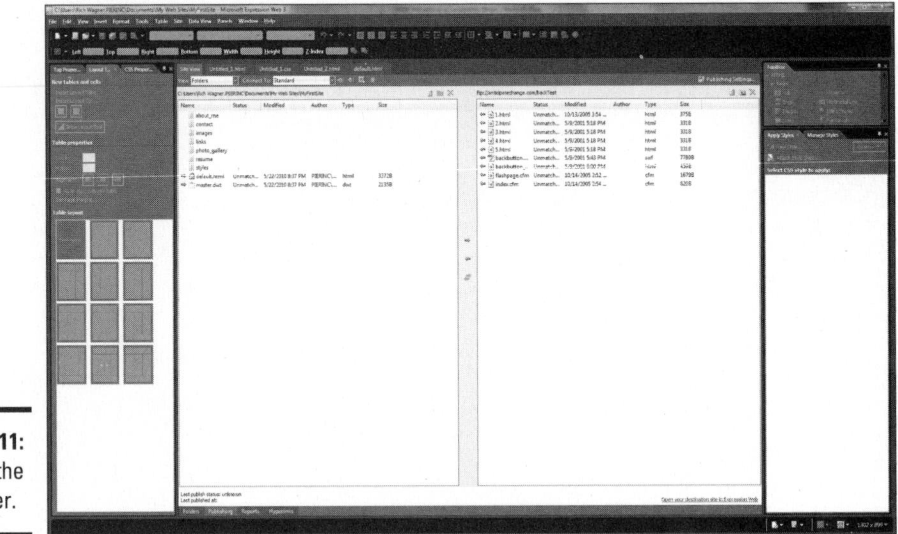

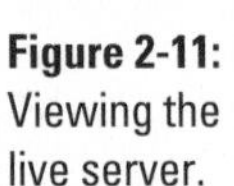

Figure 2-11: Viewing the live server.

9. **From the local view, select the files in which you want to publish and click the Publish Files to the Destination Site button.**

   Expression Web displays the results of the transfer in the Status pane. If the upload was successful, congratulations! You published your first site using Microsoft Expression Web.

Be sure to upload all of the images and other files that are used by your Web site, not just the pages themselves. One of the most common mistakes when building a Web site is to forget about these support files when you publish.

When you need to republish your files at a later date, select the files and click the Publish Files to the Destination Site button. The files upload using the settings you've previously defined.

Importing a Site into Expression Web

Perhaps you have an existing site that you'd like to import into Expression Web so you can begin using it. To import a Web site, follow these steps:

1. **Choose Site⇨Import⇨Import Site Wizard.**

   The Import Web Site Wizard dialog box appears, as shown in Figure 2-12.

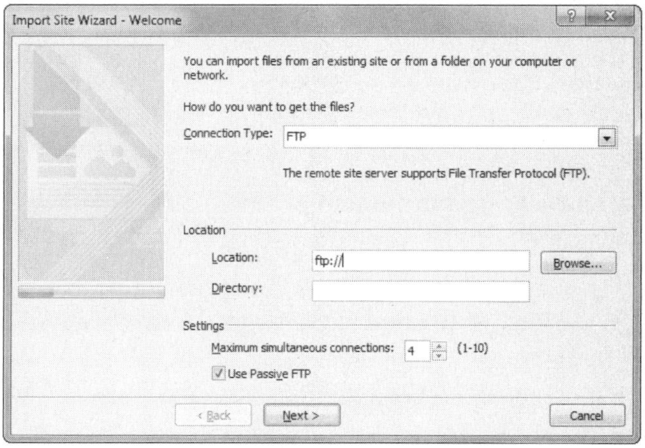

Import Site Wizard - Welcome

You can import files from an existing site or from a folder on your computer or network.

How do you want to get the files?

Connection Type: FTP

The remote site server supports File Transfer Protocol (FTP).

Location

Location: ftp://

Directory:

Settings

Maximum simultaneous connections: 4 (1-10)

Use Passive FTP

< Back | Next > | Cancel

Figure 2-12: You can get a head start by importing work you've already done with another Web tool.

2. **Select the transmission method in which you would like to retrieve the files.**

   - *FTP:* If you're importing an old site of yours that you have on a Web server, select FTP (if you have your username and password information).
   - *HTTP:* For everything else, select HTTP.

3. **Specify the address in the Location field.**
4. **If you're using FTP, specify the Directory.**
5. **Click Next to begin.**

   Expression Web connects to the remote server (requesting your username and password if those are needed). If Expression Web is able to connect, the next page in the wizard is shown (see Figure 2-13).

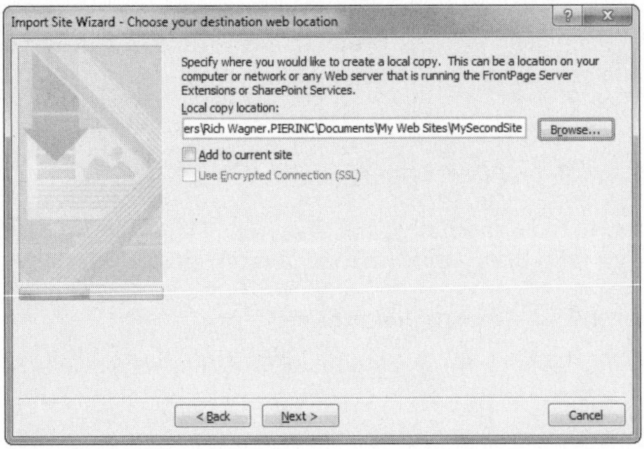

Figure 2-13: Enter the local folder in which you want to store the imported files.

6. **Enter the folder where you'd like to place your Web site files and click Next.**

   A final dialog box appears.

7. **Click Finish to start the import process.**

   Expression Web opens the Remote Web Site view in the Web Site window.

8. **Select the Remote to Local radio button in the Publish All Changed Pages group.**

9. **Click the Publish Web Site button.**

   Expression Web connects to the Web server and begins the transfer process. The status of the transfer is shown as the files are retrieved from the remote server.

10. **When the transfer process is complete, click the Folders view button at the bottom of the Editing window.**

    The local files on the Web site are listed. You can now select and edit any of the site files shown.

Chapter 3: Working with Text, Graphics, and Links

In This Chapter

- **Inserting and formatting text**
- **Working with images**
- **Adding links**

It's all about the content. A Web site should be attractive and easy to navigate. If your site visitors are going to come back again and again, you need to have something for them to see — the content.

Much of the content you'll be working with on your Web site consists of three basic types: text, graphics, and links. You arrange and style these pieces of content in a variety of ways by using HTML (Hypertext Markup Language) and CSS (Cascading Style Sheets), but having a solid grasp on the basics is important. You explore how to work with text, pictures, and links in this chapter.

Expression Web doesn't take you too far into HTML or CSS. But if you're interested in discovering more about those tools, I discuss HTML in Book III and CSS in Book IV.

Adding and Editing Text in Your Pages

If you've used Microsoft Word before, you already have a pretty good idea how to work with text inside Expression Web. Although the underlying technologies are different, many of the ways how you format and edit your text are consistent between Word and Expression Web. This synergy makes your transition to the Web all that much easier.

Adding text

To add text to your page, just click in the Editing window at the place where you want text, and start typing. If you're not in any other element (besides the body of the page), Expression Web adds a paragraph (`<p>`) element for you around your text, automatically.

Expression Web performs much like Microsoft Word when you enter text:

✦ The text wraps when you reach the end of a line.

✦ Pressing Enter closes the paragraph and creates a new one.

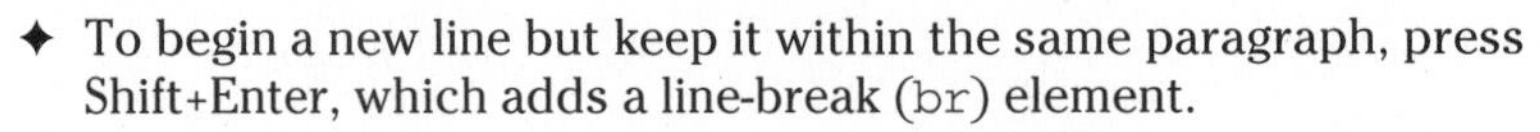

✦ To begin a new line but keep it within the same paragraph, press Shift+Enter, which adds a line-break (`br`) element.

✦ You can also add a line break by double-clicking the Break tag in the Toolbox.

After you enter your text, you can format it in two ways: directly and with styles.

Directly formatting text

You can format your text in Expression Web by directly formatting it from the Common toolbar, as shown in Figure 3-1. You do this exactly as you've likely always done in Microsoft Word.

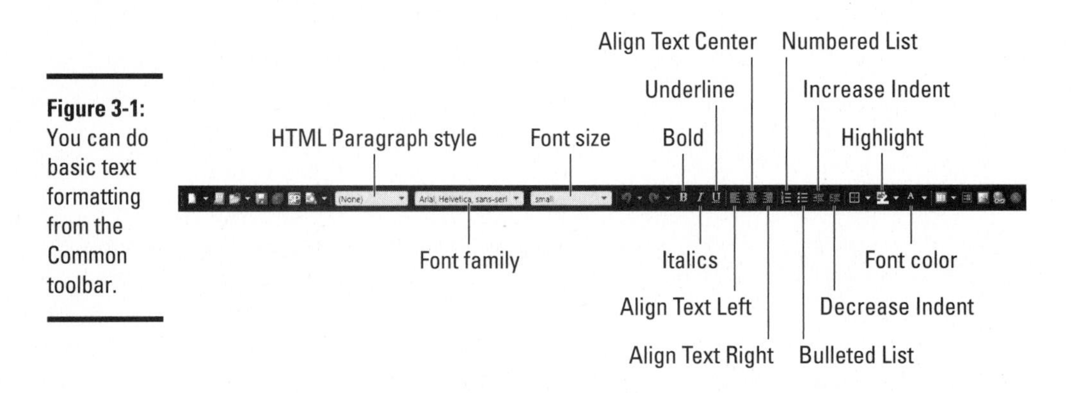

Figure 3-1: You can do basic text formatting from the Common toolbar.

The HTML paragraph style is a setting for the entire paragraph (you indicate where it goes by positioning the text cursor somewhere inside the paragraph), but the remaining formatting options are applied to text you've selected with your mouse.

Here are some of the more commonly used formatting options:

✦ **Style:** The Style drop-down list displays the traditional HTML paragraph styles of text:

- *Paragraph* (the default)
- *Heading 1* (largest header) *through Heading 6* (smallest header)

- *Preformatted* (monospaced)
- *A series of list and definition styles*

  The list styles can also be applied using the Bulleted and Numbered list buttons.

✦ **Font:** The Font drop-down list shows the fonts that you can apply to your text. Web fonts are usually applied as a *family* (a prioritized list of font faces, separated by commas). The most common font families are shown at the top of the list.

✦ **Size:** The Size drop-down list displays a list of possible font sizes. You can use various sizing measurements:

- *xx-small* to *xx-large*
- *Smaller* (one size smaller than previously defined) and *Larger* (one size larger than previously defined)

✦ **Basic word processing styles:** The Common toolbar also has formatting buttons that perform just as Microsoft Word does, including Bold, Italic, Alignment, Bulleted List, Numbered List, Decrease Indent, and Increase Indent.

✦ **Highlight:** The Highlight button is a carryover from the word processor world. To highlight text, you use a tool such as a colored highlighter.

✦ **Font Color:** The Font Color box allows you to select a text color from the drop-down box that appears.

The Format menu also has access to several dialog boxes for direct formatting of text, particularly the Format⇨Font and Format⇨Paragraph commands. Once again, you'll find these dialog boxes basically the same as in Microsoft Word.

Formatting with CSS styles

Expression Web also allows you to format your text by using CSS styles. The way you work with styles in Expression Web is loosely based on the ways you apply and manage styles in Microsoft Word. If you've worked with Word styles before, you will find yourself with a head start. However, CSS styles are far more powerful (and complex) than Word styles are.

See Book IV for all of the ins and outs of CSS.

Applying CSS styles to your text

To format your text using styles, display the Apply Styles panel (see Figure 3-2). If it's not visible already, choose Panels⇨Apply Styles.

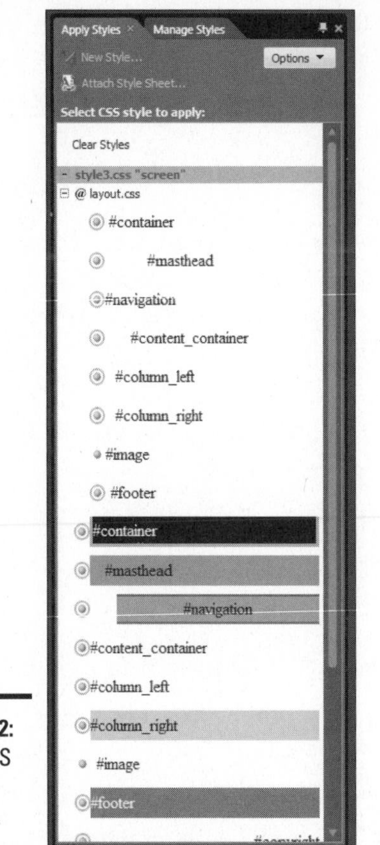

Figure 3-2: Apply CSS styles to your text.

The Apply Styles panel displays all the styles that are accessible from the opened document. The styles are defined in the document itself or from external style sheets linked into the document with a `<link>` tag. Each is displayed in a way that emulates the look of the style. Here's how the style list is organized by default:

- **Class-based and `id`-based styles** are listed according to their source document (current or external `.css` file).
- **Element-based styles** are listed in the Contextual Selectors section.
- **Inline styles** are listed in the Inline Styles section.

For details on these different styles, see Book IV, Chapter 2.

The Options button at the top of the panel is where you can modify the sorting and the styles that are displayed.

To apply a style, position the cursor or select the text in which you want to apply the style and then click the style from the Apply Styles panel.

Managing CSS styles

You can manage your CSS styles from both the Manage Styles and the Apply Styles panels, although the Manage Styles panel (see Figure 3-3) is generally preferred.

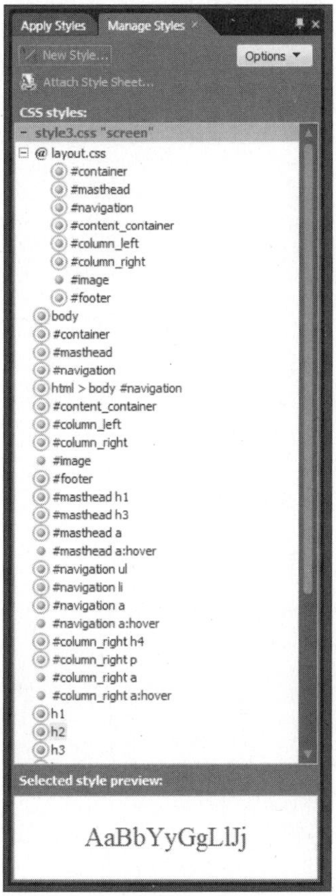

Figure 3-3: Managing CSS styles from here.

Here are some of the typical tasks that you'll want to perform with CSS styles:

- ✦ **Define a new style.** Click the New Style link to define a new style. The New Style dialog box appears, as shown in Figure 3-4. In the Selector field, enter the pound sign (#) and a unique identifier for an `id` selector, a period (.) and a class name for a class selector, or select an element name from the list. Next, define the location in which the class should be defined in the Define In field. After that, format the style according to the dialog-box settings. Click OK to save.

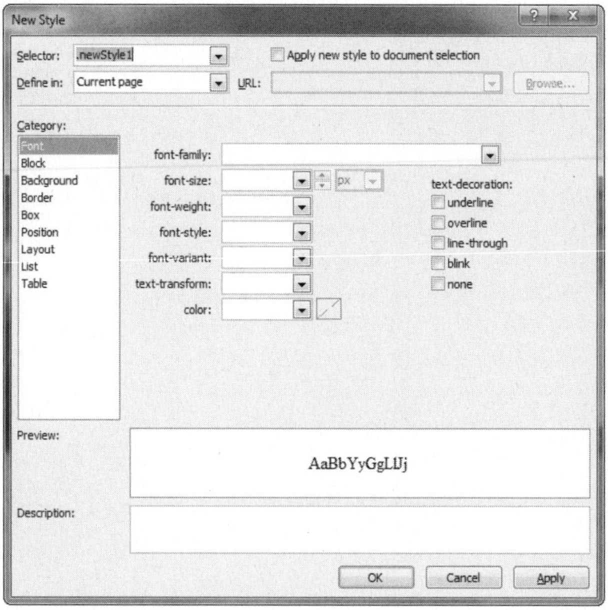

Figure 3-4: Defining a new CSS style.

- ✦ **Attach a style sheet.** Click the Attach Style Sheet link to attach an external `.css` file to the current document (or optionally to all HTML pages in the site).
- ✦ **Edit an existing style.** You can edit an existing style by selecting it from the CSS Styles list, right-clicking, and then choosing Modify Style from its pop-up menu. The Modify Style dialog box appears.
- ✦ **Jump to a style's CSS code.** If you are comfortable with CSS code, you can jump directly to a style's CSS definition code by double-clicking the style from the list.

Working with Pictures

Pictures are the second staple of any Web site. Here's how to work with them inside Expression Web.

Adding a picture to your page

To insert an image, perform the following steps:

1. **In the Editing window, position your cursor at the place on-screen where you'd like to insert an image.**
2. **Click the Insert Picture from File button from the Common toolbar.**

   You can also choose Insert➪Picture➪From File, if you prefer.

   The Picture dialog box (shown in Figure 3-5) appears.

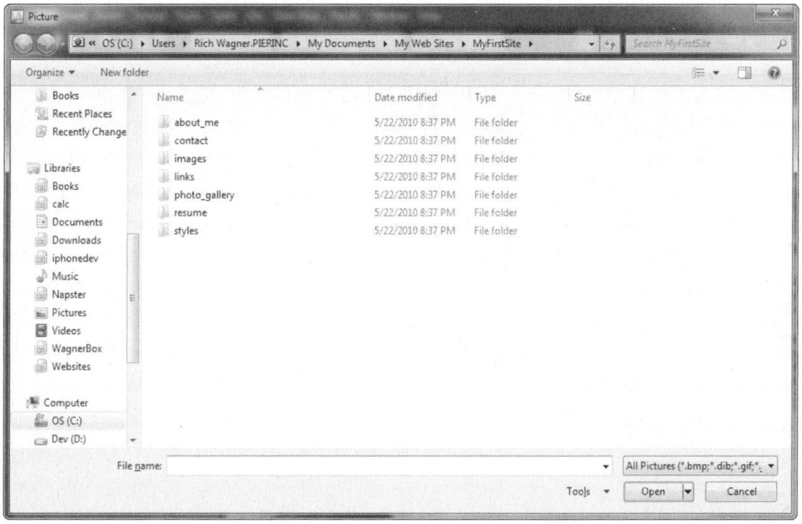

Figure 3-5: Select an image to place a picture into your document.

3. **Select the desired image.**
4. **Click Open.**

   The Accessibility Properties dialog box appears (see Figure 3-6). Providing alternate text for your images ensures that visually impaired persons will be better able to understand your Web site.

Figure 3-6: Providing alternate text for your images.

Accessibility Properties

Alternate text:

Long description: Browse...

Show this prompt when inserting images OK Cancel

5. **Enter a description of the image in the Alternate Text field.**

   Alternate text is vital for visually impaired visitors of your site.

6. **Click OK.**

   The image is now available on your Web page, as shown in Figure 3-7.

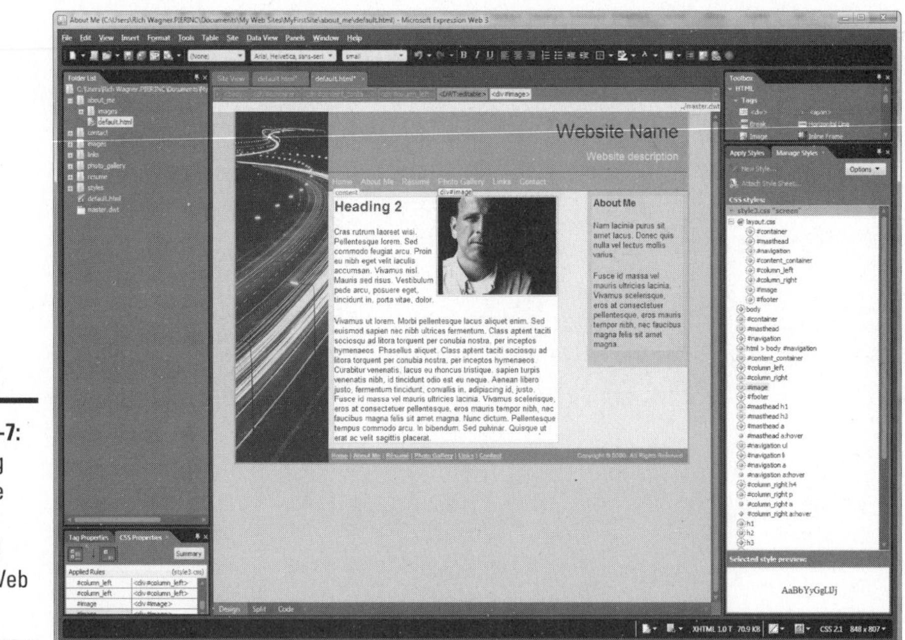

Figure 3-7: Inserting a picture of some hayseed onto a Web page.

If the image isn't already located inside the folder of the current site, Expression Web displays a Save Embedded Files dialog box (see Figure 3-8) when you save the document. Use this dialog box to add the picture to your images folder of your site.

Figure 3-8: Saving the picture into a site folder.

Modifying a picture

You can modify the properties of an image by double-clicking the image in the Editing window, which opens the Picture Properties dialog box. This dialog box has two tabs: the General tab (see Figure 3-9) and the Appearance tab (see Figure 3-10).

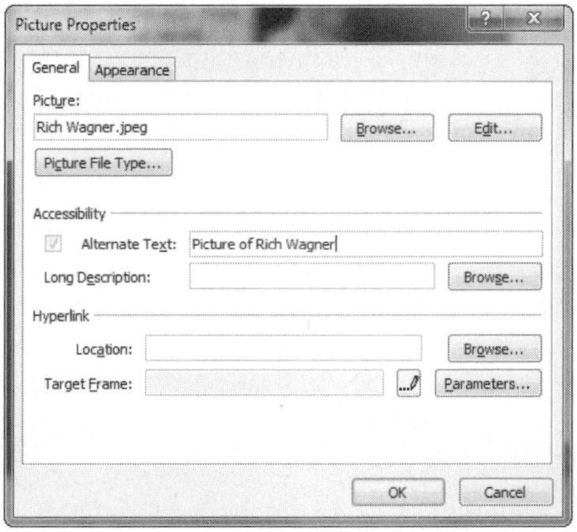

Figure 3-9: Edit image attributes here.

In the following sections, I walk you through some of the changes you might want to make to an image's properties.

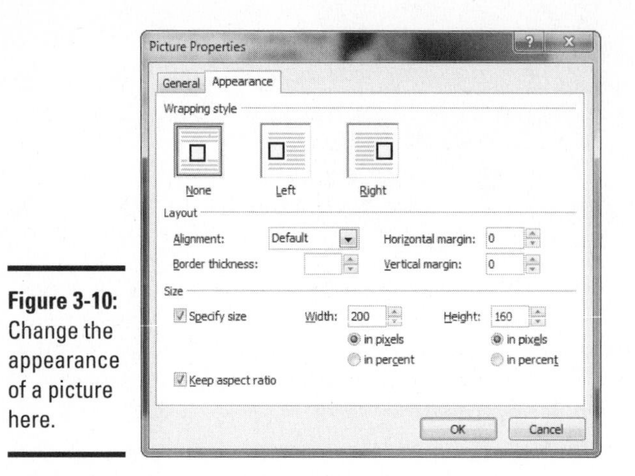

Figure 3-10: Change the appearance of a picture here.

Changing the image file type

Expression Web enables you to convert your existing image into another format type when you click the Picture File Type button on the General tab. You can convert the format to GIF, JPEG, PNG-8, or PNG-24. (See Book VI for full details on the pros and cons of these different formats.)

If you have an image editor, such as Photoshop, you probably want to do most of your image conversion there because that way you have greater control over the quality of the conversion. However, if you don't have access to other software, the conversion utility built into Expression Web can come in handy.

Aligning and wrapping the picture

By default, when you insert a picture into a paragraph, the image is added directly in the paragraph itself. However, in most cases, you want to wrap the text around the image instead. In the Picture Properties dialog box, use the Wrapping Style options on the Appearance tab to specify the type of wrapping you'd like to use: None, Left, or Right. You can also specify the position from the Alignment drop-down list.

Padding the image

In the Picture Properties dialog box, the Horizontal Margin and Vertical Margin fields allow you to specify the padding (in pixels) that you'd like to add around the image. (Five pixels is often a good rule.)

Adding a border

You can add a border by entering a pixel value in the Border Thickness field in the Picture Properties dialog box.

Sizing the image

Expression Web places the actual dimensions (in pixels) of the image in the Width and Height fields. If you want to shrink, expand, or skew the image, enter new values in the Picture Properties dialog box.

You can also directly resize the image inside the Editing window by clicking the image and dragging one of the border boxes. When you do so, a Picture Action drop-down list appears when the picture is selected. Then you can specify whether you want to modify the HTML size attributes or have Expression Web resize the image for you, using those specified dimensions. (However, when you resize your image in this manner, the file size remains the same. Therefore, I recommend resizing your image only in an image-editing software program like Photoshop.)

Editing the image

Much like Microsoft Word, Expression Web provides image-editing functionality within the editor itself, in a Pictures toolbar (shown in Figure 3-11). To access the toolbar, choose View⇨Toolbars⇨Pictures. The toolbar has a series of commands for editing the image.

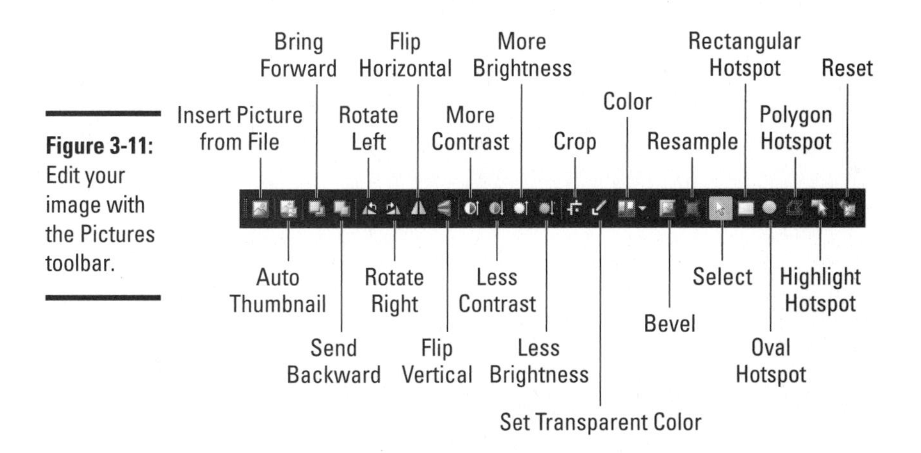

Figure 3-11: Edit your image with the Pictures toolbar.

Some commonly used features include

- ✦ **Auto Thumbnail:** Clicking this button creates a small thumbnail version of the selected picture. The thumbnail image is then linked to the larger image. When you save the page, Expression Web asks you to save the new thumbnail image.
- ✦ **Brightness and Contrast:** Click the Brightness and Contrast buttons to tweak these image settings.

✦ **Crop:** Click the Crop button to trim the size of the image directly on your page. These changes are made to the image file itself.

✦ **Resample:** Click the Resample button to save the image based on current dimensions.

✦ **Reset:** Click the Reset button to restore the original image dimensions of the picture.

Working with Hyperlinks

Hyperlinks, quite literally, make the Web what it is today. Not surprisingly, one of the most common practices you'll find yourself doing is adding links here, adding links there, adding links everywhere.

Creating a hyperlink

To insert a link, follow these steps:

1. **Select the text or picture you want to serve as the link.**
2. **Click the Insert Hyperlink button on the Common toolbar.**

   You can also choose Insert⇨Hyperlink.

   The Insert Hyperlink dialog box appears (see Figure 3-12).

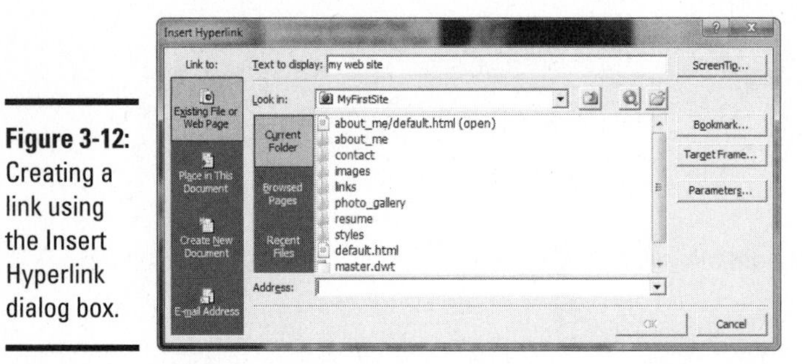

Figure 3-12: Creating a link using the Insert Hyperlink dialog box.

3. **(Optional) Edit the link text in the Text to Display field.**
4. **Select the desired option from the Link To list.**

   The options are as follows:

   • *Existing File or Web Page* links to a file in your site or to a URL on the Internet.

   • *Place in This Document* links to a bookmark previously defined within the current document.

- *Create New Document* links to a new document that you subsequently create.
- *E-mail Address* links to an e-mail address.

The dialog box updates to put into effect the selection you make.

5. **If you're linking to an existing file or Web page, navigate to the selected file or type the URL in the Address field.**
6. **(Optional) To specify the target window for the linked document, click the Target Frame button.**

   You can specify the window or frame that the linked page should display in the Target Frame dialog box. You can choose the following options:

   - *Page Default (none)* makes no changes.
   - *Same Frame (`_self`)* displays the document in the same window that sent the link.
   - *Whole Page (`_top`)* opens the returning document in the top-level window (replacing any frames).
   - *New Window (`_blank`)* opens the returning document in a new window.
   - *Parent Frame (`_parent`)* displays the document in the parent window of the current one.
7. **Click OK to create the link.**

Removing a hyperlink

You can delete a link that you previously created by selecting the text or the image that the link is assigned to. Right-click and choose Hyperlink Properties from the pop-up menu. Then, in the Edit Hyperlink dialog box, click the Remove Link button.

You can also simply remove the URL value from the `href` property in the Tag Properties panel.

Creating an image map and hotspots

To link different portions of an image to different URLs, click the Hotspot buttons on the Pictures toolbar (refer to Figure 3-11) to create an image map.

You can create hyperlinks to images just like you can for text so that when the image is clicked, the user is taken to a new URL. However, you can also define regions inside of an image *(hotspots)* and assign each region a specific URL to go to when those are clicked. An image that contains hotspots is an *image map.*

To create an image map, follow these steps:

1. **Select the image to which you'd like to add hotspots.**
2. **From the Pictures toolbar, select the desired hotspot tool that matches the shape you'd like to create.**

   For most uses, the Rectangular Hotspot tool works just dandy.
3. **Drag your mouse over the image to set the hotspot in the dimensions you desire. Release the mouse when you're satisfied with the size.**

   Expression Web displays the Insert Hyperlink dialog box.
4. **Enter the URL you want to associate with the clickable region in the Address field. Or navigate to the file of your choice via the dialog box.**
5. **Click OK to add the link.**
6. **Repeat Steps 2–5 for each hotspot you want to add.**

If you want to resize, reposition, or remove a hotspot after it's added, click it with your mouse inside of the Editing window and manipulate it according to the desired action.

Chapter 4: Laying Out Your Page with Expression Web

In This Chapter

- **Working with div elements**
- **Using layout tables for page design**

It seems much like ancient history now for those who lived through it, but back in the 1980s, there was a memorable scene from a U.S. vice-presidential debate between Senators Dan Quayle and Lloyd Bentsen. After Quayle compared himself to Kennedy, Bentsen retorted, "Senator, I served with Jack Kennedy. I knew Jack Kennedy. Jack Kennedy was a friend of mine. Senator, you are no Jack Kennedy." That line became one of the more popular political quotes of the late 20th century.

That quote came to mind when I began recalling the constant comparisons that I've been making between Microsoft Word and Expression Web throughout this minibook. After all, for many normal tasks, they could just as well be the same product. However, the pages that emerge from the two products should *not* look the same. If you're going to create a well-designed Web site, you want to do more than populate it with online versions of word-processing documents. Instead, use the tools available in Expression Web to create sophisticated, standards-based page layouts.

In the end, you'll want to be able to look at the Microsoft Word icon and tell it, "I worked with Expression Web to create my Web site. Expression Web was a friend of mine. Word, you are no Expression Web." (However, if you do so, I recommend not speaking out loud while others are present or you could wind up on YouTube.)

In this chapter, I show you how to work with the most important page-layout tools inside Expression Web, including `div` elements and layout tables.

Working with div Elements

The `div` element is the most important component in HTML for laying out Web pages. The `div` element, by itself, isn't visible by default and does little more than serve as a rectangular container for blocks of content. However, when you combine div elements with Cascading Style Sheets (CSS), you can position them exactly as you want on your page to create a visual masterpiece of splendorific satisfaction. Okay, maybe I'm getting carried away, but you can find well-designed sites around the Web that make effective use of div blocks.

Before starting out this section, you need at least a basic knowledge of what CSS positioning is. See Book IV for more on positioning div elements using CSS.

Adding a div element

You can add a div element onto a page by double-clicking the <div> tag in the Toolbox panel. (Or you can choose Insert➪HTML➪<div>.) The div element, displayed as a dotted rectangular box, is added at the current cursor position. See Figure 4-1. Note that Expression Web doesn't let you insert a div element inside a paragraph.

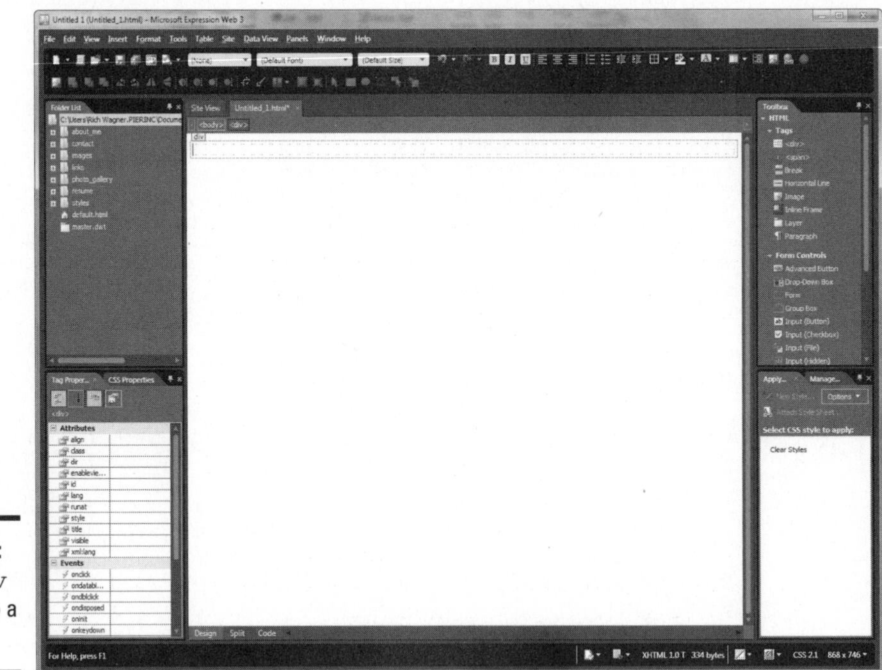

Figure 4-1: Add a div element to a page.

You can add content to the div element or position it. To add content, simply begin typing just as you would in the document body.

Sizing and positioning a div element

You can resize the `div` directly by selecting it and then using the handles on its border to change its dimensions. However, the kind of positioning that you can perform using your mouse is limited — that's because you're working within a flow-based environment in which everything normally is positioned in a left-to-right, top-down manner. Think of how text flows in a word processor like Microsoft Word.

Therefore, to position your `div`, you want to use CSS. If you already have a style defined in a style sheet for your `div`, you can use the Apply Styles panel to apply a style. However, if you don't have a style already created, follow these steps:

1. **Choose Format⇨Position.**

   The Position dialog box appears (see Figure 4-2).

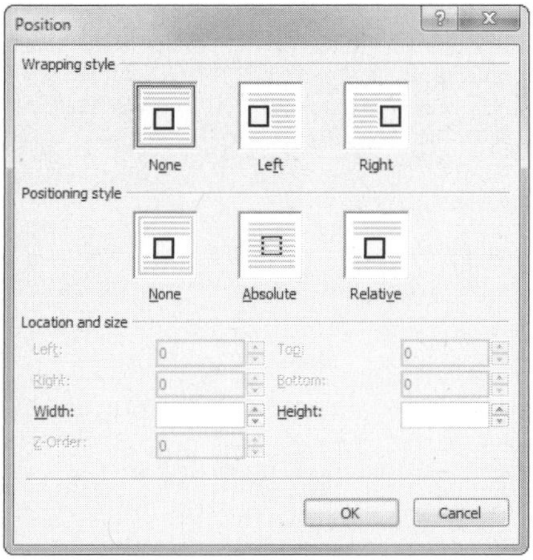

Figure 4-2: Setting the position and size of a div element.

2. **In the Wrapping Style section, specify the type of wrapping you'd like the `div` to have, relative to the document's normal text.**

   The Left and Right settings add a float CSS property to the `div`.

3. **In the Positioning Style section, indicate whether the `div` should be positioned in an absolute, fixed position or placed relative to other elements around it. Or, if you don't want to specify, click None.**

   If you choose Absolute, the `div` element is not wrapped around other elements — which means the `div` element might be overlain above or beneath other content.

In most cases, you want to position the div relative to other elements on the page to ensure that they don't overlap.

4. **If you choose Absolute in Step 3, indicate the Left, Right, Top, and Bottom values in the spaces provided.**

   These values are not used when the div is relatively positioned.

5. **Indicate the desired dimensions of the block in the Width and Height fields.**

6. **Click OK.**

   The div is repositioned and resized to match your settings. Figure 4-3 shows a right-wrapped block sized to 150 x 300 pixels.

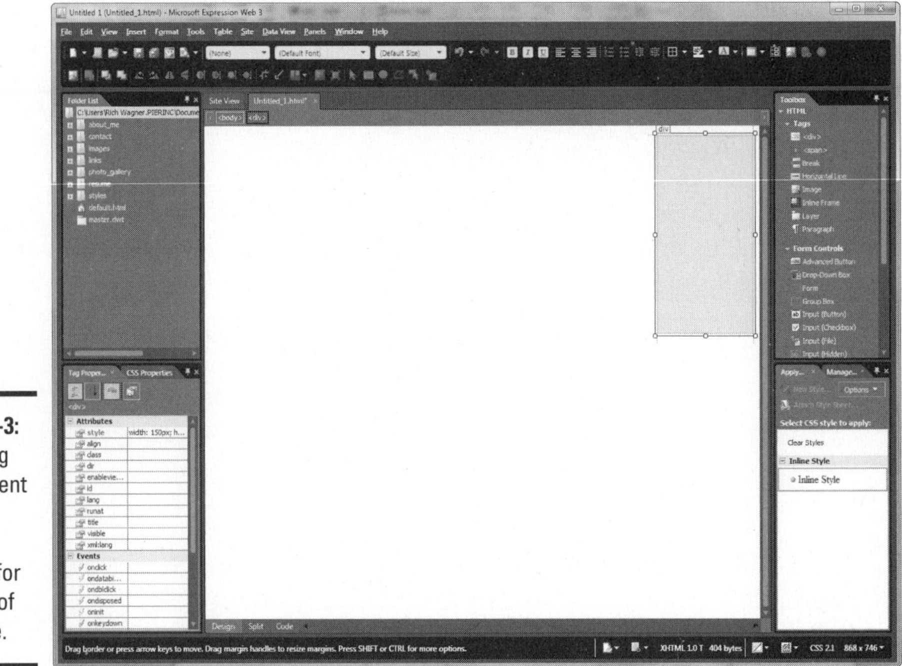

Figure 4-3: A floating div element makes a useful sidebar for the rest of the page.

In addition, as Figure 4-3 shows, the Tag Properties panel displays the properties you set. You can use the panel to tweak these positioning values, if desired.

The Positioning toolbar, as shown in Figure 4-4, is useful for tweaking various aspects of the position and size settings. You can access this by choosing View⇨Toolbars⇨Positioning.

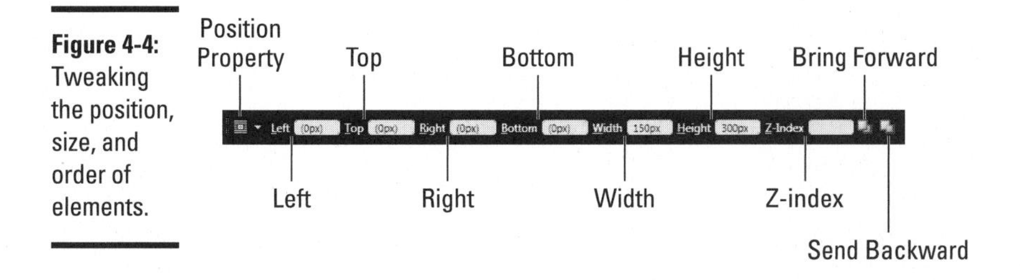

Figure 4-4: Tweaking the position, size, and order of elements.

Formatting a div element

Because a div element is a blocked container of content, it has no "appearance" to it other than the content that is packaged inside it. However, you can use CSS to apply formatting to it — giving it a background, border, margins, and padding.

As you get more and more comfortable with creating CSS style sheets (see Book IV), you can create class-based styles for your div elements so they look uniform throughout your Web site.

However, you can also apply formatting directly to div elements. Here's how:

1. **Select a div element in the Editing window.**

   Figure 4-5 shows the div element that I'll modify.

2. **Activate the CSS Properties panel.**

   If the panel is not visible, choose Format⇨CSS Properties.

   Be sure that the Summary view isn't enabled, or else you can't see all the formatting properties. If the list shows only a handful of properties, click the Summary button to see the full list. (See Figure 4-6.)

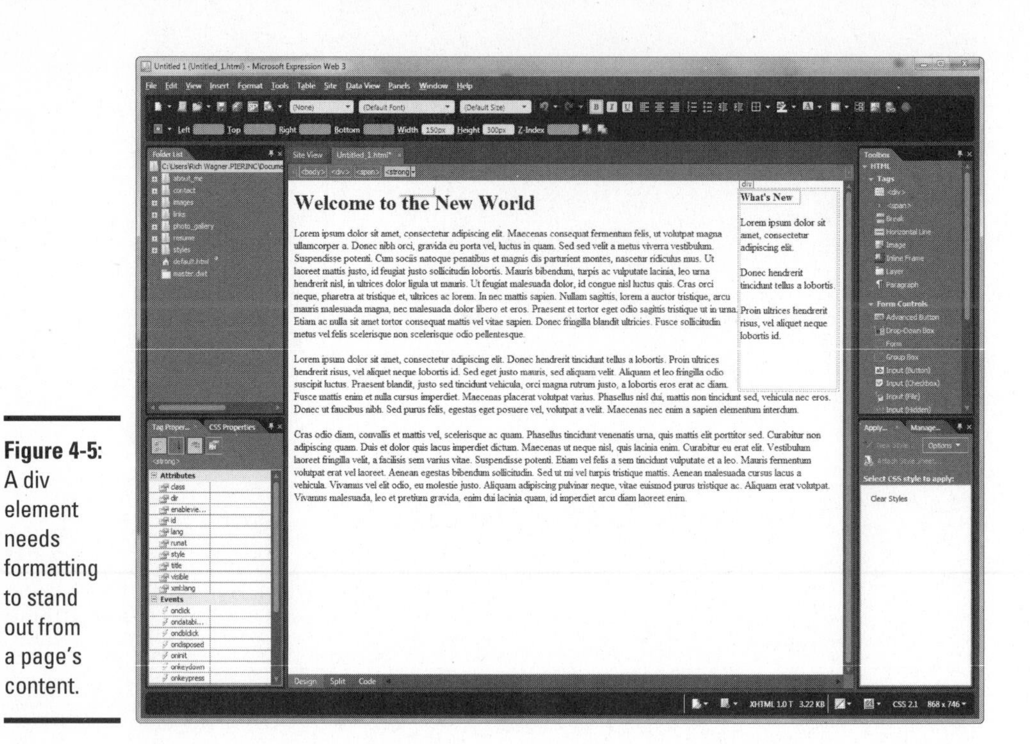

Figure 4-5: A div element needs formatting to stand out from a page's content.

3. **Click the Show Categorized List button on the CSS Properties panel.**
4. **In the Background category, set a background color by choosing a color from the drop-down list.**

   Alternatively, you could specify a background image instead.

5. **In the Border category, expand the `border` property and define its three subproperties.**

   This example sets `border-width` to `thin`, `border-color` to black (`#000000`), and `border-style` to `solid`.

6. **In the Box category, specify the `margin` properties to offset the `div` element from other elements on the page.**

   To move the `div` down from the top of the page, use the `margin-top` property. For this example, I specified `50px`.

   To offset the `div` from the rest of the page content, I defined the left and bottom margins to be `10px`.

I didn't specify the `margin-right` property because I'd like it to be aligned to the side of the page.

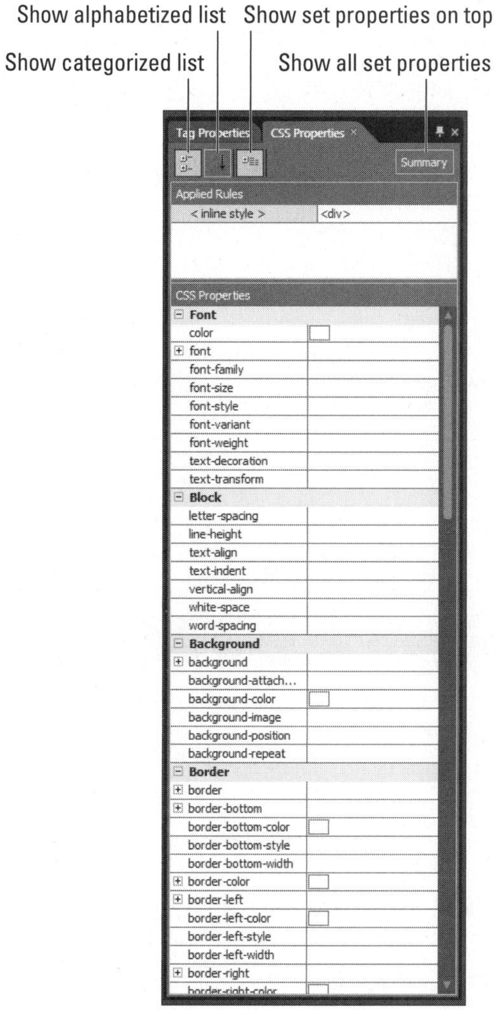

Show alphabetized list Show set properties on top

Show categorized list Show all set properties

Figure 4-6: The CSS Properties panel.

7. **In the Box category, specify the padding properties to offset the content of the `div` with its border.**

   Typing **5px** in the padding property defines the same value for all four sides.

Figure 4-7 shows a newly formatted `div` element.

Figure 4-7: Formatting a div element from the CSS Properties panel.

The CSS Properties panel provides a full list of formatting properties. Glance through the list for a better understanding of the `div`-formatting capabilities of CSS.

Working with Layout Tables

In the earlier days of the Web — before `div` elements — tables were the main ingredient of any page-design recipe. And although `div` elements are now strongly preferred by Web designers as a way to lay out pages, Expression Web does provide layout tables as an alternative for page design.

A *layout table* is just like a normal HTML table you define. However, it has special formatting capabilities inside Expression Web that aren't available with normal tables.

A layout table is designed to have a fixed width rather than a width that varies relative to the size of the browser window.

Inserting a layout table

To add a layout table to your Web page, choose Table➪Layout Tables. The Layout Tables panel appears, as shown in Figure 4-8.

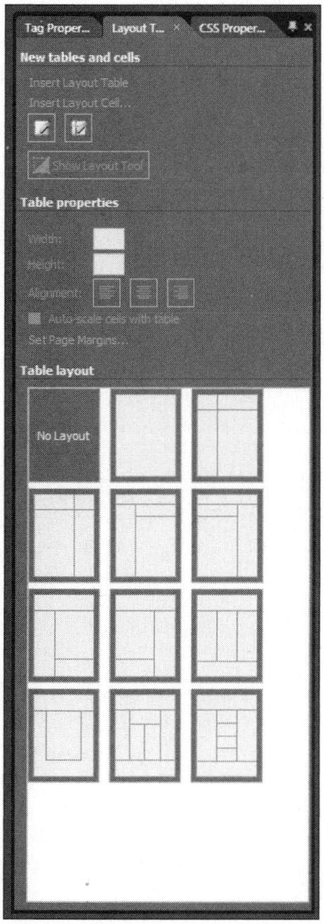

Figure 4-8: The Layout Tables panel.

The Layout Tables panel is where you can draw your table and cells manually, using the Insert Layout Table link and the drawing tools in the New Tables and Cells section. When you add a cell in the desired location, the layout tool adds the appropriate rows and columns automatically to position your cell.

If you prefer, you can use a predefined layout template from the Table Layout list. For most purposes, you can find a layout that suits your needs in the Table Layout list. When you select a layout option, its surrounding border becomes lighter. After you decide on one, click it to insert into the current page, as shown in Figure 4-9.

Figure 4-9: A layout table looks like this when added to the current document.

The layout table is inserted and displayed with the Layout Tool turned on. When the table is selected in the Tag Selector, the dimensions of the various cells are shown in labels surrounding the cells.

TIP

Use the Show Layout Tool button on the Layout Tables panel to toggle between normal Table view and enhanced Layout view.

TIP

Use the Layout Tables panel to specify basic table properties, including width, height, and alignment. Selecting the Auto-Scale Cells with Table check box causes the cells to expand and collapse based on the table size.

Editing layout cells

You can perform several different tasks when in Layout mode:

- **Resize cells.** You can also resize the various table cells by dragging the borders to the desired size with your mouse and then moving them into a new position.

  Resizing your layout table directly with your mouse is arguably the handiest aspect of the Layout Tables feature.

- **Adjust row and column properties.** With the entire table selected (or a single cell), the row/column sizes are shown on-screen in label boxes. Click the down arrow on a box to specify various column and row options.

- **Insert a layout cell.** Click the Insert Layout Cell link to add a new cell to the layout table. You can specify the size and location of the new cell in the Insert Layout Cell dialog box. You can also add a layout cell by clicking the Draw Layout Cell button and using your mouse to draw the cell.

- **Delete a layout cell.** To remove a cell from the layout table, select the cell and then right-click. From the pop-up menu, choose Delete⇨Delete Cells.

Chapter 5: "Been There, Formatted That" with Dynamic Web Templates

In This Chapter

- **Understanding Dynamic Web Templates**
- **Creating a new Dynamic Web Template**
- **Marking editable regions**
- **Attaching and detaching Dynamic Web Templates**

We humans just don't like to repeat something we've already done. "Been there, done that" is the familiar saying. That's why Microsoft Word, for example, has its ubiquitous `Normal.dot` template that allows you to specify the default formatting of new documents you create. Or, if you're really adventurous, you can create your own customized templates for more specialized needs.

Not to be outdone, Expression Web has its own version of "been there, formatted that." In this chapter, you'll discover how to work with Dynamic Web Templates to help you maintain a consistent page design throughout your site.

Understanding Dynamic Web Templates

A *Dynamic Web Template* in Expression Web is an HTML document that contains a page layout, formatting, and page elements. After you create a Dynamic Web Template, you can attach it to new pages. The new documents take on these settings and layout. Later, when you want to make changes, edit the template; all the created documents are updated.

Keep the following in mind when working with Dynamic Web Templates:

- ✦ You can create your own customized Dynamic Web Template or use a premade one when you create a new site from a template.
- ✦ A Dynamic Web Template file has a `.dwt` extension and is normally stored in a site's root folder.

✦ A Dynamic Web Template is divided into editable and non-editable regions. You can specify which regions in your template can be edited or have content added. Other parts of the page are locked.

If you look at the source code of the template, editable regions are enclosed with <!-- #BeginEditable --> and <!-- #EndEditable --> comments.

✦ The document head has a section that you can modify by going into Code view.

✦ You can also go into Code view to modify any of the non-editable regions. However, when you return to Design view, Expression Web notifies you of what you did and asks whether to discard these changes the next time the document is updated from the template.

Creating a Dynamic Web Template

Because a Dynamic Web Template is a special kind of HTML document, creating one is quite similar to creating an ordinary Web page. Here's how to create one:

1. **Choose File⇨New⇨Page.**

   The New dialog box appears, as shown in Figure 5-1.

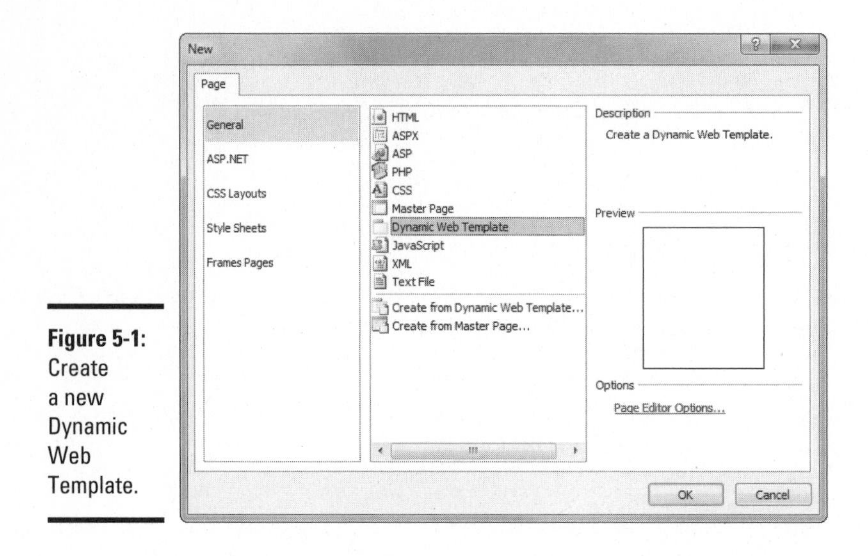

Figure 5-1: Create a new Dynamic Web Template.

2. **From the General group, choose the Dynamic Web Template item from the list.**

3. **Click OK.**

   The `Untitled_1.dwt` document appears in the Editing window (see Figure 5-2).

   Expression Web adds a `div` element to the document body and marks it as an editable region.

   If you find the `div` element helpful, use it. Otherwise feel free to delete it and mark your editable regions later.

Figure 5-2: A new template document is now ready for customizing.

4. **Edit the design and layout of your Dynamic Web Template.**

   With `div` elements or layout tables, organize your template into non-editable and editable zones.

5. **Add content and features that you'd like to appear on every page created from the Dynamic Web Template.**

6. **Add placeholder text in a region that you intend to mark as editable.**

7. **Select the editable region (`div`, table cell, text selection, paragraph, and so on) with your mouse.**

8. **Right-click and choose Manage Editable Regions from the pop-up menu.**

   The Editable Regions dialog box appears, as shown in Figure 5-3.

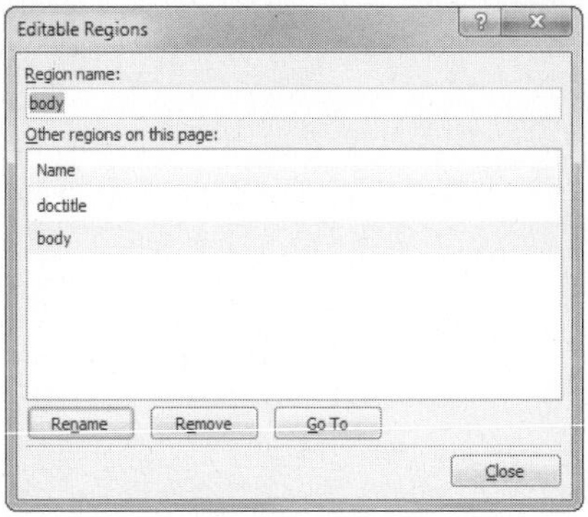

Figure 5-3: Add a new editable region.

9. **Enter the name of the editable region in the Region Name field.**
10. **Click Close.**

    Expression Web marks the selection as an editable region. If the region has no content, the region's name is added in parentheses as canned text.
11. **Repeat Steps 6–10 for each editable region on your page.**

    Note that any areas you don't mark as editable can't be edited.

    Your basic Dynamic Web Template is ready to go.
12. **Choose File⇨Save.**

    The Save As dialog box appears.
13. **Navigate to the desired site folder you want to add the template to.**
14. **Enter a name in the File Name field.**
15. **Click Save.**

    Expression Web saves the Dynamic Web Template, adding a `.dwt` extension.

You can also transform an HTML document you have already created into a Dynamic Web Template. To create a template from an existing page, follow these steps:

1. **Open an existing page into the editing window.**
2. **Remove any content that you don't want to be part of the Dynamic Web Template.**
3. **Select the content region that you want to be editable.**

4. **Right-click and choose Manage Editable Regions from the pop-up menu.**

   The Editable Regions dialog box appears.

5. **Enter the name of the editable region in the Region Name field.**

6. **Click Add.**

   Expression Web marks the selection as an editable region. If the region has no content, the region's name is added in parentheses as canned text.

7. **Repeat Steps 3–6 for each editable region you'd like to define.**

   Your basic Dynamic Web Template is ready to go.

8. **Choose File⇨Save As.**

   The Save As dialog box appears.

9. **From the Save as Type drop-down list, choose Dynamic Web Template (*.dwt).**

10. **Navigate to the desired folder in the Folder box.**

11. **Add a name in the File Name field.**

12. **Click Save.**

    Expression Web saves the document as a template and adds a `.dwt` extension to it.

Using a Dynamic Web Template to Create a New Page

After you build your template, you're ready to create new pages based on it. To do so, follow these steps:

1. **Choose File⇨New Page.**

   The New dialog box appears.

2. **From the General category, click the Create from Dynamic Web Template item.**

   Figure 5-4 shows the dialog box.

3. **Click OK.**

   The Attach Dynamic Web Template dialog box is shown.

4. **Locate the desired `.dwt` file in the Folder box.**

Figure 5-4: Create a new document from a Dynamic Web Template.

5. **Click Open.**

   A new document based on the Dynamic Web Template appears in the Editing window.

6. **Modify the content inside of the editable regions of the page.**

   You can't modify the content of non-editable regions unless you go into Code view.

7. **Choose File⇨Save.**

   Save your document as you would a normal Web page.

Making Changes to Your Dynamic Web Template

The "dynamic" part of the Dynamic Web Template is the linkage maintained between a template and the documents created from it. As a result, when you modify a template and then save it, Expression Web asks you whether you want to update all related documents as well.

Be careful making changes to the template; any updates change all of the Web pages on your site that are based on that template. To modify a template and then update all documents attached to that template, follow these steps:

1. **Choose File⇨Open to open the Dynamic Web Template `.dwt` file in the Editing window.**

   Alternatively, you can open the template by using one of two other options:

- *If you have the site open that contains your template:* Click the Web Site button on the Editing window's tabbed pane and then double-click the template in the folder list.
- *If you have a Web page open in the Editing window that is already attached to the template:* Choose Format⇨Dynamic Web Templates⇨Open Attached Dynamic Web Template.

The Dynamic Web Template opens in the Editing window.

2. **Edit the document.**
3. **Choose File⇨Save.**

   A message box appears. It asks whether you would like to update the attached documents at this time.

4. **Click Yes to confirm the update action. If you don't want to confirm the update (for whatever reason), click No.**

   If you click Yes, Expression Web goes through all the attached documents and updates them as needed. Changes are reflected the next time you open them.

REMEMBER

Upload the changed files to the Web server.

Attaching and Detaching a Dynamic Web Template

As you can see in the earlier "Using a Dynamic Web Template to Create a New Page" section, when you create a new document based on a Dynamic Web Template, you attach the template to the page. However, Expression Web also allows you to attach a template to an existing page.

To attach a template to an opened document, follow these steps:

1. **Choose Format⇨Dynamic Web Template⇨Attach Dynamic Web Template.**

   The Attach Template dialog box appears.

2. **Choose the desired template.**
3. **Click Open.**

   Expression Web evaluates the editable regions of the current document with the Dynamic Web Template and seeks to map between the two. When the two don't match, the Match Editable Regions dialog box appears (as shown in Figure 5-5).

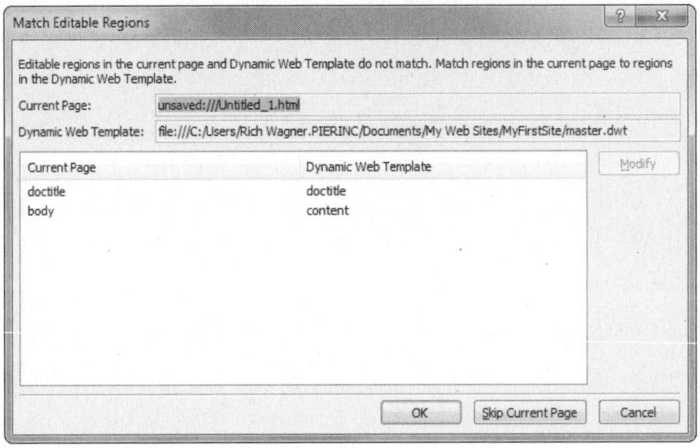

Figure 5-5: "Match-maker, match-maker, make me a match. . . ."

4. **Match the regions as best as possible to retain the existing content.**
5. **Click OK.**

   Expression Web attaches the Dynamic Web Template and makes the appropriate changes.

If you need to detach a document from a Dynamic Web Template, choose Dynamic Web Template⇨Detach Dynamic Web Template from the menu. Expression Web breaks the link and removes all traces of the former Dynamic Web Template.

Book VIII

Adobe Dreamweaver

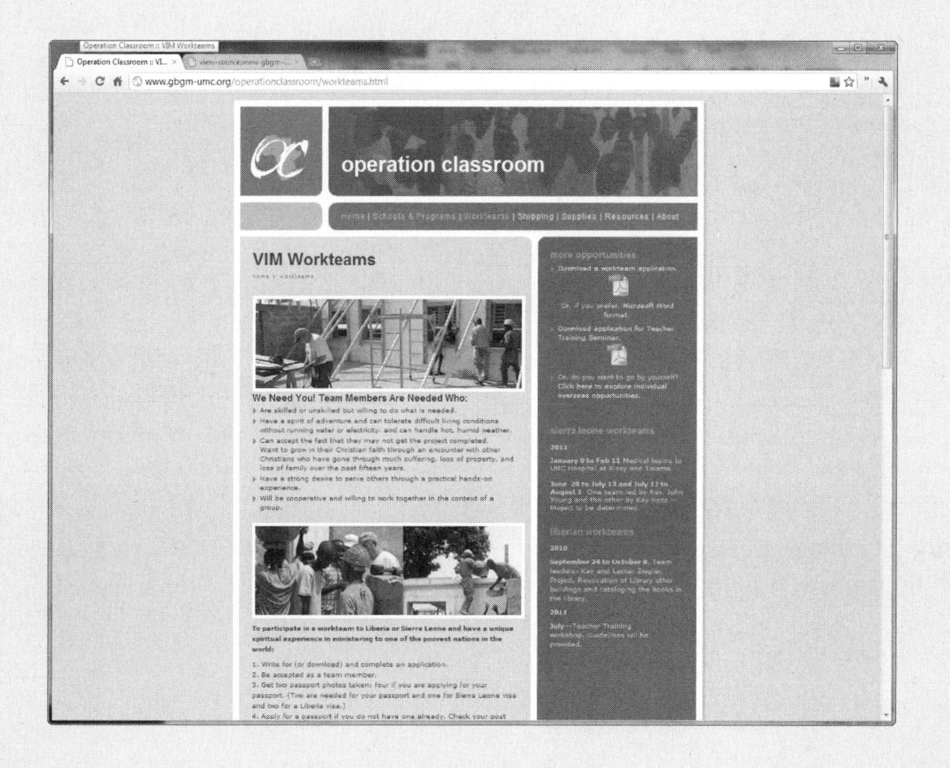

Contents at a Glance

Chapter 1: Getting to Know Dreamweaver

In This Chapter

- **Working with the Dreamweaver workspace**
- **Exploring the Document window**
- **Using toolbars, inspectors, and panels**
- **Customizing the workspace**

Adobe Dreamweaver CS5 is the *de facto* standard Web-site design tool for both Microsoft Windows and Mac OS X. Web professionals use Dreamweaver because of its power, features, and extensibility. If you're a beginner with the product, don't feel shellshocked. You can quickly become productive in the Dreamweaver visual environment, all while gradually discovering the many capabilities it has to offer.

This chapter introduces you to Dreamweaver CS5 and gives you a guided tour around the major features of its workspace. I don't talk yet about how to use Dreamweaver to create Web pages. First I want you to "kick the tires" of Dreamweaver and get comfortable with its working environment.

Introducing the Dreamweaver Workspace

When you launch Dreamweaver, a welcome screen is displayed, as shown in Figure 1-1. From this screen, you can start creating a new page or open an existing file.

By default, the welcome screen appears every time you start Dreamweaver. To bypass this window, select the Don't Show Again check box before proceeding.

Click the HTML button under the Create New section, or click any other option you want to select. The new file is created inside the Dreamweaver workspace (see Figure 1-2).

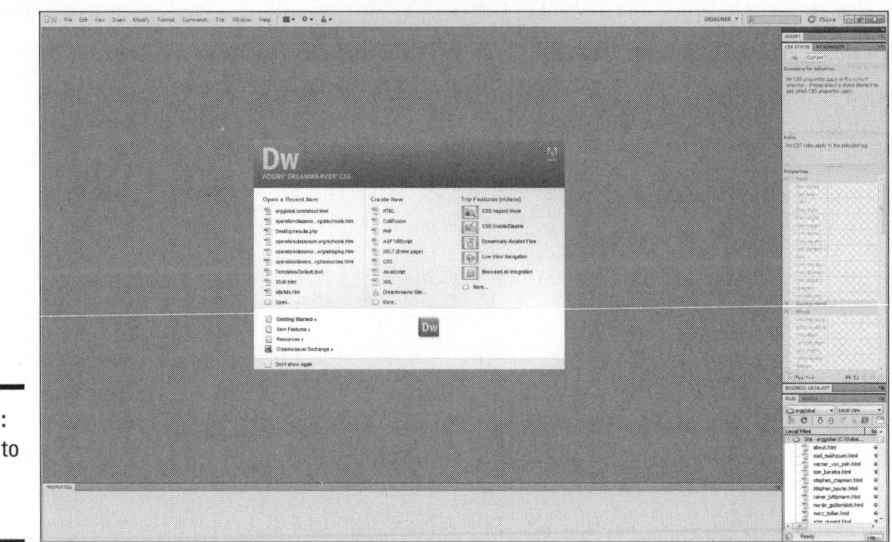

Figure 1-1: Welcome to Dreamweaver.

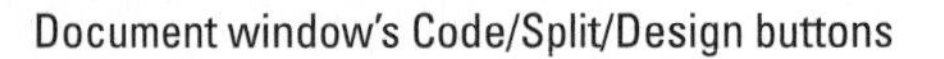

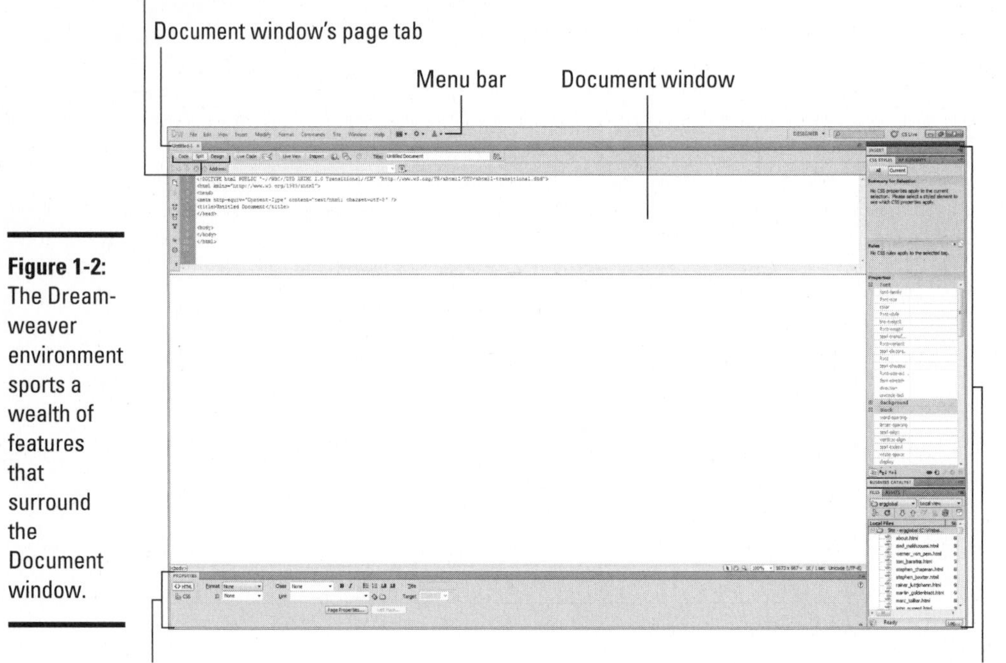

Figure 1-2: The Dreamweaver environment sports a wealth of features that surround the Document window.

Windows and Mac versions: Any difference?

The Windows and Mac versions of Dreamweaver are nearly identical in functionality. In fact, the only noticeable difference between the two is arguably that the Windows version keeps the panels, the toolbars, and the Document window inside the main Dreamweaver application window. However, following Mac interface conventions, the Mac version has no main application window. The Insert panel, Document window, and panels all float around the desktop.

You compose and design your Web pages in the Document window. The bars, inspectors, and panel windows that surround the document help you construct or manage your document or site.

Exploring the Document Window

The Document window is where you spend almost your time as you work in Dreamweaver. As you get started, familiarize yourself with several parts of the document environment. Figure 1-3 highlights the major features.

Perhaps the most important feature to notice as you begin to work with Dreamweaver is the use of Code, Split, and Design buttons on the top Document bar. You use these buttons to select which mode to work in:

- **Code:** The document can be viewed in Code mode, which reveals the HTML code of the page (see Figure 1-4). Don't worry if this code looks intimidating; you can avoid this mode for now, if you like. After you read Book III, you'll probably spend more time working in Code view.
- **Split:** By default, Dreamweaver displays Split mode (refer Figure 1-3), which displays both Design and Code views.
- **Design:** Design mode is a visually oriented look at the page, which is similar to (but not exactly) how it will appear in the browser.

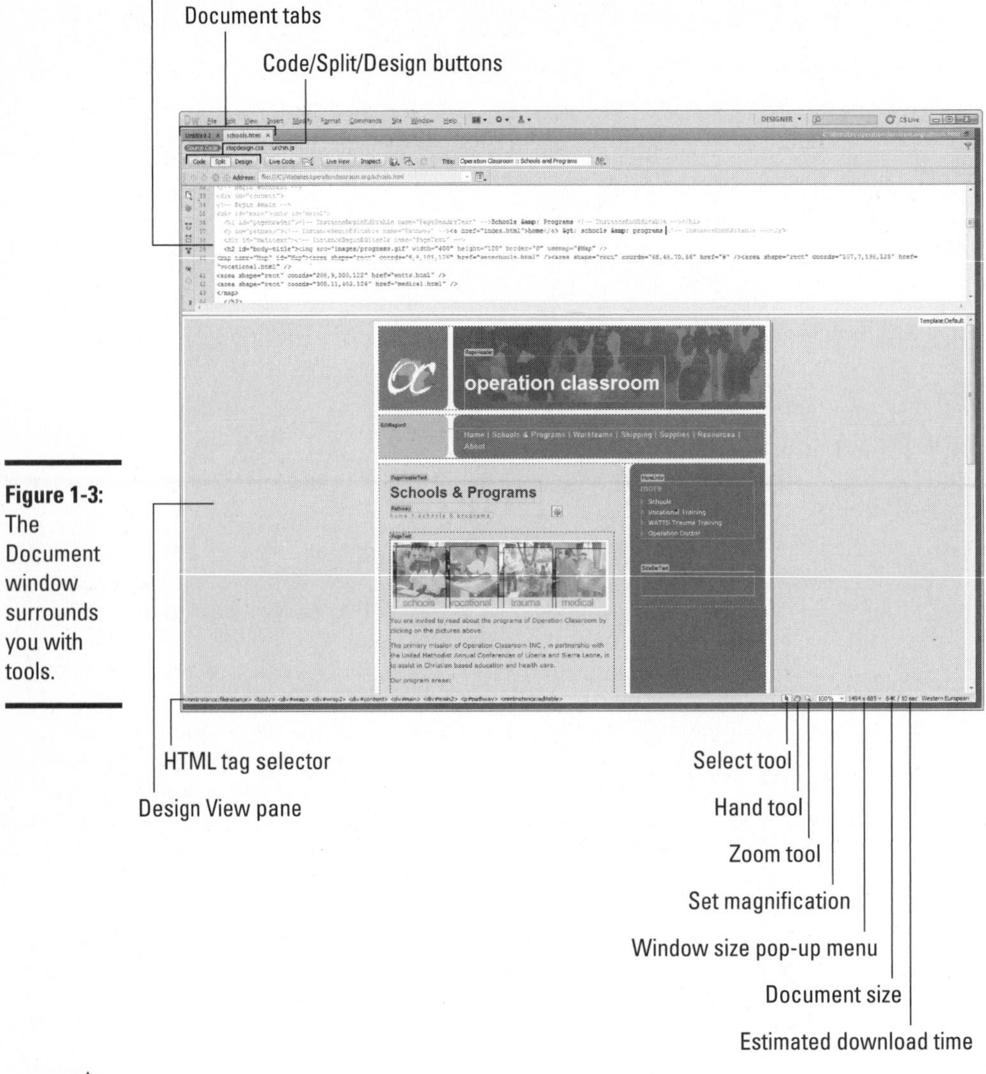

Figure 1-3: The Document window surrounds you with tools.

You can also access these views by choosing View⇨Code, View⇨Design, or View⇨Code and Design.

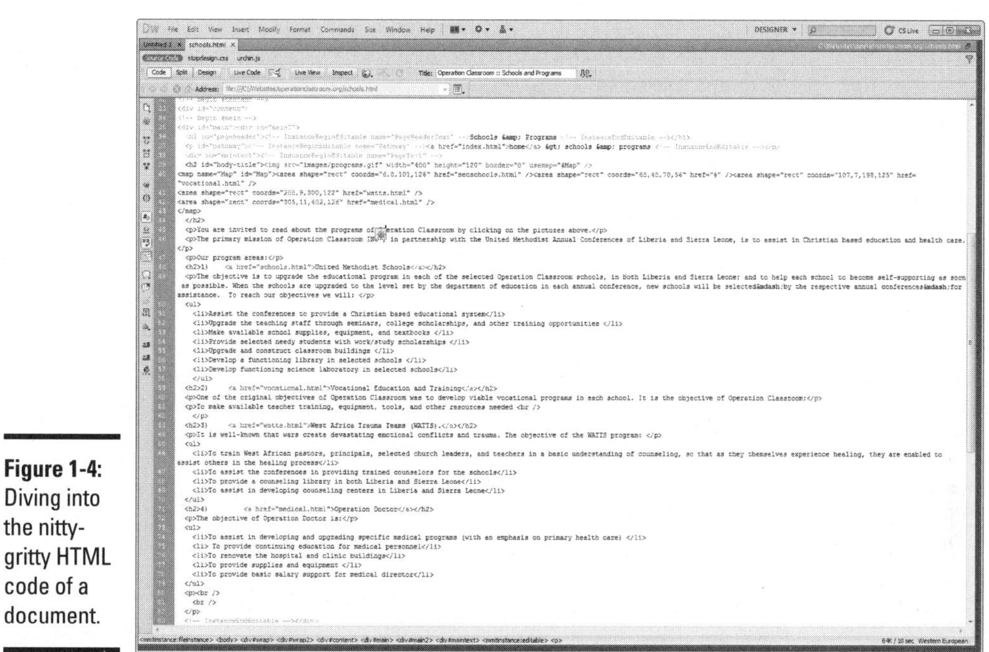

Figure 1-4: Diving into the nitty-gritty HTML code of a document.

Working with the Toolbars

When you first start using Dreamweaver, you may be overwhelmed by the sheer number of menus, bars, inspectors, panels, and other controls that can surround the Document window. You make sense of them all as you work within Dreamweaver — but in this section, I outline the three key toolbars.

The Document window displays three toolbars:

✦ **Document:** This toolbar (see Figure 1-5) is used to control basic document-level functionality. (Chapter 2 in this minibook shows you how to work with several of these commands.)

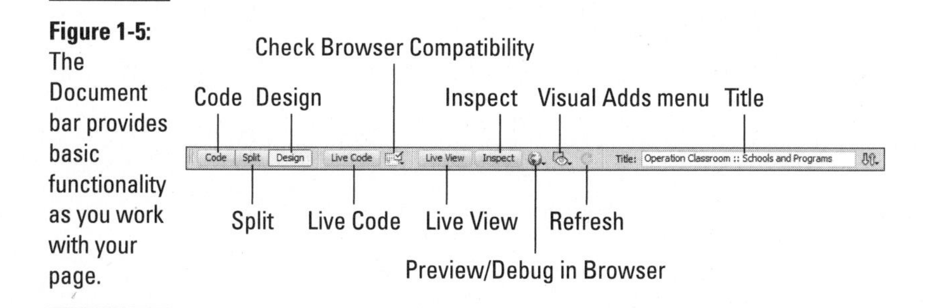

Figure 1-5: The Document bar provides basic functionality as you work with your page.

✦ **Standard:** This toolbar, shown in Figure 1-6, works much like the basic toolbar in Microsoft Word: You can create a new file, save the existing one, and perform standard editing operations (such as cut, copy, paste, and undo).

Browse in Bridge
Cut
Redo
New
Save All
Paste
Open
Print
Undo
Save
Copy

Figure 1-6: Stop the presses. Basic commands are available on the Standard toolbar.

✦ **Style Rendering:** You can use this toolbar (see to Figure 1-7) to specify different CSS style sheets if you're outputting your Web page to multiple devices (standard Web, handheld, printer, or TV).

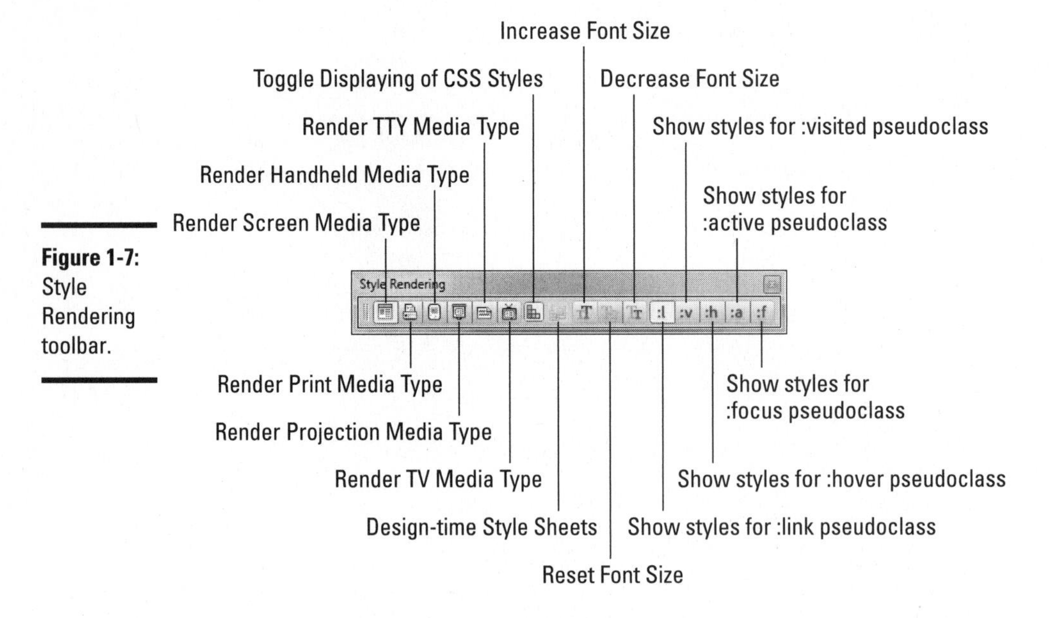

Figure 1-7: Style Rendering toolbar.

By default, the Standard and Style Rendering toolbars are hidden; you have to make them visible before you can use them. You can show or hide any of the toolbars by choosing View⇨Toolbars and then selecting or deselecting a toolbar from the list.

Alternatively, if a toolbar is displayed, right-click (Ctrl-click on the Mac) it to display the Toolbar pop-up menu and then toggle the toolbar of your choice.

Checking Out the Properties Inspector

You use the Properties inspector for viewing and setting the most common properties (or attributes) of the selected element inside the active document. Because every page element you work with has different attributes, the Properties inspector is updated each time you select a different element.

The Properties inspector has two modes: Basic and Expanded. Figures 1-8 and 1-9 show Basic and Expanded modes, respectively, for an image element. Basic mode shows the core set of properties, and Expanded mode displays an additional set of lesser used properties. You can toggle between these modes by clicking the expander arrow in the lower-right corner of the Properties inspector.

Figure 1-8: Basic properties in the Properties inspector.

Figure 1-9: Expanded properties in the Properties inspector.

Toggle the visibility of the Properties inspector by choosing Window⇨Properties. Windows users can also press Ctrl+F3, and Mac users can press ⌘+F3.

The Insert Panel

One of the most common of the panels that you will use is the Insert panel (shown in Figure 1-10). You can use it to add various elements to your page. It's visually separate from the Document window, although it always acts on the active document.

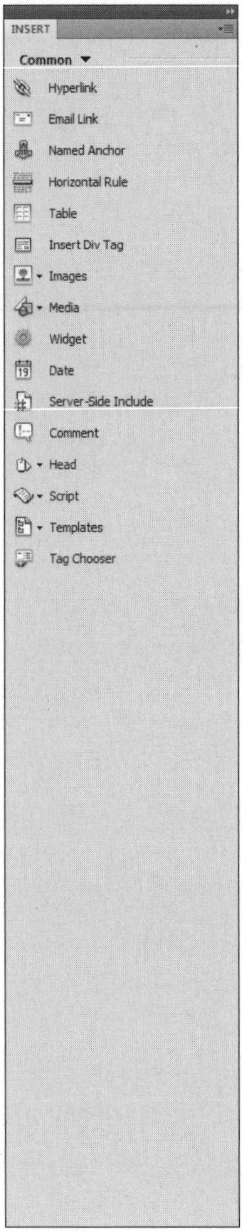

Figure 1-10: Use the Insert panel to add elements to your page.

The Insert panel has eight groups:

- ✦ **Common:** These elements are the most common elements you drop on most pages, including links, images, and tables.
- ✦ **Layout:** These elements are related to the layout of a page, including `div` and `table` elements. (Check out Chapter 4 in this minibook for full details on working with the layout controls.)
- ✦ **Forms:** All elements that you can place and work with in forms are located in this section. (Chapter 5 in this minibook covers how to work with forms in Dreamweaver.)
- ✦ **Data:** These elements relate to displaying server-side data inside a Web page. (Most of the functionality in this section of the Insert panel is beyond the scope of this book.)
- ✦ **Spry:** *Spry* is a framework for the Ajax technology, which allows you to incorporate XML data into your pages without refreshing the entire page. The elements in this section all place Spry widgets in your page. (Again, because of the complexities of working with Ajax, I don't cover it in nitpicky detail — though you can find out more about Ajax in Book V, Chapter 7; for a deeper plunge into the subject, try *Ajax For Dummies,* by Steve Holzner, PhD.)
- ✦ **InContext Editing:** Ignore this panel. These elements are used for creating editable and repeatable regions on your page that can be integrated with Adobe's now-discontinued InContext Editing service.
- ✦ **Text:** These elements are for formatting text inside your page. You find bold, italic, headings, and all the usual text suspects here. (Check out Chapter 3 in this minibook for more on working with text.)
- ✦ **Favorites:** The Favorites section is a handy depository for you to place all the elements you use most.

To add or remove elements, right-click (or Ctrl-click on the Mac) the Favorites tab and choose Customize Favorites from the pop-up menu. The Customize Favorite Objects dialog box is displayed. Use the controls in the dialog box to set the elements, and then click OK.

Working with Panels

Dreamweaver sports several panels that provide additional functionality to help you in designing and managing your Web site. You can display these panels in their own, floating window or grouped into panel groups. When a panel is docked with a group, it appears as a tab inside the panel group window.

Here are some panels you're likely to find particularly useful as you get started with Dreamweaver:

✦ **CSS Styles (see Figure 1-11):** View and edit the CSS rules and properties of an element or page. (See Chapter 6 in this minibook for more on working with CSS style sheets in Dreamweaver.)

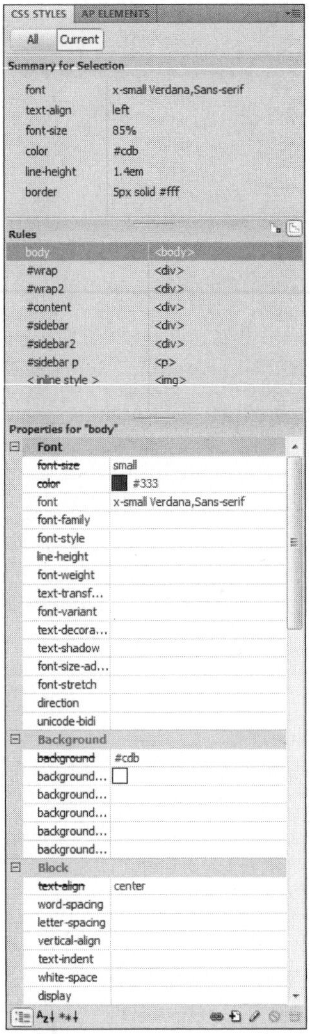

Figure 1-11: The CSS Styles panel provides a visual way to work with style sheets.

✦ **Files (see Figure 1-12):** Use the Files panel to view and manage the files of your Dreamweaver site. When working on individual Web pages, you can work with the Files panel in much the same way you work with a standard file-system dialog box. However, when you work with sites in Dreamweaver (see Chapter 8 in this minibook), you can use the Files panel to work with files on both local and remote sites.

FILES

operationclassroom | Local view

Local Files	Size	Type	Modified	Checke
Site - operationclassr...		Folder	6/24/2010 11:19 PM	-
index.html	9KB	HTML File	6/24/2010 11:19 PM	
workteams.html	10KB	HTML File	6/24/2010 11:15 PM	
application52520...	18KB	Microsoft...	5/25/2010 11:25 PM	
slschools.html	18KB	HTML File	4/28/2010 12:06 ...	
Kissy-Nutrition-Pr...	72KB	Adobe A...	4/28/2010 12:00 ...	
kissy_needs.pdf	56KB	Adobe A...	4/27/2010 11:58 PM	
schools.html	7KB	HTML File	4/4/2010 9:23 PM	
watts.html	5KB	HTML File	4/4/2010 9:22 PM	
vocational.html	5KB	HTML File	4/4/2010 9:22 PM	
supplies.html	4KB	HTML File	4/4/2010 9:22 PM	
speakers.html	4KB	HTML File	4/4/2010 9:22 PM	
shipping.html	14KB	HTML File	4/4/2010 9:22 PM	
secschools.html	4KB	HTML File	4/4/2010 9:22 PM	
resources.html	6KB	HTML File	4/4/2010 9:22 PM	
palaver.html	9KB	HTML File	4/4/2010 9:22 PM	
medical.html	9KB	HTML File	4/4/2010 9:22 PM	
localvol.html	5KB	HTML File	4/4/2010 9:22 PM	
libschools.html	13KB	HTML File	4/4/2010 9:22 PM	
kits.html	8KB	HTML File	4/4/2010 9:22 PM	
individual.html	4KB	HTML File	4/4/2010 9:22 PM	
about.html	7KB	HTML File	4/4/2010 9:22 PM	
2010vbs.pdf	28KB	Adobe A...	4/4/2010 9:11 PM	
2010-ingathering...	51KB	Adobe A...	4/4/2010 8:35 PM	
vision-2020-strat...	181KB	Adobe A...	3/26/2010 7:16 AM	
lent-offering.pdf	40KB	Adobe A...	1/26/2010 11:05 ...	
vimapp.pdf	10KB	Adobe A...	1/21/2010 12:17 ...	
teacherapp.pdf	11KB	Adobe A...	1/18/2010 11:12 PM	
alternative_to_c...	72KB	Adobe A...	11/13/2009 10:1...	
alternative-09.pdf	72KB	Adobe A...	11/13/2009 10:1...	
nutritional_report...	47KB	Adobe A...	8/31/2009 8:31 PM	
ganta_needs.pdf	44KB	Adobe A...	8/31/2009 8:28 PM	
ganta_report.pdf	193KB	Adobe A...	8/31/2009 8:23 PM	
2009_05_01_hp_...	13KB	HTML File	6/11/2009 9:17 PM	
2009_04_01_hp_...	12KB	HTML File	6/11/2009 9:17 PM	
2009_03_01_hp_...	13KB	HTML File	6/11/2009 9:17 PM	
2009_02_01_hp_...	13KB	HTML File	6/11/2009 9:17 PM	
2009_01_01_hp_...	27KB	HTML File	6/11/2009 9:17 PM	
2008_12_01_hp_...	12KB	HTML File	6/11/2009 9:17 PM	
2008_11_01_hp_...	11KB	HTML File	6/11/2009 9:17 PM	
2008_10_01_hp_...	11KB	HTML File	6/11/2009 9:17 PM	
2008_09_01_hp_...	15KB	HTML File	6/11/2009 9:17 PM	
2008_08_01_hp_...	13KB	HTML File	6/11/2009 9:17 PM	
2008_07_01_hp_...	13KB	HTML File	6/11/2009 9:17 PM	
2008_06_01_hp_...	13KB	HTML File	6/11/2009 9:17 PM	
2008_05_01_hp_...	14KB	HTML File	6/11/2009 9:17 PM	
2008_04_01_hp_...	14KB	HTML File	6/11/2009 9:17 PM	
2008_03_01_hp_...	14KB	HTML File	6/11/2009 9:17 PM	

File activity complete. | Log...

Figure 1-12: Files provides quick access to your site files.

- **Tag inspector (see Figure 1-13):** View and edit attributes of the current HTML element in your document. You can think of the Tag inspector as something like the Properties inspector "on steroids" because it lists every attribute in a categorized (or, optionally, alphabetical) list.

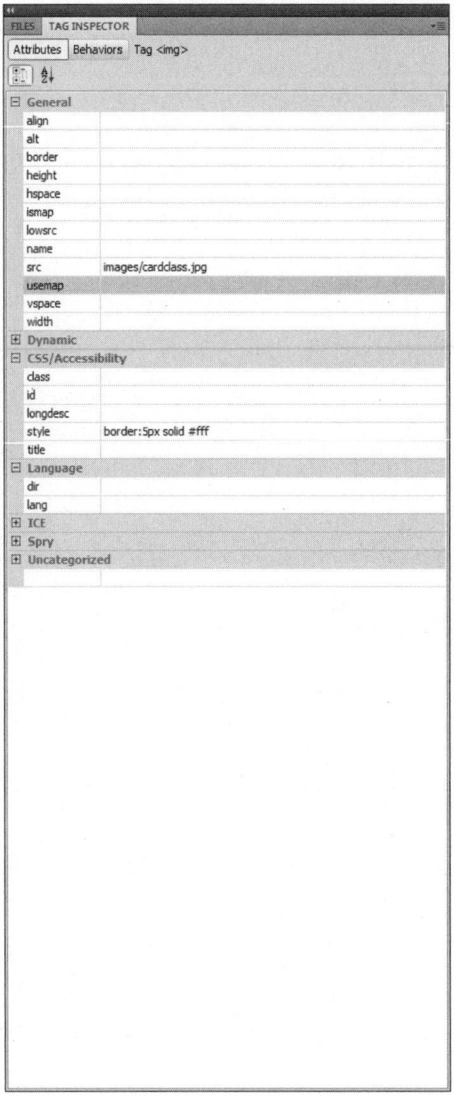

Figure 1-13: Get the full lowdown on any element with the Tag inspector.

When you're starting out, you'll probably find the Properties inspector easier to work with. However, the Tag inspector is a helpful place to look for hard-to-remember properties.

- **Results:** The Results panel (see Figure 1-14) displays the results of searches and other reporting tools, such as the Browser Compatibility Check, Link Checker, and FTP Log. By default, the Results panel is displayed in the bottom of the window, under the Properties inspector.

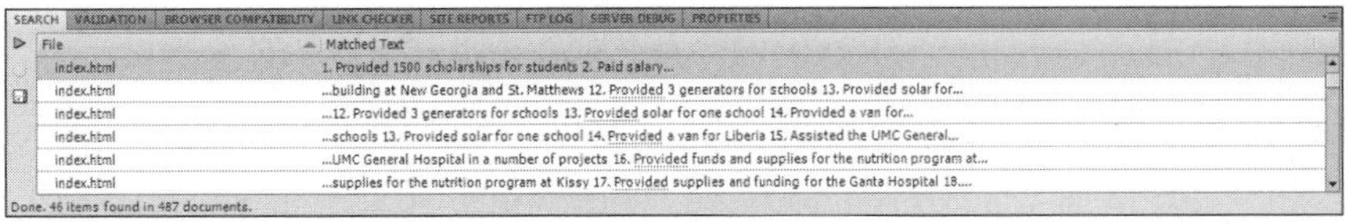

Figure 1-14: The Results panel displays results of searches.

- **Reference (see Figure 1-15):** The Reference panel is your home base for online reference documentation for HTML, CSS, JavaScript, and other Web technologies.

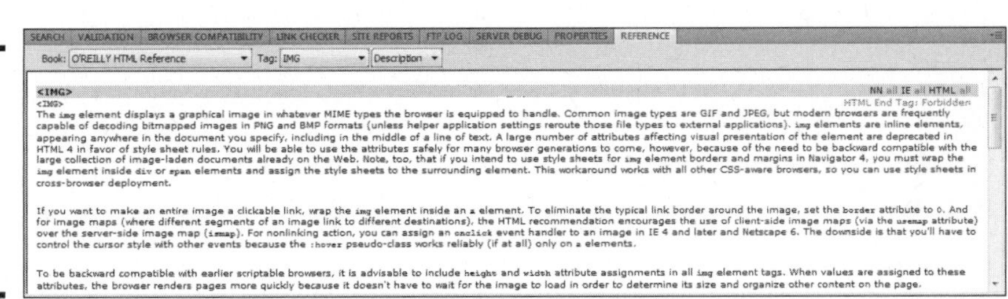

Figure 1-15: Become a Web expert inside the Reference panel.

By default, the Reference panel is part of the Results panel, but you can move it elsewhere by grouping it with another panel group (or by itself in a new group).

- **History (see Figure 1-16):** Think of the History panel as a beefed-up Undo/Redo list. You can use it to retrace your steps to undo changes you made to the document. If you want to get fancy, you can retrace your steps or even copy a series of steps and use them again.

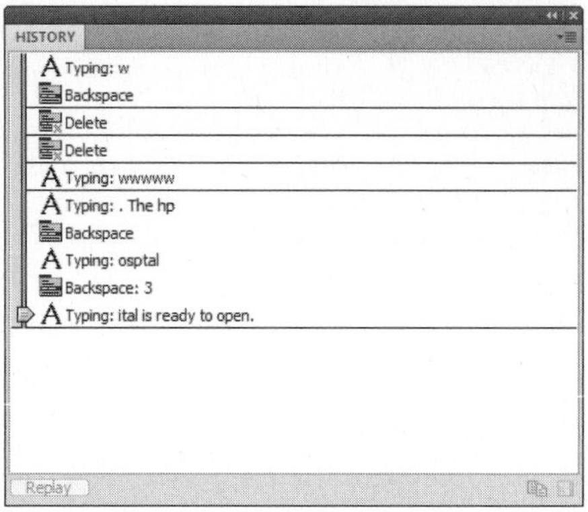

Figure 1-16: History will teach you something.

✦ **Code inspector (see Figure 1-17):** The Code inspector pops up a mini-window that displays the HTML code of the document. The active element that you're working with is selected for you in the window.

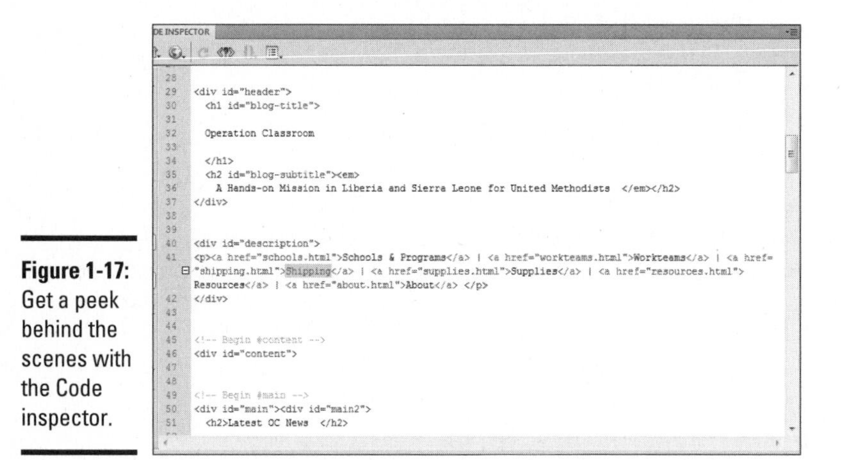

Figure 1-17: Get a peek behind the scenes with the Code inspector.

Customizing Your Workspace

Perhaps the biggest attraction of Dreamweaver is the wealth of features at your disposal as you're creating your Web site. However, because you can display so many elements in panel groups and toolbars, you can quickly clutter your work area with a set of features you never use. Fortunately, in Dreamweaver, you can tweak your working environment just the way you like it and then save your workspace for future use.

Showing and hiding a panel

You can access all panels from the Window menu. You can show or hide a panel by selecting its menu item from the list. You can also hide a panel that's open by right-clicking its tab and choosing the Close *PanelName group* command from the pop-up menu.

Press F4 to toggle the visibility of all panels and inspectors. This keyboard shortcut is useful for temporarily eliminating distractions as you work on your Web page.

Undocking and docking a panel group

In the Windows version of Dreamweaver, panel groups are normally docked at one side of the application window. To undock a panel group and create a floating panel group, click the dotted bar in the upper-left area of the panel group's title bar and drag it onto the Document window. The panel group undocks and floats on top of the workspace.

To redock, drag the panel group to the side of the application window to which you want to dock the group. Dreamweaver recognizes your intention and redocks the group to that part of the window.

Note that in the Mac version, panel groups always float.

Removing a panel from a group

To move a panel from a panel group, right-click the Panel tab and choose the Group *PanelName* With menu item. The submenu displays other panel groups. Choose one of them (or choose the New Panel Group item if you want the group to go off on its own). For an even easier method, drag the panel tab and drop it to a new location.

Saving a workspace layout

After you arrange the panels, toolbars, and inspectors the way you want them, choose Window➪Workspace Layout➪Save Current. In the Save Workspace Layout dialog box, give your new, customized workspace a name and click OK. The new layout is added to the Workspace Layout list. Dreamweaver uses this new layout each time it starts until you change it. You can display these panels in their own floating windows or grouped into panel groups. When a panel is docked with a group, it appears as a tab inside that panel group's window.

You can customize your workspace layout to make effective use of the available screen space. If you have a small monitor, you can eliminate all the extras and focus on the bare essentials for creating a Web site. However, if you have a larger screen, you can take advantage of the extra space to create the ultimate Web-site design environment, such as the one shown in Figure 1-18.

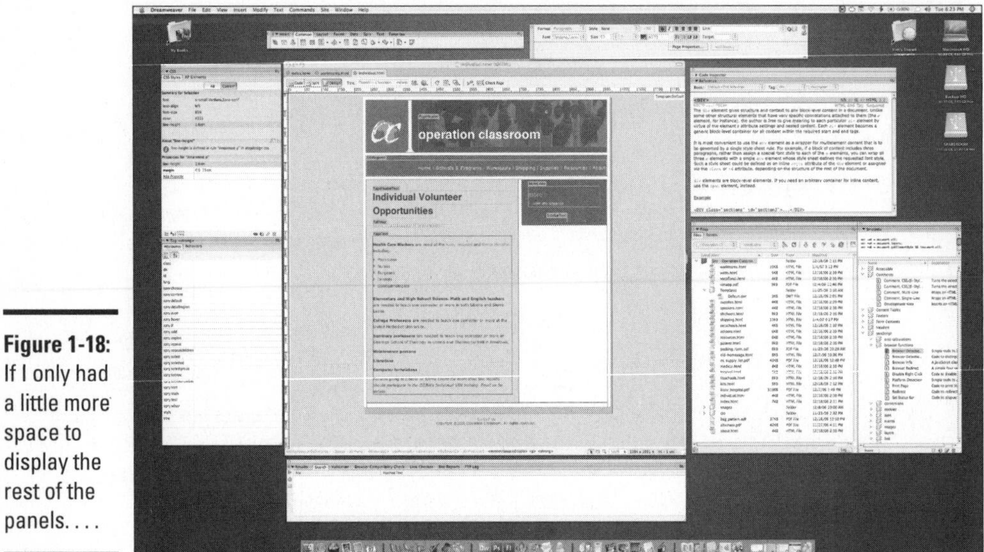

Figure 1-18: If I only had a little more space to display the rest of the panels. . . .

Chapter 2: Nuts and Bolts: Creating Your First Dreamweaver Web Site

In This Chapter

- **Creating a new Web site and document**
- **Adding content to a Web page**
- **Previewing a document in your browser**
- **Publishing your site**

Chapter 1 in this minibook gives you the showroom tour of Dreamweaver, giving you a chance to kick its tires. In this chapter, you take a test drive to see how this baby runs in the real world. I walk you through the basic steps of creating and publishing a simple one-page Web site. You can use the rest of the chapters in this minibook to begin to develop more complex pages and sites.

Because you publish your Web site to a remote server at the end of this chapter, I assume that you already have an established account with a Web-hosting provider. If you don't, skip the "Publishing Your Site" section.

Launch Dreamweaver and let's rock and roll.

Creating a New Site

You can create individual Web pages inside Dreamweaver, but the tool is really suited for working with sites. When you create Web pages inside a site, you can take advantage of many site-related features, such as a site map and a link checker.

When you create a new site in Dreamweaver, you're asked to pick a particular folder on your computer to store all the pages and assets of the site.

An *asset* is any file that's used by a Web page, such as an image, Flash file, style sheet, or JavaScript file.

To create a new site, follow these steps:

1. **Choose Site➪New Site.**

   The Site Setup dialog box appears, as shown in Figure 2-1.

Figure 2-1: Creating a basic Dreamweaver site is a snap.

2. **Enter a descriptive name for your site in the space provided.**

   Dreamweaver uses this name to label the folder and uses the name inside the application itself. The name isn't used when you publish your site on a real Web server.

3. **Enter the local directory in which you'd like to create your files.**

   You can optionally use the Browse button to navigate to the local directory.

4. **Click Save.**

   Dreamweaver creates the site for you and displays it as the active site in the Files panel, as shown in Figure 2-2.

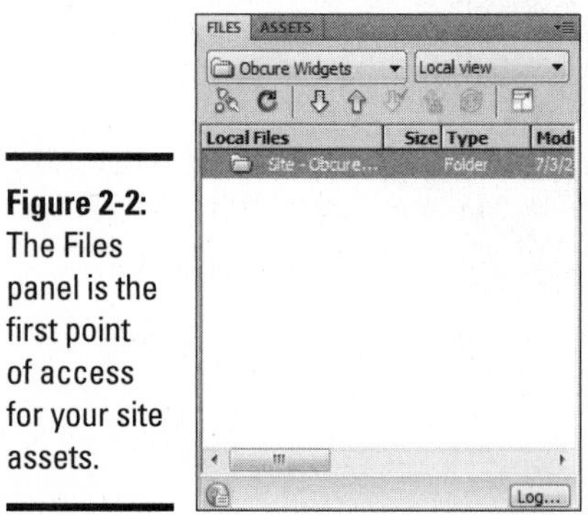

Figure 2-2: The Files panel is the first point of access for your site assets.

You can specify more site details and options by choosing Site⇨Manage Sites. In the Manage Sites dialog box, select the new site and click Edit. The Site Definition dialog box appears. Check out Chapter 8 in this minibook for complete details on managing your site.

Creating a New Document

After your site is created, you're ready to add a Web page to the site. To create a Web page, follow these steps:

1. **Choose File⇨New.**

   The New Document dialog box appears, as shown in Figure 2-3.

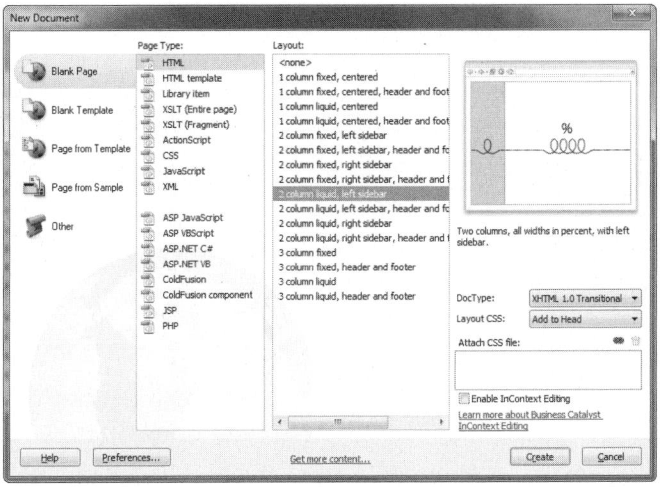

Figure 2-3: The New Document dialog box is your gateway to action, adventure, and new documents.

2. **Select HTML from the Page Type list.**

   You can create other document types later, but for now, stick with good ol' HTML.

3. **Select a layout from the Layout list.**

   The Layout list provides a large set of Web page layouts you can choose from. Or, if you would rather start with a blank page, click <none>.

   I picked the 2 column liquid, left sidebar option for this example.

4. **Select XHTML 1.0 Transition from the DocType drop-down list.**

   See Book III for more on the different document types and versions of HTML.

5. **Select Add to Head from the Layout CSS drop-down list.**

   In Chapter 6 in this minibook, I talk more about using separate style sheets, but for now, stick with the default option.

6. **Click the Create button.**

   A new document, named Untitled-1, is created for you and appears in the Document window.

   Figure 2-4 shows the document that's created by using the 2 column liquid, left sidebar layout.

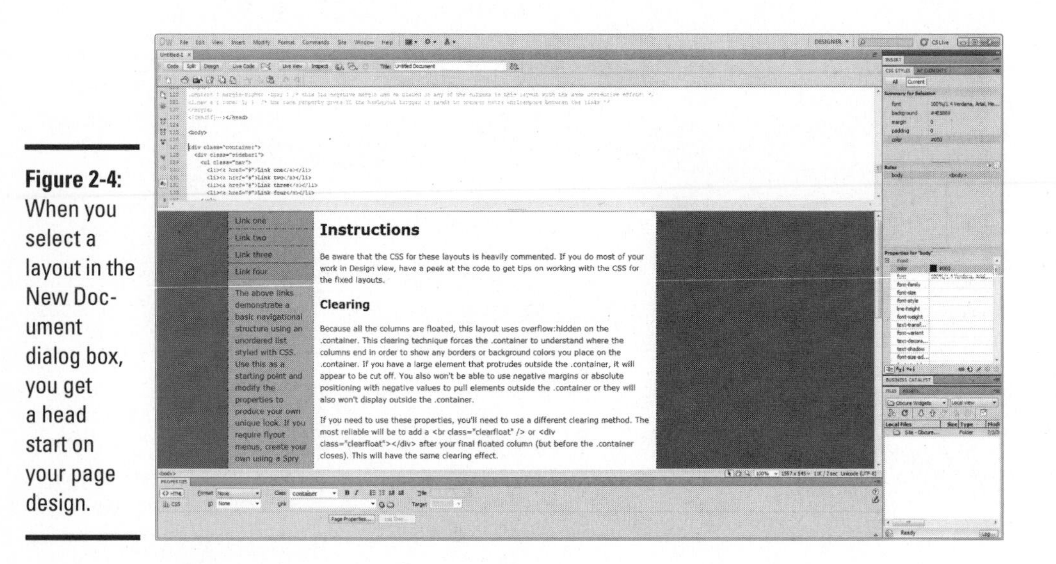

Figure 2-4: When you select a layout in the New Document dialog box, you get a head start on your page design.

Adding Content to Your Page

Much of your time in Dreamweaver is spent sitting in front of the Document window and either tweaking the page layout or adding content. Chapters 3 through 7 of this minibook focus on these tasks; for now, I keep the discussion straightforward.

To add content, follow these steps:

1. **Click the cursor at the location you want in the document and type away.**

   If you used one of the default layouts, you have to remove some canned text — unless you have a particular fondness for greeked text.

2. **(Optional) Add a link.**

   Select text that you want to link, and then enter the URL you want to link to in the Link box of the Properties inspector.

3. **(Optional) Add an image.**

   Position the cursor at the location in which you want the image to appear. Click the Images button on the Common Insert panel and select the image you want to insert in the dialog box that appears. Click OK.

4. **Add a title to your page.**

   In the Title box of the Document toolbar, add a descriptive title for your page.

I don't provide much instruction here for working with text, links, and images. I save that discussion for Chapter 3 in this minibook.

Saving a Page

As you'd do with any other document you work with on your computer, you have to save your Web page in Dreamweaver before it can be of much use. To save your document, follow these steps:

1. **Choose File⇨Save.**

   The Save As dialog box appears. The default location is your site folder.

2. **Enter a name for the file.**

   If you're creating your home page, name the file **index.html**.

3. **Click Save.**

Previewing Your Page in a Browser

Although Dreamweaver's Design mode is visual, it isn't identical to how the page will appear inside a browser. As a result, before publishing your site to your Web server, you should always preview your page *and* your entire site in a browser to see how they look and to test how they perform.

To preview a document, follow these steps:

1. **Click the Preview in Browser button on the Document toolbar.**

   A list of browsers installed on your computer appears. See Figure 2-5.

   You can also choose File⇨Preview in Browser.

Figure 2-5: Previewing your document inside a browser.

2. **Select a browser from the list.**

   Dreamweaver opens your page in the browser for you to preview.

You can edit the browser list by choosing Edit Browser List from the drop-down list to display the Preferences dialog box. From there, you can add and remove browsers and assign keyboard shortcuts to them.

Setting Up Your Site for Publishing

Before you can publish your site to a server and have it viewable on the World Wide Web, you first need to add your server information to the Site configuration.

Before proceeding with this step, you'll first need to have an account set up with a Web-hosting provider or have the ability to publish to your company's Web server. Once you have login details in hand, you are ready to continue.

1. **Choose Site ➪ Manage Sites.**

   The Manage Sites dialog box appears, as shown in Figure 2-6.

Figure 2-6: Managing your sites.

2. **Select your Web site and click the Edit button.**

   The Site Setup dialog box for your site appears.

3. **Click the Servers item on the left side list.**

   The Servers tab appears, as shown in Figure 2-7.

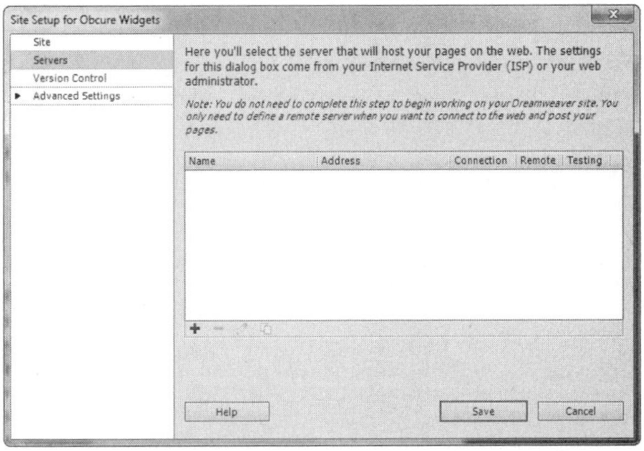

Figure 2-7: Working with servers for publishing.

4. **Click the + button to add a new server.**

   The Server Configuration dialog box appears, as shown in Figure 2-8.

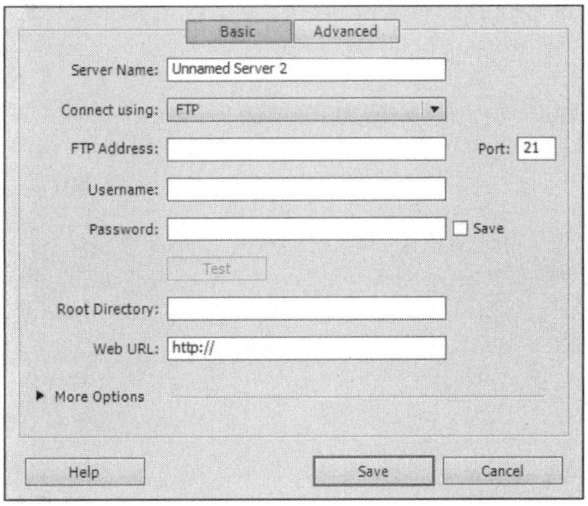

Figure 2-8: Adding a new server.

5. **Enter a descriptive name for your server in the Server Name box.**
6. **From the Connect Using drop-down list, select the way in which you connect to the remote Web server.**

   If you have a typical Web-hosting provider, you use FTP (the default option) to connect to the server. (If you're using another option, fill in the settings and then skip to Step 10.)
7. **Enter the FTP server information for your hosting provider in the text boxes.**

   If you're like me, you probably scribbled this information on a sticky note months ago and can't find it now.
8. **After you enter the information, click the Test button to ensure that the information is correct.**
9. **If necessary, add the name of the directory in which you want to publish your site in the Root Directory box.**
10. **Click the Save button to save your settings.**

    You are now ready to publish to this server.

Publishing Your Site

After you preview your site and have defined your server information, you're ready to publish your document to the Web-hosting server. After you do this, the world can view your Web page.

Here's how to publish your page:

1. **Click the File Management button on the Document toolbar.**

   A drop-down list of options appears, as shown in Figure 2-9.

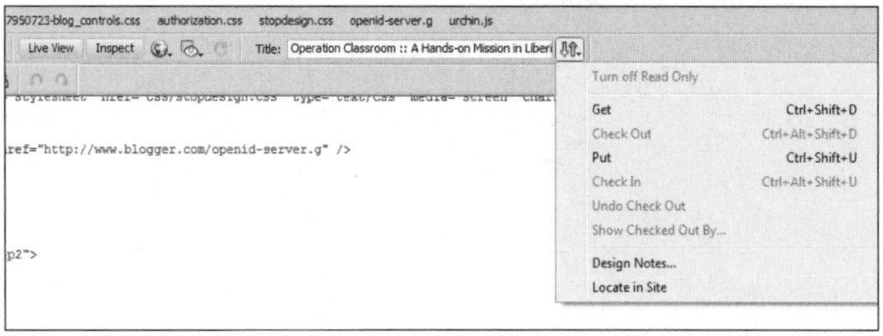

Figure 2-9: Publishing a document directly from the Document window.

2. **Select Put.**

   Dreamweaver uploads the document and all dependent files to the server.

From the Document window, you publish only the active document (and any dependent files). However, thumb over to Chapter 8 in this minibook to see you how you can publish the entire site from the Files panel.

Chapter 3: Formatting and Layout Basics

In This Chapter

- **Inserting and formatting text**
- **Inserting images**
- **Adding links**
- **Inserting tables**
- **Creating div elements**

Much of the time you work with Dreamweaver is spent inside the Document window. You create a layout. Add content to fill it in. Format the content to look good *and* be easy to read. In this chapter, you explore the basic aspects of formatting and laying out your Web page. I start by focusing on the big three: text, images, and links. After that, I explore how to work with key layout elements, including tables and `div` elements.

Working with Text

Images and multimedia may get all the acclaim, but text is the meat and potatoes of every Web page. Dreamweaver allows you to work with text inside your document in much the same way you would if you were using Microsoft Word or another word processor.

Inserting text

To insert text, click the location in the Document window in which you want to type. Just like in a word processor, text automatically wraps to the next line when you reach the edge of the line.

When you press the Return (or Enter) key, Dreamweaver begins a new paragraph (the `p` element). Or to begin a new line without creating a new paragraph, you can add a line break (the `br` element). To do so, either press Shift+Return (or Shift+Enter) or add a `br` element by clicking the Line Break button on the Text Insert panel.

Changing the text formatting

Entering text is the easy, no-brainer part of working with text. Much of the work you do with text involves formatting it. You can modify either a text selection (by selecting text with your mouse) or an entire paragraph (by positioning the text cursor anywhere inside the paragraph). When you do, the text properties are displayed in the Properties inspector. The inspector shows two different sets of properties: HTML (see Figure 3-1) and CSS (see Figure 3-2).

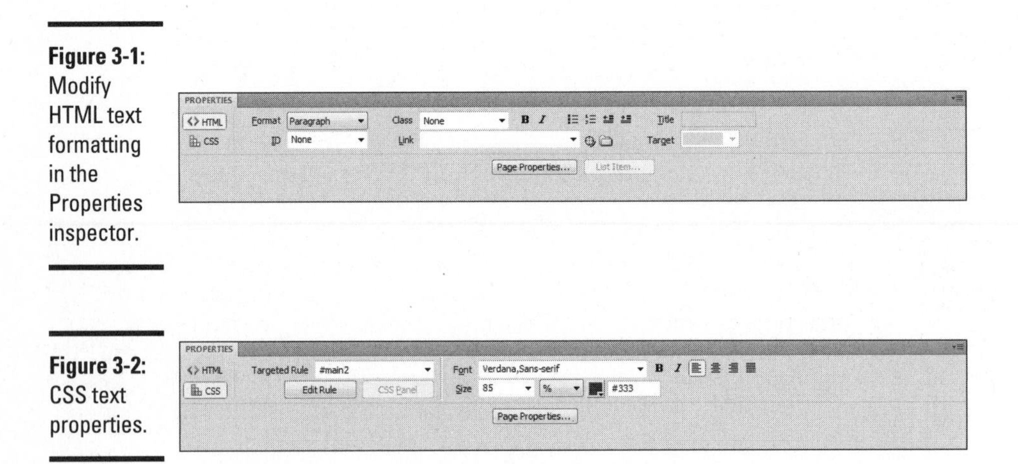

Figure 3-1: Modify HTML text formatting in the Properties inspector.

Figure 3-2: CSS text properties.

Some of the properties work on a text selection but not on the entire paragraph. Therefore, if you set the font size when no text is selected, the font size is turned on at the insertion point but has no effect on the current paragraph.

Although several formatting options are available, here are some of the ones you'll probably be working with right away:

✦ **Paragraph Format:** To format based on traditional HTML styles, use the Format drop-down box on the HTML tab of the Properties inspector. It displays the traditional HTML paragraph "styles" of text:

  - Paragraph (the default)
  - Heading 1 (largest header) through Heading 6 (smallest header)
  - Preformatted (monospaced)

  Figure 3-3 shows the formatting styles.

Figure 3-3: HTML paragraph styles provide a way to structure your document with headings and normal sections.

Heading 1
Heading 2
Heading 3
Heading 4
Heading 5
Heading 6
Paragraph
Preformatted

CSS enables you to customize the formatting of each of these HTML styles. As a result, you can use the built-in heading hierarchy that these paragraph styles give you but still use CSS. (See Book IV for more on CSS.)

✦ **Font:** In the CSS tab of the Properties inspector, the Font drop-down list displays the font faces you want to assign to your selection. Fonts are usually arranged in families (a list of font faces separated by commas). The first font is used if it's available on the user's machine. If not, the next font is chosen, and so on.

  Select Default Font when you don't want to apply any specific font formatting. When you do so, the browser uses the default font setting defined elsewhere when it renders the document.

✦ **Size:** In the CSS tab, the Size drop-down list displays a list of possible font sizes. You can use various sizing measurements:

  - *Sizes ranging from 9 to 36:* Specify the numeric size of the font. Use the drop-down box beside it to specify the measurement unit (typically points, pixels, or picas).
  - *xx-small to xx-large:* A collection of constants (`xx-small`, `x-small`, `small`, `medium`, `large`, `x-large`, `xx-large`) to define as an absolute sized font.
  - *Smaller, Larger:* One size smaller or larger, respectively, than previously defined.

  Figure 3-4 displays various font-size options.

9 point	9 pixels	xx-small	Smaller
10 point	10 pixels	x-small	Normal
12 point	12 pixels	small	Larger
14 point	14 pixels	medium	
16 point	16 pixels	large	
18 point	18 pixels	x-large	
24 point	24 pixels	xx-large	
36 point	36 pixels		

Figure 3-4: You can size your font by using relative and absolute measurements.

- **Color:** Use the color box on the CSS tab to select a text color from the palette that appears. You can also specify an HTML color code in the box that's provided.
- **Basic word processing styles:** The CSS tab in the Properties inspector also has several buttons that format text just as a standard word processor does: Bold, Italic, Align Left and Right, Align Justify, and Align Center (see Figure 3-5).

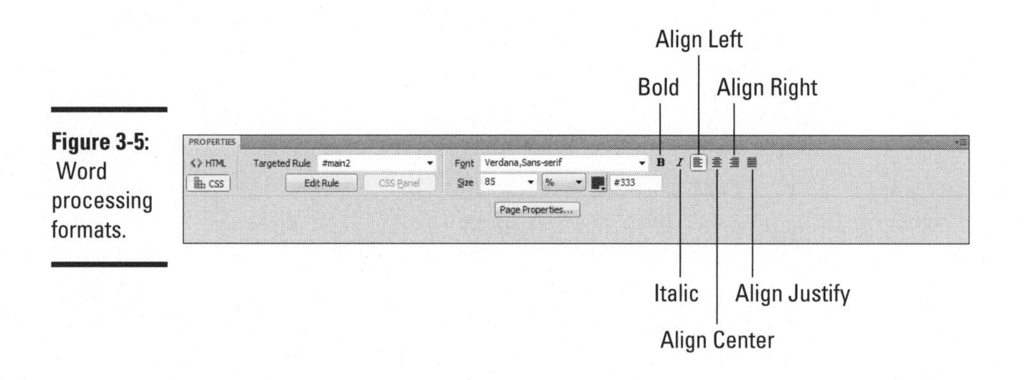

Figure 3-5: Word processing formats.

- **CSS Class and Rule:** The Class drop-down list on the HTML tab and the Targeted Rule drop-down list on the CSS tab are the two main spots to define CSS styles to your text. After you define your styles and link your CSS style sheet to the current document (see Chapter 5 in this minibook), you can simply select a style from the list.

If you need to modify a style, the Edit Rule button on the CSS tab is a quick way to display the CSS Rule Definition dialog box.

Working with Images

If text is the meat and potatoes of any Web page, images are the appetizers, desserts, and fancy drinks all rolled into one. In other words, they usually give a Web page pizzazz and character.

Inserting an image

To insert an image, follow these steps:

1. **In the Document window, position the cursor at the location in which you want to insert an image.**
2. **Click the Image button on the Common Insert panel.**

   Or, choose Insert➪Image.

   In either case, the Select Image Source dialog box appears.
3. **Navigate to the image in the Select Image Source dialog box.**
4. **Click OK (Windows) or Choose (Mac).**

   If the image isn't already located inside the folder of the current site, Dreamweaver asks whether you want to copy the image into the site's root folder (see Figure 3-6). Click Yes to have Dreamweaver perform this process. In the Copy File As dialog box, you can specify a new filename for the image, if you want.

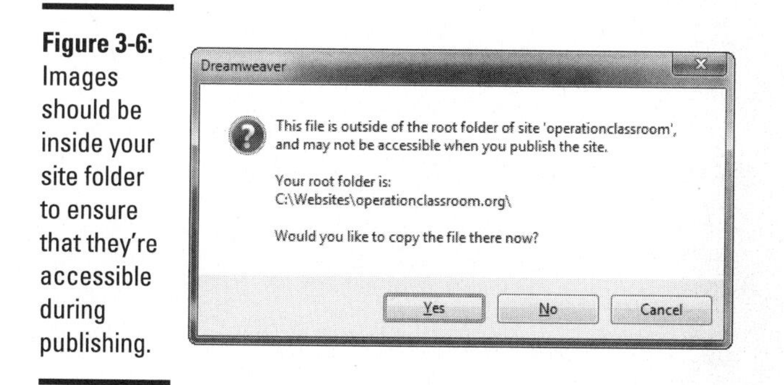

Figure 3-6: Images should be inside your site folder to ensure that they're accessible during publishing.

The Image Tag Accessibility Attributes dialog box appears (see Figure 3-7) after this step has been completed.

Image Tag Accessibility Attributes

Alternate text:

Long description: http://

If you don't want to enter this information when inserting objects, change the Accessibility preferences.

OK

Cancel

Help

Figure 3-7: Be sure to provide alternative text for your images.

5. **Enter a description of the image in the Alternate text box.**

   Alternative text is important for users who are visually impaired and use a screen reader for browsing your site. It's also useful for people who have disabled images in their browsers.

6. **Click OK.**

   If the image isn't already located inside the folder of the current site, Dreamweaver copies the image into the site's image folder.

   The image is now available on your Web page.

Modifying an image

You can modify the properties of images by selecting the image in the Document window and then working with the Properties inspector (see Figure 3-8).

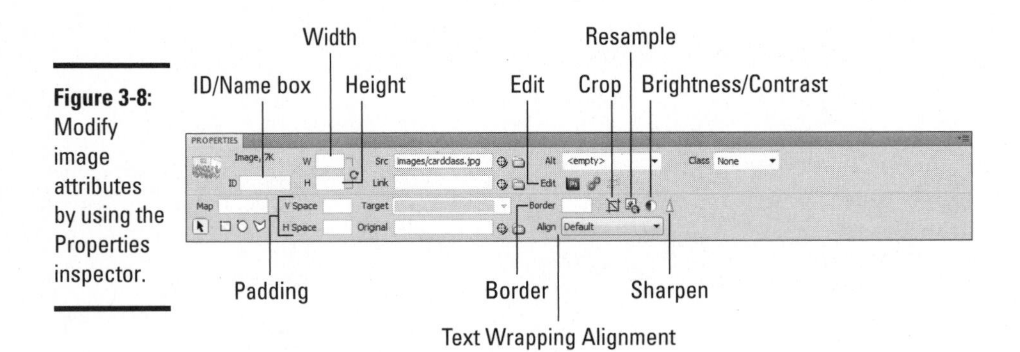

Figure 3-8: Modify image attributes by using the Properties inspector.

You can perform a variety of tasks from the Properties inspector. I cover them in the following sections.

Adding an id attribute

Enter a text value in the box beside the thumbnail image to assign a unique identifier to the image. Dreamweaver adds this text as an `id` attribute to the image.

Sizing the image

Dreamweaver places the width and height (in pixels) in the W and H boxes, respectively. If you want to shrink, expand, or skew the image, enter new values.

For an even easier method, you can directly resize the image inside the Document window with your mouse by clicking the image and dragging one of the border boxes. The W and H values are updated automatically.

If you want to change the dimensions of your image, use an image-editing program. Don't rely on the W and H values to do the resizing for you. If you do, then you force the browser to do the image resizing, which usually gives weaker results than an image-editing program.

Adding a border

You can add a border by entering a width value (in pixels) in the Border box.

Even better, you can modify this setting by using CSS instead, which is discussed in Book IV, Chapter 4.

Padding the image

Use the V Space and H Space boxes to specify the padding (in pixels) that you want to add around the image.

You can modify this setting by using the CSS `padding` property, if you prefer. The `padding` property, discussed in Book IV, Chapter 4, provides much greater precision than the built-in HTML attributes.

Aligning the image

When you insert an image into a paragraph of text, the image is added directly in the paragraph itself, right alongside of the text. The line spacing expands automatically to account for the size of the image. However, in most cases, you wrap the text around the image instead. Use the Align drop-down box to set a text-wrapping option.

Alternatively, if you prefer to align the image to the page (no text wrapping), select the desired setting from the Align drop-down box in the Properties inspector.

Editing the image

The Edit portion of the Properties inspector has a series of commands that you can access for editing the image:

- **Edit:** Click the Edit button to work with the image by using an external image-editing program. In File Types/Editors, you can specify which editor you want to use.
- **Edit Image Settings:** Click the Edit Image Settings button to display the Image Preview dialog box (see Figure 3-9). While Photoshop is preferred, you don't have to use Photoshop or another editor to tweak the size or quality of the image; you can do so right inside Dreamweaver.

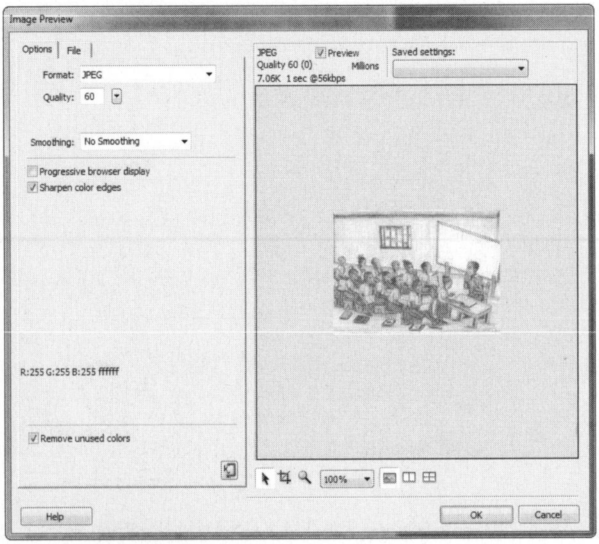

Figure 3-9: Optimize your image right inside Dreamweaver. Nothing could be easier.

- **Crop:** Click the Crop button to trim the size of the image directly on your page. These changes are made to the image file itself.
- **Resample:** Click the Resample button to enhance the image quality.
- **Brightness and Contrast:** Click the Brightness and Contrast button to change these image settings.
- **Sharpen:** Click the Sharpen button to improve the quality of blurry images.

Connecting the Dots: Adding Links

You often want to link text, images, and other elements to other pages on the Web. To insert a link, select the text or image and then look for the Link box in the Properties inspector (see Figure 3-10).

Figure 3-10: Creating a link.

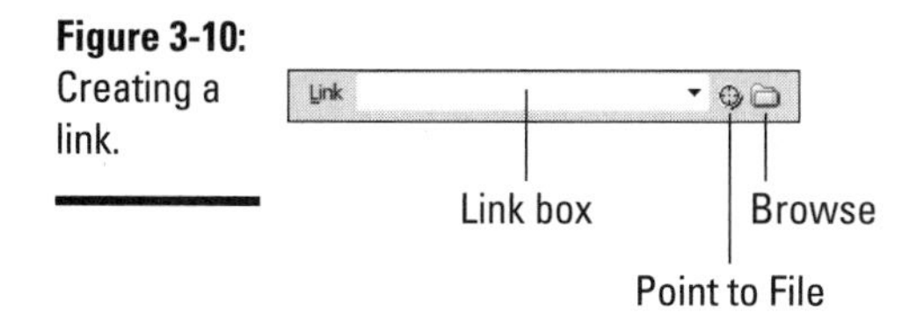

Creating and deleting a link

You have three ways to specify the link:

- **Manually:** Enter the URL in the box provided.
- **Browse:** If the file you're linking to is in your site, click the Browse button to specify the document in the Select File dialog box.
- **Point and click:** If the Files panel is opened, the easiest (and coolest) way to create a link is to click the Point to File button and then drag the mouse pointer to the file in the Files panel in which you want to link. Dreamweaver displays an arrow as you perform this process (see Figure 3-11). Release the mouse button over the file you want, and Dreamweaver creates the link.

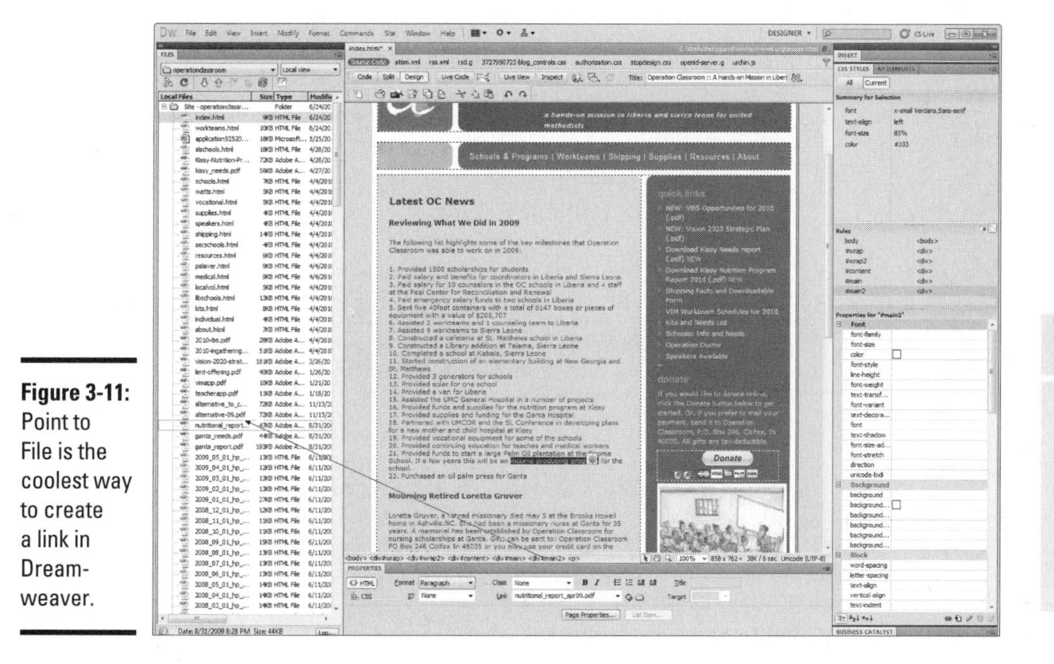

Figure 3-11: Point to File is the coolest way to create a link in Dreamweaver.

You can delete a link that you created by selecting the text or the image that the link is assigned to. In the Properties inspector, remove the text in the Link box.

Specifying the target window

You can use the Target drop-down list in the Properties inspector to specify the window or frame in which the linked page should be displayed. You can select from these options:

- `_blank` opens the returning document in a new window.
- `_parent` displays the document in the parent window of the current one.
- `_self` displays the document in the same window that sent the form. This is the default.
- `_top` opens the returning document in the top-level window (replacing any frames).

Using named anchors

To create a link to another spot on the current page (or to a particular location on another page), you need to create a named anchor. A *named anchor* is a bookmark to a specific location on the page.

Creating a named anchor

To create a named anchor, follow these steps:

1. **In the Document window, position the cursor at the location in which you want to insert the named anchor.**
2. **Choose Insert⇨Named Anchor.**
3. **Specify a name for the anchor in the Named Anchor dialog box.**

   This name isn't displayed in the text, but is used for behind-the-scenes purposes.
4. **Click OK.**

   The anchor is added at the current cursor position. An anchor icon appears in your document to represent the invisible bookmark.

Linking to a named anchor

To link to a named anchor, select the text or image you want to link from and then display the Properties inspector.

To link to an anchor on the same page, in the Link box, enter a pound sign (#) and then the exact name of the named anchor. Alternatively, you can use the Point to File button and drag the mouse pointer to the named anchor in your document.

To link to an anchor on another page, follow the instructions in the "Creating and deleting a link" section, earlier in this chapter, but add a # and the name of the named anchor at the end of the URL. For example, to link to the `section2` named anchor at `www.digitalwalk.net/intro`, you enter **www.digitalwalk.net/intro#section2**.

Creating an image map and hotspots

If you want to link different portions of an image to different URLs, you can use the Hotspot tools in the Image Properties inspector (see Figure 3-12) to create an image map.

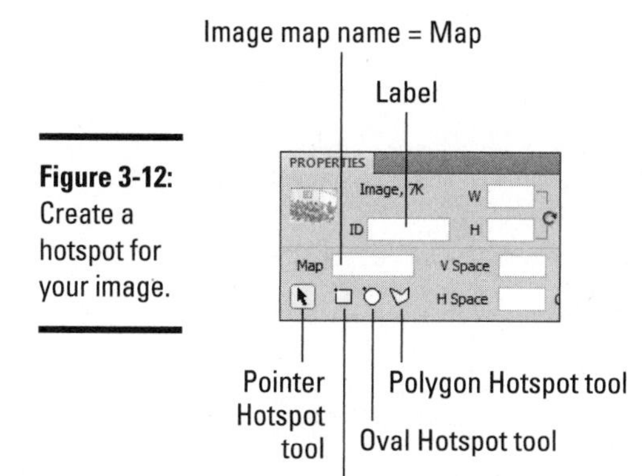

Figure 3-12: Create a hotspot for your image.

A *hotspot* is a clickable region of an image that is assigned a URL. An *image map* is an image that contains hotspots.

To create an image map with hotspots, follow these steps:

1. **Select the image to which you want to add hotspots.**

   The Image Properties inspector appears. (If not, choose Window⇨Properties.)

2. **Assign a unique name to the image map in the Map box.**

3. **From the Properties inspector, select a hotspot tool based on the shape you want to create.**

   Normally, you use the Rectangular Hotspot tool.

4. **Drag your mouse pointer over the image to set the hotspot in the dimensions you want. Release the mouse button when you're satisfied with the size.**

   Dreamweaver prompts you to specify alternative text for the hotspot from the Hotspot Properties inspector.

5. **Enter alternative text in the Alt box.**
6. **Enter the URL you want to associate with the clickable region in the Link box.**
7. **Repeat Steps 4 through 6 for each hotspot you want to add to the image map.**

Figure 3-13 shows an image map with four hotspots.

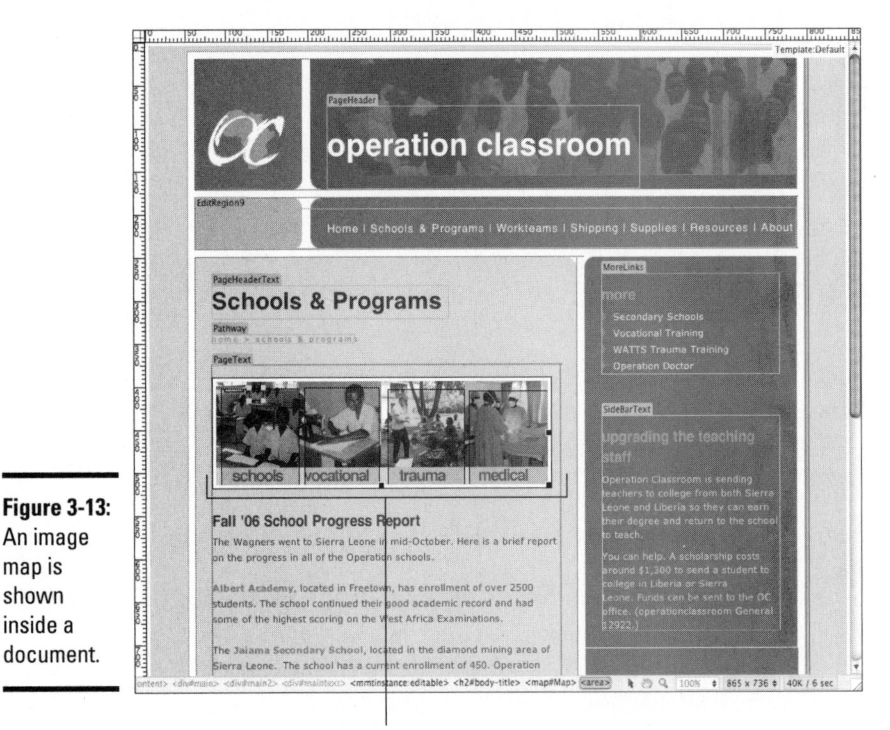

Figure 3-13: An image map is shown inside a document.

You can resize and reposition hotspots by directly manipulating them with your mouse pointer inside the Document window.

Working with Tables

A decade ago, tables were the underpinning of almost every well-designed Web page. To position elements in exact positions on the page, designers were forced to assemble a complex arrangement of tables to achieve the look they were striving for. Fortunately, `div` elements have been introduced over the past few years, and they largely eliminate the need to use HTML tables as layout tools. As a result, tables can go back to their original purpose — as a way to display tabular data.

Choose Insert➪Table to add a table. You can also click the Table button on the Common Insert panel. The Table dialog box appears, as shown in Figure 3-14.

Figure 3-14: Adding a table.

Fill out these options in the dialog box:

- **Rows and Columns:** Enter numbers for the basic dimensions of the table.
- **Table Width:** Enter a value that specifies the total width of the table. The value can be either fixed (in pixels) or relative (as a percent of the total browser width).
- **Border Thickness:** Specify the pixel size of the surrounding table border. If you choose 0, no border appears.

If no value is entered, most browsers default to a value of 1.

- **Cell Padding and Cell Spacing:** Enter values (in pixels) to determine the padding and spacing of the table cells. *Padding* is the space between the edge of a cell and its contents. *Spacing* is the space between cells.

  If no values are specified, browsers typically display the cell padding as 1 and the cell spacing as 2.

- **Header:** If you want to add a heading, click to select a style (left, top, or both).

  Headers are especially helpful for visually impaired people who use screen readers.

- **Caption:** Enter text if you want a caption displayed next to the table.
- **Summary:** To summarize the table (a feature often used by screen readers), enter text in the Summary box.

Click OK and the table is inserted in your document.

If you want to delete a table, click the border of the table to select it. Press Delete (or Backspace).

Divide and Conquer: Using div Elements

The `div` element is a relative newcomer to the HTML world but has proven to be an important part of modern Web pages. The `div` element is used in combination with CSS to create blocks of content that can be positioned precisely on a page.

Be sure that you have a well-rounded understanding of CSS before working with `div` elements. See Book IV for full details on how to use CSS to position `div` elements.

Adding a div element

You can add a `div` element by clicking the Insert Div Tag button on the Layout Insert panel. The Insert Div Tag dialog box appears, as shown in Figure 3-15.

Figure 3-15: Adding a div element.

You see these options in the dialog box:

- **Insert:** You can decide whether you want to insert the `div` element at the insertion point or before or after a specific element in your document.
- **Class:** Select the CSS class that you want to attach to the `div`.
- **ID:** Choose from `div` IDs defined in an attached style sheet, or add a new ID.

Click OK and the `div` is added at the specified location, with placeholder text added to it.

Adding an AP div

Dreamweaver also enables you to "draw" an absolutely positioned (AP) `div` element to your page. An *AP* `div` is a `div` element that has a fixed position assigned to it.

Unlike other `div` elements, which normally wrap around other elements, an AP `div` is a different beast. It's placed in specific screen coordinates and appears either above or below regular page content (depending on its `z-index` property in the Properties inspector).

To add an AP `div`, follow these steps:

1. **Click the Draw AP Div button on the Layout Insert panel.**
2. **In the Document window, position the mouse cursor in the upper-left corner in which you want to add the AP `div`.**

   Notice how the cursor changes to a crosshair pointer.
3. **Click the mouse button and hold it down while you drag the mouse cursor to the lower-right corner of the `div` element.**

   A blue box is created as you move your mouse.
4. **Release the mouse button when you're satisfied with the dimensions of the `div`.**

   Your result should look something like what's shown in Figure 3-16.
5. **Add content inside the `div` element.**

If you want to move the AP `div`, you can select the element and then grab the blue box handle in its upper-left corner. Drag the element to a new location.

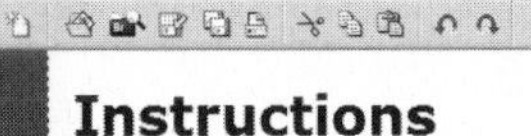

Figure 3-16: You can use an AP div to position content absolutely.

Chapter 4: Enhanced Page Elements: Flash Controls and Spry Widgets

In This Chapter

- **Enriching the user experience with Flash media and interface controls**
- **Enhancing page functionality with Spry widgets**

Dreamweaver provides built-in support for making sophisticated user interfaces. You can add not only Adobe Flash media to your Web page but also Flash-powered controls and Spry widgets (a combination of HTML, CSS, and JavaScript) to create highly interactive pages — without writing a single line of JavaScript code.

In this chapter, I show you how to work with Flash media and controls. Then I set your sights on how to add the three most useful Spry widgets to your Web site.

Working with Flash Controls

You can add a Flash media file to your Web page to provide a richer user experience for your site visitors. However, in addition to Flash media that you create yourself (see Book IX) or obtain from another source, you can work with special Flash page elements that come with Dreamweaver.

You can add normal Flash SWF or FLV content to your Web page in much the same way you'd add an image. Here are the steps:

1. **In the Document window, position the cursor at the location in which you want to insert Flash media.**
2. **Click the Media button on the Common Insert panel, and select the SWF or FLV item from its pop-up menu.**

   Or, choose Insert⇨Media⇨SWF (or Insert⇨Media⇨FLV).

   In either case, the Select File dialog box appears.

3. **Navigate to the Flash media file in the Select File dialog box.**
4. **Click OK (Windows) or Choose (Mac).**

   If the Flash file isn't already located inside the folder of the current site, Dreamweaver asks whether you want to copy the file into the site's root folder. Click Yes to have Dreamweaver perform this process. In the Copy File As dialog box, you can specify a new filename for the Flash file if you want.

   The Object Tag Accessibility Attributes dialog box appears (see Figure 4-1) after this step has been completed.

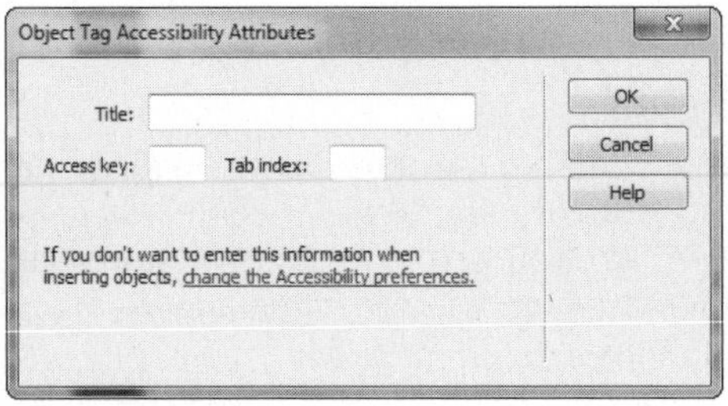

Figure 4-1: Even Flash media should use accessibility settings for the visually impaired.

5. **Enter a description of the media in the Title box.**
6. **(Optional) Add tab-index and access-key options.**
7. **Click OK.**

   The Flash media file is now available on your Web page.

You can set various Flash-related options by selecting the Flash file from the Properties inspector, as shown in Figure 4-2.

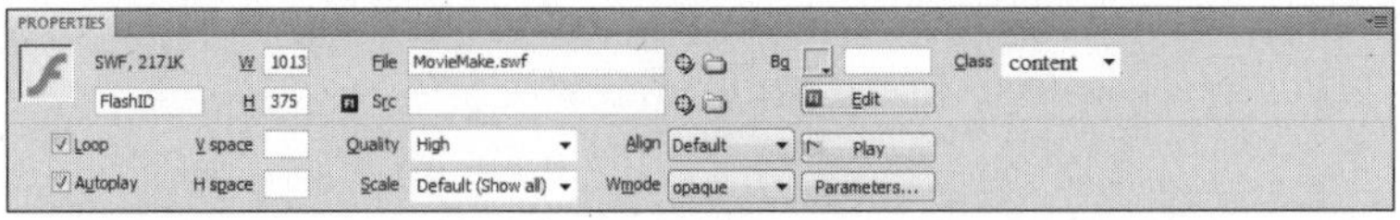

Figure 4-2: Working with a Flash media file inside Dreamweaver.

Working with Spry Widgets

A *Spry widget* is a page element you can drop into your page to provide enhanced functionality that normal HTML elements can't provide by themselves. Examples of widgets are tabbed controls, menu bars, collapsible panels, and self-validating form elements. To perform their magic, Spry widgets combine a variety of Web technologies (HTML, CSS, JavaScript, and XML).

In the past, to achieve some of these effects, you had to either hand-code the source yourself or copy and paste a lot of HTML and JavaScript code from a third party. However, Dreamweaver enables you to work with Spry widgets visually — directly inside the Document window — and set their properties by using the Properties inspector.

Be careful when you're using Spry widgets: You can break them if you aren't careful. Consider, for example, Flash media files. You can insert, delete, or modify a Flash file's properties — nothing more. In contrast, Spry widgets aren't standalone, "black box" objects. You still work with HTML in your page — with CSS and JavaScript simply "hooked up" to it. As a result, you can accidentally break something about the widget when you're working in the Document window, particularly in Source view. Here's a good rule: If the widget code gets corrupted, delete that widget and then reinsert it from scratch. It's yet another good reason to be sure you back up your Web pages regularly — to ensure that you don't lose your Spry widget settings.

Unfortunately, to customize the look of the Spry widgets, you need to roll up your sleeves and work with the underlying CSS style sheets. Dreamweaver doesn't have access to the formatting properties from the Properties inspector. To locate the rule you want to modify, click the Customize This Widget link in the Properties inspector.

To access Spry widgets, choose Insert⇨Spry or use the Layout, Forms, and Spry sections of the Insert panel. Start with the widgets on the Layout Insert panel, as shown in Figure 4-3.

Some Spry widgets are for more advanced purposes, such as working with XML data. Three layout widgets, however, are particularly handy for everyday use: the Spry Menu Bar, Spry Tabbed Panels, and Spry Collapsible Panel. The Spry Accordion is also available, although this control is less common on the Web.

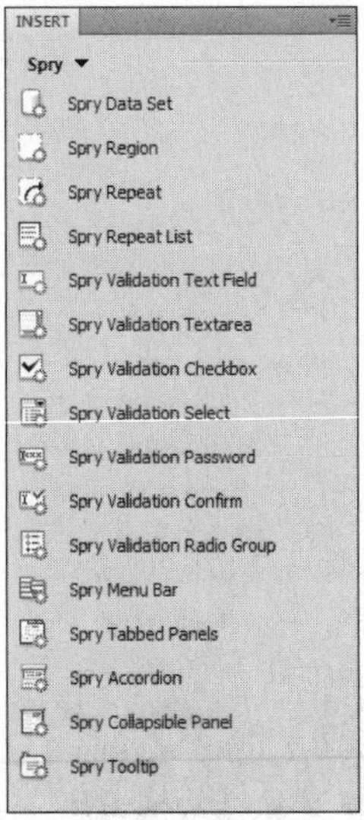

Figure 4-3: Spry Insert panel.

Adding a Spry Menu Bar

A menu bar is one of the most common elements of any Web site, yet (because it combines HTML, CSS, and JavaScript) it can be a pain to create from scratch. That's the beauty of the Spry Menu Bar: You can create a basic menu bar by simply dropping a widget onto the page and adding links from the Properties inspector.

To add a Spry Menu Bar, follow these steps:

1. **In the Document window, position the cursor at the location in which you want to insert the menu bar.**
2. **Click the Spry Menu Bar button on the Layout Insert panel.**

   Or, choose Insert⇨Spry⇨Spry Menu Bar.

   The Spry Menu Bar dialog box appears (see Figure 4-4).

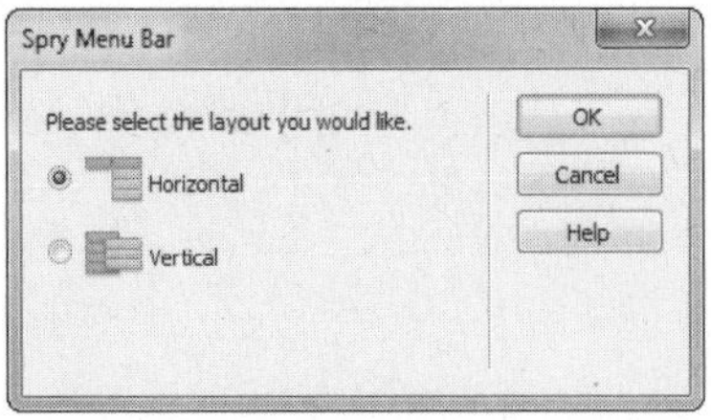

Figure 4-4: You can create a horizontal or vertical menu bar.

3. **Click to select an orientation (horizontal or vertical) for the menu bar.**
4. **Click OK.**

   The menu bar is added to your page, as shown in Figure 4-5.

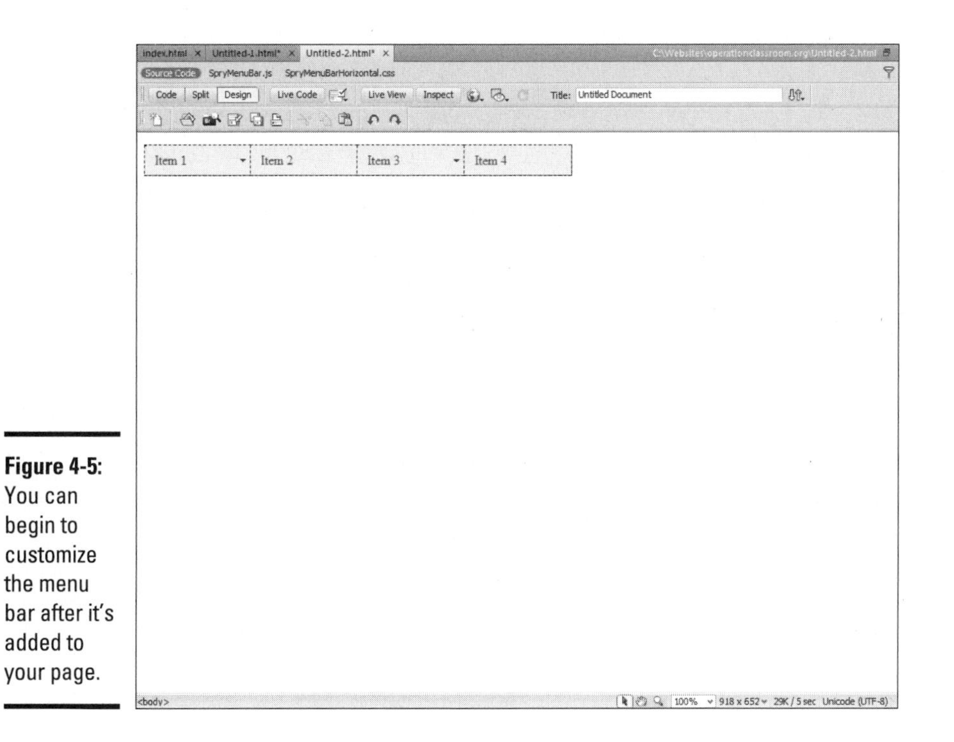

Figure 4-5: You can begin to customize the menu bar after it's added to your page.

5. **Select the menu bar to display its properties.**

   Figure 4-6 displays the Spry Menu Bar Properties inspector.

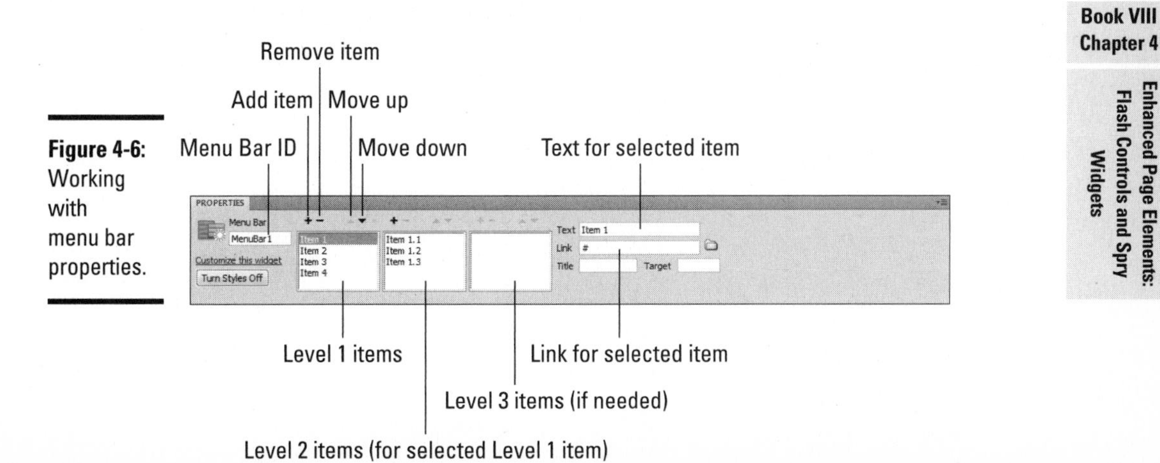

Figure 4-6: Working with menu bar properties.

6. **Create a multi-level menu structure by using the controls provided in the Properties inspector.**

   The second and third levels are always under the item selected in the level above them.

   a. *Click the plus sign (+) button to create a new item on the associated level. Or click the minus sign (–) button to remove the current selection.*

   b. *Enter the text label and URL link in the Text and Link boxes, respectively.*

   The Title box is used for accessibility purposes.

   Figure 4-7 shows the Properties inspector with a menu bar defined.

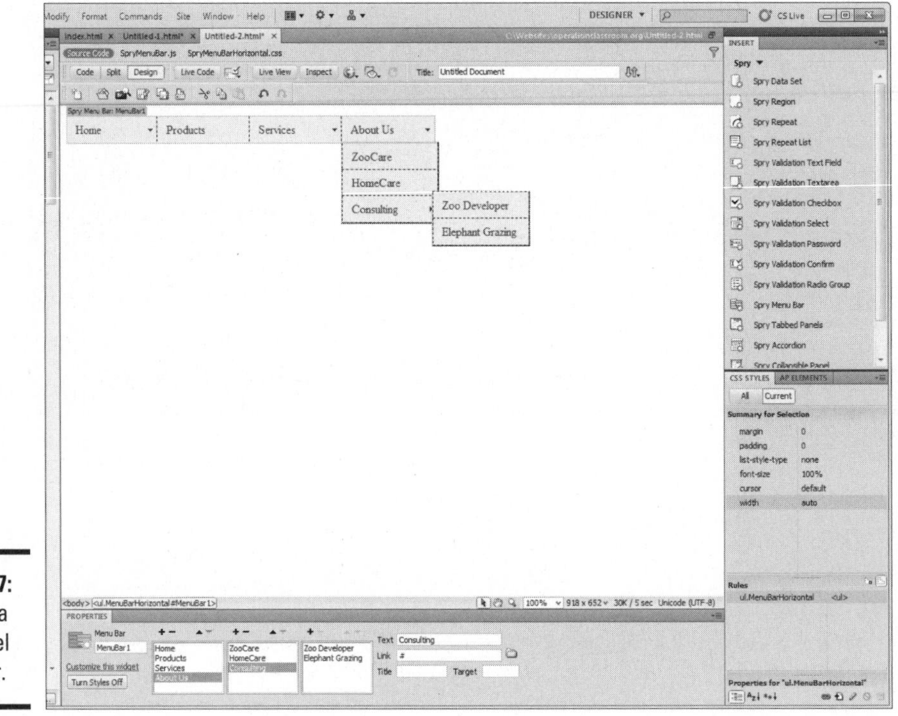

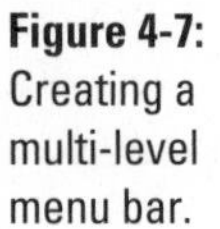

Figure 4-7: Creating a multi-level menu bar.

Figure 4-8 shows the finished menu bar in a browser.

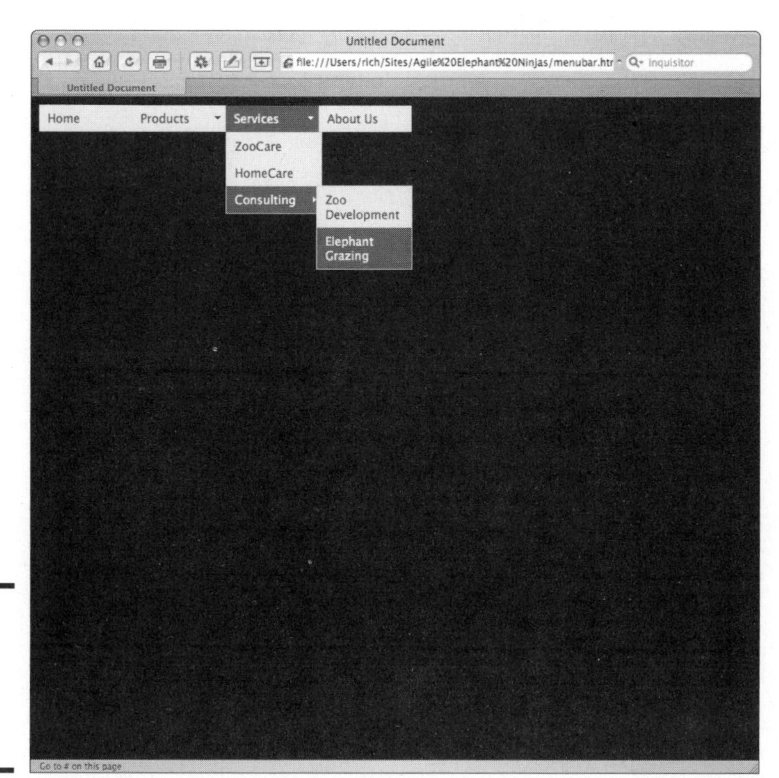

Figure 4-8: The Spry Menu Bar inside a browser.

Adding a Spry Tabbed Panel

The Spry Tabbed Panels widget provides a way to display multiple overlapping panels of content, each panel associated with a tab.

REMEMBER

The tabbed panel isn't intended to be used as a tabbed menu bar. Instead, it's meant to be used inside a single Web page.

To add a Spry Tabbed Panel, follow these steps:

1. **In the Document window, position the cursor at the location in which you want to insert the tabbed panel.**

2. **Click the Spry Tabbed Panel button on the Layout Insert panel.**

   An alternate method: Choose Insert➪Spry➪Spry Tabbed Panel.

   The tabbed panel is added to your page, as shown in Figure 4-9.

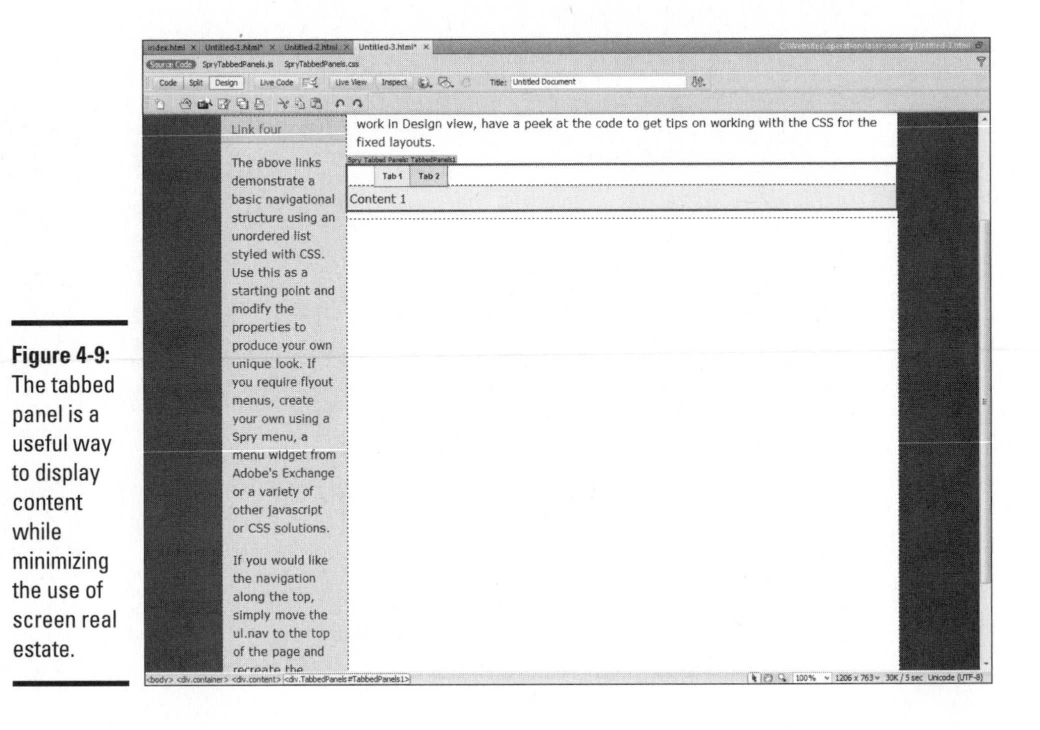

Figure 4-9: The tabbed panel is a useful way to display content while minimizing the use of screen real estate.

3. **Select the tabbed panel with the mouse to display its properties.**

   Figure 4-10 displays the Spry Tabbed Panel Properties inspector.

Figure 4-10: Setting up the properties of a tabbed control.

4. **Use the + and – buttons to add the number of tabs you want.**

   Unlike with the menu bar, you don't label the tabs in the Properties inspector. You label each tab directly in the document.

5. **In the Document window, click the left side of the tab you want and then enter the new name.**

   Figure 4-11 shows the renamed tabs.

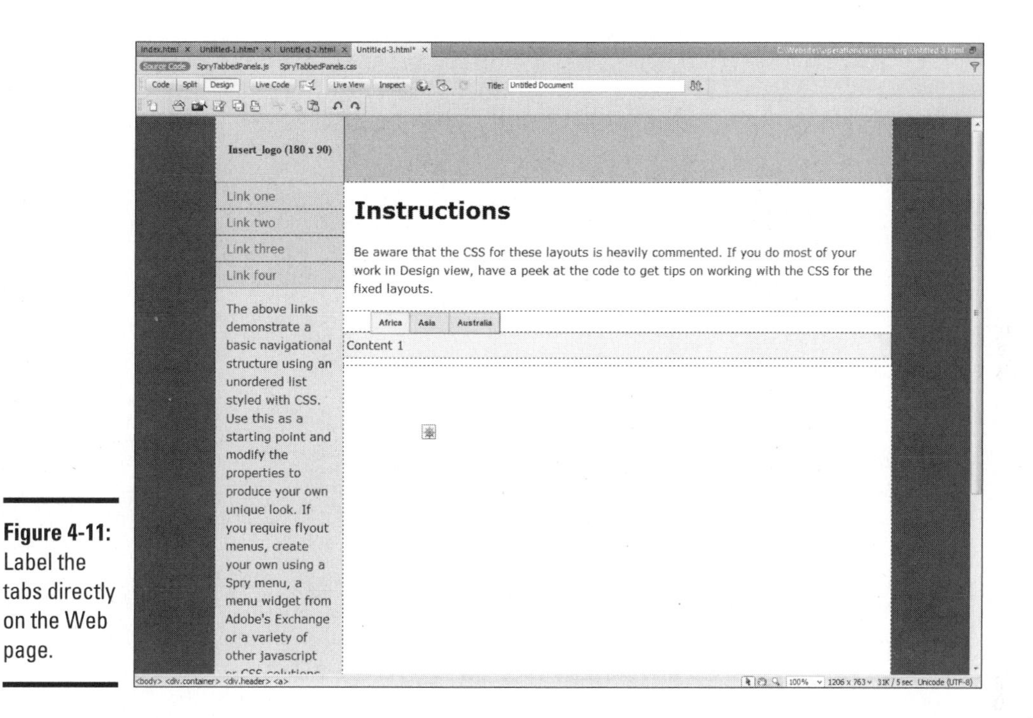

Figure 4-11: Label the tabs directly on the Web page.

6. **Select a tab to view its content by hovering the mouse pointer over the right side of the tab.**

   As Figure 4-12 shows, an eye icon appears on the tab.

7. **Add content to the selected tab panel.**

   Figure 4-13 shows the finished tabbed panel as it looks inside a browser.

Adding a Spry Collapsible Panel

The Spry Collapsible Panel is a handy way to display content that you want a user to be able to expand or collapse as needed. To add a collapsible panel, follow these steps:

1. **In the Document window, position the cursor at the location in which you want to insert the collapsible panel.**

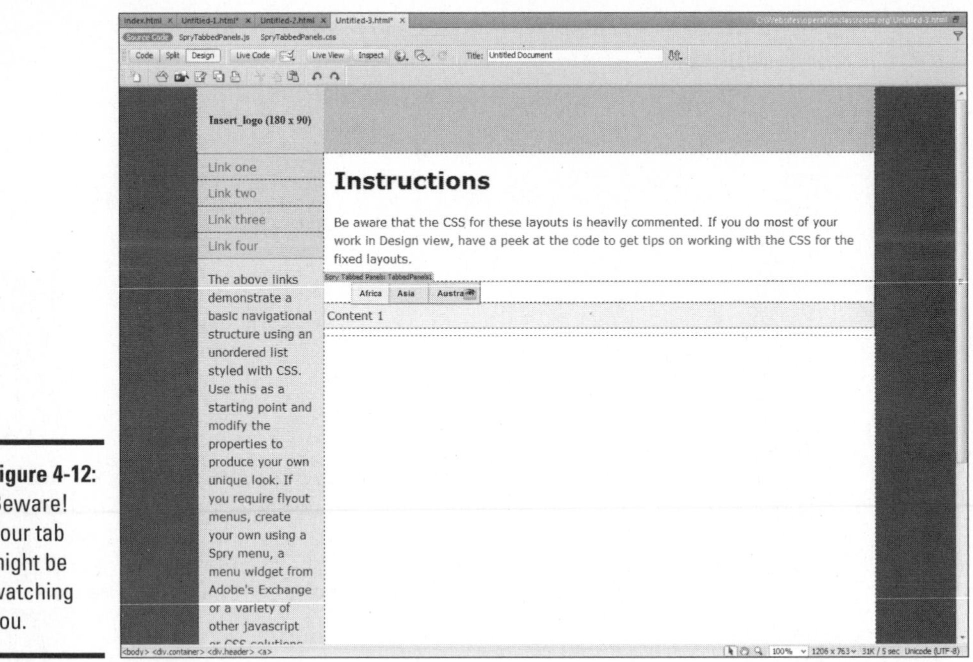

Figure 4-12: Beware! Your tab might be watching you.

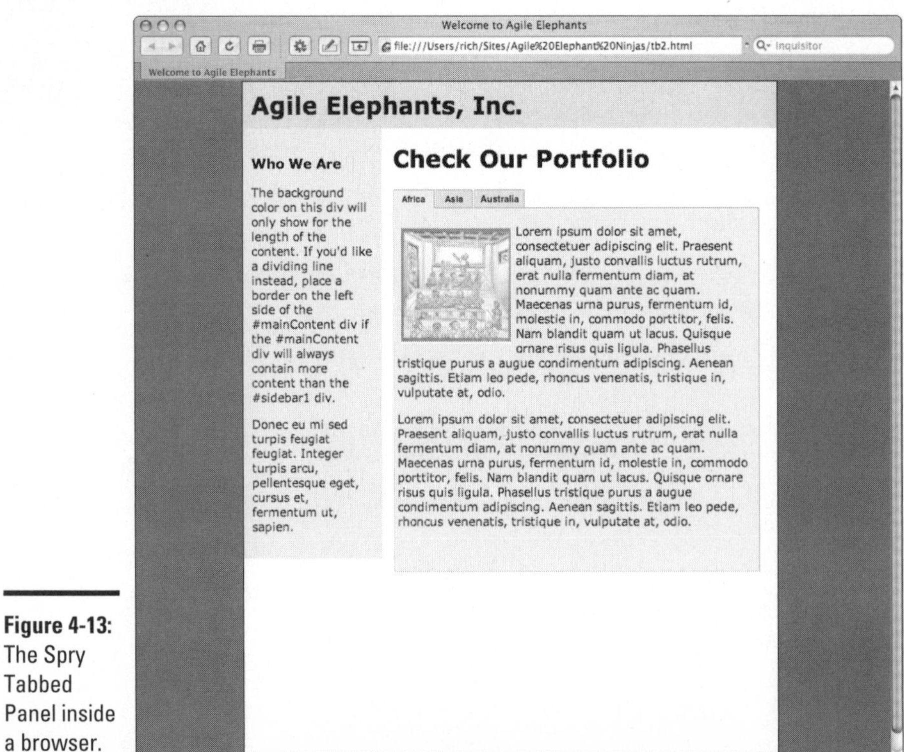

Figure 4-13: The Spry Tabbed Panel inside a browser.

2. **Click the Spry Collapsible Panel button on the Layout Insert panel.**

   Or choose Insert⇨Spry⇨Spry Collapsible Panel.

   The collapsible panel is added to your page, as shown in Figure 4-14.

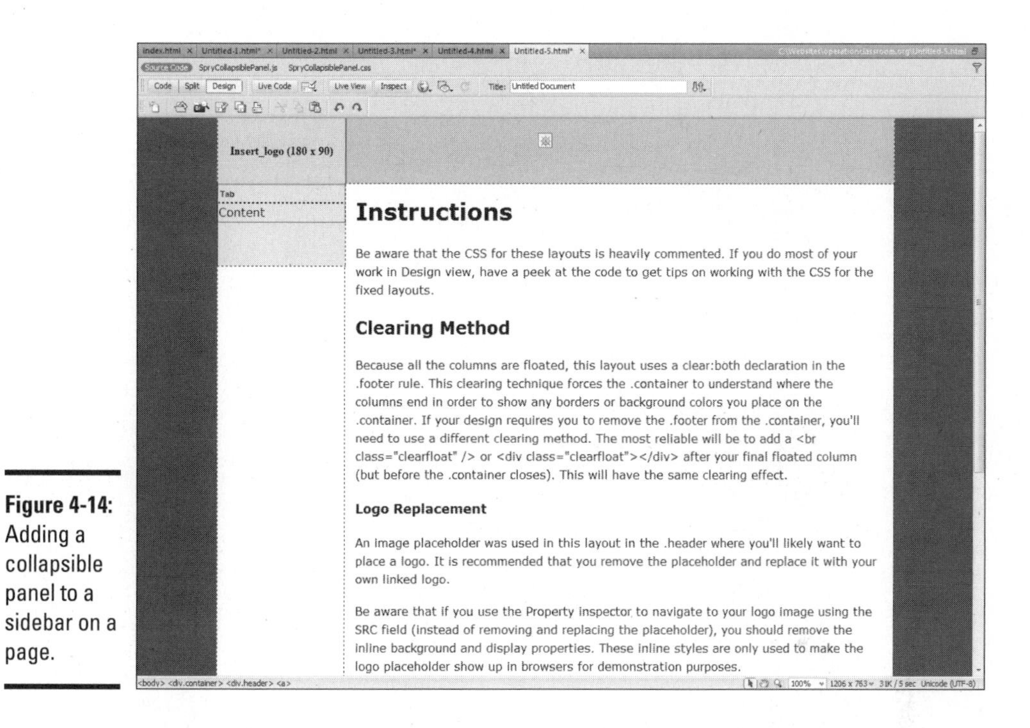

Figure 4-14: Adding a collapsible panel to a sidebar on a page.

3. **Select the collapsible panel with the mouse to display the panel's properties.**

   Figure 4-15 displays the Spry Collapsible Panel Properties inspector.

Figure 4-15: Setting up the properties of a collapsible panel.

4. In the Display drop-down box, specify the state of the panel in Design view.

5. In the Default State drop-down box, indicate whether the panel should be open or closed by default.

6. If you want to animate the collapse-and-expand process, select the Enable Animation check box.

I recommend it. It's cool!

7. Add content to the collapsible panel by selecting the panel and typing away.

If the panel is collapsed, press the eye icon to the right of the header.

Figures 4-16 and 4-17 show the collapsible panel in both states.

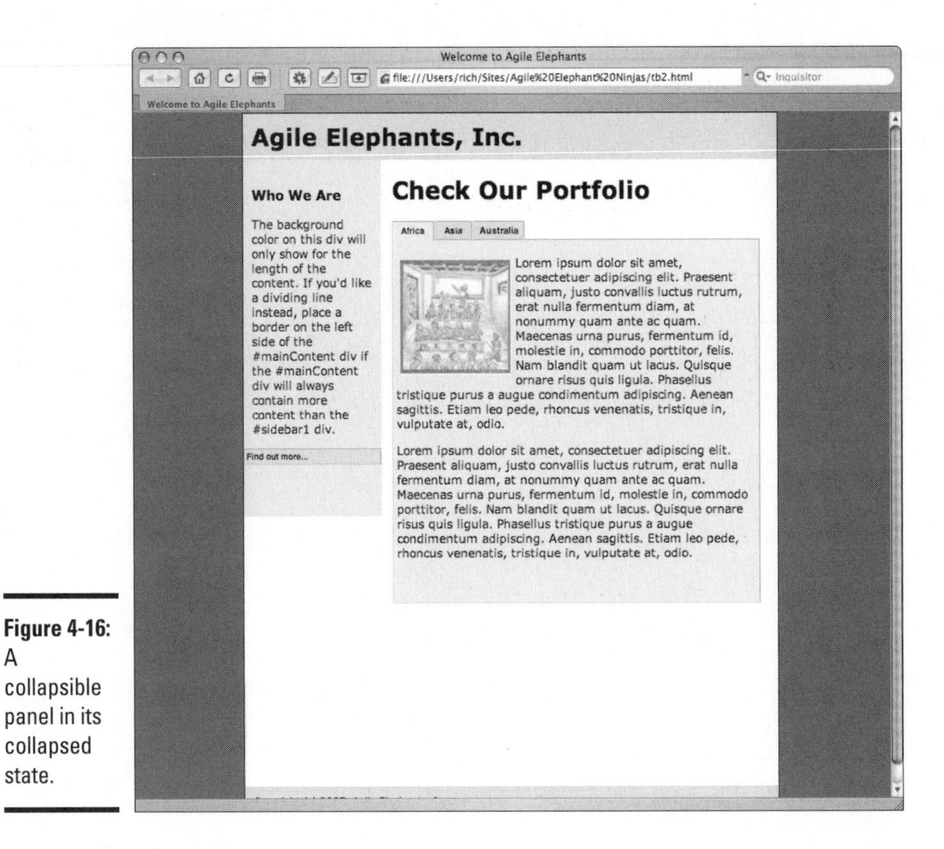

Figure 4-16: A collapsible panel in its collapsed state.

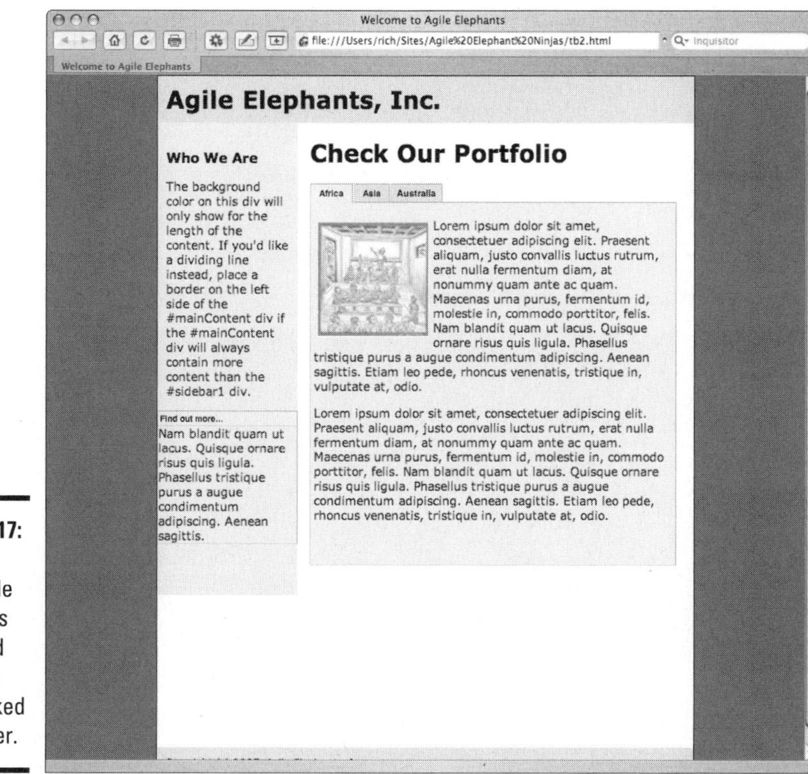

Figure 4-17: This collapsible panel was expanded when the user clicked the header.

Chapter 5: Forms Follow Function

In This Chapter

- **Working with HTML forms in Dreamweaver**
- **Making accessible forms**
- **Adding text fields, check boxes, lists, and other controls**
- **Adding a jump menu**

Forms are the primary vehicle in HTML to enable site visitors to interact with your Web site. It doesn't matter whether they're typing in a search box or entering all their personal details on an order form, an HTML form is used to collect data and send it to a remote server.

In this chapter, I show you how to set up forms in Dreamweaver. Keep in mind, however, a form isn't a standalone module. It always works with a CGI (Common Gateway Interface) program running on the server to process the input. Therefore, make sure that you have the URL and assorted details to connect your form to the server program.

If you want a primer on HTML forms, thumb through Book III.

Adding a Form

Although the `form` element in HTML doesn't show up on the Web page itself, it contains the other form elements that users interact with, such as text boxes and buttons. The `form` element also contains the information necessary to connect with the CGI program on the server.

To add a form, follow these steps:

1. **Click the Forms tab on the Insert panel (shown in Figure 5-1), and then click the Form button.**

   You can also choose Insert➪Form➪Form.

   An empty `form` container is added to your document. As Figure 5-2 shows, the container appears as a rectangular box with a red dotted outline.

Figure 5-1: The Forms Insert panel provides quick access to form elements.

2. **Click the form to display its properties in the Properties inspector, as shown in Figure 5-3.**
3. **Enter a unique name in the Form ID box.**

   Use normal alphabetical and numerical characters, without spaces or special characters.
4. **In the Action box, enter the URL for the CGI program that resides on the server.**

   Often these programs end up in a `cgi-bin` subdirectory on your Web server; for example, `http://www.myserver.com/cgi-bin/fprocess.pl`.
5. **Select a transmit method (`Default`, `GET`, `POST`) in the Method drop-down list.**
   - `GET` appends the form data to the request URL. As a result, users can see this information in the browser's address box.
   - `POST` embeds the form data in the HTTP request, which is hidden from the user when the form is sent.
   - `Default` uses the default setting in the browser, which is usually the `GET` method.

Figure 5-2: A form is added to a Web page as an empty, rectangular container.

Figure 5-3: Selecting a form displays its properties.

Check the details of the CGI program you're using to see which transmit method it's expecting.

6. **(Optional) To specify the window to display the data returned by the CGI form processor, select a value from the Target drop-down box. Or, leave this box blank (which is more typical).**

   - `_blank` opens the returning document in a new window.
   - `_parent` displays the document in the parent window of the current one.
   - `_self` displays the document in the same window that sent the form.
   - `_top` opens the returning document in the top-level window (replacing any frames).

7. **Select a MIME encoding type from the Enctype drop-down list if your CGI program requires it.**

   The `application/x-www-form-urlencode` value is usually used with the `POST` method.

   If you're uploading a file as part of the form submittal, use `multipart/form-data` value.

   Otherwise, you can leave this box blank.

At this point, the basic shell of your form is ready to go. You're ready to add elements to it.

Making Your Form Elements Accessible

Accessibility is a key issue to consider as you create your forms; you must ensure that they can be used by all visitors to your site, even those folks who use nontraditional browsers. By default, Dreamweaver provides support for these accessibility features.

When you add a `form` element to your document by using the Forms Insert panel, the Input Tag Accessibility Attributes dialog box automatically appears by default, as shown in Figure 5-4.

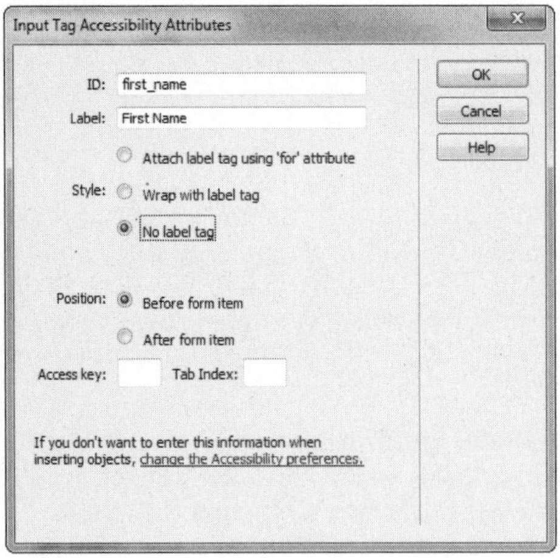

Figure 5-4: Accessibility matters! Make your forms work for everyone.

Here's how to fill out the dialog box to make the element accessible:

1. **Add a unique ID value in the ID box.**

   Add a name that effectively describes the data you're capturing, such as `first_name` for a First Name text box.

2. **(Optional) Enter a descriptive label in the Label box.**

   Dreamweaver uses this text as the label for your field.

3. **In the Style option group, choose the way in which you want to associate the label with the field.**

   Here are your options:

   - *Wrap with Label Tag:* Wraps an HTML `label` element around the text field. Normally, this option is the easiest to work with.
   - *Attach with Label Tag Using "for" Attribute:* Associates a `label` element with the text field by using the `label` tag's `for` attribute.
   - *No Label Tag:* Omits a `label` element. You have to add your own text or `label` element later if you want to identify the field for users.

4. **In the Position option group, decide whether the label should be placed before or after the field.**

   If you choose the No Label Tag option in Step 3, you can skip this step.

5. **Enter a single letter in the Access Key text box if you want to add a hotkey for keyboard access to the text field.**

   To select the text field, Windows users press Alt+*letter;* Mac users press Control+*letter.*

   If you add an access key, be sure to let users know explicitly about this shortcut. Otherwise it's never used.

6. **Enter in the Tab Index text box a number value that indicates the order in which you want this field to be selected when a user presses the Tab key.**

7. **Click OK.**

If you prefer not to have the Input Tag Accessibility Attributes dialog box displayed when you add a form element, click the Change the Accessibility Preferences link in the dialog box to display the Preferences dialog box. In the Accessibility category, deselect the Form Elements check box and click OK.

Adding Form Elements

HTML provides several different types of elements for capturing data from a user and sending it to the remote server for processing. Table 5-1 lists the common HTML elements according to the type of data they capture.

Table 5-1 Common HTML Elements by Type

Type of Information	*HTML Elements*
Text	Text field (single line), Textarea (multi-line), Password field (masked input)
Yes/No	Check box
Multiple choice	Select list, Radio group
Hidden	Hidden field
File upload	File field
Action buttons	Submit button, Reset button, Push button

Capturing text

The most common type of data you capture is plain-text input. HTML provides three types of text elements:

- **Text field** captures single lines of text.
- **Textarea** provides space for multiple lines of text.
- **Password field** allows a *masked control* for entering sensitive passwords. An asterisk or dot appears in the control for each character the user enters.

To add a text field, follow these steps:

1. **In the Document window, position the text cursor at the spot in which you want to place the new field inside your form.**

   Don't worry if you haven't created a form yet. Dreamweaver asks whether you want to create one when it adds the text field.

2. **Click the Text Field button on the Forms Insert panel.**

   By default, the Input Tag Accessibility Options dialog box appears.

3. **Enter accessibility options.**

   See the section, "Making Your Form Elements Accessible," earlier in this chapter, to fill in the dialog box. When you close the Input Tag Accessibility Options dialog box, the text box is added to the form.

4. **Select the text box with your mouse to display the TextField properties on the Properties inspector.**

   Figure 5-5 shows the Properties inspector.

5. **Specify the type of text field in the Type option group: single line, multi-line, or password.**

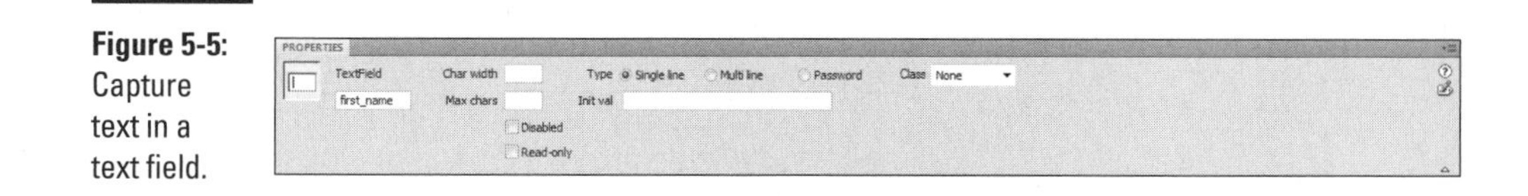

Figure 5-5: Capture text in a text field.

6. **Enter a value in the TextField box if this box is blank.**

   If you entered an ID value in the Input Tag Accessibility Options dialog box, this value is already displayed.

7. **If you want to adjust the default visible width of the text box, enter a value in the Char Width box.**

   The width is approximately the number of characters that can be displayed in the box.

8. **(Optional) Enter a value in either the Max Chars (Single Line, Password) or Num Lines (Multi Line) box.**

   If you selected Single line or Password in the Type group, you can enter a value in the Max Chars box. If this field is blank, users can enter as many characters as they want. If you enter a value, users are limited to the number of characters you specify. For example, for a U.S. state field, you can limit the size to two characters.

   If you selected Multi Line in the Type group, you can specify the number of lines that should be displayed in the box.

9. **If you selected Multi Line in the Type group, you can specify how to wrap text in the Wrap drop-down list. Otherwise skip to Step 10.**

   - `Off` and `Default` prevent users from wrapping text to the next line.
   - `Virtual` shows word wrap in the text element but sends the data to the server as a single string.
   - `Physical` wraps text in the text element and sends the data to the server in the same format.

10. **If you want to specify an initial value inside the element, enter it in the Init Value box.**

Creating a drop-down list box

A *drop-down list box* (or *drop-down menu*) gives you a way to get multiple-choice values from users without taking up much real estate on your form. Here's how to add one of these elements to your form:

1. **In the Document window, position your text cursor at the spot in which you want to place the new drop-down list box inside your form.**

   Dreamweaver asks whether you want to create a list box when it adds the text field.

2. **Click the List/Menu button on the Forms Insert panel.**

   By default, the Input Tag Accessibility Options dialog box appears.

3. **Enter accessibility options.**

   See the section, "Making Your Form Elements Accessible," earlier in this chapter to fill in the dialog box. When you close the Input Tag Accessibility Options dialog box, the drop-down list box is added to the form.

4. **Select the list with your mouse to display the List/Menu properties on the Properties bar.**

5. **Click the List Values button to display the List Values dialog box.**

   Figure 5-6 shows the List Values dialog box.

Figure 5-6: Entering list-box values.

6. **Click the + button to add a new list item in the List Values dialog box.**

7. **In the Item Label column, enter the text you want displayed in the list box.**

8. **Press Tab to move the cursor to the Value column.**

9. **In the Value column, enter a value that you want to send to the server program when this item is selected.**

10. **Repeat Steps 6 through 9 for each item in your list.**

11. **Click OK when your list is ready to go.**

12. **By default, Menu is selected in the Type group for a drop-down list box. However, if you want to display a full list, choose List.**

    Although the List type isn't often used, it allows a user to select multiple items inside the list box when the Allow Multiple check box is selected.

13. **If you want to select a default value, select an item from the Initially Selected list.**

Adding a check box

A *check box* is the simplest HTML control because it's used for capturing yes/no (Boolean) values. If the check box is selected, a checked value is sent to the server.

To add a check box, follow these steps:

1. **In the Document window, position the text cursor at the spot in which you want to place the new check box inside your form.**
2. **Click the Check Box button on the Forms Insert panel.**

   By default, the Input Tag Accessibility Options dialog box appears.
3. **Enter accessibility options.**

   See the section, "Making Your Form Elements Accessible," earlier in this chapter, to fill in the dialog box. When you close the Input Tag Accessibility Options dialog box, a check box is added to the form.
4. **Select the check box with your mouse to display the Checkbox properties on the Properties inspector.**
5. **In the Checked Value box, enter the value that you want to be sent to the server.**
6. **Indicate the default value of the check box in the Initial State group.**

Adding a radio group

A drop-down list box (see the section "Creating a drop-down list box," earlier in this chapter) is perhaps the most popular way to display a multiple-choice list of items in a form. However, you can also display a set of mutually exclusive items by using a *radio group* (from which the user selects an option by clicking a radio button).

To add a radio group, follow these steps:

1. **Position the text cursor at the spot in which you want to place the new radio group.**
2. **Click the Radio Group button on the Forms Insert panel.**

   The Radio Group dialog box appears, as shown in Figure 5-7.
3. **Click the first default item in the Label column. Enter text that you want to be displayed beside the button.**
4. **Press Tab to move the cursor to the Value column.**
5. **In the Value column, enter a value that you want to send to the remote server when this radio option is selected.**
6. **Repeat Steps 3 through 5 for the second default item.**

Figure 5-7: Say what you will — radio buttons are an exclusive set to be around.

7. **Click the + button to add more items, if needed.**
8. **Repeat Steps 3 through 7 for each item in your list.**
9. **Choose the layout of the radio group from the Lay Out Using options:**

   You have two ways of separating the options in the radio group:

   - *To place each entry on a separate line:* Select the Link Breaks (
 Tags) option.
   - *To place each entry in its own cell in a table:* Choose Table.

10. **Click OK.**

    The radio group is added to your form.

You can configure each individual radio button (for example, setting its initial state) by selecting it with your mouse and then modifying its properties by using the Properties inspector. Note, however, that you can't use the Properties inspector to view the properties of the radio group as a whole after you create the group.

Powering up with buttons

The `form` element links the form to the remote program, and the input controls, such as text field or drop-down list box, capture the data. The final pieces of the puzzle are button controls, which give the form power by telling the `form` element to send the data to the server.

You can use one of three buttons:

- The **Submit** button tells the form to submit the form data to the server.
- The **Reset** button clears all data entered on the form.
- The **Push** button does nothing with the server, but can be programmed by using JavaScript to perform a specified action. (See Book V for more on JavaScript.)

TECHNICAL STUFF

Validating form values

You can use JavaScript to validate the values that users enter on your form. Using JavaScript form validation, you can check for required fields as well as for the correctness or validity of the data being sent *before* transmitting the data. (See Book V for details on how to add validity-checking scripts to forms.)

You can also consider using the Spry validation widgets, found on the Forms Insert panel: Spry Validation Text Field, Textarea, Checkbox, and Select.

To add a button, follow these steps:

1. **In the Document window, position the text cursor at the spot in which you want to place the new button inside your form.**

   If the cursor isn't inside a form, Dreamweaver asks whether you want to create one when it adds the button.

2. **Click the Button button on the Forms Insert panel.**

   By default, the Input Tag Accessibility Options dialog box appears.

3. **Enter accessibility options.**

   See the section, "Making Your Form Elements Accessible," earlier in this chapter, to fill in the dialog box. When you close the Input Tag Accessibility Options dialog box, a button is added to the form.

   A Submit button is created by default.

4. **Select the button with your mouse to display the Button properties on the Properties inspector.**

5. **Select a button type based on the value of the Action group.**

   Use Submit Form for Submit buttons. Use Reset Form for Reset buttons. Use None for plain push buttons.

6. **If you want to change the button text, enter a value in the Value box.**

Creating a Jump Menu

Although a jump menu isn't an element you would see on a normal data-entry form, it's one of the most practical uses of a drop-down list box. A *jump menu* is a list of links in which a user goes to a URL that corresponds to a selection in the list box. You can create a jump menu the hard way, by using JavaScript and a normal drop-down list box — but you don't have to. Dreamweaver simplifies this process with its Jump Menu control. Here's how to use it to add a jump menu to your page:

1. **In the Document window, position the text cursor at the spot in which you want to place the new jump menu inside your page.**
2. **Click the Jump Menu button on the Forms Insert panel.**

   The Insert Jump Menu dialog box appears, as shown in Figure 5-8.

Figure 5-8: Dreamweaver makes it easy to create a handy-dandy jump menu.

3. **Enter the display text of your first link in the Text box.**

   You may want to add a `(Jump to)` or `(Choose one)` prompt as the first item in the list.
4. **Enter the URL of the first link in the When Selected, Go to URL box.**
5. **Click the + button to add a new jump entry.**
6. **Repeat Steps 3 through 5 as needed until your list of jumps is completed.**
7. **If you want a Go button to appear alongside the jump menu, select the Insert Go Button after Menu check box.**
8. **If your first item is a prompt, such as `Jump to`, select the Select First Item after URL Change check box.**
9. **Click OK.**

   Dreamweaver adds the drop-down jump menu and JavaScript code automatically to your Web page.

After the jump menu is inserted, Dreamweaver treats that element just like a traditional drop-down list box.

Chapter 6: Working with CSS

In This Chapter

- Working with the CSS Styles panel
- Creating CSS rules visually rather than in plain code
- Creating an external CSS style sheet
- Linking your document to an external style sheet

Cascading Style Sheets (CSS) is a companion technology to HTML that provides a far more powerful way to control the formatting and layout of your Web page than using HTML alone.

In this chapter, I show you how to work with CSS inside the Dreamweaver environment. In particular, you explore how the use of the Dreamweaver enhanced CSS features is much easier and more productive than working with the CSS source code alone.

Because this chapter focuses on using CSS in Dreamweaver, it doesn't attempt to explain what CSS is. Therefore, before you read this chapter, thumb through Book IV to get a handle on the general information about CSS rules, the workings of the `style` element, and the basics of linking external style sheets (`.css` files) into a document.

Managing Styles with the CSS Styles Panel

Although CSS enables you to create visually appealing Web pages, CSS is, on its own, somewhat technical to work with. Therefore, unless you prefer to get your hands dirty with raw Cascading Style Sheet code, you'll find the CSS Styles panel to be your styling guru inside Dreamweaver. You can use the CSS Styles panel to keep track of the CSS rules associated with either the selected (or current) element or the entire document. To view the CSS Styles panel, choose Window➪CSS Styles.

Working with styles of the selected element

When you click the Current button at the top of the CSS Styles panel, you toggle the display to Current mode, as shown in Figure 6-1.

The Current mode panel is divided into three panes: Summary for Selection pane, Rules pane, and Properties pane. I describe each of these panes in the following sections.

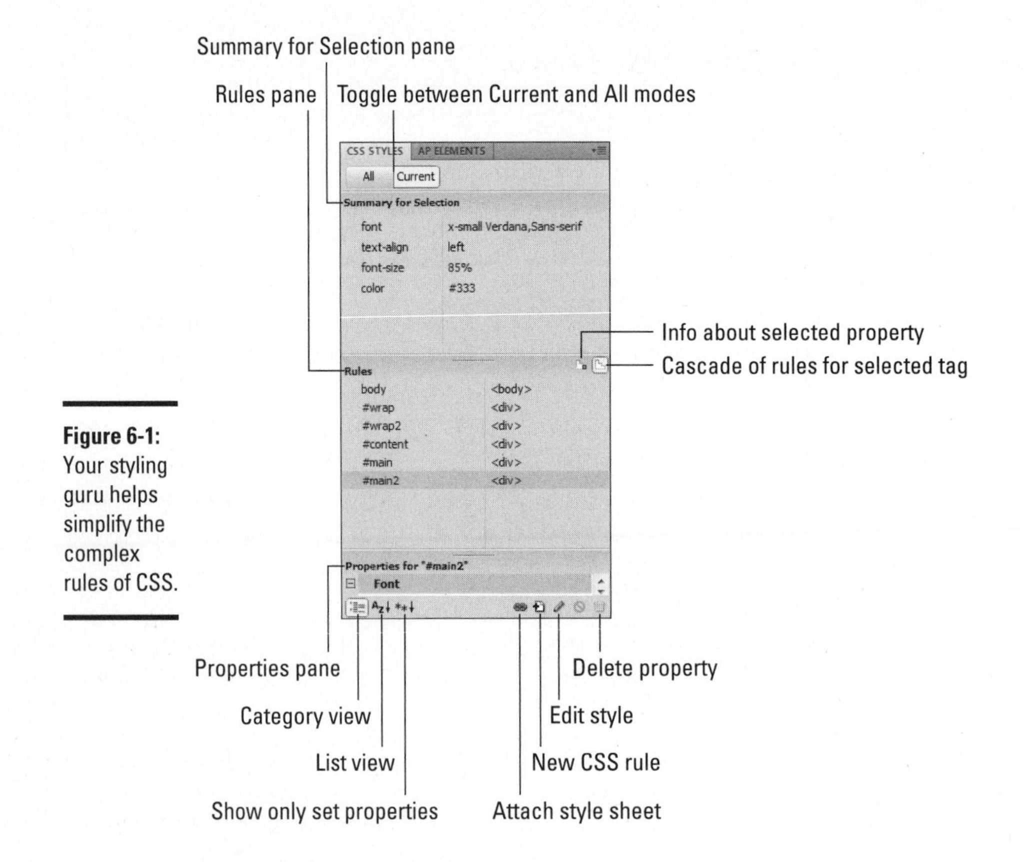

Figure 6-1: Your styling guru helps simplify the complex rules of CSS.

Summary for Selection pane

The Summary for Selection pane displays the CSS properties for the selected element in a rule-value list. The summary pane is read-only, although you can double-click it to display a dialog box for editing the rule.

When you select a property, the Rules and Properties panes are updated to display property information associated with its rule.

Rules pane

The Rules pane either tells you where the selected property is defined in your source code or lists the cascade of rules for the selected element. The buttons to the right of the pane toggle between these two modes.

Given the cascading nature of CSS, the Rules pane can be extremely helpful in tracking down a style rule.

Properties pane

The Properties pane provides a way to edit the style properties of the selected rule. By default, the properties shown in the list are explicitly set in your CSS code. You can then tweak a property by selecting a new value from its drop-down list or typing your own.

The Properties pane has two other modes, each of which you can access from the button set on the left side of the status bar (refer to Figure 6-1).

✦ **Category** view shows all possible properties arranged in categories. Set properties are placed at the top of each category and are shown in blue text.

✦ **List** view lists possible properties in alphabetical order. Set properties are displayed in blue text at the top of the list.

  List view, although complete, can make quite a long list to have to scroll down and navigate to a specific property.

Working with all styles

The CSS Styles panel can also toggle to All mode, to work with rules in the whole document. As shown in Figure 6-2, the panel is divided into an All Rules pane and a Properties pane.

The All Rules pane displays in a tree-like structure all CSS rules associated with the document. Rules are organized by their containers — either a `style` element inside the document or an external style sheet attached to the HTML file.

The Properties pane acts the same way as it does in Current mode. (See the "Working with styles of the selected element" section, earlier in this chapter.) The pane provides a way to edit the properties of the CSS rule selected in the All Rules pane. You can also view the Properties pane in Category and List views.

Creating a New CSS Rule

Rather than sending you to the document source to create a new CSS rule, Dreamweaver provides a visual way to do that from within the CSS Styles panel. Follow these instructions to add a CSS rule to your document or style sheet:

1. **Click the New CSS Rule icon (see Figure 6-3), in the lower-right corner of the CSS Styles panel.**

   The New CSS Rule dialog box appears, as shown in Figure 6-4.

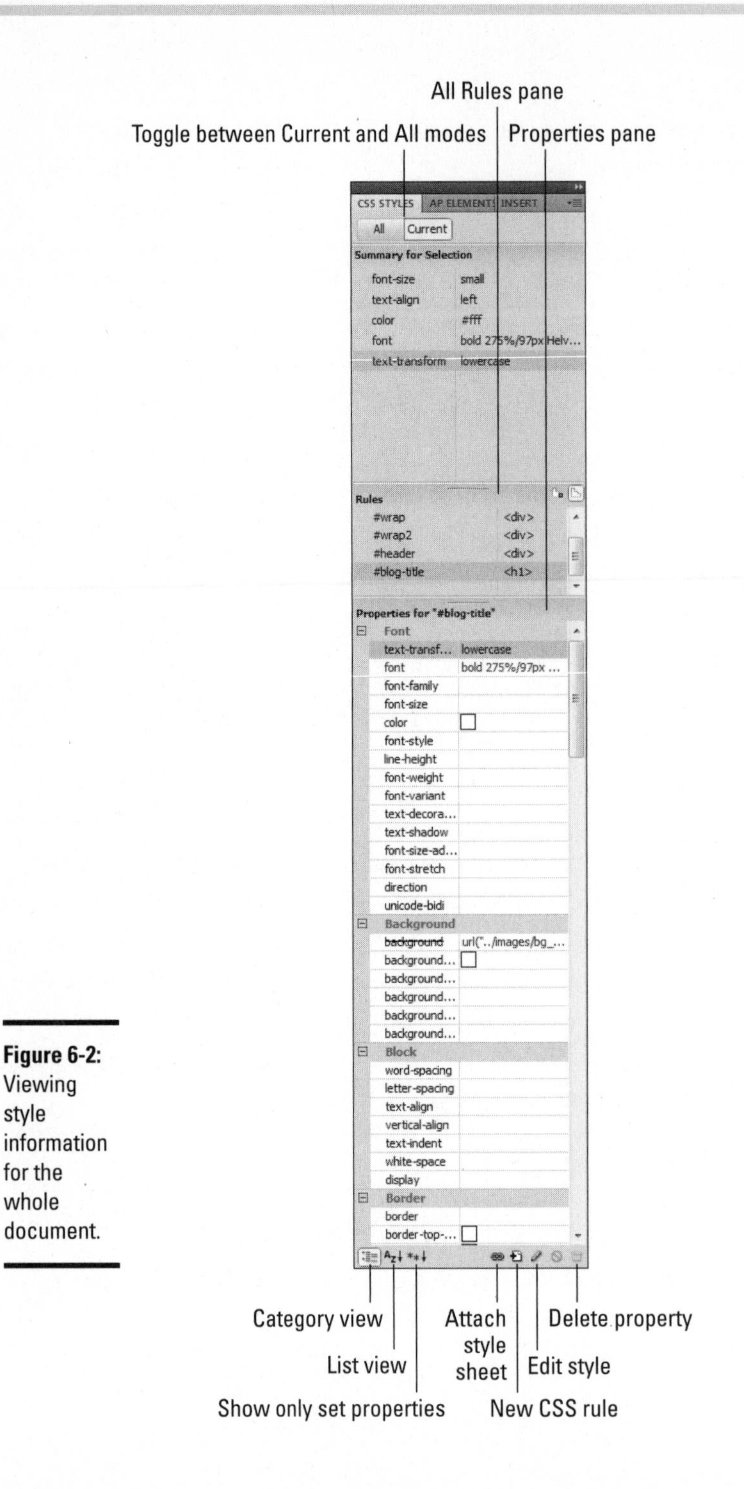

Figure 6-2: Viewing style information for the whole document.

Figure 6-3: Adding a new rule from the CSS Styles panel.

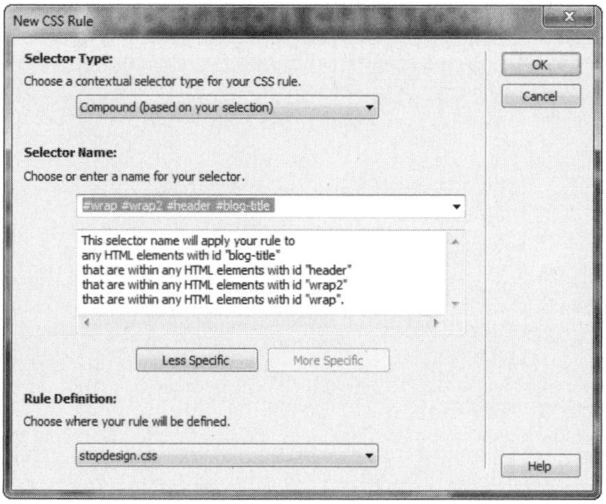

New CSS rule

Figure 6-4: Rules, rules, rules. Even style sheets need some structure.

New CSS Rule

Selector Type:

Choose a contextual selector type for your CSS rule.

Compound (based on your selection)

Selector Name:

Choose or enter a name for your selector.

#wrap #wrap2 #header #blog-title

This selector name will apply your rule to any HTML elements with id "blog-title" that are within any HTML elements with id "header" that are within any HTML elements with id "wrap2" that are within any HTML elements with id "wrap".

Less Specific | More Specific

Rule Definition:

Choose where your rule will be defined.

stopdesign.css

OK | Cancel | Help

2. **Choose the type of selector from the Selector Type options.**

   Your options are described in this list:

   - *Class:* Use Class when you want to apply the style rule by using the `class` attribute of the elements.
   - *ID:* Use ID when you want to apply the style rule to just one element using the `id` attribute.
   - *Tag:* Use Tag when you want to add to or redefine an existing HTML tag's properties.
   - *Combined:* Use Combined when you need to apply the rule based on the current selection.

3. **Enter the appropriate value in the text box based on your selection from Step 2.**

   - If you choose Class, enter a period followed by the class name in the box. Remember that a valid class selector begins with a period.
   - If you choose ID, select an ID from the drop-down list.
   - If you choose Tag, select an HTML tag from the drop-down list.
   - If you choose Combined, enter the selector value.

4. **Choose the location in which you want to add this new rule.**

   Here are your options:

   - *Existing style sheet:* If you choose this option, select a style sheet file that you already created.
   - *New style sheet:* Select the (New Style Sheet file) item from the Define In drop-down list.
   - *Current document:* Select the This Document Only option if you want to embed the style rule inside a `style` element of the current document.

5. **Click OK.**

   The CSS Rule Definition dialog box appears, as shown in Figure 6-5.

Figure 6-5: Define your style rule in the comfort of your own CSS Rule Definition dialog box.

6. **Modify all the properties you want to set inside the dialog box.**

   One of the greatest benefits to using Dreamweaver for creating style rules is that this dialog box gives you full access to all possible properties at your disposal. Feel free to go to town. Leave no stone unturned. Leave no CSS property overlooked.

   See Book IV for more details on these specific properties.

7. **Click OK.**

   Your style rule is created in the location you specified.

Editing Style Properties and Rules

You can edit style properties *and* complete rules in the CSS Styles panel. To edit a property of the selected rule, simply use the Property pane in the CSS Styles panel.

To edit a rule

- **If you're in Current mode:** Double-click a property in the Summary for Section pane to display the rule in which the property is defined. Or click the Edit Style icon on the bottom of the panel.
- **If you're in All mode:** Double-click a rule in the All Rules pane (or select the rule and click the Edit Style icon).

The CSS Rule Definition dialog box appears (refer to Figure 6-5). Make the changes you want and then click OK.

When you change a style here, it affects all of the elements that have this style, not just the current element you are working with.

Creating an External Style Sheet in Dreamweaver

Because a Cascading Style Sheet is a code-oriented document, you work with a style sheet in the Document window only in Code view. (Code-oriented documents have no Design view.) If you're comfortable with CSS code, you'll feel at home writing style rules by hand. However, if you prefer not to stare at a source-code file with strange-looking CSS syntax, you can use the CSS Styles panel as a visual interface as you define your style sheet.

Here's how to create a CSS style sheet in Dreamweaver:

1. **Choose File⇨New.**

   The New Document dialog box appears (see Figure 6-6). ***Remember:*** You get no frills in the Layout or Preview boxes because a style sheet is all text based.

2. **Select CSS from the Page Type list.**
3. **Click Create.**

   An untitled style sheet is created and displayed in the Document window (see Figure 6-7).

4. **Add CSS style rules to the style sheet.**

   You can use the CSS Styles panel with a style sheet, freeing you from dealing directly with the source code. See the "Creating a New CSS Rule" section, earlier in this chapter, for more details on using the CSS Styles panel to create new rules.

5. **Choose File⇨Save.**

   Save the style sheet in the location you want it to occupy in your site.

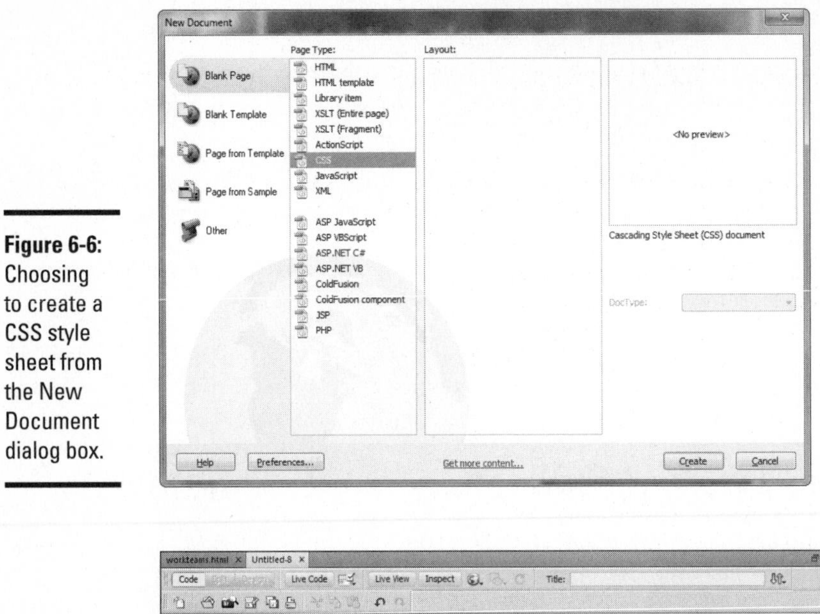

Figure 6-6: Choosing to create a CSS style sheet from the New Document dialog box.

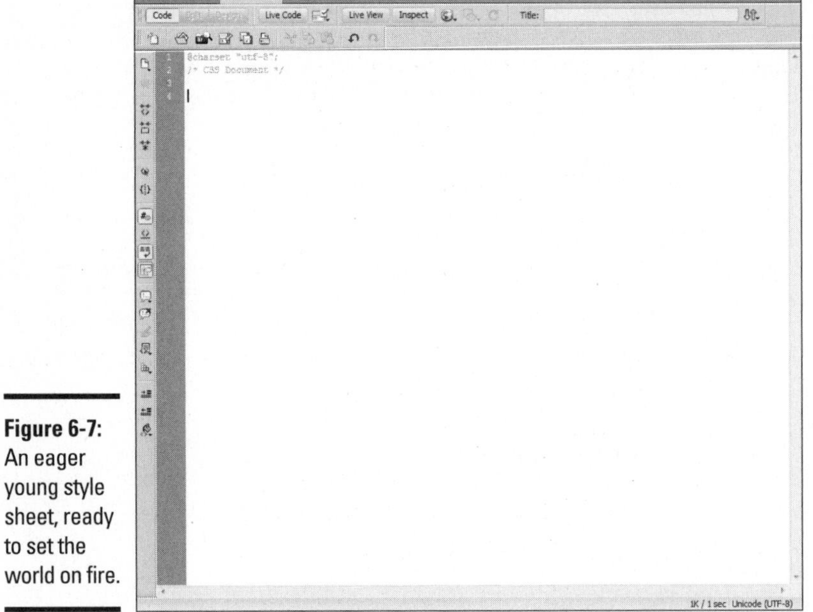

Figure 6-7: An eager young style sheet, ready to set the world on fire.

Applying and Removing a Style in Your Document

After styles are defined in your style sheets, you're ready to apply them to elements in your Web pages. If you're comfortable working with HTML, you can apply a style by making source-code changes. But, if you prefer to work with the Dreamweaver visual editor, here's how to apply a style in Design view:

1. **Select the text or element that you want to apply a style to.**
2. **Click the Style drop-down list in the Properties inspector.**

   Alternatively, you can choose Text➪CSS Styles to perform the same task.

   Figure 6-8 shows the list of styles available in my document.

Figure 6-8: Listing styles in the Properties inspector.

3. **Select the style you want to use.**

   Your selection is then updated to reflect the new style properties.

If you want to remove a style, select the text or element and choose the None option from the Style drop-down list in the Properties inspector.

Linking to an External Style Sheet

You can link to an external style sheet by following these steps:

1. **Choose Format➪CSS Styles➪Attach Style Sheet.**

   The Attach External Style Sheet dialog box appears, as shown in Figure 6-9.
2. **Enter the style sheet you want to attach in the File/URL box.**
3. **Click the Link option to attach the style sheet in the typical way.**

   Alternatively, if you want to nest style sheets, use the Import option.

   You can use the advanced technique known as *nesting* to reference a `.css` style sheet from another style sheet using an `@import url( "stylesheet.css" )` command in the CSS code.

Figure 6-9: Hear the wedding bells ring — wedding a style sheet to an HTML document.

4. **Select the screen item from the Media drop-down list.**

   If the style sheet you're attaching is for a specific type of device (such as a handheld device or a printer), select the appropriate alternative.

5. **Click OK.**

It's important to keep in mind that, when working with external style sheets, you need to publish your `.css` file with your HTML page.

Getting a Kick-Start with Sample Styles

Dreamweaver has several sample style sheets you can access by clicking the Sample Style Sheets link in the Attach External Style Sheet dialog box (refer to Figure 6-9). The Sample Style Sheets dialog box appears (see Figure 6-10). None of the styles in these samples will set the world on fire with its innovation or high-level design flair. However, they're all good tools that can give you a kick-start as you work with styles in Dreamweaver.

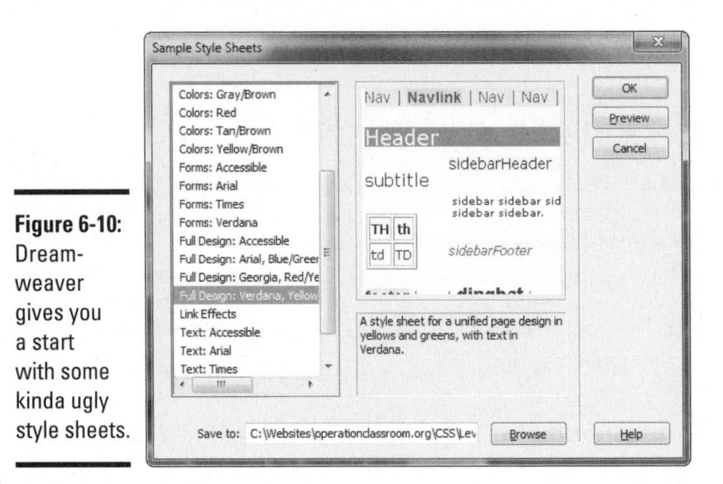

Figure 6-10: Dreamweaver gives you a start with some kinda ugly style sheets.

Chapter 7: When DWT Calls: Using Templates for a Consistent Look

In This Chapter

- ✓ **Grasping the key concepts of templates**
- ✓ **Creating a template from scratch**
- ✓ **Transforming an existing document into a template**
- ✓ **Creating a new document based on a template**

After you develop a killer page design and your text and layout formatting are exactly the way you want them, you should reproduce this common look throughout your Web site. The old-fashioned way was to create a master HTML file and then use it as the basis for starting each new document you create. Although that method can still work, its shortcomings become clear when you want to make a change to the master file. To do so, you have to open each of your documents and make the change.

Templates solve this problem. They provide an easy way to create a master document, but at the same time maintain a link with the created documents. Therefore, any time you tweak the template, you can update all the documents created with it as well.

In this chapter, you discover how to use templates to simplify managing your Web pages and help maintain a consistent look across your site.

Understanding Dreamweaver Templates

A *template* in Dreamweaver is a special file that serves as a master model of a document for site pages. Here are the key concepts to understand when working with Dreamweaver templates:

- **A Dreamweaver template is a Web document with Dreamweaver-specific instructions inside it.** A template file for an HTML document has a `.dwt` extension and is used only inside Dreamweaver, not on your live Web site.
- **A template page is divided into editable (unlocked) and non-editable (locked) regions.** A non-editable region helps you ensure that content or layout code is consistent and unaltered on all template-based pages. The editable regions give you a way to provide custom content for individual pages.

- **When editing a template, you edit both the editable and non-editable regions.** When you're working with a document created from the template, however, you can make changes only in the editable regions.
- **Inside the document body of a template-based page, only editable regions can be edited.** Inside the document head, Dreamweaver automatically creates an editable section for you for adding scripts and style instructions, for example.
- **A template is always enclosed inside a Dreamweaver site, and its file is stored in a special Templates subfolder, under the site's root folder.**

If you don't want to create a template yourself, you can find many pre-made templates available on the Web, although most of them are commercial products. You can check out `www.dreamweaver-templates.org` for reviews of both free and commercial templates.

Creating a Template

The process of creating a template is much like creating a normal Web page, except that you define editable and non-editable regions for the document. I show you two ways.

From scratch

Here's how to create a template from scratch:

1. **Choose File⇨New.**

   The New Document dialog box appears.
2. **Click the Blank Template button on the left.**

   Figure 7-1 shows the template selections.
3. **Select HTML Template from the Template Type list.**

   Or, if you feel a hankering for Web programming, you can select one of the other template types.
4. **Select a layout from the Layout list.**

   The layouts are identical to the ones you can choose from when creating an ordinary HTML document. Select <None> if you prefer to start from a blank page.
5. **Select a document type in the DocType drop-down list.**
6. **Select from the Layout CSS drop-down list the location where you want to place CSS style information.**
7. **Click the Create button.**

   The template you created is shown in the Document window.

8. **Edit the design and layout of your template.**

   Using `div` elements or tables, organize your template by dividing it into non-editable and editable zones.

9. **Add content and features that you want to appear on every template-created page.**

   Company logos, navigation bars, and footers are typical examples of "global" content that is locked in non-editable regions.

10. **Add placeholder text in the regions that you intend to mark as editable.**

11. **Select the placeholder content with your mouse.**

    You can make almost anything an editable region: a single word, phrase, paragraph, image, `div` element, table, or individual table cell.

12. **Choose Insert⇨Template Objects⇨Editable Region.**

    Or, you can click the Templates drop-down button on the Common tab of the Insert panel and then choose the Editable Region menu item.

    The New Editable Region dialog box is shown (see Figure 7-2).

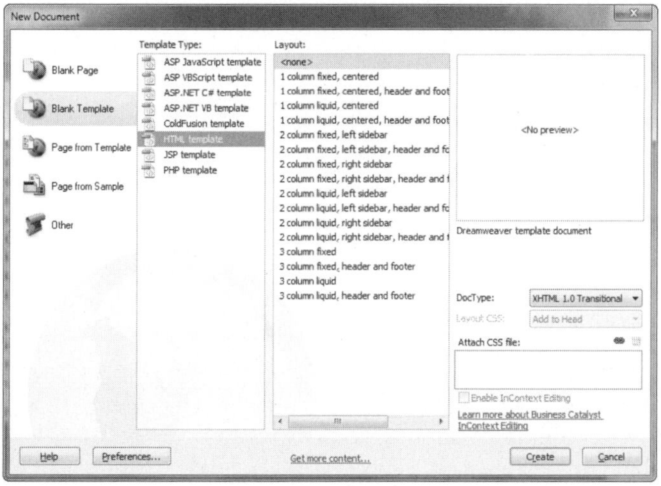

Figure 7-1: Creating a new template.

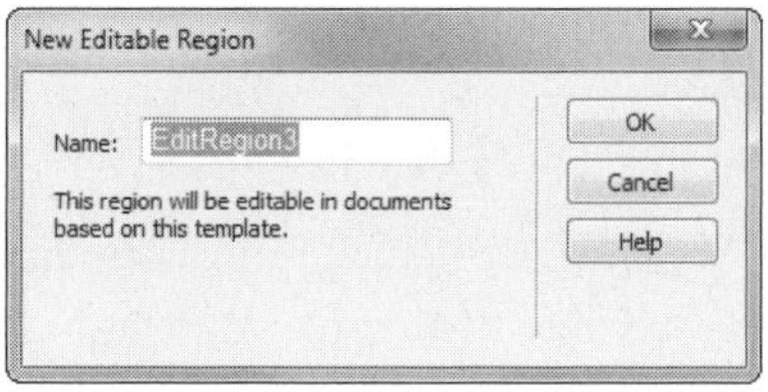

Figure 7-2: Add an editable region to a template.

13. **Name the region and click OK.**

    Dreamweaver marks the selection as an editable region, as shown in Figure 7-3.

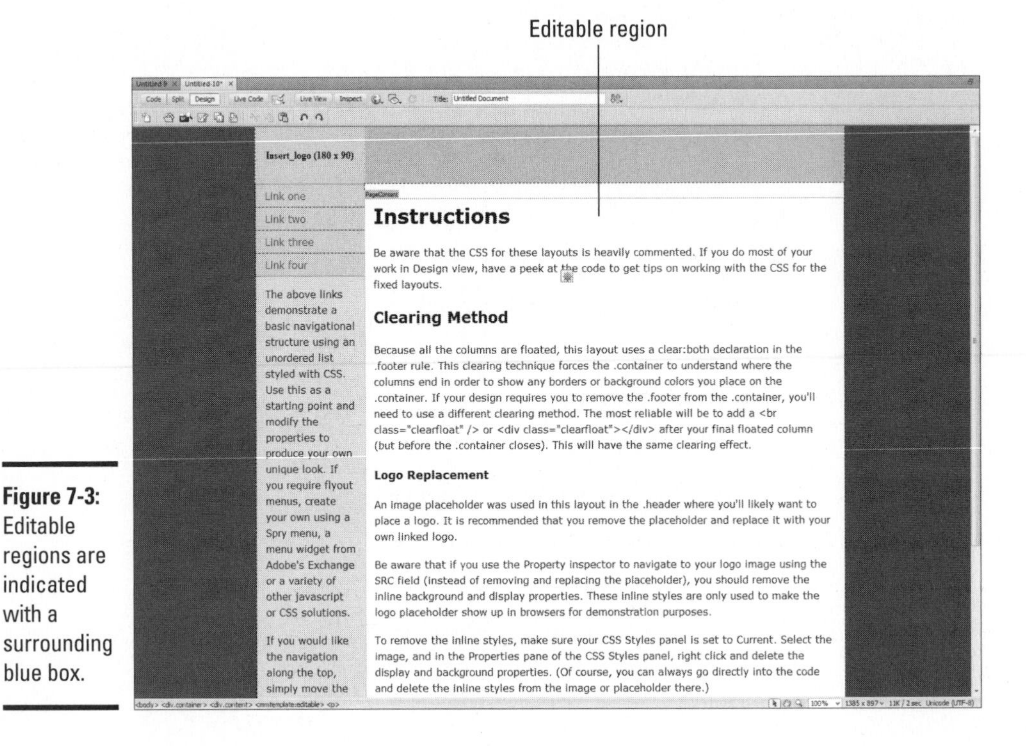

Figure 7-3: Editable regions are indicated with a surrounding blue box.

Your basic template is ready to go.

14. **Choose File➪Save.**

    The Save As Template dialog box (shown in Figure 7-4) appears.

15. **Select from the Site drop-down list the site you want to add the template to.**

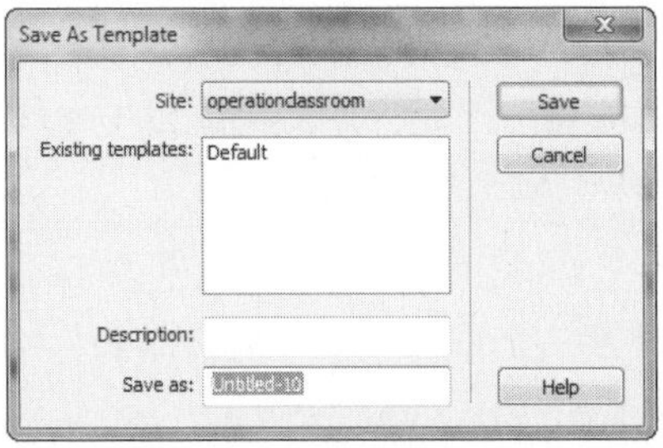

Save As Template
Site: operationclassroom
Existing templates: Default
Description:
Save as: Untitled-10
Save
Cancel
Help

Figure 7-4: Saving a template for later use.

16. **Add a name in the Save As box.**
17. **Click Save.**

    Dreamweaver saves the template in the Templates folder of the selected site and adds a `.dwt` extension.

Defining document-relative links in your template can be tricky. Dreamweaver expects the document-relative link to be based on the path *from* the Templates subfolder *to* the linked document. It's *not* the path from the template-based document to the linked page. You can help make sure that the correct path is stored by using the folder icon or the Point to File icon in the Properties inspector as you create the link.

From an existing page

In addition to allowing you to create a template from scratch, Dreamweaver enables you to transform an existing Web page into a template. Here's how:

1. **Open an existing page in the Document window.**

   After you save the document as a template, none of the existing content or layout is editable. Therefore you need to define editable regions before you save a file as a template.
2. **Select the content that you want to be editable.**
3. **Choose Insert⇨Template Objects⇨Editable Region.**

   The New Editable Region dialog box is shown (refer to Figure 7-2).
4. **Name the region and click OK.**

   Dreamweaver marks the selection as an editable region.
5. **Repeat Steps 2 through 4 for any other areas of your page that you want to be unlocked for editing.**
6. **Choose File⇨Save As Template.**

   The Save As Template dialog box appears.
7. **Select from the Site drop-down list the site you want to add the template to.**
8. **Add a name in the Save As box.**
9. **Click Save.**

   Dreamweaver saves the template in the template folder of the selected site and adds a `.dwt` extension.

Using a Template to Create a New Page

After your template is built, you're ready to create new pages based on it. To do so, follow these steps:

1. **Choose File⇨New.**

   The New Document dialog box appears.

2. **Click the Page from Template button.**

   The page is updated to display a list of sites, as shown in Figure 7-5.

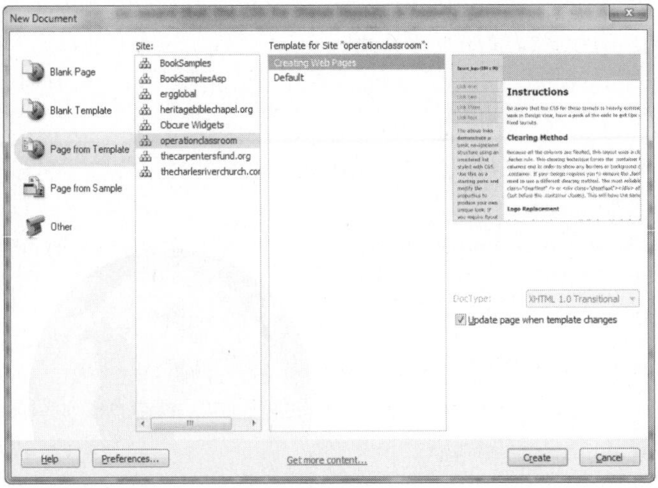

Figure 7-5: The New Document dialog box gives you access to all your templates.

3. **Select the site that contains the template you want to use.**
4. **Select a template from the template list box.**

   The preview box displays a thumbnail version of the template.

5. **Select the Update Page When Template Changes check box to maintain a link with the template.**

   If you select the check box, any changes you make in the template are updated in the new document.

   If you deselect the box, the link between the template and the document isn't preserved.

6. **Click Create.**

   A new page based on the template appears in the Document window.

7. **Edit the editable regions of the page.**

   Notice that the locked regions can't be edited or deleted, in either Design or Source view.

8. **Choose File⇨Save.**

   Save your document as you would save a normal Web page.

The Ripple Effect: Making a Change to Your Template

Templates provide a quick way to create a new document based on a prebuilt page layout. However, the real power of templates comes into play when you need to tweak the original template. Because the template maintains a connection with the documents created from it, you can apply changes automatically to all those pages by simply changing the master file. (You can also decide not to update the pages, if you want.)

To change a template and update all documents based on that template, follow these instructions:

1. **Open the template file.**

   You have three options:

   - If you're traditional, choose File⇨Open to display the Open dialog box. Navigate to the template file you want to modify and click Open.
   - If you're already working with the site that contains your template, save some time and head to the Files panel, and then double-click the template in the Templates folder.
   - Even better, if you have a document open that's attached to the template, choose Modify⇨Templates⇨Open Attached Template.

   The template is opened in the Document window.

2. **Modify the template the way you want.**

   Because you're working with the original template, you can make changes to both editable and non-editable regions.

3. **Choose File⇨Save.**

   The Update Template Files dialog box appears. It lists all files that are attached to the template.

4. **Click the Update button to update the document list.**

   Or, if you don't want to update, click the Don't Update button.

   If you choose to update, Dreamweaver works through each of the files in the list and makes the appropriate changes.

Attaching and Detaching a Template

When you create a document based on a template, you automatically attach the template to the new page. However, you can also attach a template to an existing page. When the page is attached, Dreamweaver applies the content of the template to the existing content.

To attach a template to an opened document, follow these steps:

1. **Choose Modify➪Templates➪Apply Template to Page.**

   The Select Template dialog box appears.

2. **Select a template.**
3. **Click Select.**

Bringing the template structure into an existing document can cause unexpected changes to the existing formatting. That's why I recommend creating a new file from the template and then copying and pasting the text from the original document.

Alternatively, you can detach a file from its template. When you do so, Dreamweaver unlocks all the non-editable regions, enabling you to make any changes you so desire. To detach a template from an open document, choose Modify➪Templates➪Detach from Template.

Chapter 8: Think Outside the Page: Managing Your Web Site

In This Chapter

- Creating a site
- Configuring site settings
- Working with the Files panel
- Transferring local and remote files
- Using the site map
- Checking site links

The first seven chapters in this minibook focus on how to work with the Adobe software package to create well-designed, attractive Web pages. However, it's time to think "outside the page" and focus on the Web site as a whole. Besides sporting a top-notch document editor, Dreamweaver serves as an ideal tool for managing your Web site. In this chapter, I show you how to use Dreamweaver to simplify the process of managing and working with local and remote files.

Creating and Configuring a Site

In Chapter 2 of this minibook, I walk you through a step-by-step example of creating a basic site in Dreamweaver. In this section, I show you how to do a more advanced setup and configuration.

To create a site, follow these steps:

1. **Choose Site⇨New Site.**

   The Site Definition dialog box appears.

2. **Enter a descriptive name for your site in the Site Name box.**
3. **In the Local Root Folder box, specify a location on your hard drive for storing site files.**

   Your local root folder is the working directory for your site.

4. **Click the Advanced Settings item.**

   Figure 8-1 shows the Advanced Settings section with the Local Info page selected.

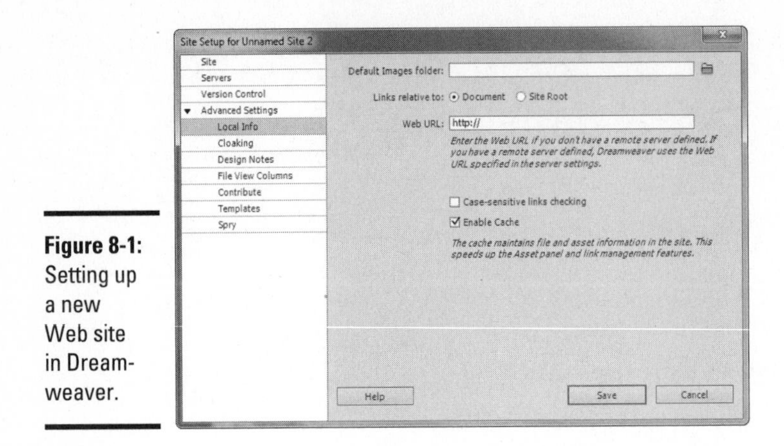

Figure 8-1: Setting up a new Web site in Dreamweaver.

5. **In the Default Images Folder box, give the default location in which you want to place site images.**

   It's often an images subfolder under your root.

6. **Specify how you want Dreamweaver to handle relative links in the Links Relative To option group.**

   If you select Document (the default), Dreamweaver creates document-relative links to another file on your site. If you select Site Root, Dreamweaver prefixes the full site's root URL before each link.

7. **Enter the URL for your Web site in the Web URL box.**

   This setting is used primarily when you specify Site Root in Step 6, but it comes in handy when you're verifying absolute URLs in the Dreamweaver link checker.

8. **Select the Case-Sensitive Links Checking check box if you want the link checker to check for case.**

   If your Web host uses a Unix server, be sure to select this option.

9. **Select the Enable Cache check box (the default) to enable Dreamweaver to store a site-based cache.**

   A cache helps to improve the performance of site-management tasks and to enable the Assets panel.

   The local settings of your site are ready. It's time to move to the remote server settings.

10. **Click the Servers item.**
11. **Enter the + button to add a new server definition.**
12. **Enter a descriptive name in the Server Name box.**
13. **Select an access method from the Connect Using drop-down box.**

FTP is the typical method if your site is hosted by an ISP or on a server you access over the Web. Some ISPs may offer Secure FTP (SFTP).

Here are the other, more advanced options:

- *Local/Network:* Use Local/Network if your Web server is on the same machine or local-area network that you use.
- *RDS:* Use RDS if you're connecting to a ColdFusion server.
- *WebDav:* Use WebDav if you connect to a server using Web-based Distributed Authoring and Versioning (WebDav) protocol.

Figure 8-2 shows the Remote Info page for FTP access.

Basic | Advanced

Server Name: Unnamed Server 2

Connect using: FTP

FTP Address: Port: 21

Username:

Password: Save

Test

Root Directory:

Web URL: http://

▸ More Options

Help | Save | Cancel

Figure 8-2: Most users configure their sites for FTP access.

14. **Enter remote-server details for the access method you selected in Step 12.**
15. **Click the Advanced tab.**
16. **Select the Maintain Synchronization Information check box if you want to keep the local and remote files in sync.**

    You do the synchronization process on the Files panel.
17. **Select the Automatically Upload Files to Server on Save check box if you want Dreamweaver to publish your local files each time you save them.**
18. **Select the Enable File Check Out check box if you plan to use Dreamweaver's multi-user file-management capabilities.**

    Your remote server settings are all gathered.
19. **Click Save.**

    You are returned to the Site Settings dialog box.
20. **Click Save again.**

    Your Web site is created. Dreamweaver opens the new site in the Files panel.

Editing Site Settings

All the site settings are made within the Site Definition dialog box. You can access the Site Definition dialog box for a site by performing these steps:

1. **Choose Site⇨Manage Sites.**

   The Manage Sites dialog box (shown in Figure 8-3) appears.

Figure 8-3: Choose any of your sites to edit.

2. **Select your site from the list.**
3. **Click the Edit button.**

   The Site Definition dialog box appears.

Note that as a shortcut, you can quickly display the Site Definition dialog box of your active site by double-clicking the site name in the Site drop-down list, located on the Files panel toolbar. Much easier!

Working with the Files Panel

The Files panel is your command-and-control center for your Dreamweaver site. You perform most site management tasks there. Figure 8-4 shows the Files panel in its normal mode.

Managing local files

Use the Files panel hierarchical directory to manage your site files. You can use this window much as you would a Windows Explorer or Mac Finder window to open, move, rename, and delete files.

Managing remote files

Although the default display of the Files panel shows the local files, Dreamweaver enables you to connect to the remote server to display a live view of the server files as well.

Put files

Get files

Check out

Refresh view

Check in

Connect to remote server

Synchronize

List of sites

View

Expand to show local/remote sites

FILES

operationclassr | Local view

Local Files	Size	Type	Modified	Checked Out
Site - operationclassr...		Folder	7/3/2010 10:48 PM	-
index.html	9KB	HTML File	6/24/2010 11:19 PM	
workteams.html	10KB	HTML File	6/24/2010 11:15 PM	
application52520...	18KB	Microsoft...	5/25/2010 11:25 PM	
slschools.html	18KB	HTML File	4/28/2010 12:06 ...	
Kissy-Nutrition-Pr...	72KB	Adobe A...	4/28/2010 12:00 ...	
kissy_needs.pdf	56KB	Adobe A...	4/27/2010 11:58 PM	
schools.html	7KB	HTML File	4/4/2010 9:23 PM	
watts.html	5KB	HTML File	4/4/2010 9:22 PM	
vocational.html	5KB	HTML File	4/4/2010 9:22 PM	
supplies.html	4KB	HTML File	4/4/2010 9:22 PM	
speakers.html	4KB	HTML File	4/4/2010 9:22 PM	
shipping.html	14KB	HTML File	4/4/2010 9:22 PM	
secschools.html	4KB	HTML File	4/4/2010 9:22 PM	
resources.html	6KB	HTML File	4/4/2010 9:22 PM	
palaver.html	9KB	HTML File	4/4/2010 9:22 PM	
medical.html	9KB	HTML File	4/4/2010 9:22 PM	
localvol.html	5KB	HTML File	4/4/2010 9:22 PM	
libschools.html	13KB	HTML File	4/4/2010 9:22 PM	
kits.html	8KB	HTML File	4/4/2010 9:22 PM	
individual.html	4KB	HTML File	4/4/2010 9:22 PM	
about.html	7KB	HTML File	4/4/2010 9:22 PM	
2010vbs.pdf	28KB	Adobe A...	4/4/2010 9:11 PM	
2010-ingathering...	51KB	Adobe A...	4/4/2010 8:35 PM	
vision-2020-strat...	181KB	Adobe A...	3/26/2010 7:16 AM	
lent-offering.pdf	40KB	Adobe A...	1/26/2010 11:05 ...	
vimapp.pdf	10KB	Adobe A...	1/21/2010 12:17 ...	
teacherapp.pdf	11KB	Adobe A...	1/18/2010 11:12 PM	
alternative_to_c...	72KB	Adobe A...	11/13/2009 10:1...	
alternative-09.pdf	72KB	Adobe A...	11/13/2009 10:1...	
nutritional_report...	47KB	Adobe A...	8/31/2009 8:31 PM	
ganta_needs.pdf	44KB	Adobe A...	8/31/2009 8:28 PM	
ganta_report.pdf	193KB	Adobe A...	8/31/2009 8:23 PM	
2009_05_01_hp_...	13KB	HTML File	6/11/2009 9:17 PM	
2009_04_01_hp_...	12KB	HTML File	6/11/2009 9:17 PM	
2009_03_01_hp_...	13KB	HTML File	6/11/2009 9:17 PM	
2009_02_01_hp_...	13KB	HTML File	6/11/2009 9:17 PM	
2009_01_01_hp_...	27KB	HTML File	6/11/2009 9:17 PM	
2008_12_01_hp_...	12KB	HTML File	6/11/2009 9:17 PM	
2008_11_01_hp_...	11KB	HTML File	6/11/2009 9:17 PM	
2008_10_01_hp_...	11KB	HTML File	6/11/2009 9:17 PM	
2008_09_01_hp_...	15KB	HTML File	6/11/2009 9:17 PM	
2008_08_01_hp_...	13KB	HTML File	6/11/2009 9:17 PM	
2008_07_01_hp_...	13KB	HTML File	6/11/2009 9:17 PM	
2008_06_01_hp_...	13KB	HTML File	6/11/2009 9:17 PM	
2008_05_01_hp_...	14KB	HTML File	6/11/2009 9:17 PM	
2008_04_01_hp_...	14KB	HTML File	6/11/2009 9:17 PM	
2008_03_01_hp_...	14KB	HTML File	6/11/2009 9:17 PM	
2008_02_01_hp_...	13KB	HTML File	6/11/2009 9:17 PM	
2008_01_01_hp_...	21KB	HTML File	6/11/2009 9:17 PM	
2007_12_01_hp_...	15KB	HTML File	6/11/2009 9:17 PM	
2007_11_01_hp_...	13KB	HTML File	6/11/2009 9:17 PM	
2007_10_01_hp_...	12KB	HTML File	6/11/2009 9:17 PM	
2007_08_01_hp_...	14KB	HTML File	6/11/2009 9:17 PM	
2007_05_01_hp_...	13KB	HTML File	6/11/2009 9:17 PM	
2007_04_01_hp_...	12KB	HTML File	6/11/2009 9:17 PM	

Date: 4/4/2010 8:35 PM Size: 51KB Log...

Click to show File Activity window

Figure 8-4: The Files panel is used for site-management tasks.

You can view the remote server files in one of two ways:

✦ **Select Remote view from the View list on the Files panel toolbar.** The local view is replaced with a live view of the server.

✦ **Click the Expand/Contract button on the Files panel toolbar, and then click the Connect to Remote Host button.** The expanded view displays a side-by-side view of the local and remote directories, as shown in Figure 8-5.

When you're done working with the remote files, you can click the Disconnect from Remote Host button on the Files panel toolbar.

Customizing Files Panel view

If you want to customize the columns that appear in the Files panel, follow these steps:

1. **Choose Site⇨Manage Sites.**
2. **Select your site from the list.**
3. **Click the Edit button.**

   The Site Definition dialog box appears.
4. **Click the File View Columns item in the Category list.**
5. **On the File View Columns page, modify the columns the way you want.**
6. **Click OK.**

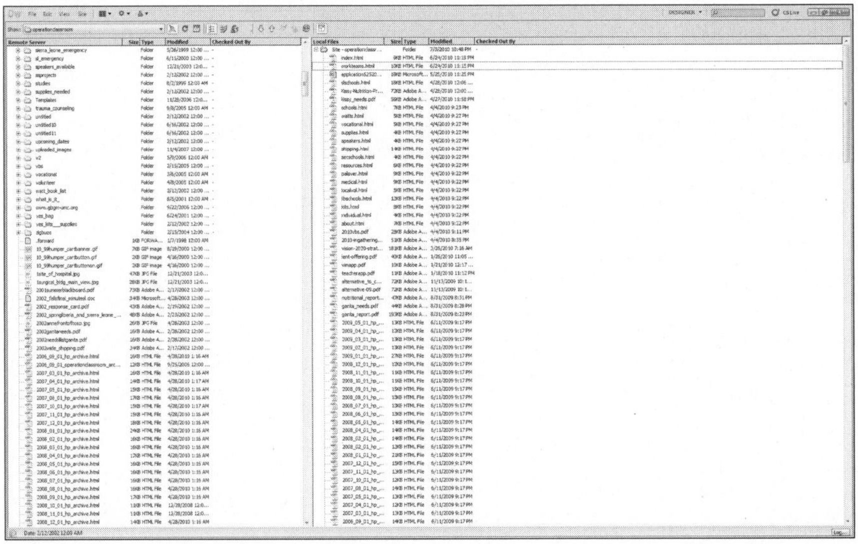

Figure 8-5: Viewing remote and local files side by side.

Working with the Assets Panel

An *asset* is any resource that your Web site uses — such as images, Flash files, script files, and even links. Dreamweaver provides a centralized location for managing these various types of assets in the Assets panel.

To access the panel, choose Window➪Assets or press F11 (or Alt+F11 on a Mac). Or, if your Files panel is visible, you normally find the Assets panel as a tab in the same panel group. The Assets panel is shown in Figure 8-6.

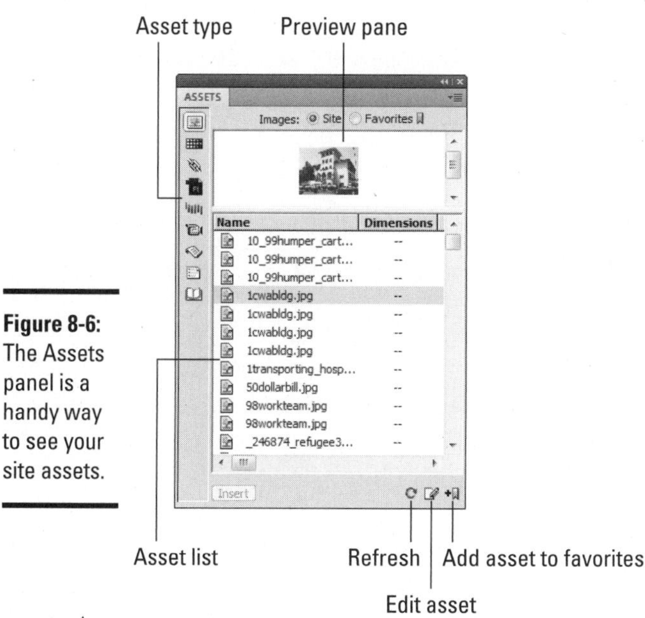

Figure 8-6: The Assets panel is a handy way to see your site assets.

Here are the most useful tasks you can perform in the Assets panel:

- **Drag and drop assets to your pages.** You can drag and drop a file-based asset, such as an image of a Flash file, from the Assets panel to your document.
- **Create a library of favorite assets.** Most Web designers use certain assets repeatedly — perhaps a bullet image, color scheme, or script file. You can click the Add to Favorites button in the Assets panel or right-click and choose Add to Favorites from the pop-up menu. You then have the asset readily available, no matter which site you open.
- **Copy an asset to another site.** You can also copy an asset from your current site to another site by right-clicking it and choosing a site from the Copy to Site pop-up menu.

Managing Local and Remote Files

Because the typical Web site in the Dreamweaver environment involves both local files (for designing and testing) and remote files (on a live server), most of your site-management responsibilities normally focus on making sure these two versions are working together properly with each other.

Transferring files

The most common action you perform when working with your site files is to upload (that is, put) a local file on the remote server. If you want a document you're working on to go to the remote server, click the File Management button on the Document toolbar (see Figure 8-7) and then select Put from the drop-down list of options.

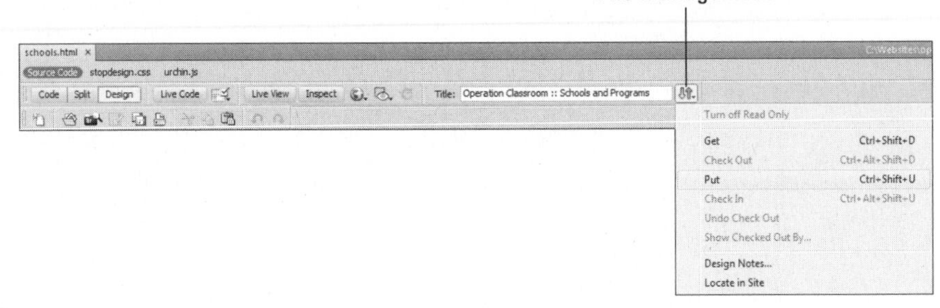

Figure 8-7: Quickly upload the file you're working on by using the Put drop-down menu command.

Alternatively, you can upload a local file by selecting it in the Files panel and then clicking the Put button on the toolbar.

If you want to copy your entire set of local files to the remote server, select the site's root folder in the Files panel and then click the Put button. Dreamweaver uploads all the site's pages and other assets to the server.

You can also retrieve a file that's on your remote server and copy it back to your local computer. To do so, open the Files panel in Remote view (see the "Managing remote files" section, earlier in this chapter). Select the file or files you want to download, and then click the Get button on the Files panel toolbar.

Automatically uploading files to the server

You usually manually upload your local files to the Web server after you test and proof them thoroughly. However, Dreamweaver allows you to upload your local files automatically, every time you save them.

To do so, follow these steps:

1. **Choose Site➪Manage Sites.**
2. **Select your site from the list.**
3. **Click the Edit button.**

   The Site Settings dialog box appears.
4. **Click the Servers item.**

   The Server list appears.
5. **Double-click the server from the list.**
6. **Click the Advanced tab.**
7. **Select the Automatically Upload Files to Server on Save check box.**
8. **Click Save.**
9. **Click Save again.**

The option to upload files automatically to the server helps ensure that your local and remote files are always in synch. However, you run the risk of "putting up" a file that is a work in progress that is not ready for live viewing yet.

Managing Links

Dreamweaver manages site links for you so you can verify and make global changes.

To check the links in your site, choose Site➪Check Links Sitewide. Dreamweaver begins checking the links throughout your site's pages and displays the results in the Link Checker panel.

Suppose you linked to a page from various locations throughout your site but now you need to change that page's filename or location. Instead of slogging manually through each page and changing the link one page at a time, you can make the global change by using the Change Link Sitewide command.

To change a link sitewide, follow these steps:

1. **Choose Site➪Change Link Sitewide.**

   The Change Link Sitewide dialog box appears, as shown in Figure 8-8.
2. **In the Change All Links To box, enter the URL you want to modify.**

   Use the Browse button if you want to locate it in your site.
3. **Enter the new URL in the Into Links To box.**
4. **Click OK.**

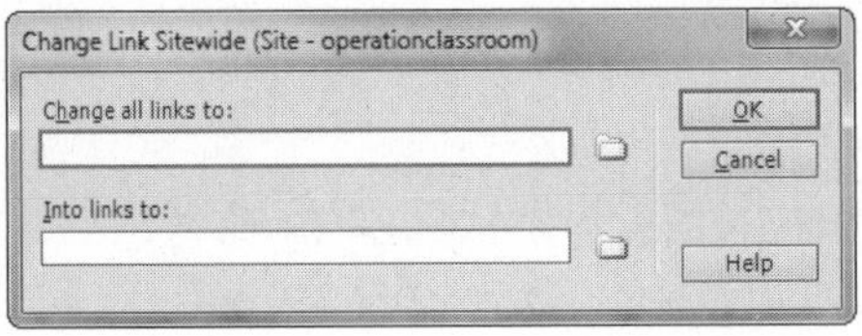

Figure 8-8: The Change Link Sitewide dialog box saves you time searching through your Web site for link changes.

Book IX

Adobe Flash

"Is this really the best use of Flash animation on our e-commerce Web site? A bad wheel on the shopping cart icon that squeaks, wobbles, and pulls to the left?"

Contents at a Glance

Chapter 1: Getting to Know Adobe Flash

In This Chapter

- **Understanding how Flash differs from other Web technologies**
- **Exploring the Flash environment**
- **Introducing Flash tools**
- **Exploring the Properties inspector and panels**
- **Customizing your Flash workspace**

Vive la différence! That's the expression that Web-site designers and users have long used about Adobe Flash. In an environment that has long demanded standards-based solutions (HTML, CSS, and JavaScript, for example) while shunning proprietary technologies, Flash stands alone. It's proprietary. It doesn't do much with HTML or JavaScript or CSS. Yet, because it can play multimedia over the Web and provide a great user experience, Flash movies are as much a part of the Web as HTML is.

It's time, therefore, for you to jump on board and embrace Flash to help you create your Web site. You can use this chapter as a jumping-off point. I start by taking you on a guided tour through the various parts of the Flash development environment.

Like Dreamweaver (see Book VIII), Flash is available for both the Microsoft Windows and Mac OS X platforms. The screen shots in this book show the Windows version, but all the instructions are for both operating systems.

A Matter of Timing: Making the Mind Shift to Flash

The expression *Vive la différence!* is not only appropriate for Web-site visitors but also suitable for you as you design and create Web sites. Flash is definitely much different from the other technologies you explore in this book.

HTML is designed to display content on the Web. CSS comes alongside and helps you present that content in a user-friendly manner. Enter JavaScript. It can be used to perform certain interactive actions when an event on the page is triggered. However, even though these technologies, when added together, form a more complex solution, they are each fairly linear in how you create them.

Flash, however, introduces you to the added dimension of time. Everything that you work with in a Flash movie is coordinated with time. Animations, movie loops, sound effects — a Flash movie introduces each of these elements according to a Timeline you manipulate.

As with a motion picture, a Flash movie is a series of frames that are displayed rapidly in succession (often 12 frames per second), giving the appearance of animation or motion. Suppose you place an image in a different position for each frame of a movie. When the movie is played back, the image gives the illusion of being in motion.

This added element of time is a factor that you need to wrap your mind around as you begin to work with Flash. For many people, this concept takes some getting used to.

Introducing the Flash Workspace

When you first launch Flash, you see a Welcome screen, like the one shown in Figure 1-1. From this screen, you can get started in creating a new Flash file, opening an existing file, or creating a new file based on a sample.

By default, the Welcome screen appears every time you start Flash. To bypass this window, however, select the Don't Show Again check box before proceeding.

Click either the ActionScript 3.0 button under the Create New section or any other option you want to select. The new file is created inside the Flash workspace (see Figure 1-2).

Figure 1-1: Welcome to Flash. I hope you enjoy your stay.

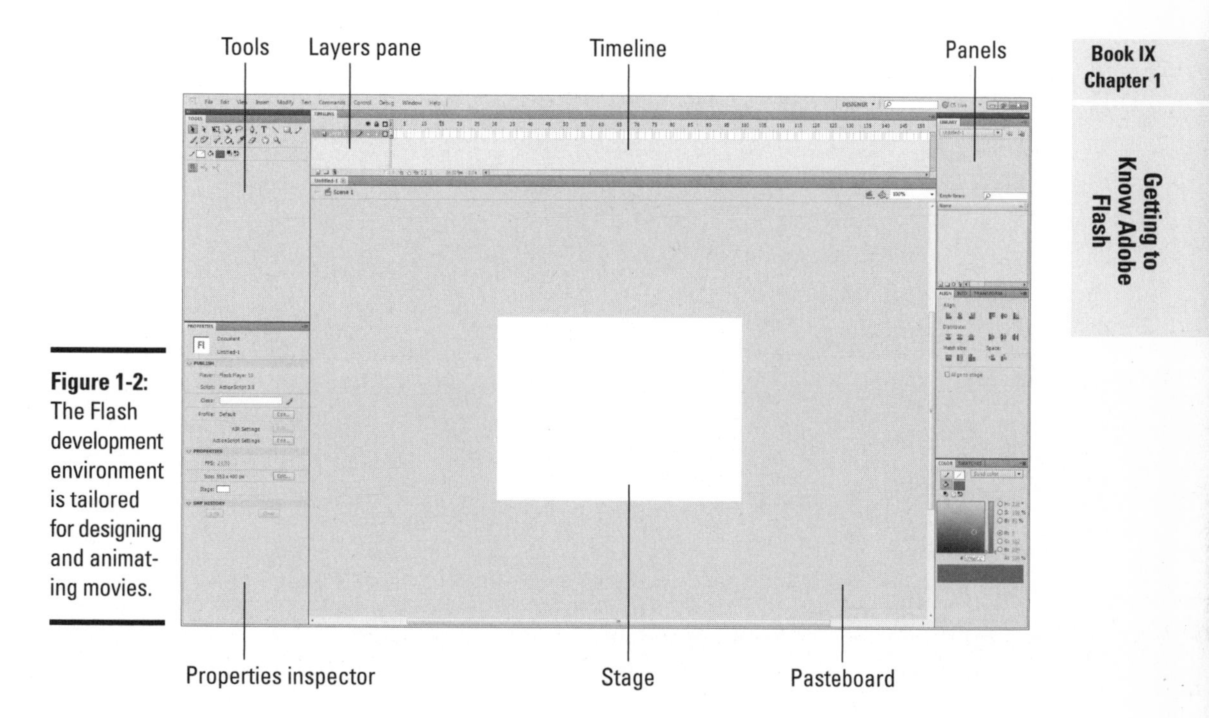

Figure 1-2: The Flash development environment is tailored for designing and animating movies.

You compose and design layers for your Flash movie by drawing or inserting objects into the Stage, which is a drawing area. (See Chapter 2 in this minibook for more on the Stage.) These layers are then added to the Timeline as frames. Each panel that surrounds the Stage window is used in the development of your movies.

Exploring the Flash Drawing Tools

To create or modify drawings, images, and text in the Stage, you work with the drawing tools in the Tools panel (shown in Figure 1-3). Some buttons have drop-down arrows that display additional tools. When you select a tool, the Options section at the bottom of the Tools panel is updated to provide options for the selected tool.

Table 1-1 lists the available tools and describes what they do.

If you have worked with Adobe Photoshop, you have a head start. Many Flash tools are similar to what you already use in Photoshop.

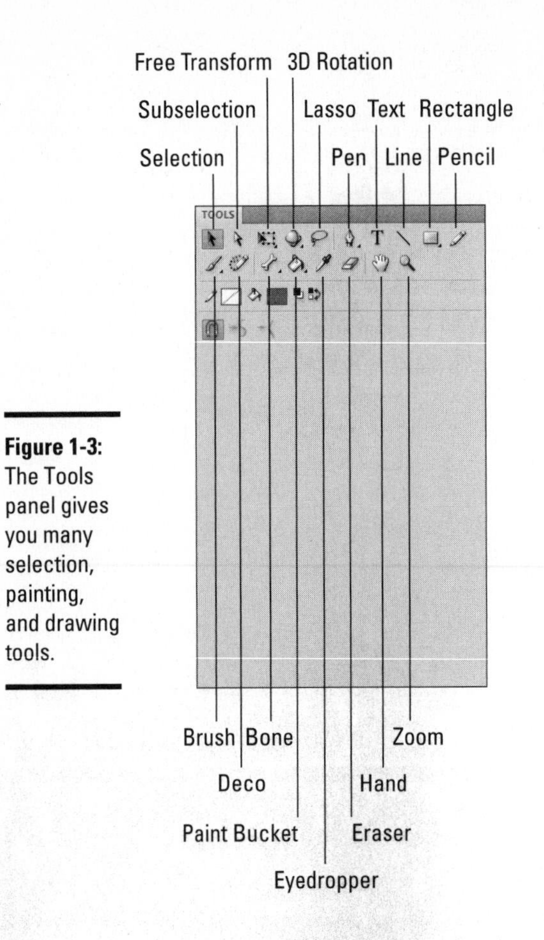

Figure 1-3: The Tools panel gives you many selection, painting, and drawing tools.

Table 1-1 Flash Tools

Tool	*What You Use It For*
Selection	Select an object in the Stage.
Subselection	Select, drag, and reshape an object by using anchor points and handles.
Free Transform	Transform (scale, rotate, skew, or distort) an object.
Gradient Transform	Transform a gradient or bitmap fill object.
3D Rotation	Rotate in 3D space.
3D Translation	Move clip along x, y, and z axes.
Lasso	Select an object by drawing a lasso around it.
Pen	Draw straight lines and curves.
Add Anchor Point	Add an anchor point for drawing.

Tool	What You Use It For
Delete Anchor Point	Remove an anchor point.
Convert Anchor Point	Convert an anchor point for drawing.
Text	Create text.
Line	Draw straight lines.
Rectangle	Draw rectangles.
Oval	Draw ovals.
Rectangle Primitive	Draw primitive rectangles.
Oval Primitive	Draw primitive ovals.
Polystar	Draw a polygon or a star.
Pencil	Draw lines and shapes.
Brush	Paint brush strokes.
Ink Bottle	Change the color, width, or style of lines or shape outlines.
Paint Bucket	Fill a closed shape with a solid color or gradient.
Eye dropper	Copy the color of an object and apply it to another one.
Eraser	Erase strokes, lines, and fills.
Hand	Move the entire movie area in the Paste board.
Zoom	Change the magnification level of the Stage.

Exploring the Properties Inspector

The Properties inspector, shown in Figure 1-4, displays the properties of the document or the selected object in the Stage.

Exploring the Flash Panels

Surrounding the Stage and Timeline window are several panels that perform a variety of tasks in the movie-creation process. These panels can be displayed in their own floating windows or grouped together; when you create a *panel group,* any panel that's docked with the group appears as a tab inside the panel group's window. You can access each of those panels from the Window menu.

Each panel has a drop-down menu on its right side that displays various available commands related to the panel.

Flash has more panels than you can shake a stick at. The following sections describe the ones you most commonly work with, organized by purpose.

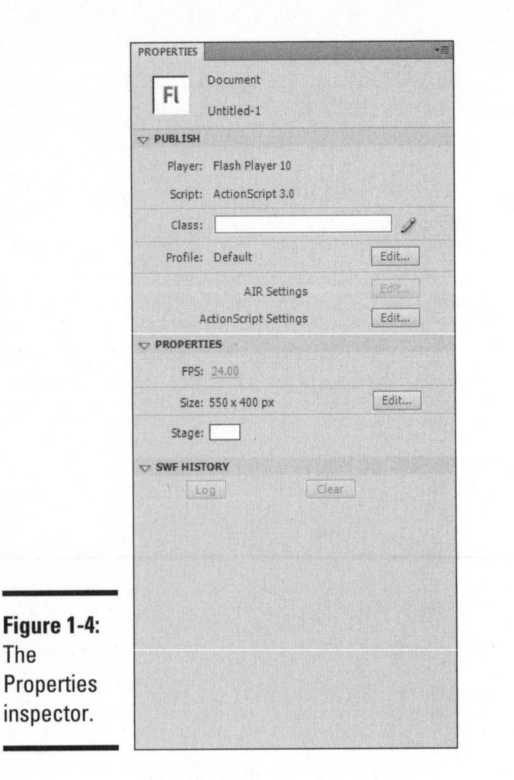

Figure 1-4: The Properties inspector.

Media components and elements panels

The three panels used for working with assets of a movie are described in this list:

- **Components:** Use the Components panel (shown in Figure 1-5) to add various user interface, multimedia, or data controls to your movie.
- **Movie Explorer:** The Movie Explorer (see Figure 1-6) provides a visual hierarchical tree display of your movie, showing the various elements (text, buttons, movie clips, and graphics, for example) that are in use. The Movie Explorer can be used as a handy way to take a big-picture look at a Flash movie (to see all the elements included in it) or as a way to search for a particular element.
- **Library:** The Library (see Figure 1-7) contains media assets (movie clips, sounds, graphics) that you either create or import. It can also contain *symbols* — graphics, buttons, or movie clips that you create once and then reuse. You can use the Library to manage the assets.

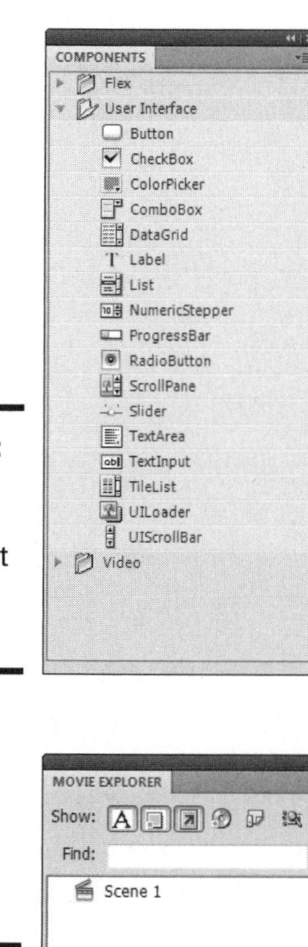

Figure 1-5: Drag and drop your component onto the Stage.

Figure 1-6: The Movie Explorer gives you a big-picture view of your movie components.

Design panels

Five main panels are used as aids in the design process (see Figure 1-8):

✦ **Color:** Use the Color panel for setting the Stroke or Fill color.

✦ **Info:** The Info panel provides size and *x,y* position information about the selected object.

✦ **Swatches:** The Swatches panel helps you manage color sets.

- **Align:** Use the Align panel to align, distribute, and match the size and spacing of selected groups of objects.
- **Transform:** Use the Transform panel for rotating, skewing, or scaling the selected object.

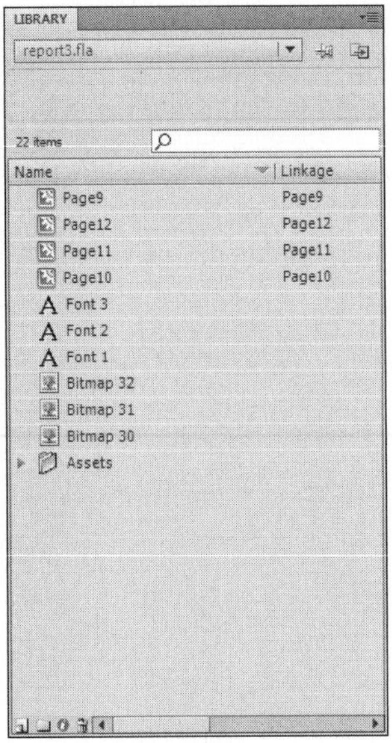

Figure 1-7: The Library stores your media assets.

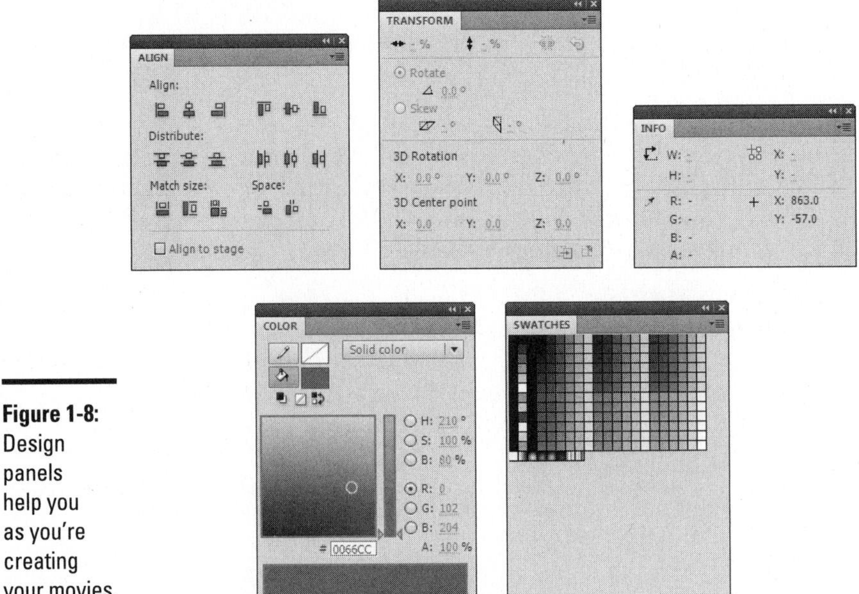

Figure 1-8: Design panels help you as you're creating your movies.

Scripting panels

Two panels are related to scripting your movie:

- **Actions:** Use the Actions panel (shown in Figure 1-9) for working with ActionScript scripts within a movie.
- **Behaviors:** The Behaviors panel contains predefined scripts that you can use to add animation to your movie.

Figure 1-9: ActionScript can add power and interactivity to your Flash movie.

Customizing Your Workspace

The sheer number of available panels and windows in Flash can make your workspace difficult to manage. However, like Dreamweaver (discussed in Book VIII), Flash provides ways to customize your working environment and position windows just the way you like. Then you can save your workspace, arranged just that way, for future use.

Showing and hiding a panel

You can access all the panels from the Window menu. You can show or hide a panel by selecting its menu item from a list. You can also hide a panel that's open by clicking its Close button.

Pressing F4 toggles the visibility of all panels and inspectors. This shortcut is useful when you want to eliminate distractions as you create, test, or preview your Flash movie.

Adding a panel to (or removing a panel from) a panel group

Each panel can be combined with others to form a panel group. You can also arrange a panel group as tabs; an example is the panel group shown in Figure 1-10. To add a panel as a tab, simply drag the panel on top of another panel. When you release the mouse, Flash adds the panel as a new tab.

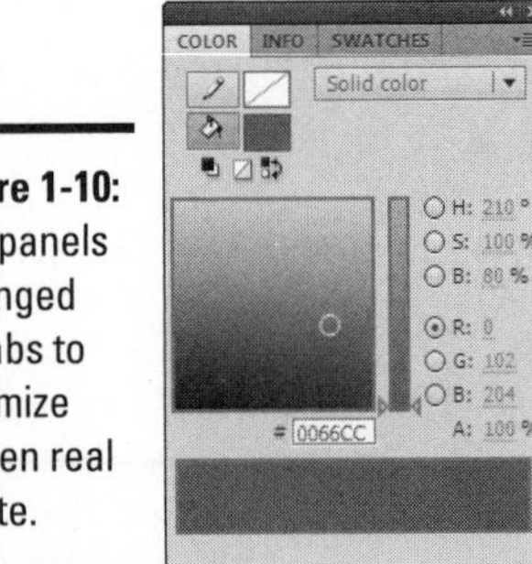

Figure 1-10: Use panels arranged as tabs to minimize screen real estate.

Alternatively, you can arrange panels on top of each other (as with the design panels shown in Figure 1-2). To add a panel above or below another panel, drag a panel onto the second panel's top or bottom border. When you release the mouse button, the panel is docked in the new position.

To move a panel from a panel group, drag the panel's tab and drop it in a new location.

Undocking and docking a panel group

In the Mac version of Flash, panel groups always float. However, in the Windows version, panel groups are normally docked at one side of the application window. To undock and create a floating panel group, simply drag the group into the Document window. The panel group undocks and floats on top of the workspace.

To redock the panel group, drag it to the side of the application window that you want to dock. Flash then redocks it.

Saving a workspace layout

After you arrange the workspace the way you want, choose Window➪Workspace➪Save Current. In the Save Workspace Layout dialog box, give your new, customized workspace a name and then click OK. The new layout is added to the Workspace list.

To use a workspace, choose Window➪Workspace and select a layout from the list.

Chapter 2: Working with the Stage and Layers

In This Chapter

- **Introducing the Stage**
- **Exploring the Timeline**
- **Working with layers**
- **Adding content to the Stage**

Because Flash is a tool for creating movies, it also uses, appropriately, movie-oriented terminology inside the workspace — stages, scenes, frames, temperamental actors, and needless violence. Okay, I made up the last two, but you get the idea that Flash introduces a whole new vocabulary to us non-Hollywood types.

In this chapter, you get started by focusing on perhaps the most important of these movie-sounding terms: the Stage. As you do so, you also explore how to work with layers that are placed on top of it.

Exploring the Stage

The *Stage* is the rectangular design canvas on which you create a Flash movie. The Stage, which is shown in Figure 2-1, looks just like the familiar rectangular shape of a Flash movie file that you see embedded inside a Web page.

You can work with several design aids in the Stage, all available from the View menu:

- **Ruler:** An on-screen tool used, as you might expect, for measuring in pixels, inches, or other units.
- **Grid:** This option displays an overlay grid on the Stage, which gives you a more precise sense of where things are on-screen.
- **Guide:** A horizontal or vertical line that you can drag from the ruler to the Stage.
- **Snapping:** These options allow you to attach on-screen objects quickly and firmly (that is, “snap” them) to grids, guides, pixels, or objects.

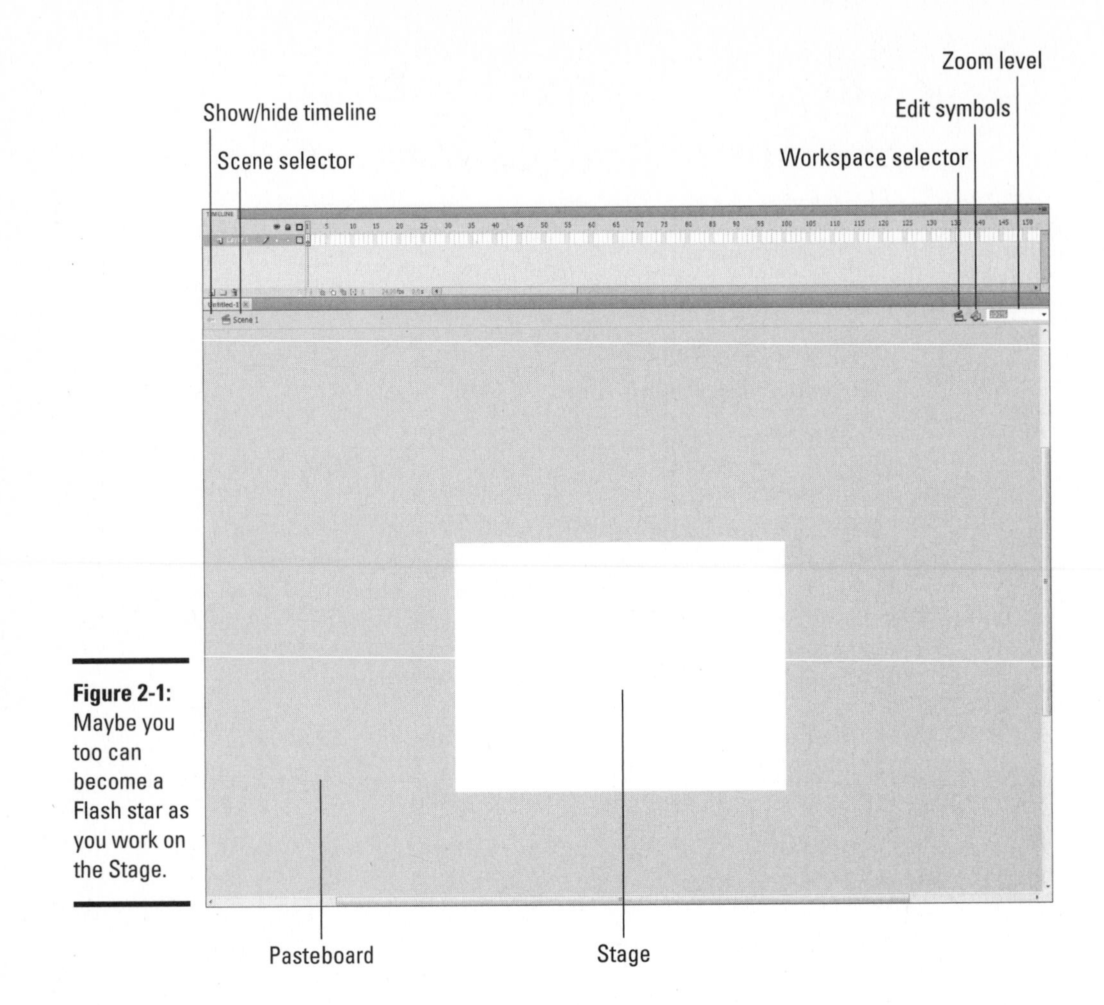

Figure 2-1: Maybe you too can become a Flash star as you work on the Stage.

Exploring the Timeline and Layers

The *Timeline* is the filmstrip-like panel that's displayed above the Stage. In the Timeline (see Figure 2-2), you work with layers and frames. The Timeline consists of two components: the Layers pane on the left side and the Frame timeline on the right.

A *frame* is the basic unit of time inside a Flash movie. It's just like the individual frames in a long strip of film stock. A *layer* is a transparent sheet, displayed on the Stage, that contains elements. A Flash movie can (and usually does) contain multiple layers of content, stacked on top of each other. The advantage of working with layers rather than placing everything on one canvas is that you can hide, show, and animate individual layers at various times inside a movie.

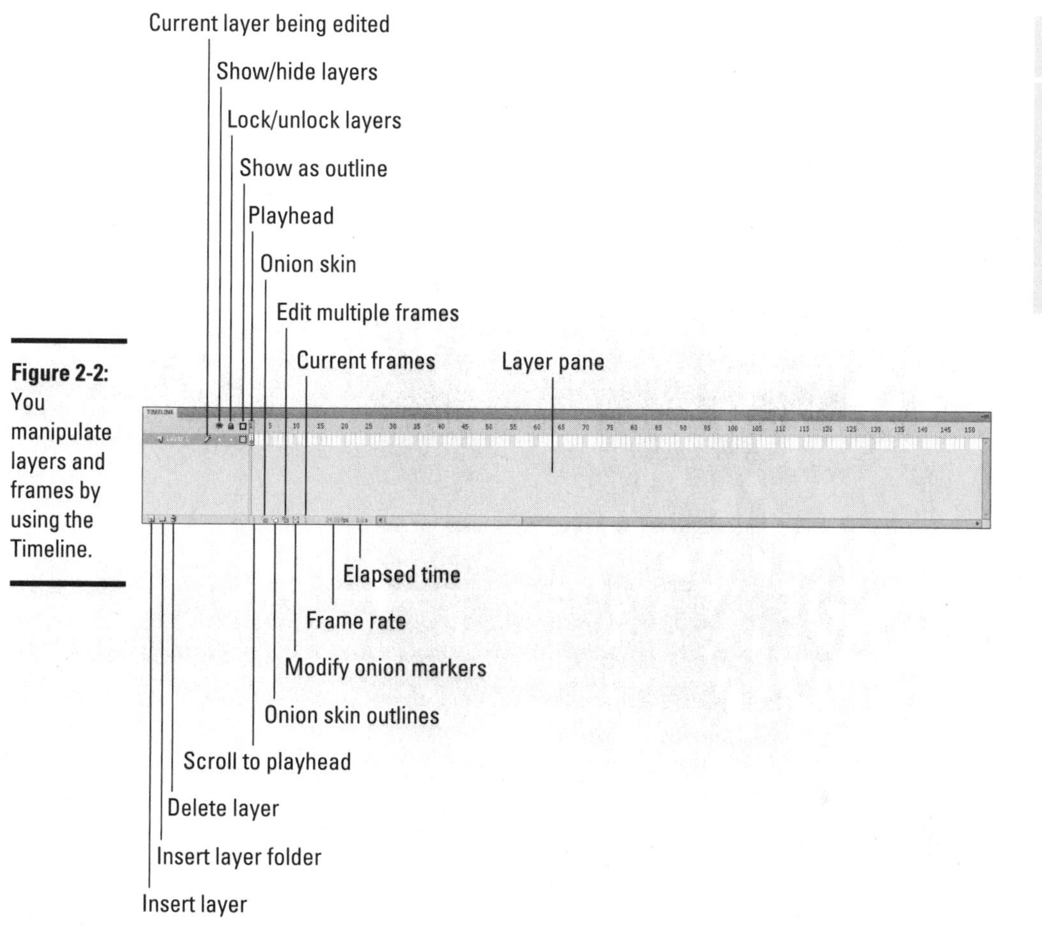

Figure 2-2: You manipulate layers and frames by using the Timeline.

If you've worked with Photoshop, you're already familiar with the concept of layers. You work with Flash layers in much the same way.

Creating a layer

To create a layer, click the Insert Layer button in the lower-left corner of the Timeline window (refer to Figure 2-2). Or you can choose Insert➪Timeline➪Layer.

The new layer appears on top of the previous one (as shown in Figure 2-3) and becomes the active layer.

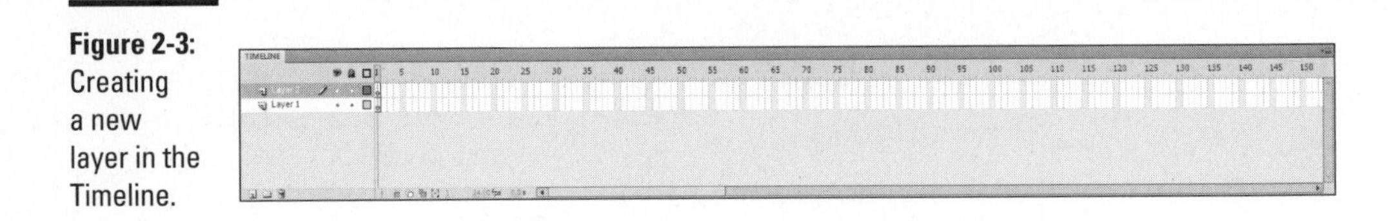

Figure 2-3: Creating a new layer in the Timeline.

Working with layers

The only disadvantage to using layers is that they take some time to get used to. Because elements you place on different layers all appear in the Stage area at the same time, you can become confused about which layer's element you're manipulating. Therefore, the Layers pane is your handy window because it always tells you which layer is active: The Pencil icon appears next to the layer name. (When the pencil icon has a slash through it, the layer is active but can't be edited — usually that happens when the layer has been locked.)

Here are some common tasks that you perform with layers:

- **Select a layer:** You can select a layer by using one of these methods:
  - Click an object on the stage. The layer that contains the object is automatically selected.
  - Click the layer in the Layers pane.
  - Click inside a frame of the Timeline on the layer row.
- **Change the order of a layer:** The order in which the layers appear in the Layers pane indicates their display order. In other words, the top layer is shown on top of all other layers, and the bottom layer is on the bottom of the pecking order. You can change a layer by selecting it with your mouse and then dragging it to a new location in the list.
- **Show or hide a layer:** In the Layers pane, you can toggle the visibility of a layer by clicking the dot under the Eye icon. Or, to show or hide all layers at one time, click the Eye icon.
- **Lock or unlock a layer:** When you lock a layer, you prevent any editing from taking place in the Stage. To lock a layer, click the dot under the Padlock icon. You can lock all layers at one time by clicking the Padlock icon.
- **View a layer as an outline:** Click the colored box beside the layer name to view the layer as an outline in the Stage. You can set the outline color by double-clicking the colored box and setting a new color in the Layer Properties dialog box.
- **Rename a layer:** You can rename a layer by double-clicking its name in the Layers pane. After the name is selected, enter a new name.
- **Delete a layer:** You can delete a layer by selecting it in the Layers pane and then dragging it on top of the garbage-can icon.

Using guide layers

In addition to the design aids discussed in the section "Exploring the Stage," earlier in this chapter, you can define *guide layers* in Flash to help you position or size elements on the Stage. Guide layers are for use only during design-time; they aren't included in the published movie.

To create a guide layer, follow these steps:

1. **Click the Insert Layer button to add a new layer to the movie.**
2. **Right-click the new layer and choose Guide from the pop-up menu.**

   The page icon in the Layers pane beside the layer is replaced with a ruler icon.

A *motion guide layer* is a special type of guide layer that you use to define a path for motion-tweened animations. (For more about tweens, see Chapter 4 in this minibook.)

Adding Movie Elements to the Stage

You can add artwork, text, graphics, components, and symbols to the Stage for use in your movie. Each time you add an element, you add to the active layer. The following sections describe some of the ways in which you can add content.

Adding lines, shapes, and text from the Tools panel

The Tools panel, discussed in Chapter 1 of this minibook, has several tools for adding text, shapes, and lines to a layer. For example, by using the Text tool, you can add text to a layer, as shown in Figure 2-4.

Inserting external graphics and media

You can insert video files, bitmapped graphics (such as JPG, PNG, GIF, and Photoshop PSD files), and vector graphics (such as Adobe Illustrator files) into Flash. You can either import the file directly onto the Stage or into the Library.

You can add external media into Flash in three different ways:

- Choose File⇨Import.
- Drag and drop an image or media file from an Explorer (Windows) or Finder (Mac) window.
- Paste from the Clipboard by choosing Edit⇨Paste in Center.

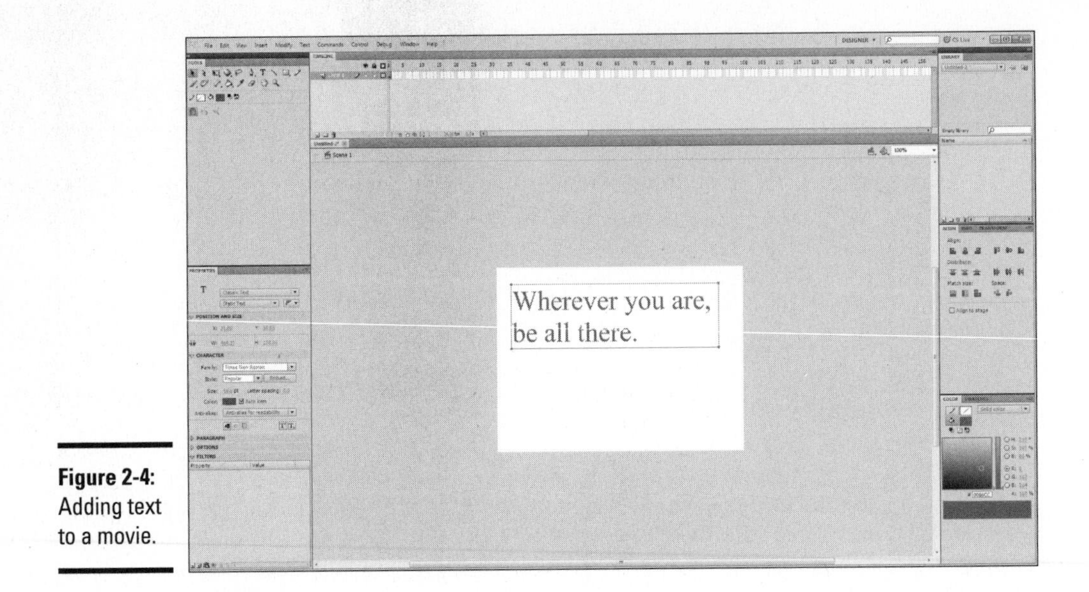

Figure 2-4: Adding text to a movie.

Adding user interface and video components

Flash comes with a variety of components you can add to your Stage, including user interface components, such as push buttons, edit boxes, drop-down list boxes, and other data-entry controls. It also has video control components, such as a volume bar and forward and backward buttons. You can add these components from the Components panel, which you access by choosing Window➪Components.

Figure 2-5 shows user interface components added to the Stage.

Adding symbols

For Flash purposes, a *symbol* is an image, button, or movie clip that you create inside Flash and then insert onto the Stage as one or more instances. Symbols are an important topic, however, so I save that discussion for Chapter 3 in this minibook.

Working with Movie Elements

When you draw or add a movie element on the Stage, you can use the Selection tool to select and move the element. When an element is selected, its properties appear in the Properties inspector. For example, Figure 2-6 shows the properties of a text element.

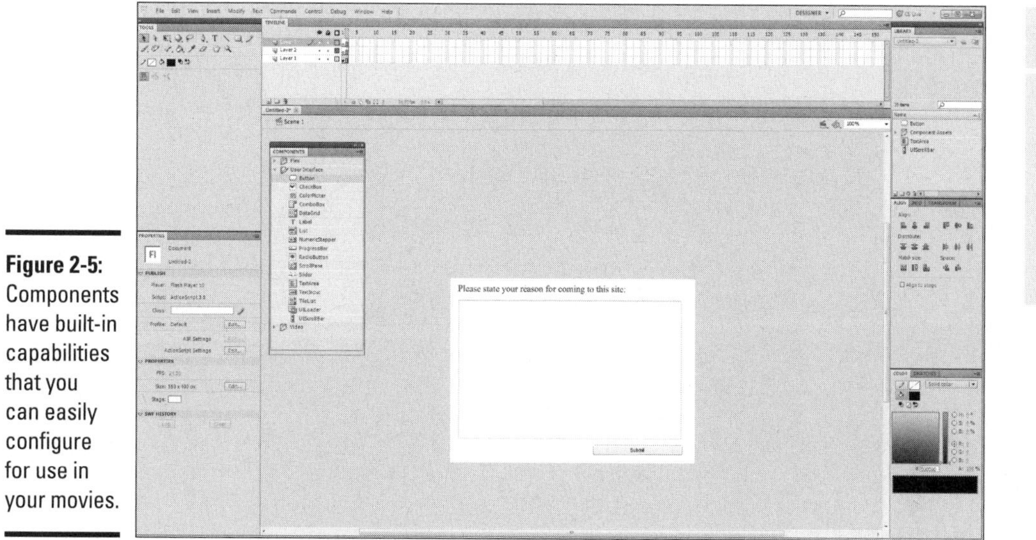

Figure 2-5: Components have built-in capabilities that you can easily configure for use in your movies.

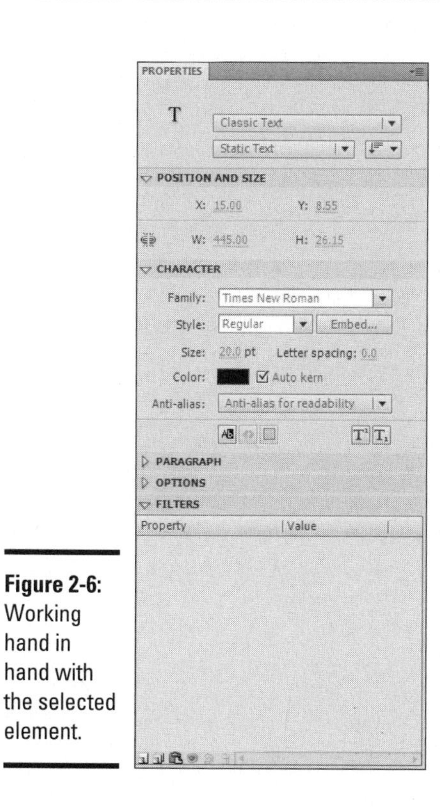

Figure 2-6: Working hand in hand with the selected element.

If you're working with a component from the Components panel, you can tweak the component in the Parameters panel, shown in Figure 2-7. All the properties you can configure that are specific to the component you're using are displayed there.

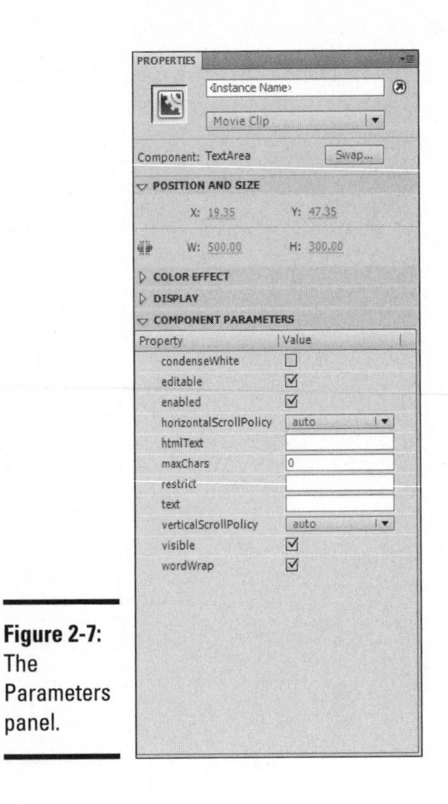

Figure 2-7: The Parameters panel.

Chapter 3: Working with Symbols

In This Chapter

- **Exploring symbols and instances**
- **Creating symbols from scratch and from existing media elements**
- **Adding instances of symbols to your Flash movie**
- **Working with the Library and Common Libraries**

In this chapter, you discover how to use symbols. No, I am sorry, you don't get to learn how to play in the percussion section of the band. That's what *Cymbals For Dummies* would talk about. I am talking about Flash symbols, which are handy thingamajigs that you frequently use as you author Flash movies. In this chapter, you see how to create and work with symbols, instances of symbols, and the Library.

Understanding Symbols and Instances

As I mention in Chapter 1 of this minibook, *symbols* are graphical images, buttons, or movie clips that you create once and then reuse in your movie file. An *instance* is a "copy" of the symbol that's added to the Stage.

Symbols are important because they have a major effect on the overall size of your Flash movie file. Suppose you have a 70K graphic that you're using in a Flash file that you want to put into 100 frames in a movie — which is a common scenario when you're animating an element. Without symbols, you need 7MB of disk space to store all that graphical data. When you use symbols, however, Flash stores the 70K file just once and then references it for each instance used on the Stage.

Much like when you use a template, when you edit a symbol in Flash, all instances of that symbol are automatically updated. Although an instance is a "copy" of the symbol, however, you can set properties that are specific to that particular instance.

Symbols are normally added to the Library of the active Flash movie file. However, Flash supports shared symbols in its Shared Library.

Flash has three main types of symbols:

- **Graphics:** A graphical symbol is used for still-image graphics and works inside the main timeline of the Flash movie.
- **Movie clips:** A movie clip symbol is used for reusing an animation, video, or audio clip. However, a movie clip has its own mini-timeline that's independent of the main Flash movie Timeline. You can also insert a movie clip inside a button symbol (explained in the following bullet) to create an animated button.
- **Buttons:** A button symbol is used to create "rollover-like" buttons that interact with the mouse. You can define various graphics associated with the four main button states (mouse up, mouse over, mouse down, and mouse hit). A button also has its own mini-timeline, consisting of four frames (one for each of the button states). You can then attach code to the button to respond to the button when it's clicked.

Creating a New Symbol

You can create a symbol by either converting an existing media element into a symbol or creating one from scratch.

Creating a symbol from an existing element

To convert an existing element, follow these steps:

1. **Import a graphical image or other media element onto your Stage.**

   A quick way is to drag a media file from Explorer (Windows) or Finder (Mac) onto the Stage.

   Figure 3-1 shows a JPG image added to the Stage. Notice how the Properties inspector treats the image as an instance of the `.jpg` file.

2. **Select the element and choose Modify⇨Convert to Symbol.**

   The Convert to Symbol dialog box (shown in Figure 3-2) opens.

3. **Enter a name for the symbol in the Name field.**

   I named my symbol `Box`.

4. **Select a symbol type: movie clip, graphic, or button.**
5. **If needed, adjust the registration point for the symbol.**

   The *registration point* is the index point that's used when you're rotating or transforming an element. You might want to add it to the center of the symbol rather than to the upper-left corner.

6. **Click OK.**

   The symbol is added to the movie file's library (see Figure 3-3), and the element on the Stage is automatically converted to an instance of the new symbol (see Figure 3-4).

Figure 3-1: Dropping an image onto the Stage.

A .jpg graphic is added to the Stage.

The graphic is treated as an instance of the .jpg file.

Figure 3-2: Converting an image into a symbol.

Convert to Symbol

Name: Symbol 1

Type: Movie Clip | Registration:

Folder: Library root

Advanced

OK

Cancel

Figure 3-3: If you're looking for a symbol, go to your friendly neighbor-hood library.

LIBRARY

Untitled-3

4 items

Name | Linkage

Box

buttons bar

IMG_0525.JPG

MyFileFolder

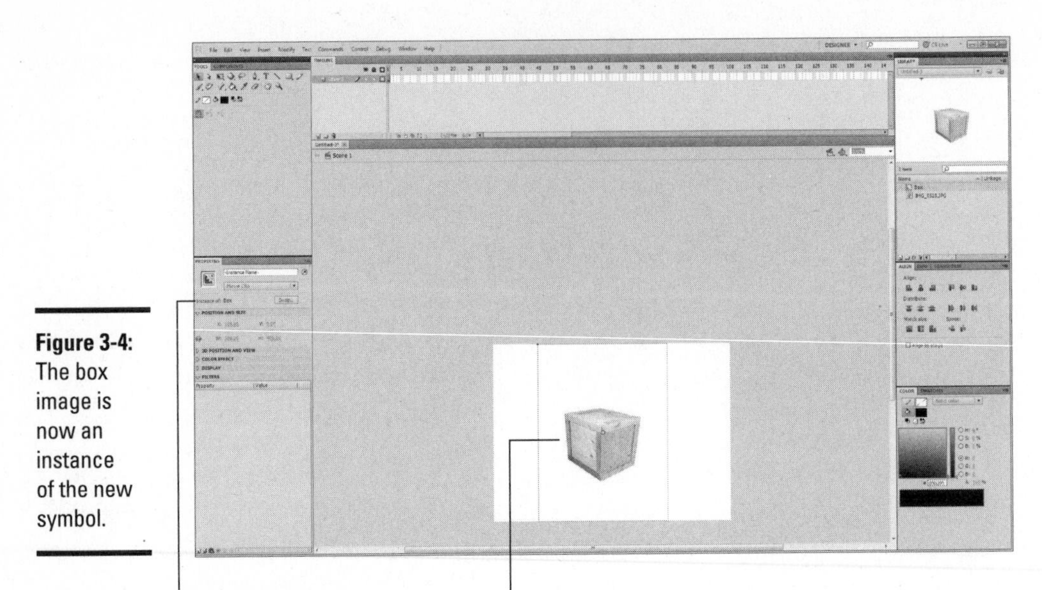
The Instance Of area
The element is now an instance of the new symbol.

Figure 3-4: The box image is now an instance of the new symbol.

Creating a symbol from scratch

To create a new symbol from scratch, follow these steps:

1. **Choose Insert⇨New Symbol.**

   You can also click the Create New Symbol button in the Library panel.

   The Create New Symbol dialog box appears.

2. **Enter a name for the symbol in the Name field.**
3. **Select a symbol type: movie clip, graphic, or button.**
4. **Click OK.**

   The symbol is added to the Library, and then something unexpected happens on the Stage: The normal document-editing mode gives way to symbol-editing mode with an empty Stage. In the example, I named the symbol `MyFileFolder` (see Figure 3-5).

   The crosshairs in the middle of the window comprise the registration point for the symbol.

5. **Draw content in, or add content to, the symbol in the Symbol Editor.**

   You can, for example, drag a graphics file to the Symbol Editor.

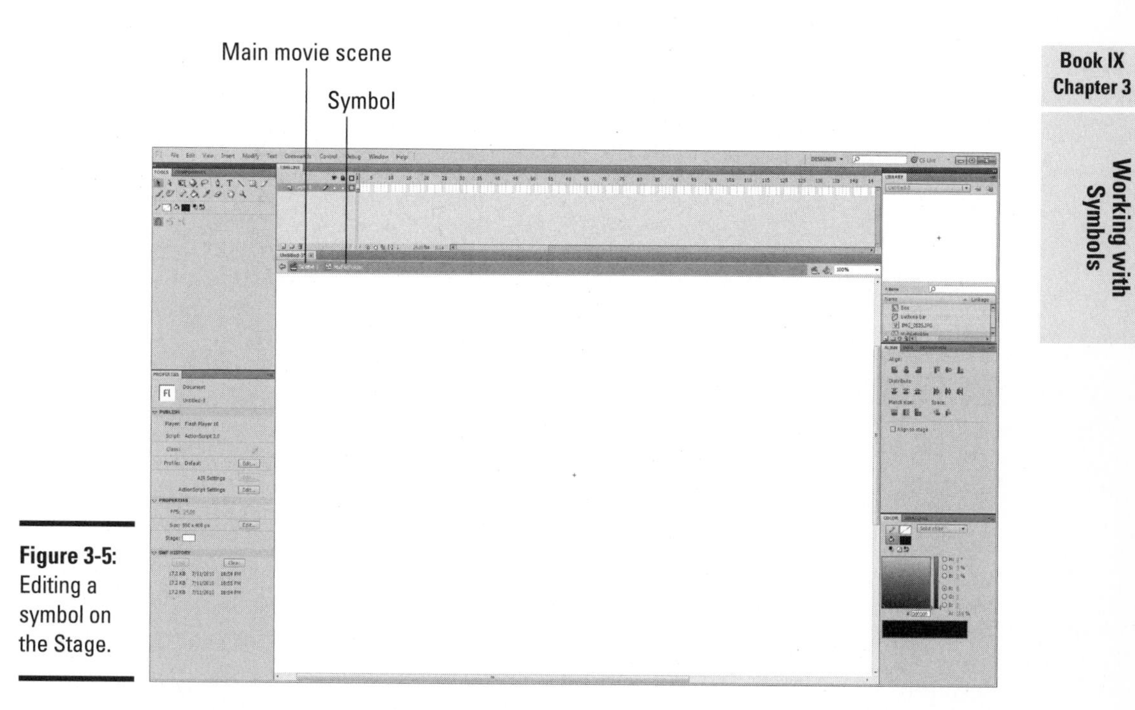

Figure 3-5: Editing a symbol on the Stage.

6. **When you finish editing the symbol, click the name of the main scene (Scene1 in the example) at the top of the Stage window.**

   You can also choose Edit⇨Edit Document.

   The normal document-editing Stage appears again.

Working with Symbols in the Library

The Library panel displays the symbols that have been added to the current Flash document (see Figure 3-6). The preview pane at the top displays the selected item in the Library.

To create a new instance of the symbol:

1. **Select the symbol from the Library.**
2. **Drag the symbol to the Stage with your mouse.**

   The instance is added to the active layer in the Timeline.

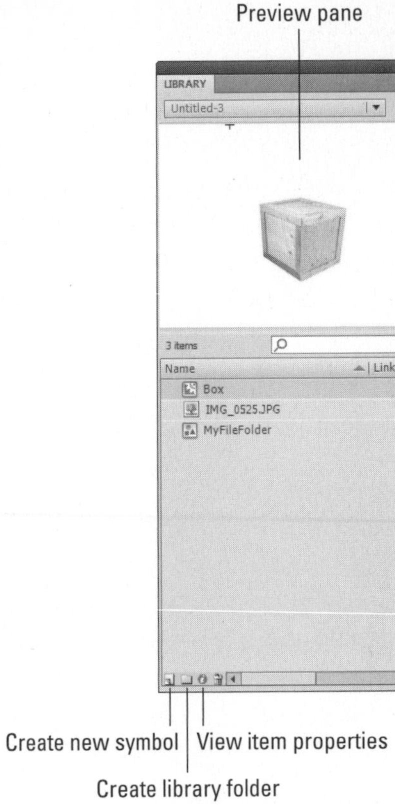

Preview pane

Create new symbol | View item properties

Create library folder

Figure 3-6: You can easily identify different types of symbols by their icons.

To edit the contents of the symbol, follow these steps:

1. **Double-click the symbol in the Library panel.**

   The Stage area displays the symbol inside symbol-editing mode.

2. **Modify the symbol the way you want.**

Although you can modify the properties of symbol instances, you might sometimes want to duplicate a symbol and make changes to it. To duplicate a symbol, follow these steps:

1. **Right-click the symbol in the Library panel, and choose Duplicate from the pop-up menu.**

   The Duplicate Symbol dialog box appears.

2. **In the Duplicate Symbol dialog box, provide a name for the new symbol and click OK.**

   The newly cloned symbol has no linkage to the symbol it originated from.

Working with Common Library Buttons

Even though you can create your own button symbols, Flash comes with a set of button symbols as part of the Common Libraries. You might find that these buttons provide exactly what you need inside your Flash files.

To add a button symbol from the Common Libraries, follow these steps:

1. **Choose Window➪Common Libraries➪Buttons.**

   A special, Common Library panel appears, as shown in Figure 3-7.

2. **Expand the folder of the button symbol set that interests you.**

   In the example, I clicked the `buttons bar` folder.

3. **Select the button symbol you want from the folder and drag it to the Stage.**

   I selected the `bar blue` button (see Figure 3-8). A new instance of it is added to the Stage.

   A button isn't useful unless it *does* something when you click it, so I show you one way to add functionality to it. However, before doing so, you need to make a change in your Flash publish settings.

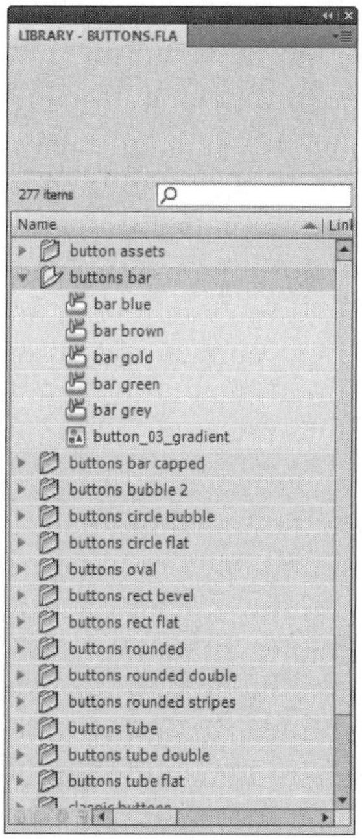

Figure 3-7: Flash features a common library packed with more buttons than a political convention.

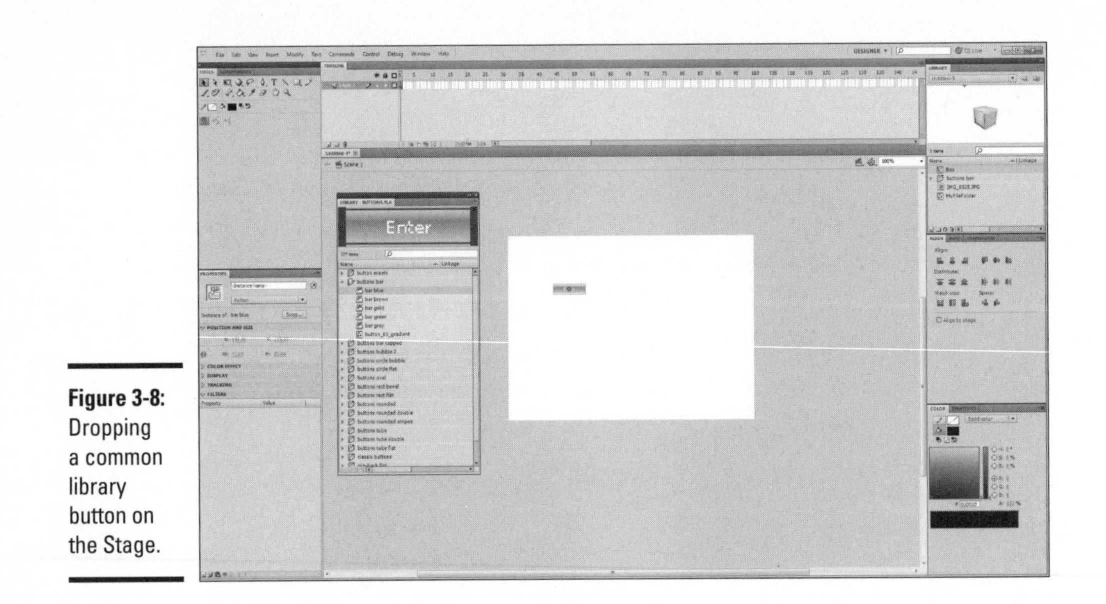

Figure 3-8: Dropping a common library button on the Stage.

4. **Choose File⇨Publish Settings.**

   The Publish Settings dialog box appears.

5. **Click the Flash tab.**
6. **Choose ActionScript 2.0 from the ActionScript Version drop-down list.**

   Note: ActionScript 3.0 doesn't support behaviors, which I use in this example.

7. **Click OK.**
8. **Choose Window⇨Behaviors to display the Behaviors panel.**
9. **Select the button instance and click the Add Behavior drop-down button.**

   A menu of behaviors appears.

10. **Choose Web⇨Go to Web Page.**

    This behavior causes the browser to go to a specified URL.

    The Go to URL dialog box appears (see Figure 3-9).

Figure 3-9: Jumping to the specified URL.

11. **Type a Web address to go to in the URL box.**
12. **Click OK.**

    The behavior is added to the button and appears in the Behaviors panel (see Figure 3-10).
13. **Choose Control⇨Test Movie.**

    Flash compiles the movie and displays it in a Flash window (see Figure 3-11).
14. **Test the button functionality when the mouse moves over the button.**
15. **Click the button to jump to the URL in your browser.**

Figure 3-10: The Behaviors panel displays behaviors defined for the selected element on the Stage.

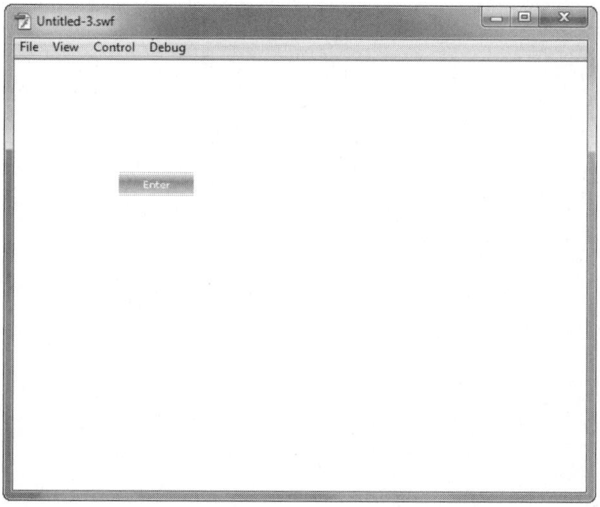

Figure 3-11: Testing the button.

16. **Close the test window to return to the Flash authoring environment.**

You can double-click a button to enter symbol-editing mode, as shown in Figure 3-12. The button symbol has a Timeline of four keyframes: Up, Over, Down, and Hit.

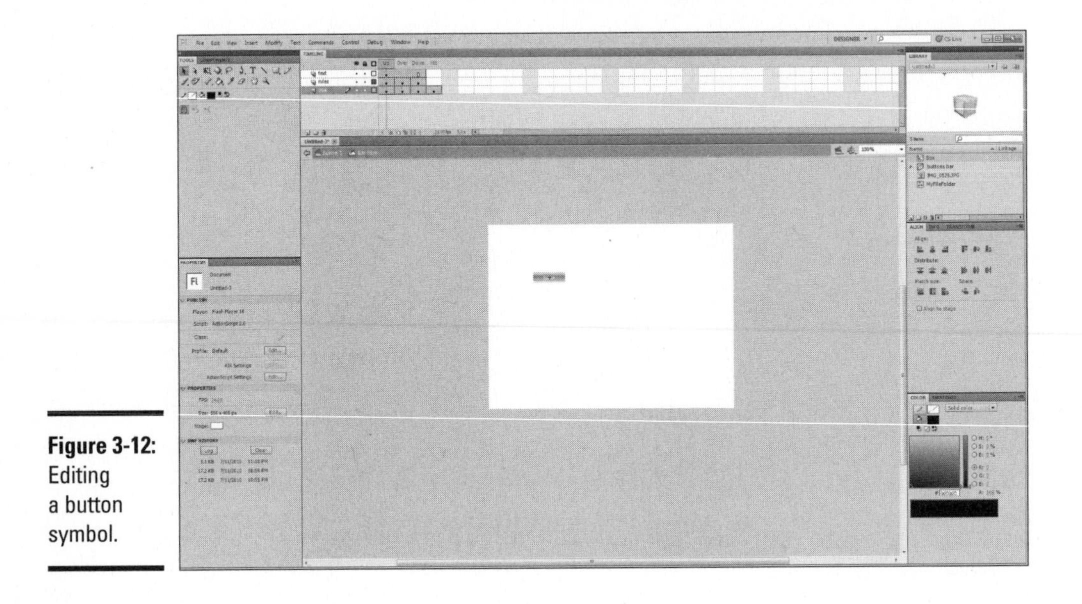

Figure 3-12: Editing a button symbol.

Chapter 4: Making Movies

In This Chapter

- Exploring Flash animation
- Creating frame-by-frame animations
- Creating tweened motion and shape animations
- Introducing behaviors and actions
- Adding sounds to your movies and buttons

In the first three chapters of this minibook, I show you how to work with the Stage, layers on the Stage, and media elements and symbols inside the layers. However, I saved one key aspect of the Flash authoring environment for this chapter: the Timeline. The Timeline is at the heart of any Flash movie. As you begin to master working with frames inside the Timeline, you can create animations and interactive Flash movies.

Creating Animations in Your Movie

You can use two types of animation techniques in Flash:

- **Frame-by-frame animation** adjusts the contents of the Stage for every individual frame. This type of animation is much like a children's flip book. When you flip the pages, the effect is an animation. (It's also the way that the first animated films, such as the early Disney films, were made, except that the "flipping" was done on reels of film rather than on pages of a book.)
- In **tweened animation,** you define an element (or group of elements) in a starting frame and then make changes to it (for example, a different location or properties) in the ending frame. Flash then automatically generates all the frames between these two points.

The changes you make in an animation are made in special frames called *keyframes.* Each frame in a frame-by-frame animation is a keyframe. In tweened animation, however, you define keyframes only in the frames in which something changes (at least the starting and ending frames) in the Timeline.

Frame-by-frame animation

When you create frame-by-frame animation, the Stage changes in every frame. Frame-by-frame animation works well for highly detailed animations, but it increases the file size because Flash has to store data for every frame of the animation.

To create a frame-by-frame animation of a layer you already created, follow these steps:

1. **Select a layer from the Layers pane of the Timeline (see Figure 4-1).**
2. **Add to the Stage the content that you want to animate.**

   Use symbols (see Chapter 3 in this minibook) to minimize storage space.

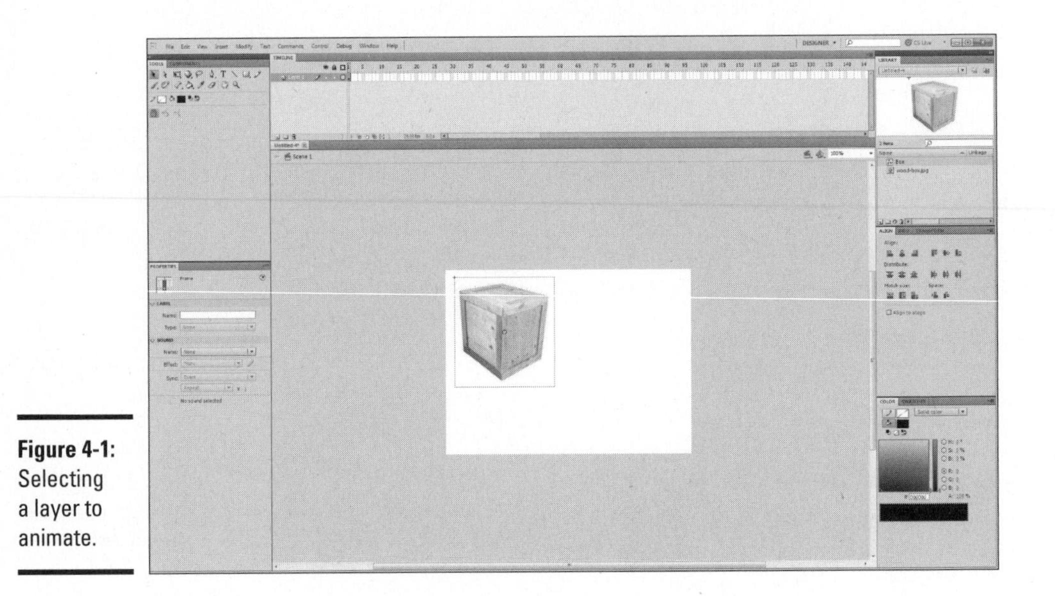

Figure 4-1: Selecting a layer to animate.

3. **In the Timeline, right-click the frame in which you want to start the animation.**

   The pop-up menu appears.
4. **Choose Insert Keyframe from the pop-up menu.**

   A round dot is added to the frame, to represent the keyframe (see Figure 4-2).
5. **Select the second frame in the Timeline, and right-click it to display its pop-up menu.**
6. **Choose Insert Keyframe from the pop-up menu.**
7. **Edit the contents of the Stage slightly as the first step in the animation.**
8. **Repeat Steps 3 through 7 as needed until you finish your animation.**

   Figure 4-3 shows the final keyframe of a 12-frame animation.

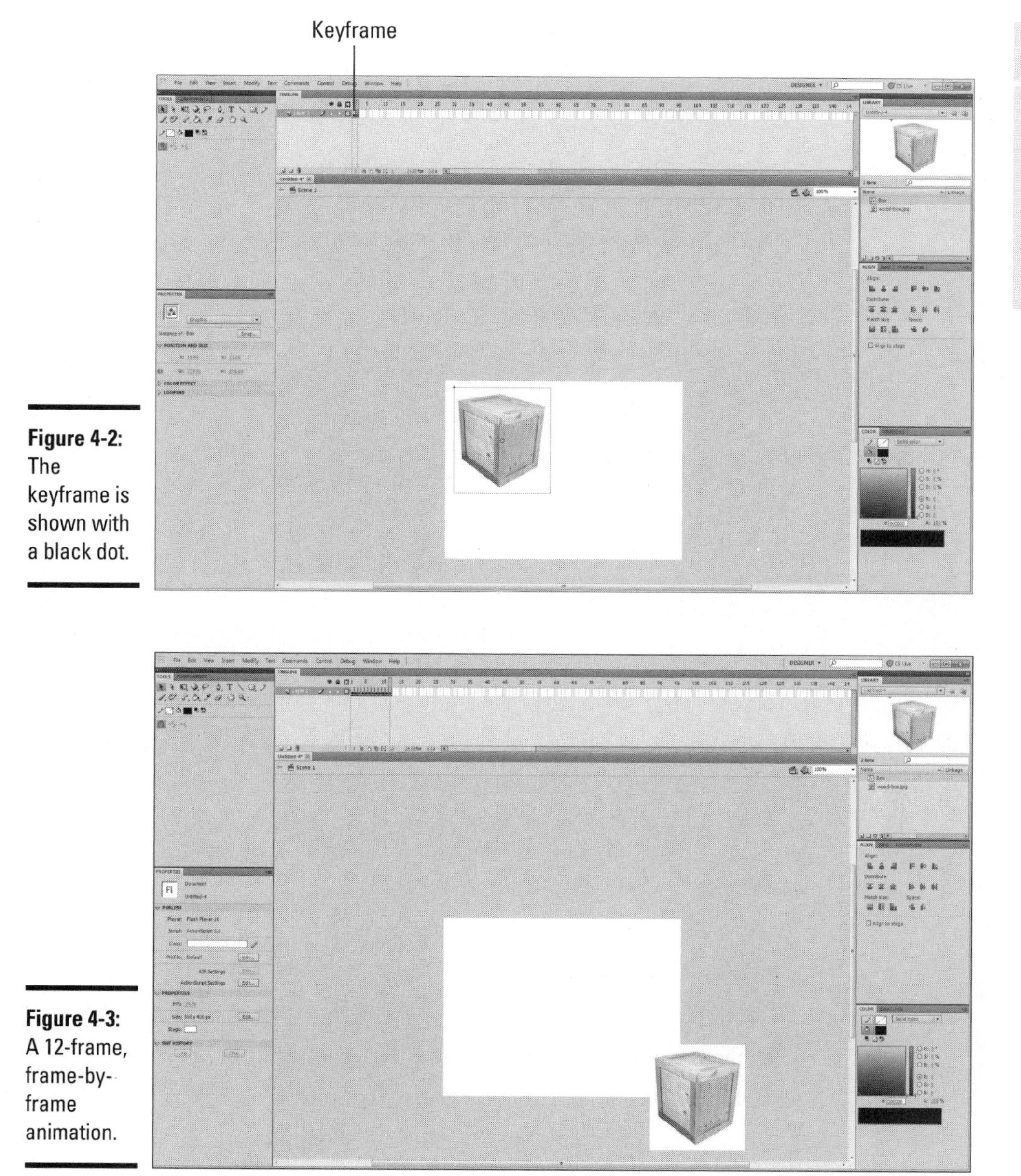

Figure 4-2: The keyframe is shown with a black dot.

Figure 4-3: A 12-frame, frame-by-frame animation.

9. **Test the animation in the authoring environment by choosing Control➪Play or pressing Enter (Windows) or Return (Mac).**

   Or, to see the animation in the compiled version, choose Control➪Test Movie.

If you're satisfied with the animation, you can stop now. If you want to make tweaks, continue.

10. **Keep the same layer selected and click a frame in the Timeline to modify its contents on the Stage.**
11. **Adjust the contents of the Stage as needed to improve the animation effect.**
12. **Test the animation again by choosing Control⇨Play.**

Tweened animation

Flash has two types of tweened animation:

- **Motion tweening:** Deals with changing the properties or location of an element from start to finish.
- **Shape tweening:** Focuses on a starting shape and then a different finishing shape. Flash creates the gradual transformation in the frames between them, thus giving the appearance of animation.

Motion tweens

To create a motion-tweened animation, follow these steps:

1. **Select a layer from the Layers pane of the Timeline.**
2. **If it isn't already selected, click the first frame in the Timeline.**
3. **Add to the Stage the content that you want to animate.**

   Be sure to convert your artwork to a symbol (see Chapter 3 in this minibook) by choosing Modify⇨Convert to Symbol. Symbols are required for creating a motion tween.

   Figure 4-4 shows a nifty little box on the Stage.
4. **Select the frame in the Timeline in which you want the animation to end.**

   In honor of the former TV hero Jack Bauer, I chose the 24th frame.

5. **Right-click the frame and choose Insert Keyframe from its pop-up menu.**

   Pressing F6 is a handy shortcut for inserting a keyframe.
6. **Change the content of the Stage in the ending keyframe.**

   You can relocate the element to another location in the Stage. Or you can change its size, rotation, skew, or other visual property.

   In the example, I used the Free Transform Tool to rotate it (see Figure 4-5) and shrunk its width and height using the Properties inspector.

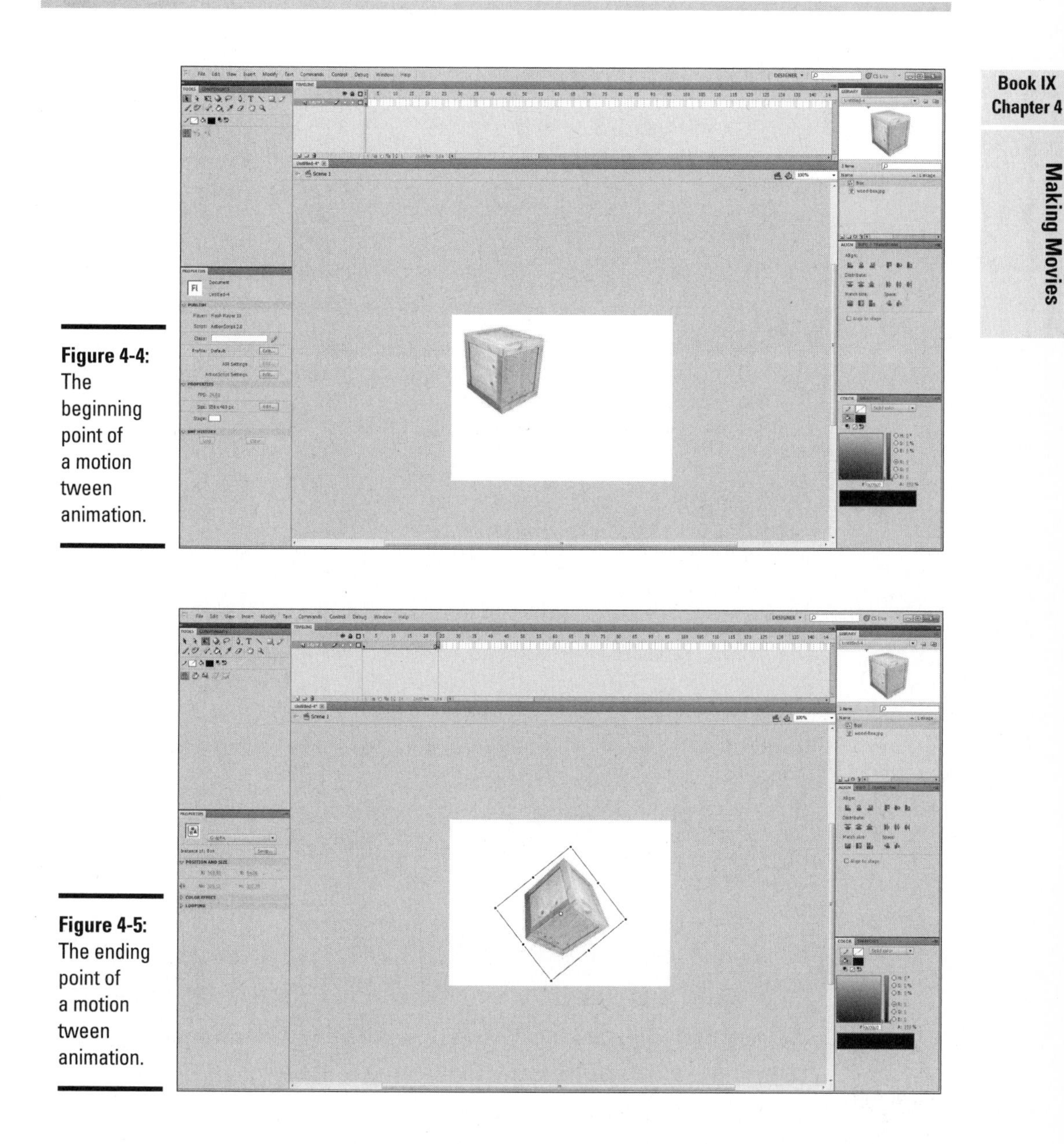

Figure 4-4: The beginning point of a motion tween animation.

Figure 4-5: The ending point of a motion tween animation.

7. **Right-click the ending keyframe and choose Create Motion Tween from its pop-up menu.**

   A motion tween is created.

8. **Choose Window➪Motion Editor to display the Motion Editor.**

   The Motion Editor is shown in Figure 4-6.

   The Motion Editor is the place in which you can edit your motion tweens.

9. **Click the + plus button on the Color Effect line and choose Brightness from its pop-up menu.**

10. **Choose the Simple (Slow) item from the Brightness drop-down menu.**

    The brightness will slowly change with this new transformation.

11. **Choose Control➪Play to test the animation.**

Use the Motion Editor to tweak and edit the type of motions and transformations in which you'd like your animation to display.

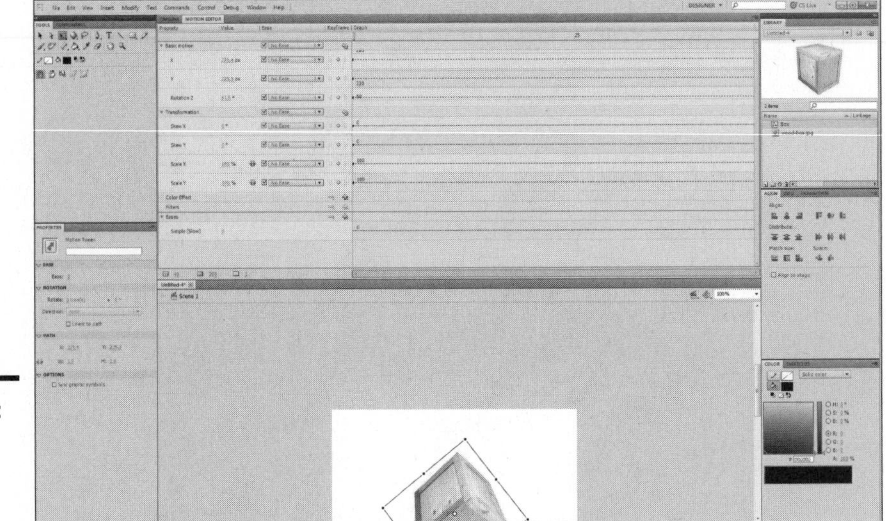

Figure 4-6: Editing a motion tween.

Shape tweens

You can use shape tweens to *morph* (smoothly transform) one shape into another.

Unlike motion tweens, the elements you morph *cannot* be symbols.

Here's how to set up a shape tween animation:

1. **Select a layer from the Layers pane of the Timeline.**
2. **If the first frame in the Timeline isn't already selected, click it.**

3. **Add to the Stage the shape that you want to animate by using the drawing tools from the Tools panel.**

   Figure 4-7 shows a rectangular shape in the keyframe.

4. **Select the frame in the Timeline in which you want the morphing to end.**

   I chose the 24th frame.

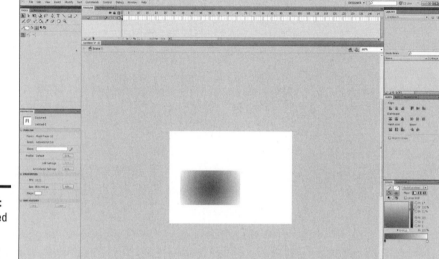

Figure 4-7: It all started with a rectangle.

5. **Right-click the frame and choose Insert Keyframe from its pop-up menu.**
6. **Delete the artwork that you previously added in the first keyframe.**
7. **Create a new object in the Stage in the ending keyframe.**

   In the example, I created an oval shape (see Figure 4-8).

8. **Right-click the ending keyframe and choose Create Shape Tween from its pop-up menu.**

   A motion tween is created. Keep the ending keyframe selected and continue.

9. **From the Properties inspector, select the desired blending option from the Blend drop-down list. See Figure 4-9.**

   The Distributive option better smoothes the intermediate shapes. Angular better sharpens the intermediate shapes.

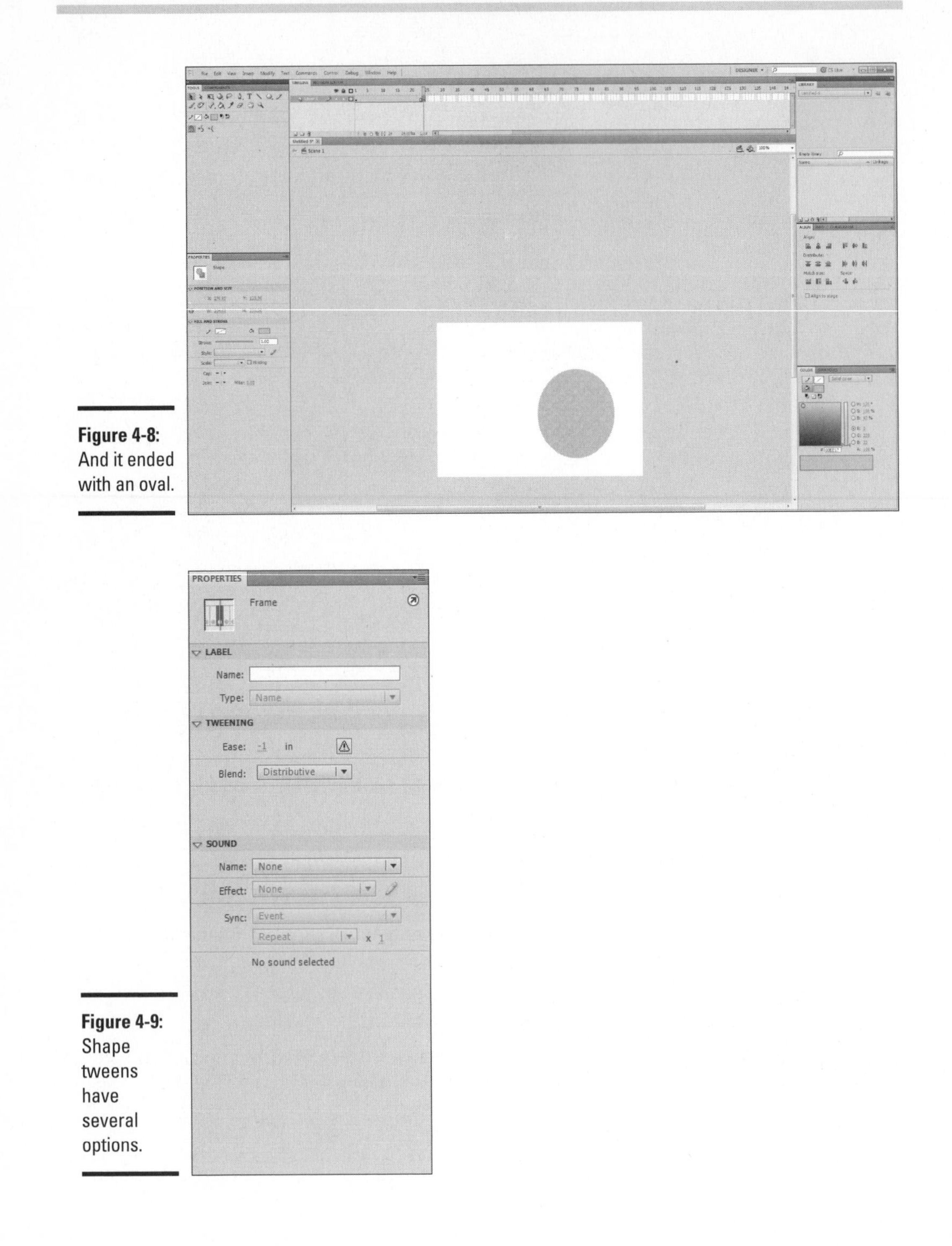

Figure 4-8: And it ended with an oval.

Figure 4-9: Shape tweens have several options.

10. **Set an ease value by using the Ease slider.**

    The 0 default setting causes the motion to be constant. A positive value (1 through 100) begins the tweened animation quickly and slows it as it nears the end. A negative value (–1 through –100) begins the tween slowly and speeds it up toward the end.

11. **Choose Control⇨Play to test the movie.**

Involving the User: Interactive Flash Movies

Flash movies aren't meant as just gizmos for users to watch. You can add interactivity to them, such as going to a URL when a user clicks a button or moving an element when the user's mouse pointer hovers over it. You can add interactivity to your Flash movie by using behaviors and actions:

- **Behaviors:** You can attach these easy-to-use predefined scripts to objects in your movie. You access behaviors by using the Behaviors panel (Window⇨Behaviors).
- **Actions:** These programming scripts are for more advanced users. The code is written in ActionScript, the Flash scripting language; it looks similar to JavaScript. You can work with actions in the Actions panel (Window⇨Actions).

Behaviors aren't compatible with ActionScript 3.0, which is the Flash scripting language. Therefore, if you plan to use Behaviors in your Flash movie, specify ActionScript 2.0 (or ActionScript 1.0) as your ActionScript version. This setting is on the Flash tab of the Publish Settings dialog box. (Choose File⇨Publish Settings.)

When you're beginning to work with Flash interactivity, behaviors are a good place to start. Then, when you feel comfortable with them, you can begin to work with actions.

See Chapter 3 in this minibook for an example of adding a behavior to a button symbol.

Adding sound to your movie

In addition to being able to add graphics and video clips, you can add sound effects or sound clips into your movie in Flash. You can add audio in two different ways. For short sound effects, such as a blip sound when a button is pressed, you can download the entire audio clip before it's played. Or, for large audio files, you can stream them. When you stream an audio file, Flash downloads the beginning of the song or audio clip and then begins playing in synch with the Timeline of the movie.

Importing an audio file

Before you can work with an audio file, you must add it to your Flash library by choosing File⇨Import⇨Import to Library. In the dialog box that appears, add one or more sound files and click the Import to Library button. Go to the Library panel for your movie; the files are displayed there.

Flash supports AIFF, MP3, and WAV sound files.

However, if the audio file is large, you can increase performance by linking to an external audio file rather than embedding it into the Flash file.

Adding an audio clip to your movie

To add a soundtrack or audio clip to your movie, follow these steps:

1. **Import an audio file into Flash.**

   See the preceding section.

2. **Insert a new layer in the Timeline by clicking the Insert Layer button at the bottom of the Timeline window (or by choosing Insert Timeline⇨Layer).**

3. **From the Library panel, drag the sound file you want to include and drop it on top of the layer name in the Layers pane of the Timeline.**

   The audio clip is added.

4. **(Optional) Add an effect (such as a fade-in) by selecting an option from the Effect drop-down list in the layer's Properties inspector.**

   If you want to get fancy, click the Edit button to customize the sound wave.

5. **Pick a synchronization option from the Sync drop-down list:**

   - *Event:* Synchronizes the sound to an event.
   - *Start:* Begins playing the sound (as does Event), except that if the sound is already playing, it doesn't start again.
   - *Stop:* Halts playing the sound.
   - *Stream:* Ensures that the animation of the movie is in synch with streamed audio.

6. **Determine the number of times the sound should loop or whether it should be continuous. Use the Repeat drop-down list and the box beside it.**

   If you want the sound to play throughout the entire animation, be sure to enter a value large enough to last the length of your movie.

   You can have multiple sounds per film. Therefore, if you want to have additional sounds (overlapping each other), repeat Steps 1 through 6.

7. **Choose Edit⇨Edit Document to return to document-editing mode.**
8. **Choose Control⇨Test Movie to test your new sound.**

Adding a sound effect to a button

To add a sound effect to a button, follow these steps:

1. **Import an audio file into Flash.**

   See the section "Importing an audio file," earlier in this chapter.
2. **Double-click the button on the Stage to enter symbol-editing mode.**

   The four-frame Button Timeline appears.
3. **Insert a new layer in the button's Timeline by clicking the Insert Layer button at the bottom of the Timeline window (or choosing Insert Timeline⇨Layer).**
4. **Double-click the layer's name and rename the layer as** Sound.
5. **In the Timeline, click the Sound layer's frame under the button state you want to assign the sound to: Up, Over, Down, or Hit.**
6. **Insert a keyframe by pressing F6 (or right-clicking the frame and choosing Insert Keyframe from the pop-up menu).**
7. **Select the new keyframe and view the Properties inspector.**
8. **Select the sound clip you want to attach from the Sound drop-down list.**
9. **(Optional) Add an effect from the Effect drop-down list.**
10. **Pick a synchronization option from the Sync drop-down list:**
    - *Event:* Synchronizes the sound to an event.
    - *Start:* Begins playing the sound (as does Event), except that if the sound is already playing, it doesn't start again.
    - *Stop:* Halts playing the sound.
    - *Stream:* Ensures that the animation of the movie is in synch with streamed audio.
11. **Determine the number of times the sound should loop or whether it should be continuous. Use the Repeat drop-down list and the box beside it.**
12. **Choose Edit⇨Edit Document to return to document-editing mode.**
13. **Choose Control⇨Test Movie to check out your new sound-enabled button.**

Chapter 5: Publishing Your Movie

In This Chapter

- **Optimizing the size of your movie file**
- **Profiling download performance**
- **Publishing your movie in Flash format for the Web**

After you create and test your Flash movie, you're ready to go live with it. Before doing so, of course, first you have to publish the movie so it can be viewed inside browsers. So I begin this chapter by showing you how to optimize your movie to decrease its file size (that way it loads faster). After that, I show you how to publish the movie. Finally, you explore how to export your movie file to different formats.

For Best Results: Optimizing Your Movie

As you create your Flash movie, be mindful of the size of the movie you're creating. Even with broadband connections, visitors still get impatient and frustrated with your Web site if they have to wait too long for a Flash movie to download.

Optimization tips

Here are several tips to keep in mind to optimize your movie:

- **Use symbols.** If you have an element, such as a video clip or graphic, that appears more than once in the movie, be sure to use a symbol for it. When you use symbols, elements are stored once and Flash uses instances of those elements every time they occur in the movie. See Chapter 3 in this minibook to use symbols.
- **Use tweened animation.** Tweened animation occupies much less space than does frame-by-frame animation. Flash needs to store information for only the two keyframes rather than for every frame. See Chapter 4 in this minibook to create tweened animations.
- **Optimize curves.** Curves that you create with the pencil and other tools are stored as miniature line segments. You can optimize the number of line segments used by Flash by choosing Modify⇨Shape⇨Optimize. The Smoothing slider determines how much the shape is smoothed.

- **Optimize text.** When you work with fonts, you can use either device fonts or embedded fonts. If you use a device font, Flash looks for the closest matching font installed on the user's system, much the same way a browser does when displaying a Web page. An embedded font, on the other hand, is stored as part of the Flash file. The font takes up more space but ensures that the text looks exactly as you intended. The decision about whether to use embedded fonts is ultimately a cost-benefit issue: design versus download speed.
- **Draw and paint wisely.** Although optimization issues shouldn't limit your creativity, keep in mind how your artwork can affect file size. Pencil strokes take less space than brush strokes. Solid lines take less information to create than do dotted and dashed lines. Grouped elements take up less space than ungrouped ones.
- **Compress the movie and embedded bitmapped graphics when you publish.** Flash provides several optimization settings that further compress the movie when you publish. See the section "Outputting Your Movie for the Web," a little later in this chapter, for more information.
- **Link instead of embed.** If you are embedding video or audio clips, you can increase performance by linking to them as external files rather than embedding them.

Profiling download performance

As you're testing your movie (choose Control➪Test Movie), you can test the download performance and even profile the specific frames of the animation that cause the greatest download delays. Follow these steps:

1. **Choose View➪Bandwidth Profiler from the test mode's menu.**

   If you don't see this menu item on the View menu, choose Control➪Test Movie and then continue.

2. **Choose View➪Download Settings to specify the simulated download rate to use in the testing.**
3. **Enable the View➪Simulate Download setting to perform a simulated download based on the download speed you set before running the movie.**

   The Bandwidth Profiler appears on top of the Flash movie window (see Figure 5-1). As the movie plays, Flash tests its performance.

The left side of the Profiler displays overall statistics about the movie, including its size and the length of time it took to download before playing.

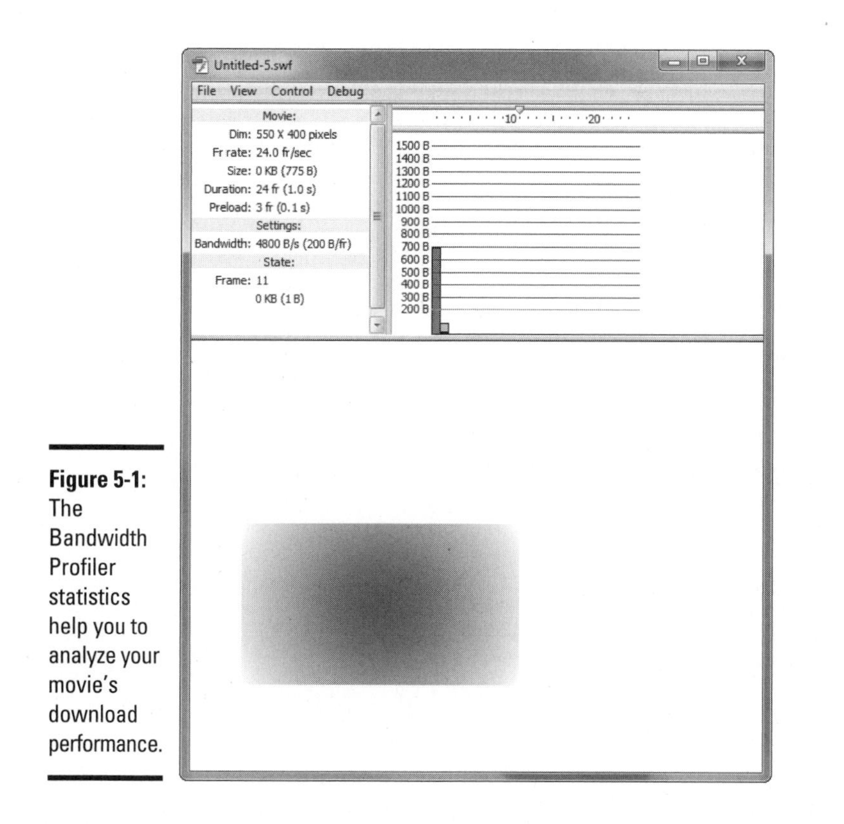

Figure 5-1: The Bandwidth Profiler statistics help you to analyze your movie's download performance.

The right side displays a timeline and graph. The graph can display either streaming data (choose View➪Streaming Graph) or a frame-by-frame look (choose View➪Frame-By-Frame Graph). The Streaming Graph displays all frames that cause slowdowns. The Frame-By-Frame Graph displays the size of every frame in the movie. Frames that are above the red line cause the movie to load more slowly, making them good targets for optimization. Click the bar to view the specific frame.

Outputting Your Movie for the Web

When you create, design, and test a Web page in Dreamweaver, Expression Web, or another software tool, you're working with the HTML files that you'll publish to your remote server. So when you speak of "publishing a Web page," that term is roughly synonymous with "uploading." Note, however, that Flash is a different story.

When you create a Flash movie inside the Flash environment, you're working with an editable `.fla` file. However, `.fla` files must be transformed into a different non-editable file format before they can be played back over the Web in a browser. This conversion process is known as *publishing*.

To publish a Flash movie that's open inside the Flash design environment, follow these steps:

1. **Choose File⇨Publish Settings.**

   The Publish Settings dialog box appears, as shown in Figure 5-2.

Figure 5-2: Specifying the formats in which you intend to publish the movie.

2. **Click the Formats tab and select all the file formats that you want to publish; Flash (`.swf`) and HTML (`.html`) are selected by default:**

   - *Flash:* The actual movie file; required for viewing inside a browser over the Web.

- *HTML:* Creates an HTML document with the .swf file already embedded into it. If you plan to insert your Flash movie inside a Web page you already built, you can deselect this option.

Because you're likely to insert the Flash file you created into a Web page you've built previously, you may be tempted simply to discard this option. However, by enabling this option and working with the HTML publishing settings, you can see all the tasks that are possible when adding a Flash movie to a Web page.

- *GIF Image, JPEG Image, PNG Image:* Create a single image version of your movie clip.
- *Windows Projector, Macintosh Projector:* Create a standalone application that can be run on a local Windows or Mac computer outside a browser.

Note that for every file format that you enable, a new tab is added to the dialog box for publishing settings.

3. **In the File section, specify a filename for each of the file formats you selected.**
4. **Click the Browse button beside the filename box to navigate to a specific output folder.**

   Otherwise, the file is published in the same location as the .fla file.

5. **Click the Flash tab (see Figure 5-3) and specify the publishing settings for the Flash movie.**

   Here's a short list of noteworthy options:

   - *Player:* Sets playback for older Flash players.
   - *JPEG quality:* Sets the compression ratio that's applied to bitmapped images inside the movie. If you're trying to minimize the size of your movie file, experiment with various settings on the slider to determine which value gives you adequate image quality while maximizing compression.
   - *Audio stream, Audio event:* Use this to set the sound quality for streams and events.
   - *Generate size report:* Helpful in determining movie download performance and even pinpointing specific frames that are causing slowdowns. The report is generated in the same location as the .swf file.
   - *Protect from import:* Ensures that no one can import your .swf file into the Flash environment and edit it.
   - *Omit trace actions:* Should be checked when you have a final movie ready to go. Trace actions are used in debugging ActionScript.
   - *Compress movie:* Reduces file size, but compressed .swf output cannot be played in earlier versions of the Flash player.

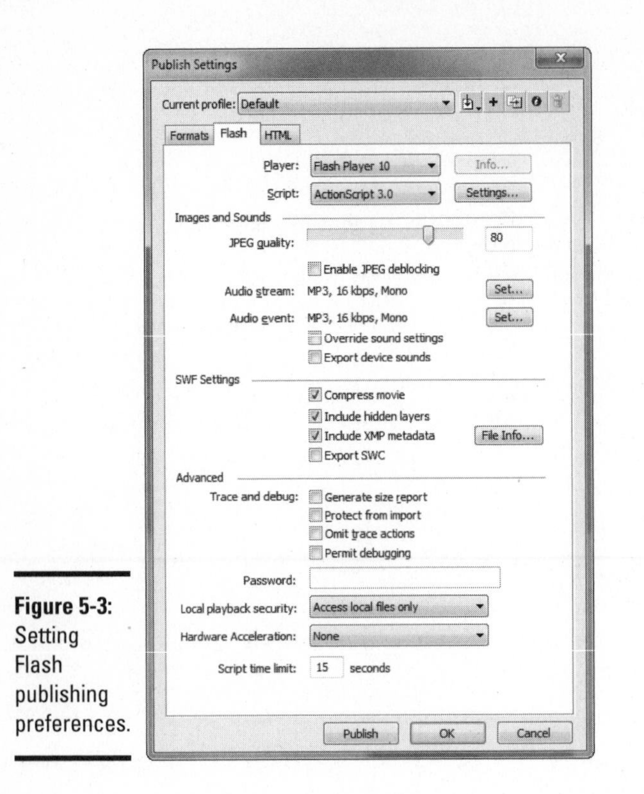

Figure 5-3: Setting Flash publishing preferences.

6. **Click the appropriate tab to specify the publish settings for HTML and any other output formats you selected.**

   If you checked HTML output, here are some notable preferences (shown in Figure 5-4):

   - *Template:* Specifies a specific template used to create the document. For each setting, click the Info button to see a description summary of what the template provides.
   - *Dimensions:* Specifies the width and height of the Flash object inside the Web page.
   - *Playback:* Provides four common options related to the playback of the movie in the Web page. *Paused at Start* requires a user to manually start the movie. *Display Menu* displays the Flash pop-up menu when the movie is right-clicked. *Loop* plays the movie continually. *Device Font* substitutes an anti-aliased system font when it can't locate a particular font on the computer.
   - *Quality:* Specifies the amount of anti-aliasing applied to the movie.
   - *HTML Alignment, Flash Alignment:* Specify the positioning of the control inside the document body.

Choose File➪Publish Preview when you're testing different publishing settings for any of the formats.

7. **Click the Publish button to publish the movie.**

   Flash generates output files for each of the file formats specified on the Formats tab.

After you configure the publishing settings, you can publish a Flash movie quickly by choosing File➪Publish.

Figure 5-4: You have a variety of options for displaying a Flash movie inside an HTML document.

Index

• Special Characters and Numerics •

• A •

• B •

• D •

• E •

• F •

• G •

• H •

• I •

• J •

• K •

• L •

• M •

• O •

• P •

• S •

• U •

• V •

• W •

• X •

• Y •

• Z •

Apple & Macs

iPad For Dummies
978-0-470-58027-1

iPhone For Dummies, 4th Edition
978-0-470-87870-5

MacBook For Dummies, 3rd Edition
978-0-470-76918-8

Mac OS X Snow Leopard For Dummies
978-0-470-43543-4

Business

Bookkeeping For Dummies
978-0-7645-9848-7

Job Interviews For Dummies, 3rd Edition
978-0-470-17748-8

Resumes For Dummies, 5th Edition
978-0-470-08037-5

Starting an Online Business For Dummies, 6th Edition
978-0-470-60210-2

Stock Investing For Dummies, 3rd Edition
978-0-470-40114-9

Successful Time Management For Dummies
978-0-470-29034-7

Computer Hardware

BlackBerry For Dummies, 4th Edition
978-0-470-60700-8

Computers For Seniors For Dummies, 2nd Edition
978-0-470-53483-0

PCs For Dummies, Windows 7 Edition
978-0-470-46542-4

Laptops For Dummies, 4th Edition
978-0-470-57829-2

Cooking & Entertaining

Cooking Basics For Dummies, 3rd Edition
978-0-7645-7206-7

Wine For Dummies, 4th Edition
978-0-470-04579-4

Diet & Nutrition

Dieting For Dummies, 2nd Edition
978-0-7645-4149-0

Nutrition For Dummies, 4th Edition
978-0-471-79868-2

Weight Training For Dummies, 3rd Edition
978-0-471-76845-6

Digital Photography

Digital SLR Cameras & Photography For Dummies, 3rd Edition
978-0-470-46606-3

Photoshop Elements 8 For Dummies
978-0-470-52967-6

Gardening

Gardening Basics For Dummies
978-0-470-03749-2

Organic Gardening For Dummies, 2nd Edition
978-0-470-43067-5

Green/Sustainable

Raising Chickens For Dummies
978-0-470-46544-8

Green Cleaning For Dummies
978-0-470-39106-8

Health

Diabetes For Dummies, 3rd Edition
978-0-470-27086-8

Food Allergies For Dummies
978-0-470-09584-3

Living Gluten-Free For Dummies, 2nd Edition
978-0-470-58589-4

Hobbies/General

Chess For Dummies, 2nd Edition
978-0-7645-8404-6

Drawing Cartoons & Comics For Dummies
978-0-470-42683-8

Knitting For Dummies, 2nd Edition
978-0-470-28747-7

Organizing For Dummies
978-0-7645-5300-4

Su Doku For Dummies
978-0-470-01892-7

Home Improvement

Home Maintenance For Dummies, 2nd Edition
978-0-470-43063-7

Home Theater For Dummies, 3rd Edition
978-0-470-41189-6

Living the Country Lifestyle All-in-One For Dummies
978-0-470-43061-3

Solar Power Your Home For Dummies, 2nd Edition
978-0-470-59678-4

Available wherever books are sold. For more information or to order direct: U.S. customers visit www.dummies.com or call 1-877-762-2974. U.K. customers visit www.wileyeurope.com or call (0) 1243 843291. Canadian customers visit www.wiley.ca or call 1-800-567-4797.

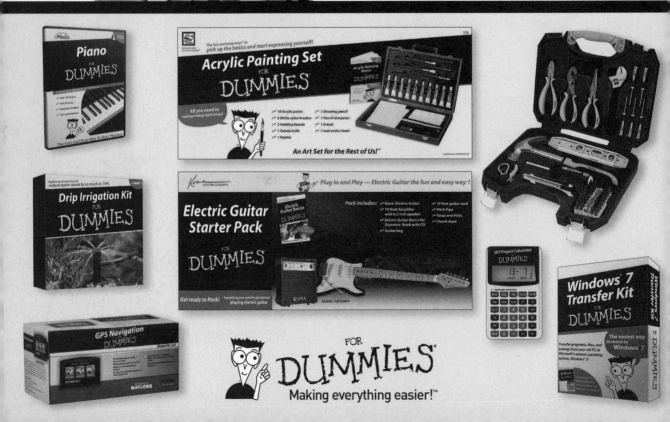